Economics for Business and Management

Visit the *Economics for Business and Management, third edition* Companion Website at **www.pearsoned.co.uk/griffithswall** to find valuable **student** learning material including:

- A list of topics cross referenced to the book to enable you to read more in the text
- 'Are you ready?' quizzes to test how much you already know and indicate where you need further practice
- A variety of activities containing interactive exercises to practise and test your understanding
- Multiple choice, data response and essay type questions similar to the types of questions you may face in an exam
- Links to relevant sites on the web
- Key definitions used in the chapters.

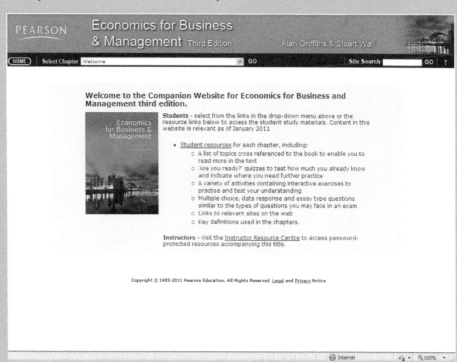

PEARSON

Economics for Business & Management Third Edition   Alan Griffiths & Stuart Wall

HOME | Select Chapter Welcome   GO   Site Search   GO | ?

Welcome to the Companion Website for Economics for Business and Management third edition.

Students - select from the links in the drop-down menu above or the resource links below to access the student study materials. Content in this website is relevant as of January 2011

- Student resources for each chapter, including:
  - A list of topics cross referenced to the book to enable you to read more in the text
  - 'Are you ready?' quizzes to test how much you already know and indicate where you need further practice
  - A variety of activities containing interactive exercises to practise and test your understanding
  - Multiple choice, data response and essay type questions similar to the types of questions you may face in an exam
  - Links to relevant sites on the web
  - Key definitions used in the chapters.

Instructors - visit the Instructor Resource Centre to access password-protected resources accompanying this title.

PEARSON

We work with leading authors to develop the strongest
educational materials in economics, bringing cutting-edge
thinking and best learning practice to a global market.

Under a range of well-known imprints, including
Financial Times Prentice Hall, we craft high quality print
and electronic publications which help readers to
understand and apply their content, whether studying
or at work.

To find out more about the complete range of our
publishing, please visit us on the World Wide Web at:
www.pearsoned.co.uk

Economics for Business and Management

Third Edition

Alan Griffiths and Stuart Wall

**Financial Times
Prentice Hall**
is an imprint of

PEARSON

Harlow, England • London • New York • Boston • San Francisco • Toronto
Sydney • Tokyo • Singapore • Hong Kong • Seoul • Taipei • New Delhi
Cape Town • Madrid • Mexico City • Amsterdam • Munich • Paris • Milan

Pearson Education Limited
Edinburgh Gate
Harlow
Essex CM20 2JE
England

and Associated Companies throughout the world

Visit us on the World Wide Web at:
www.pearsoned.co.uk

First published 2005
Second edition published 2008
Third edition published 2011

ISBN: 978-0-273-73524-3

British Library Cataloguing-in-Publication Data
A catalogue record for this book is available from the British Library

Library of Congress Cataloging-in-Publication Data

Griffiths, Alan, 1944–
  Economics for business and management / Alan Griffiths and Stuart Wall. -- 3rd ed.
      p. cm.
  Rev. ed. of: Economics for business and management / Alan Griffiths, Stuart Wall
(eds.). 2nd ed. 2008.
  Includes bibliographical references and index.
  ISBN 978-0-273-73524-3 (pbk.)
  1. Managerial economics. 2. Economics. 3. Business. 4. Management. I. Wall,
Stuart, 1946– II. Economics for business and management. III. Title.
  HD30.22.E257 2011
  338.5024'658--dc22

                                                                    2010037863

ARP impression 98

Typeset in 9/12.5 pt Stone Serif by 73
Printed and bound by Ashford Colour Press Ltd

Brief contents

Supporting resources

Visit **www.pearsoned.co.uk/griffithswall** to find valuable online resources

Companion Website for students

- A list of topics cross referenced to the book to enable you to read more in the text
- 'Are you ready?' quizzes to test how much you already know and indicate where you need further practice
- A variety of activities containing interactive exercises to practise and test your understanding
- Multiple choice, data response and essay type questions similar to the types of questions you may face in an exam
- Links to relevant sites on the web
- Key definitions used in the chapters.

For instructors

- Complete, downloadable Instructor's Manual
- PowerPoint slides that can be downloaded and used as OHTs
- Testbank of customisable questions for formative or summative assessment

Also: The [regularly maintained] Companion Website provides the following features:

- Search tool to help locate specific items of content
- E-mail results and profile tools to send results of quizzes to instructors
- Online help and support to assist with website usage and troubleshooting

For more information please contact your local Pearson Education sales representative or visit **www.pearsoned.co.uk/griffithswall**

Contents

14 Strategies in a globalised business environment   470

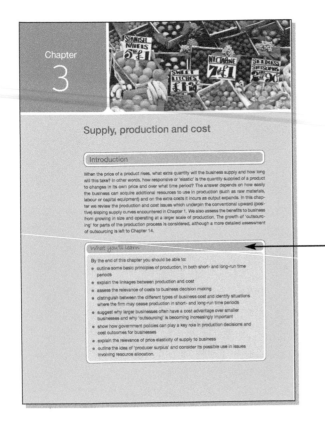

What you'll learn – each chapter starts with a list of learning objectives and outcomes, to prepare you for what you will cover.

Quote – highlighted throughout each chapter, thought-provoking quotes set the scene and provide a relevant and historical context for the theory.

Check the net – refers you to useful websites for further reading, showing you where you can find the most up-to-date and relevant information online.

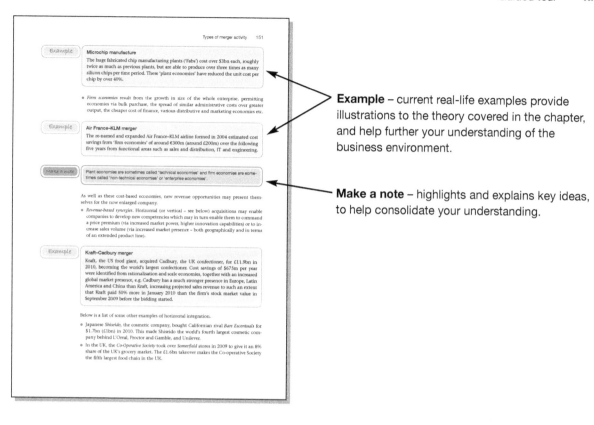

Example – current real-life examples provide illustrations to the theory covered in the chapter, and help further your understanding of the business environment.

Make a note – highlights and explains key ideas, to help consolidate your understanding.

You try – provides a variety of exercises and activities, giving you the chance to apply your own knowledge and practise your learning.

Case study – Includes topical examples, data and scenarios from the real world to show you why this subject really matters to everyday life, accompanied by open-ended questions to aid discussion.

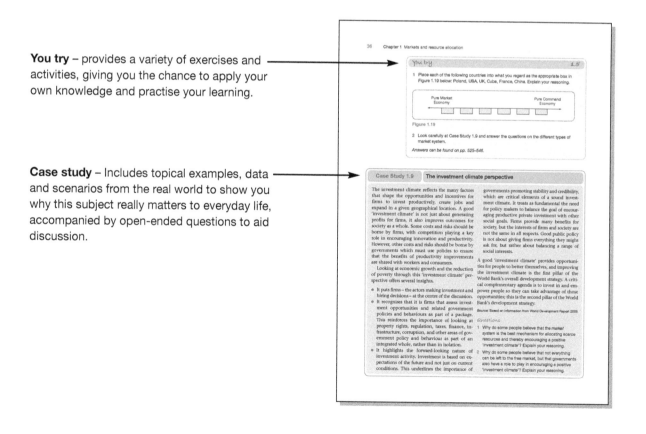

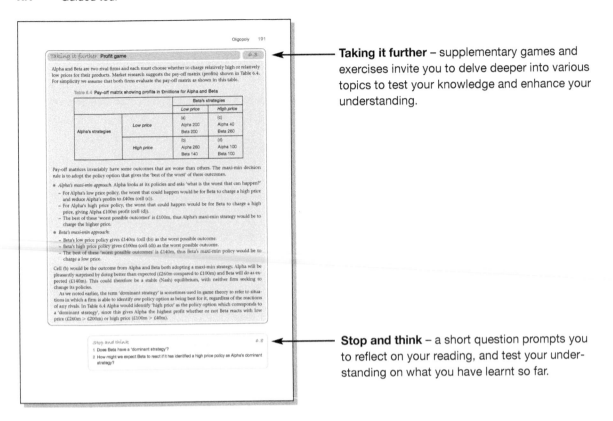

Taking it further – supplementary games and exercises invite you to delve deeper into various topics to test your knowledge and enhance your understanding.

Stop and think – a short question prompts you to reflect on your reading, and test your understanding on what you have learnt so far.

Recap – a short summary at the end of each chapter allows you to check up on your understanding at frequent intervals, and is an ideal revision tool.

Key terms – a concise list of definitions of key terms are provided for quick reference at the end of each chapter.

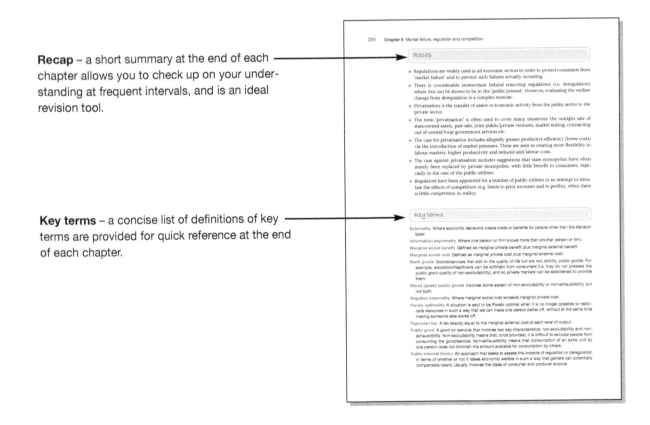

Guide to the main focus of case studies

Chapter	Page number	Title	Subject	Organisation/ business person	Country/ region
Chapter 1 Markets and resource allocation	8	1.1 Google takes networking fight to Facebook	Social networking and demand factors	Google, Facebook	Global
	10	1.2 Small cars, big question	Small cars and demand factors	Ford, General Motors, Chrysler	US
	16	1.3 Warning over battery bubble	Electric car batteries and supply factors	Major car producers	US and global
	17	1.4 Dyson relocates production to South East Asia	Supply chain	Dyson	Malaysia, UK, US
	23	1.5 Markets and global impacts	Cotton, milk and car components	Textile federation, Chinese government, Mazda	US, China, EU, Japan
	26	1.6 The drug war	Cocaine: demand, supply and price	Drug cartels	Colombia, US, EU
	29	1.7 Oiling the wheels	Price of oil	OPEC	Middle East and global
	35	1.8 Food crisis worsens amid call for 'green' reform	Price of lentils (pulses)	Indian government and Indian Farmers Forum	India
	36	1.9 The investment climate perspective	Market systems	World Bank	Global
Chapter 2 Demand, revenue and consumer behaviour	43	2.1 Pricing shampoo and conditioners	Price elasticity of demand and setting prices for shampoo	Producers of female and male grooming products	EU
	50	2.2 Taxing smokers	Price elasticity of demand and tax policy	French government and BAT	France
	52	2.3 Moves towards Beijing pollution tax	Tax policy and pollution	Chinese government and Chinese agriculture	China
	59	2.4 Transport and elasticities of demand	Price, income and cross elasticities of demand and road transport	Road users and governments	UK
	61	2.5 'Top-up fees' and the 'Veblen effect'	Consumer behaviour	Universities, student representatives, government	UK

Chapter	Page number	Title	Subject	Organisation/ business person	Country/ region
	66	2.6 What is time worth?	Consumer and occupational group behaviour	Occupational groups	UK
	67	2.7 Utility and happiness	Consumer behaviour	Students	Global
	68	2.8 Changing tastes over time	Consumer behaviour	National population	UK
Chapter 3 Supply, production and cost	78	3.1 Small oil explorers eye big role in North Sea	Costs of oil production	Smaller oil producing companies	UK and global
	81	3.2 Theatre costs in the West End	Costs and price setting	Theatre companies	UK
	84	3.3 Sony pulls ultra-thin TV in Japan	Costs, technology and TVs	Sony	Japan
	87	3.4 Head Office – some easy economies?	Administrative costs	Multinationals	US/EU
	91	3.5 Scale economies in the skies	Cost advantages of large planes	Boeing, Airbus, WTO	US/EU
	98	3.6 Outsourcing: South Korea looks to China	Cost advantages of outsourcing	Hyundai car production	South Korea, China
Chapter 4 Business organisation, objectives and behaviour	111	4.1 Britain should not fear foreign ownership	Business organisation	Cadbury, Kraft	UK/US
	117	4.2 RBS links new tougher pay schemes to bank's profits	Business objectives and remuneration	Royal Bank of Scotland (RBS)	UK
	124	4.3 Drive to link pay to sustainability begins	Business objectives and remuneration	TNT, DSM	Netherlands
	133	4.4 In the eye: Minority shareholders are aggrieved	Business organisation	Novartis, Alcon	Switzerland
Chapter 5 Firm size, mergers and the 'public interest'	140	5.1 Entrepreneurship and SMEs	Factors influencing entrepreneurial behaviour	SMEs	Global
	143	5.2 The Alternative Investment Market (AIM)	Access to funds	SMEs	UK
	148	5.3 Mergers – for managers or shareholders?	Principal-agent problem	AOL, Time Warner	US
	155	5.4 Premium car deal fills a hole at Geely	Cross border mergers	Geely, Volvo	China, Sweden
	158	5.5 Return of the Chaebol	Conglomerate integration	Samsung, Hyundai	South Korea

Chapter	Page number	Title	Subject	Organisation/ business person	Country/ region
Chapter 6 Market structures	171	6.1 Perfect competition and the Internet	Absence of barriers to entry	Internet organisations	US
	174	6.2 New entry and the banking system	Presence of barriers to entry	UK major banks	UK
	192	6.3 Pricing models for e-book sales	Price setting in oligopoly markets	E-book producers/ consumers	US/EU
	198	6.4 Price discrimination in pharmaceuticals	Price setting in oligopoly markets	Pharmaceutical industries and Napp	UK
Chapter 7 Labour and other factor markets	209	7.1 Increasing wage inequality	Sources of wage variation	Executive wage earners	UK
	211	7.2 DSM to link managers' pay with green credentials and staff morale	Pay and sustainability	Executive wage earners	UK
	214	7.3 The National Minimum Wage and business	Setting a legal minimum wage	Employers, employees and Government	UK
	219	7.4 Daimler turns to temporary staff to boost flexibility	Job flexibility in car production	Daimler	Germany
Chapter 8 Market failure, regulation and competition	232	8.1 The London Congestion Charge	Impacts of regulation	London transport	UK
	233	8.2 Stern report on climate change	Market intervention: global warming	Citizens, governments, businesses	Global
	238	8.3 Businesses face emissions law shock	Regulating pollution	Business government	UK
	240	8.4 Forced rhubarb gains recognition at last	Regulating production	Rhubarb producers	UK
	250	8.5 Welfare impact of mergers	Consumer and producer surplus and mergers	Competition Commission (UK)	UK
	251	8.6 Fined for sharing price data	Restrictive practices	Office of Fair Trading	UK
	255	8.7 Antitrust in the European Union	Restrictive practices	Cartels	EU
Chapter 9 National income determination	263	9.1 Look after the cents	Consumer behaviour	Savings of US citizens	US
	272	9.2 Comparing standards of living	Measuring living standards	United Nations Human Development Index	Global
	279	9.3 US capital productivity decline must be reversed	Return on investment	US businesses	US

Chapter	Page number	Title	Subject	Organisation/ business person	Country/ region
	285	9.4 Consumer behaviour, indebtedness and the sub-prime market	Consumer function	US/UK Financial institutions	US/UK and global
	295	9.5 The multiplier and the London Olympics	National Income multiplier	London Olympic Committee	UK
Chapter 10 Government policies: instruments and objectives	310	10.1 Global budgetary problems and the 'credit crunch'	Fiscal policy	G20 group of countries	Global
	329	10.2 German hyperinflation	Price inflation	German businesses and citizens	Germany
	335	10.3 Productivity, employment and unemployment	Labour productivity	Employers, Trade Union and Governments	US, EU and global
	340	10.4 Weak pound boosts UK shares	Exchange rates and share prices	FTSE	UK and global
	341	10.5 Exchange rates and burgers	Exchange rates and 'Big-Mac'	McDonalds	Global
	345	10.6 Risk needs a human touch	Automated risk management techniques	Basel Committee	Global
	347	10.7 Sovereign debt ratings	National insolvency	Governments and business	Greece and global
Chapter 11 Political, legal, ecological and technological environment	354	11.1 The politics of rum: Sir Henry's legacy	Micropolitical risk	Governments and business	Greece and global
	357	11.2 Political risk for business in Russia	Macropolitical risk	Yukos and Russian Government	Russia
	364	11.3 Milk regulations	Regulations: milk	Chinese Government and milk consumers	China
	365	11.4 Kettle company wins damages in China	Intellectual property rights	Strix and Kettle producers	China and Isle of Man
	367	11.5 Copyright and wrong	Intellectual property rights	Government and businesses	UK and US
	372	11.6 Beijing census exposes high levels of pollution	Ecological environment	Chinese agricultural sector	China
	372	11.7 Biofuels subsidies criticised	Ecological environment	OECD, Friends of the	Global
	376	11.8 Games guru puts his finger on chart success	iPhone Apps	Apple	US

Chapter	Page number	Title	Subject	Organisation/ business person	Country/ region
Chapter 12 Functions of management: domestic business environment	385	12.1 A better burger thanks to data crunching	Market research	Business and data analysts	Global
	392	12.2 Asos aims to wrest the web crown from Next	Marketing function	Asos, on-line fashion retailing	UK
	395	12.3 HRM and Royal Bank of Scotland	Human resource function	Royal Bank of Scotland (RBS)	UK
	400	12.4 HRM and flexible working	Human resource function	KPMG, Centrica	UK
	405	12.5 Fooled again	Accounting function	Lehman Brothers, Anglo Irish Bank	UK/Eire
Chapter 13 International business environment	423	13.1 Internationalisation of Portuguese firms	Internationalisation	Portuguese former colonies	Portugal
	435	13.2 IHRM and cultural characteristics	Cultural characteristics and Hofstede	Multinationals operating in Greece	Greece
	439	13.3 'IKEA – flat pack success!'	Market entry and development	IKEA	Global
	444	13.4 Perils of blundering into India's cultural minefield	Marketing and culture	Luxury products	India
	456	13.5 China groups eye production in India	Outsourcing	Mobile phone handsets	China, India
	457	13.6 China, exchange rates and exports	International trade	World exports from China	China
	466	13.7 High cost of anti-dumping tariffs	Trade protection	Tariffs on non-EU imports into EU	EU
Chapter 14 Strategies in a globalised business environment	476	14.1 The pharmaceutical market and GlaxoSmithKline	Mergers and alliances	GlaxoSmithKline and pharmaceutical sector	Global
	485	14.2 IKEA and growth strategies	Porter's Five Forces	IKEA	Global
	496	14.3 Outsourcing: Competing in a globalised economy	Outsourcing	Daewoo and shipbuilding	Global
	503	14.4 Daimler and Renault-Nissan create strategic alliance	Alliances	Daimler and Renault-Nissan	Germany, France, Japan

About the authors

Alan Griffiths, BA, MSc is Reader in Economics at Ashcroft International Business School, Anglia Ruskin University, having previously been Tutor in Economics at the University College of Wales, Aberystwyth. He has acted as a visiting fellow of the Japan Foundation at Sophia University, Tokyo and as Research Officer at the Research Institute for the National Economy at Yokohama University. He is author of a wide range of books and articles.

Stuart Wall, BA, MSc is Professor of Business and Economic Education at Ashcroft International Business School, Anglia Ruskin University, and has been a visiting lecturer, supervisor and examiner at Cambridge University. He has acted as a consultant to the OECD Directorate for Science, Technology and Industry, and as a member of a number of degree awarding bodies in Business and Economics in the UK. He is author of a wide range of books and articles.

Contributors

Margaret O'Quigley, BA, MSc lectures in economics at the Ashcroft International Business School, Anglia Ruskin University, with special reference to macroeconomic modules such as monetary economics and international economics. Research interests include financial bubbles and football finance. Responsible for Chapters 9 and 10.

Jonathan Wilson, MA lectures in international marketing at the Ashcroft International Business School, Anglia Ruskin University. His research interests include UK/Chinese business-to-business relationships and he has presented papers at various international conferences including that of the Chinese Economic Association. He has also published in the *Asia Pacific Journal of Marketing and Logistics*. Responsible for Chapter 13.

We would also like to acknowledge the major contributor of George Carrol to Chapter 6. We have all been saddened by his untimely death.

Preface: using this book

This book is written for students beginning undergraduate or equivalent courses with an economics, business or management focus. It adopts a highly interactive approach throughout, seeking to engage students in a broad range of case study and self-check exercises and activities, rather than present unbroken stretches of text more suited to passive reading. The book will be relevant to a wide range of modules which emphasise the business environment and economic perspectives needed to understand the various functional and strategic areas of business and management, including the many debates and challenges to conventional theories and institutional structures stemming from the impacts and origins of the global 'credit crunch'. The key principles of microeconomics and macroeconomics are presented and applied to a wide variety of situations encountered by decision makers in the contemporary global economy. Detailed consideration is also given to the political, legal, demographic, socio-cultural, ethical and environmental dimensions which characterise the business environment in which decision makers must operate.

A wide variety of up-to-date case study materials, drawn from many business sectors, are presented and discussed in all chapters of the text. Although the UK provides the setting for some of the applied materials, the global contexts of business activity are extensively discussed, together with the regulatory and institutional environment facing national and international businesses. The contemporary debates on appropriate regulatory and supervisory environment and structures post 'credit crunch' are reviewed and assessed.

Students can find answers and responses to all the You try and Stop and think activities on pages 525–46. Students will also find a range of 'Assessment Practice' questions for each chapter on the companion website, together with outline answers and responses to all these questions. Additional exercises, activities and questions are also provided, to support the teaching process, in the accompanying Instructor's Manual (IM). Where core modules have large numbers of students and where many lecturers are involved in seminars/tutorials, a structured programme can be readily devised from these case study and test bank materials to assist overstretched teaching resources.

Although the distinction between micro and macro business environments is somewhat artificial, with the effective analysis of many issues requiring both micro and macro perspectives, Part I of the book contains eight chapters with a broadly micro business orientation and Part II a further six chapters with a broadly macro business orientation.

Each chapter concentrates on a particular topic area and begins with a set of learning objectives, which provide a useful guide to the chapter content, and concludes with a summary of the key points raised in the chapter and definitions of the key terms used. Other features related to each chapter include the following.

- You try and Stop and think. At different points in each chapter students will encounter a variety of these to self-check their understanding of the materials presented. Answers and responses to all these are to be found on pages 525–46.
- Case study materials. A number of carefully selected and up-to-date case studies are presented in all chapters, putting into practice many of the ideas encountered.

Questions are set at the end of each case study to guide students' thinking, and outline answers and responses are provided in the Instructor's Manual accompanying the text.

- **Assessment practice.** For each chapter you will find on the companion student website a structured set of multiple choice questions, data response and stimulus-based questions, matching pair and true/false questions, as well as essay-based questions. These will check your understanding of the materials presented throughout the chapter and give you valuable practice in preparing for examinations and assignments. Outline answers and responses are provided to all these questions in the companion student website.

- **Companion student website.** As already noted you can find extra questions and activities (with answers) on the companion student website, together with annotated weblinks and further up-to-date reading lists.

- **Companion lecturer website.** On this secure, password-protected website can be found an electronic downloadable version of the Instructor's Manual (IM) containing a wide range of additional teaching materials, extra case studies for download, a test bank of additional questions (with answers) which may be used for formative or summative assessment, PowerPoint slides for use in lectures are provided together with full solutions and responses to all Case Study questions in the text.

Acknowledgements

Authors' acknowledgements

Alan Griffiths and Stuart Wall are indebted to the colleagues who have contributed chapters to this title, namely Margaret O'Quigley (Chapters 9 and 10) and Jonathan Wilson (Chapter 13). We would also like to acknowledge the major contribution of George Carrol to Chapter 6 and we have all been saddened by his untimely death. All other chapters have been written by ourselves.

We would also like to acknowledge the major contribution to this title made by Eleanor Wall of the Ashcroft International Business School who has played a key role in developing our wide range of up-to-date case and website materials.

Publisher's acknowledgements

We are grateful to the following for permission to reproduce copyright material:

Figures

Figure 5.1 from Global Entrepreneurship Monitor: GEM 2006 Summary Results. State of SMEs and Entrepreneurship in Finland. Anglia Ruskin University, Oct 24th–25th 2007 Jukka Siltanen, ProAcademy/TAMK, TAMK University of Applied Sciences, p.11 Global Entrepreneurship Monitor, 2006; Figure 5.2 from Global Entrepreneurship Monitor, 2007 Global Report on High-Growth Entrepreneurship. State of SMEs and Entrepreneurship in Finland Anglia Ruskin University, Oct 24th–25th 2007 Jukka Siltanen, ProAcademy/ TAMK, TAMK University of Applied Sciences. p. 15 Global Entrepreneurship Monitor, 2007; Figure 8.2 from *Applied Economics*, 11 ed. Financial Times/Prentice Hall imprint published by Pearson Education (Griffiths, A., and Wall, S. 2007); Figure 12.2 adapted from *Motivation and Personality,* 3rd Edition, by permission of Pearson Education, Inc., Upper Saddle River, NJ (Maslow, Abraham H.; Frager, Robert D.; Fadiman, James,), Copyright 1987; Figure 13.4 adapted from *International Business,* 6th Edition, by permission of Pearson Education, Inc., Upper Saddle River, NJ (Griffin, Ricky W; Pustay, Michael), Copyright 2010, p. 104; Figure 14.1 adapted from *Strategic Management,* 11 ed., McGraw-Hill (Thompson, A., and Strickland A. 1999) The five tests of strategic management, reproduced with permission of The McGraw-Hill Companies.; Figure 14.2a from *Harvard Business Review,* Porter's generic strategies; Figure 14.2b from Strategies of diversification, *Harvard Business Review*, 25(5), 113–25 (Ansoff, H.I. 1957), The Harvard Business School Publishing Corporation. All rights reserved.; Figure 14.4 adapted with the permission of The Free Press, a Division of Simon & Schuster, Inc., from *Competitive Strategy* by Michael E. Porter. Copyright © 1998 by Michael E. Porter. All rights reserved.; Figure 14.5 from the Product Portfolio Matrix © 1970, The Boston Consulting Group; Figure 14.6 from *The Competitive Advantage of Nations*, Palgrave Macmillan (Porter, M., 1990); Figure 14.8 used with the permission of The Free Press, a Division of Simon & Schuster, Inc., from *Competitive Advantage: Creating and Sustaining Superior Performance* by Michael E. Porter. Copyright © 1985 by Michael E. Porter. All rights reserved.

Tables

Table on page 30 adapted from The World Factbook 2010, https://www.cia.gov/library/publications/the-world-factbook/index.html, Washington, DC: Central Intelligence Agency, 2010; Table 2.3 from *Principals of Economics*, 8 ed., Palgrave Macmillan (Marshall, A. 1920); Table 2.6 adapted from Gooding, P, 15/03/2010, Office of National Statistics (2010), Crown Copyright material is reproduced with permission under the terms of the Click-Use License; Table on page 113 adapted from UK Business: Activity, Size and Locations 2009. Office of National Statistics, Crown Copyright material is reproduced with permission under the terms of the Click-Use License; Table on page 122 from Primary Objectives in British Manufacturing, *Journal of Industrial Economics*, 29 (1981), Copyright 1981 Blackwell Publishing. Reproduced with permission of Blackwell Publishing Ltd.; Table 5.2 adapted from Enterprise Directorate (2010) SME Statistics for the UK and Regions, and European Commission (2009) Annual Report on EU Small- and Medium-Sized Enterprises, Crown Copyright material is reproduced with permission under the terms of the Click-Use License; Table 5.4 adapted from Enterprise Directorate (2010) SME Statistics (UK and Regions) Table 2a, Crown Copyright material is reproduced with permission under the terms of the Click-Use License; Table on page 214 from Low Pay Commission (2010) www.lowpay.gov.uk. Direct Gov. (2010) Newroom, March 25, Crown Copyright material is reproduced with permission under the terms of the Click-Use License; Table 7.2 adapted from Poor returns, winners and losers in the job market, *Equal Opportunities Commission, Working Paper Series*, 52 (Jones, P., and Dickerson, A. 2007); Table on page 250 adapted from Competition Commission 2006, 'Estimated costs to consumers of the mergers against which the CC took action between March 2005 and March 2006' Analysis: Evaluation Reports, July 9 (4 pp). http://www.competition-commission.org.uk/our_role/analysis/estimated_costs_to_consumers_of_the_mergers.pdf; Table 9.1 from Statistical Annex, *European Economy 2009*, Spring (2010), © European Union, 1995–2010; Table 9.2 adapted from Human Development Report (2009), UN; World Development Report (2010); Table on page 321 adapted from ONS (2009), The Effects of Taxes and Benefits on Household Income, Crown Copyright material is reproduced with permission under the terms of the Click-Use License; Table 10.1 from Treasury (2010) Budget Report; Table 10.2 from HM Treasury (2010) Budget Report 2010, Press notice 2, Crown Copyright material is reproduced with permission under the terms of the Click-Use License; Table 10.4 adapted from HM Treasury (2010) Budget in Graphics, March, Crown Copyright material is reproduced with permission under the terms of the Click-Use License; Table 10.5 from Gooding, P. 15/03/2010, ONS, Consumer Prices and Retails Prices index, 2010 Basket of Goods and Services, Crown Copyright material is reproduced with permission under the terms of the Click-Use License; Table 10.9 adapted from *UK Balance of Payments; The Pink Book 2009 edition*, ONS (2009), Crown Copyright material is reproduced with permission under the terms of the Click-Use License; Table 11.3 adapted from UK Patent Office, www.patent.gov.uk, Crown Copyright material is reproduced with permission under the terms of the Click-Use License; Table 13.5 from Distribution of IKEA sales, purchasing and workforce, 2009 (%) Inter IKEA Systems B.V. 2010, www.ikea.com

Text

Case Study 1.2 from 'Small cars, big question', www.economist.com, © The Economist Newspaper Ltd, London (21/01/2010); Case Study 4.1 from 'Britain should not fear foreign ownership', *Financial Times*, 22/02/2010 (Carlin, W. and Mayer, C.); Case Study 6.2 from Britain's Banking Market, 'A breath of fresh air', www.economist.com © The Economist Newspaper Ltd, London (08/04/2010); Case Study 6.3 from 'E-publish or perish', www.economist.com, © The Economist Newspaper Ltd, London (31/03/2010); Case Study 10.3 from Productivity growth, 'Slash and earn', www.economist.com © The

Economist Newspaper Ltd, London (18/03/2010); Case Study 11.5 adapted from Protecting creativity, 'Copyright and wrong', www.economist.com © The Economist Newspaper Ltd, London (08/04/2010); Case Study 12.1 from 'A better burger thanks to data crunching', *Financial Times*, 06/09/2007 (Matthews, R.); Case Study 13.3 adapted from Copyright Inter Ikea Systems B.V. 2010, www.idea.com

The Financial Times
Case Study 1.1 from Google takes networking fight to Facebook, *Financial Times*, 10/02/2010 (Waters, R.), © The Financial Times Ltd; Case Study 1.3 from Warning over battery bubble, *Financial Times*, 22/02/2010 (Reed, J.), © The Financial Times Ltd; Case Study 1.5 from Cotton at two-year peak after fall in China crop, *Financial Times*, 02/03/2010 (Meyer, G.), © The Financial Times Ltd; Case Study 1.8 from Food crisis amid call for 'green' reform, *Financial Times*, 10/02/2010 (Kazmin, A), © The Financial Times Ltd; Case Study 2.3 from Beijing considers pollution tax, *Financial Times*, 10/02/2010 (Harvey, F), © The Financial Times Ltd; Case Study 3.1 from Small oil explorers eye big role in North Sea, *Financial Times*, 08/03/2010 (Johnson, M.), © The Financial Times Ltd; Case Study 3.3 from Sony pulls ultra-thin TV in Japan after demand drops, *Financial Times*, 17/02/2010 (Harding, R.), © The Financial Times Ltd; Case Study 3.6 adapted from Seoul sleepwalk: Why an Asian export champion is at risk of losing its way, *Financial Times*, 19/03/2007 (Fifield, A.), © The Financial Times Ltd; Case Study 4.2 from RBS links new tougher pay schemes to bank's profits, *Financial Times*, 19/03/2010 (Goff, S. and Jones, A.), © The Financial Times Ltd; Case Study 4.3 from Drive to link pay to sustainability begins, *Financial Times*, 24/02/2010 (Milne, R), © The Financial Times Ltd; Case Study 5.4 from Premium car deal fills a hole at Geely, *Financial Times*, 29/03/2010 (Waldmeir, P.), © The Financial Times Ltd; Case Study 7.2 from DMS to link managers' pay with green credentials and staff morale, *Financial Times*, 24/02/2010 (Milne, R., and Steen, M), © The Financial Times Ltd; Case Study 7.4 from Daimler turns to temporary staff to boost flexibility, *Financial Times*, 15/03/2010 (Schafer, D), © The Financial Times Ltd; Case Study 8.3 from Businesses face emissions law shock, *Financial Times*, 05/03/2010 (Harvey, F.), © The Financial Times Ltd; Case Study 8.4 from Forced rhubarb gains recognition at last, *Financial Times*, 26/02/2010 (Bounds, A.), © The Financial Times Ltd; Case Study 8.6 from RBS fined for $28m for sharing price data, *Financial Times*, 31/03/2010 (Peel, M., and Goff, S.), © The Financial Times Ltd; Case Study 10.4 from Weak pound boost UK shares, *Financial Times*, 06/03/2010 (Kelleher, E.), © The Financial Times Ltd; Case Study 10.6 from Risk needs a human touch but models hold the whip hand, *Financial Times*, 23/01/2009 (Davies, P.), © The Financial Times Ltd; Figure 10.15 from SIV managers dig out their manuals, *Financial Times*, 30/08/2007 (Davies, P.), © The Financial Times Ltd; Activity 11.2 from Sugar beet sweetens India's output prospects, *Financial Times*, 20/08/2007 (Leahy, J.), © The Financial Times Ltd; Case Study 11.4 from Kettle company wins damages in China, *Financial Times*, 01/02/2010 (Mitchell, T), © The Financial Times Ltd; Case Study 11.6 from Beijing considers pollution tax, *Financial Times*, 10/02/2010 (Harvey, F.), © The Financial Times Ltd; Case Study 11.7 adapted from OECD slams biofuels subsidies for sparking food inflation price, *Financial Times*, 11/09/2007 (Bounds, A.), © The Financial Times Ltd; Case Study 11.8 from Games guru puts his finger on chart success, *Financial Times*, 22/12/2009 (Menn, J), © The Financial Times Ltd; Case Study 12.2 from Asos founder turns to online homeware, *Financial Times*, 28/06/2010 (Kuchler, H), © The Financial Times Ltd.; Case Study 12.4 from A different way of working, *Financial Times*, 23/03/2010 (Maitland, A.), © The Financial Times Ltd; Case Study 12.5 from Fooled again, *Financial Times*, 19/03/2010 (Hughes, J.), © The Financial Times Ltd; Case Study on page 450 from China's wary shoppers set store by Western brands, *Financial Times*, 04/09/2010 (Dyer, G.), © The Financial Times Ltd; Case Study 13.4

from Perils of blundering into India's cultural minefield, *Financial Times*, 19/03/2010 (Kazmin, A.), © The Financial Times Ltd.; Case Study 13.5 from Chinese headset groups look to India, *Financial Times*, 17/02/2010 (Hille, K.), © The Financial Times Ltd; Case Study 13.7 from Mandelson warns on hidden cost of anti-dumping tariffs, *Financial Times*, 04/09/2007 (Bounds, A.), © The Financial Times Ltd; Case Study 14.2 from An Empire Built on a Flat-Pack, *Financial Times*, 24/11/2003, 12 (Brown-Humes, C.), © The Financial Times Ltd.; Case Study 14.3 adapted from Korean shipbuilders struggle to keep Chinese in their wake, *Financial Times*, 27/07/2007 (Fifield, A.), © The Financial Times Ltd.

In some instances we have been unable to trace the owners of copyright material, and we would appreciate any information that would enable us to do so.

Part I

MICRO BUSINESS ENVIRONMENT

Markets and resource allocation

Introduction

Why has Facebook, the social networking website, more than doubled its membership in just one year, from 200 million in April 2009 to over 400 million in April 2010 and for the first time recorded more internet visits to its website than the search engine Google? To understand how the market for social networking (or any other market) operates you must study the contents of this chapter which looks at the role of demand and supply in determining prices and outputs. Prices give vital signals to both buyers and sellers and play a key role in the allocation of resources, including factor inputs such as land, labour and capital required in production.

What you'll learn

By the end of this chapter you should be able to:

- outline key ideas such as scarcity, choice and opportunity cost
- explain the reasons for movements along and shifts in a demand curve
- explain the reasons for movements along and shifts in a supply curve
- show how demand and supply curves determine price in a market
- examine the role of price in allocating resources
- review the allocation of resources under different types of economic system.

Chapters 2 and 3 will go on to consider the behaviour of consumers and producers in rather more detail.

Wants, limited resources and choice

A problem facing all consumers is that while our wants (desires) may be unlimited, our means (resources) to satisfy those wants are limited, with the result that we must choose between the various alternatives. For example, this year we might want to buy a second-hand ('starter') car and have a holiday overseas but our limited income may force us to choose between these two alternatives. If we choose the car, then we forgo the holiday, or vice versa. The 'next best alternative forgone' is referred to as the opportunity cost of our choice.

This central problem of scarcity, which then results in choice, is not confined to consumers. Producers must also choose how to allocate their scarce resources of raw materials, labour, capital equipment and land between the different outputs that these resources can produce.

Production possibility curve

Figure 1.1 usefully illustrates this situation with a small recording studio having the capacity to produce a certain number of *albums* per year (OA) if all its resources are fully used. However, if it used all its capacity for *singles* instead, then rather more can be produced per year (OS). Of course, it might choose to produce both albums and singles, the various possibilities being shown by the curve AS. We call AS the production possibility curve (or frontier) and consider its precise shape in Chapter 3 (p. 76). If the recording studio chooses to be at point R on the curve, then it is seeking to produce OA_1 albums and OS_1 singles per year. You try 1.1 gives you some practice in using the production possibility curve.

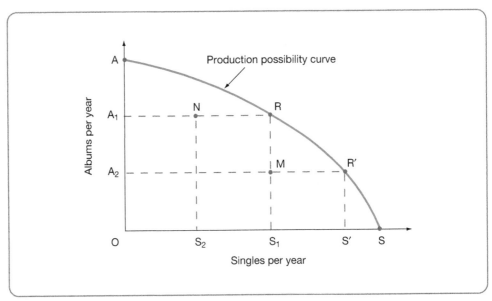

Figure 1.1 The production possibility curve

Demand curves and functions

Demand is the amount of a product (good or service) consumers are willing and able to purchase at a given price. Demand is a *flow* concept, relating quantity to time (e.g. CDs per month). The term 'effective demand' indicates that there is not just a desire to purchase, but desire supported by the means of purchase. For example, I might desire to purchase a private aeroplane, but unless I have the income to support that potential purchase it is not an 'effective demand', just wishful thinking.

Make a note From this point onwards, whenever we use the term 'demand' we shall mean 'effective demand'.

Demand curve

The **demand curve** in Figure 1.2(a) is a visual representation of how much of the product consumers are willing and able to purchase at different prices. The demand curve (D) slopes downwards from left to right, suggesting that when the price of X falls, more of product X is demanded, but when the price of X rises, less of product X is demanded. Of course, we are assuming that only the price of the product changes, sometimes called the *ceteris paribus* (other things equal) assumption. In this case changes in the price of the product will result in *movements along* the demand curve, either an *expansion* (movement down and to the right) or a *contraction* (movement up and to the left).

For example, suppose in Figure 1.2(a) product X is CDs. If the price of CDs falls from P_1 to P_2, the demand for CDs will *expand* from Q_1 to Q_2 (other things equal) because CDs will now be cheaper than other substitutes in consumption (e.g. cassettes, mini disks, vinyl records etc.). We can expect some individuals to switch towards CDs and away from these now relatively more expensive **substitutes in consumption**. Even if the alternative to purchasing the CD is downloading 'free' music from the Internet, rather than one of these

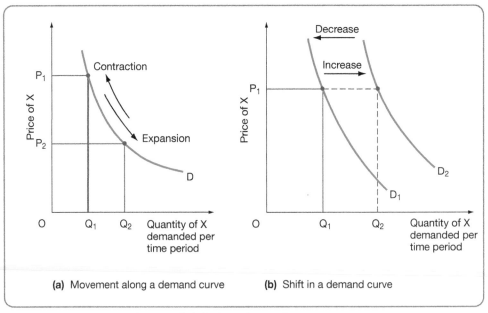

(a) Movement along a demand curve   **(b)** Shift in a demand curve

Figure 1.2 **Movements along and shifts in a demand curve**

Check the net

You can find more information on the music industry at websites such as:

www.emimusic.com
www.virginrecords.com

other substitutes in consumption, the time and effort required to download various tracks can now be set against a cheaper CD, and some consumers may choose to purchase the now lower-priced CD.

If the price of CDs rises from P_2 to P_1 then, for the opposite reasons, we can expect the demand for CDs to *contract* from Q_2 to Q_1 (other things equal).

Conditions of demand

Of course, other things may not remain equal! This brings us to the **conditions of demand** which refer to the factors that cause the demand curve for product X to *shift* either to the right or to the left.

In Figure 1.2(b):

- A shift to the right from D_1 to D_2 (*increase*) means more of product X is demanded at any given price. For example, at price P_1 demand increases from Q_1 to Q_2.
- A shift to the left from D_2 to D_1 (*decrease*) means less of product X is demanded at any given price. For example, at price P_1 demand decreases from Q_2 to Q_1.

Make a note

It is really important that you try to use the correct terms to distinguish between *movements along* a demand curve (expansion/contraction) and *shifts in* a demand curve (increase/decrease). Otherwise it is easy to confuse the two.

Variables within the 'conditions of demand' include the price of other products (P_o), the real income of households (Y), the tastes of households (T), advertising expenditure on product X and so on.

To understand more about these 'conditions of demand' it will help if you are familiar with a number of terms.

Useful terminology in demand analysis

- *Substitutes in consumption.* Used when two (or more) products are seen by consumers as alternatives, possessing broadly similar characteristics, e.g. different brands of washing powder are substitutes in consumption.

- *Complements in consumption.* Used when two (or more) products are seen by consumers as fitting together, in the sense that purchasing one product will usually involve purchasing the other(s). Personal computers and printers are obvious examples of complements in consumption, as are tennis rackets and tennis balls.

- *Real income* refers to the actual purchasing power of the consumers. If money income doubles but average prices also double, then the consumer will only be able to purchase the same as before, so that real income will be unchanged. However, if money income rises by a larger percentage than average prices, then the consumer can actually purchase more than before, so real income has risen.

- *Normal products* (often called normal goods) refer to goods or services for which demand tends to consistently increase (shift to the right) as the real income of the consumer rises, and decrease (shift to the left) as the real income of the consumer falls. Most products come under this heading, with some products tending to be more responsive to changes in real income than others. For example, as real incomes increase, the demand for education, for health services, for travel and for tourism all tend to increase quite sharply.

- *Inferior products* (or inferior goods) refer to goods or services which are cheaper but poorer quality substitutes for other goods or services. As a result, consumer demand for the inferior product may at first increase as real income rises, as this is all that can be afforded, but as real income continues to rise then the more expensive but better quality substitute may eventually come within the purchasing power of the consumer. The consumer may now switch away from the inferior product with further rises in real income, so that demand for the inferior product decreases (shifts to the left). Cheaper but poorer quality butter, margarine and coffee products are possible examples of inferior products.

Links

This brings into play the idea of *income elasticity of demand* – see Chapter 2, p. 55.

Examples

Substitutes and complements in beverage consumption

- Nintendo Wii, Microsoft Xbox 360 and Sony PlayStation 3 are gaming consoles which are *substitutes in consumption*. During 2009/10 Sony's PlayStation 3 increased global sales by 22% after a price cut (movement along the demand curve), capturing market share from the other consoles. Mobile, web-based and second-hand games are substitutes for all the consoles mentioned above, and during 2009 increasing numbers of people used these, rather than consoles, for their games.

- Video games are *complements in consumption,* in that new and attractive video games will result in more people playing these games and requiring more consoles (and other media devices) on which to play them. In 2009 the biggest hit was *Modern Warfare 2* which became the fastest selling video game ever, with 7 million copies sold on the first day of its release in November 2009.

Taking it further 1.1 gives you some practice in applying these various 'conditions of demand' to a situation involving an *increase* in demand.

Taking it further **Variables causing an increase in demand**   1.1

Here we consider briefly the major variables that might cause an *increase in demand* for a good or service. For simplicity we consider an increase in the demand for oranges, but we could apply the same reasoning to any other good or service.

- *A rise in the price of a substitute in consumption.* Substitutes for oranges might be apples, bananas or pears. If any of these substitutes rise in price, then oranges become more attractive to the household. At any given price the household can be expected to buy more oranges and less of the substitutes, so that the whole demand curve for oranges shifts bodily to the right, from D_1 to D_2 in Figure 1.2(b).

- *A fall in the price of a complement in consumption.* Suppose our household buys oranges mainly for making (sweetened) orange squash or marmalade, so that it buys sugar whenever it buys oranges. We would then say that oranges and sugar are complements in consumption for this household, i.e. products that are bought together. A fall in the price of sugar, the complement, might encourage our household to buy more oranges at any given price, since both orange squash and marmalade would now be cheaper to make. Again the whole demand curve for oranges would shift bodily to the right, from D_1 to D_2 in Figure 1.2(b).

- *A rise in income.* Most products are what economists refer to as normal goods, i.e. more is bought when income rises. It is quite likely that oranges would come into this category. A rise in income would cause the demand curve for oranges to shift bodily to the right, from D_1 to D_2 in Figure 1.2(b).

- *A change in tastes of the household in favour of oranges.* If the tastes of the household altered so that it now preferred oranges to other types of fruit, this would shift the demand curve for oranges from D_1 to D_2 in Figure 1.2(b), with more oranges bought at any given price.

- *A rise in advertising expenditure on oranges.* Suppose the 'orange growers' federation' or a major orange grower (e.g. Outspan oranges) undertakes an advertising campaign stressing the health and other benefits of eating oranges. The extra advertising may influence consumer perceptions and tastes in favour of oranges, shifting the demand curve for oranges to the right from D_1 to D_2 in Figure 1.2(b).

Stop and think   1.1

Now write down the variables that might cause a *decrease in demand* for oranges, i.e. a *leftward* shift in the demand curve.

Answers can be found on pp. 525–546.

Case Study 1.1 examines attempts by Google to *increase* the demand curve for its social networking services, i.e. shift the demand curve to the right.

Case Study 1.1   **Google takes networking fight to Facebook**   **FT**

Google has mounted its most ambitious assault on the booming social networking business in an attempt to win back ground lost to fast-growing Facebook. The group is seeking to use its core search engine technology to sift the flood of social media and filter out distracting or irrelevant information for users of Google Buzz, its latest service. 'We will have access to those things you're interested in, those posts you read,' said Sergey Brin, co-founder. 'We think we'll be able to make those things useful to you.' The launch of Buzz follows a series of unsuccessful attempts to

Case Study 1.1 *continued*

strengthen its foothold in social networking, including a service called Orkut, which pre-dated Facebook and a Twitter-like service known as Jaiku.

As Google has fallen behind, Facebook has in the past year become the first place to which many internet users turn to find information or communicate with their friends. The leading social network site has more than 400m users.

In a change of tack, Google said it would apply some of its core assets to the fightback. It would not only deploy search algorithms, but also integrate Buzz closely with Gmail, its web-based e-mail service, so it would be possible to see friends add comments to a post in real time from inside an e-mail.

Gmail had 176m monthly unique users at the end of last year, according to ComScore. Google also showed off ways to use Buzz from a smartphone, taking advantage of advanced features of its Android mobile software, such as voice recognition

for dictating messages. At first, Google said it would ask users to comment on items which they found interesting on Buzz and use these to learn about their interests and refine how information is presented. Mr Brin said the company would eventually have access to much more information and use this to improve the service.

Google employees have used Buzz for the past six months, and executives singled out its potential as a tool for business users rather than just for entertainment and talking to friends.

Source: from Google takes networking fight to Facebook, *Financial Times*, 10/02/2010 (Waters, R.), © The Financial Times Ltd

Questions

1 Which variables in the 'conditions of demand' are being targeted by Google in seeking to increase the demand for its social networking services?

2 What other variables might Google seek to target in order to increase demand?

Demand function

It will be useful at this stage to introduce *all* the variables that might be involved in movements along the demand curve or in shifting the demand curve to the right or left. This is what the **demand function** does by expressing the relationship between the quantity of product X demanded per unit of time (Q_x) and a number of possible variables. These include the own price of product X (P_x), and a number of other variables known collectively as the 'conditions of demand'.

The demand function is often shown as a shorthand expression:

$$Q_x = F(P_x, P_o, Y, T, A_x \ldots)$$

This can be read as meaning that the quantity demanded of product X (Q_x) *depends upon* its own price (P_x), the price of other products (P_o), real household income (Y), household tastes (T), advertising expenditure on product X (A_x) and so on.

Make a note

- Any change in the product's own price P_x (other things equal) will result in a *movement along* a demand curve.
- Any change in a variable within the 'conditions of demand' will cause a *shift* in a demand curve.

Case Study 1.2 will help you to apply the ideas of movement along and shifts in a demand curve to an actual market situation involving the car industry.

Case Study 1.2   Small cars, big question

Detroit's annual motor show provides a good indication of the state of America's car industry. In January 2009 the industry grappled with its biggest crisis in living memory and at least two of Detroit's Big Three carmakers were on the brink of collapse, and the usual razzmatazz was replaced by fear and foreboding. In 2010 hope had returned, but accompanied by deep uncertainty.

Hope, because both Ford, which avoided bankruptcy, and General Motors, which did not, had attractive new vehicles on display amid signs that the market is picking up, and could reach sales of 12m vehicles in America in 2010. Uncertainty, because the vehicles on which Detroit is pinning its future, and which dominated the show, are smallish cars of the kind that have long been the bedrock of the European market, but which Americans have always regarded as poor man's vehicles.

There are several reasons for Detroit's conversion to small cars. The biggest is the pressure that every big carmaker is under to meet increasingly tough rules on fuel economy and emissions. In the middle of 2009 Barack Obama announced that the new 35mpg CARE (corporate average fuel economy) standard would come into force in 2016 rather than 2020. Instead of protesting noisily, as in the past, Detroit praised his wisdom. With their survival dependent on federal bail-out funds, BM and Chrysler had little choice other than to grin and nod, but Ford was just as keen. All three had been badly burned by the near doubling of petrol prices in 2008 and were convinced that even though petrol was cheap again, a business model built on it staying that way was broken.

That led to another inescapable conclusion. Although some Americans will refuse to be parted from their pickup trucks and muscle cars, catering to American automotive tastes was no longer an option. The new CARE standard meant that cars would have to be hitting 42 mpg (26 mpg for trucks) in less time that it typically takes to develop new car models. The carmakers would have no choice but to try to sell to Americans the cars developed for Europe and Asia. Furthermore, only by using the same platforms all over the world could the carmakers begin to compensate for the loss of the fat profits that used to come from selling big vehicles.

That is why Ford's chief executive, Alan Mulally, set out in early 2007, controversially at the time, to remake the firm around his 'One Ford' global design and development strategy. That is also why GM belatedly realised that selling its European arm, Opel-Vauxhall, would have been a fatal error and stopped the proposed deal just in time! And that is why the idea of Fiat saving Chrysler is not as crazy as it first seemed. But the question which nobody can yet answer is whether Americans will pay enough for smaller cars to make them even modestly profitable.

The first company to find out will be Ford. Having just won both the North American car and truck of the year awards with, respectively, the Fusion Hybrid and the Transit Connect van, it unveiled the star of the Detroit show, the new Focus. It is a handsome and technology-laden compact car that will be sold (and made) in a very big world market from next year with only small tweaks to suit local conditions and tastes.

However, whereas the Focus that Ford currently sells in America for around $20,000 is a stripped-down version of a car that was replaced in Europe five years ago, the new Focus will have to sell in the US and elsewhere for prices closer to the much higher prices that Europeans are accustomed to paying if it is to make a profit for Ford. That suggests a US price of at least $30,000 before taxes for a mid-range version.

Well before the Focus hits the market, Ford will launch the new Fiesta in America this summer. This slickly styled smaller car has been a top seller in Europe since late 2008. There is a lot riding on the Fiesta, not just for Ford, but for the whole industry. Jim Farley, the marketing guru Ford poached from Toyota, has been planning its launch for nearly two years. Mr Farley has used social media and viral marketing techniques to generate excitement and name recognition. But even he does not believe Ford will be able to sell the Fiesta in the US for anything like the kind of prices – €17,250 ($24,700) for the top-of-the-range versions that accounted for 30% of sales last year – that Europeans are willing to pay.

The Fiesta may set new class standards for refinement and handling, but it is still a small car. Ford will offer the Fiesta in the US from about $14,000 for the basic version to around $20,000 with all the extras – around the same prices Honda charges for the Fit, a capable but less dynamically accomplished smaller car. At those prices, Ford will struggle to make much profit even if buyers choose lots of extras.

Case Study 1.2 *continued*

Ford is on a roll thanks to its improving product quality and the halo effect of having avoided bankruptcy. But the Ford brand is still best-known for rugged F-150 pickup trucks and hulking SUVs. Critically, it is far from certain whether Ford's dealers will even know how to sell such a smaller car.

A wave of great small cars is about to hit the forecourts of American dealers – none better than the European-developed cars that Ford will be offering. The big question now is whether Americans can be persuaded to pay enough for them to give the industry a viable future.

Source: Small cars big question, www.economist.com,
© The Economist Newspaper Ltd, London (21/01/2010)

Questions

1 In the market for small cars, what evidence is there for a 'movement along' the demand curve?

2 Can you find any evidence for a 'shift' in the demand curve for small cars? Identify the variables in the 'conditions of demand' that might be involved here.

3 Use the case study and your own knowledge to identify:

(a) reasons for both Ford and General Motors being confident about the future of smaller cars;

(b) reasons for both Ford and General Motors being concerned about the future of smaller cars.

Our demand function may contain a number of variables which are often omitted from standard textbook presentations. Here we consider three such variables, technology, advertising and credit.

Technology (T_n)

Although, as we shall see, *new technology* is more often associated with shifts in supply, it can also bring about shifts in demand.

Example

Technology and shifts in demand

Teenagers are using Internet technology to instantly message their friends with their verdict on new films – even as they are watching them, often contradicting expensive promotional claims for the blockbusters. Whereas, a few years ago, the average audience drop-off between a film's opening weekend and its second weekend was 40%, today that drop-off is over 55%, with the movie moguls blaming the technology of hand-held text message devices.

Advertising (A_x, A_s, A_c)

Advertising expenditure on product X itself (A_x), on a substitute in consumption for X (A_s) and/or a complement in consumption for X (A_c) may all contribute to a shift in the demand curve for product X. As we see in Chapter 6, advertising expenditure is particularly important in oligopoly markets dominated by a few large firms, each seeking to differentiate its product offerings from those of its rivals.

Example

Advertising and shifts in demand

Innovative advertising campaigns are using location-specific information on the whereabouts of individuals to sell products linked to these locations. Google launched a service called 'Latitude' in 2009 that allows friends to track one another's movements and Buzz, its recently launched social networking service, also allows users to tag messages with information about their location. Local service providers can, for example, use such location specific information to target the promotion of their products to specific individuals via ads on their mobiles. A forecast in 2010 by Juniper Research predicts that global revenues from location-based advertising could soar to $12.7 billion by 2014, up from $3 billion in 2009.

Links

We consider the idea of advertising elasticity of demand in Chapter 2, p. 57.

Of course, if those producing *substitutes* for your product spend more on their advertising (A_S), then the demand curve for X may shift to the left (decrease). However, if those producing *complements* for your product X spend more on their advertising (A_C), then the demand curve for X may shift to the right (increase).

Credit availability (C_A) and price (C_P)

Two important but often neglected variables can exert an important influence on the demand for a product, namely the availability of credit (C_A) and price of credit (C_P). This is especially important in countries such as the UK, where there is a substantial 'debt over-hang'; for example, the value of personal and business borrowing in the UK in 2010 is higher than the gross national product of the country. This means that any reduction in access to credit or any increase in the cost of securing such credit will have a major impact on the ability of individuals and businesses to pay off their debt and to continue to spend.

Example

Scarce and expensive credit!

In the period 2008–10, banks in the UK and US saw the value of the assets they held fall by over 30%, due to the loss of investor confidence in securities linked to the 'sub-prime' property market (see Chapter 9, p. 285). This loss of capital value signif-icantly reduced the ability of banks to lend to customers, as any extra monies were used by the banks to restore their capital (asset value) base, rather than lend to busi-nesses. Even when such lending did occur it was usually at higher interest rates. For example, the IMF pointed out that the average interest rate charged to borrowers in the UK and US in the period since 2008 is 1.5% higher than in the period before the 'credit crunch' of 2008 for borrowers with the same credit rating.

This reduction in the availability of credit and increase in the cost of credit will result in a leftward shift (decrease) in the demand curves for a whole range of products, and especially those with high income elasticities of demand (see Chapter 2, p. 55).

You try 1.2 will help to check your understanding of movements along and shifts in a demand curve.

You try 1.2

1 Look carefully at Figure 1.3.

We start at price P_1 with quantity Q_1 of product X demanded on demand curve D_1. Select 'True' or 'False' for each of the following statements.

(a) A move from point A to B represents an expansion of demand. True/False

(b) A move from point A to C represents an increase of demand. True/False

(c) A move from point C to A represents an increase of demand. True/False

(d) A move from point B to A represents a decrease of demand. True/False

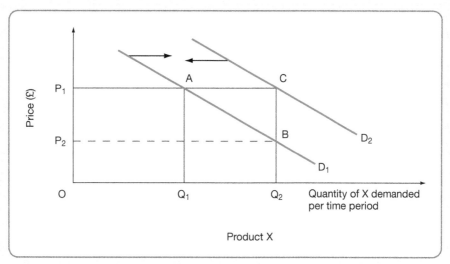

Figure 1.3

2 This question checks your understanding of the variables in the 'conditions of demand' which can shift the demand curve to the right (increase) or to the left (decrease).

For an *increase in demand*, insert letter I.

For a *decrease in demand*, insert letter D.

Changes in variable	Letter (I or D)
Rise in real income (for a normal good)	
Fall in price of a substitute in consumption	
Fall in price of a complement in consumption	
Change of tastes in favour of the product	
Fall in real income (for a normal good)	
Rise in price of a substitute in consumption	
Rise in price of a complement in consumption	
Change of tastes against the product	

3 This question checks your understanding of *normal goods* and *inferior goods* and of *substitutes in consumption* and *complements in consumption*, all of which often appear in discussions about demand.

(a) The demand for a normal good will always increase as real incomes rise and decrease as real incomes fall.   True/False

(b) An inferior good is often a cheap but poor quality substitute for some other good.   True/False

(c) A complement in consumption refers to a product that is a rival to another product.   True/False

(d) The demand for an inferior good may increase at first as real incomes rise but may decrease as real incomes rise beyond a certain level.   True/False

(e) A substitute in consumption refers to a product that is consumed jointly with another product.   True/False

Answers can be found on pp. 525–546.

Supply curves and functions

The **supply curve** in Figure 1.4(a) is a visual representation of how much of the product sellers are willing and able to supply at different prices. The supply curve slopes upwards from left to right, suggesting that at a higher price more will be supplied, and at a lower price less will be supplied.

For example, suppose product X is CDs, if the price of CDs rises from P_1 to P_2, the supply of CDs will *expand* from Q_1 to Q_2 (other things equal) because producers of CDs will now be making higher profits and so will have both the incentive and the ability to buy in the extra resources to raise output.

If the price of CDs falls from P_2 to P_1 then, for the opposite reasons, we can expect the supply of CDs to *contract* from Q_2 to Q_1 (other things equal).

Changes in the price of the product will (other things equal) result in *movements along* the supply curve, either an *expansion* (movement up and to the right) or a *contraction* (movement down and to the left).

Conditions of supply

Of course, other things may not remain equal! This brings us to the **conditions of supply** which refer to the factors that cause the supply curve for product X to *shift* either to the right or to the left.

In Figure 1.4(b):

- A shift to the right from S_1 to S_2 (*increase*) means more of product X is supplied at any given price. For example, at price P_1 supply *increases* from Q_1 to Q_2.
- A shift to the left from S_2 to S_1 (*decrease*) means less of product X is supplied at any given price. For example, at price P_1 supply *decreases* from Q_2 to Q_1.

Variables within the 'conditions of supply' include the price of other products (P_o), the costs of production (C), tax rates (T_x), tastes of producers (T_p) and so on.

To understand more about these 'conditions of supply' it will help if you are familiar with a number of terms.

Useful terminology in supply analysis

- *Substitutes in production.* Used when another product (O) could have been produced with the *same resources* (land, labour, capital, raw materials, etc.) as those used for

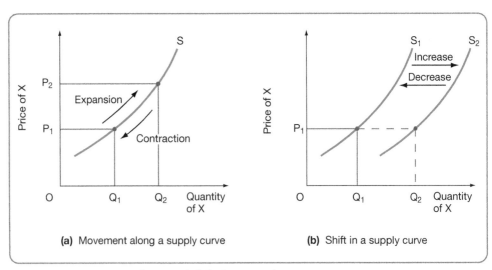

(a) Movement along a supply curve   (b) Shift in a supply curve

Figure 1.4 **Movements along and shifts in a supply curve**

product X. Suppose product X is wheat, then barley, rye and rape seed are other agricultural products that need similar types of soil, climate and other factor inputs and so can be regarded as **substitutes in production** for wheat.

- *Complements in production.* Used when the process of production for X yields a by-product. In producing mutton or lamb (X) the fleece of the sheep also yields wool (O), which can be regarded as a by-product for X. These **complements in production** are also known as *jointly supplied products.*

- *Lump-sum tax* is a tax of a constant absolute amount per unit, e.g. £1 a unit.

- *Ad valorem tax* is a tax which varies in absolute amount at different prices. A percentage tax such as VAT is an ad valorem tax as 20% of a higher price will give a greater absolute amount in tax revenue.

Examples

Substitutes and complements in sports-wear production

- Nike faced a crucial decision in 1987, namely whether to continue allocating its finance, factory and warehousing space, labour, raw materials and sales resources across a wide range of athletic and non-athletic shoes (*substitutes in production*) or whether to focus all its limited resources on the then newly developed air-technology sports trainer. It chose the latter and its *Air Max* sports shoes catapulted Nike into market leadership of the sports trainer industry.

- Some of the moulds used by Reebok in producing more tennis shoes can also be used for producing more generalised leisure footwear (*complements in production*).

Taking it further 1.2 gives you some practice in applying these various 'conditions of supply' to a situation involving an *increase* in supply.

Taking it further **Variables causing an increase in supply**   1.2

Let us consider briefly what might cause an *increase in supply* of product X, i.e. a shift in the supply curve for X from S_1 to S_2 in Figure 1.4(b) on p. 14. Here we take product X to be wheat, though the idea can be applied to any good or service.

- *A fall in the price of a substitute in production.* If barley, rye or rape seed (O) falls in price, then wheat (X) becomes relatively more attractive, and the farmer may choose to grow wheat on land previously used to grow these other products, so that more wheat is supplied at the given price, P_1.

- *A rise in the price of a complement in production.* When wheat (X) is harvested the grain is separated from the dried stalks, which are known as straw (O). The combine harvester threshes and bags the grain as it is cut, leaving the straw behind in the field. Straw is clearly a by-product (complement) of wheat production, and has many uses. It can be used as bedding or fodder for animals, and manure (fertiliser). If straw (O) rises in price, so that the farmer can sell it for more profit, then this might even encourage him to grow more wheat (X). In other words, a rise in the price of the complement in production (straw) may lead to an increase in the supply of wheat (X), more wheat being supplied at each and every price.

- *A fall in the costs of production.* A fall in the costs of production of wheat could lead to an increase in the supply of wheat. You can think of this in either of two ways: at *any given price* the farmer will now be able to supply more wheat (A to B in Figure 1.5, p. 19), or *any given quantity* of wheat can now be supplied at a lower price (A to C in Figure 1.5, p. 19). In other words, a *rightward* shift of the supply curve is the same as a *downward* shift of the supply curve. In both cases supply increases.

- *Changes in the tastes of producers in favour of X.* The farmer may now *prefer* to produce wheat rather than to engage in other types of farming. We call this a change of the producer's tastes in favour of wheat.

Taking it further 1.2 continued

- *Tax reductions.* Taxes have an effect on supply. When the government removes or reduces a tax on a good, this has exactly the same effect as a fall in the costs of production. A tax cut on products therefore increases supply, i.e. shifts the supply curve from S_1 to S_2 in Figure 1.5, p. 19.

- *Subsidies.* A subsidy has exactly the same effect as a tax cut. It will tend to increase supply, i.e. shift the supply curve from S_1 to S_2 in Figure 1.5, p. 19. This is because a subsidy of, say, 5% has the same effect as a 5% reduction in costs of production.

- *Favourable weather conditions.* For most agricultural commodities the weather might have a major influence on supply. Favourable weather conditions will produce a bumper harvest and will tend to increase the supply of wheat.

Stop and think   1.2

Now write down the factors that might cause a *decrease* in supply of wheat, i.e. a *leftward* shift in the supply curve.

Case Study 1.3 examines attempts by governments and businesses to increase the supply of special batteries to power the expected rapid growth in electric and hybrid (electric and petrol) cars.

| Case Study 1.3 | Warning over battery bubble | FT |

A costly technology bubble is forming around the lithium-ion batteries that will power a forthcoming wave of electric and rechargeable hybrid cars, a leading industry consultancy warned. Battery producers now building factories in the US, Asia and Europe – some with generous government subsidies – will by 2015 'conservatively' end up with twice the capacity they need to supply plug-in cars, said Roland Berger Strategy Consultants. The capacity glut will result in a shake-out of battery producers, according to the group, which claims that just six to eight of the 20 or so global players will survive the next five to seven years.

It warned of 'massive investment risks'. 'It's a little bit like some of the internet hype,' said Wolfgang Bernhart, a partner with Roland Berger, who wrote the report. 'At the end of the day, there will be only a few companies that can make it.' An oversupply of battery facilities would mirror the chronic problems of underused plants among carmakers themselves, exposing the newly developed car battery industry to the same downward pressure on prices and profits as their car producing customers. The research contrasts with many analysts' bullishness about the battery industry, which Deutsche Bank recently forecast could have sales worth $66bn by 2020.

Many battery producers' share prices have surged over the past year on expectations that they would grow rapidly and struggle to keep up with demand. It will add further to the uncertainty surrounding plug-in cars among carmakers developing them during a severe industry downturn and governments that have devoted huge sums to vehicle electrification.

In the US, President Barack Obama's administration in 2009 set aside $2bn of stimulus money for the development of advanced batteries. In Europe, Britain and Portugal have offered Nissan large loans and grants for battery plants to supply its forthcoming Leaf electric car. The US and Europe have also encouraged their carmakers to develop more plug-in models by favouring low emission technology in the billions of dollars of low-interest loans extended to the sector since the crisis began in late 2008. All of the world's big carmakers, including BMW, Daimler, PSA Peugeot Citroen, Toyota, Honda, General Motors and Ford Motor, plan to launch electric or rechargeable cars this decade, in spite of uncertainty about demand.

Source: from Warning over battery bubble, *Financial Times*, 22/02/2010 (Reed, J.), © The Financial Times Ltd

Case Study 1.3 *continued*

Questions

1 Which variables in the 'conditions of supply' are being targeted by those seeking to increase the supply of lithium-ion batteries?

2 What other variables might government target in order to increase supply?

3 Why is there concern that such policies aimed at increasing supply may be inappropriate?

Supply function

It will be useful at this stage to introduce *all* the variables that might be involved in movements along the supply curve or in shifting the supply curve to the right or left. This is what the **supply function** does by expressing the relationship between the quantity of product X supplied per unit of time (Q_x) and a number of possible variables. These include the own price of product X (P_x), and a number of other variables known collectively as the 'conditions of supply'.

The supply function is often shown as a shorthand expression:

$$Q_x = F(P_x, P_o, C, T_n, T_x, T_p \ldots)$$

This can be read as meaning that the quantity supplied of product X (Q_x) *depends upon* its own price (P_x), the price of other products (P_o), costs of production (C), technology (T_n), tax rates (T_x), tastes of producers (T_p) and so on.

Make a note

- Any change in the product's own price P_x (other things equal) will result in a *movement along* a supply curve.
- Any change in a variable within the 'conditions of supply' will cause a *shift* in a supply curve.

Case Study 1.4 uses an actual example involving Dyson, the well-known producer of vacuum cleaners, hand dryers and other innovative products, to consider further some of these supply-related issues.

Case Study 1.4   ## Dyson relocates production to South East Asia

In October 2009 Dyson launched yet another innovative product, its 'Air Multiplier Fan', the first desktop cooling fan without airblades. This followed its hugely successful launch of the 'Dyson Airblade' in 2006, the first hygienic hand dryer, which is 83% more energy efficient that its competitors. In the same year the Dyson dual cyclone bagless cleaner had outsold Hoover in terms of sales value in its own US 'backyard', despite Hoover being a household name in vacuum cleaner production since 1908. Dyson is now the US market leader, with around 21% of the US cleaner market, ahead of Hoover's 16%. Although Hoover sells more vacuum cleaners by volume the higher technology Dyson cleaners command a premium price, giving greater sales value from lower volume sales. James Dyson points to some key decisions several years earlier as the foundation for this success.

Despite these innovative success stories Dyson, like most dynamic companies, has felt compelled to continually review the global supply chain location of its various manufacturing, administrative and research and development activities. In fact in 2006 Dyson had announced that it was moving production of its washing machines from the UK to Malaysia, which followed its earlier decision in 2002 to shift production of its revolutionary dual cyclone bagless vacuum cleaner to Malaysia with the loss of over 800 jobs at the Dyson factory in

Case Study 1.4 *continued*

Malmesbury, Wiltshire, which had produced some 8,000 vacuum cleaners per day.

Dyson was keen to point out that since the day the first Dyson dual cyclone vacuum cleaner went on sale in 1993, the company had been operating in a price-cutting market in which its competitors were able to pass on to their customers the lower costs from manufacturing outside the UK. In contrast, Dyson had faced the further problems of rises in UK labour costs, land prices, taxation and other overhead costs while still trying to substantially increase its investment in new technology. For example, direct labour costs in Britain had doubled over the previous ten years, partly because of the need to pay high wages in an area around Swindon with almost zero unemployment.

Dyson claimed that the sums no longer added up and it faced going out of business if it continued manufacturing its products in the UK. As of September 2002 all vacuum cleaner production had shifted to Malaysia. The company argued that its production costs would benefit from the much lower wages in Malaysia, the equivalent to £1.50 per hour as compared to the then minimum wage of £4.50 per hour in the UK. Indeed the company estimated that lower wages would reduce its unit production costs by around 30%. Further cost savings would also come from now having most of its component suppliers nearby (South East Asian component suppliers having progressively replaced those from the UK) and from now being much closer to emerging new markets in Japan, Australia and the Far East. In addition, the Malaysian government had offered various 'subsidies' in the form of grants for setting up the Dyson factories there, lower taxes and other benefits.

While lamenting the loss of UK jobs, the consolation to Dyson in moving his vacuum cleaner manufacturing to Malaysia was that it would now generate enough cash to maintain the company's commitment to reinvesting up to 20% of turnover in research and development (R&D). Dyson believed that it was the technological advantages secured by R&D that would keep the company alive and ensure that 1,150 other jobs in Malmesbury were safe, more than 300 of which involved engineers, scientists, designers and testers – the brains that ensure Dyson products remain a step ahead of the rest. Dyson claims to have exported the brawn, keeping the higher-level value-added parts at home, since Dyson's comparative advantage lies in researching and designing new products to ensure the company stays two steps ahead of its rivals, most of whom manufacture in the Far East. Indeed he claimed that to have followed the rest of British industry, which invests an average of only 2% of turnover, would have been to neglect Dyson's engineering and technological heritage and to follow in the footsteps of Britain's car, television and other domestic appliances.

As noted above, Dyson's decision to switch production away from the UK was closely related to increasing supply but at lower cost, with labour costs and office rents in Malaysia in 2010 still at a third of the UK level. Production in Asia also meant that the costs of exporting to large markets in this area were minimised, which enabled Dyson to compete globally with such companies as Electrolux of Sweden, Glen Dimplex of Ireland and Candy of Italy. The 'credit crunch' has further impacted Dyson's global locational strategies. After its profits had grown at an average rate of 73% per year between 2002 and 2007, they dipped in 2008/9 as the recession reduced incomes and demand in many of its market, and a strategic decision was made to further decrease the company's work force in Wiltshire. In January 2010 Dyson announced it would expand its facilities in Malaysia and increase the amount of R&D and product development spent in the Far East, establishing a 'Centre of Engineering Excellence' for its R&D activities at its Senai plant in Malaysia. This would result in some of the company's design engineering moving to Malaysia, with extra employment and training of local Malaysian and South East Asian engineers.

Questions

1 In the market for vacuum cleaners, how did moving to Malaysia help to shift Dyson's supply curve to the right (*increase*)?

2 If Dyson had not moved to Malaysia, why does it believe that staying in the UK would have meant that its supply curve would have shifted to the left (*decrease*)?

3 What is the basis for Dyson's argument that shifting production to Malaysia is in the best interests of British workers?

4 Do the recent developments in the global supply chain location of Dyson have any relevance to your arguments in question 3 above?

You try 1.3 will help you check your understanding of movements along and shifts in a supply curve.

Look carefully at Figure 1.5.

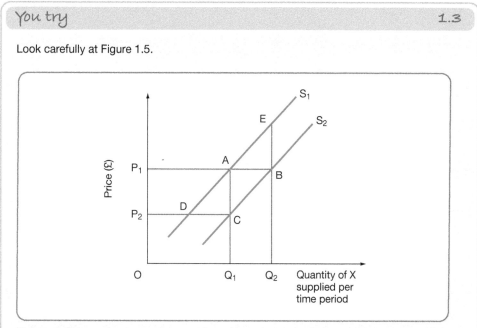

Figure 1.5

1 Match the *number* of each term on the left with the correct *letter* for its movement in Figure 1.5 on the right.

Terminology	Movement
(i) Expansion in supply of X	(a) A to B
(ii) Contraction in supply of X	(b) C to D
(iii) Increase in supply of X	(c) A to E
(iv) Decrease in supply of X	(d) A to D

2 If product X in Figure 1.5 is *petrol* then the move from A to B could be caused by which *two* of the following:

(i) Existing oil fields running dry

(ii) New oil fields being discovered

(iii) An effective blockade of oil terminals

(iv) New technology reducing the costs of 'cracking' oil into petroleum products

3 If product X in Figure 1.5 is again *petrol*, then the move from B to E could be caused by which *two* of the following:

(i) A fall in tax on petrol

(ii) A rise in tax on petrol

(iii) OPEC (Oil Producing and Exporting Countries) raising quotas for each member country

(iv) OPEC cutting quotas for each member country

4 Match the *letter* of each description on the left with the *number* for its correct term on the right.

You try 1.3 continued

Description

(a) Sometimes called a 'complement in production' with the production process for one product automatically resulting in more output of the other product (i.e. the by-product).

(b) Where the factors of production (land, labour, capital) could be used to produce either product.

(c) Has the effect of shifting the supply curve upwards and to the left (decrease in supply) by a constant amount (i.e. a parallel shift).

(d) Has the effect of shifting the supply curve upwards and to the left (decrease in supply) by a non-constant amount (i.e. a non-parallel shift).

(e) More can now be supplied at any given price or the same quantity can now be supplied at a lower price (increase in supply).

Terms

(i)   Fall in costs of production

(ii) Imposing or raising a lump-sum tax

(iii) Substitute in production

(iv) Imposing or raising a percentage tax (e.g. VAT)

(v)   Jointly supplied product

Answers can be found on pp. 525–546.

Price determination

We shall initially assume that we have a *free market*, i.e. one in which demand and supply alone determine the price. Since our demand and supply curves have the same axes, i.e. price and quantity, we can put them on the same diagram. We do this in Figure 1.6 and we can see that at price P_1 the demand and supply curves intersect at the same quantity, Q_1. We call this price P_1 and quantity Q_1 the **equilibrium** price and quantity. Equilibrium means 'at rest', with 'no tendency to change'.

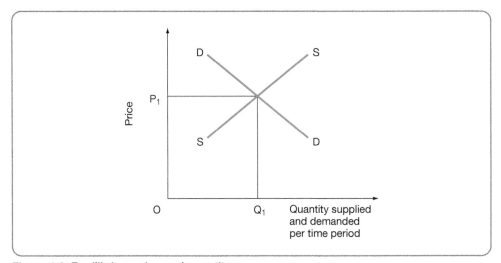

Figure 1.6 Equilibrium price and quantity

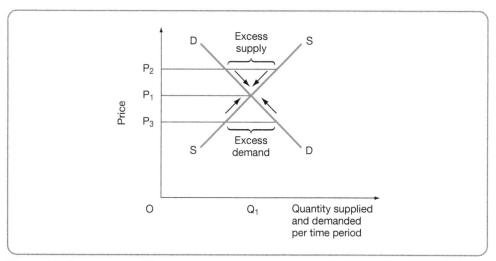

Figure 1.7 **Restoring equilibrium price and quantity in a free market**

Restoring equilibrium price

At any price other than P_1 there will clearly be a tendency for change.

Excess supply

Suppose price is higher than P_1, then supply will exceed demand. At price P_2 in Figure 1.7 there is an *excess supply*. In a free market this excess supply will cause price to fall as suppliers try to dispose of their surplus stock.

- *As price falls* consumers find the product more attractive than substitutes in consumption and some will switch away from those substitutes so that we move rightwards along the demand curve D (expansion of demand).
- *As price falls* producers find the product less attractive than any substitutes in production and may switch resources to these alternatives so that we move leftwards along the supply curve (contraction of supply).

Price will continue to fall until we reach price P_1, where sellers and buyers are in harmony, with all that is offered for sale being purchased, i.e. we have equilibrium in the market.

Excess demand

Suppose price is lower than P_1, then demand exceeds supply. At price P_3 in Figure 1.7 there is an *excess demand*. In a free market excess demand will cause prices to be bid up, as at an auction, since there are more buyers than units of the product available.

- *As price rises*, consumers find the product less attractive than the substitutes in consumption and some will switch into those substitutes so that we move leftwards along the demand curve D (contraction of demand).
- *As price rises*, producers find the product more attractive than any substitutes in production and may switch resources to this product so that we move rightwards along the supply curve S (expansion of supply).

Prices will continue to rise until we reach price P_1 where sellers and buyers are again in harmony,with all that is offered for sale being purchased, i.e. we have equilibrium in the market.

Make a note

Price is acting as a *signal* to buyers and to sellers and helps direct them to take actions (expand or contract demand or supply) which bring about an equilibrium (balance) in the market.

Changes in market price and quantity

We have seen that changes in the conditions of demand or supply will *shift* the demand or supply curves. This in turn will cause changes in the equilibrium price and quantity in the market. It will be useful to consider how increases and decreases in both demand and supply will influence equilibrium price and quantity.

Increase in demand

We have seen that the demand curve may shift to the right (increase) for a number of reasons: a rise in the price of a substitute in consumption; a fall in the price of a complement in consumption; a rise in income for a normal product; a change of consumer tastes in favour of the product, etc.

In Figure 1.8 demand increases from D to D', so that the original equilibrium price–quantity P_1–Q_1 can no longer continue. At price P_1 we now have a situation of *excess demand*. In a free market, price will be bid up. As price rises, supply *expands* along S and demand *contracts* along D' until we reach the higher price P_2 at which demand and supply are again equal at Q_2. We call P_2–Q_2 the new price and quantity equilibrium.

Make a note   An increase in demand will raise equilibrium price and quantity.

Decrease in demand

In the opposite case (Figure 1.9), where demand shifts leftwards from D to D'', we find the new price–quantity equilibrium to be P_2–Q_2. At price P_1 we now have a situation of *excess supply*. In a free market price will fall. As price falls, demand *expands* along the new demand curve D'' and supply *contracts* along S until we reach the lower price P_2 at which demand and supply are again equal at Q_2.

Make a note   A decrease in demand will reduce equilibrium price and quantity.

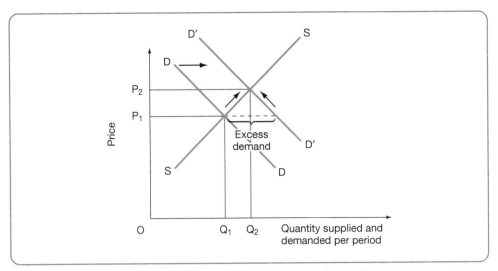

Figure 1.8 **Increase in demand: rise in equilibrium price and quantity**

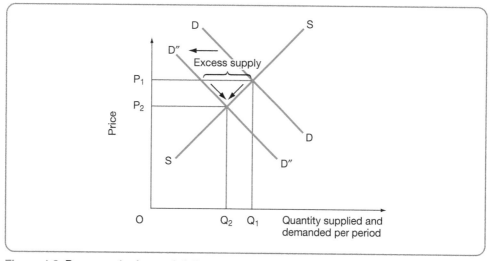

Figure 1.9 **Decrease in demand: fall in equilibrium price and quantity**

Case Study 1.5 looks at the impacts of global events on the market price and quantity of various products.

Case Study 1.5   **Markets and global impacts**

Volatile cotton prices

Almost two years to the day after a massive price jump destabilised global cotton markets, the price of cotton is again surging. The benchmark cotton contract soared in March 2010 to 84.60 cents a pound (weight), the highest level in two years and one breached on only five days in the past 15 years. The increase has revived uneasy feelings among US cotton merchants recalling the dramatic rise in March 2008 that cost them hundreds of millions of dollars, forcing some old industry names out of business.

Merchants – middlemen between growers and mills – are playing safe this time after the buying juggernaut that pushed cotton briefly to about $1 a pound (weight) two years ago. Jordan Lea, chairman of Eastern Trading, a US cotton merchant, says: 'It just looks and feels a bit like March '08, not to mention it is literally the anniversary of the event. Nobody has a sense of restored confidence in this market yet.'

Cotton's latest surge came after China, the largest producer and consumer of the plant, said in March 2010 that its 2009 crop had fallen 14.6% to 6.4m tonnes. The figure was weaker than estimates from the US Department of Agriculture – considered the

gold standard in crop forecasting – and will tighten the global supply and demand balance. The USDA already predicts the 2009–10 growing season will mark the third straight year of declining global production as farmers cut planting due to higher costs and land ceded to plantings of corn and soyabeans. The agency says demand will grow by 5% in the year ending this July, marking a fourth straight year in which demand outstrips supply.

Cotton, like most commodities, is a volatile market. But, as with copper, economists say the fibre serves as a barometer of macroeconomic conditions. 'Strong growth in cotton consumption is characteristic of periods of economic recovery, as restocking of inventories throughout the textile supply chain magnifies the effect of a rebound in retail demand,' US Department of Agriculture analysts said in a speech in February 2010. China has reopened its doors to cotton imports after restrictions last year cut into inventories and pushed prices above $1 a pound (weight). This is likely to lead to roughly a third more cotton imports this growing year, the USDA said.

For US textile mills, which have lost out to cheaper rivals, the price rise is 'having a terrible effect', says Cass Johnson, president of the National

Council of Textile Organizations. 'They have very little pricing power for their finished products and yet raw materials are going up.'

Source: from Cotton at two-year peak after fall in China crop, *Financial Times*, 02/03/2010 (Meyer, G.), © The Financial Times Ltd

Questions

1 Identify the demand and supply factors behind the sharp rise in cotton prices in early 2010. Use diagrams to illustrate your answer.

2 Why are US textile firms so concerned about these developments in the market for cotton?

Chinese consumers and EU milk prices

In late 2007, EU consumers became only too well aware of how globalisation transmits market 'shocks' to all corners of the world. A drive by the Chinese government to provide all Chinese children with half a litre of milk a day had caused demand for milk to increase dramatically by around 25% a year, with around one-third of all the worldwide production of milk now exported to China. The price of a litre of milk in the EU rose by over 25% in one week alone in August 2007, with substantial price increases in dairy-based products such as cheese, butter and yogurt following closely behind. For example, Kraft raised the prices of its cheese-based products by 12% in 2007, linking the price rise explicitly to higher milk costs.

However, others blame over-regulation in the EU, rather than globalisation, for milk-based inflation. They argue that it is the excessive milk quotas imposed by the EU in 1984 and due to last until 2015 that have prevented the supply side of the EU market for milk from adjusting to this surge of Chinese demand. Even so some market adjustment is taking place, if only slowly. For example, EU dairy farmers are breeding high-performance milk cows and selling these to Chinese farmers, who have little or no tradition of dairy farming. Increased Chinese production of milk is also being helped by Chinese government subsidies for farmers who switch to dairy farming.

Questions

1 Use demand and supply diagrams to explain:
   (a) Why the price of EU milk rose by over 25% in 2007.
   (b) Why the price of EU milk may rise less rapidly in the future.

   (c) Why Kraft raised the price of its cheese-based products by 12% in 2007.

2 Why do some argue that it is not so much globalisation as over-regulation of markets by EU governments that caused the sharp rise in milk prices in 2007?

New technology cuts car costs

Mazda announced in October 2007 that it had developed a catalyst that used up to 90% less platinum and palladium in its manufacture than existing catalysts and helped to boost its cost competitiveness at a time when raw materials and metals prices were rising rapidly.

Mazda, which is 33.4% owned by Ford, said that it had developed the first catalyst for cars using technology that allowed it to cut the use of the expensive metals while maintaining performance. Nissan had made a similar announcement earlier in 2007 stating that it had developed new technologies to reduce the use of precious metals in catalysts. In addition to the high cost of precious metals used in catalysts, there is concern about dwindling sources of palladium.

Palladium prices, which have soared over the past year, fell with the news of these developments, which came at a time when car makers have been rushing to cut their materials costs amid a demand surge that has pushed up world commodity prices. Vehicle makers are also reviewing their spending on other materials in an attempt to develop low-cost cars for emerging markets.

Japanese vehicle makers are renowned for their low-cost production, but Tata, the Indian group, had developed a $2,500 car in 2007/8 which had put pressure on Japanese groups to reduce costs even more.

Questions

1 Use demand and supply diagrams to explain why the price of the metal palladium fell on news of the technological breakthrough in the production of catalysts for cars.

2 Use demand and supply diagrams to explain how this and other technological breakthroughs might have helped Mazda and Nissan compete against the low-cost producers such as the Tata group which produced the $2,500 car.

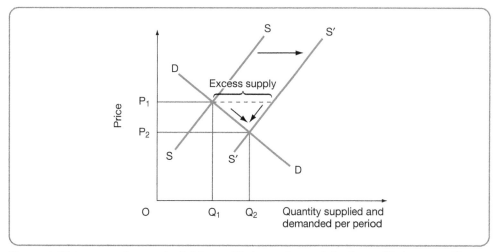

Figure 1.10 **Increase in supply: fall in equilibrium price and rise in equilibrium quantity**

Increase in supply

We have seen that the supply curve may shift to the right (increase) for a number of reasons: a fall in the price of a substitute in production; a rise in the price of a complement in production; a fall in costs of production; a reduction in tax on the product etc.

In Figure 1.10 supply shifts from S to S′ so that the original equilibrium price–quantity P_1–Q_1 can no longer continue. At price P_1 we now have a situation of *excess supply*. In a free market, price will fall as producers try to dispose of surplus stock. As price falls, supply *contracts* along S′ and demand *expands* along D until we reach the lower price P_2, at which demand and supply are again equal at Q_2.

Make a note   An increase in supply will lower equilibrium price but raise equilibrium quantity.

Decrease in supply

In the opposite case (Figure 1.11), where supply shifts leftwards from S to S″, we find the new price–quantity equilibrium to be P_2–Q_2. At price P_1 we now have a situation of *excess demand*. In a free market price will be bid upwards. As price rises, supply *expands* along

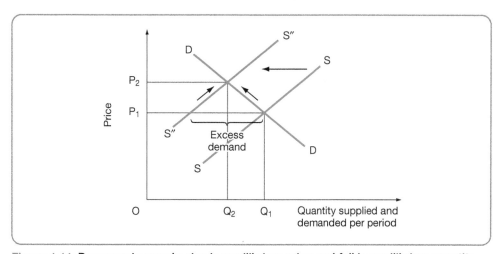

Figure 1.11 **Decrease in supply: rise in equilibrium price and fall in equilibrium quantity**

the new supply curve S″ and demand *contracts* along D until we reach the higher price P_2 at which demand and supply are again equal at Q_2.

Make a note	A decrease in supply will raise equilibrium price but reduce equilibrium quantity.

Case Study 1.6 examines the use of demand and supply analysis in discussing policies aimed at combating drug use.

Case Study 1.6   **The drug war**

There is a debate in the USA and in Europe as to how to influence the market for drugs such as cocaine. Some argue that the answer is to *reduce the supply* of drugs from Colombia – which would otherwise eventually find their way onto the world markets – by giving aid to the Colombian government to fight the drug suppliers. If this is successful, it will drive up the price of cocaine on the streets. Higher prices mean that fewer people will be willing and able to buy drugs, resulting in a fall in demand.

This scenario can be seen in Figure 1.12(a) where a successful anti-drug policy in Colombia would decrease supply, i.e. shift the supply curve for cocaine upwards and to the left so that there is an *excess demand* for cocaine at price P. This will result in a rise in the equilibrium price of cocaine from P to P_1. The quantity demanded will contract along the demand curve D from Q to Q_1 as price rises from P to P_1. Critics of these ideas argue that programmes designed to reduce the supply of cocaine from Colombia have failed in the past because the high price of drugs makes them very profitable to produce in other areas outside Colombia.

Some argue that the answer is to *reduce the demand* for illegal drugs by various means such as improved education, or by advertising the damaging effects of drugs such as cocaine. This can be seen in Figure 1.12(b) where a successful education policy decreases demand, i.e. shifts the demand curve D downwards and to the left, so that there is an *excess supply* of cocaine at price P. This will result in a fall in the equilibrium price from P to P_1 and in quantity from Q to Q_1.

Another solution would be to *legalise the consumption of cocaine*. This would arguably increase supply, i.e. shift the supply curve downwards and to the right as in Figure 1.12(c), substantially reducing the price of cocaine in the streets from P to P_1. Proponents of legalisation argue that the very high price of cocaine forces many people into criminal activity to support their habit, so that the

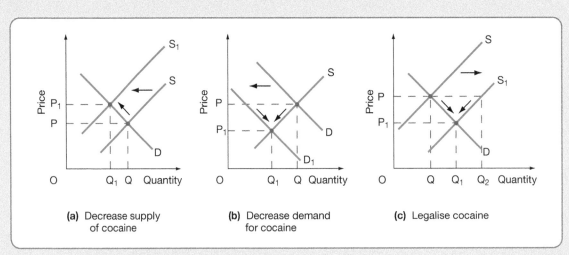

(a) Decrease supply of cocaine

(b) Decrease demand for cocaine

(c) Legalise cocaine

Figure 1.12 Supply and demand for cocaine

lowering of the price of cocaine after legalisation would reduce the pressure on addicts to use criminal activity to buy the drug.

However, it is often admitted that in the short run the equilibrium quantity of cocaine in use will rise from Q to Q_1 as the price of cocaine falls from P to P_1. Others argue that the legalisation of the drug will reduce the 'thrill' of engaging in what is currently an illegal, anti-establishment activity by taking drugs. If so, this would cause the demand curve D to decrease, shifting downwards and to the left of D. If this did happen the price of cocaine would fall below P_1 and the equilibrium quantity of cocaine use might fall below the original level Q if demand decreased sufficiently.

Further, if the lower price of cocaine squeezed the profits of suppliers, then they might use their resources elsewhere so that the supply curve decreased, shifting to the left from S_1.

Although the answer to this policy dilemma for governments is neither easy nor wholly clear, at least supply and demand analysis helps to put the fundamentals of the debate into perspective.

Questions

1 Use Figure 1.12(c) to show the extent to which the demand for cocaine must decrease to result in less cocaine being used *after* legalisation as compared to *before* legalisation.

2 How might the outcome in question 1 be affected by the now lower price for cocaine squeezing the profits of suppliers, so that supply decreases from the level S_1 reached immediately after legalisation?

3 How might the steepness of the demand and supply curves for cocaine be relevant to the outcome of legalisation?

4 What other issues might be raised by a policy of legalisation of cocaine use?

5 A major study from Loughborough University argued that, whatever their faults, the Taliban had been effective in their policy of decreasing the supply of poppy growing and therefore of heroin and cocaine (over 50% of the world supply of the poppies for these products comes from Afghanistan). Which of the three diagrams in Figure 1.12 best represents how they achieved this policy?

Maximum and minimum prices

Links

Maximum and minimum prices are sometimes referred to as 'market failure' since the market mechanism is prevented from using price signals to eliminate an excess demand or supply. A number of other types of 'market failure' are considered in some detail in Chapter 8 (pp. 227–231).

Of course, in reality governments or regulatory bodies may intervene in markets, as for example in setting maximum or minimum prices. In these cases prices are *prevented* from acting as the signals which guide buyers and sellers to an equilibrium outcome.

Maximum price

The government or agency may seek to establish a **maximum price** in the market, i.e. a *ceiling* above which price will not be allowed to rise. Again we can use demand and supply diagrams as in Figure 1.13 to show what will then happen.

If the maximum price were set *above* the equilibrium price P_1, then the market would still be able to reach the equilibrium outcome of price P_1 and quantity Q_1. However, the market mechanisms would not be able to reach this equilibrium outcome if the maximum price (P^*) was set *below* the equilibrium price P_1. At price P^* there is an excess demand and price would have risen in a free market to P_1, encouraging producers to expand supply from Q_2 to Q_1 and discouraging consumers so that demand contracts from Q_3 to Q_1, until the equilibrium P_1–Q_1 was established. Here, however, price is prevented from providing such signals to sellers and buyers to bring their decisions into harmony, and we may be left with the **disequilibrium** outcome P^* in which excess demand persists.

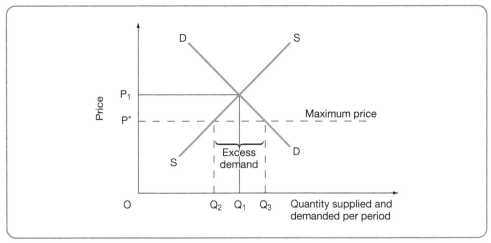

Figure 1.13 A maximum price P* set below the equilibrium price P₁

ᴛᴀᴋɪɴɢ ɪᴛ ꜰᴜʀᴛʜᴇʀ 1.3 considers some of the possible ways in which resources might be allocated in the case of a maximum price set below the equilibrium price.

ᴛᴀᴋɪɴɢ ɪᴛ ꜰᴜʀᴛʜᴇʀ Non-market mechanisms and resource allocation   1.3

How then will resources be allocated in a situation where excess demand exists?

- *Rationing.* Vouchers or coupons could be issued so that everyone got at least some of the quantity (Q₂) of the product available. The government or agency must still decide who qualifies for vouchers and how much product each voucher holder receives. Rationing is also costly to administer, with vouchers having to be printed, distributed, taken in, etc.

- *First come, first served.* In other words, some sort of queuing system may be used to allocate the product available. Time is wasted by having to queue.

- *Ballots.* The limited supply of the product may be shared among potential purchasers by some sort of ballot. 'Tickets' may be issued and a draw made, with 'successful' individuals able to purchase the product at price P*. Again ballots can be costly to administer and are arguably less fair than rationing.

- *'Black market'.* Although not strictly a mechanism for allocating resources, a 'black market' invariably operates whenever a maximum price results in excess demand. In Figure 1.13, the demand curve DD tells us that some people are 'willing to pay' a very high price for the product, well in excess of P*. This, of course, is the basis for ticket touts being able to sell tickets to popular events at a price well above the official price of the ticket.

Minimum price

The government or agency may seek to establish a **minimum price** in the market, i.e. a *floor* below which the price will not be allowed to fall. We can use our familiar demand and supply diagrams as in Figure 1.14 to show what will happen in these circumstances.

Suppose now that the government imposes a minimum price, P*, below which the price will not be allowed to fall. If that minimum price is set *below* the equilibrium price P₁ then there will be no problem. The market will already have reached its equilibrium at price P₁, and there will be no reason for P₁ to change. If, however, the minimum price is set *above* the equilibrium price P₁, then price will have to rise from P₁ to the new minimum, P*. We can see from Figure 1.14 that there will then be an excess supply at P* of Q₃–Q₂ units.

If the market had remained free, the excess supply would have been removed by the price system. However, the important point here is that the market is not free! Price

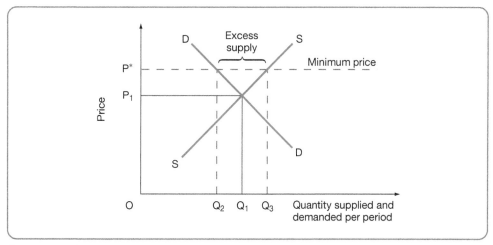

Figure 1.14 **A minimum price P* set above the equilibrium price P$_1$**

cannot fall below the minimum that has been set, P*. The excess supply will therefore remain and the price system will not be able to remove it. Sellers will be unable to dispose of their surplus stocks, which will have to be stored, destroyed or disposed of in less orthodox ways which prevent the price falling below P*.

Stop and think   1.3

Can you think of what these 'less orthodox ways' might be?

Case Study 1.7 investigates the market for oil to consider how changes in the conditions of demand and supply for oil have influenced the world price of oil.

Case Study 1.7   Oiling the wheels

In April 2010 the widely used measure for the price of crude oil, the West Texas Spot-rate, stood at $80 per barrel, more than twice the $38 per barrel price of April 2004. The price of oil fluctuated wildly in the first decade of the millennium, from a low of $19 a barrel in December 2001 to a high of $134 per barrel in June 2008. Why has there been such volatility in price? Close examination of demand and supply conditions for oil may give us some clues!

Crude oil is refined into a vast number of products via the chemical process of 'cracking'. However, just three, namely petrol, diesel and fuel oil, account for around 75% of oil derivative products and are mainly used in transport and electricity-generating activities. Of course, the demand for transport and electricity is closely linked to economic growth; for example, every 1% rise in US national income has been estimated as raising US demand for crude oil by nine-tenths of 1%.

Few immediate substitutes exist for crude oil derivatives in transport and energy. Natural gas is perhaps the closest substitute and provides around 25% of total global energy. Estimates suggest that a 1% fall in price of natural gas leads to a three-quarters of 1% fall in demand for crude oil. However, other, less obvious substitutes for oil are becoming more important. For example, all types of renewable energy sources (wind, water, sun etc.) are increasingly seen as more environmentally desirable (if more expensive) substitutes for oil in energy production in that they do not emit the carbon dioxide (CO_2) and other greenhouse gases which result from using oil-based products. The scientific linkage of these emissions with global warming led to 93 countries (but not the USA) having ratified the Kyoto Protocol by 2010, with the developed countries committing themselves to an overall 5% reduction in the emissions of greenhouse gases by 2012.

Case Study 1.7 *continued*

Top 10 oil producers (million barrels per day)		Top 10 oil consumers (million barrels per day)	
Saudi Arabia (OPEC)	10.8	USA	19.5
Russia (non OPEC)	9.8	China	8.9
USA (non OPEC)	8.5	Japan	4.8
Iran (OPEC)	4.1	Russia	2.8
China (non OPEC)	3.8	Germany	2.7
Mexico (non OPEC)	3.7	India	2.6
Canada (non OPEC)	3.4	Canada	2.5
United Arab Emirates (OPEC)	3.2	Brazil	2.4
Venezuela (OPEC)	3.0	South Korea	2.3
Norway (non OPEC)	2.6	Saudi Arabia	2.2

Source: Adapted from CIA (2010) *The Factbook*

Climate itself can also influence the demand for oil. The OECD noted that in 2002 the Northern Hemisphere recorded the warmest-ever first quarter of the year, and linked this to demand for crude oil from countries in the Northern Hemisphere falling by 1.1 million barrels per year.

While the demand for oil is capable of significant shifts, so too is the supply. Around one-third of total supply of crude oil is in the hands of a small group of twelve well-organised oil producing and exporting countries (OPEC). Members of OPEC include Saudi Arabia, Ecuador, Angola, Algeria, Iraq, Iran, Qatar, Libya, Kuwait, United Arab Emirates, Nigeria, and Venezuela. These countries meet regularly to decide on the total supply they should collectively produce, seeking to limit the total supply in order to keep the world price of crude oil at a 'reasonable' level. Having fixed the total supply, OPEC then allocates a *quota* to each member state which specifies their maximum oil production in that year.

When OPEC increases or decreases the agreed total supply of oil, this clearly has a major impact on the oil price. It was the sharp cuts in OPEC oil production that resulted in the major world 'oil crises' of 1967 and 1973, with rapid rises in the oil price leading to global recession. However, another unpredictable variable has been added to oil supply in recent years, namely the growing contribution of *non-OPEC* oil-producing countries. For example, Russia and the US are outside OPEC but each produces almost as much oil as the world's largest oil producer, Saudi Arabia, and many new oil resources in the former Soviet Republics such as Azerbaijan and Kazakhstan are now on stream. The top ten producers and consumers of oil are listed above, with the OPEC and non-OPEC producers identified.

It is not only actual events but *possible future events* that can influence the price of oil. For example, in the months before the second Iraq War in 2003, it was claimed that there was a 'war risk premium' of $5 a barrel built into the then current price of over $30 a barrel and Wall Street analysts suggested that uncertainties created by events in Iraq, Iran and Venezuela in 2006 added a $10–$20 risk premium on raising the 2006 price to over $70 a barrel.

Questions

1 (a) Discuss some of the factors suggested in the case study that might cause an *increase* in the world demand for oil.

(b) Now discuss possible reasons for a *decrease* in the world demand for oil.

(c) Can you think of reasons why there might be a fall in the equilibrium price of oil but a rise in the equilibrium quantity?

2 We have seen that OPEC has tried to restrict the total supply of crude oil from its member countries to keep the world price at a 'reasonable' level. Suppose it now aims for a higher world price per barrel.

(a) How might it achieve this new target? (You could use a diagram here.)

(b) What problems might OPEC encounter in trying to achieve this higher oil price?

3 Can you explain what was meant by those who argued that a 'war risk premium' raised the price of oil to over $30 a barrel before the second Iraq War in 2003?

You try 1.4 gives you more practice in price determination.

You try   *1.4*

1 Look at Figure 1.15 and answer the following questions.

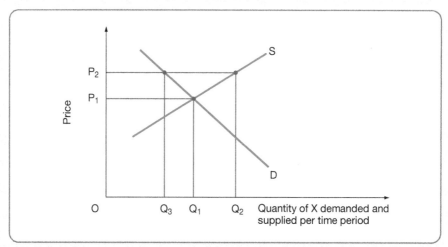

Figure 1.15

(a) Price P$_2$ is an 'equilibrium price'.   True/False
(b) At price P$_2$ demand exceeds supply.   True/False
(c) At price P$_2$ excess supply is the amount Q$_2$ − Q$_3$.   True/False
(d) If the initial price is P$_2$, in a free market price will rise.   True/False
(e) As price moves from P$_2$ towards the equilibrium price,
     demand will expand.   True/False
(f) As price moves from P$_2$ towards the equilibrium price,
     supply will decrease.   True/False
(g) In moving to an equilibrium, price is acting as a 'signal'
     to bring the decisions of producers and consumers into
     balance (harmony) with each other.   True/False
(h) If price falls below P$_1$ then excess demand will result
     in price moving back to P$_1$.   True/False

2 The market for designer trainers is currently in equilibrium. Other things equal, what will
   be the likely impact of each of the following events?

You try 1.4 continued

Event	Change in equilibrium price	Change in equilibrium quantity
(a) Successful TV advertising for designer trainers	Rise/Fall	Rise/Fall
(b) Report indicates foot damage from wearing designer trainers	Rise/Fall	Rise/Fall
(c) New factories in developing countries reduce costs of producing designer trainers while retaining quality	Rise/Fall	Rise/Fall
(d) Higher rate of VAT applied to designer trainers	Rise/Fall	Rise/Fall

3 Look carefully at Figure 1.16, which shows an increase in demand for Microsoft (X Box). Can you explain what is happening as regards Sony (PlayStation 2) in (b) and why?

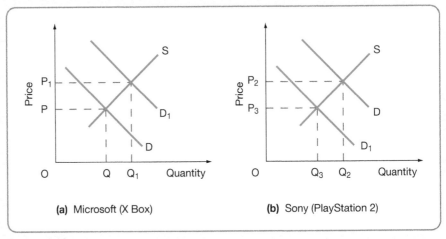

(a) Microsoft (X Box)   **(b)** Sony (PlayStation 2)

Figure 1.16

4 Look carefully at Figure 1.17, which shows an increase in demand for wool in (a). Can you explain what is happening to mutton in (b) and why?

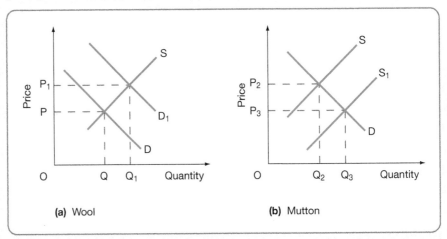

(a) Wool   **(b)** Mutton

Figure 1.17

You try 1.4 continued

5   Look carefully at Figure 1.18 which shows an increase in demand for cars in (a). Can you explain what is happening to tyres in (b) and why?

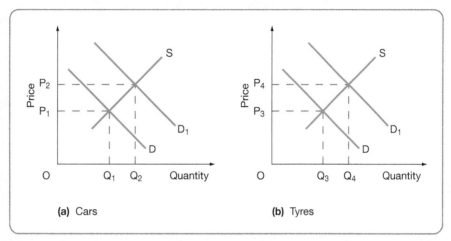

(a) Cars   **(b) Tyres**

Figure 1.18

Answers can be found on pp. 525–546.

Resource allocation in different economic systems

Although we have mainly considered resource allocation through the *market mechanism*, there are in fact different types of economic system for allocating resources. Three particular types of economic system are often discussed in the literature.

● Pure market economy

● Pure command economy

● Mixed economy.

We briefly review the characteristics of each type below, together with their advantages and disadvantages.

Make a note

Of course, in reality most economies might more accurately be located somewhere along a *spectrum* running from the pure market economy at one extreme to the pure command economy at the other extreme.

Pure market economy

● Markets alone are used to allocate scarce resources of land, labour and capital.

● Prices (determined on markets) act as 'signals' to producers and consumers, bringing supply and demand into balance (equilibrium).

- No direct role for governments in resource allocation – their main task is to provide the infrastructure needed to allow markets to work (e.g. law and order, defence etc.).
- *Advantages* – markets coordinate (via price) the activities of millions of buyers and sellers without any need for an expensive bureaucracy of decision makers.
- *Disadvantages* – 'market failures' (see Chapter 8, p. 226) can result in a misallocation of resources.

It was the role of prices within the market mechanism that Adam Smith was referring to when, in his *Wealth of Nations* in 1776, he observed that each individual was

Quote

led by an invisible hand to promote an end which was no part of his intention.

Pure command economy

- Governments, not markets, allocate scarce resources of land, labour and capital.
- Comprehensive plans are drawn up to decide which products are to be produced and in what quantities.
- Prices, if they exist, are determined by governments. If there is excess demand at the ruling price, then 'rationing' may be used. If there is excess supply, then unwanted product may simply be stored or even destroyed.
- Governments retain ownership of the means of production (little or no private ownership).
- *Advantages* – production and consumption can be based on 'social' rather than 'private' needs and wants.
- *Disadvantages* – expensive bureaucracy needed to allocate resources; inappropriate decisions often made by bureaucrats, resulting in excess supply for unwanted products or excess demand for wanted products.

Mixed economy

Check the net

You can find up-to-date information on the US economy from the Economics Statistics Briefing Room of the White House at:

http://www.whitehouse.gov/infocus/economy

Data on other advanced industrialised market economies can be found at:

http://www.oecd.org

Data on the transition economies can be found from the European Bank for Reconstruction and Development website at:

www.ebrd.com

- Uses both markets and government intervention to allocate scarce resources of land, labour and capital.
- Government intervention can be direct (e.g. nationalised industries, public sector services) and/or indirect (e.g. regulations, tax policies).
- Most modern economies are mixed – e.g. around 40% of UK expenditure and output involves the public sector.
- *Advantages* – government intervention can help offset various types of 'market failure' (see Chapter 8, p. 231); markets and prices can be used to co-ordinate large numbers of independent decisions.
- *Disadvantages* – high taxes may be needed to provide the revenues to support government intervention; these may reduce incentives and discourage output, investment and employment.

Case Study 1.8 gives a brief outline of the workings of the Indian agricultural markets to establish a case for a mixed economy with government intervention in certain circumstances.

Case Study 1.8   Food crisis worsens amid call for 'green' reform

At New Delhi's Bhogal Market, pushcarts are piled high with fresh fruit and vegetables and small shops are lined with burlap sacks filled with lentils. But for 40-year-old Jamilla Khan, who has to feed three hungry teenagers on the Rs5,000 ($107, £69) her husband earns each month as a driver, such foods are rare treats. As lentil prices have tripled over the past two years, the family has gone from eating 10 kg of pulses a month to only two or three. Their consumption of vegetables and meat – which have also shot up in price – has plunged. Many of their meals consist only of rotis, a flatbread, and spicy pickle. 'The kids say, "I want milk, I want ghee", but how can I buy it for them?' Mrs Khan asks. 'How can I fill their stomachs? Even I used to have three cups of tea a day. Now I have one.'

Policy makers have long considered growth as the way to fight India's problems of poverty, hunger and malnutrition. But while the economy has grown, agricultural production has stagnated. That has led to rocketing prices for nutritious foods. So while Indians with links to the new economy eat better than ever, many urban working-class families, who spend up to 55% of their household budgets on food, are being squeezed. 'The price of food is the most serious political issue facing the government of India today,' says Manpreet Singh Badal, finance minister of northern Punjab, often called the granary of India. 'We have . . . food sitting in our warehouses but that is only rice and wheat. India is malnourished. We need something more than rice and wheat.'

Spiralling food prices have provided debate about whether the Reserve Bank of India will have to raise interest rates to try to cool the economy. But P.K. Joshi, director of the National Academy of Agricultural Research Management, says the underlying issue can be addressed only by helping India's farmers. 'Incomes are increasing and people can afford to eat more but the increase in supply is less than the rate of increase in demand,' he says. 'Naturally prices will increase.'

Lentils are the main protein source in India, where many are vegetarian and meat is consumed only in small quantities. India consumes about 18m tonnes of pulses a year, though analysts say latent demand is far higher since many families cannot afford to eat as much as they should. Yet India's pulse production was 15m tonnes in 2008, and its productivity is below global averages. New Delhi has been bridging the shortfall with imports.

With the food crisis deepening, Pratibha Patil, India's president, has called for a 'second green revolution', which would boost farmers' yields and incomes with improved seeds, better water management and more scientific farming. But many question whether New Delhi has the will for the large-scale investment and reforms. 'This crisis has been festering for so many years,' says Ajay Jakhar, chairman of the Bharat Krishak Samaj, or Indian Farmer's Forum. India's 1970s-era green revolution, which introduced high-yielding seeds for rice and wheat, transformed India from heavy dependence on imported grains to being a rice exporter. However the pulse market has never been properly regulated or supported by the government. India's failure to boost its pulse yields could send global prices spiralling. This year, global sugar prices reached a 29-year high owing to the collapse of India's domestic sugar production. Gyanendra Shukla, Monsanto's director of corporate affairs in India, says, 'When India goes to buy even a small amount of rice, cereal or sugar, global prices rise.'

Source: from Food crisis amid call for 'green' reform, *Financial Times*, 10/02/2010 (Kazmin, A), © The Financial Times Ltd

Questions

1 Use demand and supply diagrams and analysis to explain why prices of pulses (e.g. lentils) are rising so rapidly.

2 Can you find any clues in the case study to explain how and why government intervention might help in the market for pulses?

3 What would you consider to be the potential advantages to the global economy of a well regulated Indian agricultural sector?

You try 1.5 provides opportunities to think more about these different types of economic system.

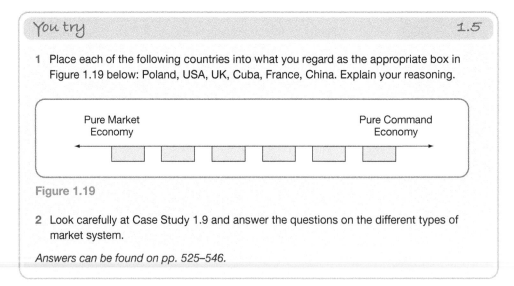

You try   1.5

1   Place each of the following countries into what you regard as the appropriate box in Figure 1.19 below: Poland, USA, UK, Cuba, France, China. Explain your reasoning.

Pure Market Economy   Pure Command Economy

Figure 1.19

2   Look carefully at Case Study 1.9 and answer the questions on the different types of market system.

Answers can be found on pp. 525–546.

Case Study 1.9   The investment climate perspective

The investment climate reflects the many factors that shape the opportunities and incentives for firms to invest productively, create jobs and expand in a given geographical location. A good 'investment climate' is not just about generating profits for firms, it also improves outcomes for society as a whole. Some costs and risks should be borne by firms, with competition playing a key role in encouraging innovation and productivity. However, other costs and risks should be borne by governments which must use policies to ensure that the benefits of productivity improvements are shared with workers and consumers.

Looking at economic growth and the reduction of poverty through this 'investment climate' perspective offers several insights.

● It puts firms – the actors making investment and hiring decisions – at the centre of the discussion.
● It recognises that it is firms that assess investment opportunities and related government policies and behaviours as part of a package. This reinforces the importance of looking at property rights, regulation, taxes, finance, infrastructure, corruption, and other areas of government policy and behaviour as part of an integrated whole, rather than in isolation.
● It highlights the forward-looking nature of investment activity. Investment is based on expectations of the future and not just on current conditions. This underlines the importance of governments promoting stability and credibility, which are critical elements of a sound investment climate. It treats as fundamental the need for policy makers to balance the goal of encouraging productive private investment with other social goals. Firms provide many benefits for society, but the interests of firms and society are not the same in all respects. Good public policy is not about giving firms everything they might ask for, but rather about balancing a range of social interests.

A good 'investment climate' provides opportunities for people to better themselves, and improving the investment climate is the first pillar of the World Bank's overall development strategy. A critical complementary agenda is to invest in and empower people so they can take advantage of those opportunities; this is the second pillar of the World Bank's development strategy.

Source: Based on information from World Development Report 2005

Questions

1   Why do some people believe that the *market system* is the best mechanism for allocating scarce resources and thereby encouraging a positive 'investment climate'? Explain your reasoning.

2   Why do some people believe that not everything can be left to the free market, but that governments also have a role to play in encouraging a positive 'investment climate'? Explain your reasoning.

Make a note

> Wherever appropriate, using demand/supply diagrams can help to clarify your answer to many assignments and exam questions on the topic areas of this chapter. However, do make sure that you draw the diagram neatly (use a rule!), label the diagram fully and, most important of all, write about the diagram in the text of your answer.

Recap

- In a free market system, price coordinates the decisions of buyers and sellers to bring them into balance (equilibrium).
- Prices act as 'signals' to consumers – e.g. a higher price for X means that substitutes in consumption are now relatively more attractive, so that demand for X contracts.
- Prices act as 'signals' to producers – e.g. a higher price for X means that substitutes in production are now relatively less attractive, so that supply of X expands.
- Excess demand at any price can be expected to raise market price.
- Excess supply at any price can be expected to reduce market price.
- A change in the product's own price (other things equal) will result in a movement along the demand or supply curve (expansion or contraction).
- A change in the conditions of demand or supply will cause the respective curves to shift (increase or decrease).
- 'Market failures', such as maximum or minimum prices, may prevent the price mechanism from allocating resources, so that 'non-price' mechanisms for resource allocation are needed.
- In a 'mixed economy' both markets and governments play a role in the allocation of scarce resources (e.g. land, labour and capital).

Key terms

Complements in consumption Where consuming more of one product results in consuming more of some other product.

Complements in production Where producing more of one product automatically results in producing more of some other product (by-product). Sometimes called 'jointly supplied' products.

Conditions of demand The variables which result in the demand curve shifting to the right (increase) or left (decrease).

Conditions of supply The variables which result in the supply curve shifting to the right (increase) or left (decrease).

Demand curve Maps the relationship between the quantity demanded of some product and changes in its own price.

Demand function Expresses the relationship between the quantity demanded of some product and the main variables that influence that demand.

Disequilibrium A situation which is not stable and must therefore change.

Equilibrium A state of balance or harmony. Equilibrium price is that price for which demand and supply are equal and there is no tendency for the price to change.

Inferior goods Cheap but poor-quality substitutes for other goods. As real incomes rise above a certain 'threshold', consumers tend to substitute more expensive but better-quality alternatives for certain products. In other words, inferior goods have negative income elasticities of demand over certain ranges of income.

Market failure Where one or more conditions prevent the market, via the price mechanism, from allocating resources in the best possible way.

Maximum price The market will not be allowed to set a price higher than this.

Minimum price The market will not be allowed to set a price lower than this.

Normal goods One for which a rise in real income will always lead to an increase in demand.

Opportunity cost The next best alternative foregone, in a situation characterised by scarcity and choice.

Production possibility curve (or frontier) Maps the different output combinations from fully using all the resources available.

Real income The money income adjusted for changes in the price level; if money income doubles but prices double, then real income (i.e. purchasing power) is unchanged.

Scarcity The central 'economic problem', arising from the fact that wants are unlimited but the means to satisfy those wants are limited.

Substitutes in consumption Where the products are alternative purchases for consumers.

Substitutes in production Where the factors of production could produce either product.

Supply curve Maps the relationship between the quantity supplied of some product and changes in its own price.

Supply function Expresses the relationship between the quantity supplied of some product and the main variables that influence supply.

Demand, revenue and consumer behaviour

Introduction

In this chapter we take further our discussions on the demand curve in Chapter 1. Why do some businesses claim that cutting prices is vital to their future prospects, while others insist on raising prices? How should a business respond to the price cuts or price rises of a rival? Is there any reason to link the future prospects of the business to changes in household or national income? We shall see that the 'elasticity' concept as applied to demand plays a key role in determining the firm's response to such questions and will help you understand the economic and business principles which influence many of the revenue-based strategies adopted by individual firms. The chapter concludes by examining those aspects of consumer behaviour which underpin the so-called 'law of demand' which predicts a rise in consumer purchases of a product as its price falls.

What you'll learn

By the end of this chapter you should be able to:

- explain the meaning of price elasticity of demand and identify the factors influencing its value
- relate price elasticity of demand to business turnover (revenue)
- show how the impact on price from taxing a product (i.e. tax incidence) depends on the price elasticity of demand for that product
- outline other types of 'elasticity' of demand (such as cross elasticity and income elasticity) and assess their importance to a business
- consider the relevance of the 'Veblen effect' to consumer behaviour
- understand the relevance of utility to consumer behaviour, as in explaining the downward sloping demand curve (i.e. the 'law of demand')
- define and apply the idea of consumer surplus.

Price elasticity of demand (PED)

In Chapter 1 the demand curve for a product X was drawn sloping downwards from left to right, indicating a sensitivity of demand for the product to changes in its own price. But will demand for X change substantially or hardly at all as the price of X varies? It will obviously be helpful to have a broadly accepted *measure* of such responsiveness.

Price elasticity of demand (PED) is a measure of the responsiveness of demand for a product to a change in its own price. PED assumes that as the price of X changes, other things (the conditions of demand) remain equal, so it involves *movements along* the demand curve (expansion/contraction) rather than shifts in the demand curve (increase/decrease).

The PED for product X is given by the equation:

$$\text{PED} = \frac{\%\ \text{change in quantity demanded of X}}{\%\ \text{change in price of X}}$$

Strictly speaking, the sign of PED for a product is negative, since a fall in price of X will lead to an expansion of demand for X $(+/- = -)$. For example, if a 2% fall in price of X results in a 6% expansion in demand, then PED is $+6/-2 = -3$. However, we usually ignore the sign of PED when expressing the numerical values.

Table 2.1 outlines the different numerical values (ignoring the sign) for price elasticity of demand, together with the terminology used and what it actually means.

Figure 2.1 gives a visual impression of each of these price elasticity situations.

Factors affecting PED

The numerical value of PED depends on a number of factors, including:

1 *The availability of substitutes in consumption.* The more numerous and closer the substitutes available, the more elastic the demand. A small percentage change in price of X can then lead to a large percentage change in the quantity demanded of X as consumers switch towards or away from these substitutes in consumption.

2 *The nature of the need satisfied by the product.* The more possible it is to classify the need as being in the luxury category, the more price sensitive consumers tend to be and the more elastic the demand. The more basic or necessary the need, the less price sensitive consumers tend to be and the less elastic the demand.

Table 2.1 **Price elasticity of demand: numerical value, terminology and description**

Numerical value	Terminology	Description
0	Perfectly inelastic demand	Whatever the % change in price no change in quantity demanded (Figure 2.1a)
>0 <1	Relatively inelastic demand	A given % change in price leads to a smaller % change in quantity demanded (Figure 2.1b)
1	Unit elastic demand	A given % change in price leads to exactly the same % change in quantity demanded (Figure 2.1c)
>1 <∞	Relatively elastic demand	A given % change in price leads to a larger % change in quantity demanded (Figure 2.1d)
∞ (infinity)	Perfectly elastic demand	An infinitely small % change in price leads to an infinitely large % change in quantity demanded (Figure 2.1e)

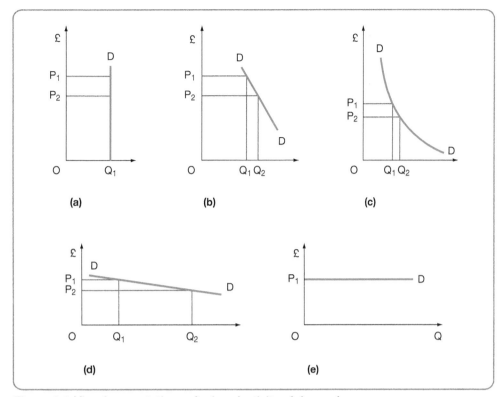

Figure 2.1 **Visual presentations of price elasticity of demand**

Stop and think   2.1

Can you suggest why relying on visual presentation alone in Figures 2.1(b) and (d) might give a misleading impression of the true price elasticity of demand?

3 *The time period.* The longer the time period, the more elastic the demand (consumers take time to adjust their consumption patterns to a change in price).

4 *The proportion of income spent on the product.* The greater the proportion of income spent on the product, the more elastic the demand will tend to be. A given percentage change in the price of a product which plays an important role in the consumer's total spending pattern is more likely to be noticed by the consumer and thereby to influence future purchasing intentions (see also the idea of 'income effect', p. 514).

Check the net

The Business Owner's Toolkit has a section on pricing and elasticity:

www.toolkit.com

5 *The number of uses available to the product.* The greater the flexibility of the product in terms of the number of uses to which it can be put, the more elastic the demand. Of course, the greater the number of uses available to the product, the more substitute products there will tend to be (point 1 above).

Price elasticity of demand (PED) and revenue

For a business to make sensible decisions as to the price it should charge, it will help to be aware of the linkage between PED and total revenue (**turnover**). The 'box' diagram shown in Figure 2.2 helps explain this linkage using a straight line (linear) demand curve (DD).

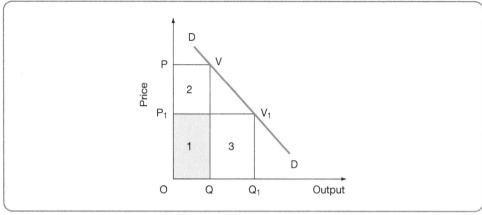

Figure 2.2 **Box diagram to show how revenue varies with output for a linear demand curve**

We can see that with the initial price at OP, total revenue (price X quantity) is shown by area OPVQ. A fall in price to OP_1 will lead to an expansion of demand to OQ_1 and a new total revenue indicated by area $OP_1V_1Q_1$. Clearly Area 1 is common to both total revenue situations, but here Area 2 is lost and Area 3 gained. The loss of Area 2 is due to selling the original OQ units at a now lower price; the gain of Area 3 is due to the lower price attracting new $(Q–Q_1)$ consumers for the product.

> **Make a note**

In this and other chapters of this book you will come across various signs which it is important to be familiar with.

>   greater than
≥   greater than or equal to
<   less than
≤   less than or equal to
∞   infinity

The relationships listed in Table 2.2 will hold true for the box diagram. We can now use these relationships to make a number of predictions involving price changes and total revenue.

Price changes and total revenue

● For *price reductions* along a **unit elastic demand** curve (PED = 1) or segment of a demand curve, there will be no change in total revenue (Area 3 = Area 2).

Table 2.2 **PED and revenue**

Numerical value of PED	Relationship between Area 2 and Area 3
1	Area 3 = Area 2
>1	Area 3 > Area 2
<1	Area 3 < Area 2

- For *price reductions* along a relatively elastic demand curve (PED $> 1 < \infty$) or segment of a demand curve, total revenue will increase as there is a more than proportionate response of extra consumers to the now lower price (Area 3 > Area 2).

- For *price reductions* along a relatively inelastic demand curve (PED $> 0 < 1$) or segment of a demand curve, total revenue will decrease as there is a less than proportionate response of extra consumers to the now lower price (Area 3 < Area 2).

Stop and think   2.2

Now rework these predictions for a price increase in each of the three situations.

Examples

Price elastic demand

Rhapsody, the music service provider, cut the download price of its songs from 99 cents to only 50 cents, and reported a 600% rise in sales volume and a substantial rise in sales value. With a PED of around 12, we would clearly predict that the price reduction would increase total revenue.

Price inelastic demand

It was in early 2010 that the revenue and profit of British American Tobacco (BAT) had risen despite a policy of increasing the price of its premium brands such as *Kent* and *Lucky Strike*. While prices had risen by over 6%, like-for-like volumes fell by 3% over the year, with the result that both revenue and profits had risen.

Case Study 2.1 shows how the link between price elasticity of demand and revenue is an important consideration when setting prices for shampoos and conditioners.

Case Study 2.1   Pricing shampoo and conditioners

There is considerable evidence that the global recession of 2008–2010 has increased the price elasticity of demand (PED) for shampoo and conditioners and indeed for grooming and beauty products in general. Mintel, the data/research group, reported in 2009 that an estimated 60% of shampoos and conditioners were bought on discount or multiple buy offers in the UK. Mintel also reported that 25% of women in the UK now wait until the brand they usually buy is on special offer before making a purchase. The Marketing Magazine also reported in 2009 that 10% of women in the UK had switched to a lower priced brand, including own labels, in a three-month survey conducted by the magazine to February 2009.

Nor is this sensitivity to price for beauty/grooming products restricted to women only. A 2010 survey by Mintel suggested that half of all men in the UK admit to worries that the recession has left them looking worn out. Nearly three-quarters of men said looking groomed increased their confidence in the workplace and one in four men now used facial moisturisers. Around 82% of those using grooming products regularly regarded shampoo as a 'must have' buy (46% for conditioners). The same survey found that UK men spend around €48 on grooming products per year in the UK with Spain €55, France €42, Germany €38 and Italy €30. Price was found to be relevant to the choice of grooming product *within* each category (shampoo, shaving preparations, facial moisturiser, conditioners, fragrances, etc.)

Question

Use your knowledge of price elasticity of demand to advise companies producing shampoos and conditioners on the pricing policy they might adopt for their products.

Measuring price elasticity of demand (PED)

It is clearly vital that the firm has an accurate estimate of price elasticity of demand over the relevant segment of its demand curve if it is to correctly forecast the revenue consequences of any proposed price change.

So far we have tended to suppose that the *whole* demand curve is relatively elastic, relatively inelastic or unit elastic. However, this is rarely the case, except for the three situations of perfectly inelastic demand, unit elastic demand and perfectly elastic demand curves shown earlier in Figure 2.1 (a), (c) and (e) respectively.

In most cases price elasticity of demand *varies along different segments* of the same demand curve. *Taking it further* 2.1 presents the reasoning behind this important observation.

Taking it further **Variations in PED along a demand curve**   2.1

For simplicity we assume a straight-line (linear) demand curve, as in Figure 2.3(a).

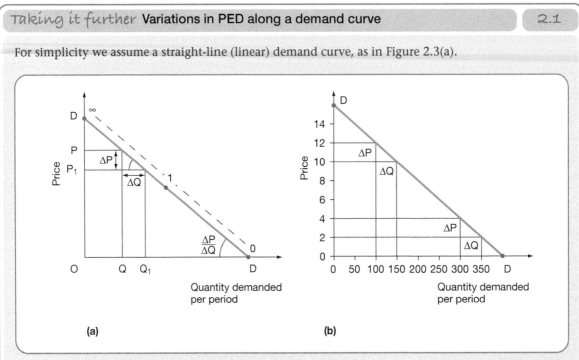

(a)   **(b)**

Figure 2.3 **PED varies along the linear demand curve**

P Q is the initial price and quantity

$P_1 Q_1$ is the new price and quantity

Δ indicates the absolute change in the price or quantity

$$\text{PED} = \frac{\text{percentage change in quantity demanded}}{\text{percentage change in price}}$$

$$= \frac{(\Delta Q/Q) \times 100}{(\Delta P/P) \times 100}$$

$$= \frac{\Delta Q}{Q} \div \frac{\Delta P}{P} \quad \text{(100s cancel out)}$$

$$= \frac{\Delta Q}{Q} \times \frac{P}{\Delta P} \quad \text{(change} \div \text{to} \times\text{)}$$

$$= \frac{P}{Q} \times \frac{\Delta Q}{\Delta P} \quad \text{(rearranging)}$$

Taking it further 2.1 *continued*

$$PED = \frac{P}{Q} \times K \quad \text{(a constant)}$$

Note that we are multiplying the ratio P/Q by a *constant value* (K), since the slope of the demand curve does not change over its entire length.*

We can use this expression to show that the value of price elasticity will vary all the way along the demand curve DD, from infinity (∞) to zero as we move down the demand curve from left to right.

- At the top end of the demand curve (DD), the ratio P/Q is close to infinity where the demand curve cuts the vertical axis (large P, infinitely small Q), and infinity times a constant (K) is infinity.
- At the bottom end of the demand curve (DD), the ratio P/Q is close to zero where the demand curve cuts the horizontal axis (infinitely small P, large Q), and zero times a constant (K) is zero.

We can apply our analysis to the actual demand curve shown in Figure 2.3(b).

For the straight-line demand curve, $\Delta Q/\Delta P$ is a constant at $+50/-2 = (-)25$

- When P = 12, PED $= \frac{12}{100} \times (-)25 = (-)3$
- When P = 4, PED $= \frac{4}{300} \times (-)25 = (-)\frac{1}{3}$

*Note that $\dfrac{\Delta Q}{\Delta P} = 1 \div \dfrac{\Delta P}{\Delta Q}$ i.e. 1 ÷ the slope of the demand curve and 1 divided by a constant is itself a constant (K)

Make a note

For a straight-line demand curve, PED falls from infinity to zero as price falls, since the ratio P/Q falls and the ratio $\Delta Q/\Delta P$ is a constant.

Non-linear demand curve

If the demand curve is *not* a straight line (i.e. it is non-linear) then we have a further problem since the ratio $\Delta Q/\Delta P$ will no longer be a constant. Clearly the ratio $\Delta Q/\Delta P$ in Figure 2.4 will now vary depending on the *magnitude* of the price change from P and the *direction* of the price change from P. This is one of the reasons why alternative measures of price elasticity of demand are used, namely 'arc elasticity' and 'point elasticity'.

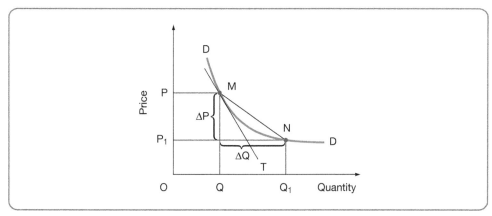

Figure 2.4 **Arc and point elasticities for the non-linear demand curve**

Arc elasticity of demand

As is shown in Figure 2.4, **arc elasticity of demand** is a type of 'average' elasticity between two points (i.e. two different price and quantity situations) on a demand curve. It is particularly useful when the demand curve is not a straight line.

Instead of using only the initial price and quantity values in measuring PED, the concept of *arc elasticity* uses the average of the initial and final values. If, using Figure 2.4, P and Q are the initial price and quantity respectively and P_1 and Q_1 are the final price and quantity, then we can write:

$$\text{Arc elasticity of demand} = \frac{\frac{P + P_1}{2}}{\frac{Q + Q_1}{2}} \times \frac{\Delta Q}{\Delta P} \quad \text{(2s cancel out)}$$

$$\boxed{\text{Arc elasticity of demand} = \frac{P + P_1}{Q + Q_1} \times \frac{\Delta Q}{\Delta P}}$$

The arc elasticity is a measure of *average* elasticity. In Figure 2.4 it is the elasticity at the mid-point of the chord connecting the two points (M and N) on the demand curve corresponding to the initial and final price levels.

Clearly, arc elasticity is only an approximation to the true elasticity over a particular segment (MN) of the demand curve. The greater the curvature of the segment of the demand curve being measured, the less accurate will this approximation of the true elasticity be. *Taking it further* 2.2 provides an example of arc elasticity.

Taking it further **Example of arc elasticity**   2.2

Suppose that demand for widgets is non-linear and that in 2010, at a price of £4 per widget, the demand was 10 million widgets per annum. In 2011 let us suppose that the price falls to £2 and, other things being equal, the demand expands to 13 million widgets per annum.

To find arc elasticity of demand we can use the following formula.

$$e_p = \frac{P + P_1}{Q + Q_1} \times \frac{\Delta Q}{\Delta P}$$

e_p = arc elasticity of demand

P = the original price in 2010 (£)

P_1 = the new price in 2011 (£)

Q = the original quantity demanded in 2010 (in millions)

Q_1 = the new quantity demanded in 2011 (in millions)

Δ = absolute change

Thus the calculation is as follows:

$$e_p = \frac{4 + 2}{10 + 13} \times \frac{3}{-2}$$

$$= \frac{18}{-46}$$

$$= (-)0.39$$

Demand is relatively inelastic with respect to price and hence we can expect total revenue to fall as price falls, which indeed it does from £40m to £26m.

Point elasticity of demand

As is also shown in Figure 2.4, this is a measure of the price elasticity of demand *at a single point* (i.e. a single price and quantity situation) on a demand curve. Again it is a particularly useful measure when the demand curve is not a straight line. It involves finding the slope $(-)\dfrac{\Delta Q}{\Delta P}$ of the straight line that just touches the demand curve at that point (i.e. the slope of the *tangent* MT) as given by the angle formed at point M in Figure 2.4. Then, using our formula from *Taking it further* 2.1 (p. 45), we multiply this slope by the price/quantity ratio.

Make a note

Point elasticity of demand $= \dfrac{P}{Q} \times$ slope of tangent at point M.

Example

Suppose we wish to estimate *point elasticity of demand* at the original price (P) in our widget example from *Taking it further* 2.2. The slope of the tangent MT at point M (sometimes referred to as dQ/dP) is, say, (−)0.5.

$$\text{Point elasticity of demand} = \frac{4}{10} \times (-)0.5 = (-)0.2$$

The point elasticity of demand is even less elastic than arc elasticity of demand.

Total, average and marginal revenue

We have already mentioned total revenue (turnover) and linked this to price elasticity of demand. It may be useful at this stage to look a little more carefully at three widely used definitions of revenue, namely total, average and marginal revenue, before linking all of them to price elasticity of demand.

Total revenue

The firm's *total revenue* is its total earnings from the sale of its product. Where the firm's product is sold to all consumers at the *same* price, then total revenue is simply price (P) multiplied by quantity sold (Q).

$$\textbf{Total revenue} = \textbf{price} \times \textbf{quantity}$$
$$\text{TR} = \text{P} \times \text{Q}$$

Average revenue

The firm's *average revenue* is simply total revenue (TR) divided by quantity sold (Q). When the firm sells all its output at the same price, then price (P) and average revenue (AR) are identical.

$$\textbf{Average revenue} = \frac{\textbf{Total revenue}}{\textbf{Total output}}$$
$$\text{AR} = \frac{\text{TR}}{\text{Q}} = \frac{\text{P} \times \text{Q}}{\text{Q}} = \text{P}$$

It follows that in this situation the demand curve of the firm is the average revenue (AR) curve, since it tells us the price (AR) consumers are willing to pay for any given quantity of the product.

Marginal revenue

The firm's *marginal revenue* is the addition to total revenue from selling the last unit of output. Marginal revenue can also be defined as the rate of change of total revenue. As we see from Question 1 in *You try* 2.1 later in the chapter (p. 53), the MR curve will lie inside a downward sloping demand (AR) curve.

> **Example**
>
> Suppose 5 units of product can be sold at £100 per unit and 6 units of product can be sold at £90 per unit.
>
> - The *total revenue* from 5 units (TR_5) would be £500 ($P \times Q$) and the *average revenue* (P) £100.
> - The *total revenue* from 6 units (TR_6) would be £540 ($P \times Q$) and the *average revenue* (P) £90.
> - The *marginal revenue* from selling the 6th unit (MR_6) would be £540 (TR_6) − £500 (TR_5) = £40. In other words selling the last (6th) unit of output adds £40 to total revenue.

More generally, as regards the nth unit:

$$MR_n = TR_n - TR_{n-1}$$

> **Check the net**
>
> You can visit individual company websites to see how they project their future demand, revenue and pricing situations. For example:
>
> Virgin's website is **www.Virgin.com** Procter & Gamble's website is **www.pg.com** Coca-Cola is **www.cocacola.com** McDonald's website is **www.mcdonalds.com**

PED and tax incidence

Having introduced the idea of price elasticity of demand (PED), it will be useful to consider its role in determining the extent to which a tax on a product (indirect tax) can be passed on to the consumer as a higher price. This is often referred to as the **tax incidence** of the tax on the consumer.

Types of tax

We saw in Chapter 1 (p. 25) that an increase in tax on a product will shift the supply vertically upwards (and to the left), i.e. a decrease in supply. This is because the producer will need to charge a *higher* price after the tax is imposed, in order to receive the same revenue per unit as was the case before the tax. In other words, any given quantity will now only be supplied at a higher price.

- *Lump-sum tax.* This is a constant absolute amount of tax (e.g. £1 per unit) irrespective of price. The supply curve shifts vertically upwards by £1 at all points, i.e. a parallel shift from S to Si in Figure 2.5(a).
- *Percentage (ad valorem) tax.* This is where the absolute amount of tax varies with the price of the product. For example, VAT at 20% will mean more tax is paid as the price of the product rises. The supply curve shifts vertically upwards by an increasing amount as price rises, i.e. a non-parallel shift from S to S_2 in Figure 2.5(a).

Tax and PED

In Figure 2.5(b) we assume, for simplicity, a lump-sum tax which shifts the supply curve S vertically upwards by the amount of the tax, giving the parallel curve S_1.

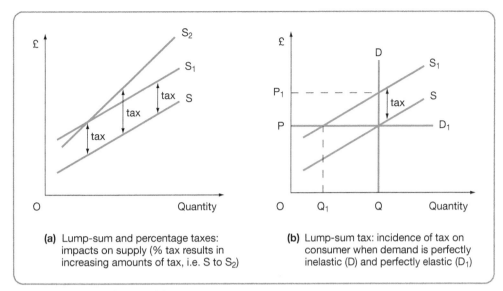

Figure 2.5 **Tax and tax incidence**

Perfectly inelastic demand

Where the demand curve is *perfectly inelastic* (D), the equilibrium price rises from P to P_1, i.e. by the full amount of the tax (equilibrium quantity is unchanged at Q).

We conclude that all the tax is passed on to the consumer, i.e.:

- 100% tax incidence on the consumer;
- 0% tax incidence on the producer.

Perfectly elastic demand

Where the demand curve is *perfectly elastic* (D_1), the equilibrium price is unchanged at P (equilibrium quantity falls to Q_1). We conclude that none of the tax is passed on to the consumer, i.e.:

- 0% tax incidence on the consumer;
- 100% tax incidence on the producer.

Relatively elastic or inelastic demand

Of course, in practice these two extreme price elasticity of demand situations are un-likely to occur. More usually the producer will be faced with *relatively inelastic demand* (Figure 2.6a) or *relatively elastic demand* (Figure 2.6b).

- Where the demand curve is *relatively inelastic* (Figure 2.6a), the producer is able to pass on the larger part of the lump sum tax *t* to the consumer in the form of a higher price. The producer only needs to absorb a small part of the tax.
- Where the demand curve is *relatively elastic* (Figure 2.6b), then the producer is less able to pass on the tax *t* to the consumer and instead the producer must absorb the larger part of the tax.

We conclude that:

- the *more inelastic* the demand, the greater the tax incidence on the consumer, and the smaller the tax incidence on the producer;
- the *more elastic* the demand, the smaller the tax incidence on the consumer, and the greater the tax incidence on the producer.

Case Study 2.2 provides some data on the impacts of higher taxes on smokers.

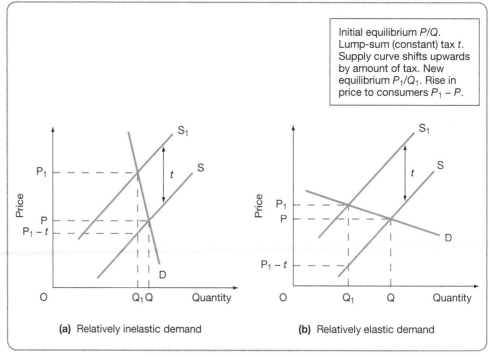

Initial equilibrium P/Q.
Lump-sum (constant) tax t.
Supply curve shifts upwards
by amount of tax. New
equilibrium P_1/Q_1. Rise in
price to consumers $P_1 - P$.

(a) Relatively inelastic demand

(b) Relatively elastic demand

Figure 2.6 Lump-sum tax: incidence of tax on consumer when demand is relatively inelastic and relatively elastic

---

Case Study 2.2   **Taxing smokers**

In recent years, tobacco taxes in France have been pushed up by over 40%, bringing a packet of 20 cigarettes bought in 2010 to around €5, one of the highest prices on the continent. The number of smokers fell at first but is now rising again, especially among teenagers. About one in three French people over 12 is a regular smoker. The French government estimates that more than a third of French adults smoke, of whom half want to stop. France also has the highest proportion of young smokers in Europe, with 53% of 15–24-year-olds counting themselves as regular smokers, compared with an EU average of 41%.

Successive French Health Ministers have bowed to pressure from health professionals and the threat of law suits from passive smokers. Smoking is held responsible for 66,000 deaths a year in France, including 6,000 people who have never smoked.

In theory smoking in all French bars and restaurants was banned as long ago as 1991, except for small, designated 'smoking' areas. In practice, the law was turned upside-down with almost entire premises marked as 'smoking areas'. This was not challenged by the French government, but from January 2008 all this changed. Increased powers to

enforce the law have been given to the police and gendarmerie as well as to the transport police and an army of inspectors. They now have the power to issue 'contravention' documents, like parking tickets, to offenders and impose fines of €68.

Campaigners regret, however, that the French government has taken so long to act decisively. The political power of France's 32,000 tobacconists, furious that French cigarettes are now the most expensive in the EU after those sold in the UK, had prompted the French prime minister to promise a four-year freeze on cigarette duties from 2003 to 2007. This concession to powerful *buralistes* reflected the fact that many of France's 11 million smokers pass through their local tobacconist on a regular basis, giving their owners, who often run bars and small bistros on the side, the opportunity to talk to and influence a large proportion of the French electorate.

Nor are these issues of smoking restrictions restricted to only French companies. For example British American Tobacco provided further proof in 2010 that the world's largest cigarette companies are seeking to shrug off the threat of smoking bans in the West by focusing on increased sales in emerging markets. In its 2010 Report and Accounts, BAT stated that excellent performances in emerging markets had helped it to post a 17% increase in global revenue and an 11% increase in earnings per share in 2009. The world's third largest cigarette maker (after China National Tobacco Corporation and PMI) stated that future acquisitions would concentrate on Asia and North Africa. In Asia, China is the major market for cigarettes with almost 2,200 billion sold per year, followed by Japan (259 billion), Indonesia (239 billion) and India (108 billion). Analysts say the continuing solid performance of the tobacco companies derives from strong trading in emerging markets, which account for around 75% of world volume.

Western markets are expected to continue to decline by 2 to 4% a year over the next 10 years due to health concerns and increasing regulations as more countries ban smoking. Even so, BAT was less affected by the extension of the smoking ban into England in 2007 as it had only a 6% share of the UK market. It has 17% of global market share and sells products in 184 countries, making it Europe's most diversified tobacco company in terms of geography.

Questions

1 What does the case study tell us about the price elasticity of demand for cigarettes in France?

2 Consider some of the implications of stricter enforcement of anti-smoking laws in France and elsewhere.

3 Can you identify any constraints for the French government in seeking to reduce smoking still further?

4 What do the experiences of BAT indicate?

Tax and government revenue

A possible motive for raising indirect taxes on products is, of course, for the government to generate additional tax revenue. Price elasticity of demand for the taxed product will play a key role in determining the impact of such tax increases on government revenue. As we can see from Figure 2.7, the more inelastic the demand for the product, the smaller the impact of any given lump-sum tax on the quantity of the product purchased and therefore the greater the government tax-take (tax per unit × quantity purchased). The tax-take (government revenue) is indicated by the shaded rectangle P_1 VWC, which is clearly greater when demand is relatively inelastic, as in Figure 2.7(a).

It is hardly surprising, therefore, that the Chancellor of the Exchequer has tended to impose higher taxes on goods and services such as cigarettes, alcoholic drinks and gambling, all of which have relatively inelastic demands. Not only can the Chancellor claim to be taxing unhealthy lifestyles (so-called 'sin taxes'), but he can rest assured that he will be raising much-needed revenue for the Exchequer. Or can he?

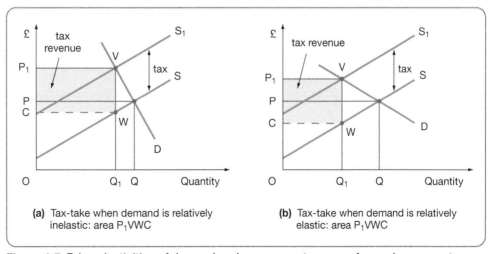

(a) Tax-take when demand is relatively inelastic: area P_1VWC

(b) Tax-take when demand is relatively elastic: area P_1VWC

Figure 2.7 Price elasticities of demand and government revenue from a lump-sum tax

It is certainly true that most empirical estimates indicate relatively inelastic demands for tobacco, drink and gambling. For example, estimates of PED for cigarettes in both the US and UK are in the range (−)0.2 to (−)0.6. However there is increasing evidence that the impacts of globalisation which are considered throughout this book (e.g. Chapter 14, pp. 490–2) may be imposing new constraints on governments seeking to raise revenue via indirect taxation, as for example through the impacts of increased levels of smuggling on the revenue raised from tobacco taxes. Tobacco smuggling features in many reports as Britain's fastest growing category of crime, with Customs and Excise estimating that around £3bn is lost in revenue each year from tobacco smuggling, including cross-Channel boot-legging, large-scale freight smuggling from outside the EU and the diversion to the home market of cigarettes officially designated for export. The VAT and excise duty lost has been estimated as equivalent to around 30% of the amount actually collected.

Taxes may also be imposed on products by governments to achieve policy objectives, as well as to raise revenue, as Case Study 2.3 on the use of taxes by China to combat pollution indicates.

| Case Study 2.3 | Moves towards Beijing pollution tax | |

China's first national census of pollution has revealed such a dire picture that the government has proposed a new tax on its sources, according to reports. The level of water pollution country-wide was found to be more than twice government estimates. Previously, the Chinese government said, it had excluded agricultural sources of pollution. Farms are revealed by the report to be the biggest single source of the main water pollutants. In 2007, the year covered by the census, more than 209bn tonnes of waste water were also discharged.

Preventing and controlling agricultural pollution would be a higher priority in future, said Zhang Lijun, vice minister of environmental protection, announcing the results of the census yesterday. Agricultural waste and the residues and 'run-off' of pesticides and fertilisers are common sources of agricultural pollution. Farmers can reduce the amount of run-off and save money, by targeting the use of chemicals rather than by spraying large areas indiscriminately.

The census found more than 63.7 trillion cubic metres of 'waste gases' were emitted that year. These included emissions of 23m tonnes of sulphur dioxide, which causes acid rain and is commonly the result of burning coal in power stations without 'scrubbers' to remove it. Wen Jiabao, the Chinese premier, admitted last month the country's pollution was 'grim'. Beijing is understood to be concerned that high levels of pollution and other forms of environmental degradation could provide social unrest.

The census will be used as the basis for policy. The data were much more comprehensive and broken down into much more detail than any information on pollutants China has published previously. But green campaigners complained the data gathered were not published in full. The census took two years, as about 6m sources of pollution – factories, farms, residential sources and others – had to be examined. Mr Zhang said: 'The census of pollution sources for the first time in the country is a significant survey on the national situation. Its operations went smoothly and its main tasks were basically completed.' Mr Zhang painted a relatively optimistic picture, forecasting pollution would soon peak and that the government could take a more targeted approach to combat pollution in future. He said discharges of industrial pollutants were concentrated in very few industries and regions. There were 'no major surprises'. China's State Council ordered the census in 2006 and $100m (£64m) was allocated to the project, which involved more than 570,000 people countrywide.

Source: from Beijing considers pollution tax, *Financial Times*, 10/02/2010 (Harvey, F), © The Financial Times Ltd

Questions

1 How might increases in taxes on pollution from agricultural production by the Chinese government help reduce pollution?

2 What other impacts might result from these higher taxes on agricultural production?

Make a note

A subsidy is essentially a negative tax, and shifts the supply curve *downwards* (to the right) by the amount of the subsidy – see Figure 2.5, p. 49. *Removing a subsidy* will have the same effect as increasing a tax. In Figure 2.5(a) introducing a subsidy t will shift the supply curve downwards from S_1 to S. However, removing the subsidy will shift the supply curve upwards from S to S_1, the same as imposing a tax t.

You try 2.1 gives you the opportunity to check your understanding of price elasticity of demand and its links to total revenue and to tax incidence.

You try 2.1

1 (a) Complete the table.

Quantity (units)	AR (£)	TR (£)	MR (£)
1	100		
2	95		
3	90		
4	85		
5	80		
6	75		
7	70		
8	65		

   (b) Draw the AR and MR curves. What do you notice?

2 In this question you'll see a lettered description of a particular situation involving PED. In each case try to match the letter for the description with the number (i) to (v) representing the correct term.

   Descriptions

   (a) A 5% fall in the price of beer leads to a 3% expansion in the amount of beer consumed.

   (b) A 10% rise in the price of books leads to a 15% contraction in the number of books purchased.

   (c) A 6% fall in the price of package tours leads to a 6% expansion in the number of package tours purchased.

   (d) An infinitely small percentage change in the price of wheat leads to an infinitely large percentage change in world demand for wheat.

   (e) A 10% rise in the price of kidney transplants in private sector hospitals leads to no change in demand for these transplants.

   Terms

   (i) Perfectly inelastic demand

   (ii) Relatively inelastic demand

   (iii) Unit elastic demand

   (iv) Relatively elastic demand

   (v) Perfectly elastic demand

3 **True or false**

   (a) Demand for coach travel is relatively elastic, so lower fares can be expected to raise total revenue for the coach company.   True/False

You try 2.1 continued

(b) Demand for rail transport is relatively inelastic so a rise in fares can be expected to reduce total revenue for the train operating company. True/False

(c) Price elasticity of demand for air travel has a numerical value (ignoring sign) of 3, so a 1% cut in price will lead to a 3% expansion of demand and a rise in total revenue. True/False

(d) A certain make of shoes has been found to have a unit elastic demand. A 5% rise in price can be expected to result in a 5% contraction of demand and an unchanged total revenue. True/False

4 **Multiple choice questions**

(a) Which *two* of these examples involve 'price elasticity of demand'?

(i) A fall in the price of beer has resulted in higher beer sales on campus.

(ii) The higher prices of books means that students are going to the cinema less often.

(iii) A fall in student income has led to fewer books being bought.

(iv) Rents in halls of residence have increased so less students are now applying for this type of accommodation.

(b) Which *one* of these statements is true?

(i) Price elasticity of demand tells us about shifts in the demand curve.

(ii) Price elasticity of demand tells us how demand for a product responds to changes in the price of substitutes in consumption.

(iii) Price elasticity of demand tells us about movements along the demand curve.

(iv) Price elasticity of demand tells us how demand for a product responds to changes in the price of complements in consumption.

(c) Which *two* of these statements are true?

(i) Strictly speaking, the sign of price elasticity of demand is negative.

(ii) Strictly speaking, the sign of price elasticity of demand is positive.

(iii) If a 5% fall in price results in a 10% expansion in quantity demanded, then demand is 'relatively inelastic'.

(iv) If a 5% fall in price results in a 10% expansion in quantity demanded, then demand is 'relatively elastic'.

(d) Which *one* of the following would be likely to result in a small percentage fall in price of Levi jeans, leading to a large percentage expansion in quantity of Levi jeans demanded.

(i) Few alternative makes of jeans are available to consumers.

(ii) Many alternative makes of jeans are available to consumers.

(iii) Levi jeans are withdrawn from high street shops and can only now be purchased by mail order.

(iv) The advertising budget for Levi jeans is sharply reduced.

(e) Which *one* of these statements is true?

(i) The more inelastic the demand, the greater the incidence of a tax on the producer.

(ii) The more elastic the demand, the smaller the incidence of a tax on the consumer.

(iii) If demand is perfectly inelastic, the whole incidence of the tax will be on the producer.

(iv) If demand is perfectly elastic, the whole incidence of the tax will be on the consumer.

Answers can be found on pp. 525–546.

Other elasticities of demand

Here we consider a number of other elasticities which can have important impacts on the demand for a product.

Cross-elasticity of demand

Cross-elasticity of demand (CED) is a measure of the responsiveness of demand for a product (X) to a change in price of *some other product* (Y). It involves shifts in a demand curve (increase/decrease) for X rather than movements along a demand curve (expansion/contraction).

The CED for product X is given by the equation:

$$CED = \frac{\%\text{ change in quantity demanded of X}}{\%\text{ change in the price of Y}}$$

- The *sign* of CED will indicate the direction of the shift in demand for X (D_X) in response to a change in the price of Y (P_Y), which in turn will depend upon the relationship in consumption between products X and Y.

  (i) Where X and Y are **substitutes in consumption**, a fall in P_Y will result in an expansion of demand for Y and a decrease in demand for X, i.e. a leftward shift in D_X as some consumers switch to the now relatively cheaper substitute for X. Here the sign of CED will be positive $(-/-=+)$.

  (ii) Where X and Y are **complements in consumption**, a fall in P_Y will result in an expansion of demand for Y and an increase in demand for X, i.e. a rightward shift in D_X as consumers require more of X to complement their extra purchases of Y. Here the sign of CED will be negative $(+/-=-)$.

- The *magnitude* of the shift in D_X will depend upon how close X and Y are as substitutes or complements in consumption. The closer the two products are as substitutes or complements, the greater will be the numerical value of cross-elasticity of demand. In other words, a given fall in price of Y will cause a larger shift to the left of D_X for close substitutes, and a larger shift to the right of D_X for close complements.

Income elasticity of demand

Income elasticity of demand (IED) is a measure of the responsiveness of demand for a product to a change in income (household income or national income). Usually we use real *income* rather than nominal income for this measurement. IED involves shifts in a demand curve (increase/decrease) rather than movements along a demand curve (expansion/contraction).

The IED for product X is given by the equation:

$$IED = \frac{\%\text{ change in quantity demanded of X}}{\%\text{ change in income}}$$

- For a *normal product* the sign of IED will be positive: for example, a rise in income increases demand for X, i.e. a rightward shift in D_X, with more of X demanded at any given price.

- For an *inferior* product the sign will be negative over certain ranges of income: for example, a rise in income beyond a certain 'threshold' level may decrease demand for X as consumers use some of the higher income to switch away from the relatively cheap but poor quality product X to a more expensive, better quality substitute.

As a broad rule of thumb, some people regard income elasticity of demand as useful in classifying products into 'luxury' and 'necessity' groupings. A product is often considered a luxury if IED is > 1 and a necessity if IED is significantly < 1.

Factors affecting IED

Factors affecting the numerical value of IED for a commodity include the following:

1 *The nature of the need satisfied by the commodity.* For some basic needs, e.g. certain types of foodstuffs, the proportion of household income spent on products satisfying these needs falls as income increases. For other needs, the proportion of household income spent on products satisfying these needs rises as income increases, e.g. services such as healthcare and education.

2 *The time period.* The longer the time period, the more likely it is that consumer expenditure patterns will have adjusted to a change in income, implying a higher IED.

3 *The initial level of national income.* At low levels of national income, certain products will still be largely unattainable for the majority of the population. Changes in national income around such a low level will therefore have little effect on the demand for these products, implying a lower IED.

Taking it further 2.3 provides a useful outline of some of the earliest work on income elasticity of demand.

Taking it further **Income elasticity and Ernst Engel (1821–96)**   2.3

Engel was appointed director of the Bureau of Statistics in Prussia and outlined what became known as Engel's Law in a paper published in 1857. The essential idea is that the proportion of income spent on food declines as income rises. In other words, food was being regarded as a necessity with an income elasticity of demand less than 1. Table 2.3 presents data on the spending patterns of 153 Belgian families he studied in 1853. This cross-sectional evidence has subsequently been verified in a range of time-series (longitudinal) data, and cross-country data. For example, in nineteenth-century America people spent some 50% of their incomes on food compared to less than 20% today. Again, people in the less developed countries spend higher proportions of their income on food than do people in, say, the advanced industrialised countries of the OECD.

Engel himself was extremely cautious in interpreting his results at the time. Certainly the table data give early support for services of various forms having high income elasticities of demand.

Table 2.3 **Percentage of total expenditure on various items by Belgian families in 1853**

	Annual income		
Expenditure item	$225–$300	$450–$600	$750–$1,000
Food	62.0%	55.0%	50.0%
Clothing	16.0	18.0	18.0
Lodging, light and fuel	17.0	17.0	17.0
Services (education, legal, health)	4.0	7.5	11.5
Comfort and recreation	1.0	2.5	3.5
Total	100.0	100.0	100.0

Note: Some items have been aggregated.

Source: A. Marshall, *Principles of Economics*, 8th edn, 1920, Macmillan: London, reproduced with permission of Palgrave Macmillan

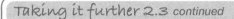

Taking it further 2.3 continued

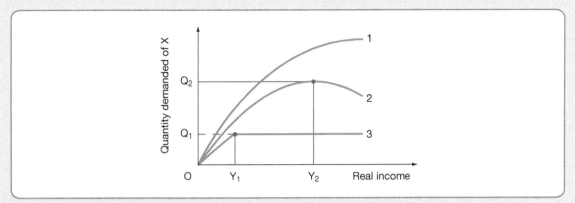

Figure 2.8 **Engel curves**

Engel's relationship between income and the quantity demand of a product has been generalised and brought up to date in the so-called Engel curves shown in Figure 2.8.

These Engel curves relate quantity demanded of a product to real income.

- Curve 1: a rise in real income increases demand for product X at all levels of income. X is a 'normal good'.

- Curve 2: a rise in real income increases demand for product X, but only up to the level of real income Y_2. Further rises in real income beyond Y_2 result in a decrease in demand for X. Product X is an 'inferior good'.

- Curve 3: a rise in real income increases demand for product X, but only up to the level of real income Y_1. Further rises in real income beyond Y_1 result in no change in demand for X. We say that demand for this product is 'fully satisfied' or 'satiated' at a relatively low level of real income.

Advertising elasticity of demand (AED)

This is a measure of the responsiveness of demand for product X to a change in advertising expenditure on the product. The intention of most forms of advertising is to reinforce the attachment of existing consumers to the product and to attract new consumers. In this latter case the advertising is seeking to change consumer tastes in favour of the product, i.e. shift the demand curve to the right with more of X bought at any given price.

$$AED = \frac{\% \text{ change in quantity demanded of X}}{\% \text{ change in advertising expenditure on X}}$$

A firm may also be interested in *cross-advertising elasticity*, which measures the responsiveness of demand for product X to a change in advertising expenditure on some other product Y. If X and Y are substitutes in consumption and extra advertising on the rival Y decreases demand for X substantially, then some counter-strategy by X to restore its fortunes (i.e. shift its demand curve to the right) might be of high priority, perhaps including an aggressive advertising campaign of its own.

Make a note

So many questions depend on your knowledge of PED and these other elasticities. Do make sure that you are familiar with the 'box diagram' (Figure 2.2, p. 42) and that, should price be changed, you can relate the numerical value of PED to changes in total revenue.

You try 2.2 uses a number of questions to check your understanding of these other elasticities of demand.

You try   2.2

1 Which *two* of the following statements are true?

   (a) A small rise in the price of student accommodation means that fewer books are bought, which suggests that the price elasticity of demand for books is high.

   (b) A small rise in the price of student accommodation results in far fewer books bought, which suggests that there may be a high cross-elasticity of demand between the two items.

   (c) The sign of the cross-elasticity of demand between two products can help indicate whether they are substitutes in consumption or complements in consumption.

   (d) Cross-elasticity of demand involves movements along the demand curve for a product, not shifts in the demand curve for that product.

2 Which *two* of the following statements refer to 'income elasticity of demand'?

   (a) A 1% rise in the UK's GNP will result in a 2% increase in demand for travel.

   (b) A 1% fall in the price of travel will lead to a 2% expansion in the demand for travel.

   (c) A 1% fall in the UK's GNP will result in a 3% decrease in demand for healthcare products.

   (d) A 1% rise in the price of prescription drugs will lead to a 3% contraction in demand.

3 In this question you'll see a lettered description of a particular situation involving CED. In each case try to match the letter for the description with the number (i) to (v) representing the correct term.

   Description

   (a) The purchase of books from the campus bookshop falls dramatically every time the price of beer rises.

   (b) A fall in the price of CDs has had no effect on the quantity of books sold.

   (c) Every time the price of designer jeans falls there is a large increase in the sales of higher-quality trainers.

   (d) A 5% rise in the price of cinema admissions leads to a 1% decrease in ice cream sales in the cinema.

   (e) A 10% fall in the price of cigarettes leads to a 1% decrease in the purchase of cigars.

   Terms

   (i)   Large negative value for CED

   (ii) Large positive value for CED

   (iii) Small negative value for CED

   (iv) Small positive value for CED

   (v) Zero value for CED

4 Which of the following situations would be most favourable for a company with an income elasticity of demand for its product of +3 to plan for an increase in output?

   (a) Money incomes to rise by 2% and prices by 2%.

   (b) Money incomes to rise by 3% and prices by 4%.

You try 2.2 continued

(c) Money incomes to rise by 4% and prices by 2%.

(d) Money incomes to rise by 5% and prices by 6%.

(e) Money incomes to rise by 6% and prices by 5%.

5 Football socks are found to have a cross-elasticity of demand of −2 with respect to product Y. Which of the following products is most likely to be product Y?

(a) Rugby boots

(b) Football boots

(c) Tennis socks

(d) Tennis shoes

(e) Cricket boots

6 Lager is found to have a cross-elasticity of demand of +2 with respect to product Y. Which of the following products is most likely to be product Y?

(a) Crisps

(b) Vodka

(c) Pub lunches

(d) Beer

(e) Wine

Answers can be found on pp. 525–546.

The following case study uses transport to see how these different elasticity concepts can be relevant to practical policy making.

Case Study 2.4   Transport and elasticities of demand

In the 2010 budget, the tax on petrol was raised yet again, this time by 3 pence per litre, the fifth time the government has increased petrol tax in 18 months since January 2009. Motorists and organisations such as the AA and RAC point to the fact that over 80% of the price paid at the pump for petrol now goes to the Treasury in tax, a dramatic rise on the much smaller 44% of the petrol price which went to the Treasury as recently as 1980.

Evidence from the developed economies suggests that for every 10% increase in real fuel prices, the demand for fuel will fall by around 6%. This consumer response to higher fuel prices may take several years to fully work through.

The demand for car ownership and for travel (and therefore the derived demand for fuel) is also closely related to the level of household income.

Again, studies suggest that for every 10% increase in real income the demand for fuel eventually increases by around 12% within two years of the rise in real income.

Of course, the demand for fuel does not only depend on its own price and the level of real household income, but also on other factors. For example, whereas the real cost of motoring per kilometre travelled (fuel costs, car purchase, repairs, road tax etc.) has barely changed over the past 20 years (e.g. more efficient engines result in more kilometres per litre of petrol), the real costs of rail and bus per kilometre travelled have risen by more than 30% and 35% respectively over the same 20-year period. Clearly this change in *relative* costs has given a boost to demand for car ownership and travel, and therefore to the demand for fuel.

Case Study 2.4 continued

Many people argue that fuel taxes should rise even higher than they are now, since the private motorist imposes costs on society that he or she does not actually pay for. Extra motorists bring about congestion on our roads and increased journey times, increase the need for more road building with the inevitable loss of countryside, result in more carbon dioxide (CO_2) and other toxic gas emissions which damage the ozone layer and lead to global warming. In other words, many believe that the *private costs* of the motorist do not fully reflect the *social costs* imposed by the motorist.

Higher taxes on fuel will, as we have seen, raise the price of motoring and discourage road travel. For example, it has been estimated that a 10% increase in the price of fuel will lead to an extra 1% of rail passengers on rail services and an extra 0.5% of bus passengers on bus services.

Of course, demand for some products may actually *decrease* as fuel prices rise. With less car usage there may be a decrease in demand for garage-related services and products.

The *net* effect of a rise in fuel prices will depend on the sign and size of all these elasticities, namely own-price, income and cross-elasticities of demand.

Questions

1 Can you calculate any own-price, income and cross-elasticities of demand from the information given in the case study?

2 Why do some people believe that fuel taxes and fuel prices are too low?

3 Can you suggest why governments might be wary of making the motorist pay the full private and social costs of any journey?

The 'Veblen effect' and consumer behaviour

So far we have assumed that a fall in price will lead to an expansion of demand, and vice versa; in other words, that the demand curve slopes downwards from left to right. Later in this chapter and in Appendix 1 (p. 507) we use indifference curves to explain why this so-called 'law of demand' generally applies to most products.

However, it is worth noting at this point that there has long been a recognition that in some circumstances, the demand curve might actually slope upwards from left to right. In other words, that a rise in price results in an expansion of demand, and a fall in price a contraction of demand. For example, Thorstein Veblen, in his book *Theory of the Leisure Class* in 1899, pointed out that the key characteristic of some products is that they are ostentatious ('showy') and intended to impress. For such 'conspicuous consumption products', the satisfaction derived from their consumption derives largely from the effect this has on other people rather than from any inherent utility in the product itself.

What has become known as the 'Veblen effect' refers to the psychological association of price with quality by consumers, with a fall in price taken to imply a reduction in quality and therefore greater reluctance to purchase. Instead of expansion of demand, the fall in price may therefore result in a contraction of demand, giving us an upward-sloping demand curve. The 'Veblen effect' is more likely to operate for high-priced products in 'prestige' markets where accurate information on the true quality of these products is highly imperfect.

Case Study 2.5 looks at the issue of 'top-up fees' which have been used in English universities from 2006 onwards and the suggestion that universities charging less than the maximum £3,070 per annum fee permitted in 2007 for a course (or less than the £3,290 maximum of 2010/11) may be deemed, by prospective students, to be offering poorer quality courses even where that is not, objectively, the case.

Case Study 2.5   'Top-up fees' and the 'Veblen effect'

In 2010/11 universities in England are able to charge top-up fees ranging from £0 to £3,290. In fact, since September 2006 universities in England have been able to charge such 'variable top-up fees', so-called because the charge can vary between different courses in a given university and for the same course in different universities. Students can borrow the funds to cover these fees and other living expenses. In 2010 the average first-year student loan exceeded £7,000, but the loan is only repayable once students are in employment and earn over £15,000 per year. An interest rate is charged on the loan which is much lower than commercial rates and is only intended to cover the rate of inflation.

In fact, most universities are charging the full £3,290 annual tuition fee, though initially some universities and some courses chose to charge lower fees.

A number of potential pricing (charging) principles were actively discussed by universities in deciding upon what fees to charge.

Cost-plus pricing

Here top-up fees are higher where the costs of course/subject delivery are higher. For example, science-based courses need expensive laboratories and equipment.

Revenue-based pricing

Here top-up fees are higher for those courses/subjects where demand is greatest. This often means courses/subjects which are the most popular with students, sometimes because they are expected to increase employment opportunities the most and therefore raise the expected lifetime income from studying that course.

Let us first review some studies indicating lifetime returns on undergraduate study. Considerable evidence exists to suggest that projected student lifetime returns and other benefits (e.g. lifetime employment prospects) are greater, on average, for graduates than for non-graduates.

The *average* lifetime return for graduates vis-à-vis non-graduates has been calculated at various times in the recent past.

- In 1988 the UK government claimed that the annual rate of return on human capital investment in the form of a degree – reflecting the additional lifetime earnings a graduate will accrue over and above those of a non-graduate – was around 25%. In 1996, the Dearing Report brought this 'rate of return' estimate down to between 11% and 15%.
- In 2001 the OECD estimated that the annual 'rate of return' on a UK degree was some 17% vis-à-vis non-graduates (higher than that in any of the ten countries studied, such as the 15% of France and 10% of the Netherlands).
- The UK government has in the past used a figure of £400,000 as the additional lifetime earnings for the average graduate vis-à-vis the average non-graduate. Data from the Department for Education and Skills focuses on comparing the lifetime earnings of those with a degree with a more specific comparator group than the 'average non-graduate'. When comparing the lifetime earnings of graduates with those who 'have the qualifications to get into higher education but choose not to go to university', the earnings premium falls from £400,000 to £120,000 over the average working lifetime.
- Universities UK[1] (2007) usefully reviewed variations in lifetime returns by subject/courses studied. While it found the average extra lifetime earnings associated with a degree was in the order of £160,000, this varied from over £340,000 for subjects such as medicine and dentistry to around £35,000 for subjects linked to the arts.
- Dorsett *et al.*[2] (2010) find that upgrading qualifications to degree or equivalent level increases lifelong earnings significantly, for example by 12.2% for males aged 25 years or over at the time of graduation.

The lifetime *employability* of graduates has also been emphasised in studies by the Council for Industry and Higher Education in 2003, which indicate that the overall demand for graduates is likely to exceed the growing number emerging with degrees, even should the 50% target for graduates in the UK be achieved.

[1]Universities UK (2007) *The Economic Benefits of a Degree*.
[2]Dorsett, R., Lui, S. and Weale, M. (2010) 'Economic Benefits of Lifelong Learning', NIESR Discussion Paper, No. 352.

Case Study 2.5 *continued*

Prestige pricing

Here price is itself associated with *quality* by users of the product. In situations where the information available to users is imperfect, price is often used as a proxy variable for quality. Student and parent assessment of educational courses characterised by differential top-up fees is an obvious candidate for such a 'Veblen' effect, reinforced by the fact that the 'older' universities (widely perceived by the general public to be of the highest quality) will be seen to charge the full £3,290 annual tuition fee for most of their courses.

A major cross-country study into higher education by IDP Education Australia in association with the British Council strongly supported the existence of this Veblen effect as regards international student demand for higher education. Senior researcher Anthony Bohm commented: 'Students cannot make an informed choice about the exact quality of comparable products, so they use price as a proxy for understanding the value they will get out of an international programme.'

Questions

1 Suppose you were responsible for setting the top-up fees to be charged for the course you are studying. Use the ideas in the case study to suggest how you might go about making your decision.

2 Can you explain how the case study might provide some support for an upward sloping demand curve for higher education?

Consumer surplus

Links

Pricing policies are discussed in many chapters of this book. However, Chapter 12 (pp. 388–9) brings these various pricing approaches together in one section.

Before leaving our discussion of consumer behaviour, it is useful to consider the idea of **consumer surplus**. In its most widely used form it measures in value terms the difference between the amount of money that a consumer *actually pays* to buy a certain quantity of product X and the amount that he/she would be *willing to pay* for this quantity of X. In Figure 2.9 it is given by the area APC, where quantity X_1 is purchased at price P.

As we shall see in other parts of this book, the idea of consumer surplus is sometimes used when trying to put a value on the *economic welfare* from using resources in a particular way (e.g. Chapter 8, p. 250).

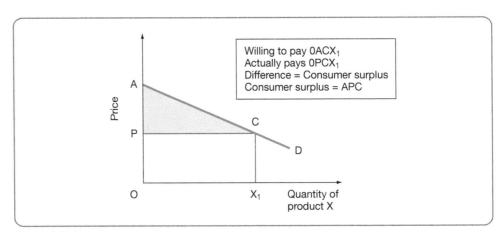

Figure 2.9 **Consumer surplus**

Utility and consumer behaviour

Utility refers to the satisfaction consumers derive from the consumption of goods and services (products). Utility is important because only those products which possess utility, i.e. which provide satisfaction, will be demanded. Of course, the amount of utility or satisfaction gained from consuming a product is different for different people. Nevertheless, to begin with, we simplify the situation by assuming that utility can be measured in 'units of satisfaction' as in Table 2.4.

Total and marginal utility

- **Total utility** represents the overall satisfaction from consuming a given amount of a product.
- **Marginal utility** represents the change in satisfaction from consuming an extra unit of the product.

Table 2.4 shows the different levels of total and marginal utility from consuming different amounts of drink. We can see that *total utility* rises up to seven drinks consumed, remains unchanged for the eighth drink and actually falls for the ninth drink.

Figure 2.10 plots the data of Table 2.4 on a diagram showing the *total utility curve* and the marginal utility curve.

Stop and think   2.3

Comment on the relationship between total and marginal utility:

  (a) when total utility is rising;

  (b) when total utility is a maximum;

  (c) when total utility is falling.

Table 2.4 **An individual's utility schedule**

Drinks consumed	Total utility (units of satisfaction)	Marginal utility (units of satisfaction)
0	0	–
1	27	27
2	39	12
3	47	8
4	52	5
5	55	3
6	57	2
7	58	1
8	58	0
9	56	-2

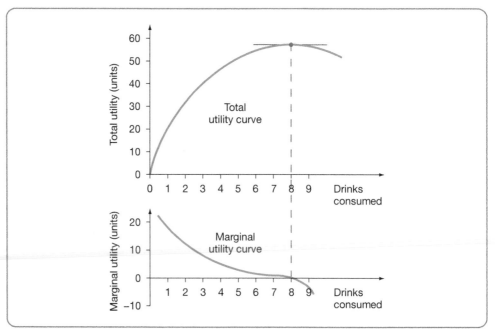

Figure 2.10 **Total and marginal utility curves**

Law of diminishing marginal utility

This simply states that as extra units of a product are consumed, each extra (marginal) unit adds less and less to total utility (satisfaction). The second cold drink on a hot day may certainly increase your satisfaction, but *by less* than you gained from consuming the first cold drink! In other words, the marginal utility of the second cold drink was less than the first, and so on. Indeed the marginal utility of the eighth drink is zero in Table 2.4 and that of the ninth drink is actually negative (i.e. results in *disutility*.)

Utility and the demand curve

The law of diminishing marginal utility helps to explain the general relationship between an individual's demand for a good or service and the price of that good or service. If each extra unit of a product gives less satisfaction to an individual than the previous unit, then it follows that the individual will often need the incentive of a lower price if he or she is to be encouraged to consume an extra unit. Because of this it is reasonable to assume that for an individual, as the price of a good or service falls, the amount demanded will rise (expand).

> **Make a note**
>
> We are moving along a given demand curve as the price of the product changes – so we use the terms *expand* or *contract*.

A further assumption about utility is usually made, namely that consumers will choose between the different goods and services they might purchase in order to gain as much utility as possible, i.e. *maximise total utility*. Of course, the different combinations of goods and services actually available to the consumers will depend upon their levels of income and the prices of the goods and services.

Taking it further 2.4 presents a more formal explanation of this linkage between marginal utility and the downward sloping demand curve.

Taking it further Marginal utility and demand   2.4

Since consumers aim to maximise their total utility, it follows that consumer equilibrium exists when a consumer cannot increase total utility by reallocating his/her expenditure. This occurs when the following condition is satisfied:

$$\frac{MU_A}{P_A} = \frac{MU_B}{P_B} = \dots \frac{MU_n}{P_n}$$

In other words, when the ratios of marginal utility and price are equal for all products consumed.

When this condition is satisfied, it is impossible for the consumer to increase total utility by rearranging his/her purchases because the last pound spent on each product yields the same addition to total utility in all cases. This must maximise total utility because, for example, if the last pound spent on product B yielded more utility than the last pound spent on product A, then the consumer could increase total utility by buying more of B and less of A. This is impossible when the ratios of marginal utility and price are equal (see Table 2.5).

Table 2.5 Marginal utility and demand

| Quantity consumed | Product A | | | Product B | | |
	Price (£)	Total utility	Marginal utility	Price (£)	Total utility	Marginal utility
1	2	15	15	4	25	25
2	2	27	12	4	48	23
3	2	37	10	4	68	20
4	2	46	9	4	86	18
5	2	53	7	4	102	16
6	2	56	3	4	116	14
7	2	57	1	4	128	12
8	2	55	-2	4	139	11

It is assumed that only two products, A which costs £2 per unit and B which costs £4 per unit, are available, and that the consumer has a total budget of £18.

Given the consumer's budget, the existing prices and the levels of utility available from consumption, equilibrium is achieved when 3 units of product A and 3 units of product B are purchased.

$$\frac{MU_A}{P_A} = \frac{MU_B}{P_B} \text{ with } \frac{10}{2} = \frac{20}{4}$$

With a budget of £18 it is impossible to achieve a higher level of utility.

Stop and think   2.4

Suppose the price of product B now falls from £4 to £2 per unit, other things equal; use the equilibrium condition to show that demand for B expands.

While there are many problems in doing so, modern approaches are trying to measure the utility of different products to different people. Case Study 2.6 looks at recent attempts to put a value on a particular 'product' (namely time) as between different people.

Case Study 2.6   What is time worth?

Putting a value on time

Some recent calculations suggest that the average British minute is worth just over 10p to men and 8p to women. A mathematical formula for the monetary value of every minute of a person's working life has been devised by researchers at Warwick University, showing the precise cost of a lie-in, an extra hour at the office or even brushing one's teeth.

The equation, according to its inventors, will allow people to work out whether they are getting a fair rate for overtime, as well as helping them to decide whether it is worth spending extra cash to save time. It can judge the financial cost of a takeaway meal against the time taken to cook dinner, or the relative benefits of paying for a taxi or saving money by taking the bus, and comes up with very different answers according to where people live and how much they earn.

The formula, which has been calculated by Ian Walker, a professor of economics at Warwick University, is

$$V = W \frac{\left(\dfrac{100 - t}{100}\right)}{C}$$

where V is the value of an hour, W is a person's hourly wage, t is the tax rate and C is an index of the local cost of living.

This means that an hour of a man on average earnings in 2010 was valued at £8.32, or 14p a minute, while an hour of a woman on average earnings in 2010 was valued at £6.59 or almost 11p per minute. An hour is most valuable to men in London, where it averages £10.81, and least valuable to women in the north of England, at £5.55.

People who earn the same amount of money, however, can find their time worth significantly more or less in different parts of the country. In the north of England, where the cost of living is lowest, someone with a salary of £20,000 puts a value of £6.80 on an hour compared with just £5.15 in London.

Professor Walker said that the formula would help people to work out whether they would benefit by spending money to save time, for example by employing a cleaner or by taking taxis. If the amount one pays for a service is less than the value of the time you would take to do it yourself, it is generally worth spending the money on buying the service.

For example, an accountant living in London on a salary of £60,000 with a cost of living index (C) of 1.32 will value each hour at £13.64 and each minute at 23p. It will cost the accountant 69p (3 minutes) to brush his/her teeth and £11.50 (50 minutes) to cook dinner. In contrast, an office worker on a salary of £20,000 in Sunderland with a cost of living (C) of 1.00 will value each hour at £6.80 and each minute at 11p. It will cost 33p to brush his/her teeth and £5.50 to cook dinner.

'This research is the first of its kind to take into account the overall picture of how highly our time is being valued,' he said. 'Traditionally, wages or salaries have given an indication of how we are valued at work; however, by looking at salaries against taxation, the cost of living and regional variations we can see how much an hour of our time is worth whether at work or home.' Ian Barber of Barclaycard, which commissioned the research, said: 'What this formula can do is help us to think about how to value and use our time more effectively, vital in an age when many people feel as though they have less time to spend in the way they want to.'

Questions

1 Why is it suggested that for people earning the same amount the value of an hour is worth more in the North than in London?

2 What does it mean when C (index of the local cost of living) is stated as being 1.32 in London but 1.00 in the North?

3 Does the case study suggest that we can have a 'unit of utility' for time that is common to everyone?

You try 2.3 checks your understanding of total and marginal utility.

You try   2.3

1 Which *two* of these examples illustrate the idea of diminishing marginal utility?

   (a) The third ice cream raises total utility by the same amount as the second ice cream.

   (b) The third ice cream raises total utility by more than the second ice cream.

   (c) The third ice cream raises total utility by less than the second ice cream.

   (d) The addition to total utility from the second ice cream is more than the addition to total utility from the third ice cream.

   (e) The addition to total utility from the second ice cream is less than the addition to total utility from the third ice cream.

2 Which *one* of these examples illustrates the idea of constant marginal utility?

   (a) The third ice cream raises total utility by the same amount as the second ice cream.

   (b) The third ice cream raises total utility by more than the second ice cream.

   (c) The third ice cream raises total utility by less than the second ice cream.

   (d) The addition to total utility from the second ice cream is more than the addition to total utility from the third ice cream.

   (e) The addition to total utility from the second ice cream is less than the addition to total utility from the third ice cream.

3 Which *two* of the following refer to situations in which total utility is a maximum?

   (a) Marginal utility is positive.

   (b) Marginal utility is negative.

   (c) Marginal utility is zero.

   (d) The ratios of prices and marginal utilities are different for all the products consumed by an individual.

   (e) The ratios of prices and marginal utilities are equal for all the products consumed by an individual.

Answers can be found on pp. 525–546.

Even though we have sought to place a value on time in Case Study 2.6, it is unclear whether an increase in the value placed on our time will inevitably increase our 'happiness'. Some linkages between utility and happiness are explored further in Case Study 2.7.

| Case Study 2.7 | Utility and happiness |

Richard Layard, in his book *Happiness*,* argues that extra income does make us happier because we are able to satisfy certain basic wants. But once incomes are above $20,000 a year, the relationship breaks down. What is more, it is clear that while a boost to our spending power makes us feel good for a while, the effect soon wears off as we become used to our new income level. The impact of getting a pay rise is dulled if everyone else at work gets one too.

An experiment conducted at Harvard and cited by Layard makes the point. Students were asked to choose between two imaginary worlds: in the first they would earn $50,000 a year while the average for everybody else would be $25,000, while in the

*Layard, R. (2005) *Happiness*, Allen Lane.

Case Study 2.7 *continued*

second they would earn $100,000 against an average of $250,000. Conventional economics would suggest that any rational individual would choose the latter option since they would be twice as well off. Actually, a majority chose the former; they were happier to be poorer if that meant they were higher in the pecking order.

Interestingly, the same did not apply when the researchers looked at holidays. In one world, students would have two weeks off while others had one week's holiday; in the second they would have four weeks off and everybody else would have eight. This time only 20% of the students chose the first option, suggesting that they valued extra leisure more highly than they valued extra income.

The picture, according to Layard, is not a pretty one. He says that a study of 50 countries has found that six factors can account for 80% of the variations in happiness. These are the divorce rate, the unemployment rate, the level of trust, membership of non-religious organisations, the quality of government and the fraction of the population that believes in God. Divorce and unemployment are higher than they were 40 years ago, the levels of trust, memberships of societies and religious belief are down. We live in a rich but barren environment, insecure about our jobs and worried about crime. So what is to be done? Layard says happiness should become the overarching goal of government policy and comes up with a number of novel ideas for how this might be done, including compulsory classes on parenting in schools, lessons on emotional intelligence from the age of five, greater security from losing your job, and a more sceptical approach to the whole question of labour market flexibility.

Questions

1 What influences happiness in this study?

2 What implications are there for government policy?

So far we have assumed that we can actually measure satisfaction (i.e. that utility is cardinal). In practice, many observers believe that there is no such thing as a 'unit of satisfaction (utility)' that is common to everybody, so that utility cannot be measured. If that is the case then we need a different approach to consumer behaviour. An alternative approach can also explain the downward sloping demand curve but using the much 'weaker' and more realistic assumption that consumers need only be able to *order* their preferences between different combinations (bundles) of products, preferring some bundles to other alternative bundles (i.e. utility is ordinal). This is the essential feature of indifference curve analysis, which is considered in detail in Appendix 1 (pp. 507–517).

Links

If your course involves indifference curves and budget lines, then turn to Appendix 1 (pp. 507–517) for an analysis of the 'law of demand' using these techniques.

Whatever our approach to utility, what is clear is that the tastes of consumers have changed considerably over time and continue to change. The resulting shifts in demand curves for various goods and services have had significant effects on patterns of output and employment in the UK. Case Study 2.8 documents some of the changes in tastes of UK consumers over the past 50 years or so.

Case Study 2.8   Changing tastes over time

We have seen that an indifference curve captures the different bundles of products that give the consumer a constant level of utility. There is no doubt that the bundles of products that yielded a certain amount of utility in the past are very different from the bundles that give a similar amount of utility today!

For example, each year the Office for National Statistics (ONS) monitors the most popular products in the nation's shopping baskets in the UK. The basket in 2010 contained 650 goods and services that a typical household bought over the last 12 months, and each year the basket is adjusted to reflect changing consumer behaviour.

Case Study 2.8 *continued*

Table 2.6 **Changes in the UK 'shopping basket' 2010**

New item	Dropped item
Garlic bread	Pitta bread
Cereal bars	Men's training shoes/casual footwear
Frozen fish in breadcrumbs/batter	Squash court hire
Powdered baby formula	Baby food
Fruit drink, bottle	Fruit drink carton
Still mineral water, small bottle	Fizzy canned drink
Allergy tablets	Gas call-out charge
Blu-ray players	Gas service charge
Computer games with accessories	Disposable camera
Electric hair straighteners/tongs	Hairdryer
Lip gloss	Lipstick
Liquid soap	Individual bar of toilet soap

Source: Gooding, P. (2010) 'Consumer Prices Index and Retail Index: The Basket of Goods and Services', *ONS*, March 15, Tables 3 and 4. Crown copyright material is reproduced with the permission of the Controller of HMSO and the Queen's Printer for Scotland under the Click-Use Licence.

Table 2.6 presents the products that were included for the first time in 2010, and those products that were excluded.

The shopping basket was first introduced in 1947 as a basis for accurately calculating the rate of inflation. In the 1960s the products entering included sliced bread, fish fingers, crisps, jams and 'meals out' in restaurants. During the 1970s in came frozen foods, aluminium foil, wine, hardboard for home improvements and the cost of visiting stately homes. The 1980s saw the introduction of microwaves, video recorders, CDs and CD players and low alcohol lager and the 1990s included for the first time the Internet, satellite dishes, camcorders, computer games, CD-Roms, Internet subscriptions and foreign holidays.

During the first decade of the millennium various higher-technology products replaced those of an earlier vintage, with flat-panel TVs, satellite navigation systems, digital radios, DVDs and mobile downloads replacing various types of earlier TV, radio and music technologies. Similarly, higher-priced, 'luxury'-type food and drinks (e.g. broccoli, courgettes, pro-biotic drinks, coffee latte) have replaced many cheaper convenience foods, with expenditure on such foods having risen by 40% over the past five years, and joining vegetarian and reduced-calorie ready meals which appeared for the first time in the early part of the decade. Spending on healthcare is also rising rapidly in the UK and even pre-prepared pet food is now in, replacing the effort previously made in preparing home-made foods for pets.

The changes in the contents of the basket for 2010 continue to reflect new purchasing trends. For example, the importance of new technology is seen in the inclusion of Blu-ray disc players and computer games (with accessories), reflecting in part the decrease in prices of new Blu-ray technology and the growing popularity of computer games. In terms of food, the inclusion of 'frozen fish in breadcrumbs' was designed to improve the coverage of fish, which was under-represented in the previous basket of goods. The substitution of fizzy canned drinks by small bottles of still water reflect the 'on the go' drinks market where consumers buy small bottles for journeys and for consumption at work.

Questions

1 Look again at Table 2.6. Can you explain any of the patterns and trends in the UK which might help explain why some products are 'in' and some 'out' of the typical shopping basket?

2 Does your answer to Q.1 help explain the products in the shopping basket observed in the earlier decades of the 1960s, 1970s, 1980s and 1990s?

3 What products might you expect to appear in, and disappear from, the typical shopping basket over the next ten years? Explain your reasoning.

> ### Recap
>
> - The numerical value of price elasticity of demand (PED) indicates to the business the likely impact of a change in the price of its product on total revenue.
> - 'Arc elasticity of demand' is an *average* measure of PED over a range of the demand curve. 'Point elasticity of demand' is a measure of PED at a particular point on a demand curve.
> - The incidence of a tax on a product will fall more on the consumer (and less on the producer) the less elastic is the demand for the product.
> - The sign and size of cross-elasticity of demand (CED) indicates the closeness of substitutes or complements in consumption for product X. It tells us the direction and magnitude of shift in the demand curve for product X when some other product Y changes its price.
> - The sign and size of income elasticity of demand (IED) tells us the direction and magnitude of shift in the demand curve for product X when real incomes rise.
> - The law of 'diminishing marginal utility' can be used to help explain why the demand curve is negatively sloped (i.e. the 'law of demand').

> ### Key terms
>
> **Arc elasticity of demand** A measure of price elasticity of demand which uses the average of the initial and final values for price and quantity. It is the elasticity at the mid-point of the chord connecting the two points on the demand curve corresponding to the initial and final price levels.
>
> **Cardinal utility** The cardinalist school supposed that utility could be measured, either in terms of some abstract quantity (e.g. utils) or in terms of money. In the latter case, utility is expressed in terms of the amount of money a consumer is willing to sacrifice for an additional unit of a commodity.
>
> **Consumer surplus** An area representing the benefit to consumers from paying a price lower than the price they were willing to pay.
>
> **Cross-elasticity of demand (CED)** Indicates the responsiveness of demand for a product to changes in the price of some other product.
>
> $$CED = \frac{\% \text{ change in quantity demanded of X}}{\% \text{ change in price of Y}}$$
>
> The CED for *substitutes in consumption* is positive (−/−). The CED for *complements in consumption* is negative (+/−). CED involves shifts in demand.
>
> **Income elasticity of demand (IED)** The responsiveness of demand for a product to changes in consumer (national) income. Here, as for CED, we are considering shifts in the demand curve of the product.
>
> $$IED = \frac{\% \text{ change in quantity demanded of X}}{\% \text{ change in real income}}$$
>
> **Indifference curve** The different combinations of purchases of the products which give the same level of utility.
>
> **Marginal utility** The addition to total utility from consuming the last unit of a product.
>
> **Ordinal utility** The ordinalist approach does not assume that consumer utility be measurable, merely that consumer preferences can be ranked in order of importance.

Price elasticity of demand (PED) A measure of the responsiveness of demand for a product to changes in its own price.

PED indicates the extent of movement along the demand curve for X in response to a change in price of X.

$$PED = \frac{\% \text{ change in quantity demanded of X}}{\% \text{ change in price of X}}$$

Relatively elastic demand Where a given % change in own-price of a product leads to a larger % change in quantity demanded of that product.

Relatively inelastic demand Where a given % change in own-price of a product leads to a smaller % change in quantity demanded of that product.

Tax incidence This involves measuring the proportion of any tax increase that is paid for by the consumer (in higher prices) or by the producer. For example, the tax incidence would be 100% on the consumer and 0% on the producer should the whole of the tax increase be passed on to the consumer (e.g. perfectly inelastic demand).

Total utility The total satisfaction to consumers.

Turnover A term which refers to the total sales revenue of a business.

Unit elastic demand Where a given % change in own-price of a product leads to exactly the same % change in the quantity demanded of that product.

Veblen effect The psychological association of price with quality.

Supply, production and cost

Introduction

When the price of a product rises, what extra quantity will the business supply and how long will this take? In other words, how responsive or 'elastic' is the quantity supplied of a product to changes in its own price and over what time period? The answer depends on how easily the business can acquire additional resources to use in production (such as raw materials, labour or capital equipment) and on the extra costs it incurs as output expands. In this chapter we review the production and cost issues which underpin the conventional upward (positive) sloping supply curves encountered in Chapter 1. We also assess the benefits to business from growing in size and operating at a larger scale of production. The growth of 'outsourcing' for parts of the production process is considered, although a more detailed assessment of outsourcing is left to Chapter 14.

What you'll learn

By the end of this chapter you should be able to:

- outline some basic principles of production, in both short- and long-run time periods
- explain the linkages between production and cost
- assess the relevance of costs to business decision making
- distinguish between the different types of business cost and identify situations where the firm may cease production in short- and long-run time periods
- suggest why larger businesses often have a cost advantage over smaller businesses and why 'outsourcing' is becoming increasingly important
- show how government policies can play a key role in production decisions and cost outcomes for businesses
- explain the relevance of price elasticity of supply to business
- outline the idea of 'producer surplus' and consider its possible use in issues involving resource allocation.

We begin the chapter by outlining the factors of production and identifying some well-established 'laws' of production in both short- and long-run time periods.

- *Short-run time period* is that period of time in which at least one factor of production is fixed and cannot be changed. The length of this time period will depend on the economic activity under consideration. It may take 20 years or more to plan, locate and make operational a new nuclear power station but only a few months to plan, locate and make operational a workshop producing knitwear or other types of clothing.

- *Long-run time period* is that period of time in which *all* factors of production can be varied. In our example above, the long run would be 20 years plus for the nuclear power sector since its capital infrastructure cannot be changed in less than that time period. However, the long run would only be a few months for our knitwear or clothing sector.

The factors of production

Factors of production are those inputs required to produce a particular product, and are often thought to include land, labour, capital and enterprise.

Land

This was defined by early economists to include 'all the free gifts of nature', i.e. all the natural resources with some economic value which do not exist as a result of any effort by human beings. It therefore includes the surface area of the planet as well as its mineral and ore deposits. These natural resources are sometimes classified as renewable and non-renewable. *Renewable* resources include sunlight, wind, water and other power sources which can be reproduced. *Non-renewable* resources include coal, oil, gas and other power sources which, once used, cannot be reused. As a factor of production, land has special characteristics as it cannot be moved from one place to another.

Labour

Labour not only refers to the number of people available for the production of goods or services, but also includes their physical and intellectual abilities. The *labour force* of a country is the number of people in employment plus the number unemployed. The size of the labour force depends on the age distribution of the population and the proportion of any age group actually engaged in work (i.e. the *participation rate*). An interesting issue is how best to organise work in order to get the most output from the available workforce.

Division of labour

'Division of labour' or 'specialisation' refers to the way in which economic activities are broken down into their various component parts so that each worker performs only a small part of the entire operation. The idea was developed as early as 1776 by Adam Smith in his *Wealth of Nations* when he demonstrated how the production of pins could be greatly increased by splitting the process down into separate tasks, each performed by a single person.

Advantages of division of labour

- *Increased productivity.* Division of labour leads to a greater average product per worker being achieved than is possible in the absence of specialisation. But why is this increase in productivity possible?

    - Someone who performs the same task every day becomes very skilled at it and is able to work much faster.
    - Most of the worker's day is spent on a particular task so that less time is wasted in moving from work area to work area or in changing one set of tools for another.
    - Workers can be trained more quickly since there are fewer skills to learn.
    - Breaking production down to a small number of repetitive tasks makes possible the use of specialist machinery which, in combination with the worker, can raise productivity (e.g. output per person hour).
    - Workers can specialise in performing tasks for which they have a particular aptitude.

- *Increased standard of living.* The greater levels of productivity achieved through division of labour have led to an increase in the volume and value of output per person, raising levels of money income and helping to reduce prices (raising 'real' income still higher).

- *Increased range of goods available.* The greater output, higher money incomes and lower prices achieved by division of labour have increased the range of goods and services available to most people.

Disadvantages of division of labour

Despite these advantages, the division of labour has several disadvantages.

- *Increased boredom.* Greater specialisation results in boredom as workers perform the same tasks throughout the working day. This can lead to low morale, which in turn leads to poor labour relations, higher absenteeism as well as carelessness and an increased number of accidents.

- *Lack of variety.* Output is standardised and large numbers of identical products are produced.

- *Worker interdependence.* Specialisation leads to interdependence, with each worker in the production process depending upon all other workers in the production process. A stoppage by a small group of workers can therefore cause considerable disruption.

- *Limited market size.* Division of labour is only possible if there is a large market. It is useless producing vast quantities of output, even at relatively low prices, if there is only a small market for what is produced.

> **Make a note** A common expression is to say that division of labour or specialisation is 'limited by the size of the market'.

Capital

This is defined by economists as any man-made asset which can be used in support of the production of further goods and services. However, it is the *use* to which a particular asset is put which determines whether or not it is regarded as capital. For example, a vehicle used by a salesman would be classed as capital, but the same vehicle used for social and domestic purposes would be classed as a consumer product.

Economists sometimes distinguish between *fixed capital* and *circulating capital*. The former can be used time and again in the production process whereas the latter can only be used once. Fixed capital therefore includes such things as machinery and factory buildings, the road and rail networks, hospital and educational buildings and so on, whereas circulating capital (also known as *working capital*) consists of raw materials and other intermediate inputs into the production process.

Capital is created from scarce resources and therefore has an **opportunity cost** (see Chapter 1, p. 4). For example, in order to create more capital, it may be necessary to consume less so that resources can be released from producing consumer products and used instead for the production of capital. In other words, to accumulate capital a community may need to forego current consumption, i.e. the community as a whole must save. This is an issue we return to in Chapters 9 and 10.

Enterprise

This factor of production may also be referred to as *entrepreneurship*. The *entrepreneur* is seen as performing two important roles:

- hiring and combining factors of production;
- risk-taking by producing goods and services in anticipation of demand which may, or may not, materialise.

While there is no universally accepted definition of the term 'entrepreneur', the *Oxford English Dictionary* defines an entrepreneur as 'a person who attempts to profit by risk and initiative'. There is considerable debate as to how to identify and develop entrepreneurial talent that can better fulfil the two roles identified.

Example

In 2010 the *Global Entrepreneurship Monitor*, the largest independent study of its kind, found that one in sixteen adults in the UK had set up their own business in 2009, a 15% jump on the figure for 2005. One in six graduates in the UK will set up their own business, males in the UK are more than twice as likely as females to start their own business and black males are twice as likely as white males to go it alone.

Combining factors of production: the laws of returns

All production requires the input of factors of production. However, these can often be combined in a variety of ways, sometimes by using more of one factor relative to another, and vice versa. Profit-maximising firms, i.e. firms which aim to make as large a profit as possible, will combine the factors of production so as to achieve the maximum output from a given amount of factor inputs or, put another way, to minimise the cost of producing any given output.

Measuring changes in output

Over time, firms vary the level of output they produce within any given period, such as a week or a month. Here we define some important concepts which are used to measure these changes in output.

- **Total product** (TP). This is simply the total output a firm produces within a given period of time. For example, the total product of a particular firm might be 1,000 units per week.

- **Average product** (AP). This is usually measured in relation to a particular factor of production, such as labour or capital.

$$\text{Average product of labour} = \frac{\text{Total product}}{\text{Total labour input}}$$

- **Marginal product** (MP). Marginal product is the change in total product when one more unit of the factor is used. For example, if total product when the firm employs 10 workers is 1,000 units per week, and this rises to 1,080 units per week when the firm employs an additional worker, then the marginal product of the last (11th) worker is 80 units per week.

$$\text{Marginal product of labour} = \frac{\text{Change in total product}}{\text{Change in labour input}}$$

> *Example*
>
> Each year, the Harbour Report provides data on the average product of labour in car assembly in North America. In 2008, it noted that the overall time taken to stamp the engine, make the transmission system and then finally assemble a car stood at 30.37 hours per car for both Toyota and Chrysler. The hours taken by the rest of the automobile companies were, in descending order of efficiency, Honda (31.33), General Motors (32.29), Nissan (32.96), Ford (33.88), Hyundai (35.10). The report also showed that the difference between the most and least productive company in assembling a car was a mere 3.5 hours. This near parity was a far cry from a few years earlier when the Japanese could out-produce the big three US companies by a ratio of 2:1.

Law of variable proportions

This 'law' applies to the short-run time period when at least one factor of production (usually capital) is fixed. It follows that as the variable factor is progressively increased, the *proportions* in which it is combined with the fixed factor will change. The result is that in the short-run time period the so-called 'law of variable proportions' applies. We can use Table 3.1 to illustrate this 'law'.

Table 3.1 **Changing nature of returns to a variable factor**

No. of workers	Total product	Average product	Marginal product
1	4	4	4
2	10	5	6
3	20	6.7	10
4	35	8.8	15
5	50	10	15
6	61	10.2	11
7	65	9.3	4
8	65	8.1	0
9	55	6.1	−10

Note: Figures rounded to one decimal place.

Increasing returns to the variable factor

The idea here is that prior to some optimum proportion of variable to fixed factor (e.g. 1 man : 1 machine), we initially have too little of the variable factor. Extra units of the variable factor, here labour, will then be highly productive, making fuller use of 'spare capacity' in the fixed factor. Output rises more than in proportion to the extra input of variable factor, and we say that *increasing returns* have set in.

Diminishing returns to the variable factor

Beyond the optimum proportion of variable to fixed factor, additional units of the variable factor, here labour, will be progressively less productive, and we now say that *diminishing returns* have set in.

As we can see from Table 3.1 where labour is the variable factor, it may be that diminishing average returns set in at a different level of input of the variable factor than is the case for diminishing marginal returns. Indeed we can see from Table 3.1 that diminishing average returns set in after six units of labour, but diminishing marginal returns set in earlier, after only five units of labour.

Figure 3.1 presents a stylised diagram to highlight some of these relationships between total, average and marginal product of the variable factor, here labour.

Now we can see visually that the marginal product of labour curve starts to fall after five units of labour, but that the average product of labour keeps rising until six units of labour are employed, after which it falls. In other words, diminishing marginal returns set in before diminishing average returns.

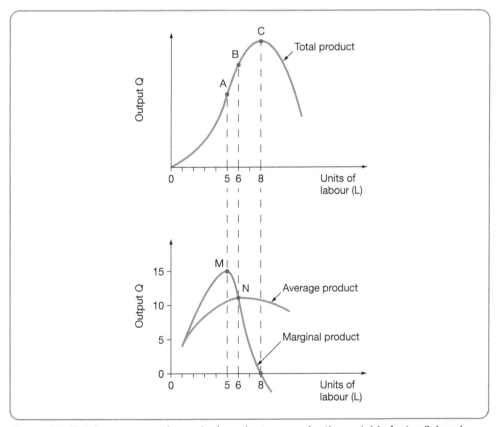

Figure 3.1 **Total, average and marginal product curves for the variable factor (labour)**

Make a note

Even though the *marginal product* of labour is falling after five units (point M), it is still above the *average product* between five and six units so the average product of labour will keep rising. Think of a game of darts; if your last (marginal) score is higher than your average score, then your average will still rise, even if your marginal scores are falling. When your marginal score exactly equals your average score (point N), the average will neither rise nor fall. When your marginal score falls below the average, then the average will fall.

Note that when the last worker neither adds to, nor subtracts from, output (i.e. the marginal product is zero), then total product is a maximum (point C).

Costs of production: short run

We shall see that the ideas we have discussed for production are important for determining costs, particularly in the **short-run** time period when the law of variable proportion applies.

In the short-run time period, costs are usually defined as either fixed or variable costs corresponding to the fixed or variable factors of production previously discussed.

Fixed costs

It is impossible to vary the input of fixed factors in the short run, therefore fixed costs do not change as output increases. Additionally, it is important to realise that fixed costs are incurred even when the firm's output is zero. Fixed costs might include mortgage or rent on premises, hire purchase repayments, business rates, insurance charges, depreciation on assets, and so on. None of these costs is directly related to output and they are all costs that are still incurred in the short run, even if the firm produces no output. They are therefore sometimes referred to as *indirect costs* or *overheads*.

Variable costs

Unlike fixed costs, variable costs are directly related to output. When firms produce no output they incur no variable costs, but as output is expanded extra variable costs are incurred. The costs that vary directly with output include costs of raw materials and components, power to drive machinery, wages of labour and so on.

Stop and think   3.1
Think of your own college, university or workplace. Can you identify the fixed and variable costs? Be as precise as you can.

| Case Study 3.1 | Small oil explorers eye big role in North Sea | **FT** |

In January 2010 Alistair Darling, the then chancellor, unveiled a multimillion pound package to encourage development of North Sea oil and gas reserves. Now many in the industry expect the UK government to introduce measures to cut the costs for smaller companies of buying ageing fields and offer incentives for new explorers. With insufficient North Sea reserves to make exploration attractive for many global operators, smaller companies argue they will be the driving force behind maximising UK production. They say, however, that high decommissioning costs for old fields and taxation issues are a deterrent and pose a threat to one of the UK's largest industries.

Britain's oil and gas reserves could last for only six years at current levels of investment, says Oil & Gas UK, the trade body. 'We are all aligned in wanting to get as much recovery from the North Sea as possible,' says Mark McAllister, chief executive of Fairfield Energy, who sits on the board of Oil & Gas UK. 'But the current situation is certainly a barrier to getting deals done, and this is an area in which government and industry need to work together to find the best solution.' One of the biggest issues facing small explorers is the liability they must take on to guarantee that older fields they buy will be cleaned up once they are exhausted. Oil & Gas UK estimates decommissioning costs will rise to more than £26bn by 2040.

When an independent explorer wants to buy a stake in a field, it has to prove to the other partners it will be able to meet its slice of the decommissioning costs. This requires the smaller company to put up a letter of credit from a bank, or cash deposit. This ties up the often small amounts of capital they have to develop fields and raises the cost of buying assets. Under present rules, if a smaller company disappears, the liability passes to the previous owners of the fields, meaning international oil companies are more wary of selling assets to independent explorers.

'The way decommissioning liabilities are structured across future, current and previous owners is often somewhat arbitrary,' says Ian Sperling-Tyler of Deloitte. While companies can offset the charge when fields are abandoned many hope the new government says the cost of abandonment will become tax deductible – freeing more cash for development.

Source: from Small oil explorers eye big role in North Sea, *Financial Times*, 08/03/2010 (Johnson, M.), © The Financial Times Ltd

Questions

1 What does the case study suggest in terms of the costs the small oil companies must take into account in their production decisions?

2 How might government policies help reduce the costs for the smaller oil companies?

3 What impacts might such cost reduction have on the supply of North Sea oil and gas, and therefore on its price?

Just as we defined total, average and marginal *product*, so it will be useful to define total, average and marginal *cost*, as can be seen from Taking it further 3.1.

Table 3.2 presents an arithmetic example of short-run changes in costs as output expands. It gives us the opportunity to calculate total, average and marginal costs respectively.

Taking it further Total, average and marginal cost   3.1

- **Total cost**

  Total cost = Total fixed cost + Total variable cost
  i.e.   TC = TFC + TVC

- **Average total cost**

  $$\text{Average total cost (ATC)} = \frac{\text{Total cost}}{\text{Total output}} = \frac{TC}{Q}$$

  i.e. $$ATC = \frac{TFC + TVC}{Q} = \frac{TFC}{Q} + \frac{TVC}{Q}$$

  ATC = AFC + AVC

- **Marginal cost** Marginal cost is the addition to total cost from producing one extra unit of output. Marginal cost is entirely variable cost.

  $$\text{Marginal cost (MC)} = \frac{\text{Change in total cost}}{\text{Change in total output}} = \frac{\Delta TC}{\Delta Q} \text{ where } \Delta Q = 1$$

Table 3.2 **Relationship between cost (£) and output in the short run**

Output	Total fixed cost	Total variable cost	Total cost	Marginal cost	Average variable cost	Average fixed cost	Average total cost
0	100	0	100		0	–	–
				50			
1	100	50	150		50	100	150
				45			
2	100	95	195		47.5	50	97.5
				40			
3	100	135	235		45	33.3	78.3
				30			
4	100	165	265		41.3	25	66.3
				15			
5	100	180	280		36	20	56
				10			
6	100	190	290		31.7	16.7	48.4
				5			
7	100	195	295		27.9	14.3	42.2
				10			
8	100	205	305		25.7	12.5	38.2
				20			
9	100	225	325		25	11.1	36.1
				40			
10	100	265	265		26.5	10	36.5
				60			
11	100	325	425		29.5	9.1	38.6
				85			
12	100	410	510		34.2	8.3	42.5

Note: Figures rounded to one decimal place.

It is often helpful to plot the values for total, average and marginal costs on diagrams. Figure 3.2 presents stylised diagrams indicating the relationships between the various curves.

Total cost curves

As we can see from Figure 3.2(a), the total cost (TC) curve is obtained by adding (vertically) the total fixed cost (TFC) and total variable cost (TVC) curves. TFC is a horizontal straight line at some given value, 'V', since the fixed costs do not vary with output. However, TVC is usually drawn as an inverted letter 'S', suggesting that increasing returns to the variable factor initially mean that total variable costs rise relatively slowly with output.

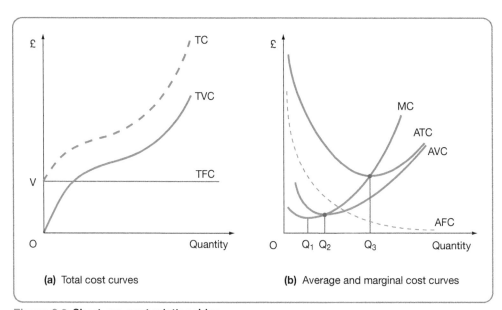

(a) Total cost curves

(b) Average and marginal cost curves

Figure 3.2 **Short-run cost relationships**

However, as *diminishing returns* set in, the total variable costs rise at an increasingly rapid rate with output.

Average and marginal cost curves

Figure 3.2(b) presents the various average cost curves and the marginal cost curve.

- Note that average fixed costs (AFC) fall continuously as we divide an unchanged TFC with a progressively increasing quantity. (This is often referred to as 'spreading the overheads'.)

- Note that the marginal cost (MC) curve slopes downwards initially, with falling marginal costs the mirror image of *increasing marginal returns* to the variable factor in the short run (see the rising part of the marginal product curve in Figure 3.1, p. 77). At output Q_1 *diminishing marginal returns* set in (see the falling part of the marginal product curve in Figure 3.1, p. 77) and the MC curve begins to rise.

- Note that we initially have increasing average returns to the variable factor with the result that AVC falls. At output Q_2 *diminishing average returns* set in (again see Figure 3.1) and the AVC curve begins to rise.

- Note that the ATC curve is the vertical sum of AFC and AVC curves and this starts to rise after output Q_3 when the rise in AVC outweighs the fall in AFC.

- Note also that, for reasons identical to those previously explained, the MC curve cuts the AVC and ATC curves at their respective minima. As soon as the marginal is above the average, then of course the average must rise; the analogy with a game being that if your last (marginal) score is greater than your average, then your average must rise.

Case Study 3.2 provides an example of fixed and variable costs and their relationship to profit.

Case Study 3.2 — Theatre costs in the West End

Some interesting data was made available on theatre costs when *Umoja*, a celebration of African music, was performed at the New London Theatre, owned by the Really Useful Theatre (RUT) company, in London. In Chapter 2 we noted how the prices charged should take into account the price elasticity of demand for the product.

However, they must also take some account of the cost structure for putting on the show. In the short run, revenue must cover the variable or running costs, and in the long run revenue must cover all costs, including 'normal profit'.

For *Umoja* the ticket prices ranged from £10 to £37.50 (average £20), depending on seating position. The New London Theatre has a seating capacity of 900 (average attendance 50%) and eight shows were performed per week. The producer of the show paid a fixed rent of £12,000 a

		% of total costs
Fixed costs	Theatre rent	Up to 50%
	'Contra' (cost of running and maintenance of theatre)	
Variable costs	Ticketmaster (booking fees)	4%
	Theatre commission per ticket	10%
	Creative team pay (commission-based contract)	4.5%
	VAT	17.5%
Profit	(depending on attendance)	14%

Case Study 3.2 *continued*

week to the New London Theatre. The 'contra' costs (i.e. the costs of running the theatre, including wages of performers, cleaning and maintenance) were estimated to be between £20,000 and £25,000 per week. Wages of performers were set by Equity, the actors' union, at a minimum of £331.52 per week, with a cast of 40 needed for *Umoja*.

A more general breakdown of the typical costs of putting on a West End show is presented in the table above, which reflects estimates of where the money received on each ticket actually goes.

Of course, as well as ticket revenue, extra revenue is possible to the producers of shows via the sales of merchandising. Even here, however, merchandising staff were required to pay a 25% commission to RUT, the owners of the New London Theatre.

Questions

1 Why are performers' wages regarded as a fixed cost in the table? Is this a usual practice?

2 Comment on the items placed under the 'variable cost' heading.

3 Look carefully at the actual figures given for *Umoja*. How do these compare with the more general percentage figures given in the table?

4 What constraints might the cost figure facing *Umoja* place on its ticket pricing strategy?

You try 3.1 gives you the opportunity to check your understanding of production and costs in the short-run time period.

You try   3.1

1 Complete the following table which shows how total product (TP) varies with the number of workers (L) employed, in the short-run time period when other factors of production are fixed. You need to work out the average product and marginal product for the variable factor, here labour.

No. of workers (L)	Total product (TP)	Average product (AP)	Marginal product (MP)
1	40		
2	140		
3	255		
4	400		
5	600		
6	720		
7	770		
8	800		
9	810		
10	750		

(a) After how many workers does:

(i) diminishing marginal returns set in?

(ii) diminishing average returns set in?

(b) Draw a diagram showing the marginal product (MP) and average product (AP) curves for the variable factor, labour.

Note: Put number of workers on the horizontal axis.

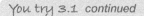

You try 3.1 *continued*

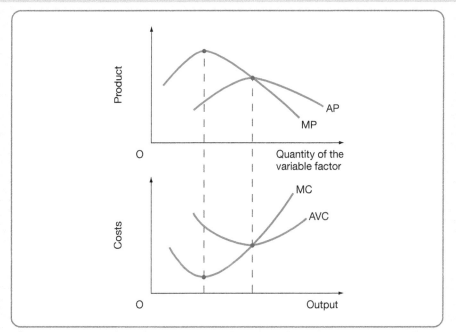

Figure 3.3

2 Look carefully at Figure 3.3 which shows production and cost curves in the short-run time period.

   (a) Explain what is happening in the top diagram where MP is marginal product and AP is average product.

   (b) Explain what is happening in the bottom diagram where MC is marginal cost and AVC is average variable cost.

   (c) How are the two diagrams linked? In other words, explain the relationship between marginal product (MP) and marginal cost (MC), and between average product (AP) and average variable cost (AVC).

3 Complete the following table.

   Note: round, where needed, to 1 decimal place.

Output	TFC	TVC	TC	AFC	AVC	ATC	MC
0	50	0					
1	50	40					
2	50	75					
3	50	108					
4	50	138					
5	50	170					
6	50	205					
7	50	243					
8	50	286					
9	50	335					
10	50	390					

Of course cost factors are often related to volume of output, and the possibilities for spreading research and development and other fixed overhead costs over a larger volume of outputs. Case Study 3.3 helps link costs to such demand factors, using the Japanese television sector.

Case Study 3.3   Sony pulls ultra-thin TV in Japan   FT

Sony announced in February 2010 that it would stop selling a ground-breaking television that uses organic light-emitting diodes (OLED) in Japan after exhausting demand for the ¥200,000 ($3,200) sets.

The 11-inch XEL-1 was the first OLED television to market in 2007 and Sir Howard Stringer, Sony's chairman and chief executive, heralded it as evidence of Sony's innovative capabilities.

'When you look at OLED, your impulse is to say 'wow'. We need that reaction from people at Sony . . . it's a statement of confidence, that there is a path to somewhere else,' Sir Howard said in December 2007.

Stopping sales of the XEL-1 in Japan without launching a long-promised 27-inch successor suggests that OLED will not be the device to rescue Sony's struggling television business.

OLED displays rely on a thin layer of chemicals that emit light when electricity passes through them. Unlike liquid crystal displays – the most common technology used – OLEDs do not need a separate light at the back so they are thinner and use less power. Sony's XEL-1 is only 3 mm thick.

A regulatory change means that Sony would have to redesign the XEL-1 in order to keep selling it in Japan after April 2010 the company said, and at today's prices the market is too small to make that worthwhile.

Sony said it would keep making the XEL-1 for sale outside of Japan and would press ahead with OLED development.

'Not only are we continuing development of mid- and large-sized OLED panels for TVs, but we also see potential for application of OLED in other devices,' the company said. Sony has hit problems with mass production of OLEDs. It makes the screens by depositing a layer of chemicals on to a glass panel but it is struggling to control the thickness of that layer. The result is a high defect rate, a low yield from the production line and high costs.

There is also an industry-wide problem with making the screens bigger. Companies are working on a solution that involves spraying OLED chemicals on to the glass like an inkjet printer. Almost every large television maker is working on OLEDs and Sony's rivals in Korea and Taiwan are catching up. In 2009 LG of Korea launched a 15-inch version of the television.

Executives at Idemitsu Kosan and Sumitomo chemical, the two largest suppliers of materials for the screens, have told the *Financial Times* they do not expect OLED televisions to take off until 2012.

Source: from Sony pulls ultra-thin TV in Japan after demand drops, *Financial Times*, 17/02/2010 (Harding, R.), © The Financial Times Ltd

Questions

1 What reasons are suggested in the case study for Sony withdrawing from ultra-thin TV production?

2 Under what circumstances might Sony return to this product range?

Costs of production: long run

The **long run** has been defined as the period of time in which all factors of production can be varied. We are now in the situation of **returns to scale**. We no longer need to add units of a variable factor to a fixed factor since, in the long run, there is no fixed factor. The average cost curves we considered in Figure 3.2(b) above were *short-run average cost* curves. How do these curves differ from **long-run average cost** curves? It is to this question that we now turn.

Long run average cost (LRAC)

Figure 3.4 shows the long-run average cost (LRAC) curve as an *envelope* to a family of short-run average cost curves (SRACs).

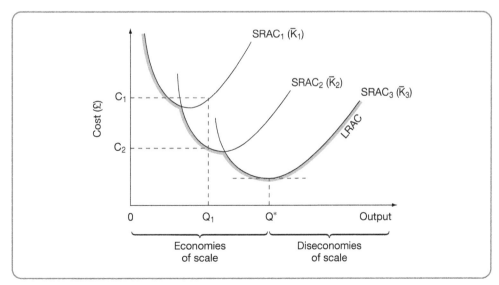

Figure 3.4 The long-run average cost (LRAC) curve as the outer 'envelope' to a family of short-run average cost (SRAC) curves

Each of the short-run average cost (SRAC) curves show how costs change with output at some given value/level of the fixed factor, here capital. For example, with capital fixed at $\overline{K}_1$, the lowest cost of producing output Q_1 would be C_t. However, in the long run we can vary *all* factors, including capital. The lowest cost of producing output Q_1 in the long run would be to change capital to $\overline{K}_2$ when it would be possible to produce Q_1 at cost C_2. So C_2 (and not C_1) is a point on the **long-run average cost curve** (LRAC) which shows the lowest cost of producing any output, given that *all* factors (here including capital, K) can be adjusted to their optimal level.

In fact, the outer envelope to the family of short-run average cost curves in Figure 3.4 will constitute the long-run average cost curve (LRAC). Up to output Q* the LRAC is falling, and we refer to **economies of scale**; beyond output Q* the LRAC is rising, and we refer to **diseconomies of scale**.

Reasons for economies of scale

In the long run the firm can increase all its factors of production and grow in size (scale) of output. This greater size may allow it to combine the factors of production in ways that reduce long-run average cost and yield economies of scale.

The economies of scale are many and varied, but they are usually grouped into certain categories.

1 Technical economies

These are related to an increase in size of the plant or production unit. Reasons include:

- *Specialisation of labour and capital* becomes more possible as output increases. Specialisation raises productivity per unit of labour/capital input, so that average variable costs fall as output increases. We have already seen that specialisation is 'limited by the size of the market' so that as output grows, more specialisation is possible.
- *'Engineers' rule'* whereby material costs increase as the square but volume (capacity) increases as the cube, so that material costs per unit of capacity fall as output increases. Wherever volume is important, as in sizes of containers, lorries, ships, aircraft etc., this 'rule' is important.
- *Dovetailing of linked processes* may only be feasible at high levels of output. For example, if the finished product needs processes A, B and C respectively, each with specialised equipment producing 10, 24, 30 items per hour, then only at an output of 120 items per hour do processes 'dovetail' in the sense that each process divides exactly into this level of output (120 is the lowest common multiple of 10, 24 and 30).
- *Indivisibility of large-scale, more efficient processes.* Certain processes of production, e.g. mass assembly techniques, can only be operated efficiently at large output volumes and cannot be operated as efficiently at lower outputs, even if all factor inputs are scaled down in proportion to one another. We call this inability to scale down the processes of production without affecting their efficiency of operation, *indivisibility* of the production process.

Make a note

Any output smaller than 120 units will incur the unnecessary cost of spare (unused) capacity. For example, if output was only 100 units per hour then we need four items of specialised equipment for process C, but only one-third of the fourth item of equipment is used.

Take, for example, the three production processes outlined in Table 3.3. For all three processes, the capital:labour ratio is the same at 1:1 and each process is a scaled-down

Table 3.3 Indivisibility in the production process

| | Factor inputs | | Output |
Type of process	L (men)	K (machines)	X (units)
A Small-scale process	1	1	1
B Medium-scale process	100	100	1,000
C Large-scale process	1,000	1,000	20,000

(or scaled-up) version of one of the other processes. However, the larger-scale processes are clearly more productive or efficient than the smaller-scale processes.

Example

Microchip production

The global microchip producers are now seeking to build huge £3bn state-of-the-art chip fabrication factories ('Fabs') that can use the 12-inch wafers (also known as 300 mm wafers) which are replacing the 8-inch versions currently in use. Where chipmakers could produce 100 chips from an 8-inch wafer, a 12-inch wafer can produce 225 chips. This means substantial reductions of around 40% in the average cost of manufacturing a chip.

2 Non-technical (enterprise) economies

These are related to an increase in size of the *enterprise as a whole* rather than simply an increase in size of the plant or production unit. Reasons include:

- *Financial economies.* Larger enterprises can raise financial capital more cheaply (lower interest rates, access to share and rights issues via Stock Exchange listings, etc.).
- *Administrative, marketing and other functional economies.* Existing functional departments can often increase throughput without a pro-rata increase in their establishment.
- *Distributive economies.* More efficient distributional and supply-chain operations become feasible with greater size (lorries, ships and other containers can be despatched with loads nearer to capacity, etc.).
- *Purchasing economies.* Bulk buying discounts are available for larger enterprises.

Case Study 3.4 looks in detail at the potential for gaining administrative economies.

Case Study 3.4   Head Office – some easy economies?

Even during the global recession of 2008/10 the cost of renting space for head offices in major cities was still rising for many companies. For example, the property consultancy CB Richard Ellis noted that office rentals had increased by 61% in Sao Paulo, by 12% in Sydney, by 11% in London, and 3% in Frankfurt. Quite apart from rental costs, a smaller head office means more money for the company's real work: producing products and services and selling them to customers. Companies with slimmer headquarters are hungrier, more focused and financially more successful. It is an attractive notion. The only problem is that there is little evidence to support it. Take a look at the size of head offices in different countries. Which part of the world would you imagine has the most streamlined corporate headquarters: the USA or Europe? Wrong. The flabby, decadent Europeans have the leanest head offices. The median American head office has 14.8 staff members for every

1,000 employees in the company. In France the median is 10 headquarters staff for every 1,000 employees. In Germany the figure is 9.3. In the Netherlands it is 7.4 – half the US figure – and in the UK 7.3. Japan, on the other hand, is true to stereotype with a mean 38.7 head office staff for every 1,000 employees.

The figures are from a recent paper by David Collis of the Harvard Business School and Michael Goold and David Young of the Ashridge Strategic Management Centre in the UK. Their survey of 600 companies reveals, however, that those national averages hide huge differences within countries. In the USA, the smallest corporate head office they looked at had seven members and the largest 13,030. In the UK the smallest corporate headquarters had 10 staff members, the largest 8,100.

The reason for the variations is that different head offices perform different tasks. Some are responsible for little more than the basic corporate functions: financial reporting, legal services, taxation and the like, with everything else handled in the operating companies. Other head offices have large research and development and information technology departments, serving the entire company.

Those familiar with Goold's earlier work – carried out with his Ashridge colleague Andrew Campbell – will be aware of his finding that differences in corporate head offices reflect more than chief executives' attitudes to staffing levels; they are often the result of entirely different approaches to running companies. In their 1987 book *Strategies and Styles*, Goold and Campbell identified three office philosophies. The first involved head offices being deeply involved in formulating operating subsidiaries' strategies and giving them time to reach their financial targets. The second philosophy was more distant – and less forgiving. Head offices did not involve themselves in their operating companies' business. They set operating managers demanding 12-month financial targets, rewarded them handsomely if they met them and got rid of them if they did not. These head offices were smaller than the first group. The third philosophy was somewhere between the first two: some financial target setting and some active interference.

The new research that Ashridge has done with Harvard builds on this work, looking at what makes different companies opt for different sorts of head offices. For example, companies whose subsidiaries are in similar businesses have bigger head offices than conglomerates whose operating companies have less in common. This is because companies whose subsidiaries are in related fields find it more convenient to provide shared services from corporate headquarters.

The most important question is whether, as many cost-cutting chief executives appear to believe, companies with smaller headquarters are financially more successful. The answer appears to be 'No'. The companies that have the highest return on capital employed have larger head offices than those that generate the lowest returns. The researchers are not altogether sure why this is. It could be because larger headquarters use their staff in ways that benefit the company, or it could be that highly profitable companies have more money to spend on head office staff. What is clear, however, is that large head offices are not necessarily a sign of corporate weakness.

That one successful company has a head office of a certain size does not mean that everyone else should have one too. 'The temptation to imitate competitors in the belief that there is a single best-demonstrated practice should be resisted,' the researchers say. 'It is more important for each company to develop a clear corporate strategy and reflect that strategy in the design of its corporate headquarters.' It may be that all those headquarters staff really are a waste of expensive space. Alternatively, strange as it seems, they may be doing something useful.

Questions

1 Why does the case study suggest that there may be fewer administrative economies available than is often supposed?

2 What policy implications follow from the case study?

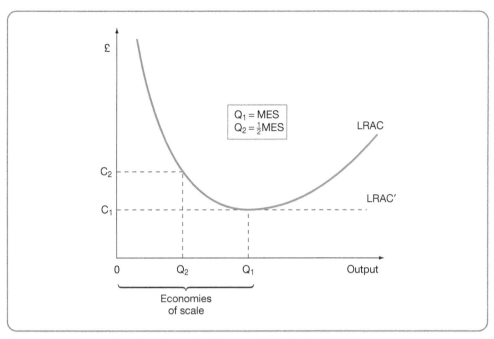

Figure 3.5 **Economies of scale and minimum efficient size (MES)**

Cost gradient

As can be seen from Figure 3.5, where economies of scale exist for these various reasons, then the long-run average cost (LRAC) curve will fall as output rises over the range $0-Q_1$. The *more substantial* these economies of scale the *steeper* the fall in the LRAC curve, which then means that any firm producing less output than Q_1 is at a considerable cost disadvantage vis-à-vis its competitors.

The **cost gradient** is an attempt to measure the steepness of the fall in LRAC up to the **minimum efficient size** or **scale (MES)**. Sometimes this 'cost gradient' is expressed over the range of the LRAC from $\frac{1}{2}$ MES to MES and sometimes from $\frac{1}{3}$ MES to MES.

For example, suppose the cost gradient for an industry is expressed as 20% from $\frac{1}{2}$ MES to MES. This means that a firm that is at output Q_2 in Figure 3.5 will have average costs at C_2 which are some 20% higher than a firm which has an output that is twice as large as Q_2 and which is benefiting from all the economies of scale available. Clearly the steeper (higher value) the cost gradient, the greater the disadvantages for a business in operating below the MES for that industry.

Also note that the larger MES (Q_1) is relative to total industry output the fewer efficient firms the industry can sustain. For example, if Q_1 is 50% of the usual UK output of glass, then arguably the UK can only sustain two efficient glass producers.

Diseconomies of scale

Some surveys suggest that if a firm attempts to produce beyond the MES (Q_1), then average costs will begin to rise and we have the 'U'-shaped LRAC curve in Figure 3.5. These higher average costs are called *diseconomies of scale* and are usually attributed to managerial problems in handling output growth efficiently.

However, other surveys suggest that while LRAC ceases to fall, there is little evidence that it actually rises for levels of output beyond Q_1. In other words, it flattens out to look less like the letter 'U' and more like the letter 'L', shown by LRAC' in Figure 3.5.

Make a note

As well as the various types of short- and long-run costs noted so far, there are other cost ideas you may encounter.

● **Opportunity cost**: the next best alternative forgone (see Chapter 1, p. 4).

● **Sunk costs**: those costs which cannot be recovered should the business fail and the assets be liquidated.

Internal and external economies of scale

● **Internal economies of scale**. These are the cost advantages from a growth in the *size of the business* itself over the long-run time period.

● **External economies of scale**. These are the cost advantages to a business from a growth in the *size of the sector of economic activity* of which the business is a part. In other words, the sources of the cost reductions are external to the business itself. For example, if a particular industry locates in a geographical area, a whole range of support services often develop to support that industry. Historically, the textile industry was located mainly in the north west of England and specialist textile markets (e.g. cotton exchanges), textile machinery suppliers, fabric and dye specialists, textile-related training and educational courses, and transport infrastructure (canals, railways, roads) were established to serve this localised industry. As the textile industry grew in size, the individual businesses which were part of that sector of economic activity benefited from these specialist support services which were often delivered at lower cost and higher quality, yielding 'external' economies of scale.

Stop and think   3.2

Can you think of any other examples of external economies of scale?

Economies of scope and experience

We have considered costs that depend mainly on the size of output and the time period in question. Here we consider two other types of cost which may be important to the business.

● Economies of scope. This refers to changes in average costs as a result of changes in the *mix* of production between two or more products. The suggestion here is that there may be benefits from the joint production of two or more products. Such economies of scope may occur in various situations:

  – *Unrelated products*, as in the joint use of inputs such as management, administration, marketing, production or storage facilities, and so on which yield cost savings for all the products produced. One head office may be able to absorb the administrative responsibilities related to several products.

  – *Related products*, as in moving towards a mix of product for which there is an element of complementarity in production, such as teaching and research, beef and hides, cars and trucks.

  – *By-products* may play a role in generating economies of scope, as with heat from energy production being used in horticulture.

● Economies of experience. This refers to a fall in average costs as *cumulative output* rises (see Figure 3.6). For example, a small firm producing an average output of 5,000 units over 20 years has a cumulative output of 100,000 units. It may have learnt many useful 'lessons' over time to help it reduce costs and compete effectively with larger rivals.

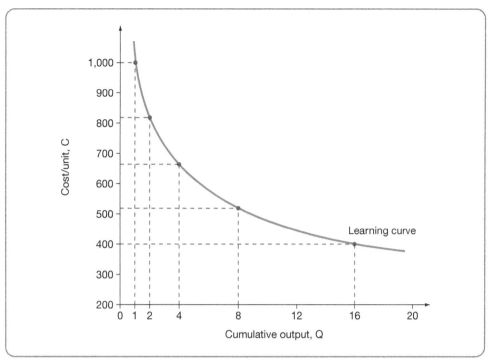

Figure 3.6 **Experience or learning curve: declining average costs as a function of cumulative output**

Make a note

Questions are regularly set in examinations and assignments which involve the reasons firms seek to grow in size and the methods they adopt (Chapter 5). It will help if you can explain economies of scale (technical and non-technical), scope and experience in some detail, using diagrams where appropriate to support your argument. Recent case-study examples will also help to 'deepen' your argument.

Case Study 3.5 looks at economies of scale in the aircraft industry.

Case Study 3.5	Scale economies in the skies

In a WTO report in March 2010, Airbus, the European consortium, and its rival, Boeing, were both criticised for 'elements of state subsidy' in their quest to dominate the global market for aircraft. In fact the huge Airbus A380 super-jumbo jet was two years behind schedule when it made its maiden commercial flight from Singapore to Sydney in October 2007. Although the absolute costs of building the 555- to 650-seater A380 super-jumbos are dramatically higher than for today's 350–400-seater jumbos, the *cost per passenger seat* is estimated to be some 15% to 20% lower than for the widely used Boeing 747-400.

How can this be? Certainly the hugely expensive $10.7 billion (£6.7 billion) programme by Airbus has required 6,000 engineers at factories in Germany, France, Spain and Britain, with an assembly hall in Toulouse more than twice the size of a football pitch! To bring all the component parts of the A380 to Toulouse from the 15 different manufacturing plants in the four countries was hugely expensive. For example, purpose-built roll-on roll-off ferries, barges and road trailers have had to be designed and built to transport to Toulouse in southern France the huge wings (from Broughton, Wales), the rear and forward fuselage (from Hamburg, northern Germany), the tail piece (from Cadiz, southern Spain) and the centre fuselage and cockpit (from St Nazaire, western France). Roads have had to be widened and secure overnight parking facilities provided (e.g. three nights of stops needed for transporting the slow-moving road convoys in France).

Nevertheless, a 'value chain' for production which involved specialising in these individual parts using firms in the different countries is thought to be cost and quality efficient and to more than compensate for the huge costs and logistical problems in transporting them for final assembly in Toulouse.

The design of the A380 has taken into account the views of numerous focus groups of potential users from many airlines. It has been designed with 20% of the airframe made from the most modern tough, lightweight plastic materials to keep within the maximum take-off weight of 560 tonnes. The basic version with 550 passengers will be able to travel some 8,000 miles without refuelling, and an extended version will carry 650 passengers an extra 1,000 miles (i.e. 9,000 miles in total).

Airbus will need to sell around 250 of these A380 jets to break even. Airbus estimate the total market for aircraft in the 400-plus seat category to be around 1,100 over the next 20 years. It also predicts that an air-freight version will be in demand, with some 300 extra customers attracted.

The annual traffic growth for air passengers has been predicted at around 4.7% per annum over the next 20 years. Whatever future scenario is chosen, much of any projected growth will involve the Asia-Pacific region, and Airbus secured relatively few orders from the major carriers in that region. Other companies also challenge the Airbus strategy, with its main rival, Boeing, believing the market will be better met by flying smaller aircraft into a wider range of smaller airports, rather than huge aircraft into a few hub-to-hub centres which will require extended runways to allow such aircraft to land. However after the 2008–10 global recession, more recent projections are for more modest growth, especially with increasing environmental concerns encouraging greater taxation and regulation of air transport to reduce its 'carbon footprint'.

Vital statistics of A380

Assembly	Toulouse
Price	$260m
Capacity	556–650 seats
Range	8,000–9,000 miles
Take-off weight	560 tonnes
Entry into service	2010/11
Programme cost	$10.7bn

Questions

1 What sources of economies of scale are helping the A380 achieve the projected 15% to 20% lower seat cost?

2 Can you identify some of the benefits and costs (e.g. risks) to Airbus in following this scale-economy strategy?

Deciding whether to produce in the short run and the long run

The distinction between fixed costs and variable costs is important in deciding whether firms should cease production. The firm is obliged to cover its fixed costs whether it undertakes production or not. For example, even when the firm produces no output it still incurs costs such as insurance charges, depreciation on assets, mortgage repayments, rent on premises, and so on. However, unlike these fixed costs, variable costs are incurred only when the firm undertakes production. When the firm produces no output it incurs no costs from purchasing raw materials, from charges for energy to drive the machinery, from overtime payments to existing workers or extra labour costs for hiring new workers, etc. All of these costs tend to rise only as output increases.

Once a firm has incurred fixed costs, its decision about whether to continue producing is therefore determined by the relationship between revenue and costs incurred over the time period in question.

Short run

- If total revenue *just covers* the total variable (running) costs incurred by producing, then the firm is neither better off nor worse off if it continues production.
- If total revenue is *greater than* total variable costs, then the firm makes at least some contribution towards covering the fixed costs already incurred by continuing in production.
- If the total revenue is *less than* total variable cost then the firm will be better off by ceasing production altogether. If the firm shuts down, its total loss is equal to its fixed cost compared with a loss equal to its fixed costs *plus* the ongoing losses from failing to cover its variable costs.

Firms will therefore undertake production, in the short run, if the *price* (average revenue) at which their product is sold is at least equal to the *average variable cost* of production. When price (average revenue) and average variable cost are equal, total revenue is exactly equal to total variable cost.

Long run

In the long run, unless *price* (average revenue) at least covers the *average total cost*, firms will experience a loss. In other words, total revenue must cover total cost in the long run, including total variable costs and total fixed costs. By definition, when prices (average revenue) *exactly equal* average total costs, firms break even.

Make a note

In the long run the total revenue of the firm must also cover 'normal profit', i.e. that level of profit regarded as just sufficient to keep a firm in that industry (line of economic activity) in the long run. Normal profit is often thought of as a long-run 'cost' of production in that if it is not made then the firm will move its scarce resources into another line of economic activity.

While they may be prepared to accept losses in the short run (as long as total variable costs are covered), firms cannot accept losses in the long run. If firms are to continue in production in the long run, the price at which their product is sold must at least equal the average total cost of production. We return to this issue in Chapter 6 (p. 167).

You try 3.2 provides an opportunity for you to check your understanding of production and costs in the short-run and long-run time periods.

You try   **3.2**

1 Look carefully at the data on economies of scale in car production shown in the tables.

Car output per plant per year	Index of unit average production costs (car)
100,000	100
250,000	83
500,000	74
1,000,000	70
2,000,000	66

You try 3.2 continued

Optimum output per year (cars)	
Advertising	1,000,000
Sales	2,000,000
Risks	1,800,000
Finance	2,500,000
Research and Development	5,000,000

What does the data suggest about the benefits of size in the car industry?

2 In this question you'll see a letter giving a description of a particular situation and a number next to a term. Try to match each description with its correct term.

Description

(a) A larger firm can reduce the costs of raising finance by using a rights issue on the London Stock Exchange.

(b) The material costs of producing cargo ships increase as the square but the capacity increases as the cube.

(c) We can cut the costs of production by using the robotic assembly line for both cars and tractors.

(d) Robotic assembly techniques are highly efficient but can only be used by firms producing over 4 million cars per year.

(e) Even though the paint company only has around 1% of the market, it has been in the paint business for over 50 years and still manages to compete.

(f) Firms in 'Silicon Fen' around Cambridge benefit from a pool of highly skilled electronic experts, with their training needs well supported by local universities and colleges.

Terms

(i)   Economy of scale: technical

(ii) Economy of scale: non-technical

(iii) Economy of scope

(iv) Economy of experience

(v)   External economy of scale

Note: one of these terms is the answer to two of the descriptions.

3 Match the letter of each description with the correct number of each term.

Description

(a) A type of cost which falls continuously as output increases.

(b) A cost which cannot be recovered if the firm is liquidated.

(c) Costs over this time period result from adding variable factors to one or more fixed factors.

(d) A cost which refers to the next best alternative forgone.

(e) The addition to total cost from producing one extra unit of output.

(f) Costs over this time period result from changing the proportions in which all factors of production are combined.

(g) Found by dividing all the running costs by total output.

You try 3.2 *continued*

Terms

(i) Opportunity cost
(ii) Marginal cost
(iii) Sunk cost
(iv) Average fixed cost
(v) Average variable cost
(vi) Short-run cost
(vii) Long-run cost

4 Which *two* of the following long-run situations might be regarded as yielding economies of scale?
   (a) Higher output results in lower average costs of production through greater specialisation of machinery and equipment.
   (b) Managers find it more difficult to cope with higher levels of output.
   (c) A firm producing containers finds that costs of production (area) increase as the square but capacity (volume) increases as the cube.
   (d) New breakthroughs in information technology allow 'miniaturisation' of the production process, so that smaller firms can now introduce the more efficient techniques previously only available to larger firms.

5 If output of the firm rises from $\frac{1}{2}$ minimum efficient size to the minimum efficient size and average costs fall by 60% in the long run, we might say that:
   (a) The cost gradient is steep, reflecting substantial economies of scale.
   (b) The cost gradient is shallow, showing little evidence of economies of scale.
   (c) Being below the minimum efficient size is of little consequence.
   (d) The firm is likely to consider demerging its activities.
   (e) Economies of scope would seem extremely attractive.

6 Which of the following is NOT a technical economy of scale?
   (a) Specialisation of labour and equipment is possible at larger output and raises factory productivity.
   (b) Dovetailing of separate but linked processes can only occur at larger outputs.
   (c) Material costs increase as the square but capacity as the cube.
   (d) The larger-scale processes of production tend to be the more productive but cannot easily be scaled down: i.e. they tend to be 'indivisible'.
   (e) Large factory output allows the firm's lorries to operate with smaller proportions of empty space.

7 A reduction in long-run average costs (LRAC) due to a different product mix being selected by the firm is an example of:
   (a) technical economies of scale
   (b) non-technical economies of scale
   (c) lower sunk costs
   (d) external economies of scale
   (e) economies of scope.

8 An increase in cumulative output of 10% reduces average costs by 5%. This is an example of:
   (a) technical economies of scale
   (b) experience economies
   (c) lower sunk costs
   (d) external economies of scale
   (e) economies of scope.

You try 3.2 *continued*

9 True/False

(a) 'Normal profit' is that profit which is more than sufficient to keep
the firm in the industry in the long run.   True/False

(b) When the 'long-run average cost' curve starts to rise we refer to
economies of scale having set in.   True/False

(c) A rise in cumulative output leading to a reduction in average
costs is an example of economies of scope.   True/False

(d) In the long run the firm will cease production unless average revenue
is at least equal to average total cost (including 'normal profit').   True/False

(e) Those who suggest that the long-run average cost curve is 'U'-shaped
usually point to diseconomies of scale resulting from managerial
inefficiencies as output rises.   True/False

Answers can be found on pp. 525–546.

Price elasticity of supply (PES)

Price elasticity of supply is a measure of the responsiveness of the supply of product X
to changes in its own price. It refers to movement along the supply curve (expansion/
contraction) rather than shifts in the supply curve (increase/decrease).

$$PES = \frac{\% \text{ change in quantity supplied of X}}{\% \text{ change in price of X}}$$

The numerical value, terminology and descriptions used for price elasticity of demand
(PED) apply equally to supply, though for supply all the signs are strictly positive, since
when the price of X rises the quantity supplied of X also rises ($+/+ = +$).

Table 3.4 presents the numerical values, terminology and descriptions for price elasticity of supply while Figure 3.7 presents diagrams to capture some of these PES situations.

Table 3.4 Price elasticity of supply, terminology and description

Numerical value of PES	Terminology	Description
0	Perfectly inelastic supply	Whatever the % change in price (Figure 3.7(a)), no change in quantity supplied
$> 0 < 1$	Relatively inelastic supply	A given % change in price leads to a smaller % change in quantity supplied
1	Unit elastic supply	A given % change in price leads to exactly the same % change in quantity supplied (Figure 3.7(b))
$> 1 < \infty$	Relatively elastic supply	A given % change in price leads to a larger % change in quantity supplied
∞ (infinity)	Perfectly elastic supply	An infinitely small % change in price leads to an infinitely large % change in quantity supplied (Figure 3.7(c))

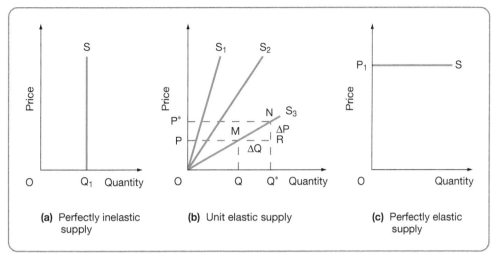

Figure 3.7 **Some important price elasticities of supply**

Factors affecting PES

Factors affecting the numerical value of PES for a product include the following:

- *The mobility of factors of production.* The more easily the factors of production can be moved between product X and the supply of other products, the more elastic the supply.

- *The time period in question.* The longer the time period under consideration, the more elastic the supply (producers take time to redirect factors of production).

- *Producer's attitude towards risk.* The less risk-averse the producer, the more elastic the supply. In other words, if producers are more willing to take risks, they will be more responsive in redirecting factors of production to alternative uses in response to price changes in product X.

- *The existence of natural constraints on production.* The less inhibited is production as regards natural constraints (such as fertile land, climate, mineral deposit, etc.), the more elastic the supply is likely to be.

The diagram representing *unit elasticity of supply*, as in Figure 3.7(b), is any straight line supply curve through the origin. *Taking it further* 3.2 explains this situation and presents more information on calculating PES.

Taking it further **Calculating price elasticity of supply (PES)**   3.2

The equivalent diagram for unit elastic demand was seen in Chapter 2 to be the rectangular hyperbola (Figure 2.1(c), p. 41). Before considering the principles behind the shape of the *unit elastic supply* curve it will be useful to follow the approach for expressing price elasticity of demand (PED) in Chapter 2 (p. 44).

We can devise an expression for price elasticity of supply (PES) in similar fashion as follows:

$$PES = \frac{P}{Q} \cdot \frac{\Delta Q}{\Delta P}$$

where P, Q refer to the original price and quantity supplied of X and ΔP, ΔQ to the change in price and quantity supplied of X.

Taking it further 3.2 *continued*

Unit elastic supply curve

We can now see why any straight-line supply curve through the origin has unit elasticity of supply. From Figure 3.7(c):

Triangles OMQ, MNR are similar; therefore ratios of corresponding sides are equal, so

$$\frac{MQ}{OQ} = \frac{NR}{MR} \quad \text{i.e.}$$

$$\frac{P}{Q} = \frac{\Delta P}{\Delta Q}$$

$$\frac{P}{Q} \cdot \frac{\Delta Q}{\Delta P} = 1 \quad \text{(rearranging)}$$

Point elasticity of supply

For a *non-linear* supply curve we can use the expression

$$PES = \frac{P}{Q} \cdot \frac{\Delta Q}{\Delta P}$$

where $\frac{\Delta Q}{\Delta P}$ is the slope of the tangent to that point on the non-linear supply curve.

Outsourcing and cost

Costs of production depend not only on the size of the production unit (plant) or enterprise (firm) but also on the geographical location of different elements of the 'value chain' (see Chapter 14, p. 492). This geographically dispersed supply chain must be carefully coordinated as it will influence the speed with which supply of the finished product can respond to changes in price (i.e. PES). In an increasingly global economy, we note in Chapter 15 that new outsourcing opportunities are available for many multinational enterprises (MNEs) which can reduce the costs of producing any given level of output. Case Study 3.6 looks at the impacts of *outsourcing* on production and costs for MNEs in South Korea.

| **Case Study 3.6** | **Outsourcing: South Korea looks to China** | **FT** |

At Hyundai Motor's noisy factory near Beijing airport, fresh-faced workers are busy attaching bumpers to Sonata sedans or mirrors to Tucson sports utility vehicles and spraying the multi-coloured Elantras that are destined to become taxis for the Chinese capital. In five different models, 68 vehicles roll off the South Korean group's production line every hour. The plant is producing 300,000 cars a year, but output will double with the completion of a second facility next year.

The 4,200 Chinese employees – average age 26 – receive a base salary equivalent to $360 (£185, €270) a month and belong to a workers' organisation whose main task seems to be to encourage harder effort rather than push for higher wages. 'The workers here are very flexible – it's the opposite to Korea, where the situation is impossible,' says Noh Jae-man, president of Beijing Hyundai. 'And because we pay our workers better than other companies, they are proud to work at Hyundai and carry out their jobs well.'

By contrast, at Hyundai's main Ulsan plant in South Korea the workers – their age averaging 41 – earn $4,580 a month, build only 55 cars an hour, refuse to produce more than three models on each production line, will not allow second shifts (which would eat into their overtime) and are heavily unionised. Last year a 25-day-long strike cost Hyundai about 7,800 vehicles or Won120bn ($127m, £65m, €95m) in lost sales.

Like other global manufacturers, Korean companies have flocked to take advantage of China's cheap productive labour and superb infrastructure. LG, the electronics and chemicals conglomerate, has such a huge presence in Nanjing, the capital of Jiangsu province, that Chinese authorities have renamed the main street 'LG Road'.

But while China represents a huge opportunity for manufacturing-dependent South Korea, it also represents a looming danger, as Chinese companies threaten not just to complement but to entirely consume Korea's industries. Hyundai may be benefiting in China but it is worried about the aggressive expansion of local carmakers such as Chery – and that many Chinese models bear a strong resemblance to the cars made by Korean and other producers. Indeed, South Korea's old economic model of imitation and manufacturing-led growth is now China's model.

Although it underwent radical restructuring and opened its market after the Asian financial crisis struck in 1997, there is a widely held belief that South Korea, one of the world's top dozen economies, needs a second wave of reforms if it is to maintain its competitive edge over emerging China and move to the next stage in its remarkable development.

Indeed, with the economy remaining dependent on manufacturing and exports – and, moreover, on just a few types of product, such as mobile phones, semiconductors and cars – concern is growing that Korea is losing its dynamism.

Many economists and business leaders in Seoul say that China is fast moving up the value chain and will soon be making the kinds of computer chips and flat-screen televisions for which Korea has become known. China's export structure, where the proportion made up of electronics and other high-technology products has grown to comprise almost 40%, much more closely resembles that of South Korea than it did a decade ago. Although most technology exports come from foreign-invested companies and the highest-tech components are still imported, the sudden change is giving Korea concern. 'Chinese manufacturing workers earn about 10% of what Korean workers

earn but the technology gap between the two countries has rapidly reduced,' Mr Kim says. 'Korea has already lost the personal computer industry and more will follow.'

Lee Kun-hee, the powerful chairman of Samsung Group – which accounts for about 20% of the country's exports – warned that Korea had to 'wake up' or risk 'economic chaos' in five to six years. Samsung might relocate its appliance division, which has posted losses since 2003, to less developed countries, he added. In shipbuilding South Korea has been the world leader for the past decade, but China is closing in so quickly that Seoul's National Intelligence service has launched investigations into technology leaks. Meanwhile, Korea's current four-year lead over Chinese manufacturers of flat-screen televisions is likely to narrow to only one year by 2010, according to the Korea Electronics Association. The Organisation for Economic Co-operation and Development says China has overtaken Japan to become the world's second biggest spender on research and development, investing $136bn this year.

South Korea's problems are worsened by the survival of uncompetitive players. The government gives credit guarantees, under which 85% of the principal is guaranteed, to banks lending to SMEs, which means that poor performers do not go bankrupt. At the same time, Korean companies with bases in China have increasingly localised their procurement of intermediate goods. Korean companies operating in China procured one-quarter of their parts locally in 1996 – but it took less than a decade before half the parts were being sourced there.

Recent OECD data shows labour productivity for South Korea at less than $20 of GDP per hour worked, well below the OECD average of $35 per hour worked and the USA's $48 per hour worked. Labour market inflexibility is also present, with the cost of firing a South Korean worker at 90 weeks of wages compared to the OECD average of only 28 weeks of wages.

Source: adapted from Seoul sleepwalk: Why an Asian export champion is at risk of losing its way, *Financial Times*, 19/03/2007 (Fifield, A.), © The Financial Times Ltd

Questions

1 Consider some of the implications of this case study for outsourcing/offshoring activities from South Korea to China.

2 Why is it suggested that the South Koreans 'are worried' about developments in China?

In fact this discussion brings into play the idea of *relative unit labour costs* (RULC) which we consider further in Chapter 14 (p. 497). Certainly we can expect service sector as well as manufacturing employment to be affected. For example, Troika, the retail financial services consultancy, predicted that over 100,000 British financial services jobs will be lost in the next five years by outsourcing back-office jobs to overseas locations, as insurers and banks struggle to cut costs. The report noted that the costs per financial or insurance policy in India and South Africa were less than £10 compared to over £30 in the UK. However, costs per policy in China are expected to fall to £0.50 per policy within five years! The report also noted that India produces 2.5 million English-speaking university graduates a year, more than the whole of Western Europe, with 70% of these graduates being IT specialists.

Even if some jobs are lost, the key idea underpinning free trade is that all countries will benefit when each country specialises in those activities in which it has a comparative advantage (see Chapter 14, p. 497) and trades the output of these activities with the rest of the world. This broader view is supported by a report from the consultants McKinsey in 2003 on outsourcing which concludes that it is a win-win arrangement for the countries involved. For example, the report estimated that for every $1 previously spent in America and now outsourced to India, there is a 'global impact' of $1.47. Of that, the USA itself receives back $1.14 – as a result of cheaper services for consumers, redeploying labour to better paid jobs, additional exports of US goods to India, etc. India also receives an extra $0.33 via new wages, extra profits and extra taxes.

Links

For more on outsourcing see Chapter 14, pp. 496–9.

Governments, location and cost

Government influence on the macro business environment and therefore over a wide range of business activities is considered in some detail in Chapters 9, 10 and 11. Here the focus is government influence on the *micro business environment*, especially where government incentives are directed explicitly towards influencing locational decisions and the cost base of businesses.

Government aid and production: UK

The UK government, as with many others, has sought to support inward foreign direct investment (fdi) by overseas firms in order to raise UK output and employment and (via exports) improve the balance of payments. A variety of grants, subsidies and incentives have been provided by the UK government, many of which are related to the business operating in a particular region of the UK.

Regional Selective Assistance (RSA)

This is the main instrument of the UK in seeking to influence locational decisions for production activities in various regions. It is a discretionary grant towards projects of any size in both the manufacturing and service sectors, is open to both domestic and international firms and is available to help with the investment costs of projects with capital expenditures above £500,000. It has three overlapping objectives:

● first, to create and safeguard jobs;

● second, to attract and retain internationally mobile investments;

● third, to contribute to improving the competitiveness of disadvantaged regions.

The RSA is usually administered either as a capital-related or job-related grant.

- *Capital-related project grants* are normally used to help cover the costs of land purchase and site preparation or the acquisition of plant and machinery.
- *Job-related project grants* are normally used to help cover the costs of hiring and training staff.

The Department for Universities, Industry and Skills (DUIS) administers the scheme and has spent over £750m over the past decade on the RSA, safeguarding or creating some 180,000 UK jobs. However, the cost per job has been estimated at around £4,000 during this period.

Example

Samsung, the Korean electronics firm, located a major manufacturing plant for electronic equipment in Teesside, UK in 1994. To encourage Samsung to locate in Teesside it received £86m of public money from the UK government, £58m in the form of RSA to support the development of infrastructure needed by the new plant, training and other project costs. It was expected that 3,000 new jobs would be created and £600m of new investment invested in a state-of-the-art electronic factory. In the event Samsung decided to close the manufacturing site in January 2004, claiming falling global prices for flat-panel screens and microwaves, two of its key projects. Samsung announced that it would disperse production to China and Slovakia, where labour costs were only 50 pence and £1 per hour respectively, compared to £5.61 per hour in Teesside.

Not all UK experiences with state aid for inward investment have been so disappointing. Nissan established its Sunderland car plant in 1969, resulting in direct employment of 4,500 people (and many more indirectly) and a major contribution to UK car exports. Nevertheless, a *Financial Times* survey in 2003 found that half the £750m of grants involved in 50 regional aid projects over the past decade went to 16 companies which have since closed or fallen well short of job creation targets promised in return for this state aid.

Links

You can find more on state aid in Chapter 8, pp. 254–5.

The issues of whether and to what extent state aid should be provided to business is important to many other countries as well as Britain.

Here we review attempts by other governments to aid business activities.

Government aid and production: global

Even countries which already have lower labour costs than the UK and other advanced industrialised economies are creating even stronger incentives for overseas businesses to locate production in their territories. For example, India has begun an aggressive drive to create special economic zones that would enable the country to compete better with China for foreign investment. India has set aside its restrictive labour laws within the country's 17 *special economic zones* (SEZs) in an attempt to reduce foreign investor concerns about India's low labour productivity. In addition, New Delhi has removed many bureaucratic obstacles to the creation of the zones. India, which has roughly half the per capita income of neighbouring China, currently attracts roughly one-tenth the foreign investment that goes to China.

Similarly government support programmes have been established in many countries to encourage inward fdi, as for example in South Africa and Egypt.

As the shortage of skilled labour is a serious constraint on becoming competitive through inward fdi, the South African government has developed several programmes aimed at improving competitive activities in all sectors. The Skills Support Programme (SSP) seeks to encourage greater investment in training, including the introduction of new advanced skills. It provides a cash grant for new projects or the expansion of existing projects, including fdi projects, for up to three years. A maximum of 50% of the training costs will be granted to companies whose training programmes are approved.

Similarly the Egyptian government has taken various measures to increase inward fdi, so as to help Egyptian industries become, or remain, globally competitive and has joined up with the private sector in an initiative known as the National Suppliers Development (NSD) Programme to boost manufacturing growth and stimulate job creation. Through this initiative, the government provides active support to companies, including multinationals, to improve the quality and cost of Egyptian goods and to tailor them to the demands of a globalised world economy. One hundred multinationals and leading exporters in Egypt have been asked to select up to 20 local suppliers for receiving technical assistance by international consultants to identify efficiency and quality shortfalls, after which they will be able to access bank loans through the NSD Programme to make the necessary improvements.

Producer surplus

Links

Check whether your course and syllabus includes the use of *isoquants* and *isocosts*. If it does then you can turn to Appendix 2 (pp. 518–21) to see how these can be used in identifying the process of production (combination of factor inputs) a firm might select to produce its target output at the lowest cost possible.

This is an idea similar to that of consumer surplus considered in Chapter 2 (p. 62). Whereas consumer surplus involves the idea of individuals being willing to pay more than the market price for units of a product, here producers are seen as being willing to offer units of the product at less than market price. In Figure 3.8 the OQ_1th unit would have been supplied at a price of P_1, but the producer actually receives the higher market price of OP, giving a producer surplus of $P - P_1$ on that unit. Over all the OQ units, the shaded area PVW corresponds to the *excess* of revenue received by producers over and above the amount required to induce them to supply OQ units of the product.

It is this excess that we call the **producer surplus**.

You try 3.3 checks some of the ideas involving price elasticity of supply and producer surplus.

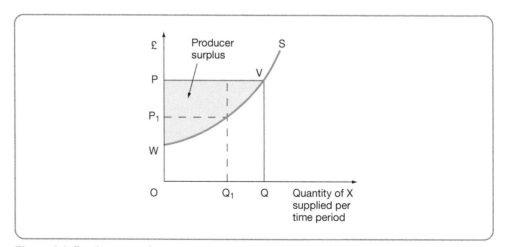

Figure 3.8 **Producer surplus**

You try   3.3

1   In this question you'll see a description of a particular situation involving PES. Try to match the letter for the description with the number for its correct term.

    Description

    (a) A 2% fall in the price of a magazine leads to a 3% contraction in the quantity supplied.

    (b) A 4% rise in the price of beer leads to a 4% expansion in the quantity supplied.

    (c) An infinitely small percentage change in the price of microprocessors leads to an infinitely large percentage change in the quantity supplied.

    (d) A 5% rise in the price of fuel leads to a 1% expansion in the quantity available at the refineries.

    Terms

    (i)   Perfectly inelastic supply

    (ii) Relatively inelastic supply

    (iii) Unit elastic supply

    (iv) Relatively elastic supply

    (v)   Perfectly elastic supply

2   'True' or 'false'

    (a) The factors of production used in brick production are highly mobile, so that they can be varied quickly and easily. Price elasticity of supply will therefore be relatively inelastic.   True/False

    (b) We would expect the price elasticity of supply to be higher in the long-run time period than in the short run.   True/False

    (c) The managing director of the firm is so cautious he is unlikely to change his methods of operation. We can therefore expect price elasticity of supply to be rather low.   True/False

    (d) Since a 4% fall in price leads to a 3% contraction of supply, the value of PES will be −0.75.   True/False

3   Price elasticity of supply for a commodity is a measure of the:

    (a) ease with which one factor of production can be substituted for another in producing that commodity

    (b) responsiveness of quantity supplied to a change in price

    (c) responsiveness of price to a change in quantity supplied

    (d) responsiveness of price to a change in quantity demanded

    (e) responsiveness of quantity demanded to a change in price.

4   A relatively elastic supply is more likely when:

    (a) factors of production are highly immobile

    (b) factors of production are highly mobile

    (c) the time period is very short

    (d) producers are highly risk-averse and therefore extremely cautious

    (e) recent natural disasters have severely constrained production.

You try 3.3 continued

5 At any given price P_1 the more inelastic the upward sloping supply curve is for all prices below P_1:

(a) the smaller will be producer surplus

(b) the smaller will be consumer surplus

(c) the greater will be producer surplus

(d) the greater will be consumer surplus

(e) will not affect either producer or consumer surplus.

Answers can be found on pp. 525–546.

Recap

- The 'law of variable proportions' involves situations in which extra units of a variable factor of production are added to one or more fixed factors.
- Diminishing average and marginal returns to the variable factor will occur in the short-run time period, when at least one factor of production is fixed.
- In the long run, when all factors are variable, average cost may fall significantly with increased output for both technical and non-technical reasons.
- As well as such 'internal' economies of scale, costs may fall because of economies of scope and experience, or because 'external' economies of scale are available.
- Costs may also fall where multinationals take advantage of 'outsourcing' opportunities.
- The more mobile the factors of production are, the greater will tend to be the responsiveness of supply to a change in product price (i.e. price elasticity of supply).

Key terms

Average product The product (output) per unit of factor input.

Cost gradient Represents the increase in costs as a result of the production (enterprise) unit being only a specified percentage of the optimum size.

Costs Includes costs in the short- and long-run time periods, and variable costs (which change with output) and fixed costs (which do not change with output).

Diminishing returns Usually refers to the short-run time period. The average marginal product curves of a variable factor will eventually decline as more of the variable factor is applied to some fixed factor.

Diseconomies of scale The suggestion that, in the long run, long-run average costs rise as output rises beyond a certain level (MES).

Economies of experience Where increases in *cumulative output* reduce the average costs of the firm. Even smaller firms in business for many years can gain from economies of experience.

Economies of scale Changes in (long-run) average cost as a result of proportionate changes in all the factors of production. It describes the downward sloping segment of the LRAC curve.

Economies of scope Changes in average costs of production as a result of changes in the mix of output.

Increasing returns Usually refers to the short-run time period. The average marginal product curves of a variable factor may at first rise as more of the variable factor is applied to some fixed factor.

Long run The period of time in which all factors of production can be varied.

Long-run average cost The average cost of production in the long-run time period.

Long-run average cost curve The curve representing the lowest cost of producing any given level of output in the long-run time period.

Marginal product The addition to total product from using one extra unit of the factor of production.

Minimum efficient size or **scale (MES)** That level of output which results in the lowest attainable average cost. Usually refers to the long-run time period.

Opportunity cost The next best alternative sacrificed as a result of making a choice.

Price elasticity of supply (PES) A measure of the responsiveness of supply of a product to changes in its own price.

$$PES = \frac{\% \text{ change in quantity supplied of X}}{\% \text{ change in price of X}}$$

Producer surplus An area representing the benefit to producers from receiving a price higher than that needed for them to supply the product.

Returns to scale The lower costs resulting from increasing the size of output in the long-run time period.

Short run That period of time in which at least one factor of production is fixed.

Sunk cost A cost of acquiring an asset, whether tangible (e.g. plant) or intangible (e.g. reputation), which cannot be recouped by selling that asset or redeploying it to some other use.

Total product The total output over a given period of time.

Chapter

4

Business organisation, objectives and behaviour

Introduction

What types of business organisation are typical in advanced industrial economies such as the UK? After considering the various types we note that most organisations, whether they are in the public sector or the private sector, have mission statements which give an indication of what the organisation wants to achieve through its operations, both in the short and long term.

This chapter examines a number of alternative objectives open to the firm. It begins with those of a *maximising* type, namely profit, sales revenue and growth maximisation, predicting firm price and output in each case. A number of *non-maximising* or behavioural objectives are then considered. The chapter also reviews recent research into actual firm behaviour, and attempts to establish which objectives are most consistent with how firms actually operate. We see that although profit is important, careful consideration must be given to a number of other objectives if we are accurately to predict firm behaviour. The need for a perspective broader than profit is reinforced when we consider current management practice in devising the corporate plan.

Issues involving corporate governance, executive remuneration and social and corporate responsibility are also reviewed.

What you'll learn

By the end of this chapter you should be able to:

- outline the advantages and disadvantages of different types of business organisation, such as sole traders, partnerships, private and public limited companies
- examine the so-called 'principal–agent' problem and its implications for firm behaviour
- identify the various types of maximising and non-maximising (behavioural) objectives the firm might pursue and assess their implications for price and output policy
- assess the empirical evidence used in support of the various firm objectives and relate these objectives to current management practice
- evaluate the suggestion that ethical, environmental and ecological considerations are increasingly influencing firm behaviour
- consider issues of corporate governance and executive remuneration
- review the impact of the 'product life cycle' on business behaviour.

Types of business organisation

Business organisations take various forms, which we now consider. However, it will be useful first to outline certain terms often used when discussing business behaviour.

- **Unincorporated businesses.** These are sole traders and partnerships. This form of ownership is called *unincorporated* because:
  - *They have no separate legal identity*. It is the owner who makes contracts on behalf of the business and it is the owner, not the business, that is liable for the debts of the company.
  - *There is unlimited liability* for business debts, which means that the owner or owners can be declared bankrupt and any personal possessions may be taken and sold to pay off the debts of the business.
  - *There are few formalities* when it comes to setting up the business.
- **Incorporated businesses.** These mainly include private and public limited companies. They are said to be *incorporated* because:
  - *They have a separate identity* from the owner and consequently can sue and be sued in their own right (i.e. under the name of the company).
  - *There is limited liability* for business debts, which means that the owners are liable only up to the amount they have themselves invested in the business. For example, if a company becomes insolvent, and a shareholder owns £1,000 of shares in the company, then he or she will only lose the £1,000 invested.
  - *There are many formalities* required to establish a company.

Sole traders

Sole traders or sole proprietors are the most common form of business organisation in the UK. Many sole traders work on their own, although they sometimes employ other people. They are to be found in all sectors of the economy, such as manufacturing, retailing and services.

Table 4.1 outlines the advantages and disadvantages of operating as a sole trader (or as self-employed).

Table 4.1 **Advantages and disadvantages of the sole trader**

Sole trader	
Advantages	Disadvantages
Needs only a small amount of capital to start up	Lack of capital can limit expansion if the trader wants to grow
Can start the business easily – no need for elaborate legal requirements	May therefore fail to benefit from any economies of scale
Trader keeps all the profit so that there is an incentive to work hard	Liability is unlimited so that the owner's personal wealth is always at risk
Can make decisions quickly and so is relatively flexible	Lack of innovative ideas for expansion because there is only one main owner
Is in sole charge of the business so it is clear who makes the decisions	Long hours and lack of continuity should the owner not be able to carry on the business

Partnerships

Partnerships have virtually the same characteristics as sole traders. This form of business relationship is usually entered into by individuals who wish to take advantage of the combined capital, managerial skills and experience of two or more people.

Ordinary partnerships

These are allowed to have up to 20 partners (see Table 4.2), although banks are not allowed to have more than 10 partners while professional firms, such as accountants and solicitors, are allowed more than 20 partners. Within a partnership there can be a 'sleeping partner', i.e. a person who invests money in the partnership but has nothing to do with the daily running of the partnership.

Most partnerships will begin with a *deed of partnership*, which is a written agreement that covers specific aspects of mutual interest to the partners. These often include:

- the amount of capital provided by the partners;
- the division of labour and profits;
- the rules for taking on new partners;
- how the partnership could be dissolved;
- the allocation of votes to each partner.

Limited partnerships

There is also a form of business organisation known as a limited partnership in which the liability of at least one of the partners is limited to the amount of money invested in the partnership. These partners have a share in the profits but have no say in the running of the business. However, at least one other partner must have unlimited liability, i.e. be liable for the debts of the partnership. Limited partnerships are rare and have to be registered with the Registrar of Companies.

Table 4.2 **Advantages and disadvantages of the ordinary partnership**

Ordinary partnerships	
Advantages	Disadvantages
Easy and cheap to set up	Unlimited liability
Financial base is greater than that of the sole trader	The capital base is still relatively small and this limits future expansion
Costs, risks and responsibility can be shared	Profits have to be shared and each partner is liable for the debts of the company, even if not responsible for those debts
No requirement to publish full financial details, so more privacy for partners	
Finances need only be declared to the income tax and VAT authorities	Partners can individually make decisions in respect of the partnership which are binding on other partners
Continuity of ownership on a day-to-day basis as partners cover for each other	Lack of continuity in that if a partner dies or resigns or is made bankrupt the partnership is automatically dissolved
No requirement to publish full financial details. More privacy for partners	
Unlike a limited company, a partnership cannot be taken over against its will by another partnership	Disagreement between partners could cause difficulties in decision making and even the break-up of the partnership

In April 2001 a *Limited Liability Partnership (LLP)* also became formally available in order to combine the benefits of limited liability with the flexibility of organising the business as a traditional partnership. However, the LLP has similar disclosure requirements to a company, including the filing of company accounts.

Limited company

The structure of a limited company is different from that of sole traders and partnerships in that ownership and control are separated. Ownership is in the hands of the shareholders (principals) who appoint directors to report, usually on an annual basis, at the Annual General Meeting (AGM). However, the directors and managers (agents) are responsible for the day-to-day running of the business and report back to the shareholders (principals) at the AGM.

A limited company (whether private or public) must issue a Memorandum of Association defining its relationship with the outside world and Articles of Association defining its internal government.

The AGM is the occasion where shareholders can elect directors and also vote to dismiss directors and auditors. Since 2003 UK shareholders have also been given the right to vote on proposed remuneration packages for senior executives, although the vote is only 'advisory' (see p. 117). Shareholders are rewarded for investing in companies by receiving a dividend on each share. In some cases, shareholders do not check the performance of managers very rigorously and managers who control the company on a day-to-day basis may have motives which are different from those of shareholders. We consider these different motives below (pp. 113–124). Here we merely note that where we have a manager disagreement resulting from the separation between ownership and control, we call this the *principal–agent problem*.

Private limited company (Ltd)

The private limited company is a company whose shares cannot be sold to the general public (see Table 4.3). The name always ends with 'Ltd'. The minimum number of members is one and the minimum number of directors is one. There is no minimum requirement for the value of issued share capital. Shareholders are usually family members, existing business partners and employees.

There is another type of private limited company, i.e. the *private company limited by guarantee* – which is a company where the members' liabilities are limited to the amount

Table 4.3 **Advantages and disadvantages of the private limited company**

Private limited company (Ltd)	
Advantages	Disadvantages
Limited liability – personal possessions of the owners are protected as they cannot lose more than they have invested	Shares cannot be sold on the open market – harder for investors to get money back if they want to sell their shares
The owners keep control and choose the shareholders	Difficult to raise much money as shares cannot be sold to the general public
The business has its own legal identity so that the survival of the company does not depend on the personal circumstance of its shareholders	There is a limit to the amount of capital that can be raised from friends and family
Accounts need only be published in summarised form, thus preserving some privacy	Unless the founder members own the majority of shares, they may lose control over the business

they have undertaken to contribute to the company's assets should it be wound up. These companies are usually formed by professional, trade or research associations and are not as common as the private limited company.

Public limited company (PLC)

A **public limited company** is a company which has its shares listed on the London Stock Exchange. The name must always end with 'PLC' (see Table 4.4). The minimum number of members is two and the minimum number of directors is two. The company must have an authorised share capital of at least £50,000. Shareholders usually include large institutions such as insurance companies, pension funds and trade unions as well as the general public.

The most important features of a public limited company are:

1 *Access to funding* – much more funding is available than is the case with a sole trader or a partnership. This makes the growth of the company more feasible.

2 *Shareholders* – jointly own the business through the purchase of shares.

3 *Limited liability* – for each shareholder.

4 *Separate legal existence* – which means the company can sue or be sued under its own name.

5 *Continuity* – the running of the business is not affected by events and the personal circumstances of the individual shareholders.

Table 4.4 **Advantages and disadvantages of the public limited company (PLC)**

Public limited company (PLC)	
Advantages	Disadvantages
Limited liability	The company must pay for an auditor to independently check the accounts
Continuous existence as the survival of the company does not depend on personal circumstances of its shareholders	Many legal formalities have to be completed before the company can be set up
Large amounts of cash can be raised in a relatively short time because of the company's size and the security it offers	Requires a solicitor to register the company and this makes it more expensive to set up than a sole trader or partnership
Can specialise by setting up separate departments etc.	Activities are closely controlled by company law
Company has a separate legal existence from its owners	The real performance of the company may not always be reflected in the price of its shares
People are willing to invest in shares because it is easy to sell their shares on the stock exchange if they want cash	Company can become too large and bureaucratic, resulting in poor communications and inefficiency
Banks are willing to lend them money	Divorce of ownership from control can lead to conflict of interest
The company is able to enjoy economies of scale	Accounts are public so this means lack of privacy
Company accounts have to be published in detail each year. Potential shareholders and those wishing to do business with them can check to see if they are financially sound	They may be subject to takeover bids as there is no way of preventing other companies buying their shares
Very large companies can compete worldwide	In practice the small shareholder has very little influence on how the company is run

Holding company

This type of business organisation operates under section 736 of the UK Companies Act 1985 and is known as a holding company. It is said to be a 'holding' or 'parent' company in that it owns a majority (over 50%) of the voting shares in a subsidiary firm or group of firms. In this way the holding company can control the management and operations of any constituent firm by having the right to appoint its board of directors.

Case Study 4.1 reviews the important question in an increasingly globalised world of business as to whether foreign takeovers and ownership of previously domestic companies should be of concern to national governments and employees.

Case Study 4.1   Britain should not fear foreign ownership

Does ownership matter? The takeover of Cadbury by Kraft in 2009 has reopened a debate that periodically emerges whenever an icon of British industry falls victim to a foreign predator. Does it matter that the confectioner is now US-owned, or that its one-time rival Rowntree was bought by a Swiss company? What does it mean to say that a company is British, American or Swiss?

For a multinational such as Cadbury, it certainly has little to do with where its production or sales are located. Cadbury operates in more than 60 countries. Globalisation has meant that companies source their production from the most cost-effective parts of the world and distribute wherever it is profitable to do so.

What about the nationality of the owners? One of the interesting facts in a fascinating presentation by Robert Carr, Cadbury's outgoing chairman at Oxford's Said Business School in February 2010 was that, prior to the bid, UK institutions controlled 28% of Cadbury and North American institutions 47% of equity and North Americans 23%. In a world of global capital markets, the ownership of large companies is highly international and it is difficult to determine their nationality on the basis of where owners reside.

So if shareholders do not determine nationality, what about the board? This is not a much clearer indicator. A study of European multinational corporations in 2005 found that, on average, 25% of directors at UK companies were foreign. Cadbury was in line with this, with a third of its board being foreign. Increasingly, boards are becoming international to bring greater diversity of experience.

So if none of production, markets, shareholders or boards establishes the nationality of a company,

what if anything does? The one serious candidate is the location of its head office. Companies in general still have single locations at which the chief personnel work and key decisions are taken. Does it matter whether it is in the UK, the US or Switzerland?

This is a critical issue for Britain because for the past 20 years it has pursued a policy of welcoming foreign direct investment. This, combined with the fact that UK companies have among the fewest defences against hostile takeovers of any country – including the US, where 'poison pills' (see Chapter 5, p. 150) and other deterrents are rampant – has made British industry particularly vulnerable. But last year foreign direct investment in Britain fell by a staggering 90%. This raises an important point about foreign ownership. It is not just that inflows are volatile; outflows could leave the UK vulnerable. During the East Asian crisis between 1996–1998, foreign-owned companies cut their investment in East Asian countries by nearly twice the amount of their domestically owned equivalents. This ratio has been mirrored in recessions elsewhere in the world.

There are two interpretations of this observation. East Asia became a less attractive location in which to site activities and multinationals could benefit by locating activities to more productive markets elsewhere. Alternatively, companies might have been under pressure from their domestic governments and employees to retrench back to their home markets when conditions were tough.

In a study of whether social and political 'influence' outweighs economic efficiency, we examined how the location of headquarters affects the investment decisions of some 5,000 subsidiaries

Case Study 4.1 *continued*

around the world. On balance, we found that foreign ownership encourages a greater focus on relative profitability in investment appraisals and so benefits rather than detracts from the quality of investment decisions. If this is correct, then the location of headquarters does matter from a resource allocation standpoint. The only thing we have to fear from foreign control is our inefficiency. The unpalatable fact about the announced closure of Cadbury's factory in Bristol may be that Britain can eat its chocolate but it cannot make it.

Continuation of UK domestic production depends on global relative efficiencies.

Source: Carlin, W. and Mayer, C. (2010) from Britain should not fear foreign ownership, *Financial Times*, 22 February

Questions

1 What do you understand by the term 'foreign ownership'?

2 Consider the advantages and disadvantages of a switch to foreign ownership.

You try 4.1 reviews some of the aspects of business organisation.

You try   4.1

1 Look around any local town or village (e.g. for sole traders and partnerships) and look through recent copies of the financial press (e.g. *Financial Times*, *The Economist* etc.) for Ltd and PLC companies. Name *five* examples of each of the following types of companies. What do you notice?

Company type	Example
Sole trader	1
	2
	3
	4
	5
Partnership	1
	2
	3
	4
	5
Private limited company (Ltd)	1
	2
	3
	4
	5
Public limited company (PLC)	1
	2
	3
	4
	5

You try 4.1 continued

2 Look carefully at the table below. What does the table suggest?

Number of VAT-based enterprises by category in the UK, 2007

Sector	Total	Sole proprietors	Partnerships	Companies and public corporations	General government and non-profit-making bodies
Agriculture	139,100	57,935	66,180	14,370	615
Production	140,580	24,740	13,010	102,305	530
Construction	289,085	78,670	26,185	183,410	815
Services	1,583,635	363,915	184,395	951,885	83,420
Total	2,152,400	525,260	289,770	1,251,990	85,380

Note: Statistics based on turnover bands.

Source: Adapted from ONS (2009) *UK Business: Activity, Size and Locations 2009*, London: HMSO. Crown copyright material is reproduced with the permission of the Controller of HMSO and the Queen's Printer for Scotland under the Click-Use Licence.

Answers can be found on pp. 525–546.

Business objectives: maximising

The objectives of an organisation can be grouped under two main headings: *maximising objectives* and *non-maximising objectives*. We shall see that marginal analysis is particularly important for maximising goals. This is often confusing to the student who, rightly, assumes that few businesses or organisations can have any detailed knowledge of marginal revenue or marginal cost. However, it should be remembered that marginal analysis does not pretend to describe *how* firms maximise profits or revenue. It simply tells us what the output and price must be if firms do succeed in maximising these items, whether by luck or by judgement.

Profit maximisation

For most firms **profit** is the major concern, with total profit defined as total revenue minus total cost. A profit objective is often the principal reason for the original formation of the company. The traditional economist's view is that firms in the private sector are profit maximisers, with each business decision based on the need to increase profits. This may be the case for small operations that are under the direct control of the owner but, as we note later, large companies may be equally concerned with objectives such as turnover, market share or growth.

Profit, however, remains an important objective because:

● it ensures the long-term survival of the business;
● it provides a source of finance for future investment;
● it provides rewards for stakeholders (dividends for shareholders, wage increases for employees, price reductions or improved products for the consumer etc.);

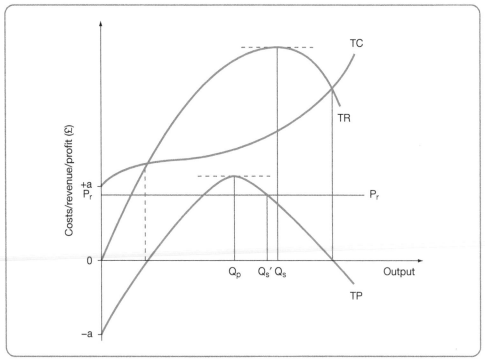

Figure 4.1 **Variation of output with firm objective**

- it provides a measure of the efficiency and effectiveness of management policies;
- it allows comparison with other forms of investment.

Figure 4.1 shows the output (Q_p) at which total profit is a maximum. We return to this diagram from time to time as we consider other maximising objectives.

Stop and think   4.1

Had the marginal revenue and marginal cost curves been presented in Figure 4.1, where would they have intersected?

It may be useful at this stage to look at *Taking it further* 4.1 which explains why profit can only be a maximum where marginal cost equals marginal revenue.

Taking it further **Profit maximisation and marginal analysis**   4.1

Does John Higgins or Ronnie O'Sullivan stop to calculate the angle of incidence and angle of reflection before trying to pot each snooker ball? Of course not, they use their experience, skill and judgement, although when they do pot the ball it will be *as if* they had made the calculation. Similarly, when a firm uses its experiences and judgement to maximise its profit it will be equating marginal cost (MC) with marginal revenue (MR). Even if it is entirely unaware of these terms, it will be acting *as if* it had made such a calculation.

In Figure 4.2 we show that total profit can only be a maximum when MR = MC.

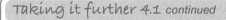

Taking it further 4.1 *continued*

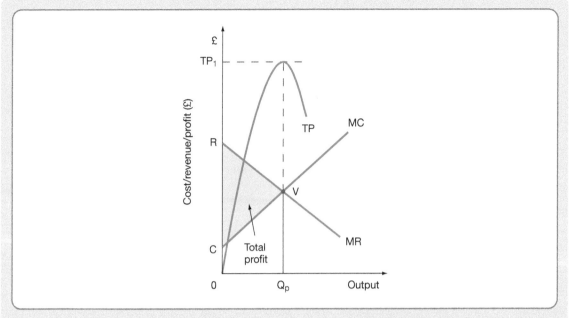

Figure 4.2 **Total profit is a maximum (RVC) at the output (Q_p) for which MR = MC**

Before using Figure 4.2 to demonstrate this point, we might note the following expressions for profit:

- Total profit = Total revenue − Total cost (TP = TR − TC)
- Average profit = Average revenue − Average total cost (AP = AR − ATC)
- Marginal profit = Marginal revenue − Marginal cost (MP = MR − MC)

In Figure 4.2, for every unit of output up to Q_P, MR is greater than MC and each unit adds something to total profit (i.e. marginal profit is positive).

For the Q_Pth unit of output, MR = MC and that unit adds nothing to total profit (i.e. marginal profit is zero).

For every unit of output beyond Q_P, MR is less than MC and each extra unit reduces total profit (i.e. marginal profit is negative).

It follows that only at output Q_P is total profit (area RVC) a maximum. If we draw the total profit (TP) curve, it will have reached a maximum value (TP_1) at output OQ_P.

Note: At output Q_P the rate of change of total profit (i.e. marginal profit) is zero. We can see this from the fact that the gradient to the TP curve is horizontal at output Q_P (i.e. TP has reached a maximum turning point).

The profit-maximising theory is based on two key assumptions: first, that owners are in control of the day-to-day management of the firm, so that there is no 'principal–agent' problem (see below); second, that the main desire of owners is for higher profit. The case for profit maximisation as 'self-evident' is, as we shall see, undermined if either of these assumptions fails to hold.

Principal–agent problem

To assume that it is the owners who control the firm neglects the fact that the dominant form of industrial organisation is the public limited company (PLC) which is usually run by managers rather than by owners. This may lead to conflict between the owners (shareholders) and the managers whenever the managers pursue goals which differ from those of the owners. This conflict is referred to as a type of **principal–agent problem** and emerges when the shareholders (principals) contract a second party, the managers (agents), to perform some tasks on their behalf. In return, the principals offer their agents some compensation (wage payments). However, because the principals are divorced from the day-to-day running of the business, the agents may be able to act as they themselves see fit. This independence of action may be due to their superior knowledge of the company as well as their ability to disguise their actions from the principals. Agents, therefore, may not always act in the manner desired by the principals.

Indeed, it may be the agents' objectives that predominate and that may shift the focus away from profit. This has led to a number of managerial theories of firm behaviour, such as sales revenue (turnover) maximisation and growth maximisation.

Sales revenue maximisation

It has been suggested that the manager-controlled firm is likely to have sales revenue (turnover) maximisation as its main goal rather than the profit maximisation favoured by shareholders. W. J. Baumol (1959) argued that the salaries of top managers and other perquisites (perks) are more closely correlated with sales revenue than with profits, giving managers an incentive to prioritise sales revenue in situations where managers had effective control of the firm.

O. E. Williamson (1963) developed a theory of 'managerial utility maximisation' which, like Baumol's, suggested that managers would seek to maximise sales revenue. Williamson's theory was, however, more broadly based, with the manager seeking to increase satisfaction through the greater expenditure on both staff levels and projects made possible by higher sales revenue. Funds for greater expenditure on staff levels and projects can come from profits, external finance and sales revenue. In Williamson's view, however, increased sales revenue is the easiest means of providing such additional funds, since higher profits have in part to be distributed to shareholders, and new sources of finance imply greater accountability. Baumol and Williamson are actually describing the same phenomenon, though they approach it from somewhat different perspectives.

If management seeks to maximise sales revenue without any thought to profit at all (i.e. *pure sales revenue maximisation*), then this would lead to output Q_s in Figure 4.1. This last (Q_sth) unit is neither raising nor lowering total revenue, i.e. its marginal revenue is zero and total revenue is a maximum.

Constrained sales revenue maximisation

Both Baumol and Williamson recognised that some constraint on managers could be exercised by shareholders. Maximum sales revenue is usually considered to occur well above the level of output that generates maximum profits. The shareholders might demand at least a certain level of distributed profit, so that sales revenue can only be maximised subject to this constraint.

The difference a profit constraint makes to firm output is shown in Figure 4.1 (p. 114):

- If P_r is the minimum profit required by shareholders, then Q'_s is the output that permits the highest total revenue while still meeting the profit constraint.
- Any output beyond Q'_s up to Q_s would raise total revenue TR – the major objective – but reduce total profit TP below the minimum required (P_r).
- Therefore Q'_s represents the **constrained sales revenue maximisation** output.

In the UK, as in other countries, there has been a rise in shareholder power and many see this as strengthening the links between executive remuneration packages and profit targets. For example, in 2003 the UK government introduced a ruling compelling a vote by shareholders at each Annual General Meeting (AGM) on executive remuneration packages proposed by PLCs for their senior executives. Although these votes are, as yet, only 'advisory', they have begun to influence company policies on executive remuneration. For example, a new pay deal had to be arranged for Jean-Pierre Garnier, the then chief executive officer (CEO) of GlaxoSmithKline (GSK) in December 2003 after shareholders voted down the original remuneration package which had offered him £22m should he choose to leave the company in the next two years even if the company's share price continued to fall. Institutional shareholders were outraged and voted against the remuneration package, seeing it as 'reward for failure'.

Case Study 4.2 usefully illustrates attempts to bring reward schemes for senior executives at the Royal Bank of Scotland (RBS) more closely into line with bank profits and performance.

Case Study 4.2   **RBS links new tougher pay schemes to bank's profits**

In March 2010 the Royal Bank of Scotland unveiled a new, tougher reward scheme for senior executives built around a range of performance measures, as the state-backed bank moved to introduce a more balanced pay structure.

The new incentive plan published in RBS's annual report could pay as much as £4.9m to Stephen Hester, chief executive. It is linked to a measure of the bank's profits as well as its share price, and is therefore more sophisticated than the two previous pay schemes, which were based purely on the shares hitting a certain level. The new scheme also scales back the maximum share award under the long-term incentives for senior executives from 450% to 400% of salary. It was developed after extensive discussions with UK Financial Investments, the body responsible for managing the governments' stakes in banks, and other shareholders.

UKFI was previously supportive of a pay scheme that focused solely on RBS's share price performance as this was aligned with the government's interest in selling its 70% stake in the bank at a profit. However, while the share price performance is still relevant, UKFI has been keen for the bank to introduce a broader set of performance criteria. Under the new scheme's terms, half the award will be linked to the bank's economic profit – which factors in its cost of capital – achieved in 2012. Another 25% will be based on the total shareholder return, a measure of the share performance relative to RBS's competitors, with the maximum for top quartile performance.

The final quarter will reflect the pure share price performance. Executives will gain a full entitlement if the shares hit 75p; fractionally higher than the 70p target of the old scheme. RBS shares are currently trading at 42p.

Source: from RBS links new tougher pay schemes to bank's profits, *Financial Times*, 19/03/2010 (Goff, S. and Jones, A.), © The Financial Times Ltd

Questions

1 What contribution might these changes in the remuneration packages for senior executives at RBS make to the principal–agent problem?

2 What are the arguments for including a target share price in the remuneration package? Why include elements other than share price performance?

Growth maximisation

Some of the main reasons for firms seeking growth include:

- *Cost savings*: firms can benefit from economies of scale.
- *Diversification of product*: reduces the risk of dependence on one product or service.

- *Diversification of market*: reduces dependence on one economy and one set of customers.
- *Market power*: increased power in the market allows firms to influence prices and to obtain better margins through reduced competition.
- *Risk reduction*: larger firms are less likely to suffer in market downturns and are less likely to be taken over by competitors. In an increasingly competitive market, firms are pressured into continually reducing costs and improving efficiency. One way of achieving this is to expand either by internal or by external growth.
- *Internal growth*: this is when the firm expands without involving other businesses. It is organic growth achieved by increasing sales of its existing products to a wider market.
- *External growth*: this can be achieved by either a takeover (gaining at least a 51% share in another firm) or a merger (two firms agreeing to join in creating a new third company).

Marris model of growth

So far we have assumed that the goals of owners (profits) have been in conflict with the goals of management (sales revenue). R. Marris, however, argues that the overriding goal which *both* managers and owners have in common is growth:

- Managers seek a growth in demand for the firm's products or services, to raise sales revenue and firm size, and thereby managerial income, power and status.
- Owners seek a growth in the capital value of the firm to increase personal wealth.

It is important to note, therefore, that it is only through the growth of the firm that the goals of both managers and owners can be achieved.

Also central to the analysis of Marris is the ratio of retained to distributed profits, i.e. the '*retention ratio*':

- If managers distribute most of the profits (*low retention ratio*), shareholders will be content and the share price will be sufficiently high to deter takeover.
- If managers distribute less profit (*high retention ratio*), then the retained profit can be used for investment, stimulating the growth of the firm. In this case shareholders may be less content, and the share price lower, thereby increasing the risk of a takeover bid.

The major objective of the firm, with which both managers and shareholders are in accord, is then seen by Marris as maximising the rate of growth of both the firm's demand and the firm's capital ('*balanced growth*'), subject to an acceptable retention ratio. Figure 4.3 shows the trade-off between higher balanced growth and the average profit rate.

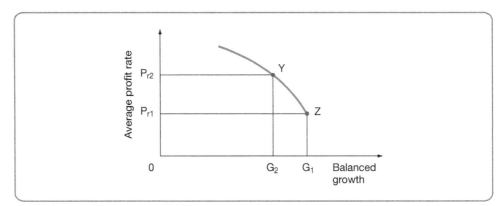

Figure 4.3 Trade-off between average profit and balanced growth

- For 'balanced growth' to increase, more and more investment in capital projects must be undertaken. Since the most profitable projects are undertaken first, any extra investment must be reducing the average profit rate.

- Point Z is where the balanced growth rate is at a maximum (G_1), with an implied retention ratio so high that all profitable investment projects have been pursued, giving an average profit rate P_{r1}.

- Risk avoidance by managers may, however, enforce a lower retention ratio with more profits distributed. Point Y is such a constrained growth-maximising position (G_2), with a lower retention ratio, lower investment and higher average profit (P_{r2}) than at point Z.

How close the firm gets to its major objective, Z, will depend on how constrained management feels by the risk of disgruntled shareholders, or a takeover bid, should the retention ratio be kept at the high rates consistent with points near to Z.

Business objectives: non-maximising behaviour

The traditional (owner control) and managerial (non-owner control) theories of the firm assume that a single goal (objective) will be pursued. The firm then attempts to achieve the highest value for that goal, whether profits, sales revenue or growth.

The **behaviouralist** viewpoint is rather different and sees the firm as an organisation with various groups, such as workers, managers, shareholders and customers, each of which has its own goal, or set of goals. The group that achieves prominence at any point of time may be able to guide the firm into promoting its 'goal set' over time. This dominant group may then be replaced by another giving greater emphasis to a totally different 'goal set'.

The traditional and managerial theories which propose the maximisation of a single goal are seen by behaviouralists as being remote from the organisational complexity of modern firms.

Satisficing theories

One of the earliest behavioural theories was that of H. A. Simon (1959) who suggested that, in practice, managers cannot identify when a marginal point has been reached, such as maximum profit with marginal cost equal to marginal revenue. Consequently, managers set themselves *minimum acceptable levels of achievement*. Firms which are satisfied in achieving such limited objectives are said to 'satisfice' rather than 'maximise'.

This is not to say that satisficing leads to some long-term performance which is less than would otherwise be achieved. The achievement of objectives has long been recognised as an incentive to improving performance and is the basis of the management technique known as management by objectives (MBO).

Figure 4.4 illustrates how the attainment of initially limited objectives might lead to an improved long-term performance. At the starting point 1, the manager sets the objective and attempts to achieve it. If, after evaluation, it is found that the objective has been achieved, then this will lead to an increase in aspirational level (3B). A new and higher objective (4B) will then emerge. Thus, by setting achievable objectives, what might be an initial minimum target turns out to be a prelude to a series of higher targets, perhaps culminating in the achievement of some maximum target or objective.

If, on the other hand, the initial objective is *not* achieved, then aspirational levels are lowered (3A) until achievable objectives (4A) are set.

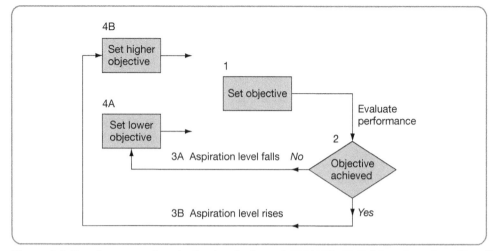

Figure 4.4 Development of aspiration levels through goal achievement

Simon's theory is one in which no single objective can be presumed to be the inevitable outcome of this organisational process. In fact, the final objective may, as we have seen, be far removed from the initial one.

Coalitions and goal formation

If a firm is 'satisficing', then who is being satificed – and how? R. M. Cyert and J. G. March (1963) were rather more specific than Simon in identifying various groups or coalitions within an organisation. A **coalition** is any group that, at a given moment, shares a consensus on the goals to be pursued.

Workers may form one coalition, wanting good wages and work conditions and some job security; managers want power and prestige as well as high salaries; shareholders want high profits. These differing goals may well result in group conflict, e.g. higher wages for workers may mean lower profits for shareholders.

The behavioural theory of Cyert and March, along with Simon, does not then view the firm as having *one* outstanding objective (e.g. profit maximisation), but rather *many*, often conflicting, objectives.

Cyert, March and others have suggested that different coalitions will be in effective control of firms (i.e. be *dominant*) at different times. For example, in times of recession the dominant coalition may be that which has formed around the cost and management accountants with the agreed objective of avoiding bankruptcy. In more prosperous times the dominant coalitions may involve marketing or promotion directors and others seeking objectives such as higher turnover, market share or growth. Clearly, different objectives may be followed depending on the coalitions that are dominant at any point in time.

The following are just some of the multiple objectives or goals which are identified by Cyert and March:

- *profit goals* (e.g. rate of return on capital employed);
- *sales goals* (e.g. growth of turnover or market share);
- *production goals* (e.g. to achieve a given level of capacity or to achieve a certain unit cost of production);
- *financial goals* (e.g. to achieve a sustainable cash flow).

Within the organisation different groups will pursue different priorities. In order to achieve success the firms' managers have to compromise and 'trade off' some goals or objectives against others. For example, a single-minded pursuit of production goals can obviously conflict with sales goals (if the production levels exceed market demand), inventory goals (if the unsold production piles up in warehouses), financial goals (if the firm's cash is tied up in unsold output) and profit goals (if, in order to sell the output, prices are slashed to below cost).

Stakeholder approaches

It is not just internal groups that need to be satisfied. There is an increasing focus by leading organisations on **stakeholders**, i.e. the range of both internal and external groups which relate to that organisation. Stakeholders have been defined as any group or individual who can affect or be affected by the achievement of the organisation's objectives. Cyert and March suggest that the aim of top management is to set goals that resolve conflict between these opposing stakeholders groups.

Does firm objective matter?

The analyst is continually seeking to predict the output and price behaviour of the firm. Figure 4.1 (p. 114) has already indicated that *firm output* does indeed depend upon firm objective, with the profit-maximising firm having a lower output than the sales-revenue-maximising firm (pure and constrained).

If we remember that price is average revenue (i.e. total revenue/total output), we can see from Figure 4.5 that *firm price* will also vary with firm objective.

$$\text{Price in the pure sales-maximising firm} = \tan \theta_s = R_1/Q_s$$
$$\text{Price in the profit-maximising firm} = \tan \theta_p = R_2/Q_p$$
$$\tan \theta_s < \tan \theta_p$$

Price of the pure sales-maximising firm is below that of the profit-maximising firm. It is clear that it really does matter what objectives we assume for the firm, since both output and price depend on that objective.

You try 4.2 gives an opportunity to self-check your understanding of material covered so far in this chapter.

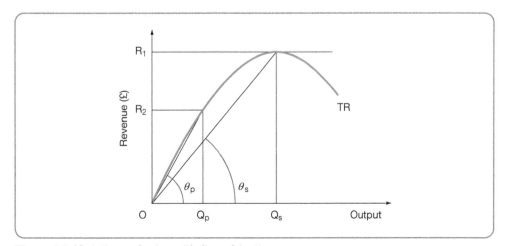

Figure 4.5 **Variations of price with firm objective**

You try   4.2

1 Look carefully at the diagram (Figure 4.6).

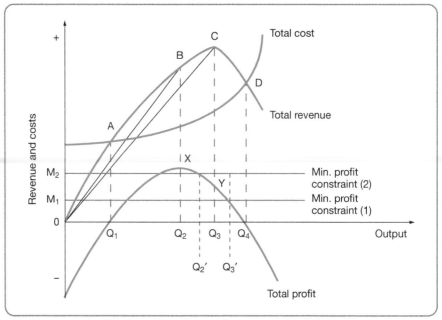

Figure 4.6

(a) At what output is total profit a maximum? What is the value of total profit at this output?

(b) At what output is total revenue a maximum? What is the value of total revenue at this output?

(c) What is the situation at both output Q_1 and Q_4?

(d) If the firm is seeking to maximise sales revenue subject to the minimum profit constraint (1), what output should it produce? Would anything change if the minimum profit constraint rises from (1) to (2)?

2 Look carefully at the table below which reflects the results of a major questionnaire survey by Shipley (1981) on business objectives. Some 728 firms responded to his questionnaire, with two particular questions giving the following results (percentages). What conclusions might you draw from these results?

	%
1 Does your firm try to achieve:	
(a) Maximum profits	47.7
(b) 'Satisfactory' profits?	52.3
2 Compared to your firm's other leading objectives, is the achievement of a target profit . . . regarded as being	
(a) of little importance	2.1
(b) fairly important	12.9
(c) very important	58.9
(d) of overriding importance?	26.1
Those responding with both 1(a) and 2(d)	15.9

Source: Adapted from Shipley, D. (1981) 'Primary objectives in British manufacturing', *Journal of Industrial Economics*, Vol. 29, 4 June. Reprinted with permission of Blackwell Publishing.

3 Which *two* of the following are characteristics of a sole trader?

(a) Limited liability.

(b) Potential lack of continuity of business.

(c) Unlimited liability.

(d) Economies of scale.

(e) Ease of access to capital.

4 Which *two* of the following are characteristics of a public limited company (PLC)?

(a) Economies of scale.

(b) Unlimited liability.

(c) Potential lack of continuity of business.

(d) Risk of takeover by other firms buying shares on the Stock Exchange.

(e) Can't sell shares to the general public.

5 Which *two* of the following are likely to be true for a firm which succeeds in maximising sales revenue?

(a) Marginal profit is zero.

(b) Marginal revenue is zero.

(c) Marginal cost is zero.

(d) At any other output, total revenue will be rising or falling.

(e) At any other output, total profit will be rising or falling.

6 Which *two* of the following are likely to be true for a firm which succeeds in maximising total profit?

(a) Marginal profit is zero.

(b) Marginal revenue is zero.

(c) Marginal cost is zero.

(d) At any other output, total revenue will be rising or falling.

(e) At any other output, total profit will be rising or falling.

7 Which *two* of the following are likely to be true for a firm which can be said to be a 'satisficer'?

(a) Marginal profit is zero.

(b) The firm will revise its objectives if achievement fails to match aspiration.

(c) The firm produces at break-even output.

(d) It is extremely difficult to predict the firm's output and pricing policy.

(e) The difference between total revenue and total cost is a maximum.

8 Which *two* of the following are characteristics of the 'principal–agent' problem?

(a) Ownership and control in hands of same people.

(b) Ownership and control in hands of different people.

(c) Shareholders and managers pursue different objectives.

(d) Shareholders and managers pursue same objectives.

(e) Sole traders are the dominant form of business organisation.

You try 4.2 continued

9   Which *two* of the following are characteristic of a constrained sales revenue maximising firm?

(a) Total profit is zero.

(b) Total revenue is the highest it can be while still meeting the profit constraint.

(c) Total profit is the highest it can be while still meeting the revenue constraint.

(d) Any extra output will raise total revenue but reduce total profit below the constraint.

(e) Any extra output will raise total profit but reduce total revenue below the constraint.

Answers can be found on pp. 525–546.

Profit, ethics and the environment

It is often suggested that firm behaviour which seeks to be more than usually ethical or to give considerable weight to environmental concerns must do so at the expense of profit. However, many firms are now seeing ethical and environmentally responsible behaviour as being in their own self-interest. Indeed, attempts are now being made to incorporate ethical and environmental considerations into formal stock exchange indices in the UK and other financial markets. A new FTSE 4 Good Index was launched in July 2001, using social and ethical criteria to rank corporate performance. All companies in three sectors were excluded, namely tobacco, weapons and nuclear power (representing 10% of all FTSE companies). Of the remaining companies, three criteria were applied for ranking purposes: environment, human rights and social issues. If a company 'fails' in any one of these criteria, it is again excluded. Of the 757 companies in the FTSE All Share Index, only 288 companies have actually made it into the index.

Check the net

KPMG has a section devoted to business ethics:
www.kpmg.com/About/CSR/

The FTSE itself has produced figures showing that if this new FTSE 4 Good Index had existed over the previous five years, it would actively have outperformed the more conventional stock exchange indices. The same has been found to be true for the Dow Jones Sustainability Group Index in the US. This is a similar ethical index introduced in the US in 1999. When backdated to 1993 it was found to have outperformed the Dow Jones Global Index by 46%.

Case Study 4.3 looks further into this linkage between social/environmental responsibility, business performance and executive remuneration.

Stop and think   4.2
Can you think of reasons why ethical/environmental considerations might actually increase, rather than reduce, business profitability?

| Case Study 4.3 | Drive to link pay to sustainability begins | **FT** |

Sustainability has been a trendy, if sometimes derided, concept for some time in business circles. Now it appears to be becoming a buzz word in executive remuneration. DSM and TNT, the Dutch life sciences group and postal operator respectively, in February 2010 joined a growing band of companies – predominantly from the Netherlands – that link part of the bonuses senior management receive to sustainability, an all-encompassing term that refers not only to the environment but to issues such as employee satisfaction and safety.

The decision raises questions such as how to measure sustainability as distinct from something more tangible such as a rise or fall in a share price, and whether it makes sense to do it. Akzo Nobel, the Dutch paint company that bought ICI of the UK three years ago, was among the pioneers. It based half of its long-term incentive scheme on its position in the Dow Jones Sustainability Index for chemical companies.

'There is a risk that if rewarding for performance is your value, you put all your eggs in one basket,' Hans Wijers, chief executive, says. It is an idea Mr Wijers has introduced at Royal Dutch Shell, the oil group at which he is head of the remuneration committee. In addition to safety, which fellow oil company BP also uses to calculate bonuses, its ranking in the Dow Jones Sustainability index will count in the future. Mr Wijers says the idea has been positively received by shareholders – Akzo's proposal was passed by 97% of investors – as well as by workers.

Carola van lamoen, a pay expert at Robeco, the Dutch investor, says it has been asking companies to include sustainability in remuneration for several years. 'We are convinced that strong corporate values, including care for the interests of employees, customers and the environment, are a precondition for stable, long-term, above-average results for a company.'

But not everyone is convinced. The VEB, the powerful Dutch retail shareholders' association, is against using sustainability in regard to pay. Jan Maarten Slagter, its director, argues performance is sufficient. Good companies, he says, know sustainability will help them to perform better than rivals. 'You can score well on three or four sustainability components and still do poorly in [forming] shareholder value. We would like to see pay

policies directed to [forming] shareholder value in the long term.'

One important challenge concerns how to measure sustainability in a concrete manner. Akzo Nobel managers receive a full bonus when the company is in the top three, out of about 90, companies in the Dow Jones Sustainability Index. They would receive some shares if the company were to be placed fourth or fifth.

Both DMS and postal operator TNT rejected using the Sustainability Index. They have instead opted to adopt a mixture of ideas to measure things such as employee and customer satisfaction, greenhouse gas reduction and energy use. A glance at DMS's greenhouse gas reduction target demonstrates the ways in which they have tried to make the targets measureable.

DMS last year reduced greenhouse gases by about 2%, once revenue growth was stripped out. Feike Sijbesma, the company's chief executive, says the proposals are still being finalised but would see an annual reduction of 1–1.5% go unrewarded; if 5–6% were to be achieved, the full bonus would be paid and there would be a sliding scale in between.

Mr Sijbesma pitches the proposal as being about more than merely business: 'It is very good to pay attention to this because we need a next generation that is going to live here. Our grandchildren will be less interested in what our returns were on the stock market in 2009 or 2010 but [they] will be [interested] in what impact we had on the planet.'

Source: from Drive to link pay to sustainability begins, *Financial Times*, 24/02/2010 (Milne, R.), © The Financial Times Ltd

Questions

1 What are the arguments for and against linking executive pay to 'sustainability'?

2 How would you define and measure 'sustainability' when seeking to relate pay to such outcomes?

Firms are increasingly aware of the benefits of aligning themselves with ethical and ecological initiatives. Various 'kitemarks' exist for firms to certify that their product conforms to ethical standards in production, as for example 'Rug-Mark' for carpets and rugs, 'Forest Stewardship Council' mark (to certify wood derived from sustainable forestry extraction methods) and 'Fairtrade' mark (guarantees a higher return to developing country producers).

Check the net

Oxfam, Make Trade Fair campaign:
www.maketradefair.com

Labour behind the Label pressure
group: **www.labourbehindthelabel.org**

Clean Clothes, European campaign:
www.cleanclothes.org

**www.Guardian.co.uk/environment/fair
trade**

At the sectoral level, many of Britain's biggest retail names have joined the *Ethical Trading Initiative* (ETI) which brings together companies, trade unions and non-governmental organisations in seeking to ensure that the products sold in their retail outlets have not been produced by 'sweatshop' labour working for next to nothing in hazardous conditions.

At the corporate level Exxon Mobil seems to be an example of a company that has accepted the linkage between ethical/environmental practices and corporate profits. It announced in late 2003 that it had been holding discreet meetings with environmentalists and human rights groups worldwide in an effort to change its unfavourable image in these respects. The charm offensive has been linked to fears at Exxon's Texas headquarters that a negative public image is threatening to damage its Esso petrol brand, which has faced 'stop Esso' boycotts in the EU and elsewhere following its being linked to supporting President Bush's boycott of the Kyoto agreement on protecting the climate.

Example

Fairtrade

It was reported in 2010 that annual sales of *Fairtrade* food and drink in Britain have reached over £500m, having grown at over 40% per year over the past decade. It has expanded from one brand of coffee ten years ago to around 1,000 foodstuffs, including chocolate, fruit, vegetables, juices, snacks, wine, tea, sugar, honey and nuts. A Mori poll found that two-thirds of UK consumers claim to be green or ethical and actively look to purchase products with an environmental/ethical association.

Business behaviour

We now turn our attention to the ways in which companies actually behave and consider some of the implications of such behaviour.

Control in practice

Profit maximisation is usually based on the assumption that firms are *owner-controlled*, whereas other theories as to firm objective often assume that there is a *separation* between ownership and control. The acceptance of these alternative theories was helped by early research into the ownership of firms.

- Studies in the US by Berle and Means in the 1930s, and by Larner in the 1960s, suggested that a substantial proportion of large firms (44% by Berle and Means and 85% by Larner) were manager-controlled rather than owner-controlled.

- Later research has, however, challenged the definition of 'owner-control' used in these early studies. Whereas Berle and Means assumed that owner-control is only present with a shareholding of more than 20% in a public limited company, Nyman and Silberston (1978) used a much lower figure of 5% after research had indicated that effective control could be exercised by owners with this level of shareholding.

- This lower figure would suggest that owner-control is far more extensive than previously thought. For example, Leech and Leahy (1991) found that 91% of British public limited companies are owner-controlled using the 5% threshold figure, whereas only 34% are owner-controlled using a 20% threshold figure.

- Clearly the degree of control by owners of firms is somewhat subjective, depending crucially on the threshold figure assigned to shareholding by owners in order to exercise effective control.

- A further aspect of owner-control involves the role of financial institutions and pension funds. Between them they now own over 76% of the shares of public companies in the UK, compared to only 36% in 1963, while individual share ownership has declined from 54% in 1963 to around 20% today.

- Financial institutions are more likely than individuals to bring influence to bear on chief executives, being experienced in the channels of communication and sensitive to indices of firm performance. The increase in share ownership of these institutions is seen by many as moving the firm towards the profit-maximising (owner-controlled) type of objective.

Profit-related behaviour

In a major study, Shipley (1981) had concluded that only 15.9% of his sample of 728 UK firms could be regarded as 'true' profit maximisers (see p. 122). A similar study by Jobber and Hooley (1987) found that 40% of their sample of nearly 1,800 firms had profit maximisation as their prime objective. In a more recent study of 77 Scottish companies by Hornby (1994), 25% responded as 'profit maximisers' to the 'Shipley test'.

Given the significance of the profit-maximising assumption in economic analysis, these results may seem surprising, with less emphasis on profits than might have been expected. However, some consideration of the decision-making process may serve to explain these low figures for profit maximisation.

Firms in practice often rely on *pre-set 'hurdle' rates of return* for projects, with managers given some minimum rate of return as a criterion for project appraisal. As a result, they may not consciously see themselves as profit maximisers, since this phrase suggests marginal analysis. Yet in setting the hurdle rates, top management will be keenly aware of the marginal cost of funding, so that this approach may in some cases relate closely to profit maximisation. In other words, the response of management to questionnaires may understate the true significance of the pursuit of profit.

Profit as part of a 'goal set'

Although few firms appear to set out specifically to maximise profit, profit is still seen (even in response to questionnaires) as an important factor in decision making. In the Shipley study the firms were asked to list their principal goal in setting price. Target profit was easily the most frequently cited, with 67% of all firms regarding it as their principal goal when setting prices. Even more firms (88%) included profit as at least part of their 'goal set'.

Profit and reward structures

There has been a great deal of concern over recent years that managers in large firms have paid too little regard to the interests of shareholders, especially as regards profit performance of the company. Indeed, a number of celebrated cases in the press have focused on the apparent lack of any link between substantial rises in the pay and bonuses of chief executives and any improvements in company performance.

The majority of empirical studies have indeed found little relationship between the remuneration of top managers and the profit performance of their companies. In the UK, Storey *et al.* (1995) found no evidence of a link between the pay of top managers and the ratio of average pre-tax profits to total assets, with similar results for studies by Jensen and Murphy (1990) and Barkema and Gomez-Meija (1998) in the US.

However, the absence of any proven link between the profitability of a firm and the reward structures it offers to its CEO and other top managers does not necessarily mean that profit-related goals are unimportant. Firms increasingly offer top managers a total remuneration 'package' which often involves bonus payments and share options as well as salary. In this case higher firm profitability, and therefore dividend earnings per share, may help raise the share price and with it the value of the total remuneration package. Indeed Ezzamel and Watson (1998) have suggested that the total remuneration package offered to CEOs is directly related to the 'going rate' for corporate profitability. It may therefore be that top management have more incentives for seeking profit-related goals than might at first be apparent.

To summarise, therefore, although there may be no open admission to profit maximisation, the strong influence of owners on managed firms, the use of preset hurdle rates and the presence of profit-related reward structures may in the end lead to an objective, or set of objectives, closely akin to profit maximisation.

Sales revenue-related behaviour

Sales revenue maximisation

Baumol's suggestion that management-controlled firms will wish to maximise sales revenue was based on the belief that the earnings of executives are more closely related to firm revenue than to firm profit. A number of studies have sought to test this belief. For example, in a study of 177 firms between 1985 and 1990, Conyon and Gregg (1994) found that the pay of top executives in large companies in the UK was most strongly related to a long-term performance measure (total shareholder returns) and not at all to current accounting profit. Furthermore, growth in sales resulting from takeovers was more highly rewarded than internal growth, despite the fact that such takeovers produced on average a lower return for shareholders and an increased liquidity risk. These findings are in line with other UK research (Gregg *et al.*, 1993; Conyon and Leech, 1994) and with a study of small UK companies by Conyon and Nicolitsas (1998) which also found sales growth to be closely correlated with the pay of top executives.

Sales revenue as part of a 'goal set'

The results of Shipley's analysis tell us little about sales revenue maximisation. Nevertheless, Shipley found that target sales revenue was the fourth-ranked principal pricing objective and that nearly half the firms included sales revenue as at least part of their set of objectives. Larger companies cited sales revenue as an objective most frequently; one-seventh of companies with over 3,000 employees gave sales revenue as a principal goal compared to only one-fourteenth of all the firms. Since larger companies have greater separation between ownership and management control, this does lend some support to Baumol's assertion. The importance of sales revenue as part of a set of policy objectives was reinforced by the study of 193 UK industrial distributors by Shipley and Bourdon (1990), which found that 88% of these companies included sales revenue as one of a number of objectives. However, we see below that the nature of planning in large organisations must also be considered and that this may temper our support for sales revenue being itself the major objective, at least in the long term.

Strategic planning and sales revenue

Current thinking on strategic planning would support the idea of short-term sales maximisation, but only as a means to other ends (e.g. profitability or growth). Research in the mid-1970s by the US Strategic Planning Institute linked market share – seen here as a proxy for sales revenue – to profitability. These studies found that high market share had a significant and beneficial effect on both return on investment and cash flow, at least in the long term. However, in the short term the high investment and marketing expenditure needed to attain high market share reduces profitability and drains cash flow. Profit has to be sacrificed in the short term if high market share, and hence future high profits, are to be achieved in the long term.

Constrained sales revenue maximisation

The fact that 88% of all companies in Shipley's original study included profit in their 'goal set' indicates the relevance of the profit constraint to other objectives, including sales revenue. The later study by Shipley and Bourdon (1990) reached a similar conclusion, finding that 93% of the UK industrial distributors surveyed included profits in their 'goal set'.

Non-maximising behaviour

We have seen that the non-maximising or behavioural theories concentrate on how firms actually operate within the constraints imposed by organisational structure and firm environment. Recent evidence on management practice broadly supports the behavioural contention, namely that it is unhelpful to seek a single firm objective as a guide to actual firm behaviour. This support, however, comes from a rather different type of analysis, that of portfolio planning.

Portfolio planning

Work in the US by the Boston Consulting Group on the relationship between market share and industry growth gave rise to an approach to corporate planning known as 'portfolio planning'. Firms, especially the larger ones, can be viewed as having a collection or 'portfolio' of different products at different stages in the product life cycle. If a product is at an early stage in its life cycle, it will require a large investment in marketing and product development in order to achieve future levels of high profitability. At the same time another product may have 'matured' and, already possessing a good share of the market, be providing high profits and substantial cash flow.

The usual strategy in portfolio planning is to attempt to balance the portfolio so that existing profitable products are providing the funds necessary to raise new products to maturity. This approach has become a classic part of strategic decision making.

If a firm is using the portfolio approach in its planning then it may be impossible to predict the firm's behaviour for individual products or market sections on the basis of a single firm objective. This is because the goals of the firm will change for a given product or market sector depending on the relative position of that product or market sector within the overall portfolio. Portfolio planning, along with other behavioural theories, suggests that no single objective is likely to be useful in explaining actual firm behaviour, at least in specific cases.

'Managing for value' (MFV)

The non-maximisation behaviour of large companies can be seen clearly in the approach taken by some large companies (Griffiths, 2000). For example, between 1997 and 2000 Cadbury Schweppes, the chocolate and confectionery multinational, explained its objectives in terms of 'managing for value' (MFV). To meet the MFV criterion the company stressed the importance of:

- increasing earnings per share by at least 10% every year;
- generating £150m of free cash flow every year;
- doubling the value of shareholders' investment in the four years to 2000;
- competing in the world's growth markets by effective internal investment and by value-enhancing acquisitions;

- developing market share by introducing innovations in product development, packaging and routes to market;
- increasing commitment to value creation in managers and employees through incentive schemes and share ownership;
- investing in key areas of air emissions, water, energy and solid waste.

From the above list it is clear that the first three preoccupations are related to the profit objectives while the fourth and fifth relate to company growth and market share. In addition, the final two objectives encompass both human resource and environmental issues. In this context, it can be seen that maximising a single corporate goal seems unrealistic in the dynamic world of multinationals.

Reviewing business behaviour

The traditional theory of the firm assumes that its sole objective is to maximise profit. The managerial theories assume that where ownership and control of the organisation are separated, the objective that guides the firm will be that which the management sets. This is usually thought to be maximisation of either sales revenue or growth. It is important to know which, if any, of the maximising objectives are being pursued, since firm output and price will be different for each objective. Behavioural theory tends to oppose the idea of the firm seeking to maximise any objective. For instance, top management may seek to hold the various stakeholder groups in balance by adopting a set of minimum targets. Even where a single group with a clear objective does become dominant within the firm, others with alternative objectives may soon replace it.

In practice, profit maximisation in the long term still appears to be important. Sales revenue seems quite important as a short-term goal, though even here a profit target may still be part of the goal set. The prominence of the profit target may be an indication that ownership is not as divorced from the control of large firms as may once have been thought. One reason why sales revenue may be pursued in the short term is found in an analysis of current strategic planning techniques, which link short-term sales revenue to long-term profit. Sales revenue may therefore be useful for explaining short-term firm behaviour.

Those who, like Marris, argue that growth is a separate objective from profit find some support in the lack of any clear relationship between growth and profitability. Growth may also be a means of securing greater stability for the firm. It may reduce internal conflict, by being an objective around which both owner-shareholders and managers can agree, and possibly reduces the risk of takeover. Also, large firms experience, if not higher profits, then less variable profits. A widely used technique in the management of larger firms, portfolio planning, would seem to support the behaviouralist view, that no single objective will usefully help predict firm behaviour in a given market.

Corporate governance

Corporate governance refers to the various arrangements within companies which provide both authority and accountability in its operations. In other words, the various rules and procedures which are in place to direct and control the running of the company. However, there has been much concern in recent years as to the ways in which the larger public limited companies (PLCs) have been governed, especially in view of high-profile company collapses such as Enron in the US in 2001 and Parmalat in Italy in 2004.

Before turning to the problems encountered by such companies and the remedies proposed, it may be useful to consider the issue of *executive remuneration* in rather more detail. This has itself been a major source of concern to shareholders and other corporate investors.

Executive remuneration

We have already reviewed (pp. 115–117) executive pay in the context of the principal–agent problem. In Europe, 84% of companies place decisions about executive pay in the hands of their compensation, or remuneration, committee, according to a survey by consultants Hewitt, Bacon and Woodrow. So, ultimately, it is remuneration committees that are as responsible as anyone when executive pay appears to bear scant relationship to corporate performance. *Pensions and Investment Research Consultants* (PIRC), the UK corporate governance watchdog, regularly reports that the pay of executive directors at FTSE 100 companies has spiralled high above inflation.

The rapid rise in executive pay, when the companies themselves have been performing modestly at best, has created widespread criticism from shareholders and others. *Stock options* have been a particular source of criticism – the practice whereby senior executives have been given the 'option' of buying company shares at a heavily discounted price (i.e. lower than the market price) and then selling them at a profit should they succeed in raising the share price above an agreed target. Often, exercising these options has given far more income to executives than their basic salaries.

So who sits on the remuneration committee which decides the executive remuneration schemes? In the UK the *Combined Code* of corporate governance states that members should be drawn 'exclusively' from non-executives due to the potential for conflicts of interest. By and large, this is so. However, says PIRC, some 14% of FTSE 100 companies continue to include executives on their remuneration committees.

Arguably, excessive executive pay is even more widespread in the US. For example, the gap between the earnings of ordinary Americans and top executives has grown far wider in the past 25 years. A statistic commonly quoted by the labour group AFL-CIO shows that a chief executive made $42 for every dollar earned by one of his or her blue-collar workers in 1980. Today, chief executives were earning $531 for every dollar taken home by a typical worker.

Corporate 'scandals'

Corporate scandals, such as those at Enron, WorldCom and Global Crossing in the USA, have become well known in the past few years. However, such problems are by no means confined to the USA, as the case of the Italian dairy company, Parmalat, clearly indicates. In little more than a fortnight in December 2003, the Italian dairy conglomerate became engulfed in Europe's biggest financial fraud as some €10bn to €13bn were found to have disappeared from its accounts. Deloitte, Parmalat's chief auditor, did not do its own checks on some big bank accounts at one of the Italian dairy group's subsidiaries that turned out to be fakes. As a result, in December 2003, a major scandal broke after the disclosure that Bonlat, a Parmalat subsidiary in the Cayman Islands, did not have accounts worth almost €4bn (£2.8bn) at Bank of America (B of A). Eventually this 'lost' money was found to be three times greater. Bonlat's auditor was Grant Thornton and B of A told it in January 2004 that a document purportedly showing accounts with cash and securities worth €3.95bn was fake. Deloitte, one of the big four global accounting firms, allegedly did not make independent checks on the authenticity of Bonlat's supposed accounts with B of A, believing it was entitled to rely on Grant Thornton's work on Bonlat, rather than do its own checks, and such an arrangement was permitted by Italian law and regulators. Even though the division of work between Deloitte, as chief auditor, and Grant Thornton, as auditor to Parmalat's subsidiaries, was allegedly agreed with the company and notified to Consob, Italy's chief financial regulator, the deficiencies in such regulation became only too apparent with the eventual collapse and prosecution of those involved.

Lessons for corporate governance

These high-profile company collapses, together with shareholder concerns as to the often 'excessive' remuneration packages of company directors in poorly performing companies, have resulted in changes in the rules of corporate governance in recent years. These have involved changes in both internal and external practices, as for example in the companies' dealings with auditors and accountants. *Taking it further* 4.2 reviews some recent changes and proposals for change in the UK and elsewhere.

Taking it further **Corporate governance**   4.2

In the UK the *Higgs Committee* in 2002 has sought to improve corporate governance in the wake of the bitter experiences for shareholders and investors in the collapse of Enron, WorldCom, Global Crossing and other high-profile companies. The Higgs proposals include the following:

- At least 50% of a company's board should consist of independent non-executive directors.
- Rigorous, formal and transparent procedures should be adopted when recruiting new directors to a board.
- Roles of Chairman and Chief Executive of a company should be separate.
- No individual should be appointed to a second chairmanship of a FTSE 100 company.

In the USA the *Sarbanes–Oxley Act* in 2002 was also directed at strengthening corporate governance.

- If officers of a company are proved to have intentionally filed false accounts, they can be sent to jail for up to 20 years and fined $5m.
- Executives will have to forfeit bonuses if their accounts have to be restated.
- A ban on company loans to its directors and executives.
- Protection for corporate whistleblowers.
- Audit committees to be made up entirely of independent people.
- Disclosure of all off-balance-sheet transactions.

Other suggestions for improving corporate governance include the following:

- The European Commission wants to ensure that group auditors take responsibility for all aspects of companies' accounts and is considering requiring each European Union member state to set up US-style accounting oversight boards.
- Italy's government wants a stronger regulator to replace Consob, the existing securities and markets authority.
- The OECD has drafted a revision of its principles of corporate governance, including calls for shareholders to be able to submit questions to auditors.
- Auditors should be seen as accountable to shareholders and not to management, as has often been the case. The draft proposals also call on boards to protect whistleblowers.

Rules on corporate governance to support efficient markets must, however, extend beyond the accounting conventions and structures adopted within boardrooms, as Case Study 4.4 indicates.

Case Study 4.4   In the eye: Minority shareholders are aggrieved

On 26 August 2010 Novartis, a pharmaceutical company, announced that it had completed its purchase of shares in Alcon, the specialist eyecare company, from its previous owner, Nestlé, giving Novartis 77% ownership of Alcon. Alcon is the world's largest and most profitable eyecare company and offers new growth opportunities from an ageing world population. However, this takeover has made it clear that, despite Switzerland being one of the world's oldest democracies, minority shareholders in Swiss firms have fewer rights than those in many other countries. The minority shareholders in Alcon – an American-listed but Swiss-based eyecare company – have discovered to their cost that some owners are more equal than others!

Nestlé, the food giant from which Novartis bought the stake, has already spent some of the $28.1 billion revenue from selling its Alcon shares on buying Kraft's American pizza business for $3.7 billion, which in turn gave Kraft the cash for its hostile takeover bid for Cadbury, a British confectioner, in 2010.

However, Alcon's remaining 23% of shareholders are less than pleased. Under most countries' takeover rules, all holders of the same class of stock must be offered the same amount of money for their shares. Yet in this case Novartis has only offered to pay Alcon's minority shareholders $153 a share for their 23% holdings instead of the $180 a share paid to the 77% majority shareholders. Even this lower valuation has only been offered in terms of the equivalent value of Novartis shares rather than in cash itself. This non-cash offer to minority shareholders turned out to be an offer of 2.8 Novartis shares for each 1 Alcon share.

This unequal treatment has caused uproar, especially among hedge funds that had bought Alcon shares hoping to profit from the difference between the price at which the shares were then trading and the expected price of shares when the projected takeover was agreed. 'Shareholders are saying that this can't be happening,' says one observer. 'They are astounded because this is not a banana republic, it is Switzerland'.

But Switzerland is not a member of the EU and is therefore not bound by the rules of the European Union's takeover Directive of 2004 which obliges all members to pass laws forcing bidders to make mandatory offers to minority shareholders at an 'equitable price'. America's rules on takeovers would also prevent this unequal treatment of minority shareholders.

Unhappily for Alcon's shareholders, however, Swiss merger law does allow bidders to pay one price to controlling shareholders and a lower price to the remainder. Indeed, some Swiss lawyers and business people defend such different treatment on the grounds that many Swiss firms are controlled by families which ought to be compensated for the additional costs they incur from being less diversified than other shareholders and because they invest more time in overseeing management.

The takeover of Alcon is further complicated because the firm is based in Switzerland but its shares trade in America, leaving investors with neither the protections afforded by American corporate law nor those of Swiss securities law, both of which would have been more favourable to Alcon's minority shareholders.

Source: Based on information from *The Economist* (2010) 9–15 January, p. 62

Questions

1 In what ways are minority shareholders in Switzerland at a disadvantage to those in other countries?

2 What changes to corporate governance rules in Switzerland might help in this situation?

3 Why do some argue that the current governance situation in Switzerland for minority shareholders is acceptable?

Product life cycle

Most products go through four stages in the product life cycle, namely introduction, growth, maturity and decline, as indicated in Figure 4.7. As we see below, business behaviour in terms of price-setting and other product-related policies will depend upon the stage the product has reached in its life cycle.

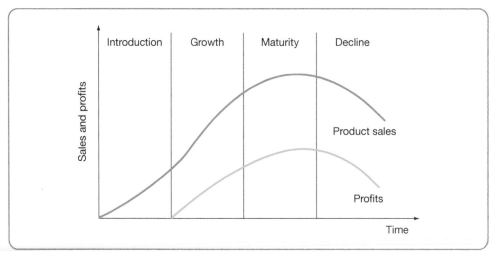

Figure 4.7 **Stages in the product life cycle**

1 *Introduction.* This is a stage in which the product is relatively unknown, sales are low, and profits are not yet being made. The promotion strategy will be designed to inform people that the product is available. The product would normally be stocked in a limited number of outlets but the firm would try to ensure that there was maximum exposure at these points of sale. Price might be relatively low at this time in an attempt to gain a market 'foothold' (**penetration pricing** strategy). Alternatively, price might be relatively high where the producer faces little competition for a new product with unique characteristics (**price skimming** strategy).

2 *Growth.* In this stage there is extremely rapid growth which attracts the first competitors to the market. Prices are likely to be lowered to attract a wider base of customers and the number of outlets likely to be increased. The firm will also be seeking the new products that will replace this one, or modifications to some existing products that will extend their life cycle. The profits which are starting to be made can be used to support such investments.

3 *Maturity.* The majority of sales are repeat orders in this stage rather than first-time purchases. Fierce competition often forces the firm to reduce prices further. Advertising seeks to persuade customers to buy this, rather than some other, brand of product. The firm will be looking to see if the product can be sold in other markets – often abroad. Refinements and cosmetic changes are introduced to provide a competitive edge and maintain sales levels. Replacement products are likely to be introduced. Economies of scale resulting from large volume production will help to keep unit costs low and profits high.

4 *Decline.* As sales decline, advertising and promotion cease. Prices may be reduced as much as possible to keep at least some sales. Eventually, as the product moves into loss, it is withdrawn from the market. However, as price is relatively inelastic for those fewer 'loyal' customers who still purchase it, prices may sometimes be increased during the decline stage for some products.

Stop and think   4.3

What might be the reasons for increasing the price of a product during its decline stage?

Table 4.5 Business behaviour and the product life cycle

Introduction	Growth	Maturity	Decline
Characteristics	*Characteristics*	*Characteristics*	*Characteristics*
• High failure rate • Little competition • Frequent modifications • Make losses	• More competitors • Rising sales • Possibly acquired by larger company	• Sales increase at reduced rate • Product line widened • Prices fall as market share is lost • Difficult for new entrants • Marginal producers drop out	• Falling industry sales • Falling product sales • Some producers abandon market • Falling profits
Strategies	*Strategies*	*Strategies*	*Strategies*
• Create product awareness • 'Skim' pricing or penetration pricing • Shake-out policy – quickly drop unsuccessful products	• Promote brand image • Acquire outlets • Obtain economies of scale	• Encourage repeat buys • Seek new customers by repositioning and brand extension strategies • Seek to hold or increase market share by greater efficiency • Use price discounting to hold or win market share • Hold on to distributors	• Strict cost control • 'Run out' sales promotion with low price to get rid of stocks prior to introduction of replacement • Higher prices charged to fewer, but still loyal, customers

Links

Business behaviour involving product, price, promotion and place for both single product and multi-product firms is considered more fully in Chapter 12, p. 386.

Table 4.5 summarises this discussion on how price and non-price behaviour of a business might vary with the product life cycle.

Recap

- Separation between ownership by shareholders (principals) and control by managers (agents) makes profit maximisation less likely.
- Maximisation of sales revenue or asset growth (as well as profit) must be considered in manager-led firms.
- The objectives pursued by the firm will influence the firm's price and output decisions.
- Different groupings (coalitions) may be dominant within a firm at different points of time. Firm objectives may therefore change as the coalitions in effective control change.
- Organisational structure may result in non-maximising behaviour; e.g. the presence of diverse stakeholders may induce the firm to set minimum targets for a range of variables as a means of reducing conflict.
- Shipley's seminal work (supported by later studies) found less than 16% of the firms studied to be 'true' profit maximisers. However, Shipley found that 88% of firms included profit as part of their 'goal set'.
- Separation between ownership and control receives empirical support, though small 'threshold' levels of shareholdings may still secure effective control in modern PLCs.
- Profit remains a useful predictor of long-term firm behaviour, though sales revenue may be better in predicting short-term firm behaviour.
- Profit maximisation may not be acknowledged as a goal by many firms, yet in setting 'hurdle rates' senior managers may implicitly be following such an objective.

- Profitability and executive pay appear to be largely unrelated, suggesting that other managerial objectives might be given priority (sales revenue, growth, etc.). However, total remuneration 'packages' for top executives may be linked to profitability, helping to align the interests of managers more closely to the interests of shareholders.

- Businesses may be able to raise revenue and profit by adopting ethical and environmentally sustainable policies.

- Business behaviour, both price and non-price, may depend on the stage the product has reached in its life cycle.

- Portfolio planning points to a variety of ever-changing objectives guiding firm activity rather than any single objective.

Key terms

Articles of Association Sets out the rules by which the company will be administered (e.g. voting rights of directors).

Behavioural objectives Objectives influenced by the dynamics of firm behaviour: often non-maximising.

Coalitions Groups which have a consensus on a particular objective/goal.

Constrained sales revenue maximisation Firm seeks to maximise sales revenue (turnover) but subject to meeting some minimum profit target.

Corporate governance The various rules and procedures used to direct and control the running of the company.

Growth This can be expressed in various forms: e.g. the rate of increase of output per annum, or rate of increase of the firms capitalised value per annum, and so on.

Managerial objectives Objectives set by managers (agents) rather than shareholders (principals). Profit will tend to be less important; sales revenue, market share, growth will tend to be more important.

Memorandum of Association Document which forms the basis of registration of a company. Lists the subscribers to the capital of the company and the number of shares they hold. May also list company objectives etc.

Partnership Unincorporated business of between 2 and 20 people who share risks and profits. Partnerships usually have unlimited liability for debts of other partners (though limited partnerships can be formed).

Penetration pricing A low-price strategy in the introduction stage of the product life cycle.

Price skimming A high-price strategy in the introduction stage of the product life cycle.

Principal–agent problem Where agents (managers) pursue different objectives from principals (shareholders).

Private limited company (Ltd) A limited number of shareholders (2–50) with limited liability. Cannot offer shares to general public.

Product life cycle The stages a typical product will go through during its 'life cycle', namely introduction, growth, maturity and decline stages.

Profit Total profit is total revenue minus total cost.

Public corporations Government owned; sometimes called nationalised industries.

Public limited company (PLC) Unlimited number of shareholders (with limited liability). Can offer shares to general public.

Sales revenue maximisation Firm seeks to maximise sales revenue (turnover).

Satisficing A theory which suggests that objectives constantly change, depending on whether previous aspirations have (or have not) been met.

Sole trader One-person business.

Stakeholders All those with an interest in the business, e.g. consumers, employees, employers, shareholders, etc.

Firm size, mergers and the 'public interest'

Introduction

How do we define small and medium-sized enterprises (SMEs)? Why has the small firm continued to survive and how important is it to the whole economy? Why do many SMEs wish to grow larger, what methods do they use and what problems do they encounter? Under what circumstances are mergers likely to be in the 'public interest' and in any case what do we mean by the 'public interest'. What patterns and trends are taking place in merger activities and why and how do governments seek to regulate such activity?

The contents of this chapter will help you to understand these issues and take further the discussions on economies of scale, scope and experience in Chapter 3. A more detailed analysis of competition policy in the UK and EU, including mergers and restrictive practices legislation, is presented in Chapter 8.

What you'll learn

By the end of this chapter you should be able to:

● outline the various definitions of SMEs and their contribution to the UK economy

● explain the reasons why small firms continue to exist

● understand why SMEs often seek to grow larger, the methods they use and the government support programmes available

● assess the contribution of larger firms to the UK economy

● identify the patterns and trends in merger activity and understand why governments seek to regulate merger activity in the 'public interest'.

Small to medium-sized enterprises (SMEs)

Before assessing the contribution of small and medium-sized enterprises (SMEs) to the UK and the EU economy, it will be helpful if we first define them.

Definition of SMEs

There are a number of different ways of defining small and medium-sized firms.

- *Bolton Committee Report of 1971*. This had recognised the difficulty of defining the small firm. Rather than depending solely on numbers of employees or other data, it suggested that the emphasis be placed on the characteristics which make the performance of small firms significantly different from those of large firms. Three such characteristics were identified as being of particular importance:
  - having a relatively small share of the market;
  - being managed by owners in a personalised way rather than via a formalised management structure;
  - being independent of larger enterprises, so that its owner-managers are free from outside control when taking their decisions.
- The *1985 Companies Act*. This was more specific and defined a company in the UK as small if it satisfied any *two* of the following:
  - turnover less than £2m;
  - net assets under £975,000;
  - fewer than 50 employees.
- *The Department of Business, Innovation and Skills*. This defines SMEs in terms of numbers of employees as follows:
  - micro firm (0–9 employees);
  - small firm (10–49 employees);
  - medium-sized firm (50–249 employees);
  - large firm (over 250 employees).
- *European Union* (EU). This definition of an SME involves four criteria, as listed in Table 5.1.

To qualify as an SME both the employees and independence criteria must be satisfied together with either the turnover or the balance sheet criteria. An SME is defined as an 'independent enterprise' when the amount of capital or voting rights in that firm held by one or more non-SME firms does not exceed 25%. The values shown in the table for turnover and balance sheet are liable to be changed over time as the absolute monetary values require adjustment because of inflation.

Table 5.1 Defining micro, small and medium-sized firms*

	Micro firm	Small firm	Medium firm
Turnover	Not exceeding €2m	Not exceeding €10m	Not exceeding €50m
Balance sheet total	Not exceeding €2m	Not exceeding €10m	Not exceeding €43m
Employees	Fewer than 10	Fewer than 50	Fewer than 250
Independence criteria	–	25% or less	25% or less

*'Headcount' includes all staff (employees and manager owners); 'turnover' refers to income from sales and services; 'balance sheet total' refers to the value of a company's main assets

Table 5.2 Shares (%) of enterprises, employment and turnover: UK and EU

	Micro (0–9)	Small (10–49)	Medium (50–249)	Large (250+)
Enterprises:				
UK	95.4	3.8	0.6	0.2
EU	91.8	6.9	1.1	0.2
Employment				
UK	26.5	11.9	10.2	51.6
EU	29.8	20.7	16.7	32.8
Turnover				
UK	20.6	14.0	13.3	52.1
EU	18.8	19.3	19.5	42.4

Sources: Adapted from Enterprise Directorate (2010) *SME Statistics for the UK and Regions* and European Commission (2009) *Annual Report on EU Small and Medium Sized Enterprises*. Crown copyright material is reproduced with the permission of the Controller of HMSO and the Queen's Printer for Scotland under the Click-Use Licence

Importance of SMEs

Table 5.2 indicates the shares of different-sized enterprises in the total number of enterprises, total employment and total turnover, both for the UK and the EU.

The 'micro' firm, employing fewer than 10 people, makes up 95.4% of all UK enterprises, provides 26.5% of all UK employment and 20.6% of all UK turnover. While the figures for the contribution of micro enterprises within total enterprises were higher in the UK than in the EU, it is interesting to note that small and medium-sized enterprises tended to contribute rather less to employment but rather more to turnover in the UK than in the EU. Table 5.2 also highlights the greater contribution that large firms make to employment and turnover in the UK as compared to the EU.

Although large firms with over 250 employees are few in number in both the UK and EU, their contribution to employment and turnover is highly significant. In the UK, while large firms are only 0.2% (i.e. 1 in 500) of all enterprises, they contribute 51.6% of UK employment and 52.1% of UK turnover. We return to consider the large firm in more detail later in this chapter (p. 146).

Small firm survival

As we saw in Chapter 3 (pp. 85–91), economic theory suggests that large firms should be more efficient than small firms owing to the existence of economies of scale. Despite this, small firms continue to survive for the following reasons.

- *Supply a small (niche) market* either geographically (e.g. corner shop) or by producing a specialist item or service.

- *Provide a personal or more flexible service*, e.g. local solicitor, accountant or builder.

- *Allow entrepreneurs the opportunity to start their own business and to test their ideas in the marketplace.* Many of these people are dissatisfied with working for large companies and desire to be their 'own boss'.

- *The owners have made a conscious decision not to grow* because they do not want to undertake the inherent risks and workload associated with growth.

- *Benefit from government support programmes* directed towards helping the small firm survive and grow.

Case Study 5.1 looks at entrepreneurship in relation to SMEs.

Case Study 5.1	**Entrepreneurship and SMEs**

In recent years there has been an increasing emphasis by governments across the world on developing attributes of 'entrepreneurship' or 'enterprise' within the workforce. Often the term 'entrepreneurship' is associated with business start-ups, with popular TV programmes such as *The Apprentice* and *Dragons' Den* capturing this enthusiasm for developing one's own business. As we note in Table 5.4 (p. 145), around 78% of all UK businesses are 'sole traders' with 0 or 1 employees, although these only account for around 14% of total employment and 8% of total turnover.

In more recent times the term 'high-expectation entrepreneurs' has come into use. This is defined by the *Global Entrepreneurship Monitor* as 'All start-ups and newly formed businesses which expect to employ at least 20 employees within five years'. Only around 14% of all start-up attempts are expected to create 20 or more jobs within the first five years, while 44% are expected to create five or more jobs. High growth entrepreneurs, sometimes termed 'gazelles', are given particular attention by national policy makers because of the significant (and disproportionate) contribution they make to national new-job creation! Figure 5.1 shows the percentage of the working age population for different countries in such high-growth expectation business start-ups (<42 months old) over the period 2004–2009. China has over 4% of its adult population engaged in high-growth expectation business

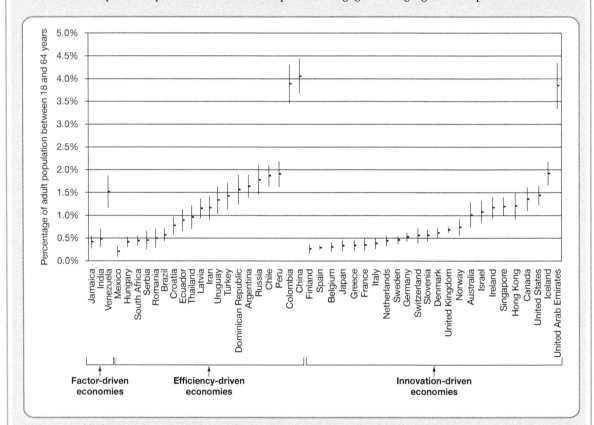

Figure 5.1 **High-growth expectation early-stage entrepreneurship (HEA), 2004–2009**

Case Study 5.1 *continued*

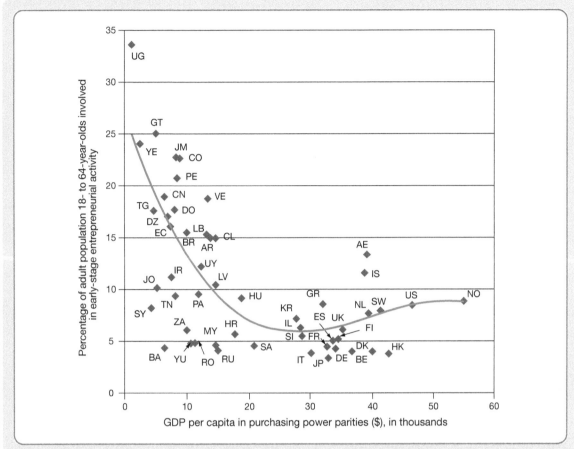

Figure 5.2 **Early-stage entrepreneurial activity rates and per capita GDP, 2009**

start-ups compared to 1.5% in the US, 0.7% in the UK, and less than 0.5% in many EU economies.

Yet another term widely used in discussions of entrepreneurship is 'early stage entrepreneurial activity', which refers to the percentage of the population aged 18–64 years which is involved in starting new businesses at any one time. As we can see from Figure 5.2, there is a wide variation across countries in this percentage, with such early-stage entrepreneurial activity seeming to be related in interesting ways to the standard of living, measured by Gross Domestic Product (GDP) per capita.

Figure 5.2 demonstrates that entrepreneurship rates are not just a function of differences in economic development (or welfare) but also other factors (R^2 only 0.39). Examples of such factors might include population growth, which can stimulate demand and the stock of existing business owner-managers, who serve as role models and who are more likely to start a business than

other individuals. Eastern European countries, with falling populations and a low stock of business owner-managers as a legacy of communism, are clusters below the trend line, while Latin American countries, with healthy population growth rates and a larger stock of business owners, tend to appear above the trend line.

Questions

1 Look carefully at Figure 5.1 and consider possible reasons why there are differences between countries in terms of high-growth expectation entrepreneurs.

  NB You might choose two specific countries which differ significantly in their scores.

2 Look carefully at Figure 5.2 and examine some of the factors which might explain the linkage between 'early-stage entrepreneurial activity' and GDP per capita.

'Problems' facing SMEs

Despite the importance of SMEs to the UK and EU economies noted in Table 5.2, they face a number of obstacles to their survival and growth.

- *Small firms and the banks.* One of the most common concerns of SMEs has been to secure adequate financial backing at reasonable interest rates. Smaller firms rely on personal savings at the start-up stage but then obtain some 60% of external finance from banks, although very small firms also use hire purchase and leasing arrangements. The relationship between smaller firms and banks is therefore of vital importance for this sector of UK industry. As has been noted in many surveys, the central problem of financial support for small firms is not necessarily the availability of finance but its cost. For example, the rate of interest for small firms employing fewer than 30 employees in the UK is currently between 3% and 5% above base rates and this is often doubled if the overdraft is exceeded, even if only briefly.

- *Debt structure.* Another issue for UK small firms relates to the structure of their debt. The dependence of UK SMEs on overdraft finance accounts for 59% of total external funding, which is above the EU average. Such dependence often restricts the ability of smaller firms to take a long-term view because overdrafts are repayable on demand. As far as the length of loans is concerned, some 24% of UK SMEs have loans of up to three years, which is similar to the EU average. On the other hand, a smaller proportion of UK SMEs have loans of three to five years, and a larger proportion of UK SMEs have loans of over five years, as compared to the EU average.

- *Lack of training.* Surveys in the past decade have shown that between 80% and 90% of small companies in the UK had no business training and received no formal preparation for company board responsibility. The continued need for such support was highlighted in a major study of 1,300 SMEs by the Centre for Business Research of Cambridge University (Cosh and Hughes, 2000). This study found that less than half of all the firms investigated had formal structures for their management organisation and less than half provided formal training within their companies.

- *Low turnover and cash flow* are frequently identified as problems in regular surveys, such as the National Westminster/SBRT Quarterly Survey of Small Business.

  - *Low turnover* was identified by almost 45% of firms as the most important problem in the immediate aftermath of the economic slowdown of the early 1990s and is still cited as such by around 25% of UK SMEs.

  - *Cashflow payments* problems are seen as the main source of concern by around 10% of UK SMEs. Sometimes the source of this problem may be high interest rates on loans or the lack of demand in times of recession. However, the linkage of cashflow problems in SMEs to late payments is sometimes exaggerated. For example, UK SMEs currently have an average payment delay of 41 days, longer than countries such as Denmark (33 days), Norway (30 days) and Germany (31 days), but shorter than France (58 days) and Italy (78 days).

- *Government regulations and paperwork.* These are cited as a problem by nearly 15% of respondents to the NatWest/SBRT surveys. Valuable time and resources are taken up responding to a host of paperwork reflecting new initiatives and directives from the UK, EU and other regulatory bodies. Nor is the problem confined only to SMEs. The Institute of Chartered Accountants estimates that such 'red tape' cost the UK economy over £6bn each year.

It may be useful to review how successive governments in the UK have introduced various support programmes, especially as the small firm has become more widely perceived as a source of growth for both national output and employment.

Government support programmes

Small firm support has focused on three main areas.

1 Easier access to equity and loan capital

- *Enterprise Finance Guarantee*. This scheme is designed to provide a government guarantee of 75% on loans which finance institutions provide to small and medium–sized firms. The government guarantees loans of between £1,000 and £1m for periods of up to ten years to qualifying UK businesses with an annual turnover of up to £25m.
- *Enterprise Investment Scheme*. This scheme encourages investors to invest in the ordinary shares (equity) of companies by providing a range of tax reliefs for investors. For example, if shares are held for a minimum of three years then a tax relief of 20% of the cost of the shares can be given. The minimum investment is £500 and the maximum is £500,000.

Other government schemes to provide funds for small businesses include Regional Venture Capital Funds, High Technology Funds, Venture Capital Trusts and support for the Alternative Investment Market (AIM). Case Study 5.2 looks in more detail at the contribution of AIM to SME financial support.

2 Increased tax allowances and grants

- *Corporation tax*. Small companies pay a reduced rate of 21% on taxable profits compared to a standard rate of 28%.
- *Enterprise grants*. For example, the Grant for Business Investment (GBI) can give assistance of between 20% and 35% of the capital expenditure of small companies (employing less than 50 employees) depending on the region in which they are located.

Other such schemes include Small Firms Training Loans (SFTL) and a host of small firm support services via Learning and Skills Councils, Chambers of Commerce, Business Links, Small Business Service etc.

3 Less government interference

Various attempts have been made to reduce 'red tape' and government bureaucracy for small firms, with mixed results.

Case Study 5.2 reviews the contribution of the Alternative Investment Market to the growth of small firms in the UK economy.

Case Study 5.2	The Alternative Investment Market (AIM)

The *Alternative Investment Market* (AIM) was opened in 1995 to meet the demand for a low-cost and accessible investment market for small and growing companies. Its trading rules are less demanding than those for a full listing on the London Stock Exchange, as indicated in Table 5.3.

In 2010 the initial fee payable by all companies seeking admission to AIM varied from £6,085 to £68,750 depending on the value of market capitalisation for the company while the equivalent fees payable on the main LSE market varied from £6,085 to £352,085. Once admitted, the annual fee payable per company on the AIM was £4,925 compared to an annual fee of between £4,005 and £39,000 on the LSE depending on the market capitalisation of the company.

Case Study 5.2 continued

Table 5.3 **The differences between the main market and AIM**

Listing criteria	Main market	AIM
% of free-floating shares	Minimum 25% in public hands	No minimum
Trading history	Three years trading record normally required	No prior trading record required
Listing fees	Companies required to pay a listing fee of between £6,085 and £352,085, depending on market capitalisation	Fee of between £6,085 and £68,750 per company depending on market capitalisation
Shareholder participation	Prior shareholder approval needed for certain transactions	No prior shareholder approval required
Reporting requirements	Required to report profits twice a year	Required to report profits twice a year
Admission documents	Pre-vetting of admission documents by the Financial Services Authority (FSA)	No pre-vetting of documents made by LSE or FSA unless a public offer of securities is made
Capitalisation	Minimum market capitalisation of £700,000	No minimum market capitalisation

By February 2010 there were 1,268 companies trading on the AIM with a combined market value of £58bn. The total money raised between 1995 and 2010 was £66bn and companies on the AIM in 2010 included Majestic Wine (drinks), Carluccio's (café/food), Young and Co Brewery (drinks), Straight plc (food waste disposal), Falkland Oil and Gas (gas exploration) and Millwall Holdings (football).

Question

How might you justify government support for the Alternative Investment Market?

It may be useful at this stage to review some survey evidence on the contribution of small firms to the UK economy.

Small firms and the UK economy

The current interest in small firms is due partly to a growing recognition of their ability to create new jobs and provide innovative products and services. However, there is a danger in placing too heavy an emphasis on the role of small firms in rebuilding the UK's industrial base. Figures from the then Department of Trade and Industry (DTI) in 2006 showed that 45% of VAT registered businesses failed to survive the first three years. Storey (1982) had already shown that most small firms stay static or die. In his study of all the new manufacturing firms started in Cleveland, County Durham and Tyne and Wear from 1965 to 1978 he found that only 774 survived out of 1,200. Of the survivors, more than half still had fewer than 10 employees in 1982, and nearly three-quarters had fewer than 25. In fact, the probability of a new business employing more than 100 people after a decade was less than 0.75%. For every new job created by a small firm in these three counties over the 13-year period, four jobs were lost from large companies employing over 1,000 persons.

Storey *et al.* (1987) found that in their survey of single-plant independent manufacturing companies in northern England, one-third of the new jobs were found in less than 4% of the new starters. Further research (Storey, 1994) also showed that it is incorrect to assume that countries which have experienced the most rapid increase in new firm formation (measured in terms of increase in self-employment) are those which have experienced the fastest growth of employment creation. The same survey also pointed out that investment in government training schemes for small company entrepreneurs at the start-up or at later stages is not necessarily related to the future success of small companies. The evidence shows that success is more closely related to the original educational attainment of the business owner. In other words, it may be more important to improve the level of the UK's general education as a whole, if small firms are to thrive.

For all these reasons, the net advantages of small firms may be less than is commonly supposed. Nevertheless, small firms are able to find market niches, especially where economies of scale are not easily obtained, as in providing specialised items for small markets, and in developing products used as components by large firms. Also, the movement towards a higher proportion of employment being in the service sector, where traditionally smaller firms have been dominant, suggests an increasingly important role for small firms in the UK economy. For example, a major report has shown that UK-based SMEs performed relatively well over the period 1988–2001 as compared to large companies when measured in terms of growth in real value added, employment and profitability (European Commission, 2002).

However, in absolute terms there are still major gaps between small and large firms. For example, in the UK at the beginning of the new millennium, the value added per occupied person (labour productivity) in small firms was still only 87% of the UK average as compared to 120% for large firms (TUC, 2000). In addition, larger firms should not be neglected since although only 1 in 500 UK firms have 250 or more employees, large firms currently contribute around 52% of total employment and 52% of total turnover in the UK.

You try 5.1 gives an opportunity to further check your understanding of SMEs.

You try   5.1

1 Look carefully at Table 5.4. What does the table suggest about the contribution of: (a) SMEs in the UK, (b) large firms in the UK?

Table 5.4 **Number of businesses, employment and turnover share by size band in the UK (2010)**

Employment size band	Number of businesses (thousands)	Share of total (%)		
		Businesses	Employment	Turnover
0–1	3,767,145	77.8	14.4	8.2
2–4	641,175	13.2	6.4	6.7
5–9	238,625	4.9	5.5	5.7
10–19	125,400	2.6	5.7	6.1
20–49	60,370	1.2	6.2	8.0
50–99	18,975	0.4	4.4	5.5
100–199	9,385	0.2	4.4	5.4
200–249	1,950	0.0	1.4	2.4
250–499	3,795	0.1	4.4	8.7
500+	4,470	0.1	47.2	43.4
Total	4,871,290	100.0	100.0	100.0

Source: Enterprise Directorate (2010) *SME Statistics (UK and Regions)* Table 2a (modified). Crown copyright material is reproduced with the permission of the Controller of HMSO and the Queen's Printer for Scotland under the Click-Use Licence

You try 5.1 *continued*

2 Which of these sectors is likely to contain the highest proportion of small firms?
   (a) Public utilities
   (b) Personal services
   (c) Manufacturing
   (d) Industrial construction
   (e) Telecommunications

3 In which type of market is a small firm most likely to survive?
   (a) Mass market
   (b) Global market
   (c) National market
   (d) Niche market
   (e) Common market

4 Which type of situation is *least favourable* to the small firm's survival?
   (a) Few economies of scale
   (b) Market involves personal services
   (c) Many small competitors exist
   (d) Considerable product differentiation (i.e. non-homogeneous product)
   (e) Substantial economies of scale

5 Which of the following is NOT a reason why small firms may want to grow?
   (a) Cost savings through economies of scale
   (b) Diversification of product portfolio to reduce risk
   (c) Diversification of market to reduce dependence on one set of customers
   (d) To ensure that ownership continues to provide control of the firm
   (e) To increase market power and, with it, control over price

Answers can be found on pp. 525–546.

Growth in firm size

Important though SMEs are, Table 5.4 shows that large firms also make a vital contribution to the UK economy. Although only 0.2% (i.e. 1 in 500) of the businesses have 250 or more employees, these large firms contribute some 51.6% of total employment and 52.1% of total turnover.

Reasons for firm growth

In Chapter 3 (pp. 85–92) we noted that there are potential cost savings from the growth in firm size. However, as Table 5.5 notes, these economies of scale are only one of a number of possible reasons why firms may seek to grow in size.

Methods of firm growth

The methods by which firms seek to grow are many and varied. It will be useful to review some of the most usual methods adopted.

Organic growth

Organic growth is where the firm uses its own resources to support growth, for example reinvesting its own profits ('ploughed-back profits'). Of course, the firm may also seek to

Table 5.5 Reasons for growth in firm size

Reasons for growth	Description
Cost savings	Firms can benefit from economies of scale, both technical and non-technical economies (see Chapter 3, pp. 85–92)
Diversification of product	Firms reduce the risk of dependence on one good or service
Diversification of market	Firms reduce their dependence on one economy and one set of customers
Market power	Firms increase their power in the market as they grow larger, which allows them to influence prices and to obtain better profit margins through reduced competition
Risk reduction	Firms of larger size with a more diversified product portfolio and market presence are less likely to suffer in market downturns and are less likely to be taken over by competitors

raise investment finance by borrowing from financial intermediaries or by issuing share or paper assets. As we noted in Chapter 4, the sources of finance available to the firm will depend on whether it is a sole trader, partnership, private limited company or public limited company.

> *Stop and think*   5.2
> What are the advantages and disadvantages of organic growth?

Franchising and licensing

- *Franchising.* Here one firm (the franchisee) purchases the right to undertake business activity from another firm (the franchisor) using that firm's name or trademark rather than any patented technology. The scale of this activity varies from so-called 'first-generation franchising' to 'second-generation franchising' in which the franchisor transfers a much more comprehensive business package to the franchisee to help establish a 'start-up position'. This may include detailed guidance on how to operate the franchise, even extending to specialist staff training.

  In *first-generation* franchising, the franchisor usually operates at a distance. However, in *second-generation* franchising, the franchisor exerts far more control on the day-to-day running of the local operations. This type of franchising is common in the hotel, fast food restaurant and vehicle rental industries, such as Holiday Inn, McDonald's and Avis respectively.

- *Licensing.* At its simplest, licensing can mean permission granted by one firm (*licensor*) to another firm (*licensee*) in the form of a contract to engage in an activity that would otherwise be legally forbidden. The licensee buys the right to exploit a fairly limited set of technologies and know-how from the licensor, who will usually have protected the intellectual property rights involved by a patent, trademark or copyright. This tends to be a low-cost strategy for growth since the licensor makes little or no resource commitment. The licensor benefits from the licensee's local knowledge and distribution channels which would otherwise be difficult and time-consuming to develop and maintain.

Mergers and acquisitions

Mergers and acquisitions have become two of the most widely used methods of firm growth in recent years, accounting for about 50% of the increase in firm assets and 60% of the increase in industrial concentration in the UK.

Links

Joint ventures and alliances may also be used as a mechanism for expanding the activity base of a firm. However, some would argue that these do not, strictly, contribute to growth of firm size. Chapter 14 (pp. 501–504) looks at the strategic benefits of joint ventures and alliances.

- *Merger*. This takes place with the mutual agreement of the management of both companies, usually through the merging firms exchanging their own shares for shares in the new legal entity. Additional funds are not usually required for the act of merging, and the new venture often reflects the name of both the companies concerned.

- *Takeover (or acquisition)*. This occurs when the management of Firm A makes a direct offer to the shareholders of Firm B and acquires a controlling interest. Usually the price offered to Firm B shareholders is substantially higher than the current share price on the stock market. In other words, a takeover involves a direct transaction between the management of the acquiring firm and the stockholders of the acquired firm. Takeovers usually require additional funds to be raised by the acquiring firm (Firm A) for the acquisition of the other firm (Firm B) and the identity of the acquired company is often subsumed within that of the purchaser.

As we consider in more detail below, it is often suggested that merger activity brings potential benefits for the new, enlarged enterprise via both cost savings and revenue opportunities.

Mergers: who benefits?

A key question, not as yet fully answered, is who exactly benefits from the regular surges in merger activity experienced throughout the world? Undoubtedly the many financial and legal advisers earn huge fees, but have the owners of the company (shareholders) found that merger activity adds value or destroys value? It is to this important issue that we now turn.

The managerial theories considered in Chapter 4 would suggest that fast-growing firms, having already adopted a growth-maximisation approach, are the ones most likely to be involved in merger activity. These theories would also suggest that fast-growing firms will give higher remuneration to managers, and will raise job security by being less prone to takeover. Is it then the managers (agents) rather than the shareholders (principals) who have most to gain from merger activity?

Case Study 5.3 considers the issue of who, if anyone, actually benefits from the frequently observed surges in mergers and acquisitions activity in the UK and elsewhere.

Case Study 5.3   Mergers – for managers or shareholders?

A number of surveys in recent years have suggested that the owners of companies, the shareholders, rarely benefit from mergers. For example, Buckingham and Atkinson (1999) note that only 17% of mergers and acquisitions produced any value for shareholders while 53% of them actually destroyed shareholder value. However, there is ample evidence (Fuller, 2007) that managers' remuneration packages may be more closely related to variables such as growth in corporate turnover and growth in company size than to corporate profitability. This misalignment of incentives between senior management seeking growth and shareholders seeking profit may be an important factor in the continued drive towards M&A as a strategic focus,

with managers seeing M&A as the quickest way to grow both turnover and company size.

Another reason for mergers often failing to increase profitability and therefore shareholder value may be put down to the overconfidence and lack of judgement of senior management and the self-interested city financiers who advise them. These flaws can show up in all three phases of any merger activity, namely the planning implementation and operational phases.

For example, in the *planning phase* the top management of the merging firms invariably see benefits from combining operations which are rarely actually achieved. Steve Case, the founder of America Online, stunned the world in 2000 by announcing his intention to acquire Time Warner, a merger completed in January 2001 with the birth of the new combined company AOL Time Warner. When AOL revealed its intention to acquire Time Warner the Internet boom was at its peak and AOL's sky-high share value gave it the paper wealth to make its £97bn offer, despite the fact that Time Warner's revenues were four times higher than AOL. The expected benefits of combining the companies were seen in terms of linking, for the first time, a major Internet company with a major media company. Ted Turner, vice chairman of the new company, said 'I have not been so excited since I first had sex 42 years ago.' Yet just two years later, in January 2003, Steve Case announced his intention to stand down as chairman, with the new company valued at less than one-quarter of the £162bn value placed on it at the time of the merger.

In the *implementation phase* culture clashes at corporate or national levels may also occur, preventing potential benefits being realised. For example, at the corporate level, acquisitions involving a traditional bureaucratic company with an innovative entrepreneurial company will invariably bring conflicts, with the result that for some employees there will be a loss of identification with, and motivation by,

the new employer. High-quality human resources are extremely mobile and key knowledge, skills, contacts and capabilities are embedded in these employees, whose loss as a result of the M&A activity will seriously diminish the prospects of the new corporate entity. The *demerger* of DaimlerChrysler in 2007 was widely attributed to cultural differences in management principles and practice between the German and US executives preventing the expected synergies from the 1998 merger from occurring.

Finally, in the *operational phase* the hoped-for economies of scale and scope may fail to materialise, for a variety of reasons, not least problems of coordination and control when new, integrated computer systems fail to work as intended. In surveying 253 horizontal mergers in manufacturing in the EU and US, Laurence Capron (1999) found that only 49% of companies believed that the implementation of the merger had created any positive net value in terms of the overall outcome.

Questions

1 How has the separation between ownership and control acted as a stimulus to merger activity?

2 Why do so few mergers seem to create extra value for shareholders?

Recent merger evidence

A study by Sara Moeller *et al.* (2004) of mergers in the USA between 1998 and 2001 also questioned whether shareholders benefit from such activity. After examining some 4,136 US mergers and acquisitions during this time, the combined stockmarket value of the merging firms was found to have fallen by an astonishing $158bn. Shareholders of the *buying firms* lost the most, the value of their shares falling by $240bn – some 12% of the purchase price.

However, this data may overstate the losses of shareholders! Moeller and her co-authors point out that the buying shareholders often used their own, over-valued shares in helping to fund the deals. In other words, they knowingly exchanged their own over-valued shares (equity) for the real assets of the companies bought, hardly a true loss of shareholder value! Further, most of the shareholder losses could be linked to 87 huge merger deals, representing less than 2% of the mergers investigated. The remaining 98% of mergers actually increased shareholder value for both buyers and sellers.

Within this broad picture, *The Economist* (2004) noted that two further patterns are identifiable:

- The value created by mergers and takeovers has been almost twice as high when there has been more than one bidder. Arguably, when the opportunities to create value are greatest, this tends to be recognised by several would-be buyers.

- The value created has been larger for mergers within the same industry than for diversifying acquisitions (see p. 152). This suggests that chief executive officers should focus on mergers within sectors of economic activity with which they are familiar.

Merger avoidance

Companies have become quite skilled in placing barriers in the way of unwanted takeover bids. Two of the most widely used involve the so-called 'poison pill' and 'staggered board' barriers.

'Poison pill' barrier

This often involves company rules that allow the shareholders to buy new shares in their company at a large discount, should that company be threatened by a hostile takeover. The now enlarged pool of shareholders makes it more difficult and more expensive for the acquiring firm to complete the takeover. In the US, some 40% of the 5,500 companies tracked by *Institutional Shareholder Service*, a research organisation, have been found to employ the 'poison pill'.

'Staggered board' barrier

These involve company rules which allow different groups of directors to be elected in different years. This is likely to deter hostile takeovers since it may be many years before the acquiring company will be able to dominate the existing boardroom of the target company. *Institutional Shareholder Service* estimate that some 60% of US companies have a staggered board. Lucian Bebchuk (2004) of Harvard Business School argues that staggered boards cost shareholders around 4–6% of their firm's market value by allowing entrenched managers and directors to resist takeover bids which would be attractive to the majority of shareholders.

Types of merger activity

Four major forms of merger activity can be identified: horizontal integration, vertical integration, the formation of conglomerate mergers, and lateral integration.

Horizontal integration

This occurs when firms combine at the same stage of production, involving similar products or services. Some 80% of mergers in the UK over the past decade have been of this type. The Hong Kong and Shanghai Banking Corporation's acquisition of Midland Bank to become HSBC in 1992, the merger of Royal Insurance and Sun Alliance to form Royal SunAlliance in 1996, the merger of Carlton and Granada broadcasting companies to form ITV PLC in 2004, and Air France merging with the Dutch carrier KLM in 2004 are all examples of horizontal mergers.

Horizontal integration may provide a number of cost-based economies at the level both of the plant (productive unit) and the firm (business unit).

- *Plant economies* may follow from the rationalisation made possible by horizontal integration. For instance, production may be concentrated at a smaller number of enlarged plants, permitting the familiar technical economies of greater specialisation, the dovetailing of separate processes at higher output, and the application of the 'engineers' rule' whereby material costs increase as the square but capacity as the cube. All these lead to a reduction in cost per unit as the size of plant output increases.

Microchip manufacture

The huge fabricated chip manufacturing plants ('Fabs') cost over $3bn each, roughly twice as much as previous plants, but are able to produce over three times as many silicon chips per time period. These 'plant economies' have reduced the unit cost per chip by over 40%.

- *Firm economies* result from the growth in size of the whole enterprise, permitting economies via bulk purchase, the spread of similar administrative costs over greater output, the cheaper cost of finance, various distributive and marketing economies etc.

Air France–KLM merger

The re-named and expanded Air France–KLM airline formed in 2004 estimated cost savings from 'firm economies' of around €300m (around £200m) over the following five years from functional areas such as sales and distribution, IT and engineering.

Plant economies are sometimes called 'technical economies' and firm economies are sometimes called 'non-technical economies' or 'enterprise economies'.

As well as these cost-based economies, new revenue opportunities may present themselves for the now enlarged company.

- *Revenue-based synergies.* Horizontal (or vertical – see below) acquisitions may enable companies to develop new competencies which may in turn enable them to command a price premium (via increased market power, higher innovation capabilities) or to increase sales volume (via increased market presence – both geographically and in terms of an extended product line).

Kraft–Cadbury merger

Kraft, the US food giant, acquired Cadbury, the UK confectioner, for £11.9bn in 2010, becoming the world's largest confectioner. Cost savings of $675m per year were identified from rationalisation and scale economies, together with an increased global market presence, e.g. Cadbury has a much stronger presence in Europe, Latin America and China than Kraft, increasing projected sales revenue to such an extent that Kraft paid 50% more in January 2010 than the firm's stock market value in September 2009 before the bidding started.

Below is a list of some other examples of horizontal integration.

- Japanese *Shiseido*, the cosmetic company, bought Californian rival *Bare Escentuals* for $1.7bn (£1bn) in 2010. This made Shiseido the world's fourth largest cosmetic company behind L'Oreal, Proctor and Gamble, and Unilever.
- In the UK, the *Co-Operative Society* took over *Somerfield* stores in 2009 to give it an 8% share of the UK's grocery market. The £1.6bn takeover makes the Co-operative Society the fifth largest food chain in the UK.

- *Lafarge SA*, the leading French global cement company, acquired the Egyptian company *Orascom Cement*, the leading cement group in the Middle East and Mediterranean for $12.8bn in 2008, in order to strengthen its presence in the region.
- *E.ON AG*, the German electricity services giant, acquired *Endesa*, the Spanish electricity and gas company, for €11.5bn in 2008.
- Belgium-based brewer *InBev* took over *Anheuser-Busch* of the US for $52bn (£35bn) to form Anheuser-Busch InBev in 2008. The new giant company sells such drinks as Budweiser, Becks, Hoegaarden and Leffe across the globe.
- *Morrisons*, the UK supermarket, acquired *Safeway*, another UK supermarket, for £3bn in 2004, almost doubling its market share to 20% in the UK.
- *British American Tobacco* (BAT) acquired *RJReynolds*, America's second largest tobacco group for $6.2bn in 2003.
- *SAB Miller*, the London-listed second largest brewer in the world, acquired *Birra Peroni*, Italy's number two brewer in 2003.

Vertical integration

This occurs when the firms combine at different stages of production of a common good or service. Only about 5% of UK mergers are of this type.

- **Backward vertical integration.** Firms might benefit by being able to exert closer control over quality and delivery of supplies if the vertical integration is 'backward', i.e. towards the source of supply. Factor inputs might also be cheaper, obtained at cost instead of cost + profit.
- **Forward vertical integration.** Of course, vertical integration could be 'forward' – towards the retail outlet. This may give the firm merging 'forward' more control of wholesale or retail pricing policy, and more direct customer contact. An example of forward vertical integration towards the market was the acquisition by the publishing company Pearson PLC of National Computer Services (NCS) in 2000 for £1.6bn. NCS was a US global information service company providing Internet links and curriculum and assessment testing facilities for schools. The takeover allowed Pearson to design integrated educational programmes for schools by providing students with customised learning and assessment testing facilities. It could also use the NCS network to reach both teachers and parents. In this way, Pearson was able to use its NCS subsidiary to sell its existing publishing products while also developing new online materials for the educational marketplace.

Vertical integration can often lead to increased control of the market, infringing monopoly legislation. This is undoubtedly one reason why they are so infrequent. Another is the fact that, as Marks & Spencer (M&S) have shown, it is not always necessary to have a controlling interest in suppliers in order to exert effective control over them. Textile suppliers of M&S send over 75% of their total output to M&S, which has been able to use this reliance to their own advantage. In return for placing long production runs with these suppliers, M&S have been able to restrict supplier profit margins while maintaining their viability. Apart from low costs of purchase, M&S are also able to insist on frequent batch delivery, cutting stockholding costs to a minimum.

Conglomerate integration

Conglomerate integration involves each firm adding different products and activities to those with which it was previously involved. The major benefit is the spreading of risk for the respective firms and shareholders. Giant conglomerates like Unilever (with interests in food, detergents, toilet preparations, chemicals, paper, plastics, packaging, animal feeds, transport and tropical plantations – in 75 separate countries), are largely cushioned against any damaging movements which are restricted to particular product groups or particular countries.

Procter & Gamble moves into beauty products

Procter & Gamble (P&G), the US multinational, is the world's largest consumer group conglomerate, owning brands such as Pringles crisps, Pampers nappies and Crest toothpaste. In recent years it has broadened its portfolio of products still further into haircare, acquiring Nioxin, a US scalp care company in 2009, Gillette hair care products in 2005, the German hair care company, Wella, in 2003 and Clairol in 2001.

The various 'firm (enterprise) economies' outlined above may also result from a conglomerate merger. P&G expects to save €300m annually from its purchase of Wella by economies from combining back-office activities, media buying, logistics and other purchasing activities.

The ability to buy companies relatively cheaply on the stock exchange and to sell parts of them off at a profit later is another important reason for some conglomerate mergers. The takeovers by Hanson PLC of the Imperial Group, Consolidated Goldfields and the Eastern Group, in 1986, 1989 and 1995 respectively, provide good examples of the growth of a large conglomerate organisation which subsequently demerged the acquired businesses. Similarly, P&G has developed a strategy of divesting itself of brands in slower growth markets and focusing on sectors with faster future growth potential, such as beauty products.

Despite these benefits of diversification, times of economic recession (e.g. the early 1990s in the UK) often result in firms reverting back to their more familiar 'core' businesses. Only some 10% of UK mergers over the past decade can be classified as conglomerate mergers and some conglomerates have moved in the opposite direction. For example, the de-merger of Hanson PLC in 1996 produced four businesses with recognisable 'core' activities, namely tobacco, chemicals, building and energy.

Lateral integration

This is sometimes given separate treatment, though in practice it is difficult to distinguish from a conglomerate merger. The term 'lateral integration' is often used when the firms that combine are involved in different products, but in products which have some element of *commonality*. This might be in terms of factor input, such as requiring similar labour skills, capital equipment or raw materials; or it might be in terms of product outlet. For example, the takeover of Churchill Insurance by the Royal Bank of Scotland (RBS) for £1.1bn in 2003 is arguably an example of lateral integration. Churchill gave RBS a presence in the *general household insurance* business for the first time, complementing its existing presence in motor insurance via its earlier acquisition of Direct Line. Direct Line dominates the market in selling insurance to careful, budget-conscious motorists, while Churchill is widely used by buyers of household insurance in which Direct Line is less strong. For example, in 2003 Direct Line insured 6 million motorists but only 1.6 million households, whereas Churchill insured 5 million households but only 2 million motorists.

The takeover of Clerical Medical, the life assurance company, by Halifax Building Society for £800m in 1996 was also an example of lateral integration, involving the linking of companies with different products but within the same financial sector. The increase in savings by an ageing population, together with a reduction in mortgage business, meant that the Halifax had surplus funds which it could now direct into insurance policies using Clerical Medical's strong presence among independent financial advisers. These advisers could also act as distribution channels for other Halifax products as well as for those of its Clerical Medical subsidiary.

However, the Swiss company TetraLaval's offer for the French company Sidel in 2001 (which was finally cleared by the EU competition authorities in 2002) provides an example of the difficulty of distinguishing the concepts of conglomerate and lateral integration. TetraLaval designs, manufactures and sells packaging for liquid food products as well as manufacturing and marketing equipment for milk and farm products. Sidel designs and sells machines used in the manufacture of plastic bottles and packaging. The European Commission regarded the merger as conglomerate in that the companies operated in different sectors of the market and were to be organised, post-merger, into three distinct entities within the TetraLavel Group. However, it was still the case that the merger would resemble a case of lateral integration in that the companies had a commonality of experience in the package and container sector.

Make a note

Mergers and acquisitions can take a variety of formal and less formal structures, with 'alliances' (see Chapter 14, pp. 501–503) sometimes a more accurate term for the emerging relationship. Microsoft and Yahoo entered into an internet search alliance in 2010, approved by US and EU regulation authorities. Daimler and Renault (pp. 503–504) entered into a cross-shareholding alliance in March 2010 to gain scale economies in small car production, as did Mazda and Toyota in 2010 to share expensive R&D investment costs for hybrid and electric cars.

Stop and think   5.3

Can you find additional examples of these four different types of integration?

Explanations of merger activity

A number of theories have been put forward to explain the underlying motives behind merger activity. However, when these various theories are tested empirically the results have often been inconsistent and contradictory.

The value discrepancy hypothesis

The **value discrepancy hypothesis** is based on a belief that two of the most common characteristics of the industrial world are imperfect information and uncertainty. Together, these help explain why different investors have different expectations of the prospects for a given firm.

The *value discrepancy hypothesis* suggests that one firm will only bid for another if it places a greater value on the firm than that placed on the firm by its current owners. If Firm B is valued at V_A by Firm A and V_B by Firm B then a takeover of Firm B will only take place if $V_A > V_B +$ costs of acquisition. The difference in valuation arises through Firm A's higher expectations of future profitability, often because A takes account of the improved efficiency with which it believes the future operations of B can be run.

It has been argued that it is in periods when technology, market conditions and share prices are changing most rapidly, that past information and experience are of least assistance in estimating future earnings. As a result, differences in valuation are likely to occur more often, leading to increased merger activity. The value discrepancy hypothesis would therefore predict high merger activity when technology change is most rapid, and when market and share price conditions are most volatile.

The valuation ratio

Another factor which may affect the likelihood of takeover is the **valuation ratio**, as defined below:

$$\text{Valuation ratio} = \frac{\text{market value}}{\text{asset value}} = \frac{\text{no. of shares} \times \text{share price}}{\text{book value of assets}}$$

If a company is 'undervalued' because its share price is low compared to the value of its assets, then it becomes a prime target for the 'asset stripper'. If a company attempts to grow rapidly it will tend to retain a high proportion of profits for reinvestment, with less profit therefore available for distribution to shareholders. The consequence may be a low share price, reducing the market value of the firm in relation to the book value of its assets, i.e. reducing the valuation ratio. It has been argued that a high valuation ratio will deter takeovers, while a low valuation ratio will increase the vulnerability of the firm to takeover. In the early 1990s, for example, the property company British Land purchased Dorothy Perkins, the womenswear chain, because its market value was seen as being low in relation to the value of its assets (prime high street sites). After stripping out all the freehold properties for resale, the remainder of the chain was sold to the Burton Group.

In recent years the asset value of some companies has been seriously underestimated for other reasons. For example, many companies have taken years to build up brand names which are therefore worth a great amount of money; but it is often the case that these are not given a money value and are thus not included in the asset value of the company. As a result, if the market value of a company is already low in relation to the book value of its assets, then the acquirer gets a double bonus. One reason why Nestlé was prepared to bid £2.5bn (regarded as a 'high' bid, in relation to its book value) for Rowntree Mackintosh in 1988 was to acquire the 'value' of its consumer brands cheaply, because they were not shown on the balance sheet. Finally, it is interesting to note that when the valuation ratio is low and a company would appear to be a 'bargain', a takeover may originate from within the company; in this case it is referred to as a management buyout (MBO).

Stop and think   *5.4*

Can you name any recent examples of management buyouts?

Case Study 5.4 looks at the merger of Geely, the Chinese car maker, with Volvo, the Swedish car maker.

| Case Study 5.4 | **Premium car deal fills a hole at Geely** | **FT** |

Successful cross-border vehicle company mergers can be counted on the fingers of one hand. When one famous car brand buys another – whether General Motors and Saab, Daimler and Chrysler, or Ford and Volvo – one of the most common by-products is buyer remorse.

Perhaps the March 2010 Geely–Volvo deal will go down in automotive history as just another mergers and acquisitions lemon – or maybe it will help make Geely, and its head Li Shufu, household names. Either way, the $1.8bn deal is likely to mark a significant shift in the global industry to the East. China has the world's largest auto markets; now it owns one of the world's best known premium car brands.

On paper, the deal makes sense: Geely makes cheap small cars; it is developing a line of new mid-sized cars; what it lacks is a premium brand, strong in all the areas where Chinese carmakers still trail: technology, research and development, service and quality. Geely planned to nearly double the loss-making Swedish carmakers' sales to

600,000 by 2015, in part by building its presence in China, the world's biggest vehicle market. Mr Li declined to give further details on Geely's plans, but a person briefed on its business plan told the FT that it was planning to build at least two car plants and one engine plant in China.

But that assumes that Geely can do what Ford could not: run Volvo profitably. In 2009 when China's small car market exploded in the wake of government tax breaks, Geely lost market share. Its sales rose 48% in 2009, to 330,000 units – but other automakers did better.

According to criteria outlined by Bain & Co, the management consultancy, in a study of why M&A deals succeed or fail, Mr Li has slim prospects with Volvo. Bain concludes that there are 'two kinds of deals that most (Chinese) auto players should walk away from', and one of them is buying stakes in US or European OEMs [original equipment manufacturers] in the hope of turning them around'. That is exactly what Geely plans to do with Volvo: run it profitably, by liberating the Volvo management from the dead hand of Ford (according to Geely insiders) and selling lots of Volvos in China.

Selling cars may be the easy part; the Swedish company sold only 22,000 vehicles in China last year, according to JD Power. Yale Zhang, of CMS Auto in Shanghai, says such entry-level luxury brands will grow very strongly in coming years.

Geely's strong connections with central government – without which no such acquisition could have been contemplated – will also help; if Volvo can be named an approved brand for government procurement that could boost sales. Freeman Shen, Geely's head of international operations, says Geely has no illusions about potential integration problems between what is in many ways the most Chinese of Chinese automakers and its absolute opposite in Sweden.

For the time being, Volvo will remain very European; R&D will remain in Sweden and the main production base will stay in Europe, says Mr Shen. 'We want to be careful not to damage the Volvo brand,' he says. 'We don't want the image of a luxury car made in a third world country. We want the image of a European luxury car, owned by a Chinese company.' Volvo sits in the 'near-luxury' or 'only-just-up-scale' part of the car market, alongside rival Swedish brand Saab and Fiat's loss-making Alfa Romeo – a sub-section of the premium market under attack from luxury leaders BMW, Mercedes-Benz and Audi since the car industry's crisis began in 2008.

The German brands' superior sales and higher prices have allowed them to outspend Volvo on research and development, and rise from the crisis in fitter shape. Volvo sold just under 335,000 vehicles worldwide in 2009, 11% fewer than 2008.

However, Volvo's reputation for building safe cars could help its business in China as safety becomes an increasing priority in the world's largest car market.

Volvo would, in turn, benefit from Geely's 'deep knowledge' of the Chinese market, Mr Li said.

In design, Volvo is moving away from making boxy, square cars into more edgily fashioned, smaller and alternative fuel models – an area where Geely, which is developing electric cars, can help it.

Source: from Premium car deal fills a hole at Geely, *Financial Times*, 29/03/2010 (Waldmeir, P.), © The Financial Times Ltd

Questions

1 What benefits does Geely expect from its linkage with Volvo and what problems might it face?

2 What benefits does Volvo expect from its linkage with Geely and what problems might it face?

The market power theory

The main motive behind merger activity may often be to increase monopoly control of the environment in which the firm operates. Increased *market power* may help the firm to withstand adverse economic conditions, and increase long-term profitability.

Three situations are particularly likely to induce merger activity aimed at increasing market power:

1 Where a fall in demand results in excess capacity and the danger of price-cutting competition. In this situation firms may merge in order to secure a better vantage point from which to rationalise the industry.

2 Where international competition threatens increased penetration of the domestic market by foreign firms. Mergers in electronics, computers and engineering have in the past produced combines large enough to fight off such foreign competition.

3 Where a tightening of legislation makes many types of linkages between companies illegal. Firms have in the past adopted many practices which involved collusion in order to control markets. Since restrictive practices legislation has made many of these practices illegal between companies, merger, by 'internalising' the practices, has allowed them to continue.

For these reasons merger activity may take place to increase a firm's market power. However, the very act of merging usually increases company size, both in absolute terms and in relation to other firms. It is clear, therefore, that increased size will be both a by-product of the quest for increased market power and itself a cause of increased market power.

Economies of scale and other synergies

It is often argued that the achievement of lower average costs (and thereby higher profits) through an increase in the scale of operation is the main motive for merger activity. As we noted in Chapter 3 (pp. 85–9) and in this chapter (pp. 151–2), such economies can be at two levels:

- first, at the level of the plant, the production unit, including the familiar technical economies of specialisation, dovetailing of processes, engineers' rule, etc;
- second, at the level of the firm, the business unit, including research, marketing, administrative, managerial and financial economies.

To these plant- and firm-level economies we might add the 'synergy' effect of merger, the so-called '2 + 2 > 4' effect, whereby merger increases the efficiency of the combined firm by more than the sum of its parts. Synergy could result from combining complementary activities as, for example, when one firm has a strong R&D team while another firm has more effective production control personnel.

Managerial theories

In all the theories considered so far, the underlying reason for merger activity has been related, in one way or another, to the pursuit of profit. For example, market power theory suggests that through control of the firm's environment, the prospects of higher revenues and therefore profit, at least in the long run, are improved. Economies of scale theory concentrates on raising profit through the reduction of cost. Managerial theories on the other hand (see also Chapter 4) lay greater stress on non-profit motives. Some theories see the growth of the firm in terms of revenue, asset size, etc. as raising managerial utility by bringing higher salaries, power, status, and job security to managers. Managers may therefore be more interested in the rate of growth of the firm than in its profit performance.

Demerging

While the focus has been on merger activity, in recent times there has been a renewed interest in the alleged benefits of demerger, a recent example being the DaimlerChrysler demerger of 2007.

Nor is it always conventional mergers and acquisitions that result in corporate success (or failure). Case Study 5.5 examines the resurgence of the conglomerate holding companies or *chaebols* in South Korea.

Case Study 5.5   Return of the chaebol

The *chaebols* of South Korea are making a comeback! These huge industrial conglomerates, controlled by rich and inscrutable families who are treated as royalty by many, have reversed the sharp downturn in their fortunes experienced during the Asian financial crisis of 1997–98.

The South Korean economy was close to collapse during that crisis and it was the *chaebols* that were widely blamed by the public, the government of the time and the IMF. South Koreans and global investors were shocked at the extent of the mismanagement subsequently revealed by investigations into the running of the *chaebols* which, in the 1960s and 1970s under the regime of Park Chung-hee, had received huge amounts of cheap government finance and relied on the government to protect them from foreign competition.

The *chaebols* had vast ambitions for industrial conquest – and they had public money to back them. Samsung was one such *chaebol* which had expanded from sugar and wool into electrical goods, chemicals and engineering. Another was Hyundai, whose founder, Chung Juyung, had started building roads and then decided to build the cars and other vehicles to drive on them.

However, many *chaebols* had overstretched themselves by the late 1990s, building up huge debts as they borrowed vast amounts to buy capital equipment to move up the technological ladder and to fund new mergers and acquisitions. South Korea's economy over-heated and its current account deficit soared. Some thought the *chaebols* had become so big the government could not let them fail, but they were wrong and many conglomerates collapsed; the closure of Daewoo in 1999 was followed by the bankruptcy of more than half of the then top 30 conglomerates. Four of the country's five carmakers went bankrupt and South Koreans, many of whom had gladly handed over their gold jewellery in a patriotic gesture to help pay off the foreign debt, were appalled at the level of government and business collusion and inefficiencies that came to light.

As a result, both business and government embarked on reform after these public failures and since 2000 *chaebol* balance sheets have improved, as has corporate governance, with increasing rights for minority shareholders and extra responsibilities for company directors. Also many of the cross-shareholdings used to disguise the weakness of subsidiaries and protect them from hostile takeovers have been replaced with more transparent holding-company structures.

Samsung Electronics provides a good example of how the *chaebols* have restored their reputation over the past decade. Samsung has become one of the world's strongest brands, known for attractive design, cutting-edge technology and good value. It has a presence in numerous electronic-related markets, producing screens of all sizes, from a few centimetres square on a mobile phone, to larger screens on laptops and giant 3D television screens. Indeed for any product with a screen, Samsung Electronics will be one of the top two firms in the world, either making the screen or the memory chips inside it. The company's global market shares are startling: more than 40% of the flash memory used in sophisticated electronics like the Apple iPhone, almost 20% of global mobile phones and around 16% of global television sets. It even makes screens for Sony's TVs. Focusing on manufacturing as its major growth strategy seems to have been successful for Samsung.

Having invested aggressively in new, mainly manufactured products, Samsung Electronics has been little troubled by the 2008–10 global financial crisis, almost doubling its operating profit in 2009, and in 2010 analysts expect it to generate record profits of over $10 billion. Sales are forecast to be about $130 billion, which is likely to confirm its lead over America's Hewlett-Packard as the world's biggest technology company by revenue. Other parts of the Samsung group have also met with considerable success, as with the construction division recently completing the tallest building in the world in Dubai and Samsung Heavy Industries being hugely successful in securing shipbuilding orders.

The often repeated saying that what is good for General Motors is good for the USA is certainly true for Samsung. What has been good for Samsung has been good for South Korea. The Samsung group's products account for about 20% of the country's GDP, and when the South Korean currency, the won, fell sharply in 2008, raising fears

Case Study 5.5 *continued*

of a currency crisis, the exporting *chaebols* such as Samsung, Hyundai and IL quickly took advantage with their customers even more willing to buy the now less expensive South Korean products in the overseas markets.

The *chaebols* are also globally diversified - only one-tenth of the country's exports go to America, with any lost sales via the 'credit crunch' there being more than compensated by extra sales in fast-growing emerging markets like China. As a result the reputation of the *chaebols* has been much improved amongst the South Korean public as

they recognise their role in helping South Korea avoid many of the problems associated with the global 'credit-crunch' of 2008–10.

Source: Based on information from *The Economist* (2010) 3–9 April, pp. 64–65

Questions

1 What factors led to the rise and fall of *chaebols* in the period from 1946 to 2000?

2 What factors have helped the *chaebols* restore their effectiveness and reputation in the first decade of the twenty-first century?

Mergers and the public interest

Although there is clearly much debate about the motivation behind merger activity, there is a broad consensus that the resulting growth in firm size will have implications for the 'public interest'. It may be helpful to consider the potential impacts of a merger on **productive efficiency** and **allocative efficiency**, which are two key elements in any definition of the 'public interest'.

● *Productive efficiency*. This involves using the most efficient combination of resources to produce a given level of output. Only when the firm is producing a given level of output with the least-cost methods of production available do we regard it as having achieved 'productive efficiency'.

● *Allocative efficiency*. This is often taken to mean setting a price which corresponds to the marginal cost of production. The idea here is that consumers pay firms exactly what it costs them to produce the last (marginal) unit of output: such a pricing strategy can be shown to be a key condition in achieving a so-called '**Pareto optimum**' resource allocation, where it is no longer possible to make someone better off without making someone else worse off. Any deviation of price away from marginal cost is then seen as resulting in 'allocative inefficiency'.

Links

Chapter 8, pp. 248–55, examines the issue of mergers and the public interest in more detail, including the approach of the UK and EU competition authorities to this issue.

What may pose problems for policy makers is that the impacts of proposed mergers may move these two aspects of economic efficiency in opposite directions. For example, economies of scale may result from the merger having increased firm size, with a lower cost of producing any given output thereby improving productive efficiency. However, the greater market power associated with increased size (see Chapter 6, p. 177) may give the enlarged firm new opportunities to raise price above (or still further above) its costs of production, including marginal costs, thereby reducing allocative efficiency.

We may need to balance the gain in productive efficiency against the loss in allocative efficiency to get a better idea of the overall impact of the merger on the 'public interest'.

You try 5.2 helps you self-check many of the issues involved in the growth of firm size.

You try   5.2

1 Match each *lettered* term to the correct *numbered* description.

   Term

   (a) Cost savings   (e) Organic growth
   (b) Diversification of product   (f) Forward vertical integration
   (c) Diversification of market   (g) Backward vertical integration
   (d) Market power

   Description

   (i)   Firm wishes to grow in order to gain control over prices and to obtain better margins through reduced competition.
   (ii)   A small shoe manufacturer acquires a leather works.
   (iii) A song-writing partnership acquires a music publishing company.
   (iv)   A firm wishes to grow in order to reduce its dependency on one good or service.
   (v)   A firm decides to increase output by 50% since it expects to benefit from both technical and non-technical economies of scale.
   (vi)   A firm decides to build a new factory rather than take over a smaller competitor.
   (vii) A firm decides to establish a subsidiary company overseas since home market demand is 'saturated'.

2 Match each *lettered* term to the correct *numbered* description.

   Term

   (a) Conglomerate integration
   (b) Lateral integration
   (c) Horizontal integration
   (d) Forward vertical integration
   (e) Backward vertical integration

   Description

   (i)   Involving a firm in the same business and at the same stage of production.
   (ii) Involving a firm in a totally unrelated business.
   (iii) Towards the final consumer.
   (iv) Towards the raw material supplier.
   (v)   Involves firms in different product areas but with some common element (e.g. common factor inputs or product outlets).

3 (a) A car battery firm acquiring a firm producing acidic materials for those batteries is an example of forward vertical integration.   True/False
   (b) A soft drinks producing firm acquiring a chain of stores to distribute its products is an example of backward vertical integration.   True/False
   (c) A car assembly firm merging with another car assembly firm is an example of conglomerate integration.   True/False
   (d) A holiday company merging with a financial services provider in order to spread risk is an example of conglomerate integration.   True/False
   (e) A ferry operator merging with a food export/import company because its ships can be used in both functions is an example of lateral integration.   True/False

You try 5.2 *continued*

(f) A company 'ploughing back' its own profits to fund new investment projects is an example of organic growth.   True/False

(g) A high **gearing ratio** means that the company is at little risk, since external borrowing is a small percentage of total capital employed.   True/False

(h) The market for personal services is one in which small firms typically operate at a competitive disadvantage.   True/False

Answers can be found on pp. 525–546.

Recap

- Across all sectors in the UK, firms with fewer than five employees account for around 90% of the total number of firms. However, such firms account for only around 20% of total employment and 15% of total turnover.

- The small firm is increasingly seen by governments as a focus of new growth and employment opportunities, therefore justifying government support. Such small firm support has focused on three main areas: easier access to equity and loan capital, increased tax allowances and grants, and less government interference.

- Banks provide the main source (59%) of external finance for small firms (via overdraft) in the UK, increasingly in the form of medium- to longer-term loans, though high exposure to such overdraft finance remains a problem in the UK.

- Small firms in the UK see interest rate policy, general macroeconomic policy and taxation policy as the governmental policies with most impact on themselves.

- Low turnover is by far the most important single problem identified by small firms in the UK.

- Types of merger activity include horizontal, vertical, conglomerate and lateral.

- Suggested reasons for merger include at least one company believing it can add value beyond the costs of merger (value discrepancy hypothesis), a low valuation of share price relative to assets (valuation ratio) and the desire for greater market power.

- Other reasons include the securing of substantial economies of scale at plant and/or enterprise level. The former would be mainly technical economies by rationalisation of production into larger plants and the latter mainly non-technical economies related to functional areas such as administration, finance, marketing, distribution, purchasing, etc.

- There is little evidence to suggest that merger activity increases shareholder value but considerable evidence to suggest that merger activity may diminish profitability and shareholder value.

Key terms

Allocative efficiency Where price is set equal to marginal cost and resources are allocated so no one can be made better off without making someone else worse off (i.e. a 'Pareto optimal' resource allocation).

Alternative Investment Market (AIM) Low-cost and accessible market for SMEs seeking to raise share capital.

Backward vertical integration Towards the raw material supplier.

Conglomerate integration Involving firms in a totally unrelated business.

Conglomerate mergers (see 'conglomerate integration')

Demergers Where a company breaks itself up into smaller units.

Economies of scale Achieving lower long-run average cost by growth in size.

Forward vertical integration Towards the final consumer.

Gearing ratio Reflects the financial risk to which the company is exposed via external borrowing. Ratio of external borrowing to total capital employed.

Horizontal integration Involves firms in the same business and at the same stage of production.

Large firm Over 250 employees.

Lateral integration Involves firms in different product areas, but with some common elements (e.g. factor inputs, product outlets).

Medium-sized firm 50–249 employees.

Micro firm 0–9 employees, includes sole traders.

Organic growth Where the firm uses its own resources (e.g. 'ploughed-back profits').

Pareto optimum A resource allocation where it is no longer possible to make someone better off without at the same time making someone worse off.

Productive efficiency Producing at the level of output where average total cost is a minimum.

Small firm 10–49 employees.

SME Small and medium-sized enterprises, include micro, small and medium-sized firms.

Valuation ratio The ratio of market value/asset value.

Value discrepancy hypothesis Suggests that one firm will only bid for another if it places a greater value on the firm than that placed on the firm by its current owners.

Vertical integration Involves firms at different stages of production.

Market structures

Introduction

We saw in Chapter 1 that prices in free markets are determined by the interaction of supply and demand. However, this does not imply that price determination is completely beyond the influence of all firms (or consumers). If firms are able to influence supply and/or demand conditions for their product, they can clearly influence the price at which that product is sold. The level of control that a particular firm has over the price of its product will depend to a large extent on the *structure* of the particular market in which it operates, i.e. on:

● the number of other firms producing that product;

● the number of other firms producing a close substitute for that product;

● the relative ease with which firms can enter or leave the market for that product.

Differences in these three market characteristics produce different market structures that are usually categorised as perfect competition, monopolistic competition, monopoly and oligopoly, all of which are reviewed in this chapter.

What you'll learn

By the end of this chapter you should be able to:

● explain why perfect competition is often suggested to be the 'ideal' form of market structure in terms of resource allocation

● understand that 'contestable market' analysis is an attempt to relate the ideas of perfect competition to actual market situations

● outline the major barriers to market entry and discuss their contribution to 'market power'

● examine the 'classical' case against monopoly (higher price/lower output than perfect competition) and identify circumstances when this may or may not apply

● compare and contrast the outcomes of monopolistic competition with those from other market structures

● evaluate the key characteristics of oligopoly markets and the relevance of competitor actions and reactions to different market outcomes.

An industry, sector or market (these terms are used interchangeably) can be defined as a group of firms that produce close substitutes, whether goods or services, as for example in the case of the cosmetics industry, the motor industry, the healthcare sector, the educational sector and so on. These industries or sectors have different numbers of firms operating within them, different levels of substitutability by other products, and different barriers (if any) to the entry of new firms. This chapter examines how these three market characteristics may affect the price and output behaviour of firms and therefore how resources are allocated under a particular market structure. As we shall see, the allocation of resources resulting from one type of market structure might, under certain circumstances, be regarded as preferable to that resulting from another type of market structure.

Figure 6.1 shows that perfect competition and monopoly fall at the opposite ends of the spectrum of market structures. Perfect competition, on the extreme left, is often said to represent the 'ideal' market structure in which producers have no control over price and resources are allocated most efficiently. The further to the right our position on the spectrum in Figure 6.1, the greater the extent to which the firm can influence price and output, and the less competitive the market structure.

We begin by reviewing the 'perfect competition' model of market structure, although we should remind ourselves that all the models of market structure described in this chapter are a simplification of reality.

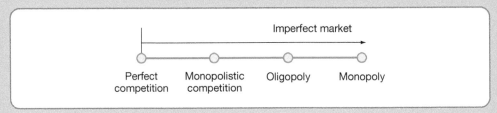

Figure 6.1 **Spectrum of market structures**

Perfect competition

In this type of market structure, there are a large number of small firms producing identical products with none of these firms having any 'market power', in the sense of being able to influence market price or output. Strictly speaking, for a market to be defined as 'perfectly competitive' a number of conditions must all be met simultaneously:

- *large number of small firms* supplying the product, none of which is able, by itself, to influence overall (market) supply;
- *each small firm is a 'price taker'* in the sense that it recognises that it is too small to influence the ruling market price, which must therefore simply be accepted;
- *large number of buyers*, none of whom is sufficiently large to influence overall (market) demand;
- *perfect information* for both sellers and buyers;
- *homogeneous product* so that the product offered by one firm is identical in all respects to the product offered by the other firms;
- *freedom of entry and exit* so that firms can either enter or leave the market at will, with no 'barriers' to discourage such entry or exit.

These assumptions are extremely restrictive and it would be difficult to find an example of a market structure that fulfils all these assumptions simultaneously. However, some markets display many of the features of perfect competition. For example, an individual

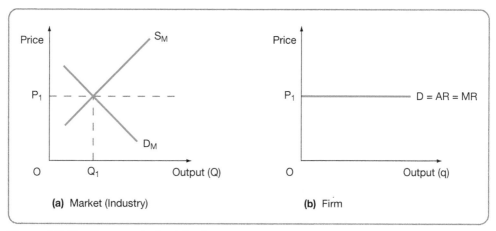

Figure 6.2 **The firm as a 'price taker'**

farmer has little influence over the price of carrots since the farmer produces only a small proportion of the total market supply. Nothing makes these carrots any different from any other farmer's carrots, and all the buyers of carrots are well informed about prices.

As we shall see, the perfectly competitive market structure makes certain predictions as to firm and industry price and output in both **short-run** and **long-run** time periods. However, before undertaking this analysis it will be useful to consider the individual firm's *demand curve* in rather more detail.

Firm's demand curve

We have noted that each perfectly competitive firm recognises that, by itself, it cannot influence market supply and therefore market price. It is therefore in the situation shown in Figure 6.2.

The equilibrium price (P_1) is determined in Figure 6.2(a) by the intersection of the market demand curve (D_M) with the market supply curve (S_M) for this identical product. At this market price P_1 the small firm can reasonably suppose that it can sell *all* its output, knowing that it is so small that any extra output will have no impact on market supply and therefore no impact on price. It is as though the firm's demand curve is perfectly elastic at the going market price P_1, as we can see in Figure 6.2(b).

When the firm sells all its product at an identical price, then the firm's demand curve tells us the revenue per unit or average revenue (AR) from any given output. When the firm's demand (D = AR) curve is horizontal or perfectly elastic (see Chapter 2, pp. 41–8), then each additional unit of output adds exactly the same amount to total revenue as did each previous unit. In other words, the marginal revenue (MR) is constant at the going market price P_1. We can say that:

$$D = AR = MR$$

Example

> **AR and MR for a 'price taker'**
>
> Suppose our small firm is faced with the following situation as it seeks to raise output from four units:
>
> | Price (AR) | Quantity (Q) | TR | MR |
> |---|---|---|---|
> | £5 | 4 units | £20 | £5 |
> | £5 | 5 units | £25 | £5 |
> | £5 | 6 units | £30 | £5 |
> | £5 | 7 units | £35 | £5 |

> The small firm is a 'price taker' at £5. Raising output from four units to five units will raise total revenue (TR) from £20 to £25. Average revenue is still £5 (TR/Q) and the marginal revenue (MR) of the fifth unit is also £5 (£25 − £20).
>   So £5 = AR = MR

This perfectly elastic demand curve for the firm will ensure that it charges an identical price for its product to that charged by other firms. Since the product is homogeneous, consumers will have no preference for a particular firm's product, so that if a firm sets a price *above* that of its competitors it will face a total loss of sales.

Alternatively, the firm has no incentive to set a price *below* that of its competitors since it can sell its entire output at the existing market price. The firm in perfect competition is therefore a 'price taker', i.e. it accepts the market price as given and beyond its control.

Firm's supply curve

In Chapter 4 we noted (p. 114) that the profit-maximising firm must equate marginal cost with marginal revenue (MC = MR). It follows that, under perfect competition, the *marginal cost curve* will, in effect, be the firm's supply curve. This is shown in Figure 6.3.

We start with market demand D_M and market supply S_M in Figure 6.3(a), giving an initial market price P_1. At this price P_1 the price-taking small firm in Figure 6.3(b) is faced with the horizontal demand curve $D_1 = AR_1 = MR_1$. The profit-maximising firm will then produce output q_1, where marginal cost equals marginal revenue.

However, should market demand increase to D'_M in Figure 6.3(a), then market price rises to P_2 and the price-taking small firm in Figure 6.3(b) is faced with the horizontal demand curve $D_2 = AR_2 = MR_2$. The profit-maximising firm will now produce output q_2, where marginal cost equals marginal revenue.

What we can see in Figure 6.3(b) is that at each price, the small firm will *supply* that output where price (= AR = MR) = marginal cost (MC). Put another way, the *firm's marginal cost curve* is the *firm's supply curve*, telling us how much output the profit-maximising firm will supply at each and every price.

Taking it further 6.1 looks at the firm's supply curve under perfect competition in the short-run and long-run time periods.

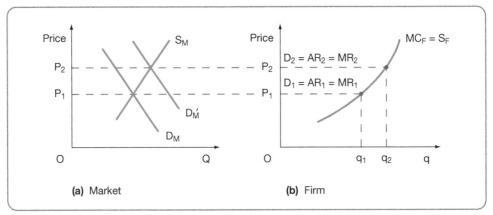

(a) Market   **(b)** Firm

Figure 6.3 Under perfect competition the firm's supply curve (S_F) is the firm's marginal cost curve (MC_F)

We noted in Chapter 3 (p. 80) that the marginal cost (MC) curve will always intersect the average variable cost (AVC), and average total cost (ATC) curves at their lowest points. Here we use this knowledge to identify the firm's short- and long-run supply curves.

Firm's short-run supply curve

In the short-run time period, the firm must at least earn enough revenue to cover its *total variable costs*, thereby making some contribution to the total fixed costs already incurred. In other words, price (AR) must be greater than or equal to average variable cost (AVC).

● At any price *below* P_1, we have AR < AVC so that TR < TVC. The firm is better off shutting down, since it is not even covering its total variable costs. No output will be supplied in the short run at prices less than P_1.

● At any price *above* P_1, we have AR > AVC so that TR > TVC and the firm is making some contribution to the total fixed costs already incurred. The firm will therefore produce output in the short run.

In Figure 6.4 the segment of the firm's marginal cost curve EG represents the firm's *short-run supply curve*.

Firm's long-run supply curve

In the long-run time period all costs, whether variable or fixed, must be covered, including the **normal profit** (see p. 168) often included in cost.

● At any price *below* P_2, AR < ATC, so that TR < TC and no supply is worthwhile.

● At any price *above* P_2, AR > ATC, so that TR > TC and supply is worthwhile.

In Figure 6.4 the segment of the firm's marginal cost curve FG represents the firm's *long-run supply curve*.

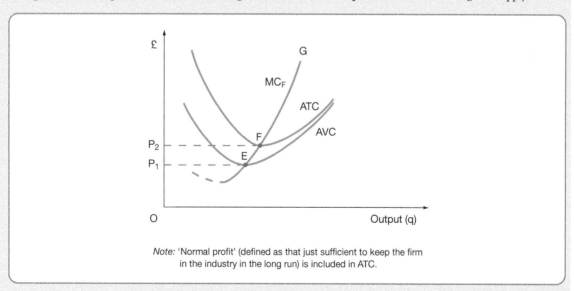

Note: 'Normal profit' (defined as that just sufficient to keep the firm in the industry in the long run) is included in ATC.

Figure 6.4 Under perfect competition EG is the firm's *short-run* supply curve and FG the firm's *long-run* supply curve

Having identified the firm's supply curve, we can now identify the industry (market) supply curve.

Industry supply curve

Clearly, segments of the MC curve of the firm constitute the supply curve of the firm, depending on the time period in question. If we aggregate the MC curves for each and every

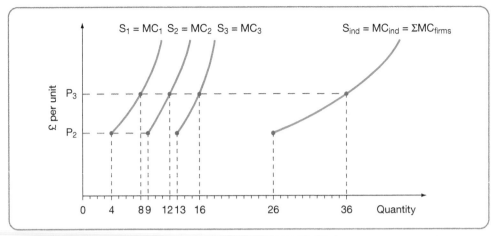

Figure 6.5 The industry supply curve is the industry MC curve, which in turn is the sum of the firm MC curves

firm (summing horizontally), we derive the industry MC curve. Since by aggregating the MC curves of each firm we are aggregating their supply curves, we also derive the industry supply curve. Figure 6.5 outlines this procedure in a simplified situation in which three firms constitute the industry.

The industry supply curve is therefore the sum of the individual firm MC curves in a competitive industry.

Short-run equilibrium

We have already defined (p. 73) the short run as that period of time in which at least one factor of production is fixed. Therefore no new firms can enter the market/industry, being unable to acquire all the factors of production needed to supply the product over this time period.

> **Make a note**
>
> *Normal profit* is the level of profit that is just enough to persuade the firm to stay in the industry in the long run, but not high enough to attract new firms. It can, therefore, be considered as a 'cost' to the firm in that this minimum acceptable rate of profit must be met if the firm is to stay in the industry in the long run.

As we shall see, in the short-run time period the market (industry) and the firm may earn either above normal (*super-normal*) or below normal (*sub-normal*) profits. Figure 6.6(a) indicates the former and Figure 6.6(b) the latter.

Making super-normal profit

In Figure 6.6(a) the profit-maximising firm equates MC with MR (see Chapter 4, p. 115), produces output q_1, earns total revenue (price × quantity) of Oq_1bP_1, incurs total cost of Oq_1ad and therefore makes a super-normal profit of abP_1d. In the short run no new firms can enter and this excess profit can be retained.

Making sub-normal profit

In Figure 6.6(b) the profit-maximising firm produces output q_2, earns total revenue of Oq_2bP_2 but incurs total costs of Oq_2ad, and therefore makes a sub-normal profit (loss) of

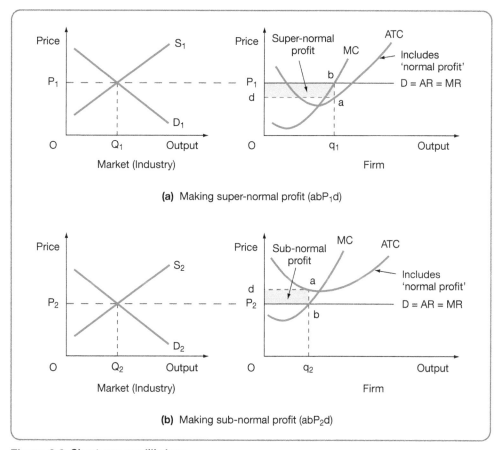

(a) Making super-normal profit (abP₁d)

(b) Making sub-normal profit (abP₂d)

Figure 6.6 **Short-run equilibrium**

abP₂d. In the short run, no existing firms exit the industry (unless they are not even covering their variable costs, see p. 167) and so these losses will remain.

In summary, in the short-run profit-maximising equilibrium

$$P = AR = MR = MC$$

Long-run equilibrium

In the long run *all* factors can be varied, new firms can enter and existing firms (*incumbents*) can leave the market/industry. It will be helpful to see how we move from our short-run equilibrium positions of super-normal and sub-normal profits, respectively, to the long-run equilibrium where only normal profits are earned.

Short-run super-normal profits

If a large number of new (small) firms are attracted into the industry by super-normal profits, then this will have an effect on the (long-run) industry supply curve, shifting it to the right in Figure 6.6(a). New firms will continue to enter the industry until any super-normal profit is competed away: i.e. only normal profit is earned.

The mechanism by which the super-normal profit is eroded is indicated in Figure 6.7 and involves the industry price falling (P_1 to P^*) as industry supply increases (S_1 to S^*). What has happened is that new firms have been encouraged to enter the industry by the super-normal profits and industry supply has increased (shifted to the right). Price will continue to fall until the super-normal profits are competed away.

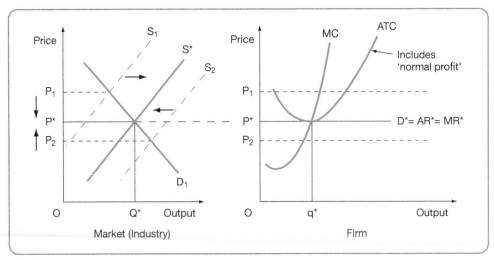

Figure 6.7 Long-run equilibrium for a profit-maximising firm in perfect competition (P*q*): normal profit earned

Long-run equilibrium will only be achieved when the profit-maximising firm (MC = MR) is just earning normal profit (ATC = AR), i.e. when the following condition holds true:

$$P = AR = MR = MC = ATC$$

This can only occur (see Figure 6.7) when the price-taking firm faces a perfectly elastic demand curve that just touches (is a tangent to) the bottom of its ATC curve. Here, and here only, is the above condition satisfied (remember MC intersects ATC from below at the lowest point of ATC). The profit-maximising firm (MC = MR) is now earning only normal profit (ATC = AR), and no further incentive exists for new firms to enter the industry. We are in *long-run equilibrium*.

Short-run sub-normal profits

In our earlier Figure 6.6(b), where firms earned sub-normal profits, a large number of (small) firms would leave the industry, shifting industry supply to the left in Figure 6.7 (S_2 to S*), raising industry price (P_2 to P*) and restoring profits to the normal level. What has happened here is that existing firms have failed to achieve the level of profit (normal profit) needed to keep them in this industry in the long run and have left the industry. Again we are in *long-run equilibrium*.

In summary, the long-run profit-maximising equilibrium will only occur when firms are neither entering nor leaving the industry. This will occur when normal profits are being earned, i.e. when the following condition is fulfilled.

$$P = AR = MR = MC = ATC$$

Perfect competition and efficiency

Some ideas of 'efficiency' were considered in Chapter 5 (p. 159) and are considered further in Chapter 8. Here we identify two types.

- *Productive efficiency.* To achieve productive efficiency (or cost efficiency) a firm must use its resources in such a way as to produce at the lowest possible cost per unit of output. Therefore, productive efficiency is achieved at the lowest point on a firm's long-run average total cost curve. In other words, costs per unit of production in the long run are as low as technically possible. Productive efficiency is achieved by the firm in Figure 6.7 at output q* (and price P*).

- *Allocative efficiency.* To achieve allocative efficiency it *should not be possible* to make someone better off by a reallocation of resources without, at the same time, making someone worse off. If you could make someone better off and no one worse off, then you should obviously reallocate resources. To achieve this situation (called a 'Pareto optimum' resource allocation, see Chapter 8, p. 159), one key condition is that price should equal marginal cost. In other words, consumers should pay a price for the last unit of output that just covers the extra cost of producing that last unit of output. Allocative efficiency is achieved by the firm in Figure 6.7 at price P* (and output q*).

In other words, the long-run equilibrium of the firm (and of the market/industry) under perfect competition results in both productive and allocative efficiency. This is why the perfectly competitive market structure is often thought to be 'ideal' in terms of resource allocation.

> **Make a note**
>
> Strictly, it can be shown that the long-run equilibrium in Figure 6.7 will be one in which the bottom of both the short-run *and* long-run average total cost curves (see Chapter 3, p. 85) just touch the perfectly elastic demand curve at P*.

We consider these 'efficiency' or resource allocation aspects of competitive markets further in Chapter 8. We also look at the impacts of various types of 'market failure' in preventing these 'efficiency' outcomes.

Case Study 6.1 applies our ideas of perfect competition to the Internet.

Case Study 6.1   Perfect competition and the Internet

It has been argued in recent years that the explosive growth of retailing on the Internet has made this form of retailing resemble an almost perfectly competitive market. Consumers appear to have perfect information about both prices and products at their fingertips by merely logging onto the net in search of the best deals. In a perfectly competitive market products are identical; there are a large number of buyers and sellers; there are no search costs; customers are perfectly informed; there is free entry into and exit out of the industry; and profit margins would be 'normal' in the long run.

The Internet does seem to have some of these attributes of a perfect market. For example, studies have shown that online retailers tend to be cheaper than conventional retailers and that they adjust prices more finely and more often. The Internet has also led to the growth of people who use 'shopbots', i.e. computer programs that search rapidly over many websites for the best deal. These provide customers with a more complete knowledge of the market, hence minimising search costs. In addition, entry and exit from Internet sites is relatively easy for sellers so there are no obvious **barriers to entry**. Under these conditions one would expect prices for the same or similar products to be virtually identical on the Internet, as under perfect competition.

However, a closer study of the Internet retail market shows that there may still be important elements of imperfection in the market. Studies in the USA by the Sloan School of Management have shown that there is still an element of price dispersion (i.e. difference between the highest and lowest prices for a given product or service) in Internet retail markets. This would tend to indicate that the Internet retail market is inefficient, with some retailers still being able to charge more than others. For example, price dispersion for identical books and for CDs and software among different online retailers can differ by as much as 33% and 25% respectively. Researchers at the Wharton School in Pennsylvania found that airline tickets from online travel agents differed by an average of 28%!

Questions

1 Why does a degree of price dispersion suggest that we do not have a perfect market?

2 What factors might explain why various retailers can still charge different prices for the same product over the Internet, despite the claim that it resembles a perfect market?

Contestable market theory

The theory of 'contestable markets' indicates how the principles we have discussed might generally apply to markets which are not, strictly, perfectly competitive. The emphasis here is on the threat of new entrants resulting in existing firms in non-perfectly competitive markets acting *as if* they were in a perfectly competitive market.

The idea of **contestable markets** broadens the application of competitive behaviour beyond the strict conditions needed for perfect competition. In other words, instead of regarding competitive behaviour as existing only in the perfectly competitive market structure, it could be exhibited in any market structure that was contestable. Generally speaking, the fewer the barriers to entry into a market, the more contestable that market. In this sense, some monopoly and oligopoly markets could be regarded as contestable.

The absence of entry barriers increases the *threat* of new firms entering the market. It is this threat which is assumed to check any tendency by incumbent (existing) firms to raise prices substantially above average costs and thereby earn super-normal profit.

> *Stop and think*　　　　　　　　　　　　　　　　　　　6.1
>
> Can you identify any product markets which have few, if any, entry barriers?

Perfectly contestable market

It may be useful to illustrate this approach by considering the extreme case of perfect contestability. In a **perfectly contestable market** there are no barriers to entry so that incumbent firms are constrained to keep prices at levels which, in relation to costs, earn only normal profits. Incumbents in perfectly contestable markets therefore earn no super-normal profits, are cost efficient, cannot cross-subsidise between products or in any way set prices below costs in order to deter new entrants.

At least three conditions must be fulfilled for a market to be perfectly contestable.

1 *An absence of sunk costs* (see p. 90). Sunk costs are the costs of acquiring an asset (tangible or intangible) which cannot be recouped by selling the asset or redeploying it in another market should the firm exit the industry. The presence of sunk costs, by increasing the costs of exiting the industry, can be assumed to make incumbent firms more determined to avoid being forced to exit the industry and therefore more aggressive towards new entrants. They might then seek to resist new entrants by adopting a variety of strategies which essentially constitute a barrier to entry.

2 *The potential entrant must be at no disadvantage compared to incumbents as regards production technology or perceived product quality*. Any lack of access to equivalent production technology utilised by incumbents might prevent new entrants competing on the same cost base or quality of product base. This would inhibit the threat of potential new entrants, thereby permitting incumbents to earn and retain super-normal profits. Similarly, perceptions of consumers (via branding etc.) as to the superiority of incumbent product quality would also inhibit the threat of new entrants and permit incumbents to earn and retain super-normal profits.

3 *The entrant must be able to engage in 'hit and run' tactics;* i.e. to enter a market, make a profit and exit before incumbents can adjust their prices downwards. Put another way, existing suppliers can only change their prices with time-lags whereas consumers respond immediately to any lower prices offered by new entrants.

Under these conditions there is a total absence of barriers to entry, and exit from the market is costless. Such a *perfectly contestable market* will ensure that incumbents are unable to earn super-normal profits in the long run, and that price will equate with long-run average total cost (including normal profit). Any rise in price above long-run average cost will attract new entrants which, by undercutting the price of incumbents, can attract their customers and make a profit before the incumbent can react by reducing price. The new entrant can exit the market at zero cost by such 'hit and run' tactics, having benefited by earning super-normal profits prior to the reaction of incumbents, namely the curbing of their prices back to long-run average cost.

Although such perfect contestability is an ideal rarely, if ever, achieved, it sets the context for competitive behaviour in all types of market structure. Even highly monopolistic or oligopolistic markets could, in principle, experience a high degree of contestability, thereby achieving a competitive-type market solution with price close to long-run average costs and profits close to normal. The policy implication of such an approach is to encourage the removal of entry barriers and the lowering of exit costs in all types of market structure in order to increase the degree of contestability.

A rather weaker, but more pragmatic, approach to contestability focuses on cost rather than price contestability. Here the suggestion is that the threat of entry may be more likely to induce incumbents to be *cost efficient* than to set prices equal to long-run average costs. By 'cost efficient' is meant the delivery of a given level of output at the lowest cost technically feasible. As we shall see (Chapter 8), the perspective of 'cost contestability' is a widely used argument in support of deregulation, i.e. the opening up of specified markets to potential new entrants as a means of securing efficiency gains via cost cutting by incumbents.

Monopoly

In this section we move the analysis to the opposite end of the spectrum from pure perfect competition to look at what happens to price and output decisions in a *monopoly* market structure.

Pure monopoly

Pure monopoly occurs in the extreme case when there is a *single* seller of the product, with no close substitute available, so that the firm is, in effect, the industry.

It follows that under 'pure monopoly' the downward sloping demand (AR) curve of the *industry* is now the downward sloping demand curve of the *firm*. As we saw in Chapter 2 (p. 48), this means that there will be a marginal revenue (MR) curve lying inside the downward sloping demand (AR) curve, as in Figure 6.8 (p. 176).

Barriers to entry

Any monopoly situation, 'pure' or otherwise, can only exist in the long run because of barriers to new firm entry. These barriers can take various forms.

- *Substantial scale economies*, so that large firms have a significant cost-advantage over smaller new entrants. In the extreme case the *minimum efficient size* (MES) of production (see p. 89) may be so large that the industry can only sustain one technically (productively) efficient firm. This is the **natural monopoly** argument, which we return to below (p. 176).
- *Control over scarce resources needed for production*, such as raw materials, key components, skilled labour etc.
- *Possession of patents or copyrights* for products or for processes of production.
- *Awarding of franchises* giving firms the exclusive rights to sell a particular good or service in a specified location.
- *Government regulations*, such as those creating the nationalised industries or other public sector bodies.

Stop and think   6.2

Choose *three* separate products and for each identify any barriers to entry that might exist.

Case Study 6.2 shows how the presence or *absence* of serious barriers to entry is likely to influence the competitive situation in the UK banking sector in the long-run time period, even when the industry has elements of market power in the sense that large-scale providers are dominant.

Case Study 6.2	New entry and the banking system

Consumer groups have long worried about a lack of competition in Britain's personal banking market. Waves of consolidation over the years have left it more concentrated than, for example, that of the United States. Consumers have remained highly reluctant to switch their current accounts (checking accounts, as Americans call them) because it can be so cumbersome, even though they have become quite used to shopping around for other utilities. This is clear from a recent Office of Fair Trading (OFT) report, whereas only 12% of UK bank customers had switched provider in the past five years, 53% of electricity and gas consumers, 43% of fixed-line phone users and 36% of mortgage holders had switched provider in the past five years. Forced mergers and takeovers during the financial crisis made things worse: the governor of the Bank of England, Mervyn King, has expressed worries that the resulting megabanks are too big to fail, and thus should be broken up.

Now, with some of the rescued banks' branches being put up for sale, and several ambitious new entrants seeking to grab a significant share of the market, there is the chance of a better choice for bank customers. On 6 April 2010 bidding closed for 318 branches of the Royal Bank of Scotland (RBS) – in which the taxpayer now has an 84% stake – that are being sold on the orders of the European Commission, as a quid pro quo for its state rescue. Depending on who wins, the sale could be a first step on the road to ending the oligopoly enjoyed by Britain's big four – RBS, HSBC, Barclays and Lloyds.

If Santander, a big Spanish bank, wins, not much may change. It has already mopped up several medium-sized British banks – Abbey and Alliance & Leicester, and the branch network of the state-rescued Bradford & Bingley – and is amalgamating their combined 1,300-odd branches into a single outfit. Another potential consolidator is National Australia Bank, which already owns the mid-sized Yorkshire and Clydesdale banks. But Santander's main domestic rival, BBVA, which so far has little presence in Britain, has also bid for the RBS branches. And so has JC Flowers, an American private-equity investor and serial buyer of banks in the Netherlands, Germany and Japan. Potentially the most significant bidder is Sir Richard Branson's Virgin Money, which recently bought a tiny regional bank, Church House Trust, to use its licence to launch a big push into personal banking. If it fails to win the RBS branches it may go after other banking operations that are coming on to the market: the still-active part of the rescued Northern Rock is to be sold, as are at least 600 branches of Lloyds, which took over the ailing HBOS during the crisis. In April 2010 it was confirmed that Wilbur Ross, an American investor, was ready to put up to £500m into the Virgin venture.

Among other new entrants to come is Metro Bank, backed by Vernon Hill, an American bank founder. It got its licence from the Financial Services Authority in March and plans to open up to 200 'customer- and dog-friendly' branches around Greater London. Walton & Co, backed by Panmure Gordon, an investment bank, is a more modest venture into family banking in selected market towns, still waiting for its licence. Sweden's Handelsbanken is also planning to increase its small branch network in Britain, and the huge Bank of China is also seeking a share of the British mortgage market.

The new competitors may struggle to loosen the existing big four's grip on the market

Given the cost and complexity of creating branch networks from scratch, and the even greater challenges involved in absorbing and integrating existing branches, with their often outdated information technology systems, the new competitors may struggle to loosen the existing big four's grip on the market. However, there are two other, far stronger, potential contenders with better chances of taking a decent share.

One is the Post Office. It does not have a banking licence of its own but provides an outlet for some of Bank of Ireland's banking services, and allows customers of 12 other banks to use the 11,500 post-office counters across Britain. The Post Bank Coalition, combining trade unions, think tanks and the Federation of Small Businesses, is pressing for the Post Office to abandon its joint ventures and become a fully-fledged, publicly owned bank for individuals and small firms, something like the mighty Japan Post.

Tesco wants a 10% share of the banking market

Another, whose plans to become big in banking are already well advanced, is Tesco, Britain's biggest retailer with almost 2,300 stores across the country. This week the firm said it was aiming eventually for a 10% share of the market for current accounts, which it will enter next year. It already offers credit cards and insurances at its stores, and plans to add mortgages too. Like the other new entrants, Tesco is finding that it is a struggle to build the information systems needed to run a full-scale bank. But it already has a strong branch network and a customer relationship with millions of consumers.

Since the failure of Northern Rock demonstrated the dangers of banks relying on the wholesale markets for their funding, they have taken a renewed interest in taking deposits from the public – though savers grumble that the rates on offer are still miserly. Several of the potential rivals to the existing big four – Virgin, Tesco and the Post Office, are trusted household names, so there is a fair chance consumers will consider them. But to get a significant slice of the banking market they will need to persuade the public to move their current accounts, not just savings accounts and credit cards. Many people remain reluctant to do this, not least because the biggest banks benefit from a stronger implicit government guarantee. The main challenge for the new contenders, then, may be to persuade them to shop around, just as they have learned in recent years to switch regularly between different providers of electricity, gas and telephone lines, to chase the best deals.

Source: Britain's banking market, 'a breath of fresh air', www.economist.com, © The Economist Newspaper Ltd, London (08/04/2010)

Questions

1 What does the above account tell us about the nature of the 'barriers to entry' in the UK banking market?

2 What will determine whether this market becomes more or less open to competitive forces?

3 How does the case study help us understand the concepts of 'normal profit' and 'super-normal profit' in an industry?

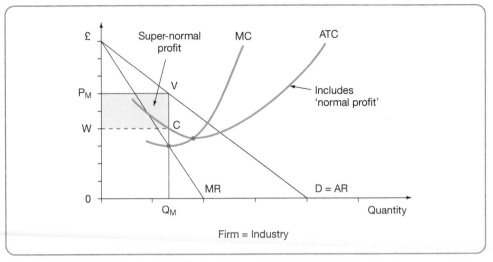

Figure 6.8 **Price (P$_M$) and output (Q$_M$) for the 'pure monopoly'**

Equilibrium price and output

Because of these barriers to entry, any super-normal profits earned in the short run can be retained in the long run. Figure 6.8 outlines the equilibrium situation for a pure monopoly setting a single price.

In Figure 6.8 the profit-maximising monopolist equates MC with MR, giving output Q$_M$ and price P$_M$ in equilibrium. Under 'pure monopoly' strict barriers to entry allow the super-normal profit (P$_M$VCW) to be retained in the long run, so this is both a short-run and a long-run equilibrium.

Notice here how, unlike perfect competition, monopoly fails to achieve either productive or allocative efficiency.

- Output (Q$_M$) is lower than that at which ATC is a minimum, so no 'productive efficiency'.
- Price (P$_M$) is higher than marginal cost (MC), so no 'allocative efficiency'.

Natural monopoly

Figure 6.9 provides a useful illustration of the **natural monopoly** argument which suggests that, in terms of our earlier analysis (Chapter 3, p. 89), the minimum efficient size (MES) is so large that only one efficient firm producing at minimum long-run average cost (LRAC) can be sustained by that particular industry.

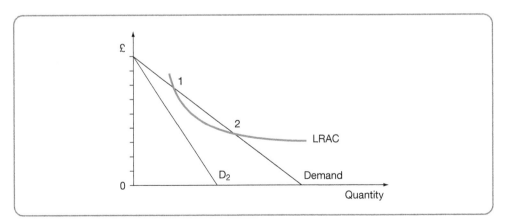

Figure 6.9 **'Natural monopoly' situation**

The falling long-run average total cost curve (LRAC) indicates that economies of scale occur as output rises. When there is only one firm operating in the market the industry and the firm's demand curve is the same. Here output can occur between points 1 and 2 profitably. Suppose a second firm enters the market and the industry demand is now divided between the two firms (in this case each firm has 50% of the market). Each firm now faces the same individual demand curve, i.e. D_2 in Figure 6.9. In this situation long-run costs (LRAC) are greater than revenue at all levels of output. Consequently, one firm must leave the market, leaving us with a single (natural) monopoly.

The 'classical' case against monopoly

The so-called 'classical' case against monopoly is that price is higher and quantity lower than under perfect competition. We now evaluate this case, for simplicity keeping our assumption of a pure monopoly.

Under perfect competition, price is determined for the industry (and for the firm) by the intersection of demand and supply, at P_C in Figure 6.10. We have already seen (p. 168) that the supply curve, S, of the perfectly competitive industry is also the marginal cost (MC) curve of the industry.

Suppose now that the industry is taken over by a single firm (pure monopoly), and that both costs and demand are initially unchanged. It follows that the marginal cost curve remains in the same position; also that the demand curve for the perfectly competitive industry now becomes the demand (and AR) curve for the monopolist. The marginal revenue (MR) curve must then lie inside the negatively sloped AR curve.

The profit-maximising price for the monopolist is P_M, corresponding to output Q_M where MC = MR. Price is higher under monopoly than under perfect competition ($P_M > P_C$) and quantity is lower ($Q_M < Q_C$). This is the so-called 'classical' case against monopoly.

Links

The natural monopoly argument is further considered in Chapter 8 (p. 245).

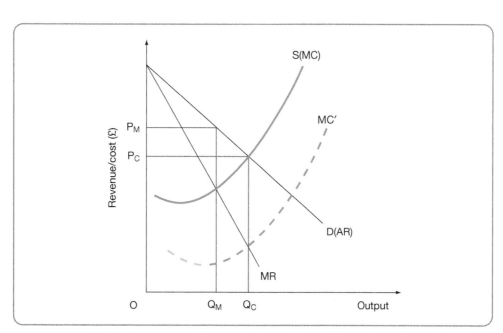

Figure 6.10 **Price under perfect competition and monopoly**

This criticism of monopoly is additional to the fact that, as we noted from Figure 6.8 (p. 176), output is *not* at minimum average total cost and price does *not* equal marginal cost, breaking the respective conditions for productive and allocative efficiency (productive and allocative inefficiency).

However, these criticisms of monopoly may not be as strong as they first appear. We have already seen that the increased size which underpins monopoly power may yield *economies of scale*, both technical and non-technical (see Chapter 3, pp. 85–9). Where these economies of scale are significant, it may even be that the 'classical' case against monopoly fails to hold true, with the firm now able to move to a lower short-run average cost curve and with it a lower marginal cost curve.

Make a note

> The marginal cost (MC) curve must cut the bottom (p. 81) of each short-run average cost curve (SRAC). If economies of scale allow the firm to move to a lower SRAC curve, then the firm will also have a lower MC curve (see Chapter 3, p. 85).

In Figure 6.10, if economies of scale were sufficiently large to lower the MC curve to MC′ then the profit-maximising monopoly price P_M and quantity Q_M would be *identical* to those achieved under perfect competition. If economies of scale were even greater, lowering the MC curve *below* MC′, then the monopoly price (P_M) would be below that of perfect competition and the monopoly output (Q_M) would be higher than that of perfect competition. The key question is therefore how substantial are the economies of scale for the monopoly industry, and it is this *empirical* question which will determine whether or not the 'classical' case against monopoly still holds true.

Stop and think   6.4

1 Why might the demand curve be different for the monopoly than for the perfectly competitive industry?

2 What might this mean for the 'classical case' against monopoly?

Throughout this discussion of monopoly we have simplified the analysis by contrasting 'pure monopoly' with perfect competition. In fact, industries in which more than one-third of the output is in the hands of a single seller or group of linked sellers can technically be called 'monopoly' in the UK. However, such 'general' monopoly situations are in practice difficult to distinguish from the oligopoly form of market structure which we consider later in the chapter.

You try 6.1 gives you the chance to self-check some of the material on perfect competition and monopoly.

You try   6.1

1 Figure 6.11 shows the cost and revenue curves of a firm under conditions of pure monopoly. Answer the following questions with reference to this figure.

(a) What would be the price and output if the market was perfectly competitive?

(b) What price would a monopolist charge if it wished to maximise profit and what output would it produce?

(c) Marginal revenue becomes negative beyond what output level?

(d) At what point on the demand curve is the price elasticity of demand equal to unity?

You try 6.1 continued

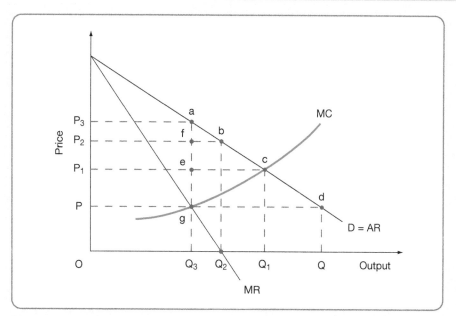

Figure 6.11

(e) If the 'classical case' against monopoly holds true, how much *consumer surplus* and how much *producer surplus* is lost as compared to the perfectly competitive equilibrium?

(f) If the monopoly was seeking to maximise *total revenue*, what price would it charge and what output would it produce?

2 Put the *letter* for each of the following types of barrier to entry in the box next to its correct description.

(a) Geographical distance

(b) Brand image

(c) Restrictive practices by incumbents

(d) Economies of scale

(e) Government regulations

(f) Ownership of resources

Type of barrier	Description
	The minimum efficient size (MES) at which average costs are a minimum may be a large output, preventing smaller firms from competing effectively
	Access to scarce raw materials or scarce intellectual property rights (patents/copyright) may be in the hands of a few large firms
	Expensive advertising has created strong consumer loyalty to products which may deter new firm entry
	The creation of nationalised industries or the imposition of tariff barriers, quota restrictions etc. may restrict competition in national markets
	High transport costs may discourage competition from outside a particular region or nation
	Existing firms may use various devices to discourage new firm entry, e.g. setting artificially low prices, parallel pricing (all set similar prices), etc.

You try 6.1 continued

3 Which *two* of the following are key assumptions of perfect competition?

(a) The firm has perfect information about the market in which it operates.

(b) Firms find it easy to leave the industry but difficult to enter.

(c) Some firms are able to influence market price by making an individual decision.

(d) Firms produce differentiated products so there is no need for advertising.

(e) Each firm faces a perfectly elastic demand curve at the going market price.

4 Which *two* features refer to a perfectly competitive firm operating in the long run?

(a) Earns super-normal profit.

(b) Earns normal profit.

(c) Produces at the technical optimum (minimum average cost).

(d) Earns sub-normal profit.

(e) Produces at an average cost above the minimum level technically feasible.

5 Which *two* of the following features will help to make a market more contestable?

(a) There are few barriers to entry.

(b) There are many barriers to entry.

(c) Incumbent firms find it easy to erect new entry barriers.

(d) Incumbent firms find it difficult to erect new entry barriers.

(e) The industry is a 'natural monopoly'.

6 Which *two* of the following characteristics apply to pure monopoly?

(a) All units of the product are sold at an identical price.

(b) The firm is the industry.

(c) The firm faces a horizontal demand curve.

(d) The firm faces a downward sloping demand curve.

(e) Price = marginal revenue = average revenue.

Answers can be found on pp. 525–546.

Monopolistic competition

This type of market structure is sometimes called 'imperfect competition'.

● It contains elements of a competitive market structure in that it assumes:

 – a large number of small firms in the industry;

 – freedom of entry into, and exit from, the industry.

● It contains elements of an 'imperfect' market structure in that it assumes:

 – each small firm supplies a product which is not homogenous but *differentiated* in some way from that of its rivals. Put another way, the product of each small firm is a close but not perfect substitute for the product of other small firms in the industry.

Examples

> There are many Chinese takeaway restaurants in most cities and towns. The menus are very similar but each one arguably cooks or presents its food in ways which differ from its rivals. Similarly, orange growers in Australia differentiate their orange juice concentrate from domestic and foreign rivals by designating the region of Australia in which the oranges were grown.

Downward sloping demand curve

Because the product is differentiated from that of its rivals, the firm's demand curve will no longer be the perfectly elastic (horizontal) demand curve of perfect competition. In fact, it will be the downward (negatively) sloping demand curve shown in Figure 6.12(a).

● If the firm lowers the price of its (differentiated) product it will capture some, but not all, consumers from other firms.

● If the firm raises its price it will lose some, but not all, of its consumers to rival firms.

Loyalty to the differentiated products of the respective firms means that price, while important, is not the sole influence on consumer choice. Hence we have a negatively sloped demand curve for the firm's products. Of course, the greater the loyalty to the firm's differentiated product, the greater the price rise needed to induce consumers to switch away from the product to that of a rival. Similarly, the greater the price cut needed to attract (loyal) consumers attached to its rival firm's products. It follows that the greater the product differentiation and consumer loyalty to the product, the *less price elastic* the demand curve for a particular firm will be, and of course the greater the monopoly power over price available to the firm.

Short-run equilibrium

In Figure 6.12(a) the profit-maximising firm (MC = MR) will, in the short run, produce output Q_S and sell this at price P_S, yielding super-normal profit P_SVWC. This excess profit will, given freedom of entry into the market, attract new entrants.

Unlike perfect competition, the new entrants do not increase the overall market supply of a single, homogenous product. Rather, the new entrants will partly erode the

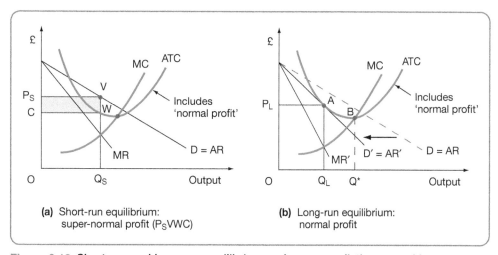

(a) Short-run equilibrium:
super-normal profit (P_SVWC)

(b) Long-run equilibrium:
normal profit

Figure 6.12 Short-run and long-run equilibrium under monopolistic competition

consumer demand for an existing firm's (differentiated) product, i.e. the new entrants will capture some of the customers of the existing firm by offering a still wider variety of differentiated products. We show this by a leftward shift (decrease) in the existing firm's demand curve in Figure 6.12(a).

Long-run equilibrium

Only when profit is reduced to normal for firms already in the market will the attraction for new entrants be removed, i.e. when ATC = AR, with normal profit included in ATC. In other words, the demand (AR) curve for the existing firm will shift leftwards until it just touches the ATC curve. This long-run equilibrium occurs in Figure 6.12(b) with demand curve D' at price P_L and output Q_L.

- If the demand curve is still to the right of D' in Figure 6.12(b) then super-normal profits will still be made and new entry will continue.
- If the demand curve has shifted to the left of D' then sub-normal profits will be made and some firms will leave the industry (bankruptcy) and the demand curve will shift back to the right.
- Only at D', when normal profits are earned, will there be no long-run tendency for firms to enter or leave the industry.

In this analysis, the firm will produce an output of Q_L and charge a price of P_L, making normal profit – there is no further entry of firms into the industry. The firm will operate where the average cost is tangential to the demand curve (point A) but technically the firm is able to operate at point B with an output of Q^*. In other words, the firm has a capacity to produce more at a lower average cost. Consequently, a criticism of monopolistic competition is that each firm is serving a market that is too small and has the capacity to serve more customers. The firm in monopolistic competition therefore operates with *excess capacity* in the long run, equivalent to the difference between Q_L and Q^* in Figure 6.12(b). The excess capacity leads to higher average costs than would exist if output were expanded and to higher consumer prices.

Monopolistic competition and efficiency

We might usefully summarise the 'efficiency' aspects of long-run equilibrium for monopolistic competition.

- *Normal profits*. Only normal profits are earned in the long run, as with perfect competition.
- *Higher price, lower output*. Price is higher and output lower than would be the case in the long run for perfect competition (which would be at the price and output corresponding to point B).
- *Productive efficiency*. ATC (at A) is higher than the minimum level technically achievable (B), so productive efficiency is *not* achieved.
- *Excess capacity*. In Figure 6.12(b) output is Q_L but for minimum ATC output should be higher at Q^*. This shortfall in actual output (Q_L) below the productively (technically) efficient output (Q^*) is often called excess capacity.
- *Allocative efficiency*. Price is higher than marginal cost, so allocative efficiency is *not* achieved.

You try 6.2 gives you the opportunity to consider further some aspects of monopolistic competition.

You try   6.2

1 Put the letter for each of the following statements in the correct box.

   (a) Downward sloping demand curve   (f) Average cost above minimum in long run

   (b) Perfectly elastic demand curve   (g) No monopoly power

   (c) Differentiated product   (h) Some monopoly power

   (d) Homogeneous product   (i) Price taker

   (e) Average cost a minimum in long run   (j) Some non-price consumer loyalty.

Perfect competition	Monopolistic competition

2 If a firm in monopolistic competition is in its long-run equilibrium position, then which one of the following is untrue?

   (a) Profits are normal

   (b) $P > MC$

   (c) $AR = AC$

   (d) AC is not at its minimum

   (e) No excess capacity.

3 Which one of the following does *not* hold true for a firm operating under monopolistic competition?

   (a) Price is the sole influence on consumer choice.

   (b) The greater the product differentiation, the more inelastic the demand.

   (c) The firm will maximise profits in the short run where $MR = MC$.

   (d) In the long run the firm will not produce at the technical optimum (minimum average cost).

   (e) Only normal profits will be earned in the long run.

4 Refer to Figure 6.13. If this profit maximising firm is in monopolistic competition, then it will produce an output level:

   (a) of 40 units

   (b) of 60 units

   (c) of 80 units

   (d) that is impossible to determine without information concerning the rival firms

   (e) that is lower than 40 units.

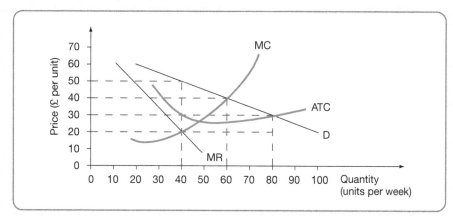

Figure 6.13

Answers can be found on pp. 525–546.

Oligopoly

Oligopoly refers to a situation in which a few firms dominate the market. Crucially, these few firms recognise their rivalry and interdependence, fully aware that any action on their part is likely to result in counter-actions by their rivals. Firms will therefore be drawn into devising strategies and counter-strategies taking into account their rivals' expected actions and reactions.

The three- and five-firm *concentration ratios* are often used as an indicator of the presence of oligopoly markets. These ratios tell us the proportion of the total value of output or of employment contributed by the three and five largest firms, respectively, in the market or industry. For example, the largest five firms in the tobacco industry in the UK contribute 99% of output and 98% of employment, clearly suggesting an oligopoly market.

Table 6.1 presents some data at the 'product group' level, showing both three- and five-firm concentration ratios in terms of product output in the UK.

Another feature of oligopoly markets is *product differentiation*. There are often many brands of a particular product, with extensive advertising by rival firms emphasising the difference between their product and that of their rivals, whether real or imagined.

As we shall see, the greater uncertainty of oligopoly markets makes it more difficult to predict short-run and long-run equilibrium situations, as we did for the previous market structures. Nevertheless, we can analyse various types of oligopoly situations, using two broad categories.

- *Non-collusive oligopoly*. Here the oligopoly firms compete against each other using strategies and counter-strategies, but do not seek to make agreements, whether formal or informal, to 'fix' the market outcome.

- *Collusive oligopoly*. Here the oligopoly firms do seek various arrangements between themselves in an attempt to remove some of the market uncertainty they face.

People of the same trade seldom meet together, even for merriment and diversion, but the conversation ends in a conspiracy against the public or in some contrivance to raises prices.

(Adam Smith, *The Wealth of Nations*, 1776)

Table 6.1 **Company shares of the UK market by sector/product, 2006***

Sector/product group	Percentage share of UK market	
	Three largest companies	Five largest companies
Cigarettes	95.6	99.5
Chocolate confectionery	80.0	86.0
DIY retail	75.3	86.4
Motor insurance	53.8	63.3
Motor cycles, scooters	45.2	64.2
Household cleaning products	44.0	62.0
Mortgage lenders	41.2	57.4
Cars	37.0	51.5
Bottled water	35.5	42.1
Luxury watches	25.6	35.5

* = 2006 or latest date

Source: Mintel International Group Ltd (2006) *Mintel Reports* (various)

Non-collusive oligopoly

First we consider situations in which each firm decides upon its strategy without any formal or even informal collusion with its rivals.

Kinked demand curve

In 1939 Hall and Hitch in the UK and Sweezy in the USA proposed a theory to explain why prices often remain stable in oligopoly markets, even when costs rise. A central feature of that theory was the existence of a *kinked demand curve*.

To illustrate this theory, we take an oligopoly market which sells similar, but not identical products, i.e. there is some measure of product differentiation. If one firm raises its price, it will then lose some, though not all, of its customers to rivals. Similarly, if the firm reduces its price it will attract some, though not all, of its rivals' customers. How many customers are lost or gained will depend partly on whether the rivals follow the initial price change.

Extensive interviews with managers of firms in oligopoly markets led Hall and Hitch to conclude that most firms have learned a common lesson from past experience of how rivals react.

● If the firm were to *raise* its price above the current level (P in Figure 6.14), its rivals *would not follow*, content to let the firm lose sales to them. The firm will then expect its demand curve to be relatively elastic (dK) for price rises.

● However, if the firm were to *reduce* its price, rivals would follow to protect their market share, so that the firm gains few extra sales. The firm will then expect its demand curve to be relatively inelastic (KD′) for price reductions.

Overall, the firm will believe that its demand curve is kinked at the current price P, as in Figure 6.14.

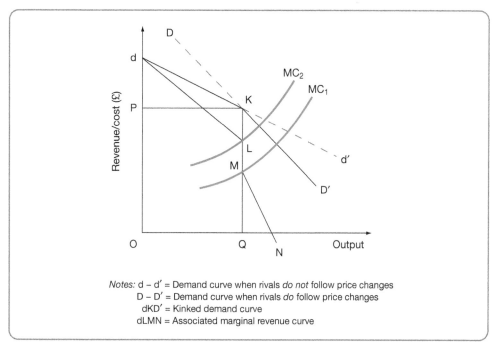

Notes: d – d′ = Demand curve when rivals *do not* follow price changes
D – D′ = Demand curve when rivals *do* follow price changes
dKD′ = Kinked demand curve
dLMN = Associated marginal revenue curve

Figure 6.14 Kinked demand curve and price stability

Make a note

Associated with each demand (AR) curve in Figure 6.14 will be an associated marginal revenue (MR) curve which lies inside it.

● For price rises *above* P, dL is the relevant marginal revenue curve.

● For price reductions *below* P, MN is the relevant marginal revenue curve.

As we can see in Figure 6.14, there is a *vertical discontinuity*, LM, in the overall marginal revenue curve dLMN. The marginal cost curve could then vary between MC$_1$ and MC$_2$ without causing the firm to alter its profit-maximising price P (or its output Q).

In the kinked demand model the firm assumes that rivals will react to its own strategies, and uses past experience to assess the form that reaction might take. In this case the firm assumes that price increases will largely be ignored but price decreases will tend to be matched.

Example

Price reductions matched by tabloid newspaper

The assumption that firms in oligopoly markets will tend to match price reductions by rivals is certainly supported by many examples of price 'warfare' as among the tabloid newspapers.

The *Daily Mirror* has around 19% of total tabloid ('popular') newspaper sales in the UK while the *Sun* (owned by Rupert Murdoch) has around 34%. They have been engaged in matching one another's price reductions for much of the past decade – though this has often damaged profitability! It was reported in 2003 that the *Daily Mirror* had lost £22m of revenue over that year alone in matching price reductions by the *Sun*.

Non-price competition

We have seen that kinked-demand theory predicts relatively stable prices in oligopoly markets, and that the assumption is made, based on past experience, that the rival will react to a price cut, but not react to a price rise.

However, instead of using past experience to assess future reactions by rivals, the firm itself could try to identify the *best possible moves* the opposition could make to each of its own strategies. The firm could then plan counter-measures if the rival reacts in these predicted ways. As we see below, this is the essence of game theory and can involve both price and non-price competition.

Game theory

This terms refers to various theories which analyse oligopoly situations as though they were 'games' in which 'players' can adopt various strategies and counter-strategies in order to improve their position. Many of these oligopoly 'games' were developed from an early, non-economic problem known as the *Prisoners' Dilemma*, which is considered in some detail in Taking it further 6.2.

Taking it further Prisoners' Dilemma   6.2

Alf and Bob (the 'players') have been caught stealing cars. The case against them is watertight and enough to imprison them for five years apiece. The police also suspect the pair of stealing the Crown Jewels – a serious crime warranting 30 years in the Tower of London. In order to get a conviction, the police need confessions, so Alf and Bob are interviewed separately and each given the following alternatives:

1 If both say nothing, each will receive a five-year sentence.

2 If one confesses to stealing the Crown Jewels but the other does not, the confessor will receive an incredibly lenient two years but his partner will get the full 30 years.

3 If both confess, both receive a reduced sentence of 10 years.

What strategy should each adopt? The options or strategies are shown in Table 6.2, which is a special table known as a *pay-off matrix*.

Table 6.2 **Pay-off matrix for the Prisoners' Dilemma**

		Bob's strategies	
		Confess	*Doesn't confess*
Alf's strategies	*Confess*	(a) Alf gets 10 years Bob gets 10 years	(c) Alf gets 2 years Bob gets 30 years
	Doesn't confess	(b) Alf gets 30 years Bob gets 2 years	(d) Alf gets 5 years Bob gets 5 years

The pay-off matrix shows all the possible outcomes (pay-offs) for each combination of strategies that Alf and Bob could choose. In this case there are four possible combinations:

1 Both confess.

2 Neither confesses.

3 Alf confesses but Bob does not.

4 Bob confesses but Alf does not.

Here, Alf's strategies are read *along* the rows, while Bob's are read *down* the columns. The intersections of rows and columns form *cells* which display the pay-off for that combination of strategies.

By convention, the player with strategies along the rows has their pay-off listed first.

Alf's point of view

If Alf decides to confess, we must read along the top row to work out his pay-offs. If Bob also confesses, the outcome in cell (a) shows us that they both can expect 10 years in prison.

Now move along the top row to cell (c) which shows the pay-off if Alf confesses but Bob remains stubbornly silent. This time Alf gets two years but poor Bob spends the next 30 years in the Tower of London.

> Stop and think   6.5
> What are the pay-offs to Alf if he doesn't confess?

Bob's point of view

Now look at the matrix from Bob's point of view and assume that he also decides to confess. This time we must read down the first column to work out Bob's pay-offs. Once again we come across cell (a) where both players receive 10 years' imprisonment. Moving down the column to cell (b) we see what happens

Taking it further 6.2 continued

when Bob confesses but Alf remains silent. We see that this time it is Bob who receives two years while silent Alf will get the full 30 years' imprisonment – the exact opposite of cell (c) when we were following Alf's pay-offs.

> **Stop and think**   6.6
> What are the pay-offs to Bob if he doesn't confess?

Arguably, the best outcome for their common good is if both don't confess and receive five years (cell (d)). This is the optimal (best possible) solution. Any other combination will either result in 10 years apiece (a) or with at least one of them serving 30 years (cells (b) and (c)).

The prisoners cannot speak to one another so cannot collude; each must make his own decision. Game theory assumes that Alf and Bob are rational human beings whose sole aim in life is to maximise their own rewards (thus to minimise their sentences) regardless of other people. Alf and Bob will also assume that their partner will act equally selfishly.

Links

Cell (d) is often called the **Pareto optimal** solution, since one prisoner cannot be made any better off without making the other prisoner worse off. We consider Pareto optimal solutions further in Chapters 5 and 8.

Looking at the matrix, we can see that remaining silent ('doesn't confess') will result in either five years or thirty years in prison. On the other hand, confessing could bring as little as two years in prison and at worst no more than ten years.

Both realise that for their common good they should both remain silent – but can they trust one another to do so? This is indeed a dilemma. Some questions and answers will help to highlight various aspects of this prisoner's dilemma.

Question   **If Alf and Bob act selfishly, as game theory predicts, what will they do?**

Answer   Alf will confess. He is prepared to let Bob spend 30 years in prison if he can get away with only two. Alf knows he may still receive 10 years if Bob confesses, but that is preferable to the 30 years he could receive if he remains silent and Bob confesses. Even if the police hinted that Bob was not talking, Alf will still confess; Alf is rational and prefers two years in prison to the five he would receive if he remained silent like his partner.

Bob will also confess – for the same selfish reasons as outlined for Alf. Thus both prisoners confess, the game is 'solved' and equilibrium is reached at (confess, confess). Each player has the same '*dominant strategy*' (see below).

What happens if Alf confesses and Bob does not? Alf serves a mere two years while Bob is in prison for 30 – surely that is not fair? But game theory is not about fairness; game theory assumes that all players act rationally and selfishly – even to the detriment of the common good.

Question   **Would the outcome be any different if Alf and Bob had agreed on a vow of silence before their arrest?**

Answer   Yes, provided they both stuck to their agreement, the outcome would be five years apiece. Collusion is in their mutual interest.

Question   **Supposing Alf and Bob return to their life of crime once they have served their 10 years. They are rearrested and face a similar scenario as before. Will they confess this time?**

Answer   This is known as a *repeated game*, a situation where we would expect players to learn from their previous mistakes. Alf and Bob should realise that silence is the best policy – but can they trust one another?

Game theory can readily be applied to firms in oligopoly situations as they also face uncertainty in terms of the actions and reactions of rivals, just like Alf and Bob. We might usefully review some important terms and definitions widely used in game theory, before turning to some business examples.

Types of game

- *Zero sum*: where any gain by one player must be matched by an equivalent loss by one or more other players. A market share game is zero sum, since only 100% is available to all players.
- *Non-zero sum*: where gains and losses need not cancel out across all players. The *Prisoners' Dilemma* was one example (the four cells in the matrix did not have the same net value) and a *profits game* is another.

Types of decision rule

- Maxi-min: where the best of the worst-possible outcomes from any strategy is selected.
- Mini-max: where the worst of the best-possible outcomes from any strategy is selected.

Dominant strategy

The term 'dominant strategy' is sometimes used in game theory. It is often used where a firm is able to identify *one* policy option as being best for it, regardless of the reactions of any rivals. In Table 6.2 Alf has 'confess' as his dominant strategy, since whatever Bob's reaction, he gets less time in prison (10 years or 2 years) than if he doesn't confess (30 years or 5 years). The same is true for Bob.

Nash equilibrium

The Nash equilibrium is said to occur where each firm is doing the best that it can in terms of its own objectives, taking into account the strategies chosen by the other firms in the market.

We can illustrate the application of game theory to business situations taking a zero-sum (market share) game involving two firms (duopoly). By its very nature, a market share game must be 'zero sum', in that any gain by one 'player' must be offset exactly by the loss of the other(s).

Example

Duopoly (two firm) market share game

Suppose Firm A is considering choosing one of two possible policies in order to raise its market share, a 20% price cut or a 10% increase in advertising expenditure. Whatever initial policy Firm A adopts, it anticipates that its rival, Firm B, will react by using either a price cut or extra advertising to defend its market share.

Firm A now evaluates the market share it can expect for each initial policy decision and each possible reaction by B. The outcomes expected by A are summarised in the pay-off matrix of Table 6.3.

Table 6.3 **Firm A's pay-off matrix**

		Firm B's strategies	
		Price cut	*Extra advertising*
Firm A's strategies	*Price cut*	60*#	70#
	Extra advertising	50*	55

*'Worst' outcome for A of each A strategy
#'Worst' outcome for B of each B strategy

If A cuts price, and B responds with a price cut, A receives 60% of the market. However, if B responds with extra advertising, A receives 70% of the market. The 'worst' outcome for A (60% of the market) will occur if B responds with a price cut.

If A uses extra advertising, then the 'worst' outcome for A (50% of the market) will again occur if B responds with a price cut.

We will assume that both players adopt a *maxi-min* decision rule, always selecting that policy which results in the best of the worst possible outcomes.

Firm A will select the price-cut policy since this gives it 60% market share rather than 50%, i.e. the best of these 'worst possible' outcomes.

If Firm B adopts the same *maxi-min* decision rule as A, and has made the same evaluation of outcomes as A, it also will adopt a price-cut strategy. For instance, if B adopts a price-cut policy, its 'worst' outcome would occur if A responds with a price cut – B then gets 40% of the market (100% minus 60%), rather than 50% if A responds with extra advertising. If B adopts extra advertising, its 'worst' outcome would again occur if A responds with a price cut – B then receives 30% rather than 45%.

The best of the 'worst possible' outcomes for B occurs if B adopts a price cut, which gives it 40% of the market rather than 30%.

In this particular game we have a **stable equilibrium**, without any resort to collusion. Both firms initially cut price, then accept the respective market shares which fulfil their maxi-min targets, i.e. 60% to A, 40% to B.

The problem with game theory is that it can equally predict unstable solutions. An unstable solution might follow if each firm, faced with the pay-off matrix of Table 6.3, adopts an entirely different decision rule. Firm B might not use the maxi-min approach of A, but a *mini-max* approach, choosing the worst of the 'best possible' outcomes.

A mini-max approach is arguably a more optimistic but riskier approach to the game. You assume your rival does not react in the worst way possible to each decision you make, but in the best way for you. You then introduce a note of caution by selecting the 'worst' of these 'best possible' outcomes.

Stop and think   6.7

What would happen in Table 6.3 if A adopts a maxi-min decision rule and B a mini-max decision rule?

An unstable solution might also follow if each firm evaluates the pay-off matrix differently from the other. Even if they then adopt the same approach to the game, one firm at least will be 'disappointed', possibly provoking action and counteraction.

If we could tell before the event which oligopoly situations would be stable, and which unstable, then the many possible outcomes of game theory would be considerably narrowed. At present this is beyond the state of the art. However, game theory has been useful in making more explicit the interdependence of oligopoly situations.

We can equally apply our terms and definitions to a *non-zero sum* game, namely a profits game. This is done in *Taking it further* 6.3.

Taking it further Profit game   6.3

Alpha and Beta are two rival firms and each must choose whether to charge relatively high or relatively low prices for their products. Market research suggests the pay-off matrix (profits) shown in Table 6.4. For simplicity we assume that both firms evaluate the pay-off matrix as shown in this table.

Table 6.4 **Pay-off matrix showing profits in £millions for Alpha and Beta**

		Beta's strategies	
		Low price	*High price*
Alpha's strategies	*Low price*	(a) Alpha 200 Beta 200	(c) Alpha 40 Beta 260
	High price	(b) Alpha 260 Beta 140	(d) Alpha 100 Beta 100

Pay-off matrices invariably have some outcomes that are worse than others. The maxi-min decision rule is to adopt the policy option that gives the 'best of the worst' of these outcomes.

- *Alpha's maxi-min approach*. Alpha looks at its policies and asks 'what is the worst that can happen?'
  - For Alpha's low price policy, the worst that could happen would be for Beta to charge a high price and reduce Alpha's profits to £40m (cell (c)).
  - For Alpha's high price policy, the worst that could happen would be for Beta to charge a high price, giving Alpha £100m profit (cell (d)).
  - The best of these 'worst possible outcomes' is £100m, thus Alpha's maxi-min strategy would be to charge the higher price.

- *Beta's maxi-min approach*:
  - Beta's low price policy gives £140m (cell (b)) as the worst possible outcome.
  - Beta's high price policy gives £100m (cell (d)) as the worst possible outcome.
  - The best of these 'worst possible outcomes' is £140m, thus Beta's maxi-min policy would be to charge a low price.

Cell (b) would be the outcome from Alpha and Beta both adopting a maxi-min strategy. Alpha will be pleasantly surprised by doing better than expected (£260m compared to £100m) and Beta will do as expected (£140m). This could therefore be a stable (Nash) equilibrium, with neither firm seeking to change its policies.

As we noted earlier, the term 'dominant strategy' is sometimes used in game theory to refer to situations in which a firm is able to identify *one* policy option as being best for it, regardless of the reactions of any rivals. In Table 6.4 Alpha would identify 'high price' as the policy option which corresponds to a 'dominant strategy', since this gives Alpha the highest profit whether or not Beta reacts with low price (£260m > £200m) or high price (£100m > £40m).

Stop and think   6.8

1 Does Beta have a 'dominant strategy'?

2 How might we expect Beta to react if it has identified a high price policy as Alpha's dominant strategy?

Collusive oligopoly

When oligopoly is non-collusive, the firm uses guesswork and calculation to handle the uncertainty of its rivals' reactions. Another way of handling that uncertainty in markets which are interdependent is by some form of *central coordination*; in other words, 'collusion'. The methods that are used to promote collusion may be formal, such as by making explicit agreements of one kind or another between the parties or even 'acting as one' as in a cartel. The methods may also be informal, via tacit understandings or arrangements.

Formal collusion: agreements

Agreements seem to have been made between 'players' in the e-book market which would suggest it would come within the collusive oligopoly category, with a considerable degree of central coordination by (legal) agreements among the parties. The market for e-books is certainly oligopolistic, dominated by a few large publishers and a few large distributors, and clear pricing models/agreements have been made which constrain the price setting behaviour of key participants in the market, both publishers and distributors, as Case Study 6.3 indicates.

Case Study 6.3 — Pricing models for e-book sales

John Grisham, a prolific author of legal thrillers, long refused to allow his books to be sold in electronic form. In a television interview last year, he lamented that e-books and heavy discounting of printed books by big retailers were 'a disaster in the long term' for the publishing industry. But last month Mr Grisham's publisher announced that the author had had a change of heart: henceforth all of his books will be available in virtual form. His timing was impeccable. On 3 April 2010 Apple began to sell the first of its iPad table computers, which are expected to give a big boost to e-book sales.

The iPad's impeding arrival has created commercial intrigue worthy of a Grisham yarn. A group of big publishers, including Macmillan and Harper Collins have been using Apples' interest in e-books to persuade Amazon, which currently dominates sales of digital books, to renegotiate its pricing model. At one point in January an angry Amazon briefly removed many of Macmillan's books from its own virtual shelves before reinstating them after some authors kicked up a fuss.

Like many other parts of the media industry, publishing is being radically reshaped by the growth of the internet. Online retailers are already among the biggest distributors of books. Now e-books threaten to undermine sales of the old-fashioned kind. In response, publishers are trying to shore up their conventional business while preparing for a future in which e-books will represent a much bigger chunk of sales.

Quite how big is the subject of much debate. PricewaterhouseCoopers, a consultancy, reckons e-books will represent about 6% of consumer book sales in North America by 2013, up from 1.5% last year. Carolyn Reidy, the boss of Simon & Schuster, another big publisher, thinks they could account for 25% of the industry's sales in America within three to five years. She may well be right if the iPad and other tablet computers take off, the prices of dedicated e-readers such as Amazon's Kindle keep falling and more consumers start reading books on smart-phones. Mobclix, an advertising outfit, reckons the number of programmes, or apps for books on Apple's iPhone recently surpassed that for games, previously the largest category.

Alert to such shifts, publishers are trying to undo a mess that is largely of their own making. For some time they have operated a 'wholesale' pricing model with Amazon under which the online retailer pays publishers for books and then decides what it charges the public for them. This has enabled it to set the price of many new e-book titles and bestsellers at $9.99, which is often less than it has paid for them. Amazon has kept prices low in order to boost demand for its Kindle, which dominates the e-reader market but faces stiff competition from Sony and others.

Case Study 6.3 *continued*

Publishers fret that this has conditioned consumers to expect lower prices for all kinds of books. And they worry that the downward spiral will further erode their already thin margins – some have had to close imprints and lay off staff in recent years – as well as bring further dismay to struggling bricks-and-mortar booksellers. Unless things change, some in the industry predict that publishers will suffer a similar fate to that of music companies, whose fortune faded when Apple turned the industry upside down by selling individual songs cheaply online.

Ironically, publishers have turned to Apple to help them twist Amazon's arm. Keen to line up lots of titles for new iPad owners, the company has agreed to an 'agency model' under which publishers get to set the price at which their e-books are sold, with Apple taking 30% of the revenue generated. Faced with these deals, Amazon has reportedly agreed similar terms with several big publishers. As a result the price of some popular e-books is expected to rise to $12.99 or $14.99.

Once Apple and Amazon have taken their cut, publishers are likely to make less money on e-books under this new arrangement than under the wholesale one – a price they seem willing to pay in order to limit Amazon's influence and bolster print sales. Yet there are good reasons to doubt whether this and other strategies, such as delaying the release of electronic versions of new books for several months after the print launch, will halt the creeping commoditisation of books.

Apple, for instance, is rumoured to have kept the option of charging much less for popular e-books if they are being heavily discounted elsewhere. Other firms, including the mighty Google, are likely to enter the market soon, which will only increase the competitive pressure.

This is particularly alarming for publishers because digital margins are almost as slender as print ones. True, e-books do not need to be printed and shipped to retailers, but these costs typically represent only a tenth of a printed book's retail price, according to Credit Suisse, an investment bank. Meanwhile, as David Young, the boss of Hachette Book Group, points out, publishers are incurring new costs in the form of investment in systems to store and distribute digital texts, as well as to protect them from piracy.

Source: E-publish or perish, www.economist.com, © The Economist Newspaper Ltd, London (31/03/2010)

Questions

1 What factors are influencing the prices consumers must pay for e-book titles?

2 Why are both publishers and distributors of e-books concerned about the future profitability of this market?

Formal collusion: cartels

Cartels involve establishing and maintaining some kind of organisation which seeks to direct the policy of its members to reach some agreed end. For example, OPEC (Oil Producing and Exporting Countries) seeks to control the output of its member countries in order to keep the oil price above a target level previously agreed.

The operation of a cartel can be illustrated in terms of Figure 6.15.

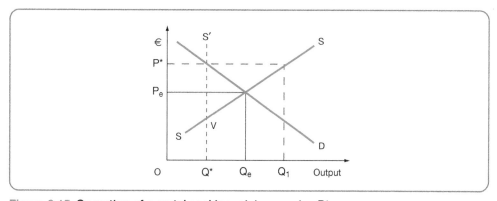

Figure 6.15 Operation of a cartel seeking minimum price P*

If no agreement is reached among suppliers, the suggestion in Figure 6.15 is that an equilibrium price P_e and quantity Q_e will result from the market. However, suppose the producers establish an organisation which seeks to prevent prices falling below P^*. In effect the cartel must prevent output rising above Q^*. It can do this by capping output at Q^*, causing the original supply curve SS to take the shape SVS', in Figure 6.15.

An obvious problem is that at price P^* the producers would (in the absence of the cartel) have supplied quantity Q_1, giving *excess supply* $Q^* - Q_1$. In order to limit the output of members to Q^*, big cartels often allocate quotas, i.e. a maximum production level for each member such that, when aggregated, no more than Q^* is produced in total. Of course, if members cheat and produce more than their quota, overall supply will rise above Q^* and price will fall below P^*.

Cartels are illegal in most countries. The EU in particular spends much time and effort in breaking up cartels and imposing fines amounting to millions of euros on the perpetrators. Fines have been restructured recently so that large firms receive a larger proportion of the fine and there has also been a move towards the US system of plea bargaining. Suggestions that the fine structure becomes more predictable have been rejected on the basis that allowing firms to calculate a cost–benefit ratio is not a sustainable policy of deterrence and zero tolerance.

One might think, therefore, that such illegal activity would be confined to shady businesses operating on the margins of society. Not at all; some of the most spectacular cases have involved high-profile household names.

The record fine to date goes to a four-firm 'lift cartel' led by ThyssenKrupp of Germany which was fined €480m, the largest fine for a single firm in EU history. The total fine for the cartel of four firms was €992m (£666.8m). Between them, the four fixed prices, rigged bids and shared out the market for lifts in four countries. Buildings affected by the market rigging include the EC headquarters and the EU courts in Luxembourg. The EC points out that the damage caused by this cartel will last many years as it not only covered the initial supply of the lifts but also their maintenance.

The governments of most advanced industrialised nations subscribe to the view that formal (or informal) agreements to restrict output are harmful and therefore have passed legislation making cartels illegal. However, certain international cartels have not been prohibited, covering commodities such as oil, tin and coffee and indeed services such as air transport and telecommunications.

> **Links**
>
> For more on the legality of cartels in the UK, see Chapter 8, p. 251.

Informal collusion

Certain forms of informal (tacit) collusion are also illegal in many countries (see Chapter 8, p. 254). However, other forms are legal, including various types of 'price leadership'. In these situations one or more firms become recognised as the main price-setters for the industry and the other firms tend to act as followers.

Three different types of **price leadership** are often identified, namely **dominant**, **barometric** and **collusive**.

1 *Dominant firm price leadership.* This is when the firm widely regarded as dominating the industry or market is acknowledged by others as the price leader. Ford has frequently acted as the dominant price leader in the motor vehicle industry by being first to announce price increases for various models of car.

2 *Barometric price leadership.* In some cases the price leader is a small firm, recognised by others to have a close knowledge of prevailing market conditions. The firm acts as a 'barometer' to others of changing market conditions, and its price changes are closely followed.

3 *Collusive price leadership.* This is a more complicated form of price leadership; essentially it is an informal cartel in which members arrange to introduce price changes almost simultaneously. Such 'parallel' price changes have been noticed in the wholesale petrol market from time to time. In practice it is often difficult to distinguish collusive price leadership from types in which firms follow price leaders very quickly. Collusive price leadership is actually illegal in many countries.

Other oligopoly practices

A number of other practices are widely associated with oligopoly.

Deterrence of new entrants by limit pricing

A major threat to long-run profit is the potential entrance of new firms into the industry. The *'limit price'* can be defined as the highest price which the established firms believe they can charge without inducing new firm entry. Its precise value will depend upon the nature and extent of the 'barriers to entry' for any particular industry. The greater the barriers to entry, the higher the 'limit price' will be.

The principle of 'limit-pricing' can be illustrated from Figure 6.16. Let us make the analysis easier by supposing that each established firm has an identical average total cost (ATC) curve, and sells an identical output, Q_F, at profit-maximising price P* which the established firms have identified as appropriate for the industry. Suppose a new firm, with an identical cost profile, is considering entering the industry, and is capable of selling E units in the first instance. Despite the initial cost disadvantage, the new firm believes it can survive.

One way of preventing the survival of the new firm, perhaps even deterring its entry, would be for the established firms to agree to reduce the industry price to P_L. Although this would reduce their own excess profits in the short run (by VW per unit), the new entrant would make a loss selling E at price P_L, since price would be less than average cost at that output. It would have needed to produce as much as output S immediately at the price P_L, even to have just covered its average costs.

The greater the barriers to the entry of new firms, the higher the 'limit price', P_L, can be, i.e. the closer P_L can be to P*. The most favourable situation for established firms would be if barriers were so great that P_L were at, or above, P*. In other words, established firms could set the joint profit-maximising price without inducing entry.

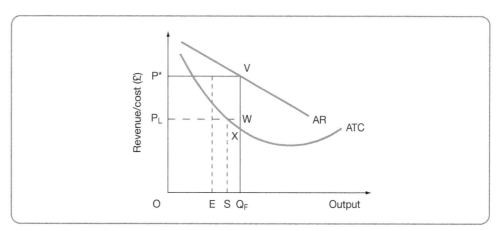

Figure 6.16 **Limit pricing as a barrier to entry**

Price discrimination

Another strategy often associated with oligopoly (though equally available to monopoly) is that of **price discrimination**. So far we have assumed that firms charge only one price for their product. In practice, firms may charge different prices for an identical product – which is what 'price discrimination' refers to. If the product is differentiated in some way, then charging different prices to reflect a different quality of good or different standard of service *is not* price discrimination. For example, price discrimination does not occur when an airline company charges a higher price for a business class seat since the price premium over an economy class seat reflects different quality of service.

Examples of price discrimination might include:

- manufacturers selling an identical product at different prices in different geographical locations (e.g. different regions of a country, different national markets, etc.);
- electricity, gas and rail companies charging higher prices at peak hours than at off-peak hours for the same service;
- cinemas, theatres and transport companies cutting prices for both younger and older customers;
- student discounts for rail travel, restaurant meals and holidays;
- hotels offering cheap weekend breaks and winter discounts.

A key reason for price discrimination is to increase revenue and profit (revenue minus cost) for the firm. Suppose that if, instead of charging the single, uniform price OP in Figure 6.17(a), the firm were to charge what each consumer is *willing to pay*, as indicated by the demand curve.

- It follows that an additional PP_WV of revenue will result. Total revenue would be OP_WVQ as compared to OPVQ with a single, uniform price OP.

> **Make a note**
>
> This type of price discrimination is capturing all the consumer surplus that occurs at price OP and converting it into revenue for the producer.

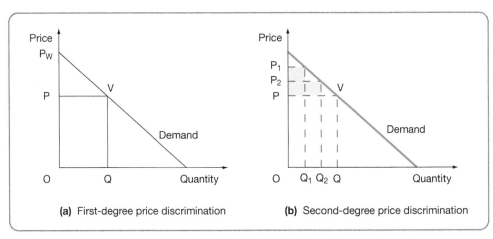

(a) First-degree price discrimination

(b) Second-degree price discrimination

Figure 6.17 **First- and second-degree price discrimination**

This type of price discrimination is sometimes called 'first degree' price discrimination. In fact, three types of price discrimination are often identified in the literature.

- *First-degree price discrimination.* Where, as in Figure 6.17(a), the firm charges a different price to every consumer, reflecting each consumer's willingness to pay.
- *Second-degree price discrimination.* Where different prices are charged for different quantities or 'blocks' of the same product. So, for example, in Figure 6.17(b) the quantity OQ is split into three equal-sized blocks (O–Q_1, Q_1–Q_2, Q_2–Q) and a different price is charged for each block (P_1, P_2, P respectively). The idea is that while consumers cannot, in practice, be identified in terms of individual willingness to pay, different prices might be charged to groups of consumers. Again, total revenue (shaded area) is greater than would have occurred with a single uniform price (OPVQ).
- *Third-degree price discrimination.* Where the market is separated into two or more groups of consumers, with a different price charged to each group. *Taking it further* 6.4 looks in more detail at this type of price discrimination.

Taking it further **Third-degree price discrimination**   *6.4*

For third-degree price discrimination to be undertaken it must be both possible and profitable to segment the market into two or more groups of consumers, with a different price charged to each group.

- *To be possible*, the firm must be able to prevent consumers moving from the higher-priced market segment to the lower-priced market segment. In other words, there must be 'barriers' separating the respective market segments. Such barriers could include geographical distance (domestic/overseas markets), time (peak/off-peak), personal identification (young/old) etc.
- *To be profitable*, the price elasticity of demand must be different in each separate market segment.

Figure 6.18 outlines the situation of third-degree price discrimination.

In Figure 6.18 we assume that the large oligopoly firm produces in one location and sells its output to two separate markets, A and B, with different price elasticities of demand in each market. Market B has a much higher price elasticity of demand than Market A. The corresponding *total market* marginal and average revenue curves are obtained by summing horizontally the *individual market* marginal and average revenue curves.

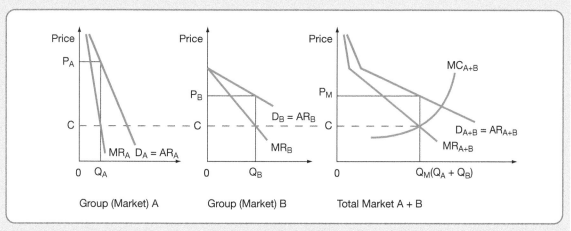

Figure 6.18 **Third-degree price discrimination: charging different prices to different groups of customers**

Taking it further 6.4 continued

With production in a single location there is one MC curve, giving the overall profit-maximising output of Q_M, which might be sold at a single price P_M. However, total profit can, in this situation, be raised by selling this output at a different price to each group (market).

The profit-maximising condition is that MC for whole output must equal MR in each separate market:

$$\text{i.e.} \quad MC_{A+B} = MR_A = MR_B$$

In Figure 6.18 total output Q_M will be allocated so that Q_A goes to group (market) A and Q_B to group (market) B, resulting in the respective prices P_A and P_B.

Any other allocation of total output Q_M must reduce total revenue and therefore, with unchanged costs, reduce total profit.

We can illustrate this by considering a single unit reallocation from market A to market B. The addition to total revenue (MR_B) of this unit when sold in market B is less than C, whereas the loss to total revenue (MR_A) of not selling this unit in market A is C. The overall change in total revenue from this unit reallocation is clearly negative, which, with total costs unchanged, must reduce total profit.

As we can see from Figure 6.18, the implication of third-degree price discrimination is a higher price in the market with lowest price elasticity of demand ($P_A > P_B$).

Case Study 6.4 looks at a particular case of third-degree price discrimination in the UK.

Case Study 6.4 | **Price discrimination in pharmaceuticals**

In April 2001 the Office of Fair Trading (OFT) in the UK imposed a penalty on Napp Pharmaceuticals Holdings Ltd, a Cambridge-based pharmaceutical company, for abuse of its dominant position in the market for a drug called MST, a slow-release morphine product used to treat severe pain in cancer patients. The company controlled 94% of the overall sales of the drug, which was sold to two distinct markets – the community segment and the hospital segment. The community segment involved MST sold to pharmacies who, in turn, supplied them to patients through GP prescriptions, while the hospital segment involved sales of MST direct to hospitals.

The OFT Report commented that GPs were strongly influenced by the reputation of the product and were reluctant to experiment with new products of which they had no direct experience. In addition, for GPs, cost seemed to be 'rarely considered in terminal care pain relief'. On the other hand, hospital doctors were found to be more willing to accept 'intra-molecular substitution' – that is, they were willing to use any brand of a single molecular product to treat their patients. The OFT Report found that the price which Napp charged for its 5 mg tablets of MST to the *community market* was 70% higher than its price to the *hospital market* – where prices were set at below average variable cost (AVC). The OFT found that Napp had engaged in anti-competitive activity and proposed that the company should immediately reduce the price of MST tablets to the community sector. It was estimated that this would save the NHS around £2m annually.

Questions

1 What indicators are there that Napp had monopoly power in the market for MST?

2 Identify the factors which would ensure that Napp could apply price discrimination policies in this market.

3 How was Napp keeping other rivals out of the market?

You try 6.3 looks at various aspects of oligopoly markets.

You try   6.3

1   Try to match the *lettered* term with the correct *numbered* description.

Terms

(a) Zero-sum game

(b) Kinked demand theory

(c) Maxi-min decision rule

(d) Mini-max decision rule

(e) Cartel

(f) Barometric leadership

(g) Parallel pricing.

Description

(i)   Where the industry strategy is set by a small firm recognised as having good market intelligence.

(ii)   Selecting the best of the worst possible outcomes.

(iii) Where any gain for one firm is offset by an equivalent loss for some other firm (or firms).

(iv)   A central body responsible for setting the industry price or output.

(v)   Selecting the worst of the best possible outcomes.

(vi)   Where any change in price by one firm is simultaneously matched by other firms.

(vii) Where rivals match the firm's price cuts but do not match the firm's price rises.

2   Which one of the following is *not* a characteristic of an oligopolistic market?

(a) Prices can become 'sticky' or rigid.

(b) There are a few sellers of a good or service.

(c) Entry is relatively easy.

(d) Firms consider the possible reactions of rivals.

(e) Firms are often drawn into game-playing situations.

3   Which of the following statements does *not* refer to a method of deterring entry into an industry?

(a) Where incumbent firms set a price that is below the average long-run costs of the potential new entrant.

(b) Where incumbent firms advertise extensively in order to make their demand curves more inelastic.

(c) Where incumbent firms agree to decrease prices almost simultaneously in response to the threat of potential new entrants.

(d) Where incumbent firms decide to leave a cartel that had previously sought to maximise joint profits.

(e) Where incumbent firms purchase all known sources of supply of a vital raw material.

4   Which of the following is a feature of a two-firm zero sum game?

(a) A loss for one firm can lead to an equivalent loss for the other firm.

(b) A gain by one firm can lead to a gain for the other firm.

Answers can be found on pp. 525–546.

You try 6.3 continued

(c) If both of the firms select the worst of the best possible outcomes for each initial strategy, they are said to be adopting a maxi-min approach to the game.

(d) In a market share duopoly game, +3% to one firm must be matched in reality by −3% to the other firm.

(e) In a profits game, +£1m to one firm is matched by +£1m to another firm.

Recap

- Concentration ratios for both product and industry groups have risen over time, implying a more oligopolistic market structure.
- 'Recognised interdependence between the few' is a key feature of oligopoly markets.
- Where firms develop their own strategies independently we speak of 'non-collusive behaviour'.
- Even in this case firms will seek to anticipate how their rivals might react to any strategy they might adopt.
- Past experience might be a guide to rival reactions, as in the 'kinked demand' model. Firms learn that rivals match price cuts but not price rises. The model predicts price stability.
- Even where there is little price competition, there may be extensive non-price competition.
- 'Game' simulations may be used to predict the outcomes of different combinations of action/reaction. Games may or may not have stable equilibriums depending on the strategies each firm adopts.
- To avoid uncertainty, collusion may occur, whether formal (cartels) or informal (tacit).
- To be successful firms must abide by the rules of a cartel, e.g. producing no more than their allocated quotas.
- Informal collusion may include various types of price leadership models as well as agreements of various kinds.

Key terms

Barometric-firm leadership Here the price leader is a small firm, recognised by others as having a close knowledge of prevailing market conditions.

Barriers to entry Various deterrents to new firm entry into a market.

Collusive price leadership Where a group of often large firms set similar prices for their products, but where no 'formal collusion' (e.g. cartel) exists.

Contestable markets Markets in which the threat of new firm entry causes incumbents to act as though such potential competition actually existed.

Dominant-price leadership Where the prices set by a single, usually dominant, firm in the market are followed by other smaller firms.

Dominant strategy One in which the respective firms seek to do the best they can in terms of the objectives set, irrespective of the possible actions/reactions of any rival(s).

Limit price The highest price which the established firms believe they can charge without attracting new firm entry.

Long-run Period of time in which all factors of production can be varied.

Maxi-min An approach in game theory whereby the firm selects from the best of the worst possible outcomes identified in a pay-off matrix.

Mini-max An approach in game theory whereby each firm selects the worst of the best possible outcomes identified in a pay-off matrix.

Monopolistic competition A market structure which contains elements of both monopoly and competitive market forms. Differentiated (or non-homogeneous) products give firms an element of market power, but the existence of large numbers of relatively small firms, with freedom of entry/exit, provides an element of competition.

Monopoly Where over 25% of the output of a product is in the hands of a single firm or group of linked firms.

Nash equilibrium Occurs when each firm is doing the best that it can in terms of its own objectives, given the strategies chosen by the other firms in the market.

Natural monopoly Situation where the minimum efficient size of the productive unit or enterprise is so large that the industry can sustain only a single operator.

Normal profit That profit just sufficient to keep the firm in the industry in the long run.

Oligopoly A market dominated by a few large firms and in which their interdependence is recognised by those firms.

Pareto optimal A resource allocation for which it is no longer possible to make anyone better off without making someone else worse off.

Perfect competition A market in which there are a large number of small firms producing an identical product and in which there is freedom of entry and exit.

Perfectly contestable market Situation in which no barriers to entry exist so that incumbent firms are constrained by the threat of new firm entry to keep prices at levels that, in relation to costs, earn only normal profits. Incumbents in perfectly contestable markets earn no super-normal profits, are cost efficient, and cannot cross-subsidise between products or set prices below costs in order to deter new entrants.

Price discrimination Situation in which different prices are charged for identical units of a product.

Price leadership Where firms tend to respond, when setting their own prices, to the prices already set by one or more other firms in the industry.

Pure monopoly A single supplier of the product.

Short-run Period of time in which at least one factor of production is fixed.

Stable equilibrium Situation in which any movement away from an equilibrium initiates changes that move the situation back towards that equilibrium.

Zero-sum game A game in which any gain for one or more players is offset by an equivalent loss for some other players.

Chapter 7

Labour and other factor markets

Introduction

In this chapter we consider how the price and output of the factors of production are determined, paying particular attention to the labour market. We begin by discussing the idea that the return to all factors of production is 'derived' from the demand for the product or service they help produce. Attention then switches exclusively to labour as a factor of production and to those elements influencing the wage rate and the level of employment for various occupations. We go on to review many of the policy issues affecting work in modern societies. These include a wide variety of attempts to impose regulations on working conditions by both national and supra-national (e.g. EU) bodies. The minimum wage, maximum working hours directives and issues involving work–life balance are among those covered in this chapter, together with ageism and gender issues in the labour market. The circumstances in which payments to some factors of production can be regarded as 'surplus' are then considered.

What you'll learn

By the end of this chapter you should be able to:

- explain the idea of 'derived demand' for a factor of production
- account for variations in earnings between different occupations
- examine the impacts on occupational earnings and employment of 'monopoly' and 'monopsony' conditions in imperfectly competitive labour markets
- evaluate the costs and benefits of various types of labour market regulation, including the minimum wage
- assess the implications for the labour market of the EU Social Chapter and various work-related Directives
- discuss issues of gender and age discrimination in labour markets
- identify the circumstances in which the returns to factors of production include an element of surplus payment ('economic rent').

Factor payments and derived demand

We noted in Chapter 3 (p. 73) that a conventional listing of factors of production often includes land, labour and capital, though some might include 'entrepreneurship' as a factor in its own right.

Derived demand

Whatever our list, what is generally true is that factors of production are not demanded for purposes of ownership, as is arguably the case with consumer goods, but rather because of the stream of services they provide. For example, in the case of labour, workers are demanded for their mental and physical contribution to the production process. We therefore say that the demand for a factor of production is a *derived demand* rather than a direct demand. It is derived from the demand for the product, whether a good or a service, which the factor helps to produce.

It may be useful to begin by outlining the *marginal productivity theory* of wages, which is often used to explain the demand for a particular occupation and therefore the wage it can command in the marketplace. As we shall see, this theory makes a number of assumptions which are broadly unrealistic (such as perfectly competitive product and labour markets), which we relax later in the chapter.

Marginal productivity theory

According to this theory, firms will continue to employ labour until the employment of the marginal worker adds as much to revenue as it does to costs. For simplicity, it is sometimes assumed that there is perfect competition in the market in which the product is sold so that firms can sell their entire output at the ruling market price.

We noted in Chapter 3 (p. 76) that the 'law of variable proportions' applies in the short run when at least one factor of production is fixed. This 'law' predicts that when labour is the variable factor being applied to some fixed factor (such as land or capital), the marginal physical product of labour at first rises but subsequently falls as the employment of workers increases, as is shown in Table 7.1.

- Marginal physical product of labour (MPP_L) refers to the additional (physical) output contributed by the last person employed. We can see from Table 7.1 that MPP_L begins to fall after the sixth worker has been employed. However, employers are less concerned with marginal physical product than with marginal revenue product.

- Marginal revenue product of labour (MRP_L) is the addition to total revenue contributed by the last person employed. In a perfectly competitive product market, MRP_L is found by multiplying the MPP_L by the price of the product; in Table 7.1 the MRP_L is calculated assuming a constant product price of £5 per unit.

$$MRP_L = MPP_L \times \text{product price}$$

Under marginal productivity theory the profit-maximising firm will continue to employ workers until the last person employed adds exactly the same value to revenue as he or she adds to costs, i.e. until MRP_L from employment = MC_L of employment.

$$MRP_L = MC_L \text{ for profit maximisation}$$

For illustrative purposes, as well as assuming a constant product price of £5, Table 7.1 assumes a constant wage rate per person of £100 so that the employer can hire as many people as he/she wants at £100 per person (i.e. $AC_L = MC_L = £100$). The only cost in Table 7.1 is labour, i.e. variable cost.

Table 7.1 **Returns to labour in the short run**

No. of workers	Total physical product	Marginal physical product (MPP$_L$)	Marginal revenue product (MRP$_L$)	Marginal cost (MC$_L$)	Total revenue product	Total variable cost	Total profit
1	12	12	60	100	60	100	−40
2	26	14	70	100	130	200	−70
3	50	24	120	100	250	300	−50
4	90	40	200	100	450	400	50
5	140	50	250	100	700	500	200
6	200	60	300	100	1,000	600	400
7	254	54	270	100	1,270	700	570
8	304	50	250	100	1,520	800	720
9	340	36	180	100	1,700	900	800
10	358	18	90	100	1,790	1,000	790
11	374	16	80	100	1,870	1,100	770
12	378	4	20	100	1,890	1,200	690

Make a note

In terms of a diagram, at a wage of £100 the supply of labour curve (S$_L$) is perfectly elastic (see Figure 7.1). It follows that £100 = wage = MC$_L$ = AC$_L$. For example, if three people are employed, total cost of labour is £300, average cost of labour is £100. If four people are employed, total cost of labour is £400, average cost of labour is £100 and the marginal cost of labour is £100 (i.e. £400 − £300).

It is clear from Table 7.1 that after the employment of the second person and up to the employment of the ninth person, each worker adds more to revenue than to cost (MRP$_L$ > MC$_L$). After the employment of the ninth worker the situation is reversed and each additional employee adds more to costs than to revenue (MRP$_L$ < MC$_L$). It follows that profit is maximised (at £800) when nine people are employed.

MRP$_L$ as the firm's demand curve for labour

The demand curve for any factor, including labour, is seen as being *derived* from the demand for the product or service it produces. Additional labour will always be required if the revenue gained from selling the output produced by the last person, the marginal revenue product of labour (MRP$_L$), is greater than the extra cost of employing that person, the marginal cost of labour (MC$_L$). In a competitive labour market (see Figure 7.1), the supply of labour (S$_L$) to each firm would be perfectly elastic at the going wage rate (W$_1$), so that the wage rate is itself both the average and the marginal cost of labour.

The profit-maximising firm would then hire people until MRP$_L$ equalled MC$_L$, i.e. L$_1$ persons in Figure 7.1.

- If *more than* L$_1$ people were hired, then the extra revenue from hiring an extra person would be less than the extra cost. Profit will rise by hiring less people.
- If *fewer than* L$_1$ people were hired, then the extra revenue from hiring an extra person would be greater than the extra cost. Profit will rise by hiring more people.

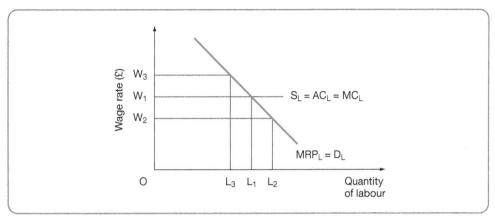

Figure 7.1 **Wage determination in a competitive market**

Example

Productivity lags in the UK

The marginal physical productivity of labour (MPP_L) is clearly a key element in labour demand. Professor Michael Porter was commissioned by the UK's then Department of Trade and Industry (now part of the Department of Business, Innovation and Skills) to investigate the UK's comparative productivity. The results of his 2003 study (which were still broadly true in 2010) showed that in Germany and France output per hour worked was some 20% higher and in the US 40% higher than in the UK. One of the key reasons, in Porter's view, was the higher capital to labour ratio in these countries; the amount of capital per hour worked being 25% lower in the UK than in the US, 32% less than in France and a remarkable 60% less than in Germany.

Under these conditions the MRP_L curve becomes the demand curve for labour (D_L), since at any given wage rate the profit-maximising firm will employ labour until MRP_L equals that wage rate. For example, if the wage rate falls to W_2 in Figure 7.1 then demand for labour expands to L_2.

Market (industry) demand for labour

If we know the number of workers each *firm* in an industry demands at any given wage rate, then we can derive the overall *market* (industry) demand for labour by adding together the individual firm's demand curves. Because each individual firm's demand for labour will vary inversely with the wage rate, the overall market demand for labour will also vary inversely with the wage rate. In other words, market demand for labour will expand as the wage rate falls (see Figure 7.1).

Of course, the firm and market demand for a *particular occupation* will be different from that for an entirely different occupation. In moving to market demand we are therefore aggregating firm demands for a particular skill level or occupational type, rather than for all skill levels or all occupational types.

Elasticity of demand for labour

As with (price) elasticity of demand for products (Chapter 2, p. 40), so we can define (price) elasticity of demand for factors such as labour.

$$\text{Elasticity of demand for labour} = \frac{\% \text{ change in quantity of labour demanded}}{\% \text{ change in price of labour}}$$

It is clearly useful to know how responsive the demand for labour will be to a change in its price (e.g. wage rate). Clearly the demand for labour will vary *inversely* with the wage rate, with the demand for labour expanding as the wage rate falls. However, as with price elasticity of demand, we usually ignore the sign. The range of numerical possibilities and terminology are in fact the same as in Table 2.1 (p. 40) for price elasticity of demand.

Influences on the elasticity of demand for labour

We can say that the elasticity of demand for labour will depend upon the following:

● *The price elasticity of demand (PED) for the product produced by labour.* If PED for the product is relatively inelastic, then elasticity of demand for labour will tend to be relatively inelastic, with a given percentage rise in the price of labour resulting in a smaller percentage fall in the demand for labour. The reasoning is that employers will be able to pass on the higher wage costs as higher product prices in the knowledge that consumer demand will be little affected.

● *The proportion of the total costs of production accounted for by labour.* Where this is relatively small, then the demand for labour will tend to be relatively inelastic. Even a large percentage rise in the price of labour will have little effect on the price of the product and therefore on the demand for labour.

● *The ease with which other factors of production can be substituted for labour.* Where it is difficult to substitute capital equipment or other factors of production for the now more expensive labour input, then elasticity of demand for labour will tend to be relatively inelastic, with any given percentage rise in the price of labour having little effect on the demand for labour in the production process.

Stop and think   7.1

Outline the situations which will tend to make the demand for labour relatively elastic.

Elasticity of supply of labour

We have seen that the equilibrium price (wage rate) and quantity of labour employed depend on both demand and supply conditions. The supply of labour to any particular industry or occupation will vary *directly* with the wage rate. At higher wage rates more workers make themselves available for employment in this particular industry or occupation and vice versa. At the higher wage, extra workers are attracted to this occupation since they now earn more than in the next best paid alternative employment.

Again it will be useful to know how responsive the supply of labour will be to a change in its price (e.g. wage rate). The (price) elasticity of supply for labour can be expressed as follows:

$$\text{Elasticity of supply for labour} = \frac{\%\text{ change in quantity of labour supplied}}{\%\text{ change in price of labour}}$$

Influences on the elasticity of supply for labour

We can say that the elasticity of supply of labour will depend upon the following:

● *The degree to which labour is mobile, both geographically and occupationally.* The less mobile a particular type of labour (e.g. occupation) is between geographical regions and occupations, then the less responsive (less elastic) will be its supply to a change in the wage rate.

• *The time period in question.* The supply of labour to all industries or occupations will tend to be less responsive (less elastic) in the short run than in the long run since it may take time for labour to acquire the new skills and experience required for many occupations. This is especially true where the nature of the work is highly skilled and requires considerable training. In this case the supply of labour to the occupation will not rise substantially, at least initially, as wage rates increase, as for example with doctors and barristers.

You try 7.1 gives you an opportunity to check your understanding of the short-run return to labour and the demand curve for labour.

You try   **7.1**

1 Look back at Table 7.1 (p. 204).

   (a) Use this table to identify and draw the *demand curve for labour* when there is perfect competition in both factor and product markets.

   (b) Use your demand curve to identify how many people would be employed at a wage rate of:

      (i) £250

      (ii) £80.

      Explain your reasoning.

   (c) Under what conditions might this demand curve for labour become *more elastic*?

   (d) Suppose the price of the product produced by labour now rises from £5 per unit to £8 per unit.

      (i) How would this affect Table 7.1?

      (ii) Would your answers in part (b) of this question remain the same?

Answers can be found on pp. 525–546.

Occupational differences in wages and employment

We now seek to apply what we have learned to the key question of why some occupations achieve higher levels of earnings and higher rates of employment than others. That differences in occupational earnings exist and are actually widening is evident from recent data.

Example

Widening gap between high earners and others

Researchers at *Incomes Data Services* reported in 2010 that pay rises for higher-earning occupations have outstripped those for the rest of the workforce. As a result of this 'skew' (to the right) in the occupational earnings distribution, the average (arithmetic mean) wage has been pulled upwards, leaving more and more occupations beneath it. In 2010 some 65% of the workforce earned less than the average weekly wage of £635 before tax, compared to only 60% in 1990.

We first approach this question assuming no imperfections in the labour market before relaxing this assumption and examining the labour market as it really is in practice.

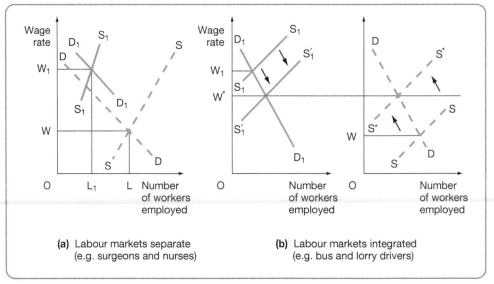

Figure 7.2 **Equilibrium wage rates and levels of employment in two competitive labour markets**

Competitive labour market

In competitive labour markets, wage rates are determined by the forces of supply and demand for labour. In these circumstances, different wage rates between occupations will reflect differences in the respective conditions of supply and demand, as in the two hypothetical labour markets shown in Figure 7.2.

In Figure 7.2(a) the higher wage rate (W_1) in one of these competitive labour markets is due to the fact that, at any given wage rate, demand for labour is greater (D_1D_1) and supply of labour is lower (S_1S_1) in this, as compared to the other competitive labour market. This wage difference can be maintained over time if the labour markets are separate, i.e. little or no mobility between the two occupations (e.g. surgeons and nurses).

However, if workers can easily move between the two occupations, then any initial wage difference is unlikely to be maintained over time (e.g. bus and lorry drivers).

Stop and think   7.2

● Use Figure 7.2(a) to explain the circumstances under which the wage rate for the occupation described by the DD and SS curves respectively might rise *above* W.

● How might the level of employment be affected at this now higher wage?

● Use Figure 7.2(b) to explain why the initially higher wage (W_1) for bus drivers may not last.

Given a competitive labour market and a particular set of supply and demand conditions for labour, we can now make a number of assertions:

● Only one wage rate is sustainable (i.e. in equilibrium), namely that which equates supply of labour with demand for labour.

● Wages in a particular industry or occupation can only change if there is a change in the conditions of supply or in the conditions of demand, or in both.

Case Study 7.1 looks at the increase in wage inequality in the UK since the early 1990s.

Case Study 7.1 | **Increasing wage inequality**

Two-thirds of the UK workforce in 2010 was earning less than the average wage as a result of soar-away pay deals for executives and directors. Pay researchers at Incomes Data Services (IDS) say that wage inequality is rising, despite the introduction of the minimum wage because top pay is increasing faster than pay for the rest of the workforce.

Since 1990 pay rises for top earners have continued to outstrip those for the rest of the workforce to such an extent that the average wage has been pulled upwards, leaving more and more employees earning beneath it. Nearly 65% of the workforce now earns less than the full-time average weekly wage in the UK of £635 a week before tax. Ten years ago, some 60% of workers earned less than the average wage.

The UK government introduced the minimum wage in April 1999, but the IDS researchers noted that while this put a floor under poverty pay and stopped the lowest 10% of workers from falling further behind the rest of the workforce, it has had little impact on wage inequality.

This is because earnings for the top 25% and particularly the top 10% have continued to grow at a much faster pace, outstripping the gains made by those at the bottom. The late 1990s shares boom led to an explosion in the remuneration packages of executives, which continued even when the markets started to fall. Executive pay rose by 18% in 2003 alone, according to a *Guardian* survey, a year when billions were wiped off the value of companies.

Male executives have pocketed the largest pay increases, a factor which contributed in 2002 to the first widening in the gender pay gap for five years.

Questions

1 Can you explain how two-thirds of UK workers can be on less than average pay?

2 What factors have contributed to these findings?

3 What policy implications are suggested for reducing such income inequality?

Of course, in reality the labour market may not be competitive at all.

Example

The Confederation of British Industry (CBI) reported in 2010 that the chief executives of the UK's largest 100 companies now earn 81 times the average pay for full-time workers, compared to 47 times higher in 2000.

We now turn to consider the impacts of different types of 'market failure' in labour markets.

Imperfectly competitive labour markets

We turn first to the presence of monopoly conditions in the supply of labour.

Monopoly in labour markets: trade unions

If the labour force is now unionised, then the *supply* of labour to the firm (or industry) may be regulated. However, even though unions bring an element of **monopoly** into labour supply, theory suggests that they can only influence price or quantity, but not both. For example, in Figure 7.3(a) the union may seek wage rate W_3, but must accept in return lower employment at L_3. Alternatively, unions may seek a level of employment L_2, but must then accept a lower wage rate at W_2. Except (see below) where unions are able

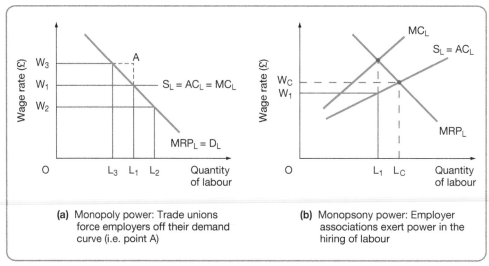

Figure 7.3 Imperfections in the labour market

to force employers off their demand curve for labour (MRP_L), unions can only raise wages at the 'cost' of reduced employment.

A given rise in wages will reduce employment by less, under the following circumstances:

1 the less elastic is final demand for the product;

2 the less easy it is to substitute other factors for the workers in question;

3 the lower the proportion of labour costs to total costs of production.

All of these circumstances, as we have already noted, will make the demand curve for labour, MRP_L, less elastic (i.e. steeper).

Unions and bargaining power

Unions may seek to force employers *off* their demand curve for labour so that they make less than maximum profits. It may then be possible for wages to rise from W_1 to W_3 with no loss of employment, i.e. point A in Figure 7.3(a). How effective unions will be in such strategies will depend upon the extent of their 'bargaining power'. Chamberlain defines union bargaining power as:

$$\text{Union bargaining power} = \frac{\text{Management costs of disagreeing (to union terms)}}{\text{Management costs of agreeing (to union terms)}}$$

Although the ratio cannot be measured, as it relies on subjective assessments, it is a useful analytical tool. If unions are to exert effective influence on management the ratio must exceed unity. That is to say, it must be more costly for management to disagree (e.g. loss of profits or loss of market share as a result of industrial action) than to agree (e.g. higher labour costs and higher employment levels) to the union's terms. The higher the ratio, the more likely it is that management will agree to the union's terms.

Example

Union density and bargaining power

The 'management costs of disagreeing' to union terms are likely to be greater, the higher the proportion of total workers in a union. For the UK as a whole this 'union density' has fallen dramatically in recent times and with it, arguably, the 'bargaining power' of unions. For example, union density in the UK reached a peak of 55% in 1979 but is only around 27% in 2010.

Monopsony in labour markets: employer associations

It may, however, be the case that market power lies not with the 'suppliers' of labour (e.g. the trade unions) but with the 'buyers' of labour. In this case we use the term monopsony to refer to market power in the hands of those who demand labour.

Employer associations are groups of employers who come together to create an element of monopoly on the *demand* side of the labour market (i.e. 'monopsony'). These associations bring together the employers of labour in order to exert greater influence in collective bargaining. Standard theory suggests that monopsony in the labour market will, by itself, reduce both wages and employment in the labour market.

> **Example**
>
> **Employer associations**
>
> Altogether there are about 150 employer associations in the UK which negotiate the national collective agreements for their industry with the trade unions concerned. Most of these belong to the *Confederation of British Industry (CBI)*.

In Figure 7.3(b), under competitive labour market conditions the equilibrium would occur where the supply of labour ($S_L = AC_L$) equalled the demand for labour (MRP_L), giving wage W_C and employment L_C. If monopsony occurs, so that employers bid the wage rate up against themselves, then it can be shown that the MC_L curve will lie *above* the $S_L = AC_L$ curve. For example, if by hiring the fourth worker, the wage (= AC_L) of all three existing workers is bid up from £5 to £6, then the AC_L for the fourth worker is £6 but the MC_L for the fourth worker is higher at £9 (£24 – £15). The profit-maximising employer will want to equate the extra revenue contributed by the last worker employed (MRP_L) to the extra cost of employing the last worker (MC_L). In Figure 7.3(b) this occurs with L_1 workers employed.

Note, however, that the employer only has to offer a wage of W_1 in order to get L_1 workers to supply themselves to the labour market. The wage W_1 is *below* the competitive wage W_C and the level of employment L_1 is *below* the competitive level of employment L_C. This is the standard case against monopsony in a labour market, namely lower wages and lower employment as compared to those in a competitive labour market.

You try 7.2 gives you the chance to review the presence of monopsony and monopoly in the labour market.

Case Study 7.2 looks at the growing tendency to link remuneration to measures of sustainability.

Case Study 7.2	**DSM to link managers' pay with green credentials and staff morale**	**FT**

Two Dutch companies have proposed linking top managers' pay to broad measures of environmental sustainability and worker and customer satisfaction, giving a novel twist to the debate on how to reward executive performance. DSM, the Dutch life sciences group, announced in February 2010 that half the bonuses for its management board will be tied to targets such as the reduction of greenhouse gas emissions and energy use, the introduction of environmentally friendly products and improvements in workforce moral. At the same time TNT, the Dutch mail operator, unveiled similar plans that also included customer satisfaction.

Feike Sijbesma, chief executive, said DSM would focus on 'the triple bottom line: people, profits, planet'. Mr Sijbesma, whose pay was €1.5m (£1.3m) in 2008, told the *Financial Times:* 'Sustainability is the key driver of our whole strategy. Remuneration is one of the ultimate expressions of your values.' The supervisory board at DSM – which makes chemicals, nutritional supplements and plastics and had sales of €9bn last year – consulted widely and is optimistic the proposal will pass at next month's annual meeting.

Case Study 7.2 *continued*

But some investors are sceptical, saying financial performance remained the best yardstick for pay. 'You lose sight of the fact that all these things lead to shareholder value itself. If you use sustainability or employee satisfaction as targets it becomes too easy and too opaque,' said Jan Maarten Slagter, director of the VEB retail shareholders' association.

Half of DSM's short-term bonuses will be determined by the number of environmentally friendly products it introduces each year, whether it reduces energy consumption and how it performs in an employee satisfaction survey. The other half will be based on financial targets such as sales and cashflow. Bonuses will be in shares, with half based on performance and the rest on how much DSM reduces emissions per unit.

Source: from DMS to link managers' pay with green credentials and staff morale, *Financial Times*, 24/02/2010 (Milne, R., and Steen, M), © The Financial Times Ltd

Questions

1 Why are companies making this linkage between sustainability and remuneration?

2 How might the labour market analysis we have considered in this chapter help explain this linkage?

UK labour market regulations

We first consider the introduction of the National Minimum Wage in the UK, before moving to a variety of other important labour market regulations.

The National Minimum Wage

In the UK the Low Pay Commission for the first time recommended the introduction of a National Minimum Wage (NMW) as from October 2000, at that time set at £3.70 per hour for those 21 years and over, with a lower 'development' wage of £3.20 for 18–21 year olds. There has been much controversy over the level at which the NMW should be set. The unions had pushed for a rate considerably above £4.00 per hour in 2000, but the Low Pay Commission eventually recommended a lower rate. By September 2010 the over-21 minimum wage rate had risen to £5.80 per hour, with a new minimum of £3.57 per hour introduced for 16–18-year-olds.

Example

China has a minimum wage in each province and in March 2010 increased the minimum wage in Guangdong, its largest export centre, by 20% in an attempt to attract workers to a province with severe skill shortages.

You try   7.2

1 Look at the following table for a monopsony labour market.

Wage rate (AC_L) (£)	Number of workers supplied (per day)	Total cost of labour (£)	Marginal cost of labour (MC_L) (£)
50	1		
60	2		
70	3		
80	4		
90	5		
100	6		
110	7		
120	8		

You try 7.2 continued

(a) Complete the table.

(b) Draw the labour supply (AC_L) curve.

(c) Draw the marginal cost of labour (MC_L) curve.

(d) What do you notice?

(e) How will your answer to (d) influence the equilibrium level of wages and employment under monopsony? Draw a sketch diagram to illustrate your answer.

2 Assume that a trade union is important in a particular labour market.

(a) Draw a sketch diagram and use it to show how the union might be able to raise wages *without* reducing employment.

(b) What will determine the ability of the union to achieve the outcome in (a)?

Answers can be found on pp. 525–546.

Figure 7.4(a) illustrates the problem of setting too high a minimum wage. If the NMW is set *above* the competitive wage (W_C) for any labour market, then there will be an excess supply of labour of $L'–L^*$, with more people supplying themselves to work in this labour market than there are jobs available. In Figure 7.4(a) the actual level of employment falls from L_C to L^*.

However, there have been a number of studies suggesting that in the USA, a higher minimum wage has actually increased *both* wages and employment, although it has been noted that many of the US studies have involved labour markets (e.g. the fast food sector) which are dominated by a few large employers of labour, i.e. *monopsonistic* labour markets.

In fact our earlier analysis of monopsony might have led us to expect this. For example if, in Figure 7.4(b), the initial monopsony equilibrium was wage W_1 and employment L_1, then setting a minimum wage of W^* would result in a rise in both wages (W_1 to W^*) and employment (L_1 to L^*). It will be helpful to explain this outcome using Figure 7.4(b).

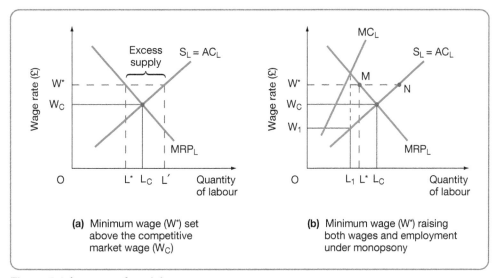

(a) Minimum wage (W^*) set above the competitive market wage (W_C)

(b) Minimum wage (W^*) raising both wages and employment under monopsony

Figure 7.4 **Impacts of a minimum wage**

Since no labour is supplied *below* the minimum wage W*, then W*NS_L becomes the effective labour supply curve. Along the horizontal segment, W*N, we then have $W^* = AC_L = MC_L$ (as in Figure 7.1). The profit-maximising situation is at point 'M' on the MRP_L curve, where the marginal cost of hiring the last person (MC_L) exactly equals the extra revenue resulting from employing that last person (MRP_L). So imposing a minimum wage on a labour market that is already imperfect (here monopsony) can increase both wages and levels of employment.

Example

Minimum wage in China

We noted earlier that in 2010 Guangdong, China's biggest export centre, announced it would raise the provincial minimum wage by over 20%. This reflects the need to attract more workers from elsewhere in China, such as agricultural sectors or non-export production, to unfilled positions in the major export manufacturing plants in Guangdong.

Case Study 7.3 reviews some recent discussions on the implications of the minimum wage for small businesses in the UK.

Case Study 7.3   The National Minimum Wage and business

The National Minimum Wage (NMW) covering minimum wages for employees over the age of 18 was introduced in the UK in April 1999 and in October 2004 the NMW was extended to cover 16- and 17-year-olds. The table below shows the increases in the rates of NMW for three categories of workers between April 1999 and October 2011.

The NMW has been revised upwards at regular intervals during this period, with the adult rate increasing by 64% between 1999 and 2010, and the Youth Development Rate (18–21 years) increasing by 61% over the same period. In 2010 for the first time a minimum wage for apprentices of £2.50 per hour was introduced.

	Aged 16–17	Aged 18–21	Aged 22 and over
April 1999–May 2000	—	£3	£3.60
June 2000–September 2000	—	£3.20	£3.60
October 2000–September 2001	—	£3.20	£3.70
October 2001–September 2002	—	£3.50	£4.10
October 2002–September 2003	—	£3.60	£4.20
October 2003–September 2004	—	£3.80	£4.50
October 2004–September 2005	£3	£4.10	£4.85
October 2005–September 2006	£3	£4.20	£5.05
October 2006–September 2007	£3.30	£4.45	£5.35
October 2007–September 2008	£3.40	£4.60	£5.52
October 2008–September 2009	£3.53	£4.77	£5.73
October 2009–September 2010	£3.57	£4.83	£5.80
October 2010–September 2011	£3.64	£4.92	£5.93

Source: Low Pay Commission (2010) www.lowpay.gov.uk. *Direct Gov. (2010) Newsroom*, March 25. Crown copyright material is reproduced with the permission of the Controller of HMSO and the Queen's Printer for Scotland under the Click-Use Licence

Figure 7.4(a) earlier illustrates the problem of setting too high a minimum wage. If the NMW is set above the competitive wage (W_c) for any labour market, then there will be an excess supply of labour with more people supplying themselves to work in this labour market than there are jobs available.

We have already noted that there have been a number of studies suggesting that in the USA, a higher minimum wage has actually increased wages and employment, although many of the US studies have involved labour markets (e.g. fast food) which are dominated by a few large employers of labour, i.e. monopsonistic labour markets. In fact our earlier analysis of monopsony in Figure 7.4(b) might have led us to expect this.

Despite the fall in the number of workers earning low wage rates in the UK since the NMW was introduced, there are still a significant number of low-paid workers in some sectors of economic activity. For example, the percentage of workers paid less than £5 per hour is higher in sectors such as Hotels and Restaurants (44% below £5 per hour), Wholesale, Retail and Motor Trades (29%), Agriculture, Hunting and Fishing (22%) and the Community, Social and Personal sectors (21%). Similarly, part-time jobs are about five times as likely to be low paid as full-time jobs, while women's jobs are three times as likely to be low paid as men's jobs.

There has been some concern as to the lack of impact of the NMW in the UK, as British law allows escape clauses from paying the minimum wage. In May 2007 Carluccio's, a restaurant chain, was denounced for paying its waiting staff only £3.75 an hour, which was £1.60 below the then minimum wage. Carluccio's actual wages were augmented by tips from customers – a practice that was legal in 2007 and which the company said virtually all other restaurants followed. Carluccio's also says that at least in their case all their tips go to the staff, whereas other restaurants keep some of the customers' tips.

Enforcement of the minimum wage in the UK has also been criticised, with only 100 compliance officers to cover the whole of the UK. In fact, HM Revenue & Customs have only prosecuted one cheating employer since 1999, whereas most EU countries have vigorous work inspectors. The UK chose a 'soft' inspection regime, afraid of employer groups, such as the CBI, criticising the NMW for adding to the already heavy 'regulatory burdens' their members faced. With £5,000 as the maximum penalty, rogue employers are not deterred.

However, in February 2010 the Department for Business Innovation and Skills (BIS) announced the formation of HM Revenue and Customs' (HMRC) New Dynamic Response Team to work on high profile and complicated National Minimum Wage cases. In addition, since October 2009 employers can no longer rely on any form of gratuity to make up the NMW for their workers, even if these are paid through the payroll and since then employers have had to pay arrears to some 14,000 workers.

Questions

1 What factors might be considered when setting the minimum wage?

2 Must a higher minimum wage mean job losses?

3 What criticisms might be made of the UK minimum wage policy?

Other UK labour market regulations

Apart from the National Minimum Wage, a number of other changes have been made in recent years to the regulations governing the UK labour market. These regulations have involved particular aspects of labour market activity.

Closed shop

This is a situation where employees obtain or retain a job only if they become a member of a specified trade union. This practice was progressively weakened by legislation in the 1980s and 1990s making unions liable to legal action from both employees and management if they tried to enforce the closed shop.

Strikes and other industrial action

- *Secondary action*. An important provision in the *Employment Act 1982* restricted 'lawful trade disputes' to those between workers and their own employer, making 'secondary action' unlawful, i.e. action against an employer who is not part of a dispute.

- *Picketing*. This is where striking workers approach non-strikers as they enter their place of work. Picketing is now restricted in law to the union members' 'place of work', often even excluding another plant of the same employer. If illegal picketing occurs, unions are now liable to pay damages in civil actions brought against them by employers.

- *Secret ballots*. Official industrial action, i.e. that approved by the union leadership, must be sanctioned by a secret ballot of the membership. The ballot must be held no more than four weeks before the event, and a majority of union members must be in favour of the action. If the action takes place without majority consent, then the union loses any legal immunity for organising industrial action that it may have enjoyed in the past. These provisions were strengthened by the *Employment Act 1988* which gave the individual union member the right not to be called out on strike without a properly held secret ballot and the right not to be disciplined by his or her union for refusing to strike or for crossing a picket line.

- *Unofficial action*. The *Employment Act 1990* and *Trade Union and Labour Relations Act 1992* took the control of union behaviour even further by requiring that the union leadership must take positive steps to repudiate 'unofficial action', i.e. actions undertaken by union members without union consent (that is, of the executive committee or president or general secretary). For instance, the union must do its best to give written notice to all members participating in the unofficial action that it does not receive the union's support. Failure by the union to take such steps could mean loss of immunity for the union, even though the action is unofficial.

- *Postal ballots*. The *Trade Union Reform and Employment Rights Act 1993* passed two main provisions relating to the organisation of industrial action. First, ballots held in support of action should be fully postal and subject to independent scrutiny, effectively restricting the ability of the 'rank-and-file' to initiate action. Second, unions are to be required to give seven days' written notice before industrial action can be taken. This gives a longer waiting period which may help in settling any dispute.

Example

Unions must be sincere in opposing unofficial strikes

Although trade unions can avoid potential liability for unofficial strikes by making it clear that the union does not support them, union officials must not behave in a manner inconsistent with the union's repudiation. For example, in 1985 the Newspaper Group Express & Star Ltd took on the printers' union, the NGA, in an early test case of the Conservatives' trade union legislation involving a strike by printers. The court held that any repudiation of unofficial action must be 'clear and unambiguous'. In this case it was ruled that the repudiation was a 'sham'. The court ruled that two officials were 'paying lip service to the order but plainly breaking it', and that it was 'inconceivable that they would do this unless encouraged from above'. The union was fined £15,000. Large unions can be fined up to £250,000 for encouraging illegal action, with the smallest unions liable for fines of up to £10,000.

Trade union democracy

The various Trade Union Acts already mentioned have also sought to strengthen trade union democracy:

- The main executive committee of a trade union must now be elected in a secret ballot of the union's members within the previous five years.
- Trade union members have the right to a postal vote in elections for all members of union-governing bodies and for key national leaders.

Recognition of trade unions

The *Employment Relations Act 1999* gives union rights to workers in organisations with at least 21 employees where a trade union has made a request to be recognised as the representative of employees for bargaining purposes. If an employer rejects the request, the union can apply to the Central Arbitration Committee (CAC) which has to decide whether the union has the support of the majority of the workforce that comprises the proposed 'bargaining unit', i.e. the group of employees to be covered by collective bargaining. If 50% or more of the bargaining unit are members of the union applying for recognition, then the CAC may award automatic recognition. If this criterion is not met, then a ballot can be held. In this case recognition will depend on the union receiving a majority of the votes in a ballot in which at least 40% of the workers entitled to vote have done so. The recognition agreement lasts for three years.

Check the net

Many interesting articles on labour issues are included in:

www.peoplemanagement.co.uk

www.tomorrowscompany.com

www.croner.co.uk

Before looking at other work-related issues in the UK, it will help to review EU legislation which itself has a major impact on the UK labour market.

EU Social Chapter

The 'Social Chapter' was the name given to the bringing together in the 1992 *Maastricht Treaty* of many work-related provisions contained in earlier EU treaties. It was made clear in the Maastricht Treaty that these provisions would be further developed by a series of 'Directives' and other EU regulations (see Chapter 11, p. 363). The idea was to provide minimum agreed working conditions for all employees in EU firms, creating a 'level playing field' when those firms compete in the Single European Market. It was expected that these minimum working conditions might then be improved throughout the EU over time.

After initially 'opting out' of the Social Chapter, the new Labour government agreed to join it shortly after its election in 1997, though reserving the right to delay implementation of certain specified Directives.

Main Directives of the Social Chapter

Over 30 Directives have so far been adopted by the EU.

- *Parental Leave Directive.* Women, regardless of length of service, are to have 14 weeks' *maternity leave* during which their jobs will be protected and firms will have to find replacements. Various rights to take time off after the birth or adoption of a child have now been extended to fathers. Prior to this Directive there was a length of service requirement with the employer of two years for full-timers and five years for part-timers. Women with over 26 weeks' service have the right to *maternity pay*.

- *Working Hours Directive*. A maximum of 48 hours is imposed on the working week (with exceptions for hospital doctors and for workers with 'autonomous decision making powers' such as managers). Other requirements include a four-week paid annual holiday, and an eight-hour limitation on shifts.

- *Part-time Workers Directive*. This extends equal rights and pro-rata benefits to part-time staff.

- *European Works Council Directive*. Companies employing over 1,000 workers, with at least 150 in two or more member states, are required to install a *transnational worker council* with information and consultation rights over the introduction of new production processes, mergers and plant closures.

- *Information and Consultation Directive*. In 2002 these rights were extended to any establishments in EU states with at least 50 employees. These now have the right to information and consultation on the performance of the business and on decisions relevant to employment, particularly where jobs are threatened. The Directive was only introduced in the UK in 2008.

- *Young Workers Directive*. There is a ban on work for those under 15. For those who are 17 or under and in education, work must be less than three hours a day: if out of education, the limit is eight hours a day; five weeks' paid holiday is also required and there is a ban on night work.

As far as the Social Chapter of the Maastricht Treaty was concerned, the UK had been opposed to many of the regulations and directives associated with the Social Chapter and secured an opt-out from its provisions. Successive Conservative governments had argued that attempting to impose regulations in such areas as works councils, maternity/paternity rights, equal pay, part-time workers' issues and so on merely increased labour costs and decreased UK competitiveness. Nevertheless, the Labour government in the UK has adopted many parts of the Social Chapter in order to provide basic minimum standards across Europe, even if this does result in some increase in labour costs. In any case, even if the UK had remained outside the Social Chapter it would still have been subject to a great deal of EU social and health and safety legislation introduced as part of other programmes for which there is no UK 'opt-out'.

We have already noted that the Working Hours Directive imposes a 48-hour limit on the number of hours worked per week. However, all Social Chapter Directives seek to set 'minimum' working conditions and individual EU countries can always impose improved working conditions. In the context of weekly hours worked, an 'improvement' would imply a still *lower limit*. France is one EU country which has done just this, imposing a 35 hours per week limit on weekly working.

The UK in 2010 has the longest working hours in the EU, with the 'usual hours worked per week' being 42 hours in the UK, compared to an average of 39.8 hours for the EU as a whole.

The UK is the only EU country to have insisted on an 'opt-out' clause for the *Working Hours Directive* whereby individual workers in any occupation can voluntarily agree to work more than 48 hours. In 2010 the EU reported that over 4 million people, or 16% of the UK workforce, claim to work over the 48-hour limit and expressed concern that many of these 'voluntary' agreements to work longer are in fact the result of pressure by employers.

Flexible working and work–life balance

The *Employment Act 2002* introduced further individual rights for employees, the most significant of which address certain 'family friendly' practices to promote 'work–life balance'. Taking it further 7.1 looks at this issue in more detail.

Taking it further Work–life balance   7.1

The changes which came into effect in the UK in April 2003 are outlined below.

- Parents of children under six have the right to ask employers to let them work flexibly.
- Employers are obliged to take their request seriously. Bosses who fail to pay proper heed to requests could face claims at employment tribunals.
- Employees have to take reasonable account of the business interests of the firm, including the size of the firm, production deadlines and so on.
- The right to ask to work flexibly applies to parents of disabled children up to the age of 18.
- Fathers are entitled to two weeks' paid paternity leave, paid at £100 a week, within eight weeks of the birth or adoption of a child.
- Entitlement to maternity leave is extended up to a year, comprising 26 weeks' paid and 26 weeks' unpaid leave.
- Standard statutory maternity pay is to be increased from £75 to £100 a week, with most firms able to reclaim the cash from the government.
- Parents adopting a child are entitled to go on leave when a child is newly placed with them.

Since April 2003, maternity leave was increased and working fathers have been given the right to two weeks' paternity leave. Employees are also able to request flexible working from their employers, such as job-sharing, flexi-time, home-working and part-time working. Employers have the right to refuse such requests, but must explain their reasons for this to the employee in writing.

Perhaps not surprisingly, there are different perspectives as to who will benefit from these new flexible working opportunities. Case Study 7.4 looks at flexible approaches to working patterns by Daimler, the German car manufacturer.

Case Study 7.4   Daimler turns to temporary staff to boost flexibility   FT

Daimler is seeking greater flexibility in car production by hiring more temporary workers and using external service groups, a move echoed by other German industrialists but which could reignite tensions with the unions.

Bobo Uebber, chief financial officer at the German premium car and truckmaker, told the *Financial Times* in March 2010 that the credit crisis had persuaded the group of the need for greater staffing flexibility. He said: 'Our European truck business has been very flexible during the crisis, while at the car business we did not have this [flexibility] as much. In the future we will have to work on that.' Mr Uebber said Daimler could achieve this with increased use of temporary workers and external service companies and through a more cautious hiring policy for permanent staff.

Mr Uebber's words highlighted how the plunge in industrial demand last year had influenced export-dependent German industry about how to cope with future demand shocks. Martin Kapp, head of VDW, the German machine tool makers' association, said: 'We will have to take an even closer look at our workforce and our flexibility. 'We will be even more cautious during the next upturn.'

Many German industrial companies released their temporary workers when the crisis started, but these were usually a small proportion of the workforce. Instead, companies from Thyssen-Krupp to Bosch to Daimler have turned to measures such as government-sponsored short-term working schemes. This has helped them to avoid releasing engineers but came at the expense of labour productivity.

In 2009, labour costs per hour shot up by 4.1% on the previous year, according to the German statistical office. Franz Fehrenbach, chief executive of Bosch, the world's largest car parts supplier by revenue, recently warned: 'German industry has lost competitiveness during the crisis and will have to catch up on productivity now. If we don't do anything about this, there will be a rude awakening because we will no longer be competitive.'

But Daimler's drive for more flexibility is set to put its management back on a collision course with its German workforce. A decision this year to move production of its E-Class sedan to the US triggered an uproar that was only resolved after the management agreed to a long-term pledge to secure jobs at its Sindelfinger plant.

Daimler's Mercedes Benz brand has been hit harder than other carmakers by the global economic crisis. Daimler piled up a €2.6bn ($3.6bn) net loss in 2009 as truck sales went into free fall and customers shunned luxury sedans such as the S-Class, Mercedes' market dominating top-class model.

Source: from Daimler turns to temporary staff to boost flexibility, *Financial Times*, 15/03/2010 (Schafer, D.), © The Financial Times Ltd

Questions

1 Why are trade unions concerned about more flexible approaches by employers to working patterns?

2 Consider the reasons for Daimler adopting more flexible working arrangements.

Gender and ageism

It will be useful at this stage to review two other issues often raised in labour market discussions, namely gender and ageism issues.

Gender issues

In the UK in 2010, the gap between the *hourly pay* of men and women narrowed to its smallest yet, with women's hourly pay at 83% of that for men. However, the gender gap for *annual earnings* was wider, with the average annual salary of women in 2010 around 73% of that for men.

> **Stop and think**   7.3
>
> Can you think of reasons why the gender gap in favour of men is greater for annual earnings than for hourly earnings?

That such a gender gap still exists would disappoint those who framed two key Acts of Parliament seeking to reduce gender inequalities in the UK.

- *Equal Pay Act* (1970): women performing similar tasks to men, or performing work of equal value to that of men, must be treated equally to men.
- *Sex Discrimination Act* (1975): men and women should have equal opportunities.

Possible reasons for lower female earnings

Of course, for any particular task, to the extent that men/women present *different characteristics* to the labour market, some of the observed pay differential might be justified, i.e. not be 'discrimination' as such.

1 *Less continuous employment* is more likely to be the experience of women than men, given child-bearing and rearing responsibilities. For example, some 28% of women graduates leave the labour force for family reasons within five years of joining it.

- Continuous employment is associated with an earnings premium of around 3% per year for both men and women in the UK.
- Continuous employment implies being more up to date with changing technologies and work practices, thereby raising marginal productivity.
- Continuous employment implies greater opportunities to receive in-firm education and training, acquiring skills which raise marginal productivity.

2 *Less geographical mobility* for women when partners'/husbands' jobs take priority. Where this is the case, an oversupply of women in a given geographical location may depress female wages.

3 *Less unionisation of women workers*, especially for the higher proportion of part-time employment, reduces female bargaining power. Statistically, union membership is associated with an hourly wage some 7% higher than for non-unionised labour.

4 *Less unsocial working hours* for women than men, with such unsocial hours receiving, on average, an extra 11% in earnings per hour in the UK.

Where these different labour market characteristics are presented by women, then it might be argued that at least some of the gender pay gap actually observed may be 'justified' rather than 'discriminatory'.

Other gender inequalities

Check the net

The Equality and Human Rights Commission is found at
www.equalityhumanrights.com

A major study (Jones and Dickerson, 2007) indicates that the so-called 'glass ceiling' for women is still with us in the UK, despite more females working than ever before. Table 7.2 presents some of the findings from this study, which examined the gender representation in the top ten jobs identified for various occupations.

Table 7.2 **Gender shares in the top ten jobs**

Occupation	Male %	Female %
Directors and chief executives of major organisations	90	10
Aircraft pilots and flight engineers	96	4
Dental practitioners	64	36
Police officers (inspectors and above)	94	6
Medical practitioners	61	39
Senior officials in national government	70	30
Financial managers and chartered secretaries	65	35
Ophthalmic opticians	51	49
IT strategy and planning professionals	86	14
Information and communication technology managers	83	17
Top 10 jobs	75	25

Source: Adapted from Jones, P. and Dickerson, A. (2007) 'Poor returns, winners and losers in the job market', *Equal Opportunities Commission, Working Paper Series*, No. 52. Reprinted with permission

Chapter 7 Labour and other factor markets

Chapter 7 Labour and other factor markets

> ### Stop and think　　　　　　　　　　　　　　　　　　7.4
> What actions might employers take to reduce gender inequalities?

Ageism issues

Until recently, the 'norm' in the UK was for men to work until 65 years and women until 60 years. However, changes in the law now permit women to work until 65 years and only at that age to qualify for the retirement pension and men no longer have to retire compulsorily at 65 years.

Nevertheless, there are still complaints of 'age discrimination' in the workplace. For example, although men can legally work beyond the age of 65 years, they have no legal rights to do so. If employers choose to dismiss workers beyond the official retirement age, then these older workers have less protection in law. Age Concern is committed to providing people over 65 years with exactly the same workplace rights and protection as those under 65 years.

Links

Demographic aspects include an increasing proportion of older people in the economies of most advanced industrialised economies.

Example

> ### No rights for over-65s – but changes are imminent!
> In 2002 John Rutherford, 72, and Samuel Bentley, 75, had won a key case for unfair dismissal by their employers. They had claimed that their dismissal from their jobs in the clothing industry on the grounds of age had been 'discriminatory' since more men than women work beyond 65. However, in October 2003 this earlier judgment in their favour was overturned by the Employment Appeals Tribunal. Nevertheless it was announced in 2010 that from April 2011, employees would have new rights in the UK to work beyond 65 years.

> ### Stop and think　　　　　　　　　　　　　　　　　　7.5
> Why might it be in the interests of employers themselves to provide more incentives for workers over 65 years?

Transfer earnings and economic rent

These ideas apply to any factor of production:

- **Transfer earnings** are defined as the payments that are absolutely necessary to keep a factor of production in its present use.
- **Economic rent** is any extra (surplus) payment to the factor over and above its transfer earnings.

For example, if David Beckham (factor – labour) currently receives £100,000 a week as a footballer but could earn £40,000 a week in his next best paid alternative employment as, say, a celebrity host on television, then we might regard £60,000 per week as *economic rent* and £40,000 per week as *transfer earnings*. If he were to receive less than £40,000 per week as a footballer he might be expected to 'transfer' to his next best paid alternative employment, i.e. celebrity host on television.

Make a note

'Economic rent' is used here to mean a surplus payment to *any* factor over and above its next best paid alternative (transfer earnings). This can be confusing since 'rent' is a word usually applied in everyday use to the return on the factor land or payment on a property let to tenants.

We can use the demand and supply diagrams of Chapter 1 to illustrate these ideas further.

In Figure 7.5(a) SS and DD represent the relevant supply and demand curves for any factor of production. In this market the equilibrium price is P. However, all but the last unit employed would have been prepared to accept a *lower price* than P to offer themselves to this factor market. In fact, the very first unit would have been supplied at a price of approximately equal to S. All units except the last unit supplied therefore receive an amount *in excess* of their supply price or transfer earnings. Because of this, the area PRS is referred to as *economic rent* (surplus) and the area OSRQ is referred to as *transfer earnings*.

Make a note

Transfer earnings refer to the payments necessary to keep the factor in its present use. *Economic rent* is any surplus payments over and above these 'transfer earnings'.

To earn relatively high reward it is necessary to possess those abilities which are in scarce supply and which are demanded by others and for which people are prepared to pay. It is, therefore, both supply and demand that account for the relatively large earnings of pop singers, film stars and some individuals from the sporting and entertainment world. Figure 7.5(b) is used to illustrate this point. Above some relatively low rate of pay, the supply of this individual's services becomes totally inelastic (at N). The actual rate of pay is determined by the intersection of supply and demand at W. Because of the inelastic supply and high level of demand, the bulk of this person's earnings consist of economic rent, equal to WRNS.

It is clear that any factor of production can earn economic rent and that the main determinant of such rent involves both the supply and demand curves for the factor of production.

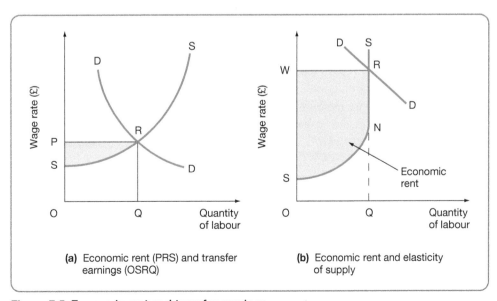

(a) Economic rent (PRS) and transfer earnings (OSRQ)

(b) Economic rent and elasticity of supply

Figure 7.5 **Economic rent and transfer earnings**

Short and long run: quasi rent

Sometimes factors of production earn economic rent in the *short run* which is eliminated in the *long run*. In this case economic rent is referred to as quasi rent.

Should economic rent be taxed?

It is often suggested that economic rent should be taxed. The reasoning behind this is that since economic rent is a surplus rather than a cost of supply, a tax on economic rent will be borne entirely by the factor of production receiving economic rent. This will leave the supply of that factor, and therefore the output it produces, unchanged.

The case for taxing economic rent is therefore a powerful one. However, there are major difficulties with implementing such a tax. In the first place, it is extremely difficult to identify economic rent. If a tax exceeds the value of the surplus, then the supply of the factor of production will be reduced and its price, along with the price of whatever it produces, will be increased. Another problem is that not all economic rent that is earned is true economic rent; it might simply be quasi rent. Quasi rent refers to income that is entirely a surplus in the short run, but part of which is transfer earning in the long run. Taxing this will reduce the long-run supply of the factor of production.

Recap

- Demand for and supply of labour will determine wage rates and levels of employment in competitive labour markets.

- Unions can usually secure higher wages only at the 'cost' of less employment unless their bargaining power is strong. If this is the case, they may be able to force employers off their labour demand curves, securing higher wages with no loss of employment.

- Chamberlain defined union 'bargaining power' as the ratio between the management costs of disagreeing and of agreeing to union terms. The larger the ratio, the greater the union bargaining power.

- A given rise in wages will usually reduce employment by less: (a) the less elastic the demand for the final product, (b) the less easy it is to substitute labour by other factors of production, (c) the lower the proportion of labour costs in total production costs.

- The government has legislated to reduce union power in various ways, e.g. removing the closed shop, imposing conditions on strikes and other union activities, deregulating the setting of wages and other working conditions and promoting trade union democracy. It has also legislated to introduce a national minimum wage.

- Where buyers of labour have market power, we refer to *monopsony* in the labour market. Monopsony can be expected to reduce both wages and employment.

- Governments may intervene in labour markets to prevent 'market failure'. For example, a national minimum wage may be introduced to protect the low paid. Both theory and evidence suggest that a higher minimum wage in monopsony labour markets might raise both wages and employment.

- The EU Social Chapter seeks to create *minimum standards* for working conditions in all member states.

Key terms

Economic rent A surplus payment to a factor of production in the sense of being over and above the minimum price at which that factor would be supplied.

Marginal physical product of labour The additional physical output contributed by the last unit of factor input.

Marginal revenue product of labour The additional value contributed by the last unit of factor input. Often refers to labour as factor input. In a perfectly competitive product market, MRP of labour is found by multiplying the MPP of labour by the price of the product.

Monopoly In the labour market context this usually refers to the presence of trade unions who seek to regulate the supply of labour in one way or another.

Monopsony Occurs when a firm is a significant purchaser of labour. Any additional hiring of labour potentially forces up the price of labour against itself.

Quasi rent That part of the earnings of a factor of production that is economic rent in the short run but transfer earnings in the long run.

Transfer earnings A necessary payment to a factor of production in that it is the minimum payment required for the factor to be supplied.

Union bargaining power The ability of unions to influence the bargaining process. Can be represented by the following ratio:

$$\frac{\text{Management costs of disagreeing (to union terms)}}{\text{Management costs of agreeing (to union terms)}}$$

Union density The proportion of the workforce who are members of a trade union.

Chapter
8

Market failure, regulation and competition

Introduction

Chapter 6 introduced elements of market failure by considering types of market structure other than perfect competition. For example, both monopoly and oligopoly market structures give producers a degree of market power, enabling them to influence price or output (but not both!). We also noted in Chapter 7 various types of market failure in the labour market, affecting both the supply (trade unions) and demand (employer confederations) for labour.

In this chapter we consider a broad range of types of market failure and the impact of these on resource allocation. Policy responses to these various types of market failure are examined, including regulation, deregulation and privatisation. The approach to competition policy in both the UK and EU is reviewed, with particular reference to the control of mergers and acquisitions and various restrictive practices.

What you'll learn

By the end of this chapter you should be able to:

● identify the various types of 'market failure'

● examine the impact of these market failures on resource allocation

● review the arguments for government intervention to 'correct' these market failures and discuss the policy instruments that might be used

● understand the case for and against deregulation and privatisation

● assess the need for and the role of the 'regulators' such as OFGAS, OFWAT and OFTEL

● explain the main features of competition policy in the UK and the EU, particularly in the context of mergers and restrictive practices.

Types of market failure

Strictly speaking, any departure from the conditions necessary for the perfectly competitive *product* markets of Chapter 6 or the perfectly competitive *factor* markets of Chapter 7 can be regarded as 'market failure'. However, four broad types of market failure are often identified, namely externalities, imperfect information, monopoly power and 'public good' types of market failure. Here we consider each of these types and their possible impacts on resource allocation.

Enhancing markets will mean reducing government but . . . we must also have the courage to recognise where markets do not work.

(Gordon Brown, former Prime Minister and former leader of the UK Labour Party)

Externalities

Externalities occur when economic decisions create costs or benefits for people other than the decision taker: these are called the *external costs* or *external benefits* of that decision.

- *External costs.* For example, a firm producing paint may discharge various chemicals into a nearby river, polluting the river, spoiling its use for leisure activities and damaging the health of those coming into contact with it. The true cost to society is then more than the (scarce) resources of labour and capital used up by the firm in producing paint. To these *private costs* of firm production, reflected by wage bills, raw material costs, lease of premises, interest payments etc., we must add any *external costs* that do not appear in the firm's balance sheet but which have resource implications for society, if we are to assess the true *social costs* of production.

$$\text{Marginal social cost} = \text{Marginal private cost} + \text{Marginal external cost}$$
$$\text{MSC} \qquad = \qquad \text{MPC} \qquad + \qquad \text{MEC}$$

- *External benefits.* For example, a firm developing a successful drug to treat motor neurone disease may spend large amounts on research but will only be able to sell the drug to the relatively few people suffering from this severe affliction. The true benefit to society is arguably more than the (small) revenue stream to the firm selling the drug. To these *private revenues* from firm production we must add any *external benefits* that do not appear in the firm's balance sheet (such as the value to society of being able to improve the quality of life of those with the disease) if we are to assess the true *social benefits* of production.

$$\text{Marginal social benefit} = \text{Marginal private benefit} + \text{Marginal external benefit}$$
$$\text{MSB} \qquad = \qquad \text{MPB} \qquad + \qquad \text{MEB}$$

Externalities and resource allocation

It will be useful to consider how the presence of externalities may distort the signals conveyed by prices in a market economy and lead to a misallocation of resources. Here we use an example where marginal social cost is higher than the marginal private cost (MSC > MPC), because of the presence of a marginal external cost (MEC > 0).

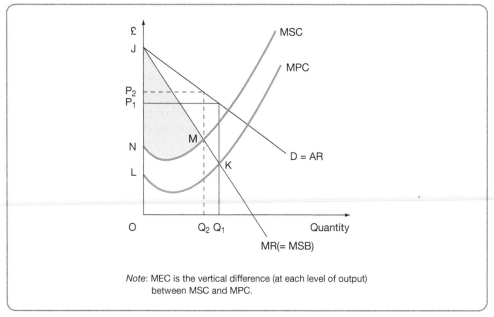

Note: MEC is the vertical difference (at each level of output) between MSC and MPC.

Figure 8.1 With negative externalities (MSC > MPC), the output Q_1 maximising private surplus (profit) differs from the output Q_2 maximising social surplus

Make a note

Although at first sight it may seem a contradiction, when marginal social cost is higher than marginal private cost (MSC > MPC) because of the existence of a *positive marginal external cost* (MEC > 0), we use the term *negative externality*. This is the situation shown in Figure 8.1 where we can see that the marginal social cost of production lies above the marginal private cost.

Negative externalities

We shall see that when negative externalities are present, the firm that seeks to maximise its *private surplus* (profit) will fail to act in the best interests of society. Put another way, when private surplus (profit) is a maximum, *social surplus* is not as high as it could be.

The profit-maximising firm in Figure 8.1 will produce output OQ_1 at price OP_1 since marginal private cost = marginal revenue (marginal private benefit) at this output. Total profit can be regarded as *total private surplus*, and this is a maximum, given by area JKL in the diagram. To produce one extra unit beyond OQ_1 would reduce total private surplus as the extra unit would incur a loss (MPC > MR); to produce one fewer unit than OQ_1 would also reduce this total private surplus, since that unit would have yielded a profit (MR > MPC) had it been produced.

Unfortunately, this output Q_1 which maximises total private surplus (profit) is *not* the output that maximises *total social surplus*. This occurs where the marginal social benefit of production, MSB (here shown as being the same as MR), equals the marginal social cost of production, MSC. This occurs at output OQ_2 with total social surplus a maximum given by area JMN, using the same reasoning as before.

Stop and think   8.1

Explain in your own words why total social surplus is a maximum at output OQ_2.

Clearly, a situation in which output Q_1 and price P_1 result will, if uncorrected, be one in which prices are conveying inappropriate signals to producers. They are leading to profit maximisers producing too much of the product and selling it at too low a price, as compared with the needs of society as a whole.

Example

CO$_2$ emissions and global warming

Excessive emissions of CO$_2$ in the use of energy by businesses and households have been linked directly to climate change, which in turn is imposing major external costs on society. For example, the *World Health Organization* (WHO) has estimated that over one million extra cases of malaria per year could be linked to an increase in global temperatures via CO$_2$ and other greenhouse gas emissions.

Externalities of both a negative (adverse) and even positive (beneficial) type can have major impacts on resource allocation if left uncorrected.

Positive externalities

You should be able to use Figure 8.1 to consider the implications of a *positive externality* (MSC < MPC) on firm output, as for example, when a firm uses its scarce resources to support some type of environmental improvement. If marginal social costs (MSC) were now *below* marginal private costs in the diagram, then the target output for society would need to be raised above OQ$_1$ if social surplus is to be a maximum, and price would need to be reduced below OP$_1$. This time, price signals, if uncorrected, are leading to profit maximisers producing too little of the product and selling it at too high a price, as compared with the needs of society as a whole.

Imperfect information

Firms may have information on their product which is not available to the purchasers. For example, a number of court cases brought by cancer sufferers have shown that cigarette companies knew from their own research about the dangers to health of smoking cigarettes decades ago but concealed this information from the general public. Similarly, recent court cases involving the mis-selling of pensions have shown that the companies involved withheld information from purchasers. Where one party has information not available to another party, this is often called 'information asymmetry'. This can again lead to a misallocation of resources.

Example

Enron deceives employees and investors

Enron, the Houston-based energy company which once dominated the market for trading of natural gas and electric power, filed for bankruptcy in December 2001 after it emerged that the company had long hidden its true financial state, eventually revealed as $67bn of outstanding debt with a $20bn 'black hole' in the accounts. Subsequently, investigations have shown how misleading information given to employees and investors alike had led to major losses for over 20,000 investors and creditors of the company, with shares falling in value by over $60bn once the true information was known.

We can again illustrate the effect of imperfect information using Figure 8.1. For example, smoking has been shown to damage the health of those who smoke (via increased risks of cancer, heart and lung diseases) and of those ('passive smokers') who inhale the air polluted by smokers. In other words, the marginal social cost of the cigarettes produced by a tobacco company is considerably higher than the marginal private costs of producing those cigarettes. We are in the *negative externality* situation of Figure 8.1, with the cigarette companies seeking to profit-maximise (MPC = MR) at output Q_1 but with society preferring output Q_2 (MSC = MSB) where *social surplus* is maximised at JMN.

Monopoly power

Chapter 6 has shown how monopoly power can lead to a higher price and lower output as compared to a perfectly competitive market structure. This is the so-called 'classical case against monopoly' (Chapter 6, p. 177). The same situation can arise under an oligopoly market structure, where a few large firms dominate the market.

Nor is the problem of 'market power' leading to a misallocation of resources confined to product markets! We noted in Chapter 7 that when the trade unions have market power over the supply of labour (monopoly), wages can be higher and employment lower than might have been the case under competitive labour market conditions (Chapter 7, p. 210). Similarly, where the purchasers of labour have market power (monopsony), the wages can be lower and employment lower than under competitive labour market conditions (Chapter 7, p. 210).

Public goods

The term 'public goods' is used to refer to goods (or services) which have particular characteristics of a type which makes it impractical for private markets to provide them. It follows that if they are to be provided, only the 'public' sector will be able to fund them out of general tax revenues, hence the name 'public good'.

Pure public goods

Two particular characteristics must be present for what is called a 'pure' public good.

● *Non-excludable*. This refers to the difficulty of excluding those who do not wish to pay for the good (or service). For example, how could you charge individuals a price for police or army protection? If you tried to use a national referendum, only charging those who say 'yes' in the referendum to wanting a police or defence force, you will encounter the so-called 'free rider' problem. This refers to people who, while they do want this protection, may vote 'no' hoping that sufficient others vote 'yes' for them still to have the protection but not have to pay for it themselves. The non-excludable condition prevents a free market developing since it is difficult to make 'free riders' actually pay for the public good, which means that it can only be provided by the 'public' sector out of tax revenue.

● *Non-exhaustible*. This refers to the fact that the marginal cost of providing the 'pure' public good is essentially zero. To protect an extra person in the country using the police or army effectively costs nothing. If marginal cost is zero, then the price set under perfect competition (see Chapter 6, p. 170) should also be zero. But private markets guided by the profit motive are hardly in the business of charging zero prices! The non-exhaustible condition implies that any price that is charged should, for 'allocative efficiency' (see also Chapter 6, p. 171), equal marginal cost and therefore be zero, which means that it can only be provided by the 'public' sector out of tax revenue.

Both conditions imply that when the market failure involves a 'pure public good', then it is best supplied by the public sector at zero price, using general tax revenue to fund provision.

Mixed (quasi) public goods

Mixed (quasi) public goods are a broader category of products (goods or services) that have elements of the characteristics of public goods, while not fully meeting the criteria for a 'pure' public good. For example, many products may be *non-exhaustible* in the sense that (at least up to the congestion point) extra people can consume that product without detracting from existing consumers' ability to benefit from it: e.g. use of a motorway, a bridge or a scenic view. However, the *non-excludable* condition may not apply, since it may be possible to exclude consumers from that product: e.g. tolls on motorways and bridges, or fencing (with admission charges) around scenic views. So a private market could be established for such a *mixed* or *quasi public good*, with a non-zero price charged.

Correcting 'market failures'

Here we consider the various policy instruments that can be used by governments to correct the four types of 'market failure' we have identified. Such corrective policies can include a number of different policy instruments.

Government intervention to correct various 'market failures' can take many different forms. It can involve the application of maximum or minimum prices, the imposition of various types of standards, taxes, quotas, procedures, directives etc., whether issued by national bodies (e.g. the UK government or its agencies) or international bodies (e.g. the EU Commission, the World Trade Organization etc.)

Correcting an externality

It may be useful to illustrate the ways in which government intervention can improve resource allocation by first considering how the *negative externality* situation might be approached.

Correcting a negative externality

Again we can illustrate the situation using Figure 8.1 (p. 228). It shows that with the firm producing a *negative externality* (MSC > MPC) society's best interests are served with an output of OQ_2 (where MSC = MSB) which maximises *social surplus* at JMN. However, the profit-maximising firm is given inappropriate 'signals' in the market, so that it seeks an output of OQ_1 (where MPC = MR) which maximises its own *private surplus* at JKL. Sometimes those who impose external costs in this way can be controlled by regulation (e.g. pollution controls such as Clean Air Acts with fines for breaches of minimum standards) or can be given incentives to reduce pollution through the tax mechanism.

● *Regulations.* The government could impose a regulation setting a *maximum level of output* of OQ_2, so that the firm is prevented from producing the extra Q_2–Q_1 output which would have raised profit still further.

● *Taxes.* The government can set a tax on the product to make the firm pay for the external cost it imposes on society. The 'ideal' tax would be one which exactly captures the marginal external cost at each level of output. This would now make the firm pay for its own internal costs *and* for the external costs it imposes. In other words, the tax policy is 'internalising the externality' so that the (previous) externality now shows up as a private cost on the firm's own balance sheet. In terms of Figure 8.1 the new MPC curve after this 'ideal' tax will be the same as the MSC curve. It follows that the profit-maximising firm will itself now want to produce output Q_2 at which the new MPC (=MSC) exactly equals MR, with both private surplus (profit) and social surplus maximised at JMN.

Make a note | This 'ideal' tax which is exactly equal to the marginal external cost is sometimes called a 'Pigouvian tax', after the economist A. C. Pigou who proposed such a tax.

An example of using a type of tax to correct a negative externality is the *London Congestion Charge* introduced in February 2003 and extended in 2007 to cover twice the original geographical area of London. It is considered further in Case Study 8.1.

Case Study 8.1   The London Congestion Charge

A congestion charge of £10 must be paid by drivers in the sixteen square mile zone in inner London. The London charging zone was first established in 2003 covering eight square miles with a £5 charge per day, rising to £8 in 2007 for an area doubled in size to 16 square miles. The current £10 charge operates from 7.00 am to 6.30 pm, Mondays to Fridays, excluding public holidays, and must be paid in advance (at selected retail outlets or by Internet or by SMS text) or by 10.00 pm on the day a vehicle entered the zone. A £120 penalty charge is imposed on those who fail to pay and have been identified by cameras recording their vehicle registration plates. This fine is reduced to £60 if paid within 14 days, but increased to £180 if unpaid after 28 days. Discounts of up to 90% are available for residents and other designated individuals (e.g. blue badge holders). Any monies received by 'Transport for London' from the charge must, by law, be spent on transport.

Twelve months after the introduction of the London Congestion Charge, some interesting results were noted:

- cars in the charging zone – down by 30%;
- journey times in the charging zone – 10–15% faster;
- bus journeys in the zone – up by 15%;
- taxi journeys in the zone – up by 20%;
- cycles entering the zone – up by 30%;
- 108,000 congestion charge payments – made each day.

Supporters of the scheme also point to less air pollution as being a further benefit of the scheme.

Although widely acclaimed, some criticisms have been made of the London Congestion Charge. The company, Capita, running the scheme had admitted that limited resources result in it identifying and sending penalty notices to only 83% of those failing to pay the fee – with the remaining 17% (around 1,650 drivers daily) not pursued. Around 25% of London traders responding to a Mori poll blamed the congestion charge for a decline in business, though some 58% regarded it as broadly positive and to be welcomed.

Nor is there much evidence to suggest that traffic congestion has increased in the areas bordering the charging zone, as critics argued would be the case. The RAC Foundation concluded that congestion outside the zone has also been reduced because fewer people are driving towards the centre of the capital. However, all is not perfect – the RAC Foundation noted that traffic is still averaging only 7.4 mph at peak hours inside the zone.

With the doubling in size of the congestion charge zone in 2007, some 60,000 residents living in the extension area now qualify for the 90% discount. Many are expected to switch back to using cars, increasing congestion in the central area by 4 to 5%.

Questions

1 The Mayor of London claimed that the London Congestion Charge has caused a change in travel habits in favour of public transport. What evidence is there to support this claim and what consequences might follow from it?

2 Why do you think London businesses claim to be broadly supportive of the scheme?

3 How might the current London congestion charge be modified if it is to move more closely towards a Pigouvian tax which charges individual drivers according to the negative externalities they themselves impose?

Currently one of the main debates involving negative externalities involves the issue of greenhouse gas emissions (such as carbon dioxide, CO_2) and the impacts of such emissions on global warming. Case Study 8.2 provides a summary of this most influential report and the policy interventions it proposes to curb the negative externality of CO_2 emissions.

Case Study 8.2   Stern Report on climate change

The Stern Report on climate change was published in late 2006, and is widely regarded as the most authoritative of its kind.

Key findings include the following.

- CO_2 in the atmosphere in about 1780, i.e. just before the Industrial Revolution, has been estimated at around 280 ppm (parts per million).
- CO_2 in 2006, however, had risen significantly to 382 ppm.
- Greenhouse gases (CO_2, methane, nitrous oxide etc.) in 2006, were even higher at 430 ppm in CO_2 equivalents.

Two key scenarios were identified in the Stern Report:

Do nothing scenario

- Temperature rise of 2 °C by 2050.
- Temperature rise of 5 °C or more by 2100.
- The damage to the global economy of such climate change from the 'do nothing' scenario is an estimated reduction in global GDP per head (i.e. income per head) of between 5% and 20% over the next two centuries. This occurs via rising temperatures, droughts, floods, water shortages and extreme weather events.

Intervene scenario

- The Stern Report advocates measures to stabilise greenhouse gas emissions at 550 ppm CO_2 equivalents by 2050.

- This requires global emissions of CO_2 to peak in the next 10 to 20 years, then fall at a rate of at least 1% to 3% per year.
- By 2050 global emissions of CO_2 must be around 25% below current levels.
- Since global GDP is expected to be around three times as high as today in 2050, the CO_2 emissions *per unit* of global GDP must be less than one-third of today's level (and sufficiently less to give the 25% reduction on today's levels).
- The Stern Report estimated the cost of stabilisation at 550 ppm CO_2 equivalents to be around 1% of current global GDP (i.e. around £200bn). This expenditure will be required *every year*, rising to £600bn per annum in 2050 if global GDP is three times higher than it is today.
- Stabilisation would limit temperature rises by 2050 to 2 °C, but not prevent them. Otherwise temperature rises well in excess of 2 °C are predicted – possibly as much as 5 °C by 2100.
- Even limiting temperature rises to 2 °C by 2050 will inflict substantial damages, especially in terms of flooding low-lying countries as the ice caps melt, but also via more extreme weather conditions in various parts of the world.

Questions

1 Why did the Stern Report not seek still tighter limits on the growth of CO_2 in the atmosphere?

2 What mechanisms might be used to achieve the stabilisation path proposed in the Stern Report?

Taking it further 8.1 examines the use of tradeable permits, seen by many as a key mechanism for restricting the impacts of pollution (i.e. restricting negative externalities).

Taking it further Tradeable permits   8.1

Another market-based solution to environmental problems could involve tradeable permits, and this mechanism is becoming widely used by governments, firms and individuals in attempting to reduce pollution. Here the polluter receives a permit to emit a specified amount of waste, whether carbon dioxide, sulphur dioxide or another pollutant. The total amount of pollutant allowed by permits issued must, of course, be within the currently accepted guidelines of 'safe' levels of emission for that

Taking it further 8.1 *continued*

pollutant. Within the overall limit of the permits issued, individual polluters can then buy and sell the permits between themselves. The distribution of pollution is then market directed even though the overall total is regulated, the expectation being that those firms which are already able to meet 'clean' standards will benefit by selling permits to those firms which currently find it too difficult or expensive to meet those standards.

Figure 8.2 provides an outline of how the tradeable permits system works. With this policy option the polluter is issued with a number of permits to emit a specified amount of pollution. The total number of permits in existence (Q_s) places a limit on the total amount of emissions allowed. Polluters can buy and sell the permits to each other, at a price agreed between the two polluters. In other words the permits are *transferable*.

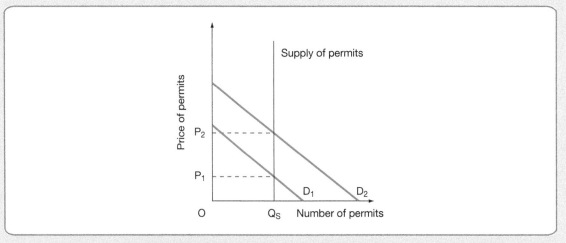

Figure 8.2 Determining the market price for permits
Source: A. Griffiths and S. Wall (eds) (2007) *Applied Economics*, 11th edn, Financial Times/Prentice Hall, p. 178.

The underlying principle of tradeable permits is that those firms which can achieve a lower level of pollution can benefit by selling permits to those firms which at present find it either too difficult or too expensive to meet the standard set. The market for permits can be illustrated by use of Figure 8.2. In order to achieve an optimum level of pollution, the agency responsible for permits may issue Q_s permits. With demand for permits at D_1 the price will be set at P_1. If new polluters enter the market the demand for permits will increase, e.g. to D_2 and the equilibrium permit price will rise to P_2.

If, for any reason, the agency wishes to relax the standard set then more permits will be issued and the supply curve for permits will shift to the right. Alternatively, the standard could be tightened, by the agency purchasing permits on the open market from polluters, which would have the effect of shifting the supply curve to the left.

The EU *Emissions Trading Scheme* uses the idea of tradeable permits in seeking to reduce greenhouse gas emissions.

The EU Emissions Trading Scheme

In the EU an Emissions Trading Scheme (ETS) is being seen as a key economic instrument in a move to reduce greenhouse gas emissions. The ETS is intended to help the EU meet its commitments as part of the Kyoto Protocol. The EU took upon itself as part of the Protocol to reduce greenhouse gas emissions by 8% (from 1990 levels) by 2008–2012. The idea behind the ETS is to ensure that those companies within certain sectors that are responsible for greenhouse gas emissions keep within specific limits by either reducing their emissions or buying *allowances* from other organisations with lower emissions. The ETS is essentially aimed at placing a cap on total greenhouse gas emissions.

Correcting a positive externality

On the other hand, firms creating positive externalities (MSB > MPB) may be rewarded by the receipt of *subsidies*. For instance, it can be argued that railways reduce road usage, creating external benefits by relieving urban congestion, pollution and traffic accidents. This is one aspect of the case for subsiding railways so that they can continue to offer some loss-making services.

Stop and think   *8.2*

Draw a diagram and use it to explain how a positive externality might be 'corrected' by a government subsidy.

Of course, the government may wish to intervene to correct market failures other than those involving externalities.

Correcting imperfect information

Regulations may force firms to give more information to consumers or to employees, or to shareholders. For example, regulations on the labelling of ingredients in foodstuffs helps increase consumer information. Other regulations may establish maximum levels for known toxins in various situations (e.g. CO_2 and other air pollutants near airports) or minimum standards to meet health and safety requirements at work (e.g. number and width of fire-exits in a building). Still other regulations require secret ballots before employees can be asked to take industrial action by unions or give rights to shareholders to vote on executive remuneration packages at Annual General Meetings.

Governments can be even more proactive in this area, as for example, in providing job centres to help those without jobs be aware of vacancies or training opportunities. In all these cases the objective is to give more information to the various parties than would otherwise be available, thereby helping reduce any 'information asymmetry' that might exist. The general approach is that better informed decisions are likely to be in both the private and public interest.

> **Links**
>
> If your course includes indifference curves, Appendix 1 (p. 507) uses these to show how imperfect information reduces consumer welfare.

Correcting monopoly power

In Chapter 5 we noted some of the benefits from increased firm size, as with various technical and non-technical economies of scale (Chapter 5, p. 150). However, we also noted the potential for increased size and greater market power in the case of monopoly and oligopoly market structures to be used to raise prices and lower outputs (Chapter 6, p. 177). Governments are well aware of the tensions created by a desire, on the one hand, to support large, efficient firms and on the other to protect consumers and employees from any abuse of such monopoly (or oligopoly) power.

To this end both the UK government and the EU have set certain rules and regulations to establish the institutions and procedures used for investigating proposed mergers and acquisitions, and the conditions under which approval is likely to be given or withheld. We consider such mergers and restrictive practices regulation for the UK and EU later in this chapter (pp. 248–55).

Correcting public and merit good situations

In recognition of the need to provide certain goods and services largely through the public sector, *general taxation* is used in the UK to support the provision of important services such as the police, the defence forces (army, navy, airforce), health and social services, education, transport and so on. Some of these are 'mixed' (quasi) public goods rather than 'pure' public goods, which means that some private market provision may take place alongside the public sector provision.

Taking it further 8.2 looks in more detail at policies involved in correcting situations of 'pure' and 'mixed' public goods.

Taking it further Public goods and policy responses   8.2

Pure public goods

We noted earlier that products which satisfy the two key characteristics of being non-excludable and non-exhaustible are called 'pure' public goods. In this case we should have a situation similar to that shown in Figure 8.3(a), with two consumers for simplicity. Strictly speaking, the marginal social cost (MSC) of providing an extra unit of the pure public good to another consumer is zero. This follows from the non-exhaustive or non-rivalry characteristic: once provided for one person, someone else can also consume that unit at no extra cost and without reducing the first person's ability to consume that same unit. In this case we can regard the MSC curve as zero, coinciding with the horizontal axis.

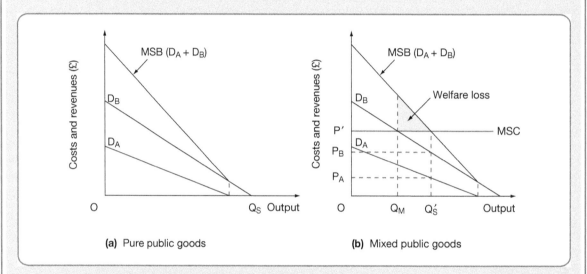

Figure 8.3 'Pure' and 'mixed' public goods and the socially optimum output

The socially optimum solution is where MSB = MSC, i.e. output Q_S in Figure 8.3(a). In this extreme case we can see that the appropriate target is the output level demanded at zero price. Clearly private markets, driven by the profit motive, will have no incentive to be established under these conditions (zero price); hence the suggestion that these are public goods. Only if general tax receipts are used to fund such products will they be provided.

Mixed (quasi) public goods

The suggestion here is that a broader category of products (goods or services) will have elements of these characteristics, while not fully meeting the criteria for a pure public good. For example, many products may be *exhaustible* in the sense that (at least up to the congestion point) extra people can consume that product without detracting from existing consumers' ability to benefit from it: e.g. use of a motorway, a bridge or a scenic view.

However, the *non-excludable* condition may not apply, since it may be possible to exclude consumers from that product: e.g. tolls on motorways and bridges, or fencing (with admission charges) around scenic views. So a market could be established for such a *mixed or quasi public good*, with a non-zero price charged. Moreover, at least beyond the congestion point, the marginal social cost of provision is also non-zero, since extra cars cause existing users to slow down on roads and bridges, and extra people hinder the enjoyment of the scenic view. As a result MSB = MSC above the horizontal axis, implying a non-zero price at P' and target output of Q_S'.

In Figure 8.3(b) the socially optimum output (MSB = MSC) occurs at Q_S' with market price P'. This price might be composed of two parts (where price discrimination is possible in the market) equivalent to the individual valuation of each consumer of output Q_S' namely P_A and P_B. Of course, there is the practical problem of identifying what sum of money each person is really willing to pay for this output. If consumers want the product but understate their true preferences in the hope that they can 'free ride', then this social optimum output Q_S' may not occur. For example, if only consumer B reveals his true preference/willingness to pay market price P' in Figure 8.3(b) (perhaps via response to a question-naire) then the market solution might be output Q_M, with the shaded area corresponding to the welfare loss resulting from the free-rider problem.

This analysis highlights one of the problems with public goods: namely, that everyone has an incentive to rely on their neighbours to provide them, rather than provide them themselves. A shipping company may desire lighthouses to guide its ships, as may other shipping companies. Unfortunately, all may delay investment decisions, hoping that a rival builds the lighthouses, on which they can then 'free ride'. Eventually perhaps one company for whom the lighthouses have most value may relent and begin construction, but the level of provision may be less than optimal. This is because it is only the (vertical) sum of the marginal valuations of all consumers of the good that can help to determine the social optimum solution. If any consumer fails to express their true marginal valuation (i.e. attempts to free ride), then we have the suboptimal type of solution shown at Q_M in Figure 8.3(b).

Merit goods

The term 'merit goods' refers to goods and services which tend to create positive externalities, i.e. benefiting society as well as the firms and individuals providing the good or service. Education is a well-used example of a merit good, since a better educated population not only benefits the *individual* (via higher lifetime earnings) but also *society* as a whole. For example, labour productivity is likely to be higher for better educated workers, raising income levels not only for the worker but for the firm (higher profits) and the government (higher tax revenue from higher employee incomes and higher corporate profits). In addition, a better educated population raises levels of employment, saving the government expenditure on unemployment and other benefits. A better educated workforce is also likely to be a healthier workforce, reducing spending on health and related services.

In all these ways, the positive externalities associated with 'merit goods' argues in favour of their receiving government support (e.g. *subsidies*) to encourage a higher output of these 'merit goods' than might otherwise occur. We are in a situation in which marginal social benefit (MSB) is greater than marginal private benefit (MR) in our earlier Figure 8.1 (p. 228).

Stop and think   8.3

Go back to Figure 8.1 and re-draw the diagram for a merit good (MSB > MR).

Regulation

In seeking to 'correct' market failures we have seen that governments can use a wide variety of policy instruments, one of which is to use *regulations*. These usually involve rules setting minimum standards for products or processes.

Types of regulation

It is very difficult to classify all the different types of regulation or rules that can be imposed on firms by the UK government or by the EU. However, two broad types are often identified:

1 regulations aimed at protecting the consumer from the consequences of market failure;

2 regulations aimed at preventing the market failure from happening in the first place.

We might illustrate these two types using regulations imposed by the EU on business. In terms of the financial sector, the *Deposit Guarantee Directive* of the EU is of the first type. This protects customers of accredited EU banks by restoring at least 90% of any losses up to £12,000 which might result from the failure of a particular bank. In part this is a response to 'asymmetric information', since customers do not have the information to evaluate the credit worthiness of a particular bank, and might not be able to interpret that information even if it were available.

The *Capital Adequacy Directive* of the EU is of the second type. This seeks to prevent market failure (such as a bank collapse) by directly relating the value of the capital a bank must hold to the riskiness of its business. The idea here is that the greater the value of capital available to a bank, the larger the 'buffer stock' it has in place should it need to absorb any losses. Various elements of the Capital Adequacy Directive force the banks to increase their capital base if the riskiness of their portfolio (indicated by various statistical measures) is deemed to have increased. In part this EU regulation is in response to the potential for negative externalities in this sector. One bank failure can invariably lead to a 'domino effect' and risk system collapse, with incalculable consequences for the banking system as a whole.

In these ways the regulatory system for EU financial markets is seeking to provide a framework within which greater competition between banks can occur, while at the same time addressing the fact that greater competition can increase the risks of bank failure. It is seeking both to protect consumers should any mishap occur and at the same time to prevent such a mishap actually occurring.

While regulations are usually imposed to protect consumers or producers from one or more types of 'market failures', businesses often complain about the time they waste filling in forms and complying with a vast number of regulations, many of which they claim are unnecessary. A National Audit Office (NAO) report on 'Better Regulation' estimated that around £11,000 a year was spent on average by small companies in the UK in implementing new regulations.

Case Study 8.3 indicates some of the uncertainties and costs associated with a regulatory approach to reducing carbon emissions from electricity usage.

| Case Study 8.3 | Businesses face emissions law shock | **FT** |

The government has underestimated by six times the number of businesses to be covered by new greenhouse gas emissions legislation, which will take effect in April 2010. Ministers have told the business community for more than a year that about 5,000 to 6,000 companies in the commercial sector will be covered by the incoming regulations, but in fact as many as 30,000 could be involved, the *Financial Times* has learned. This enormous revision to the government's estimates is likely to cause consternation among small to medium-sized businesses, thousands of which may be unaware of the new restrictions they face.

The regulations, originally called the *carbon reduction commitment* (CRC) and now known as the *CRC Energy Efficiency Scheme*, covers companies whose electricity is metered by the half hour and whose total electricity consumption exceeded 6,000 megawatt hours in 2008, requiring them to monitor and report their electricity use.

Case Study 8.3 *continued*

Officials have been preparing the rules for about four years, after the scheme was proposed by the government-funded Carbon Trust, a body that advises businesses on their emissions. However, Environmental Agency officials told the FT they had recently discovered the scope of the regulations to be far broader than had been thought. Companies covered by the regulations will be required to register from April 1 and will have until September to show that they comply. Between now and September, the Environmental Agency, which is in charge of implementing the CRC, will work on establishing exactly how many businesses must be included.

The problem of implementing the regulations is compounded by the fact that the government is relying on companies to come forward on their own initiative to register. Some companies, particularly smaller businesses, may be unaware of how much electricity they use, if bills are paid at the branch level rather than centrally. Companies covered by the scheme will include retailers, banks, owners of large offices, and hotels. Public sector bodies that operate large estates of buildings, and hospitals, universities and some large

schools are also expected to qualify. When companies have calculated and submitted details of their energy use, the government will publish a league table ranking them on their efficiency. Companies at the bottom will be penalised, with the money raised redistributed to those at the top.

The CRC is already controversial. Several companies including British Telecom have complained that the energy they take from renewable sources, such as wind turbines, is not reflected in their ranking. Another source of contention is that those companies that are already highly efficient in their energy use will lose out to rivals that have never taken efficiency measures, because the latter will be able rapidly to improve their position in the league table at minimal cost.

Source: from Businesses face emissions law shock, *Financial Times*, 05/03/2010 (Harvey, F.), © The Financial Times Ltd

Questions

1 Examine some of the advantages of using this approach to reduce carbon emissions from electricity use.

2 Examine some of the disadvantages of using this approach.

Nor do regulations always have the impact expected by those who devise them.

Example

Regulation and unintended consequences

The EU *Gender Equality Directive* of 2004 was intended to reduce gender discrimination but critics argue that it is having the opposite effect. For example, Direct Line, the insurer, argues that it now has to charge young women drivers more than before to avoid discriminating *in their favour*. Prior to the Directive the better driving record for young women allowed the actuaries (statisticians) of Direct Line to charge young women drivers lower premiums because they made fewer insurance claims for accidents. Young women drivers make 20% fewer claims in total than young men and their claims cost 40% less in value. For female drivers there are 17% fewer claims than for male drivers and these cost 32% less.

Overall, we can say that those who support any or all of these forms of government intervention, in whatever sector of the economy, usually do so in the belief that they improve the allocation of resources in situations characterised by one or more types of market failure.

Table 8.1 outlines a number of EU horticultural regulations involving fresh produce which have been widely criticised by growers and distributors.

Table 8.1 EU horticultural regulations

Product	Regulations
Bananas	Under EU regulation 2257/94 bananas must be at least 13.97 cm (5.5 inches) long and 2.96 cm (1.06 inches) round. They must not have 'abnormal curvature' as defined in an eight-page directive of 1994
Cucumbers	Any that curve more than 10 mm per 10 cm in length cannot be sold as 'Class 1'
Peaches	Must not be less than 5.6 cm in diameter between July and October to be sold as 'Class 1'
Red apples	Cannot be so described if less than 25% of the surface is red
Carrots	Cannot be less than 1.9 cm wide at the thick end, except in 'baby' varieties

However, in some circumstances producers can benefit from such regulations, as in Case Study 8.4 with the production of a particular type of rhubarb receiving the same recognition as Parma ham and champagne in the European Union.

Case Study 8.4   Forced rhubarb gains recognition at last

There were celebrations in the 'rhubarb triangle' yesterday as Yorkshire Forced Rhubarb was recognised as a delicacy on a par with Parma ham and champagne by receiving EU protected origin status.

After six years the European Union gave the product, which is grown indoors and harvested by candlelight, protected origin status. That means only plants grown by the traditional method in the triangle between Leeds, Bradford and Wakefield can be classed as *Yorkshire Forced Rhubarb*. There are just 12 producers left to enjoy the fruits of the decision. They produce pink-tinged plants – sweeter than most – in giant sheds using a process discovered almost 200 years ago. Hilary Benn, secretary of state for food, praised the 'quality of this traditionally grown product and the enthusiasm and commitment shown by all involved'.

Janet Oldroyd, of the Yorkshire Rhubarb Growers Association, said: 'To the 12 growers left in the rhubarb triangle, a future is now certain. To the hundreds of farmers long since gone this is, in part, recognition of their hard work, dedication and steadfast belief in their product that has kept this industry alive.'

The process was discovered by chance in the early nineteenth century at Chelsea Physic Garden in London, but it was Yorkshire that had the rich soil needed to grow the plant in the dark. By the turn of the century growers had made fortunes. Their businesses collapsed after the Second World War, however, with the arrival of the banana and other exotic refrigerated foods. Mrs Oldroyd says people were only too glad to give up rhubarb usually 'force-fed' to them in stodgy school meals.

The fruit has enjoyed a revival as celebrity chefs such as Rick Stein and Jamie Oliver added it to their menus. Mrs Oldroyd's farm near Leeds runs tours to visit the sheds and the local pub serves lamb and rhubarb stew and rhubarb ice cream. She sells wholesale at between £3.75–£6 a kilo depending on quantity – comparable with supermarket prices for the ordinary plant.

That is still cheaper than in the seventeenth century, when rhubarb – greatly prized as a drug to cure stomach and liver ailments – sold for three times the price of opium.

Source: from Forced rhubarb gains recognition at last, *Financial Times*, 26/02/2010 (Bounds, A.), © The Financial Times Ltd

Question

Examine the impacts on producers and consumers of a product receiving protected origin status.

You try 8.1 reviews material involving the various types of market failure and policy responses to 'correct' those failures.

You try   8.1

1 Here you will see a *lettered* description of a particular type of 'market failure' and a *numbered* list of terms. Try to match the description with its correct term.

Description

(a) Extra output of the firm emits CO_2 and pollutes the environment.

(b) The firm is aware of a design fault, the buyer is not.

(c) The firm employs almost all the labour force in a particular town.

(d) The firm finds it impossible to exclude people from consuming the product even if they don't pay.

(e) Extra output of the firm creates employment opportunities in a deprived area.

(f) The firm erects 'barriers to entry' to prevent any competition from rival firms.

Terms

(i)   Positive externality

(ii) Negative externality

(iii) Monopoly power

(iv) Monopsony power

(v)   Information asymmetry

(vi) Public good

2 Place 'M' next to those situations which might be described as leading to further market failure and 'P' next to those which might be seen as improving market efficiency.

(a) The Internet providing consumers with up-to-date information about new car prices.

(b) A report indicating that some multinationals have used child-labour to increase the production of sportswear.

(c) The UK Competition Commission preventing a merger between two companies on the basis that their combined output would be over 60% of the total supply of car batteries.

(d) New research suggesting that power lines increase the risk of developing leukaemia.

(e) A firm which already employs 40% of the labour force in a town merging with another local firm which currently employs around a quarter of the town's remaining labour force.

(f) The appointment of a new body to regulate the Financial Services industry after a report indicating the misuse of pension funds.

(g) Directors of various companies in an industry distributing copies of their proposed prices for next year to each other in order to avoid price competition.

3 Which *two* of the following might lead the government to increase tax on an activity?

(a) Marginal private cost exceeds marginal social cost.

(b) Marginal social cost exceeds marginal private cost.

(c) Marginal private benefit exceeds marginal social benefit.

(d) Marginal social benefit exceeds marginal private benefit.

(e) Marginal private benefit equals marginal social benefit.

4 Which *two* of the following might lead the government to subsidise an activity?

(a) Marginal private cost exceeds marginal social cost.

(b) Marginal social cost exceeds marginal private cost.

(c) Marginal private benefit exceeds marginal social benefit.

(d) Marginal social benefit exceeds marginal private benefit.

(e) Marginal private benefit equals marginal social benefit.

5 A negative externality can be said to occur where:

(a) private revenue falls short of private costs;

(b) private costs fall short of social costs;

(c) private costs exceed social costs;

(d) private and social costs are identical;

(e) providing extra output of the products creates a useful by-product.

Answers can be found on pp. 525–546.

Deregulation and privatisation

Governments can intervene to correct 'market failures' by imposing rules and regulation. They can also intervene by *removing* rules and regulation, i.e. by using policies of deregulation.

Deregulation

Deregulation can be supported from a number of viewpoints:

- *Opening markets up to competition.* If removing regulations helps bring more competition into a market, then consumers arguably benefit from the extra choice and lower prices that usually result.

- *Removing unnecessary obstacles to business efficiency.* Firms, small, medium and large, regularly complain about the time and money 'wasted' having to comply (e.g. form-filling) with what they regard as unnecessary bureaucratic regulations.

- *Raising economic welfare.* If regulations have themselves become so complex, time-consuming and expensive for businesses and employees to comply with, then there may be a case for removing at least some of them. 'Public interest theory' would propose removing regulations where it can be shown that 'economic welfare', defined as consumer surplus plus producer surplus, is increased by removing the regulations.

Deregulation and public interest theory

We can define *economic welfare* as consumer surplus plus producer surplus.

- The *consumer surplus* is the amount consumers are willing to pay over and above the amount they need to pay.

- The *producer surplus* is the amount producers receive over and above the amount they need for them to supply the product.

In Figure 8.4 we start with an initial demand curve DD and supply curve SS giving market equilibrium price P_1 and quantity Q_1.

Suppose that a *regulation* has been introduced whereby, in order to prevent price falling below P_2, the government has set a *quota* restricting output of the product to OQ_2.

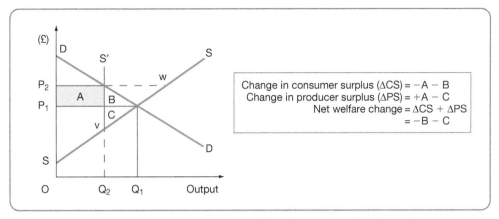

Figure 8.4 Welfare loss with a quota scheme OQ$_2$ raising price (P$_2$) above the market clearing level P$_1$

In terms of Figure 8.4, if the quota is set at Q$_2$, then the effective supply curve becomes SvS′, since no more than Q$_2$ can be supplied whatever the price.

The result is to raise the 'equilibrium' price to P$_2$ and reduce the 'equilibrium' quantity to Q$_2$.

- The quota regulation has resulted in a loss of economic welfare equivalent to the area B plus area C. The reduction in output from Q$_1$ to Q$_2$ means a loss of area B in consumer surplus and a loss of area C in producer surplus.

- However, the higher price results in a gain of area A in producer surplus which exactly offsets the loss of area A in consumer surplus.

- This means that the *net* welfare change is negative, i.e. there is a 'deadweight loss' of area B + area C.

'Public interest theory' suggests that deregulation should occur whenever the net welfare change of *removing* regulations is deemed to be positive. In terms of Figure 8.4 it might be argued that removing the regulation whereby the government restricts output to keep price artificially high at P$_2$ will give a net welfare change which is *positive*, namely a net gain of area B + area C.

In other words, allowing the free market equilibrium price P$_1$ and quantity Q$_1$ to prevail restores the previous loss of economic welfare via regulation. Put another way, public interest theory is suggesting that deregulation should occur whenever the outcome is a net welfare gain, so that those who gain can, at least potentially, more than compensate those who lose.

Privatisation

Privatisation is usually used to refer to a situation in which a good or service previously provided wholly or mainly by the public sector can now be provided by private sector firms. In the UK some important nationalised industries such as coal, telecommunications, gas, water and railways were until recently run by public corporations, not private firms. In 1979, with the election of Margaret Thatcher, these *nationalised industries* were privatised, with shares (ownership) now offered in most cases to the general public.

Privatisation in the UK has reduced the number of nationalised industries to a mere handful of enterprises accounting for less than 2% of UK GDP, around 3% of UK investment and under 1.5% of UK employment. By contrast, in 1979 the then nationalised industries

Table 8.2 **Major privatisations in the UK: a sectoral breakdown**

Mining, Oil, Agriculture and Forestry	Manufacturing, Science and Engineering
British Coal	AEA Technology
British Petroleum	British Aerospace, Short Bros, Rolls-Royce
Enterprise Oil	British Shipbuilders, Harland and Wolff
Land Settlement	British Rail Engineering
Forestry Commission	British Steel
Plant Breeding Institute	British Sugar Corporation
Distribution, Hotels, Catering	Royal Ordnance
British Rail Hotels	Jaguar, Rover Group
	Amersham International
	British Technology Group Holdings (ICL, Fairey, Ferranti, Inmos)
Transport and Communication	
British Railways	
National Freight, National and Local Bus Companies	**Electricity, Gas and Water**
Motorway Service Area Leases	British Gas
Associated British Ports, Trust Ports, Sealink	National Power, PowerGen
British Airways, British Airways Authority (and other airports)	Nuclear Electric
	Northern Ireland Electric
British Telecommunication, Cable and Wireless	Northern Ireland Generation (four companies)
	Scottish Hydro-Electric
	Scottish Power
Banking, Finance etc.	National Grid
Girobank	Regional Electricity Distribution
	Regional Water Holding Companies

were a very significant part of the economy, producing 9% of GDP, being responsible for 11.5% of UK investment and employing 7.3% of all UK employees.

The scale of the transfer of public sector businesses since 1979 to private ownership is indicated in Table 8.2, which lists the businesses privatised by their sector of operations.

We might usefully consider the arguments for and against privatisation.

Case for privatisation

1 *Greater efficiency.* The suggestion here is that breaking up the state monopoly and allowing private companies to provide the good or service makes resource allocation more efficient. Two main points are often made in this respect.
   - *Public choice theory.* This sees politicians and civil servants seeking to maximise their own interests (utility functions) in the nationalised industries. Politicians seek votes, civil servants support their departments which are lobbied by pressure groups, such as trade unions. As a result, objectives pursued in nationalised industries tend to be confused and inconsistent, resulting in inefficient management and operation of the industry.
   - *Property rights theory.* This emphasises the inability of the public to exercise control over nationalised industries. For example, the public (unlike private shareholders) have limited property rights over the company even though the public 'owns' them. In contrast, the private shareholders buying and selling shares, attending AGMs, the

threat of takeovers, all resulting from private share ownership, are thought to increase the 'efficiency' of corporate activity.

– *X-inefficiency* is the term often given to the result of these shortcomings; i.e. management failing to minimise cost in producing a given output – or failing to maximise output from a given set of resources.

2 *Greater managerial freedom.* The nationalised industries, being dependent on the Treasury for finance, had long complained of insufficient funds for investment. When the industry is privatised these constraints no longer apply, and management can now seek to raise finance for investment from the capital market (e.g. share issues).

3 *Wider share ownership.* In 1979, before the major privatisations took place, only 7% of UK adults owned shares. Today around 20% own shares, many having for the first time bought shares in some of the major privatisations. In this view, privatisation has helped create a 'property-owning democracy', resulting in more shareholders so more people sympathetic to a capitalist/market-based economy and a more committed and efficient workforce as a result of owning shares in the company.

4 *More government revenue.* The privatisation programme since 1979 has raised well over £50bn in revenue for the Treasury.

Case against privatisation

1 *Simply converts a state monopoly to a private monopoly.* The argument here is that economies of scale are so large for many of the industries and sectors privatised (see Table 8.2) that it will only ever be efficient to have one, or at most a few, large firms in those sectors. Taking it further 8.3 looks at the *natural monopoly* argument which

---

Taking it further 'Natural monopoly' argument   8.3

The *natural monopoly* argument is often advanced in favour of public ownership of certain industries. Economies of scale in railways, water, electricity and gas industries are perhaps so great that the tendency towards monopoly can be termed 'natural'. In terms of our earlier analysis (Chapter 6, p. 176) the *minimum efficient size* (MES) is so large that the nation can only sustain one efficient firm in that particular industry. It then follows that creating competition in providing such goods and services, with duplication of investment, would, in this view, be wasteful of resources.

Figure 8.5 provides a useful illustration of the natural monopoly argument. The falling long-run average total cost curve (LRAC) indicates that significant economies of scale occur as output rises.

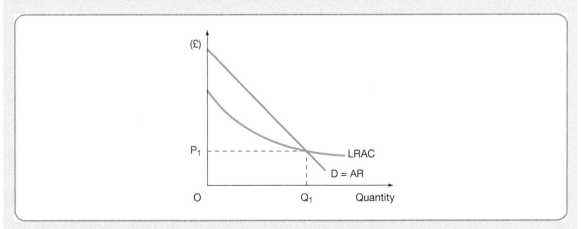

Figure 8.5 'Natural monopoly' with continuously falling long-run average cost (LRAC) curve

> *Taking it further 8.3 continued*
>
> The demand (AR) curve for the product is such that it is not possible for this industry to have even one firm producing at the minimum efficient size (MES). Output Q_1 is the highest output the nationalised industry could produce and still break even (Price = AR = AC). However, even at this output the LRAC curve is still falling. To create private sector competition in such a 'natural monopoly' situation would mean smaller outputs than OQ_1 at higher average costs and higher prices than is needed to break even, a policy hardly likely to commend itself to consumers!

suggests that only a single efficient firm may be regarded as viable in that industry. This criticism of privatisation points to the fact that one merely changes a 'state monopoly' for a 'private monopoly' by privatisation, with few if any benefits of lower price and extra choice for consumers.

2 *Need for industry regulation and extra bureaucracy.* Related to the previous point, governments have appointed industry regulators to protect the public from the market power of large private companies that have replaced the nationalised industries. So we have OFGAS, OFWAT, OFTEL, OFCOM and many other regulators who try to limit price increases and impose conditions on the operations of the now large private companies in gas, water, telecommunications and many other industries. Firms in these industries often complain of their lack of freedom to manage, excessive 'red tape' and bureaucracy from these industry regulators.

3 *Concentration of share ownership.* While more individuals own shares, the larger shareholding institutions such as pension funds, insurance companies and unit trusts have increased their shareholdings and together own almost 60% of all shares in the UK. Only those shareholders who have a significant stake in the company can, in practice, influence company policy. Having some extra individuals with a few shares each does little to bring about a true 'property-owning democracy', in this view.

4 *Loss of government revenue.* At the time of privatisation, the new shares were offered to the public at largely 'knock-down' prices to create public interest in the privatisation. This undervaluation of shares lost the Treasury considerable potential revenue at the time of these privatisations.

Regulation of privatised companies

The privatisation of public utility companies with 'natural' monopolies creates the possibility that the companies might abuse their monopoly power. In these cases UK privatisations have offered reassurance to the public in the form of regulatory offices for each privatised utility, for example, OFTEL for telecommunications and OFWAT for the water industry.

Objectives of regulators

Regulators have two fundamental objectives.

First, they attempt to create the constraints and stimuli which companies would experience in a competitive market environment. For example, companies in competitive markets must bear in mind what their competitors are doing when setting their prices and are under competitive pressure to improve their service to consumers in order to gain or retain market share. Regulations can stimulate the effects of a competitive market by setting price caps and performance standards.

Second, regulators have the longer-term objective of encouraging actual competition by easing the entry of new producers and by preventing privatised monopoly power maintaining barriers to entry.

An ideal is the creation of markets sufficiently competitive to make regulation unnecessary. The market for gas has moved substantially in this direction. British Gas, when first privatised, had an apparent classic natural monopoly in the supply of gas to industry, but by the end of 2010 the British Gas market share was below 30% for industrial users and since 1998 the company has faced nationwide competition in the supply of gas to domestic consumers. Similarly, the regulator insisted on the introduction of competition into the supply of electricity to domestic consumers as far back as 1998.

Problems facing regulators

Regulators have an unenviable role as they try to create the constraints and stimuli of a competitive market. Essentially they are arbitrating between the interests of consumers and producers. Other things being equal, attempts by regulators to achieve improvements in service levels will cause increases in costs and so lower profits, while price caps (see below) on services with price inelastic demand will also reduce profits by preventing the regulated industries raising prices and therefore revenue.

The privatised company subject to a price cap may well look for ways of lowering costs to allow profits to be at least maintained, or perhaps raised. In most organisations there are economies to be gained by reducing staffing levels, and the utility companies have dramatically reduced their numbers of employees. Investment in new technology may also enable unit costs to be lowered so that profits are greater than they otherwise would have been.

Establishing a price cap

In deciding on a price cap the regulator has in mind some 'satisfactory' rate of profit on the value of assets employed. A key issue is then the valuation of the assets. If the basis of valuation is historical, using the market value at privatisation plus an estimate of investment since that date, then the company will face a stricter price cap than if current market valuations are used for assets. This is because historical valuations will usually be much smaller than the current valuations and so will justify much smaller total profits and therefore lower prices to achieve that profit.

Price caps are often associated with job losses. In an economy with less than full employment it may then be argued that such cost savings in the privatised companies are only achieved at the expense of extra public expenditure on welfare benefit. However, a counter-argument is that lower public utility prices benefit all consumers, with lower costs of production across the economy stimulating output and creating employment.

Costs of regulation

While regulation should produce clear benefits for the consumers of each privatised company, there are inevitable costs involved in running regulatory offices and also costs for the regulated company which has to supply information and present its case to the regulator. It is likely that companies will go further than this and try to anticipate the regulator's activities, so incurring further costs.

UK competition policy

Our particular concern in this section is with mergers and acquisitions policy in the UK. We have noted in Chapter 5 the potential benefits of increased size via various economies of scale. However, we have also noted in Chapter 6 that the extra market power from increased size can lead to higher prices, lower outputs and reduced choice for consumers. Competition policy in the UK seeks to balance the potential benefits of mergers with the need to protect the public from possible excesses of market power.

Before examining how UK competition policy has been conducted, it will be helpful to review the role of some of the key institutions and bodies which are involved.

UK merger policy: key 'players'

- *Office of Fair Trading* (OFT). This is an independent statutory body which has been given the task of keeping markets under review and promoting competition. In the Enterprise Act 2002 it was given the key role in deciding which mergers should be permitted and which should be investigated further. For those mergers to be investigated further it advises the *Secretary of State for the Department of Business, Innovation and Skills* on whether, and under what conditions, the proposed mergers should be allowed.

  - Sometimes the OFT bases that advice on in-depth investigations conducted by the *Competition Commission* (CC) to which it can refer proposed mergers. For a proposed merger to be referred to the Competition Commission, two key conditions must apply, and if they do it becomes a '*relevant merger*'.

    (i) *Either* that the enterprise being taken over has a UK turnover exceeding £70m (the 'turnover test') *or* that the merged enterprises together supply at least 25% of the UK market (the 'share of supply' test). It is implicit in this criterion that at least one enterprise must trade within the UK.

    (ii) If the above condition is satisfied, the OFT will still only refer the proposed merger to the Competition Commission (CC) for further scrutiny if it is expected to result in a substantial 'lessening of competition' within the UK. 'Lessening of competition' would generally mean a situation where it is expected that product choice or quality would be reduced, prices raised, or innovation restricted as a result of the merger activity.

  - Sometimes the OFT might decide *not* to make a reference to the CC if the OFT itself believes that the 'public benefits' (e.g. higher choice, lower prices, higher quality or innovation) resulting from the merger outweigh the substantial 'lessening of competition' noted above.

- *Competition Commission* (CC). This replaced the previous Monopolies and Mergers Commission in 1998. It is an independent statutory body which conducts in-depth investigations of any potential merger situations referred to it by the OFT or the Secretary of State for the Department of Business, Innovation and Skills. The CC, when considering a merger in more depth, will weigh the 'lessening of competition' effect against the 'public benefits' effect before making its final decision.

- *Secretary of State for the Department of Business, Innovation and Skills.* This is a cabinet minister in the UK. The Enterprise Act 2002 reduced the role of the Secretary of State in mergers policy. Most decisions as to which mergers should be referred to the Competition Commission (CC) are to be made by the Office of Fair Trading following the conditions and guidelines outlined above.

- *Competition Appeal Tribunal* (CAT). There is also a new appeals mechanism giving a right to those parties involved in the merger to apply to the Competition Appeal Tribunal (CAT) for a statutory judicial review of a decision of the OFT, CC or the Secretary of State.

- *Court of Appeal.* There is also a further right of appeal (on a point of law only) to the Court of Appeal.

Putting merger policy into practice

To understand the main procedures for merger investigation in the UK, a brief account will be given here of the process.

- *First stage.* When the OFT is made aware of a proposed merger which meets its conditions (a 'relevant merger'), it may choose to undertake a 'first stage' investigation. For example, it might seek to assess the potential effect of the merger on market structure. This market structure assessment could be followed by an examination of whether the entry of new firms into the market is easy or difficult and whether any 'lessening of competition' is likely to occur.

- *Second stage.* The OFT will then make its own decision on the case without reference to the Secretary of State. The OFT will give one of three possible decisions:
  - First, the merger is given an unconditional clearance.
  - Second, the merger is given a clearance only if the parties agree to modify any behaviour identified as 'uncompetitive' or decrease their market share and market power by selling off specified businesses.
  - Third, the merger may turn out to be serious enough to refer it directly to the CC for a 'second-stage' investigation. At this point the Secretary of State can intervene in the proceedings, but under the new Enterprise Act 2002 this intervention can take place only in very specific circumstances involving mergers with media, national security or other narrowly specified implications.

- *Third stage.* If the OFT refers the merger to the CC, the Commission will consider the evidence of the OFT but will also make its own in-depth report on the merger. After consideration of the evidence and basing its views on both the 'lessening of competition' and 'customer benefits criteria', the CC will recommend that one of three possible actions be taken: (i) an unconditional clearance, or (ii) a clearance subject to conditions proposed by the CC, or (iii) an outright prohibition.
  - If the CC recommends conditional clearance then the companies involved may be asked to divest some of their assets or to ensure in some specified way that competition is maintained (e.g. giving licences to their competitors).
  - If the CC recommends prohibition of the merger, the parties can appeal to the *Competition Appeal Tribunal* (CAT). This is a three-person tribunal which seems to be an important new 'player' in mergers policy.

The OFT was concerned that the action of the Competition Appeal Tribunal would open up a 'two part' test, in that it would have to refer any proposed merger to the *Competition Commission* (a) if the OFT thought a deal might result in a 'substantial lessening of competition' or (b) if there was a possibility that the *Competition Commission* might take a different view to the OFT. In practice, almost every proposed merger would then be liable to be referred, implying huge time delays, extra costs and greater uncertainty.

In its judgment in February 2003, however, the Appeals Court rejected the need for such a 'two part' test by the OFT. However, it did criticise the OFT for making a hasty

Check the net

For information on past decisions of the UK *Competition Commission* go to:
www.competition-commission.org.uk

ill-thought-out judgment in the particular case of the iSoft and Torex proposed merger, which had then to be re-investigated. Many lawyers believe the case will have made the OFT more cautious in its assessments, perhaps resulting in a small rise in reference to the *Competition Commission*.

Case Study 8.5 examines the welfare impacts of mergers.

Case Study 8.5 | Welfare impacts of mergers

In 2006 the Competition Commission attempted to place a money value on the potential welfare losses to consumers resulting from mergers. The summary of its findings can be seen in the table below. The four merger enquiries shown in the table were carried out between March 2005 and March 2006. The SDEL–Coors merger involved the equipment used to dispense beer and some other drinks in pubs; the Somerfield–Morrisons deal involved the sale of 115 grocery stores in certain UK locations, raising the problem of local market power; the LSE–Euronext–Deutsche Borse deal involved two bids for the London Stock Exchange; and the Vue–Ster merger related to the transfer of six cinemas in the UK from Ster to Vue.

The figures in the table attempt to assess the likely price rises resulting from the lessening of competition (SLC) and the associated welfare loss of consumer surplus. The combined welfare loss to the consumers of these projected mergers was calculated to be £31.5m per annum.

Welfare costs of projected merger/acquisition activity, 2005–2006

Inquiry	Estimated costs to consumers per annum (£)
SDEL–Coors	13.9
Somerfield–Morrisons	5.5
LSE–Euronext–Deutsche Borse	11.8
Vue–Ster	0.3
Total	31.5

Source: Competition Commission (2006) www.competition-commission.org.uk/our_role/analysis/estimated_costs_05_06.pdf, last accessed 6 March 2008. Reprinted with permission

Questions

1 Explain how these estimated welfare losses might have been calculated.

2 What other welfare impacts might have been considered?

So far our concern has been with mergers policy in the UK. However, UK competition policy also includes dealing with various 'restrictive practices'.

Restrictive practices legislation

The Restrictive Trades Practices Act 1956 specified that restrictive practice operated by groups of firms had now to be registered with a *Registrar of Restrictive Practices*. It was his responsibility to bring cases to the *Restrictive Practices Court*, consisting of five judges and ten lay members with the status of a High Court.

Such restrictive practices were deemed against the public interest unless they could satisfy at least one of seven 'pathways':

1 that it protects the public against injury;

2 that it confers special benefits on consumers;

3 that it prevents local unemployment;

4 that it counters existing restrictions on competition;

5 that it maintains exports;

6 that it supports other acceptable restrictions;

7 that it assists the negotiations of fair trading terms for suppliers and buyers.

Even having satisfied one or more of the 'gateway' conditions, the firms had still to show that the overall benefits from the restrictive practice were clearly greater than the costs incurred. This 'tail piece' was largely responsible for the prohibition of many restrictive practices. Between 1956 and 2009, over 14,000 restrictive agreements have been registered. However, few of these have been brought before the court; the majority of such practices have been 'voluntarily' ended by the parties themselves in anticipation of an unfavourable decision by the court.

In 1968, 'information agreements' (i.e. agreements whereby information concerning prices, conditions etc. are formally exchanged) were for the first time considered a restrictive practice. Also in 1968 an eighth 'gateway' was added, namely 'that the agreement neither restricts nor deters competition'.

The Fair Trading Act 1973 gave permission for restrictive practices legislation to be extended to cover services as well as the production of goods. The Restrictive Practices Act 1976 consolidated previous legislation.

Despite these changes, the adequacy of restrictive practices legislation has been questioned. For example, under the Restrictive Practices Act there were no financial penalties for failing to register a restrictive agreement and many such practices were able to continue. Of particular concern was the legislation dealing with *cartels*, which has been considerably strengthened in recent years.

Cartels in the UK

The UK approach to cartels (Chapter 6, p. 193) has been considerably strengthened in recent years.

● Under the Competition Act 1998 the OFT was given civil powers to fine companies for anti-competitive behaviour involving formal or informal cartels.

● Under the Enterprise Act 2002 the OFT was given additional *criminal powers* when investigating such cartels. The OFT now has the power to investigate people suspected of price-fixing, bid-rigging or limiting production or supply of goods dishonestly. Regulators from the OFT can now use force to enter offices or homes under a search warrant and can bring in the Serious Fraud Office to prosecute any criminal offence suspected. In effect the OFT can do much more than impose fines; it can now take actions which result in the possible imprisonment of directors and others involved in cartel-related activity.

Case Study 8.6 indicates the seriousness with which information agreements are now regarded by the OFT.

Case Study 8.6	Fined for sharing price data	**FT**

The near £30m fine on Royal Bank of Scotland for breaking competition rules is a reminder of official determination to tackle a long-neglected area of corporate law. RBS's £28.6m fine for sharing loan-pricing data with Barclays employees dwarfs most Financial Services Authority sanctions and is almost as much as the punishment imposed this year on the arms dealer BAE Systems to settle a five-year criminal probe into suspected bribery.

The RBS fine is the latest in a series of cases brought by the Office of Fair Trading as it grapples with the cosy but illegal sharing of pricing information that it believes has become rooted in several big industries. Ali Nikpay, the OFT's senior director of cartels and criminal enforcement, says: 'What we are trying to do with cases like this is send a clear message that this kind of activity really does carry substantial penalties.' RBS is being fined because it admitted its staff 'unilaterally' shared information with Barclays on the pricing of loans to large law, accountancy and property firms, the OFT says. The communication took place 'on the fringes of social, client or industry events or through telephone conversations'.

The penalty is the culmination of a two-year investigation triggered when Barclays volunteered information on its role, a decision that meant the bank escaped penalties under OFT leniency rules aimed at encouraging informants.

Lawyers say the RBS penalty seems high given that the OFT has not alleged the bank was part of a full-blown cartel involving agreements to fix prices. Previous cases in which companies have been fined more – notably the £121.5m fine in 2007 imposed on British Airways for fixing fuel surcharges – have involved more serious wrongdoing. RBS said the misconduct in its case involved just two members of staff in a team of about 16. One has already left, while the other faces an internal hearing. Another notable feature of the RBS case is that the penalty is the first levied for anti-competitive behaviour on a financial services company, after OFT action against industries including supermarkets, tobacco and construction. John Fingleton, the OFT chief executive, has previously raised concerns about part of British business where 'shoddy, complacent, cosy, rotten practices' have been 'going on for years'.

For all the growing number of high-profile fines imposed by the OFT, critics say it still needs to bring on more cases and to resolve existing ones more quickly.

OFT fines

£132m	Fines on Gallaher, the tobacco company and five retailers in 2008 for inflating the cost of cigarettes
£121.5m	British Airways fine for fixing price of passenger fuel surcharges in 2007
£116m	OFT fine imposed on a group of supermarkets and dairies in December 2007 as the result of their admitted participation in a dairy cartel

The OFT's first contested criminal price-fixing prosecution involving individuals – against four past and present BA executives who deny the charges – is finally due to be heard next month, almost seven years after the watchdog acquired the powers to bring such cases. The RBS penalty is a sign from the OFT that, in the field of competition law, careless talk can cost companies money – particularly if competitors later tell the watchdog the conversations were not a good idea.

Source: from RBS fined for $28m for sharing price data, *Financial Times*, 31/03/2010 (Peel, M., and Goff, S.), © The Financial Times Ltd

Questions

1 Why are regulatory authorities paying close attention to information sharing agreements?

2 What are the strengths and weaknesses of the approach adopted with Royal Bank of Scotland (RBS)?

EU competition policy

European competition policy has been criticised for its lack of comprehensiveness, but in December 1989 the Council of Ministers agreed for the first time on specific cross-border merger regulations. The criteria for judging whether a merger should be referred to the European Commission covered three aspects.

● First, the companies concerned must have a combined world turnover of more than €5bn (though for insurance companies the figure was based on total assets rather than turnover).

● Second, at least two of the companies concerned in the merger must have an EU-wide turnover of at least €250m each.

- Third, if all parties to the merger have two-thirds of their business in one and the same member state, the merger was to be subject to national and not EU controls.

The European Commission must be notified of merger proposals which meet the criteria noted above within one week of the announcement of the bid and it will vet each proposed merger against a concept of '*a dominant position*'. Any creation or strengthening of a dominant position will be seen as incompatible with the aims of the EU if it significantly impedes '*effective competition*'.

The European Commission has one month after notification to decide whether to start proceedings and then four months to make a final decision. If a case is being investigated by the European Commission it will *not* also be investigated by national bodies such as the UK Competition Commission, for example.

Member states may prevent a merger which has already been permitted by the EU only if it involves public security or some aspects of the media or if competition in the local markets is threatened.

Links

The operation of various EU institutions is considered in more detail in Chapter 11, pp. 362–4.

Review of EU merger regulations

A number of reservations were expressed about this EU legislation on cross-border mergers and acquisitions.

First, a main aim of the legislation was to introduce a 'one-stop shop', which meant that merging companies would be liable to *either* European *or* national merger control, but not both. However, as can be seen above, in some situations national merger control could override EU control – a 'two-stop shop'!

Second, it was not clear how the rules would apply to non-EU companies. For example, it was quite possible that two US or Japanese companies, each with the required amount of sales in the EU but with no actual EU presence, could merge. While such a case would certainly fall within the EU merger rules, it was not clear how seriously the EU could exercise its powers in such cases.

Third, guidelines were needed on joint ventures.

New EU cross-border merger regulations

In March 1998 a number of amendments were made to the scope of EU cross-border merger regulations. The result of these amendments was that the three original criteria for exclusive reference to the European Commission remain, but other criteria were added to give the EU jurisdiction over smaller-sized mergers which would not be large enough to qualify under the €5bn and €250m rules described earlier.

As regards joint ventures, the new regulations also make a distinction between 'concentrative' joint ventures and 'co-operative' joint ventures, with the new European Commission rules applying to the first type (which was seen to concentrate power) but not to the second type (which was seen merely as a method to coordinate competitive behaviour).

In 2000, a review of the merger approval system was instigated by the EU. By November 2002 it was announced that a package of reforms would be introduced that would take effect from May 2004. One aspect of the reforms includes the retention of the rule that a merger is unlawful if it 'creates or strengthens a dominant position' but also adds an amendment to the merger regulation to include situations where a merger may be deemed unlawful if it creates 'collective dominance' in a market. This situation might occur when a merger results in the formation or strengthening of an oligopolistic market structure within which a few large firms can coordinate their activities to the detriment of consumers. To date, the European Commission has handled around 80 merger cases per year over the past decade.

Restrictive practices and EU legislation

As in the UK, the EU competition policy seeks to deal with much more than merger activity. The reasoning behind European competition policy is exactly that which created the original European Economic Community (EEC) over 40 years ago. Competition is viewed as bringing consumers greater choice, lower prices and higher quality goods and services.

Promoting 'fair and free' competition

The European Commission has a set of *directives* in this area which are designed to underpin 'fair and free' competition. They cover cartels (price fixing, market sharing etc.), government subsidies (direct or indirect subsidies for inefficient enterprises – state and private), the abuse of dominant market position (differential pricing in different markets, exclusive contracts, predatory pricing etc.), selective distribution (preventing consumers in one market from buying in another in order to maintain high margins in the first market), and mergers and takeovers.

Avoiding excessive use of state aid and subsidies

One of the most active areas of competition policy has involved *state aid*. The Commission has attempted to restrict the aid paid by member states to their own nationals through Articles 87 and 88 which cover various aspects of the distorting effect that subsidies can have on competition between member states. However, it is likely that the progressive implementation of Single Market arrangements will result in domestic firms increasing their attempts to obtain state aid from their own governments as a means of helping them meet greater Europe-wide competition. Overall, the amount of aid given by member states to their domestic industry has been running at around 2% of their respective GNPs during the 1990s and early years of the millennium.

However, it is not only aid and subsidies given to one's own national companies that is the target of the European Commission. The wide-ranging problems resulting from EU rulings on the legitimacy of state aid and subsidies is usefully illustrated by the experience of Ryanair, the Irish carrier. In February 2004 the European Commission ruled that Ryanair had received around £11m (€15m) in state aid from the Belgian authorities to fly to and from Charleroi airport in southern Belgium and ordered the no-frills airline to return up to £3m (€4m) of the money. According to the judgment, Ryanair's controversial benefits from the Walloon regional government which owns Charleroi included €1.92m in subsidies to launch new routes, €768,000 for pilot training, €250,000 towards hotel costs and a landing charge of only €1 per passenger, compared to the standard rate of €8 to €13.

Example

> In 2009 the European Commission found that electricity price subsidies granted by the Italian government to Alcoa for its aluminium smelters Veneto distorted the market and gave Alcoa an unfair advantage over competitors. No other justification could be found, so these subsidies are now prohibited and a major fine was imposed on Alcoa recovering most of the subsidy payment for 2006 to 2009.

Case Study 8.7 reviews the approach of the Europeans Union to mergers and restrictive practices and indicates some concerns expressed at the process and outcomes of decisions affecting the future of major firms and stakeholders in the EU.

Case Study 8.7   Antitrust in the European Union

Joaquin Alumnia became the European Union's Competition Commissioner in February 2010, with the authority to impose heavy fines on companies, force the merging companies to sell assets and even block the mergers altogether. Nor can the companies do much about his decisions if they feel they are unfair! Especially controversial is how his agency treats companies it accuses of taking part in cartels or of trying to maintain monopolies by squeezing smaller rivals. The lawyers of the firms involved often complain that the Commission acts as prosecutor, judge and jury.

This issue as to the fairness or otherwise of the anti-trust processes of the Commission has been highlighted by the EU's case against Intel in 2009 for violating Article 82 as regards the abuse of a dominant market position. Intel was found to have given hidden rebates to computer manufacturers on condition they bought Intel's chips for their central processing units and to have paid those manufacturers to halt or delay the launch of computer products using the chips of other manufacturers. Intel was fined a record €1.06 billion ($1.5 billion) in May 2009 for using these tactics to disadvantage its main rival, AMD, and prevent AMD from challenging Intel's market dominance. However, during that case it emerged that the Commission had failed to keep proper records of its own meetings with the companies involved, an oversight which confirmed suspicions that relevant evidence was not fully considered by Commission staff.

A complaint is taken up by a 'case team' of the EU Commission which, after a lengthy investigation, issues a 'statement of objections' which in effect is a legal indictment. Companies then have the right to ask for a hearing at which they can challenge the charges. But it is the Commission itself which decides whether or not the charge still stands and then itself determines the penalty, which is often sufficiently large to have a major impact on profits, even for huge corporations. The companies argue that, given the seriousness of any adverse judgments by the Commission, they should have a court-like process in which they can themselves question witnesses and introduce evidence.

These cases are often as much about settling disputes between rival firms as about upholding EC competition rules, and establishing the facts in such cases is far from straightforward. Loyalty discounts can be seen as benefiting consumers in that they help reduce prices. However they can also discourage competition, which can lead to higher prices in the long run. There are concerns that those in the Commission who are already convinced of their case may ignore evidence that doesn't fit in with their preconceived view!

Indeed, companies complain that by the time hearings take place, the case teams are already convinced of their version of events, even if they hear a strong defence, and the Commissioner, who in effect decides cases, does not always attend hearings. There is no cross-examination of witnesses and no jury to weigh the merits of opposing arguments. Whilst companies have the right to appeal against the Commissions' rulings, such appeals can take two or three years, with the panel merely assessing whether the original verdict was plausible, rather than hearing new evidence.

Cartel cases may be more clear-cut but the calls for better safeguards are just as loud, with the EU's trustbusters relying on amnesties to crack price-fixing rings: the first member of a ring to confess on its fellow price-fixers escaping prosecution. Whilst this approach has been important in America, where cartel cases are tried in court, in the European system firms may seek to implicate innocent rivals, who would not then be able to defend themselves in a proper court setting. Many believe it would be far better to target executives with criminal sanctions, in court settings with appropriate judicial safeguards.

Source: Based on information from *The Economist* (2010) 20–26 February

Questions

1 Why is the approach to competition regulation in the EU the subject of much criticism?

2 What changes/improvements might be made to this approach?

Recap

- Regulations are widely used in all economic sectors in order to protect consumers from 'market failure' and to prevent such failures actually occurring.

- There is considerable momentum behind removing regulations (i.e. deregulation) where this can be shown to be in the 'public interest'. However, evaluating the welfare change from deregulation is a complex exercise.

- Privatisation is the transfer of assets or economic activity from the public sector to the private sector.

- The term 'privatisation' is often used to cover many situations: the outright sale of state-owned assets, part-sale, joint public/private ventures, market testing, contracting out of central/local government services etc.

- The case for privatisation includes allegedly greater productive efficiency (lower costs) via the introduction of market pressures. These are seen as creating more flexibility in labour markets, higher productivity and reduced unit labour costs.

- The case against privatisation includes suggestions that state monopolies have often merely been replaced by private monopolies, with little benefit to consumers, especially in the case of the public utilities.

- Regulators have been appointed for a number of public utilities in an attempt to simulate the effects of competition (e.g. limits to price increases and to profits), when there is little competition in reality.

Key terms

Externality Where economic decisions create costs or benefits for people other than the decision taker.

Information asymmetry Where one person or firm knows more than another person or firm.

Marginal social benefit Defined as marginal private benefit plus marginal external benefit.

Marginal social cost Defined as marginal private cost plus marginal external cost.

Merit goods Goods/services that add to the quality of life but are not, strictly, public goods. For example, education/healthcare can be withheld from consumers (i.e. they do not possess the public good quality of non-excludability), and so private markets can be established to provide them.

Mixed (quasi) public goods Involves some aspect of non-excludability or non-exhaustibility, but not both.

Negative externality Where marginal social cost exceeds marginal private cost.

Pareto optimality A situation is said to be Pareto optimal when it is no longer possible to reallocate resources in such a way that we can make one person better off, without at the same time making someone else worse off.

Pigouvian tax A tax exactly equal to the marginal external cost at each level of output.

Public good A good (or service) that involves two key characteristics: non-excludability and non-exhaustibility. Non-excludability means that, once provided, it is difficult to exclude people from consuming the good/service. Non-exhaustibility means that consumption of an extra unit by one person does not diminish the amount available for consumption by others.

Public interest theory An approach that seeks to assess the impacts of regulation or deregulation in terms of whether or not it raises economic welfare in such a way that gainers can potentially compensate losers. Usually involves the ideas of consumer and producer surplus.

Part II

MACRO BUSINESS ENVIRONMENT

National income determination

Introduction

The causes and consequences of the global recession of 2008–10 and its impacts on national income are, of course, major themes throughout this chapter. Indeed the so-called 'credit crunch' forms an important context for discussion in all chapters, but particularly in Chapters 9, 10, 13 and 14.

National income is, as the name implies, the income of the whole nation. However, it can be measured in three different ways, only one of which involves income, the other two using output and expenditure. Measuring national income is important since individuals, businesses and the government all have an interest in raising the real (after inflation) value of national income. Individuals can use their higher income to purchase more goods and services and thereby improve their standard of living. Businesses will now be able to sell more output so that they can raise revenue and profit. Governments will be more likely to retain the electoral support of their citizens where they benefit from a rising standard of living and the provision of improved public services. National income is thus of vital importance to the whole country and must therefore be carefully measured and monitored.

At first sight it might appear that the material in this chapter is a little technical and complex and has little real effect on the everyday life of consumers or businesses. This is not the case at all! The ideas, components and equilibrium levels of national income are extremely important, because what we are measuring here is the total economic activity inside an economy, and this is of crucial importance to us all.

It is of such importance that almost all large companies will employ economists and analysts to examine very closely any available data that might indicate future trends in the national income. Firms want to know this information in order to be able to judge when and by how much they should change target levels of output, hire or fire workers, invest in plant and machinery, hold inventories (stocks) and so on.

To illustrate how important national income is, one only needs to think of the consequences when it fails to grow, as occurred during the period December 2007–January 2010 when UK national income fell by 4.4% and global national income fell by 0.9%. If expenditure by households falls for some reason, then output too will start to fall and fewer workers will be needed to produce that output. Unemployment may not occur immediately, as initially businesses may cut back on overtime and abandon investment plans. However, eventually, in order to remain in business, lay-offs may well become necessary and unemployment will rise and household incomes will fall. Spending may not at first fall by much but eventually may fall substantially, leading to less demand for goods and services, making output fall even further. This downward spiral of economic activity is called the *deflationary multiplier*: businesses fail, profits fall, output falls, unemployment rises. Of course, this process can be reversed and become a self-reinforcing upward spiral of recovery for output and employment, as in the case of the *expansionary multiplier*. We consider both such possibilities during the course of this chapter.

Always remember that behind national income data lie real people, and the impact of changing economic circumstances on the human beings involved should not be underestimated!

What you'll learn

By the end of this chapter you should be able to:

- understand how national income is measured and what is meant by the various definitions of national income
- outline the relevance of national income data to international comparisons of standards of living
- consider the relevance of the various components of national income for business activity
- explain the meaning of 'equilibrium' national income and show how such an equilibrium is brought about
- use both the withdrawal/injection diagram and the 45° aggregate expenditure diagram to assess changes in the equilibrium levels of national income
- explain the meaning and importance of the 'national income multiplier'
- show how the government can respond to inflationary and deflationary 'gaps'.

Chapter 10 reviews government policy instruments and objectives in still more detail. It also develops the withdrawal/injection and 45° aggregate expenditure approaches into the aggregate demand and aggregate supply analysis, which is then applied to a range of policy issues.

National income

National income is a measure of the value of the *output* of the goods and services produced by an economy over a period of time, usually one year. It is also a measure of the *incomes* which flow from that output and the *expenditure* involved in purchasing that output. It follows that all three methods can be used to measure national income and we briefly review each in turn. However, before doing so it will help to introduce the so-called 'circular flow of income' and define some terms widely used when discussing national income.

Circular flow of income: simplified

Figure 9.1 presents a simplified approach to the circular flow of income within a domestic economy characterised by firms (producers) and households (consumers). It is 'simplified'

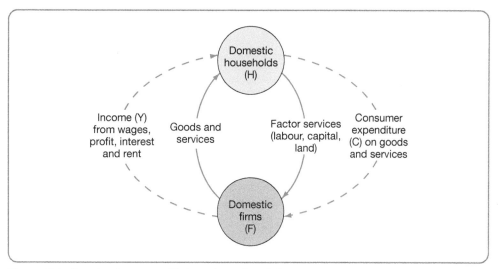

Figure 9.1 **Circular flow: no withdrawals and no injections**

in that we initially assume no savings, no investment, no government expenditure or taxation and no international trade (so no exports or imports). Nevertheless, this approach is useful in indicating that output, income and expenditure are all involved in the circular flow of income.

Make a note

We use the term 'domestic' throughout to refer to firms and households *located within* the domestic economy (e.g. within the UK).

Domestic households provide factor services (labour, loan capital, entrepreneurship, land) to domestic firms which use their services to produce an *output* of goods and services. These factor services from households are rewarded by *income* in the form of wages, dividends, interest and rent. With no savings in our simplified economy, no tax and no spending on imports, all the income received by domestic households goes in **consumption expenditure** (C) on the output of domestic firms.

In this simplified circular flow, any initial money value of income can be sustained indefinitely, since there are no withdrawals and no injections. In Figure 9.1 the dashed lines refer to 'monetary' flows, involving income and expenditure, whereas the solid lines refer to 'real' flows of factor services and the resulting output of goods and services.

It will be useful to consider a more realistic model of the circular flow of income before exploring the *three* alternative methods of measuring national income.

Circular flow of income: withdrawals and injections

We now relax our assumptions of no saving or investment, no government involvement and no international trade. As we can see from Figure 9.2, we now have certain **withdrawals** (W) from the circular flow of income, shown by a minus (−) sign, and certain **injections** (J), shown by a plus (+) sign.

Withdrawals (W)

Although it may seem over-fussy, it is very important to define carefully the terms we use in the circular flow.

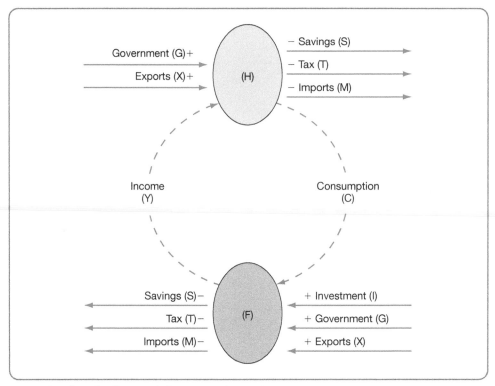

Figure 9.2 **Circular flow: withdrawals and injections**

We define a *withdrawal* (W) from the circular flow as either:

- any income received by a domestic household (H) not passed on to a domestic firm (F); or
- any income received by a domestic firm (F) not passed on to a domestic household (H).

Components of withdrawals (W)

As we see in Figure 9.2, some income received by domestic households (H) or domestic firms (F) is *not passed on* in the circular flow. In other words, it is saved (S), taxed (T) or spent on imports (M).

- *Savings* (S). These can be either personal savings by domestic households (H) or business savings (e.g. undistributed profits) by domestic firms (F).
- *Taxes* (T). These can be either taxes paid by domestic households (H), such as income tax, council tax, VAT etc. or taxes paid by domestic firms (F), such as corporation tax, business rates, VAT etc.
- *Imports* (M). These can be imports either by domestic firms (F) or domestic households (H) of goods or services from *overseas* firms or households.

In all the above cases, income received by domestic firms or households *is not passed on* in the circular flow to other domestic firms or households.

Withdrawals = Savings + Taxes + Imports

i.e.   W = S + T + M

Injections (J)

We define an *injection* (J) into the circular flow as either:

- any income received by a domestic household (H) that does not come from a domestic firm (F); or

- any income received by a domestic firm (F) that does not come from a domestic household (H).

Components of injections (J)

From Figure 9.2 we can identify investment (I), government expenditure (G) and exports (X) as meeting this definition of an injection.

- *Investment* (I). Here income is received by domestic firms (F) which does not come from domestic households (H) but from *other domestic firms* who purchase capital equipment, buildings etc. for investment purposes.

- *Government expenditure* (G). Here income is received by domestic firms (F) which does not come from domestic households (H) but from *the government* (e.g. government contracts). Alternatively, income is received by domestic households (H) which does not come from domestic firms (F) but from *the government* (e.g. public sector workers).

- *Exports* (X). Here income is received by domestic firms (F) which does not come from domestic households (H) but from *overseas households and firms*. Alternatively, income is received by domestic households (H) not from domestic firms (F) but from *overseas firms and households* (e.g. interest and dividends from overseas, consultancy overseas etc.).

Make a note | Strictly speaking, the *equals* (=) signs used previously should be *identity* (≡) signs. We use identity signs whenever we have defined a situation in such a way that the left-hand side must equal the right-hand side for *all* values of the variables.

Injections = Investment + Government expenditure + Exports

i.e.   J = I + G + X

Figure 9.2 (p. 262) brought these components of withdrawals (W) and injections (J) together on one diagram.

Case Study 9.1 | **Look after the cents**

There seems to be a contradiction between those who firmly believe that the global credit crunch can be laid at the door of profligate US consumers and others who take the opposite viewpoint, seeing the US consumer as essentially frugal during difficult times!

As long ago as 1867, Horace Greeley, a legendary American newspaper editor, described the US citizen as favouring spending: 'We are energetic, we are audacious; we are confident in our own capacities and in our national destiny; but we are not a systematic, or a frugal economical people.' On the other hand, David Blankenhorn, in his book Thrift: A Cyclopedia, argues otherwise. 'In this sweet land of liberty, one part of our inheritance . . . is thrift. [It] is more than anything else a restatement, in secular terms, of the Judaeo-Christian concept of stewardship.'

GfK Roper, a consumer behaviour analyst, notes that in every recession since 1981 American consumers have indeed been frugal, in such times going out less, whether to eat, for recreation or for holidays. According to the Pew Research Centre, which regularly polls US consumers, the global economic crisis that started in 2007 in America, has brought about a 'new creed of thrift'. From the early 1970s to 2007 its surveys found that the proportion of Americans who considered air conditioning or dishwashers a 'necessity' rose steadily, but in 2008–2010 that proportion dropped sharply!

Economists think they can explain changes in saving behaviour over time and across countries without reference to cultural norms. An IMF staff paper ascribes the enormous differences in saving rates between Americans, Germans and Japanese to demography, wealth and economic volatility. Germans and Japanese used to save more because they were older, had suffered more economic setbacks and were less wealthy, though Japanese saving rates have since come down as more people retire and draw down their savings. A model developed by Barack Obama's Council of Economic Advisers explains the American saving rate in terms of rising with wealth, rising with increased credit availability and falling with unemployment. It predicts that the US savings rate will eventually settle between 4% and 7%, having fallen from around 9% during the period 1960–2000, to only around 2% during much of the first decade of the new millennium.

Of course, political culture and national events can also influence savings rates. In 2001, after the terrorist attacks of 9/11, shopping was presented as a patriotic activity; a way for Americans to 'stick their thumb in the eye of the terrorists', as Dick Cheney, George Bush's vice-president, put it. Institutions can also influence saving behaviour. George Akerlof and Robert Shiller, in their book *Animal Spirits*, note that Singapore's sky-high saving rate can be traced to employers and employees having to pay compulsory contributions to the Central Provident Fund, created by the government in 1955.

Mr Blankenhorn blames the decline in America's 'natural tendency' to thrift on the rise of 'anti-thrift' institutions such as rent-to-own stores, cheque-cashing and chain pawn shops, indulgent credit-card companies and proliferating payday lenders. They flourished in America because voters and policy makers did not object. Belatedly, that has changed. Regulators and rulemakers now insist that lenders hold more capital and scrutinise borrowers more carefully. Whether Americans want to save more may be beside the point: they won't have much choice!

Source: Based on information from *The Economist* (2010), 3–9 April

Questions

1 Why did the US savings rate fall from 9% to less than 2% in 2008?

2 What factors are suggested as influencing the US savings rate?

3 Why are some suggesting that the US savings rate will eventually settle between 4% and 7%?

National income: definitions and measurement

Having introduced the various withdrawals from, and injections into, the circular flow, we are now in a better position to consider the different definitions of national income and the three methods for measuring national income.

National income definitions

Gross domestic product

Gross domestic product (GDP) is the value of output produced (and incomes received) by domestic residents (firms and households) using resources located within the domestic economy (e.g. within the UK).

Gross national product

Gross national product (GNP) is the value of output produced (and incomes received) by domestic residents from their *ownership of resources*, wherever these resources happen to be located, whether inside or outside the domestic economy. For example, GNP takes account of the fact that some UK residents (firms and households) earn incomes such as profits, interest and rent from owning resources located abroad. The *net* value to UK residents of such receipts from abroad and the equivalent payments abroad is called 'net property income from abroad' in the national accounts.

$$\text{GDP} + \text{Net property income from abroad} = \text{GNP}$$

Net national product

Gross national product is the total value of output produced and incomes received by UK residents in the course of a year. Unlike net national product (NNP) it therefore includes the full value of *new* plant and equipment produced during the course of the year (i.e. gross domestic fixed capital formation). However, over this period *existing* plant and equipment will have depreciated (i.e. declined in value due to wear and tear and obsolescence). In order to obtain a true measure of national income an appropriate deduction for capital depreciation must be made, i.e.

$$\text{GNP} - \text{Depreciation} = \text{NNP}$$

'Market prices' and 'factor cost'

All these measures of national income can be expressed either at 'market prices' or at 'factor cost'.

- Market prices. Here the value placed on any output uses the prices observed in the marketplace (where these are available). Such prices may, however, be distorted by taxes and subsidies. For example, the market prices of some products may be higher than they otherwise would be due to the taxes levied on them. Alternatively, the market prices may be lower than they otherwise would be due to subsidies received on them. 'Market prices' is a valuation approach which includes these impacts on price of taxes and subsidies.

- Factor cost. Here the value placed on any output seeks to *exclude* the 'distorting' impacts on the prices of product of any taxes or subsidies.
  - Taxes are subtracted from the valuation at market prices.
  - Subsidies are added to the valuation at market prices.

National income measurement

We now briefly consider the output, income and expenditure methods for measuring national income.

Strictly speaking, the national income accounts are defined in such a way that the three methods of measurement should give exactly the same result.

The output method

A country's national income can be calculated from the output figures of all firms in the economy (the 'output method'). However, this does not mean that we simply add together the value of each firm's output. To do so would give us an aggregate many times greater than the national income because of *double counting*.

- *Avoiding double counting.* The outputs of some firms are the inputs of other firms. For example, the output of the steel industry is used in part as an input for the automobile industry and so on. To avoid including the total value of the steel used in automobile production twice (double counting) we sum only the *value added* at each stage of production. Alternatively, we sum only the *final value* of output produced for the various goods and services.

Example

- A logger chops down trees and sells them to the sawmill for £500.
- At the sawmill the wood is cut into usable sizes, and sold to the timber merchant for £800.
- The timber merchant acts as the 'middleman' to B&Q and sells the wood to them for £900.
- B&Q sells the wood to the consumer for £1,500.

If we simply added all the outputs together it would add up to £3,700. But the original logging work has been added several times.

To avoid double counting we calculate the value added at each stage:

Logger	£500
Saw mill	£300
Timber merchant	£100
B&Q	£600
Total value added	£1,500

Or, we only include the value of output at the final stage, £1,500.

- *Inventories.* We must also ensure that any additions to 'stock and work in progress' (inventories) are included in the output figures for each industry, since any build-up in stock during a year must represent extra output produced during that year.

- *Public goods and merit goods.* We have already seen in Chapter 8 that the government provides many goods and services through the non-market sector, such as education, healthcare, defence, police and so on. Such goods and services are clearly part of the nation's output, but since many of these are not sold through the market sector, strictly they do not have a market price. In such cases, the value of the output is measured at resource cost or factor cost. In other words, the value of the service is assumed to be equivalent to the cost of the resources used to provide it (although since 2004 new attempts have been made to measure value added for the public sector services).

- *Self-provided commodities.* A similar problem arises in the case of self-provided commodities, such as vegetables grown in the domestic garden, car repairs and home improvements of a do-it-yourself type. Again, these represent output produced, but there is no market value of such output. The vast majority of self-provided commodities are omitted from the national income statistics.

- *Exports and imports.* Not all of the nation's output is consumed domestically. Part is sold abroad as exports. Nevertheless, GDP is the value of *domestically produced* output and so export earnings must be included in this figure. On the other hand, a great deal of domestically produced output incorporates imported raw materials and components. Hence the value of the import content of the final output must be deducted from the output figures if GDP is to be accurately measured.

● *Net property income from abroad.* This source of income to domestic residents will not be included in the output figures from firms. We have already noted that the net inflow (+) or outflow (−) of funds must be added to GDP when calculating the value of *domestically owned* output, i.e. GNP.

Make a note

If your syllabus requires a detailed treatment of the output, income and expenditure methods for measuring national income, read about these methods on pages 267–9, otherwise move on to page 269.

The income method

When calculating national product as a flow of incomes it is important to ensure that only the rewards for factor services are included. In other words, only those incomes paid in return for some productive activity and for which there is a corresponding output are included. Of course, it is the *gross value* of these factor rewards which must be aggregated, since this represents the value of output produced. Levying taxes on factor incomes reduces the amount the factors receive, but it does not reduce the value of the output produced!

● *Transfer payments.* Transfer payments are simply transfers of income within the community, and they are *not* made in respect of any productive activity. Indeed, the bulk of all transfer payments within the UK are made by the government for social reasons. Examples include social security payments, pensions, child allowances, and so on. Since no output is produced in respect of these payments they must be excluded from the aggregate of factor incomes.

● *Undistributed surpluses.* Another problem in aggregating factor incomes arises because not all factor incomes are distributed to the factors of production. For example, firms might retain part or all of their profits to finance future investment. Similarly, the profits of public bodies may accrue to the government rather than to private individuals. Care must be taken to include these undistributed surpluses as factor incomes.

● *Stock appreciation.* Care must be taken to *exclude* changes in the money value of inventory or stock caused by inflation. These are windfall gains, and do not represent a real increase in the value of output.

● *Net property income from abroad.* When moving from GDP to either GNP or NNP we have seen that it is necessary to *add* net property income from abroad to the aggregate of domestic incomes.

The expenditure method

The final method of calculating national income is as a flow of expenditure on domestic output.

● *Final output.* It is only expenditure on final output that must be aggregated, otherwise there is again a danger of double counting, with intermediate expenditure on raw materials and components being counted twice.

● *Current output.* It is only expenditure on current output that is relevant. Second-hand goods are not part of the current flow of output, and factors of production have already received payment for these goods at the time they were produced. We should note, however, that any income earned by a salesperson employed in the second-hand trade, or the profits of second-hand dealers, *are* included in the national income statistics. The service these occupations render is part of current production!

Using the symbols of Figure 9.2 (p. 262) we can say that, using the expenditure method:

$$GDP = C + I + G + X - M$$

where   C = Consumer expenditure
   I = Investment
   G = Government expenditure
   X = Exports expenditure
   M = Imports expenditure

As with the output and income methods, the value of expenditure in the economy must be adjusted if it is to measure national income accurately.

- *Consumer expenditure* (C). This is the major element in expenditure and in 2010 accounted for over 60% of GDP in the UK.

- *Investment expenditure* (I). Expenditure on fixed capital, such as plant and machinery, must obviously be included in calculations of total expenditure. Gross domestic fixed capital formation incorporates this item and in 2010 this was around 17% of GDP. What is not so obvious is that additions to stock and work in progress also represent investment. The factors of production which have produced this, as yet, unsold output will still have received factor payments. To ignore additions to stock and work in progress would therefore create an imbalance between the three aggregates of output, income and expenditure. Additions to stock and work in progress are therefore treated as though they have been purchased by firms. Care must be taken to include them in the aggregate of total domestic expenditure.

- *Government expenditure* (G). Since only domestic expenditure on goods and services is relevant, care must be taken to deduct any expenditure on transfer payments by the government or other public authorities. Transfer payments do not contribute directly to the current flow of output and, therefore, we must only include that part of government current expenditure which is spent directly on goods and services. In 2010 government (central and local) expenditure on goods and services was just over 20% of total domestic expenditure.

- *Exports* (X) *and imports* (M). We have already seen that it is important to include exports and exclude imports from our calculation of national income. Care must be taken to ensure this when aggregating total expenditures.

- *Net property income from abroad*. As before, when moving from GDP to GNP or NNP, it is important to include net property income from abroad when aggregating total expenditures.

- *Taxes and subsidies*. In measuring the value of expenditure, we are attempting to measure the value of payments made to the factors of production which have produced that output. Indirect taxes raise total expenditure on goods and services relative to the amount received by the factors of production. Subsidies have the opposite effect. In order to avoid a discrepancy between the income and expenditure totals, it is necessary to remove the effects of taxes and subsidies from the latter. The expenditure total is adjusted to *factor cost* by deducting indirect taxes and adding subsidies.

Whatever method we use to calculate national income, problems often occur when using GDP/GNP data to measure the true value of the standard of living, given the uncertainties in measuring different elements within the total.

Example

Problems in measuring public sector output

Until recently the Office for National Statistics (ONS) in the UK assumed that the output of public sector (state provided) services, such as education, health, police, fire, social services and so on, was equal to the amount of money spent on those services. In effect this meant that productivity was by definition always 1, with the value of output defined as equal to the value of input. However, new EU rules in 2006 were introduced to prevent this simplistic assumption, and statisticians in EU countries now have to find different measures to calculate the true value added of public sector services. In the UK new measures of public sector productivity (e.g. number of patients per nurse/per doctor) have changed productivity calculations for public sector workers and increased national income by around 1% per annum.

Make a note

The 'black economy'

One way in which the so-called 'black economy' can be estimated is through the difference between national income when measured by the *income* method and when measured by the *expenditure* method. Apart from errors and omissions, these are defined in the national accounts in such a way that they come to the same value. If, however, people receive income and do not declare it in tax returns, it will not appear on the income side, though expenditure will increase as the unrecorded income is spent on goods and services. In recent years the 'income' valuation – based on tax returns – has fallen short of the 'expenditure' valuation by progressively larger amounts. Some estimates have the 'black economy' as high as 10–12% of GDP.

We now turn to other problems encountered when using GDP data to make international comparisons of standards of living.

National income data: international comparisons

Real GDP per head is often used when comparing the standard of living between countries. Table 9.1 presents some recent data for the 15 members of the European Union before the various accession countries joined from 2004 onwards, making the current EU 27, together with recent data for all the EU27.

- *Absolute levels of GDP.* Clearly there is considerable variation between the EU 15, and even more so between the EU 27, with Germany, the UK, France and Italy having the four highest *absolute* levels of national income (GDP) measured in euros in 2010, with Malta in last position.

- *GDP per head.* However, when we divide by population size to get GDP per head, Luxembourg moves into first position, having a very small population, with Denmark second, Ireland third and Netherlands fourth.

- *Real GDP per head.* Although the 'real' value is not formally given in Table 9.1, we can see why we need to remove inflation from the comparison. Clearly inflation in 2010 was higher in Hungary, Slovenia and Romania than in other EU countries, so the actual *purchasing power* of the 'GDP per head' figure is overstated in these countries as compared to those with lower rates of inflation.

Table 9.1 **Standards of living in the EU, 2010**

Member country	Population (m)	GDP euro (bn)	GDP per capita euro (000s)	Inflation (%)
Belgium	10.8	345.5	32.1	1.3
Germany	81.9	2,436.0	29.8	0.6
Ireland	4.5	160.5	35.9	−0.8
Greece	11.3	243.0	21.4	1.4
Spain	46.6	1,046.0	22.5	0.8
France	64.8	1,992.0	30.8	1.1
Italy	60.4	1,573.0	26.0	1.8
Luxembourg	0.5	39.1	79.8	1.7
Netherlands	16.6	581.8	35.1	1.2
Austria	8.4	281.8	33.5	1.3
Portugal	10.7	164.1	15.4	1.3
Slovenia	2.0	36.3	17.9	3.9
Finland	5.4	180.0	30.7	1.6
Bulgaria	7.6	33.6	4.4	1.3
Czech Republic	10.5	140.9	13.4	1.4
Denmark	5.5	230.4	41.7	1.6
Estonia	1.3	13.4	10.1	0.8
Cyprus	0.8	17.8	22.1	3.3
Latvia	2.2	16.7	7.5	−3.7
Lithuania	3.5	24.7	7.4	−1.2
Hungary	10.1	98.1	1.0	4.2
Malta	0.4	5.8	13.9	1.6
Poland	38.1	327.0	8.5	2.0
Romania	21.4	122.9	5.7	3.6
Slovakia	5.4	69.5	12.8	2.3
Sweden	9.3	312.6	33.7	−1.0
United Kingdom	62.2	1,558.0	25.0	1.4
EU 27	**501.9**	**12,048.0**	**24.0**	**1.2**
EU 15	**398.7**	**11,420.0**	**27.9**	**1.1**

Notes: GDP is measured at current market prices. Inflation is measured as the private final consumption expenditure deflator.

Source: European Commission (2010) *European Economy 2009*, Statistical Annex, Spring. Reprinted with permission.

Problems in comparing international standards of living

Even when we do have the official 'real GDP per head' figure for each country, there are still problems in using this data for international comparisons.

● Aspects of one's quality of life may not be reflected in a monetary value, e.g. feelings of safety from attack, access to the countryside, freedom to express one's viewpoint without fear of retribution.

● The same income in one country does not buy the same as in another. For example, even within the EU the prices of goods vary. A recent survey by the Greek tourist board showed that the price of a cup of coffee in Athens was €3.4 while in Paris it cost €1.85.

- Needs vary between countries, for example in hot countries such as Greece and Spain the people do not need to spend as much on clothes or food as those who live in colder climates, though they might have to spend more on water or air conditioning.

Other factors that make international comparisons difficult might include variations between countries in any or all of the following:

- the level of unrecorded activity, such as activity in the informal ('black') economy;
- number of hours that people work;
- the level of public provision of goods and services;
- the distribution of national income (i.e. levels of inequality);
- the levels of negative externalities such as road congestion/pollution.

Such problems in comparing 'quality of life' increase still further when we are using real GDP per head to compare very different countries, such as the EU countries with developing economies in Africa.

Measuring 'well-being' in developing economies

We have suggested that real GDP per head is an important measure of economic well-being (standard of living). However, although this value gives an average figure for income (or output) per head of population, it is particularly unhelpful for measuring 'well-being' in developing economies.

(a) *Inappropriate exchange rates.* Unlike eurozone countries which have a common currency (the euro), converting the value of GDP expressed in a local currency into a $ equivalent using the *official exchange rate* may misrepresent the actual purchasing power in the developing economy. This is because the official exchange rate is influenced by a range of complex forces in the foreign exchange markets and may not accurately reflect the purchasing power of one country's currency in another country.

Make a note

> A more accurate picture is given if we use *purchasing power parities* (PPPs) rather than official exchange rates when making this conversion. Purchasing power parities measure how many units of one country's currency are needed to buy exactly the same basket of goods as can be bought with a given amount of another country's currency.

(b) *Differing degrees of non-market economic activity.* GDP per capita only includes the money value of recorded (market) transactions involving goods and services. Non-market transactions are excluded. For example, the output of subsistence agriculture, whereby farmers grow food for their own consumption, is excluded from GDP figures. In many less developed economies, where there is often a greater degree of non-market economic activity, this fact may lead GDP figures to underestimate the true living standards.

(c) *Varying levels of inequality.* GDP per capita gives an indication of the 'average' standard of living in a country. However, this may reflect the experience of only a small number of people in that country because its income distribution may be highly unequal, being skewed in the direction of the wealthier sections of society.

(d) *Incidence of externalities.* Externalities occur where actions by an individual or group impose costs (or benefits) on others which are not fully 'priced' (see Chapter 8). Increased pollution is a by-product of many industrial processes, reducing the quality of life for those affected. However, this negative externality may not be reflected in the GDP calculations. Similarly, the GDP figure makes no allowance for the depletion and degradation of natural resources and for the social costs these may impose, e.g. deforestation as a factor in global warming etc.

For these and other reasons (differing accounting conventions, economic and social practices etc.) there has been a move towards the use of indicators *other than* the GDP per capita figure to reflect the 'true' standard of living in developing countries. For example, various 'quality of life' indicators such as life expectancy, medical provision (number of people per doctor or nurse), educational opportunities (age of leaving school) are now widely used. The United Nations has published a Human Development Report since 1990 in which a new method of classification is presented, namely the *Human Development Index*, which incorporates both quality of life indicators and GDP per head data.

Case Study 9.2 looks in rather more detail at why official national income statistics need to be supplemented by other indicators if the true 'quality of life' of those in developing or developed countries is to be assessed. The focus here is particularly on families and children in these developing countries.

Case Study 9.2   Comparing standards of living

An interesting issue is whether the conventional GNP per capita figure can be merged with 'quality of life' indicators to give an overall index of economic well-being. A first step in this direction has in fact been made with the publication of the United Nations' Human Development Index (HDI). In Table 9.2 we present more comprehensive data for 17 countries. We also show the rank of these countries (out of 182 countries) in terms of real GNP per head using purchasing power

Table 9.2 Selected country indicators and rankings (out of 182 countries)

	(1) GNP per head ($)	(2) Real GNP per head (PPP$)	(3) Life expectancy at birth (years)	(4) Adult literacy rate (%)	(5) Enrolment ratio* (%)	(6) Human Development Index (HDI)	(7) Rank by real GNP per head (PPP$)	(8) Rank by HDI
Ethiopia	280	779	55	36	49	0.414	171	171
Cambodia	600	1,802	61	76	59	0.593	143	137
Cuba	4,870	6,876	79	100	100	0.863	95	51
Nigeria	1,160	1,969	48	72	53	0.511	175	158
India	1,070	2,753	63	66	61	0.612	128	134
China	2,940	5,383	73	93	69	0.772	102	92
Philippines	1,890	3,406	72	93	80	0.751	124	105
Brazil	7,350	9,567	72	90	87	0.813	79	75
Trinidad	18,340	23,507	69	99	61	0.837	64	90
Poland	11,880	15,887	76	99	88	0.888	53	41
Botswana	4,781	13,604	53	83	71	0.699	60	125
Germany	42,440	34,401	80	100	88	0.947	24	22
Norway	87,070	53,433	81	100	98.6	0.971	5	1
UK	45,390	35,130	79	100	89	0.947	20	21
Japan	38,210	33,632	83	100	87	0.96	26	10
USA	47,580	45,592	79	100	93	0.956	9	13
Switzerland	65,330	40,658	82	100	87	0.96	13	9

*Percentage of population at Levels 1, 2 and 3 (combined) of *OECD Literacy Survey*

Sources: Adapted from *Human Development Report* (2009), UN; *World Development Report* (2010)

Case Study 9.2 *continued*

parities and in terms of the Human Development Index. Before commenting further on these rankings it will help if we explore the background to the HDI a little further.

The Human Development Index (HDI) is based on three indicators.

- *Standard of living*, as measured by real GNP per capita (PPP$) (column 2 in Table 9.2).
- *Life expectancy at birth*, in years (column 3 in Table 9.2).
- *Educational attainment*, as measured by a weighted average of adult literacy (two-thirds weight) and enrolment ratio (one-third weight) (columns 4 and 5 respectively in Table 9.2).

Each of these three indicators is then expressed in index form, with a scale set between a minimum value (index = 0) and a maximum value (index = 1) for each indicator.

- *Standard of living*: $100 real GNP per capita (PPP$) is the minimum value (index = 0) and $40,000 is the maximum value (index = 1).
- *Life expectancy at birth*: 25 years is the minimum value (index = 0) and 85 years is the maximum value (index = 1).
- *Educational attainment*: 0% for both adult literacy and enrolment ratios are the minimum values used for calculating the weighted average (index = 0) and 100% for both adult literacy and enrolment ratios are the maximum values used for calculating the weighted average (index = 1).

An index is then calculated for each of these three indicators, and the average of these three index numbers is then calculated, as shown for each country in column 6 of Table 9.2. This average of the three separate index numbers is the Human Development Index (HDI). The closer to 1 is the value of the HDI, the closer the country is to achieving the maximum values defined for each of the three indicators.

From columns 7 and 8 of Table 9.2 we can see that the rankings of the countries (in order from 1 to 182)

do vary with the type of indicator used. In other words using a GNP per head indicator, even adjusted for purchasing power parities, gives a different ranking for countries than using the HDI index which brings quality of life aspects into the equation.

The HDI, by bringing together both economic and quality of life indicators, suggests a smaller degree of underdevelopment for some countries than is indicated by economic data alone. For example, Cuba is 95th out of 182 countries when the GNP per head data is used for ranking (column 7) but rises forty-four places to 51st when the HDI is used for ranking (column 8). For Cuba it would seem that the high life expectancy at birth and high adult literacy and enrolment ratios into education have helped raise these indicators and thereby the overall HDI. On the other hand, the HDI suggests a greater degree of under-development for some countries than is indicated by economic data alone. For example, Botswana is 60th out of 182 countries when the GNP per head data is used for ranking (column 7) but falls by sixty-five places to 125th when the HDI is used for ranking (column 8). For Botswana it would seem that the relatively low life expectancy of a country ravaged by Aids and relatively low adult literacy and enrolment ratios have lowered the overall HDI.

Although only in its infancy, it may be that classification of countries based on indices such as the HDI which bring together both economic and quality of life data, may give a more accurate picture of the level of development.

Questions

1 Comment on the strengths and weaknesses of using the Human Development Index (HDI) as a measure of comparative standards of living.

2 What other indices might be used in calculating the HDI in the future?

3 What types of policy interventions might help strengthen the possibilities of sustainable development for countries with a low HDI score?

4 Why is column 2 sometimes quite different from column 1 for the 17 countries in Table 9.2?

Despite these problems, national income data is still of great importance to governments and policy makers. We now look in more detail at the various components of the circular flow of income before examining how the equilibrium level of national income is determined in a country.

Components of the circular flow

It will be useful at this point to look at the various components of the circular flow in general terms and consider their relevance for business activity. In the next section we consider these same components rather more technically in terms of their role in determining the equilibrium value of national income.

Savings (S) and Investment (I)

Savings (S)

In the UK household savings have varied considerably over time, from around 2% of household income just after the Second World War to over 12% in the early 1980s and early 1990s. In 2010 this *household savings ratio* had fallen to around 4% of household income.

Of course, *national savings* depend on households, business and the government, all of whom may choose to save part of any extra income rather than spend it. When we aggregate all these savings, some 15% of the UK's national income is saved, which is a lower national savings ratio than that of any other OECD country today except for Turkey (13%) and Portugal (3%).

In the first instance, savings withdraws income from the circular flow, so that excessive savings may discourage business activity by reducing demand for goods and services.

Of course, should these national savings be re-injected back into the economy, as for example by being used for investment purposes, then the situation may be quite different.

Example

Thrifty Japan

Worried that the government may not be able to afford to pay for their future pensions, Japan's ageing population prefers to save rather than spend. Even with interest rates effectively 0%, this concern for the future has meant that Japanese banks are awash with savings. Unfortunately, over the past decade so few firms want to borrow these savings for investment that with so much saving and so little consumer spending the Japanese economy has barely grown.

Investment (I)

Investment expenditure is around 12% of total expenditure in the UK, i.e. around one-quarter the value of consumption expenditure (see p. 284). Nevertheless, investment is arguably one of the most significant components of total expenditure. It is highly volatile and through its impacts on productivity affects both the supply and demand sides of the economy.

Quote

In discussing the volatility of investment, John Maynard Keynes noted that expectations of business people could change dramatically at the first sign of good or bad news, using the phrase 'animal spirits' to describe the unpredictable temperament of investors. He went on to state that the prospective yields of investment projects were based on: '... partly future events which can only be forecasted with more or less confidence'.

(Keynes, 1936, p. 147)

In practice, a number of important variables may influence the firm's desire to invest in new projects. These are explored further in *Taking it further* 9.1.

Taking it further **What determines investment**   *9.1*

Rate of interest

Lower rates of interest will encourage firms to invest more since the expected returns on some projects will now exceed the costs of borrowing to fund these projects. This is the reasoning behind the so-called *marginal efficiency of investment* (MEI) theory.

The MEI approach uses a rate of discount (i) to derive the *present value* (PV) of various investment projects. Strictly, the MEI of a particular project is that rate of discount which would equate the PV of the expected future income stream from a project with its initial capital outlay (the supply price):

$$S = PV = \frac{R_1}{(1 + i)} + \frac{R_2}{(1 + i)^2} + \frac{R_3}{(1 + i)^3} + \cdots \frac{R_n}{(1 + i)^n}$$

where   S = the supply price
PV = present value
R = the expected yearly return; and
i = that rate of discount necessary to equate the present value of future income with the initial cost of the project.

The curve relating the marginal efficiency of investment (i) to the level of investment in Figure 9.3 is negatively sloped, for two main reasons.

- First, the earliest investment projects undertaken are likely to be the most profitable, i.e. offering the highest expected yearly returns (R) and therefore having the highest marginal efficiencies of investment (i). As more projects are initiated, they are likely to be less and less profitable, with lower expected yearly returns, and therefore lower MEIs.

- Second, a rise in the level of investment undertaken is, at least in the short run, likely to raise the supply price (S), which in turn will reduce the MEI. This could follow if the industries producing capital goods faced capacity constraints in their attempt to raise output in the short run.

The decision on whether to proceed with an investment project will depend on the relationship between the rate of interest (r) and the marginal efficiency of investment (i). If r is less than i then the annual cost of borrowing funds for an additional project will be less than the expected annual return on the initial capital outlay, so that the project will be profitable to undertake.

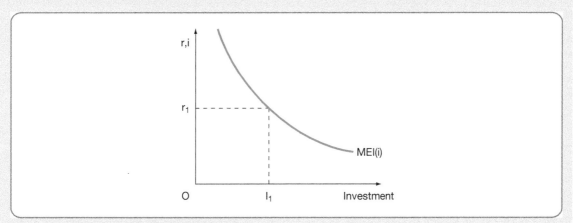

Figure 9.3 The investment demand schedule

Taking it further 9.1 continued

In Figure 9.3 with interest rate r_1 it will be profitable to invest in all projects up to I_1 with I_1 itself breaking even. The MEI schedule is therefore the *investment demand schedule*, telling us the level of investment that will be undertaken at any given rate of interest.

Expectations play an important role in this theory of investment. If, as is often the case, expectations are volatile, then the expected yearly returns (R) on any project will change, causing substantial shifts in the MEI schedule. At any given rate of interest investment demand will therefore be changing, which will reduce the closeness of any statistical fit between the interest rate and investment.

In fact, it may be via expectations that interest rates exert their major influence on investment. A fall in interest rates is often a signal to investors of better times ahead, raising expected returns, shifting the MEI curve to the right, and raising investment (and conversely).

Accelerator theory

This suggests that if the existing capital stock is being fully used, then any *change in output* (ΔY) can only be achieved by new (net) investment (I_n). It also assumes that the capital/output ratio is some constant representing the extra value of capital needed on average to secure £1 of additional output.

$$\text{i.e.}\quad I_n = a\Delta Y$$

Suppose **national output** is at **full capacity** and rises (ΔY) by £4m during the year, with £5 of new investment in capital needed, on average, for each extra £1 of output (a = 5) to be produced. New investment (I_n) will then be 5 × £4m = £20m according to this accelerator theory.

An obvious weakness is that if there is spare capacity, then new investment will not be needed to raise output.

Profitability

There are at least two reasons why changes in profitability might be associated with changes in investment.

1 Higher profits may improve business confidence and raise the expected future return on any project. An outward shift of the MEI schedule (see Figure 9.3) might then raise investment at any given rate of interest.

2 Higher profits may raise investment by reducing its cost, as funds generated internally are cheaper than those obtained from any other source.

Taxation (T) and government expenditure (G)

Taxation (T)

Around 37% of all UK national income is currently taken in various forms of taxation on household income (income tax and National Insurance payments), company income (corporation tax) and household and company expenditure (VAT, customs and excise duties) etc. Such taxes represent, at least initially, a withdrawal from the circular flow of income and the total tax take is likely to rise as household and corporate incomes and expenditures increase.

Example

National rates of taxation

The UK is only a middle-ranked country in terms of taxation. Whereas some 37% of UK national income is taken in all types of tax, the figure is much higher for countries such as Sweden (50%), Denmark (49%), Belgium (45%) and many others, although the US has a much smaller tax take at only 27% of national income.

Links

A more detailed
treatment of both
taxation and govern-
ment expenditure
can be found in
Chapter 10
(pp. 303–16).

Government expenditure (G)

Government expenditure is currently around 42% of total expenditure in the UK. Extra government spending will result in extra income for those employed in the growing public sector or for the private firms used in providing public sector goods and services. These households and firms will in turn spend some of their extra income on the output of other businesses, further raising incomes and employment (see the 'multiplier', p. 293).

Imports (M) and exports (X)

Imports (M)

Imports, like savings and taxation, are treated as a withdrawal from the circular flow since income received is not passed on as expenditure to domestic firms or households. Imports of goods and services have risen substantially in the UK in recent years, and in 2009 exceeded exports of goods and services by around £32bn. As national income rises in the UK so does consumer expenditure (see p. 284), but much of this extra spending has gone on imported goods and services. Of course, in the more recent recession imports have risen less sharply than exports from the UK, and the £32bn excess of imports over exports in 2009 is much smaller than the £54bn excess figure recorded in 2006.

It is on the goods side that imports have risen the fastest. In fact, imports exceeded exports of goods in the UK by around £82bn in 2009, whereas imports fell short of exports of services in the UK by around £49bn.

Example

Increased import penetration in goods and services

As the world becomes more globalised and trade expands, import penetration ratios have increased. For example, imports of both goods and services in the UK rose from 15.9% of total domestic expenditure in 1992, to 20% in 2000, and to 24.3% in 2010. The ratio of imports to total domestic expenditure in 2010 was similar in France (23.3%), higher in Germany (30.7%) but were much lower in Japan (9.4%) and the US (12.6%). The reason for such differences is that in the two largest economies of the US and Japan much of the domestic spending is supplied by home producers given the substantial domestic production capacity in these economies.

There is strong evidence to suggest that a high proportion of any extra national income is spent on imported goods and services, particularly the former. Estimates indicate that the income elasticity of demand (see p. 55) for imported goods and services is around +2 for the UK, suggesting that for each 1% rise in real income, total demand for imported goods and services rises by 2%.

Our assumption throughout this chapter that imports rise with national income (as do savings and taxes) is therefore quite realistic. These three items, savings, taxes and imports, comprise 'total withdrawals' in the circular flow model, since in all cases income received is *not* passed directly on to domestic households and firms.

Exports (X)

As we have already noted, exports of goods and services fell short of imports by some £32bn in the UK in 2009. As with investments and government spending, exports result in a demand for goods and services from domestic households and businesses. Therefore these three items of expenditure, together with consumer expenditure, are regarded as 'aggregate expenditure' in the circular flow model. However, these three items (I + G + X) are treated separately as 'injection' expenditures (J) which do not vary with the level of national income, unlike consumer expenditure (C) which is assumed to vary with the level of national income (see p. 284).

Equilibrium in the circular flow: W/J approach

'Equilibrium' or balance in the circular flow will occur, using this approach, when the value of withdrawals (W) from the circular flow exactly matches the value of injections (J) into the circular flow.

i.e. $W = J$ is the equilibrium condition

Make a note

This time it is strictly correct to use an equals (=) sign because W will only equal J for certain values of the variable (national income), not for all values of that variable.

Finding the equilibrium value of national income

To make the analysis simple, it is often assumed that the value of withdrawals (W) and of all its components (S, T and M) are *directly related* to the level of national income (Y). In other words, as national income (Y) rises, so does the value of savings (S), taxes (T) and imports (M) and therefore of withdrawals (W), defined as S + T + M. This situation is shown in Figure 9.4 and is further explored on pages 280–82 below.

Stop and think   *9.1*

1 Can you explain why it is reasonable to suppose that the W schedule will rise as national income (Y) rises?

2 Can you explain why the W schedule intersects the vertical axis at a negative value in Figure 9.4?

However, it is often assumed in the W/J approach that the value of injections (J) is *unrelated* to the level of national income (Y). As we can see from Figure 9.4, this means that the injections schedule (J) is shown as a horizontal straight line, suggesting that the values of investment (I), government expenditure (G) and exports (X) are unchanged as national income rises or falls.

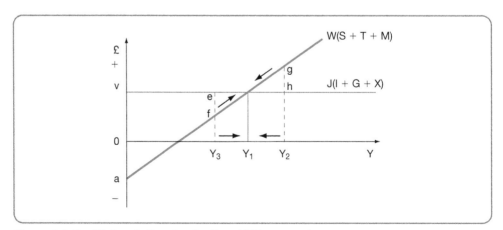

Figure 9.4 Equilibrium in the circular flow: W/J approach

Stop and think   9.2

Can you explain why this assumption for injections (J), while it helps to make the analysis easier, is actually unrealistic?

All the relationships in Figure 9.4 are assumed to be linear, so that the 'curves' can be drawn as straight lines.

In terms of the circular flow, we say that the various injections (I, G and X) are **exogenous variables**, determined outside the model, as these are independent of national income (Y). However, the various withdrawals (S, T and M) are **endogenous variables**, determined inside the model as they are dependent on national income (Y).

Before examining the individual components in Figure 9.4 more carefully, we can use the diagram to indicate why the *equilibrium* value for national income is Y_1. To do this we might look at values for national income that are *not* equilibrium values.

- *National income level Y_2.* Here withdrawals exceed injections (by g – h) so the value of the circular flow of income (Y_2) will fall. It will continue to fall until withdrawals have fallen sufficiently to exactly equal the unchanged value of injections at national income level Y_1.

- *National income level Y_3.* Here injections exceed withdrawals (by e – f) so the value of the circular flow of income (Y_3) will rise. It will continue to rise until withdrawals have risen sufficiently to exactly equal the unchanged value of injections at national income level Y_1.

Only at national income level Y_1, where W = J, is there no further tendency for national income to change. We then say we have an equilibrium (balanced) level of income at Y_1 only.

We have seen that *investment* is an important component of injections into the circular flow. However, Case Study 9.3 suggests that the return on investment is falling in the US relative to other countries.

Case Study 9.3   **US capital productivity decline must be reversed**

The biggest problem the US is facing is the decline in the productivity of capital. After the end of the Second World War it took less than $2 of investment by government, corporations and individuals to produce $1 of GDP growth. The productivity of capital continued to be impressive until 1980 when Europe had recovered and Japan was producing cars and consumer electronics products that found wide acceptance in world markets.

In a single decade of the 1980s, the productivity of capital declined from a level where it took less than $2 of investment to produce $1 of growth to one where about $3 was needed. If you assign a 30% gross profit margin to that revenue growth, the return on investment declined from 15% to 10%.

That level of return proved to be satisfactory, but in the first decade of the current century capital productivity declined seriously in the US. Because of profligate spending on over-priced housing and other assets that declined seriously, as well as deficit spending by the government, by the end of the decade it took $6 of capital to produce $1 of growth. The return on that would only be 5% and few would put money at risk for that reward.

When you look abroad to assess the US competitive position, the results are not encouraging. It is hard to put together comparable information but, based on the data I could gather, Europe was still getting $1 of growth for $2 of investment and China was getting at least $1 of growth for each dollar of investment.

If the US is to stop losing ground against other mature and developing economies, it is going to

Case Study 9.3 *continued*

have to invest money to work more effectively in terms of capital productivity. The US is still the leader in technology and scientific research and must continue to take advantage of the commercial possibilities of innovation. If the US does not reverse the current trends in capital productivity growth in the US beyond 2010 will be disappointing and the US standard of living will decline.

Questions

1 Suggest reasons for the observed decline in capital productivity in the US.

2 Examine some of the possible impacts on US National Income if this trend continues.

3 What policy measure in the US might help to reverse this trend?

It will be useful at this point to look rather more carefully at the withdrawals and injections schedules. We will come across the important ideas of *marginal propensities* and *average propensities* in this part of our analysis.

Withdrawals schedule (W)

At this stage let us consider in greater detail the *direct* relationship we have assumed to exist between each component of withdrawals (i.e. S, T and M) and the level of national income (Y).

Withdrawals (W) and national income (Y)

Here we examine in more detail the suggestion of Figure 9.5 that each component of W (i.e. S, T and M) varies directly with the level of national income (Y), i.e. rising as Y rises, falling as Y falls.

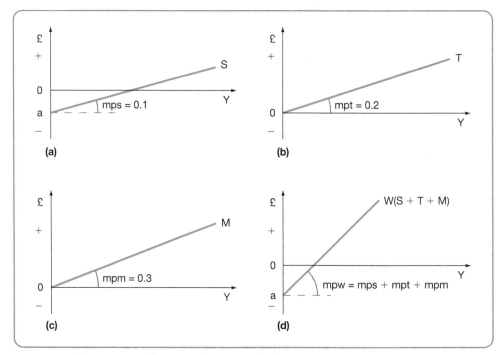

Figure 9.5 How savings (S), taxes (T), imports (M) and withdrawals (W) vary with national income (Y)

The savings (S), taxes (T) and imports (M) schedules are all drawn as straight lines, which assumes a *linear* relationship between each component and national income (Y). However, one difference is immediately apparent, namely that the savings schedule (S) does *not* go through the origin (zero). Rather Figure 9.5(a) shows S as having a negative value (−a) when national income (Y) is zero. The suggestion here is that at zero income, households will still have to spend some money on consuming various goods and services, and this can only come from running down past savings (i.e. *dissaving* or negative savings).

However, it is often assumed, as in Figure 9.5(b), that at zero income the government receives no tax revenue and, as in Figure 9.5(c), that at zero income there is no spending on imports. It follows that the T and M schedules go through the origin (zero).

In Figure 9.5(d) the withdrawals schedule (W) is shown as the aggregate of the three previous schedules (S + T + M).

For example, suppose we have the following relationships for S, T and M with respect to national income (Y).

$$S = -5 + 0.1\,Y$$
$$T = 0.2\,Y$$
$$M = 0.3\,Y$$
$$\text{Then} \quad W = -5 + 0.6\,Y$$

We can use this last relationship to explore the ideas of *marginal propensity to withdraw* and *average propensity to withdraw*. This important but rather technical material is considered in *Taking it further* 9.2.

Taking it further Marginal and average propensity to withdraw   9.2

Marginal propensity to withdraw (mpw)

This is a ratio of the change in total withdrawals (ΔW) to the change in national income (ΔY). For example, if the household withdraws 60 pence out of an extra £1 of income, then mpw = 0.6. For any straight line (linear) withdrawals schedule this is given by the slope of the line, and is a constant over its entire length.

$$\text{Marginal propensity to withdraw (mpw)} = \frac{\text{Change in Withdrawals}}{\text{Change in National Income}}$$

$$= \frac{\Delta W}{\Delta Y}$$

where Δ = 'change in'

The mpw is shown in Figure 9.5(d) as the slope of the straight line withdrawals schedule (W). We have found this to be 0.6, suggesting that for every £1 rise in national income, 60 pence is withdrawn.

Other marginal propensities

You should be able to see that:

$$\text{Marginal propensity to save (mps)} = \frac{\text{Change in Savings}}{\text{Change in National Income}} = \frac{\Delta S}{\Delta Y} = 0.1$$

$$\text{Marginal propensity to tax (mpt)} = \frac{\text{Change in Taxation}}{\text{Change in National Income}} = \frac{\Delta T}{\Delta Y} = 0.2$$

$$\text{Marginal propensity to import (mpm)} = \frac{\text{Change in Imports}}{\text{Change in National Income}} = \frac{\Delta M}{\Delta Y} = 0.3$$

$$mpw = mps + mpt + mpm$$

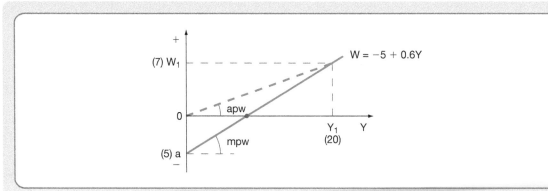

Figure 9.6 The withdrawals function (W), average propensity to withdraw (apw) and marginal propensity to withdraw (mpw)

Average propensity to withdraw (apw)

However, we are often interested in the *average* as well as marginal propensities. The difference between apw and mpw is shown in Figure 9.6.

$$\text{Average propensity to withdraw (apw)} = \frac{\text{Total Withdrawals}}{\text{Total National Income}} = \frac{W}{Y}$$

Using the withdrawals (W) schedule in Figure 9.6:

$$W = -5 + 0.6Y$$
$$\text{At, say, } Y_1 = 20$$
$$W_1 = -5 + 0.6(20)$$
$$\text{i.e.} \quad W_1 = 7$$

We can therefore say that at a level of national income (Y_1) of 20:

$$\text{apw} = \frac{7}{20} = 0.35$$

We should be able to see from Figure 9.6 that apw is the slope of the straight line drawn from the origin to the relevant point on the withdrawals schedule (W). We should also be able to see that apw (unlike mpw) will rise continuously as the level of national income rises.

Stop and think 9.3 gives you the opportunity to think about the other average propensities to save, tax and import.

Stop and think   9.3

1 Define:
   (a) average propensity to save (aps)
   (b) average propensity to tax (apt)
   (c) average propensity to import (apm).

2 Using Figure 9.5(a), (b) and (c) on p. 280, calculate the respective average propensities when national income (Y) is 20 (assume the vertical intercept is −5 in Figure 9.5 (a)).

3 Using Figure 9.5(a), (b) and (c), suggest how the following relate to each other:
   (a) mps and aps;
   (b) mpt and apt;
   (c) mpm and apm.

Injections schedule (J)

As already mentioned, we assume that each component of J (i.e. I, G and X) does *not* vary with national income, even though this may be something of an oversimplification. The injection schedule (J) is therefore drawn as a horizontal straight line at some given value v in Figure 9.4 (p. 278).

Put another way, we are treating each component of injections (i.e. I, G and X) as an *exogenous variable*, i.e. one that affects the equilibrium value of the circular flow but whose value is determined outside the circular flow.

Equilibrium in the circular flow: 45° diagram approach

An alternative approach to the W/J diagram in finding the equilibrium level of national income involves the 45° diagram. This approach makes use of the expenditure method (p. 267) of calculating national income.

The term *aggregate expenditure* (E) (or *aggregate demand*) is sometimes used to describe (C + I + G + X).

Under this approach, the equilibrium level of national income occurs where the value of aggregate expenditure (E) exactly equals the value of national output (Y).

$$E = Y$$

i.e. $C + I + G + X = Y$ in equilibrium

Figure 9.7 represents this situation, with equilibrium national income at Y_1 (where $E_1 = Y_1$). Notice that the 45° line represents all the values in the diagram for which E = Y.

Stop and think   *9.4*

Can you use the idea of a right-angled triangle to prove why E = Y at all points along the 45° diagram?

It follows that only where the aggregate expenditure schedule E *intersects* the 45° diagram do we fulfil the equilibrium condition E = Y.

● At levels of national income *above* Y_1, the value of expenditure *is less than* the value of output (i.e. E < Y), so the value of output falls.

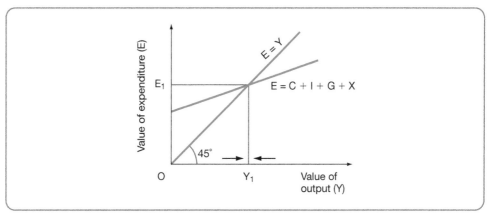

Figure 9.7 **Equilibrium in the circular flow: 45° diagram approach**

- At levels of national income *below* Y_1, the value of expenditure *is greater than* the value of output (i.e. E > Y), so the value of output rises.
- Only at Y_1 where the aggregate expenditure schedule intersects the 45° line do we have the value of expenditure *exactly equal* to the value of output, i.e. an equilibrium (E_1 = Y_1) at which the value of output does not change.

The *aggregate expenditure* schedule (E) in Figure 9.7 includes the *consumption schedule* (C), sometimes called the *consumption function*. We now consider this consumption function in rather more detail, together with the important ideas of the marginal propensity to consume (mpc) and the average propensity to consume (apc).

The consumption function

Consumption is the most important single element in aggregate expenditure in the UK, accounting for around half its total value. John Maynard Keynes related consumption to current disposable income, and his ideas are embodied in the so-called consumption function.

In the *General Theory*, Keynes argued that:

Quote

the fundamental psychological law . . . is that men are disposed, as a rule and on the average, to increase their consumption as their income increases, but not by as much as the increase in their income.

(Keynes, 1936, p. 96)

From this statement can be derived the Keynesian consumption function.

The *consumption function* shows how consumer expenditure (C) varies directly with the level of national income (Y). In Figure 9.8 we can see that at zero national income consumption (C) is +a. Consumer spending with zero income can only be achieved by running down past savings (i.e. *dissaving*), as we noted in Figure 9.5(a) previously. Again we assume a straight-line (linear) relationship between consumption (C) and national income (Y).

Case Study 9.4 looks a little more closely at the *consumption function* which plays such an important role in the circular flow of income.

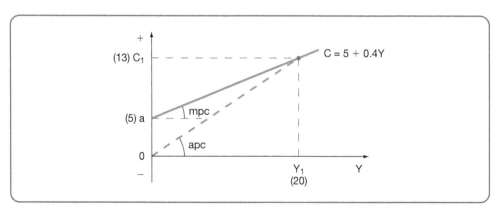

Figure 9.8 The consumption function C, average propensity to consume (apc) and marginal propensity to consume (mpc)

Case Study 9.4   Consumer behaviour, indebtedness and the sub-prime market

The 'consumption function' in Figure 9.8 (p. 284) relates consumer spending to the current level of income of individuals and the nation. As we noted above, it is assumed that consumer spending will rise as national income rises. However, in reality, consumer spending may depend on much more than the current level of national income.

Certainly the consumer has been widely seen as sustaining the UK economy by continuing to purchase goods and services, creating extra output and employment. However, there is major concern that the growing 'debt overhang' may reduce consumer spending sharply in the near future. Figures from the Bank of England in 2010 showed that the average indebted household in Britain owed around £5,000 in *unsecured debt* (hire purchase, credit cards, personal loans, overdrafts). A major concern for analysts is that any sustained future rise in interest rates will make it extremely difficult for UK households to keep up their repayments on all types of debt, both secured and unsecured. Indeed debts in the UK on mortgages, overdrafts and credit cards now exceed the annual value of UK national income.

These concerns were not helped by events in the sub-prime market in late 2007. The term 'sub-prime' is widely used to refer to excessive lending for mortgage purposes in the USA to low-income borrowers at high risk. When economic slowdown occurred in the USA in 2006/7, many of these high-risk borrowers lost their jobs and/or found themselves unable to pay the higher monthly repayments as US interest rates rose substantially in 2006/7 (by around 4% in a little over one year). Nor did these low-income/high-risk borrowers have assets to help cushion falls in their current income. As a result many have defaulted on their loans and the bad debt provisions of the lenders have soared, putting huge pressure on themselves and on other financial firms worldwide which have invested in them.

By mid-2010, US house prices had fallen by 29%, and share prices by a similar amount, from their 2007 peak. A simulation by economists at the UBS bank suggests that a 10% drop in US house and share prices would reduce US economic growth by as much as 2.6 percentage points. This cut-back in projected economic growth was linked to the expectation of a significant fall in consumer spending in the USA, given the *reversal* of the previous 'wealth effect' whereby higher house prices had played a key role in stimulating consumer borrowing and indebtedness. Indeed by mid-2010 household wealth in the US had shrunk by $12 trillion, or by 18%, since 2007.

'Contagion' is a word much feared by analysts of the sub-prime market. Many innovative financial instruments developed and used ('securitisation') to stimulate extra lending and borrowing are now viewed with much greater suspicion by the financial markets. Lending between financial intermediaries themselves has also diminished, as they have become more unsure of the true creditworthiness of the borrowers, given that there is now serious concern over the value of many of these new financial instruments in their portfolio. This reluctance of financial intermediaries to lend to each other was a key factor in the problems experienced by Northern Rock in the UK, whose business model depended on regular inter-bank loans which were no longer forthcoming. The share price of Northern Rock collapsed in late 2007, forcing the Bank of England to step in as 'lender of last resort' and to avoid a systemic banking failure in the UK.

Questions

1 What impact would higher interest rates have on the consumption function in Figure 9.8 (p. 284)?

2 How would this influence the equilibrium level of national income?

3 What do you understand by the sub-prime market? How have events in that market influenced equilibrium national income?

4 Are there any policy measures which government might take to help reduce this potential problem?

At this point it may be useful to explore the ideas of *marginal propensity to consume* and *average propensity to consume*. This important but rather technical material is considered in *Taking it further* 9.3.

> Taking it further **Marginal and average propensity to consume**   9.3

Marginal propensity to consume (mpc)

The marginal propensity to consume (mpc) is a ratio of the change in total consumption (ΔC) to the change in national income (ΔY). For example, if the consumer spends 40 pence out of an extra £1 of income, then mpc = 0.4. For any straight-line (linear) relationship this is given by the slope of the line, and is a constant over its entire length.

$$\text{Marginal propensity to consume (mpc)} = \frac{\text{Change in consumption}}{\text{Change in national income}} = \frac{\Delta C}{\Delta Y}$$

$$\text{where } \Delta = \text{'change in'}$$

The mpc is shown in Figure 9.8 as the slope of the straight-line consumption function (C), and has the value 0.4. This suggests that for every £1 rise in national income, 40 pence is consumed.

mpc and mpw

It is worth noting an important relationship between mpc and mpw (strictly speaking, this is an identity $\equiv$)

$$\text{mpc} + \text{mpw} \equiv 1$$

This must follow from our earlier Figure 9.2 (p. 262) which showed that any income received by domestic households (H) is either consumed (passed on in the circular flow) or withdrawn from the circular flow.

It follows that any change in $Y(\Delta Y)$

$$\Delta Y = \Delta C + \Delta W$$

and dividing throughout by ΔY

$$\frac{\Delta Y}{\Delta Y} = \frac{\Delta C}{\Delta Y} + \frac{\Delta W}{\Delta Y}$$

We can therefore also say that

$$1 = \text{mpc} + \text{mpw}$$

and

$$1 - \text{mpc} = \text{mpw}$$

Average propensity to consume (apc)

However, we are often interested in the average propensity to consume (apc). This is shown in Figure 9.8 (p. 284).

$$\text{Average propensity to consume (apc)} = \frac{\text{Total consumption}}{\text{Total national income}} = \frac{C}{Y}$$

Using the consumption function (C) in Figure 9.8:

$$C = 5 + 0.4\,Y$$
$$\text{At, say, } Y_1 = 20$$
$$C_1 = 5 + 0.4(20)$$
$$\text{i.e. } C_1 = 13$$

We can therefore say that at a level of national income (Y_1) of 20:

$$\text{apc} = \frac{13}{20} = 0.65$$

We should be able to see from Figure 9.8 that apc is the slope of the straight line drawn from the origin to the relevant point on the consumption function (C). We should also be able to see that apc (unlike mpc) will fall continuously as the level of national income rises.

apc and apw

$$\text{If} \quad C + W = Y \text{ (see above)}$$

$$\text{Then} \ \frac{C}{Y} + \frac{W}{Y} = \frac{Y}{Y} \ (\div \text{ by } Y)$$

$$\text{apc} + \text{apw} = 1$$

Other influences on consumer spending

As well as current income, other variables have been suggested as influencing current consumption expenditure. A number of theories have focused on the real value of *wealth* as influencing current consumption, therefore bringing other variables into play.

- *Interest rates.* If interest rates rise, then individuals are assumed to feel more secure as to the future returns from their asset holdings. If so, they may be inclined to spend more at any given level of current disposable income. In terms of Figure 9.8, the consumption function (C) will shift vertically upwards.

- *Price level.* If there is a rise in the general level of prices (inflation) then the value of people's money balances (wealth) will fall. They may therefore spend less of their current income in order to increase their money balances in an attempt to restore their initial real value. In terms of Figure 9.8, the consumption function (C) will shift vertically downwards as a result of this so-called 'real balance' effect.

Equivalence of the two approaches

Suppose we are faced with the situation shown in Table 9.3.

Table 9.3 **National income equilibrium**

National income (Y) (£bn)	Planned consumption (C) (£bn)	Planned withdrawals (W) (£bn)	Planned injections (J) (£bn)	Planned expenditure (E = C + J) (£bn)	Change in national income
0	12	−12	4	16	Increase
10	18	−8	4	22	Increase
20	24	−4	4	28	Increase
30	30	0	4	34	Increase
40	36	4	4	40	No change
50	42	8	4	46	Decrease
60	48	12	4	52	Decrease
70	54	16	4	58	Decrease
80	60	20	4	64	Decrease

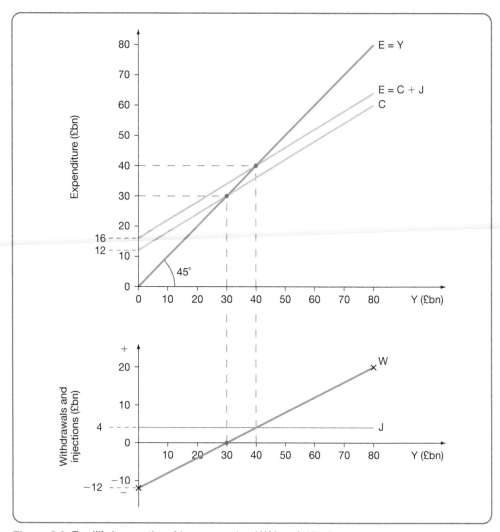

Figure 9.9 **Equilibrium national income using W/J and 45° diagrams**

Figure 9.9 presents the data in Table 9.3 using both the W/J and 45° diagrams.

- *W/J approach*
  - At all levels of national income *below* £40bn, planned injections exceed planned withdrawals (J > W). More is being added to the circular flow than is being withdrawn from it, so the value of that flow (national income) must rise.
  - At all levels of national income *above* £40bn, the opposite is true (J < W), and national income must fall.
  - At £40bn national income planned injections of £4bn exactly equal planned withdrawals of £4bn (J = W), and the level of national income is stable, i.e. in equilibrium.
- *45° diagram (aggregate expenditure) approach*
  - At all levels of national income *below* £40bn, planned aggregate expenditure (E = C + J) exceeds the national output/national income (i.e. E > Y). The value of Y must rise – either quantity of output rises or prices rise or both.
  - At all levels of national income *above* £40bn, the opposite is true (E < Y), and national income (Y) must fall.

– At £40bn national income planned aggregate expenditure of £40bn exactly equals the value of national output/income of £40bn (E = Y), and the level of national income is stable, i.e. in equilibrium.

You try 9.1 gives you the chance to self-check your understanding of the material discussed so far.

You try   9.1

1   In this question you have a description of a particular type of transaction in the circular flow of income. Try to match the *lettered* description with the correct *numbered* term.

    Descriptions

    (a) Ford, UK sells 50,000 Range Rovers to South Africa.

    (b) A successful advertising campaign by Virgin Cola results in greater sales in its domestic (UK) market.

    (c) A rise in the pound : euro exchange rate causes Toyota UK to switch from UK-based component suppliers to those located in the Eurozone.

    (d) The main GlaxoSmithKline production plant in the UK purchases new machinery from another UK firm to produce its pharmaceuticals.

    (e) A rise in UK interest rates raises the amount of money placed by domestic residents in various types of interest-bearing deposit accounts.

    (f) A government contract to build a major trunk road is withdrawn because of environmental protests.

    Terms

    (i)   Consumption expenditure (C)

    (ii)   Investment expenditure (I)

    (iii) Government expenditure (G)

    (iv)   Exports (X)

    (v)   Savings (S)

    (vi)   Taxes (T)

    (vii) Imports (M)

2   In this question you'll see a description of a particular type of measurement used for national output/income and a list of terms. Try to match the *lettered* description with its correct *numbered* term.

    Descriptions

    (a) The value of incomes received by residents located within a country (including indirect taxes and subsidies).

    (b) Pensions paid by the government to residents of that country.

    (c) The gross income received by residents minus the direct taxes they pay.

    (d) The value of incomes received by residents of a country from their ownership of resources, wherever these are located (but excluding direct taxes and subsidies).

    (e) Inward payments received by residents from their ownership of overseas property minus outward payments made by residents from their ownership of domestic property.

    (f) GNP minus the depreciation of physical assets.

You try 9.1 *continued*

Terms

(i)   Transfer payment

(ii) Net property income from abroad

(iii) GDP at market prices

(iv) GDP at factor cost

(v)   GNP at market prices

(vi) GNP at factor cost

(vii) Net national product (NNP)

(viii) Disposable income

3 The value of national income (output) can be expressed in a number of different ways. Try to match the *lettered* description with its correct *numbered* term.

Descriptions

(a) Value of output produced (and incomes received) by factors of production located within that country.

(b) Value of output produced (and incomes received) by residents of that country wherever they are located.

(c) This measure takes into account the fact that some capital equipment will have depreciated over the year via wear and tear or because technological change has made it obsolescent.

(d) Measures of national output/income which *include* indirect taxes and subsidies.

(e) Measures of national output/income which *exclude* indirect taxes and subsidies.

Terms

(i)   Factor cost

(ii) Gross national product (GNP)

(iii) Net national product (NNP)

(iv) Market prices

(v)   Gross domestic product (GDP)

4 Look carefully at the table below:

National income (Y)	Planned savings (S)	Planned taxation (T)	Planned expenditure on imports (M)	Planned investment (I)	Planned government expenditure (G)	Planned export sales (X)	Tendency to change in national income
0	−1,000	0	0	600	900	500	
1,000	−800	200	100	600	900	500	
2,000	−600	400	200	600	900	500	
3,000	−400	600	300	600	900	500	
4,000	−200	800	400	600	900	500	
5,000	0	1,000	500	600	900	500	
6,000	200	1,200	600	600	900	500	
7,000	400	1,400	700	600	900	500	
8,000	600	1,600	800	600	900	500	

You try 9.1 *continued*

(a) Fill in the last column, using *one* of the three terms 'increase', 'decrease', 'no change'.

(b) Use the information in the table to complete the following.

National income (Y)	Withdrawals (W)	Injections (J)
0		
1,000		
2,000		
3,000		
4,000		
5,000		
6,000		
7,000		
8,000		

(c) Draw the W/J diagram.

(d) Can you express each of the following as a schedule? The first has been done for you. (Check back to Figure 9.5, p. 280.)

Savings (S) $= -1000 + 0.2Y$
Taxes (T) $=$
Imports (M) $=$
Withdrawals (W) $=$

(e) Now use the information given in the table at the beginning to complete the following table:

National income (Y)	Consumption (C)	Injections (J)	Aggregate expenditure (E)
0			
1,000			
2,000			
3,000			
4,000			
5,000			
6,000			
7,000			
8,000			

Hint: Any income received by domestic households is either passed on in the circular flow (consumed) or withdrawn.

i.e. $Y = C + W$
so $Y - W = C$

(f) Draw the 45° diagram.

(g) What is equilibrium national income using this 'aggregate expenditure' approach? What do you notice?

Answers can be found on pp. 525–546.

Changes in national income

We can use our earlier Figure 9.4 (p. 278) to consider the effect of changes in withdrawals (W) or injections (J) on the *equilibrium* level of national income.

Changes in injections (J)

Increase in J (I + G + X)

As Figure 9.10(a) indicates, an *increase* in injections (ΔJ) from J_1 to J_2, will (other things equal) result in an increase in national income (ΔY) from Y_1 to Y_2. This upward shift in the injections schedule may result from an increase in investment (ΔI), government expenditure (ΔG), exports (ΔX) or in all three components.

At the original equilibrium Y_1, injections now exceed withdrawals, so the value of national income must rise. As national income rises, withdrawals rise (move along W). National income will continue to rise until withdrawals have risen sufficiently to match the new and higher level of injections (J_2). This occurs at Y_2, the new and higher equilibrium level of national income.

Decrease in J (I + G + X)

As Figure 9.10(b) indicates, a *decrease* in injections (ΔJ) from J_1 to J_2, whether from a decrease in investment (ΔI), government expenditure (ΔG), exports (ΔX) or decrease in all three components, will (other things equal) result in a *decrease* in national income (ΔY) from Y_1 to Y_2.

> *Stop and think*   *9.5*
>
> 1 Can you explain the mechanism involved in moving from the original equilibrium Y_1 to the new equilibrium Y_2 following a decrease in J from J_1 to J_2?
>
> 2 Draw a 45° diagram and use the aggregate expenditure approach in each of the following situations to show how equilibrium national income will be affected by:
>
>   (a) an increase in injections;
>
>   (b) a decrease in injections.

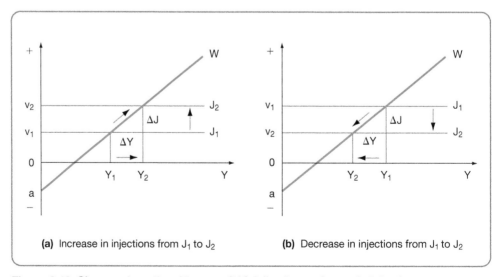

(a) Increase in injections from J_1 to J_2 (b) Decrease in injections from J_1 to J_2

Figure 9.10 Changes in national income (ΔY) following a change in injections (ΔJ = ΔI + ΔG + ΔX)

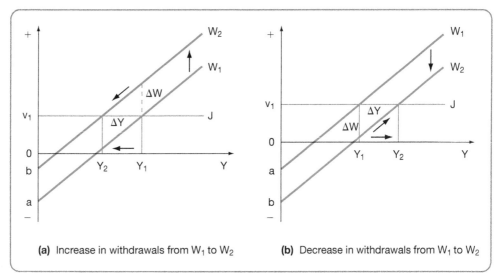

Figure 9.11 Changes in national income (ΔY) following a change in withdrawals ($\Delta W = \Delta S + \Delta T + \Delta M$)

Changes in withdrawals (W)

Increase in W (S + T + M)

As Figure 9.11(a) indicates, an *upward shift* in the withdrawals schedule from W_1 to W_2 will result in a decrease in national income (ΔY) from Y_1 to Y_2. With the new withdrawals schedule W_2 there is now a higher level of withdrawals from any given level of national income (i.e. higher apw). This may be due to an upward shift in any or all of the savings (S), taxation (T) or imports (M) schedules shown in Figure 9.5 (p. 280).

At the original equilibrium Y_1, withdrawals now exceed injections, so the value of national income must fall. As national income falls, withdrawals fall (move along W_2). National income will continue to fall until withdrawals have fallen sufficiently to match the original level of injections (J). This occurs at Y_2, the new and lower equilibrium level of national income.

Decrease in W (S + T + M)

As Figure 9.11(b) indicates, a *downward shift* in the withdrawals schedule from W_1 to W_2 will result in an *increase* in national income (ΔY) from Y_1 to Y_2.

Stop and think   9.6

1 Can you explain the mechanism involved in moving from the original equilibrium Y_1 to the new equilibrium Y_2?

2 How would a change in withdrawals be captured on the 45° diagram? For example, how would an increase in withdrawals affect the aggregate expenditure schedule (E) and why?

National income multiplier

The *national income multiplier* seeks to explain why any given change in injections (or withdrawals) may result in a change in national income which is often larger than (some multiple of) that initial change. In Figure 9.12 we see that an increase in injections of

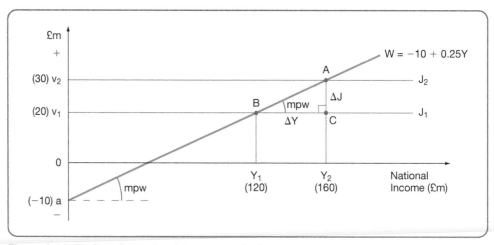

Figure 9.12 Finding the national income multiplier

£10m results in an increase in national income of £40m, suggesting a national income multiplier (K) of 4.

The original equilibrium national income is Y_1 = £120m at which withdrawals exactly equal injections at £20m.

$$W = -10 + 0.25Y$$
$$J = 20$$
$$W = J \text{ in equilibrium}$$
$$-10 + 0.25Y = 20$$
$$0.25Y = 30$$
$$Y = \frac{30}{0.25}$$
$$\underline{Y = £120m \text{ in equilibrium}}$$

Now injections rise by £10m, from £20m to £30m.

$$W = -10 + 0.25Y$$
$$J = 30$$
$$W = J \text{ in equilibrium}$$
$$-10 + 0.25Y = 30$$
$$0.25Y = 40$$
$$Y = \frac{40}{0.25}$$
$$\underline{Y = £160m \text{ in equilibrium}}$$

We define the national income multiplier (K) as:

$$K = \frac{\Delta Y}{\Delta J} = \frac{40}{10} = 4$$

Of course, the national income multiplier can work both ways:

- *raising* national income by some multiple of a given increase in injections or decrease in withdrawals (i.e. 'expansionary multiplier');
- *reducing* national income by some multiple of a given decrease in injections or increase in withdrawals (i.e. 'deflationary multiplier').

Case Study 9.5 looks at the ways in which a 'multiplier' effect can influence business activity. It looks at the London Olympic bid for 2012 and shows how incomes and employment can be raised well beyond any initial money injected into a project.

| Case Study 9.5 | The multiplier and the London Olympics |

It is important to remember that people and businesses are at the centre of the workings of the so-called national income multiplier. Studies of previous Olympic Games (e.g. Matthewman *et al.*, 2009*) show significant short- and long-run economic benefits from infrastructure and related investments, many times the value of the initial sums expended. Similarly, London's successful bid for the 2012 Olympic Games, has already resulted in a huge boost to London and surrounding areas in terms of extra income (and jobs) well beyond the initial £2.4bn of extra government spending promised for the project. The organisers have stated their intention to stage the most compact games in the history of the Olympics, with 17 of the 28 sports to be held in venues within a 15-mile radius of the Olympic Village to be constructed in Stratford, East London. Some 70,000 extra people are being hired to work in and around London before and during the games to provide support services at the various venues, all receiving an income and spending part of it on food, drink, leisure activities, accommodation, transport and so on. Those selling these goods and services to those extra workers will in turn expand output, hire new employees and generate still further employment and income.

Of course, many more firms and individuals will benefit. Barbara Cassani, the first Chairman of the London bid, said: '2012 will be a powerful catalyst for regeneration. It will lead to massive development with new sports facilities, new jobs and new housing. There will be massive benefits for the construction industry.'

One of the biggest beneficiaries of the games will be the east London borough of Newham, one of the most deprived areas in the country, where the main Olympic venues will be built, leading to major regeneration with new parks and community facilities. Once the games are over, the athletes' village will be used for affordable housing for the local community.

Around £17bn is being spent on improving road, train and underground links for the 2012 games. A new rail link from King's Cross to Stratford is being constructed for the Olympics, with the journey taking six and a half minutes. Major refurbishment work is being carried out on tube lines to Stratford while a £115m extension is being built to London City Airport in east London. The government and the Mayor of London agreed a package that allows for nearly £2.4bn of public funding, although this has since risen to £3.3bn as cost projections have risen. This will comprise £1.5bn from the National Lottery and up to £625m from an increase in the London council tax. The London Development Agency has agreed to give £250m, although there have been calls for this sum to increase since it will be the main beneficiary from rising property prices in and around the Games site in Stratford and East London.

*Matthewman, R., Kamel, K. and Bearne, M. (2009) *Economic Impacts of Olympic Games*, Locate in Kent (Kent County Council)

Questions

1 Suggest how incomes are likely to rise by much more than the £2.4bn (or revised £3.3bn) injected by the government into the games.

2 Will all the benefits of this multiplier effect occur in London?

3 What might help the final multiplier effect from the proposed government expenditure on the Olympics to be larger or smaller?

We noted above that the multiplier effect can work in both directions – upwards (expansionary multiplier) as in the case of the London Olympic bid or downwards (deflationary multiplier).

> **Example**
>
> ## Levi jeans and the deflationary multiplier
>
> The good life came to an end for workers at Levi Strauss's last two factories in America when, in October 2003, members of the 2,000-strong workforce of the plant in San Antonio, Texas, queued up to collect their last pay cheques. In the last few weeks of their employment, as well as sewing labels, zippers and rivets, they had been attending workshops and a job fair to help them prepare for life after Levi Strauss.
>
> The closure ended a momentous chapter in the history of the jeans company, established 150 years ago by a 24-year-old Bavarian immigrant to clothe miners in the goldrush. The jeans with signature red tag, considered as American as Coca-Cola, Ronald Reagan and Mom's apple pie, will from now on be made in Mexico and China. Levi Strauss, which in the 1980s had more than 60 factories in the US, has outsourced all its manufacturing to Latin America, Asia and the Caribbean in the face of fierce competition and price pressures from companies such as Wal-Mart.
>
> Around half of these workers were expected to remain unemployed and those who did get a job often found their earnings were much lower than before. Data from the Bureau of Labor Statistics in the USA shows that while around 70% of all displaced US workers find a job eventually, for manufacturing the figure is only around 35%.
>
> It was estimated that the 'ripple effects' of these job losses and earnings reductions on the whole economy of the towns affected would bring about many more job losses and threaten a downward spiral in the fortunes of these communities.

Of course, important objectives of most governments usually involve raising employment opportunities and prosperity for their populations. We consider the policy instruments which governments might use to achieve these objectives in Chapter 10.

Taking it further 9.4 looks at how we can calculate the national income multiplier.

> ## *Taking it further* Calculating the national income multiplier   *9.4*
>
> As we see in the next section, it is very important for policy purposes to be able to calculate the value of K, the national income multiplier.
>
> We defined K as the ratio $\dfrac{\Delta Y}{\Delta J}$, i.e. the ratio of the change in national income (ΔY) to the change in injections (ΔJ) which brought about that change in national income.
>
> Of course, K could equally be expressed as the ratio $K = \dfrac{\Delta Y}{\Delta W}$.
>
> Using this last expression allows us to return to Figure 9.12 (p. 294).
>
> We have seen (p. 282) that the *slope* of the withdrawals schedule (W) is the marginal propensity to withdraw (mpw). Since the withdrawals schedule (W) is a straight line, mpw is a constant along its entire length.
>
> Here we concentrate on the right-angled triangle ABC shown in Figure 9.12.
>
> From the trigonometry of right-angled triangles we can say that:
>
> $$\text{Tan of angle ABC} = \frac{\text{Side opposite}}{\text{Side adjacent}}$$
>
> $$\text{i.e. mpw} = \frac{\Delta J}{\Delta Y}$$

Taking it further 9.4 *continued*

$$\text{but } K = \frac{\Delta Y}{\Delta J}$$

$$\text{i.e. } K = 1 \div \frac{\Delta J}{\Delta Y}\left(= 1 \times \frac{\Delta Y}{\Delta J}\right)$$

$$\text{i.e. } K = \frac{1}{mpw}$$

Multiplier and the marginal propensities to save, tax and import

Remember that the marginal propensity to withdraw is the sum of the marginal propensity to save, tax and import (see p. 281).

$$\text{i.e. } mpw = mps + mpt + mpm$$

$$\text{so, } K = \frac{1}{mpw} = \frac{1}{mps + mpt + mpm}$$

For example, if mps = 0.1, mpt = 0.2 and mpm = 0.3

$$K = \frac{1}{0.1 + 0.2 + 0.3} = \frac{1}{0.6} = 1\frac{2}{3}$$

We can now find the value of the national income multiplier (K) by dividing 1 by the marginal propensity to withdraw (mpw).

In our previous example we could have calculated K directly from our knowledge of the withdrawals schedule.

$$W = -10 + 0.25Y$$

$$mpw = 0.25$$

$$K = \frac{1}{mpw} = \frac{1}{0.25} = 4$$

Make a note

As well as the national income multiplier there is also the *employment multiplier*. This compares the *total* (direct and indirect) increase in employment to the *initial* increase in employment (direct) which begins the multiplier process. Suppose a building project initially employs 100 extra people but, when all the 'ripple' effects of their extra spending works through the economy, a total of 500 extra people are employed, then the 'employment multiplier' is 5.

Inflationary and deflationary gaps

Chapter 10 looks in more detail at a variety of policy issues involving national income determination. Here, in order to illustrate our earlier analysis, we briefly review the policy issues involved for governments when seeking to 'correct' the so-called inflationary and deflationary gaps.

As already noted, most issues involving national income can be expressed in terms of either the W/J diagram or the 45° diagram. Here we use the W/J diagram by way of illustration.

Inflationary gap

When injections exceed withdrawals we suggested that the 'value' of national income will rise. Of course, using the output method, the 'value' of a given quantity of output can be found, on a market, by price × quantity.

It follows that the rise in 'value' of national income could involve:

- a rise in quantity of output;
- a rise in price of output;
- some combination of rise in price and/or quantity of output.

Links

We return to unemployment in Chapter 10, p. 330, where we see that any economy will always have a certain level of unemployment, so that 100% employment is impossible.

The extent to which a rise in national income is likely to involve *prices* rather than output will depend in part on how much (if any) spare capacity exists in the economy.

Here we use Y_F to represent the 'full employment level of output', i.e. the level of output beyond which it will be difficult to produce any extra quantity of output because of resource (here labour) constraints. In practice, Y_F need not be 100% employment! Even with, say, 96% employment (i.e. 4% unemployment) it may be difficult in practice to raise the quantity of output.

Defining the 'inflationary gap'

We can now define an 'inflationary gap', using the W/J approach as:

> **The extent to which injections exceed withdrawals at the 'full employment' level of national income (Y_F).**

In Figure 9.13(a) we have the 'full employment' level of national income (Y_F) *below* the equilibrium level (Y_1). The 'inflationary gap' in terms of our definition is represented by AB. The equilibrium level of national income will be above Y_F at Y_1, but we can expect most or all of this rise in 'value' to be due to higher prices rather than extra physical output.

Stop and think   *9.7*

How might the government seek to close the inflationary gap AB, i.e. make Y_F the equilibrium level of national income and avoid the inflationary pressures from the gap AB?

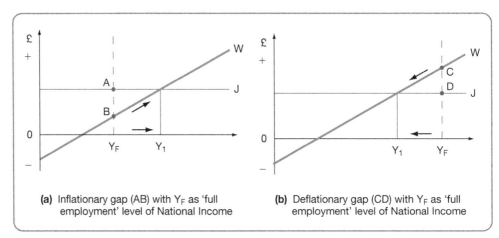

(a) Inflationary gap (AB) with Y_F as 'full employment' level of National Income

(b) Deflationary gap (CD) with Y_F as 'full employment' level of National Income

Figure 9.13 Inflationary and deflationary gaps

Deflationary gap

When injections fall short of withdrawals the value of national income will fall. This might involve a fall in quantity of output, in the prices charged for that output, or both. Terms such as 'deflation' or 'recession' are often applied to situations when the value of national income is falling.

Defining the 'deflationary gap'

We can define a 'deflationary gap', using the W/J approach as:

The extent to which injections fall short of withdrawals at the 'full employment' level of national income (Y_F).

In Figure 9.13(b), we have the 'full employment' level of national income (Y_F) *above* the equilibrium level (Y_1). The 'deflationary gap' in terms of our definition is represented by CD. The equilibrium level of national income will be below Y_F at Y_1. It may be that most of this fall in 'value' is due to less physical output rather than lower prices; for example, if employment falls below Y_F we can expect less physical output to be produced by fewer workers (at least at present levels of technology!).

Stop and think   9.8

How might the government seek to eliminate the deflationary gap CD, i.e. make Y_F the equilibrium level of national income and avoid the deflationary pressures from the gap CD?

We return to these issues of inflation and unemployment in more detail in Chapter 10, using a more realistic aggregate demand–aggregate supply model to examine their causes and consequences.

Recap

- National income can be measured using income, output, expenditure approaches.
- In the 'circular flow of income', *injections* (J) consist of investment (I), government expenditure (G) and exports (X), while *withdrawals* (W) consist of savings (S), imports (M) and taxes (T).
- 'Equilibrium' or balance in the circular flow occurs where injections into the flow (J) are exactly matched by withdrawals from the flow (W).
- 'Equilibrium' national income can be shown using *either* the withdrawals/injections diagram or the aggregate expenditure (45° diagram).
- We define aggregate expenditure (E) as consumer expenditure (C) *plus* injection expenditure (J).
- Any given change in withdrawals (W) or injections (J) will change national income by some *multiple* of the initial change in W or J.
- The national income multiplier is given by the reciprocal of (one divided by) the marginal propensity to withdraw.
- Inflationary or deflationary gaps are defined, respectively, in relation to the 'full capacity' level of national income.

Key terms

Circular flow of income A model to show how the 'equilibrium' level of national income is determined in an economy.

Consumption expenditure Where domestic households purchase the output of domestic firms.

Deflationary gap Shortfall of injections below withdrawals at the 'full capacity' level of national income.

Endogenous variable One which is determined *inside* the model or system.

Exogenous variable One which influences the system or model but which is determined *outside* that system or model.

Expenditure method Where national income is measured by expenditures on the final output of goods and services.

Factor cost The various measures of national output/income *exclude* indirect taxes and subsidies.

Full capacity That level of national income/output at which resources (land, labour, capital) are fully utilised.

Gross domestic product (GDP) Value of output produced (and incomes received) by firms and households using resources located within that country.

Gross national product (GNP) Value of output produced (and incomes received) by residents of that country from the ownership of resources, wherever those resources are located. The ownership of resources causes some UK residents to receive income from abroad (e.g. interest, dividends) or pay income abroad. In other words: GNP = GDP + *net* property income from abroad.

Income method Where national income is measured by adding incomes which correspond to productive activities.

Inflationary gap Excess of injections over withdrawals at the 'full capacity' level of national income.

Injections Additions to the circular flow of income (e.g. I, G, X).

Market prices The various measures of national output/income *include* indirect taxes and subsidies.

Multiplier The change in total national income as a multiple of the initial change in injections (or withdrawals) which brought it about. For a rise in national income the term 'expansionary multiplier' is often used, and 'deflationary multiplier' for a fall in national income.

National income Total value of income (output or expenditure) generated within the economy in a particular year.

National output *see* 'National income'.

Net national product (NNP) NNP takes into account the fact that some capital equipment will have depreciated over the year via wear and tear or because technological change has made it obsolescent. In other words: NNP = GNP − depreciation.

Net property income from abroad Inward payments received by residents from their ownership of overseas resources minus outward payments made by residents to the overseas owners of resources located in the domestic economy.

Output method Where national income is measured by taking the value added at each stage of production.

Real balance effect Where a change in the price level influences the real value of wealth holdings (including money balances) and therefore consumer spending.

Transfer payments Payments received out of tax revenue without production taking place (e.g. pensions).

Withdrawals Leakages from the circular flow of income (e.g. S, T, M).

Government policies: instruments and objectives

Introduction

This chapter takes forward the broad analysis of Chapter 9 into the more specific areas of government policy making. Such policies play a key role in shaping the macro-environment in which businesses and households must operate. Of course the whole debate on macro-economic policy, on the role and nature of financial institutions and the regulation of those institutions, has been dominated since 2008 by the adverse impacts on the national and global economies of the so-called 'credit crunch'.

Government policies on tax rates and allowances, levels and types of expenditure, interest rates and credit availability, public service provision, pension entitlement and on many other issues will have a major impact on businesses and households.

This chapter introduces the aggregate demand and aggregate supply schedules to help deepen our understanding of issues such as inflation, unemployment and economic growth. The contribution of new financial instruments and new regulatory approaches to the supply of credit are reviewed in the context of the global credit crunch and supply side issues.

What you'll learn

By the end of this chapter you should be able to:

- identify the key policy instruments available to governments in seeking to influence the macroeconomic environment and review their relative effectiveness
- consider in some detail fiscal policy, monetary policy and exchange rate policy in the UK and other economies and assess their impacts on businesses and households
- explain what is meant by 'built-in stabilisers' and show how these can help avoid excessive increases or decreases in economic activity
- understand how and why governments seek simultaneously to achieve the objective of price stability, low unemployment, balance of payments equilibrium and sustained economic growth and the implications for business and households

- use aggregate demand and aggregate supply curves to analyse issues involving inflation, unemployment and economic growth
- review the role of financial markets and financial instruments to past and present supply side and demand management policies.

We begin by looking in some detail at the use by governments of fiscal policy, paying particular attention to its role in the UK.

Fiscal policy

'Fiscal policy' is the name given to government policies which seek to influence government revenue (taxation) and/or government expenditure. We have already seen how changes in either can influence the equilibrium level of national income, with implications for output, employment and inflation.

Major changes in fiscal policy in the UK are normally announced at the time of the Budget, which in the UK traditionally takes place just before the end of the tax year on 5 April. Both revenue raising and expenditure plans are presented together at the Budget.

Budget terminology

A number of terms are often used to describe a Budget.

- **Budget deficit.** When tax revenues fall short of public expenditure ($T < G$).
- **Budget surplus.** When tax revenue exceeds public expenditure ($T > G$).
- **Balanced budget.** When tax revenue equals public expenditure ($T = G$).

Similarly, a number of terms are often used to describe the *consequences* of these budget situations.

- **Public sector borrowing requirements** (PSBR). Until recently, this term has been widely used to describe the outcome of a budget deficit, since the government will have to borrow to cover the excess of government spending over tax revenue ($G > T$), at least in the short run. This borrowing may involve issuing government bills and bonds to the financial markets.
- **Public sector net cash requirement** (PSNCR). In recent years this has been the term more usually used in the UK to refer to situations previously described by the PSBR.

Make a note | The PSNCR is sometimes described as the *public sector net borrowing* requirement (PSNBR).

Fiscal 'rules'

Further terms are often used in seeking to describe the government's fiscal policy. For example, in 1998 the Labour government committed itself to the following two important 'fiscal rules'.

- *The* 'golden rule': over the economic cycle the government will only borrow to invest and will not borrow to fund current expenditure. In effect the 'golden rule' implies that current expenditure will be covered by current revenue over the economic cycle. Put another way, any borrowing to cover the PSNCR (public sector net cash requirement) must be used only for investment purposes, in effect for spending on infrastructure, such as roads and railways, capital equipment and so on.

- *The* 'public debt rule': over the economic cycle the ratio of public debt to national income will be held at a 'stable and prudent' level. The 'public debt rule' is rather less clear in that the phrase 'stable and prudent' is somewhat ambiguous. However, taken together with the 'golden rule' it essentially means that, as an *average* over the economic cycle, the ratio of PSNCR to national income cannot exceed the ratio of investment to national income. Given that, historically, government investment has been no more than 2% to 3% of national income, then clearly the PSNCR as a percentage of national income must be kept within strict limits.

These fiscal rules seemed to work well until the sub-prime mortgage problem in the US (p. 285) and resulting bank failures which ushered in a world recession after 2007. This meant that the UK government's budget deficit as measured by the PSNCR rose rapidly to £163.8bn by 2010 as it borrowed more to bail out the banking system. The emphasis is now on limiting the growth of the public sector borrowing rather than following such fiscal rules, which illustrates the problems of using 'rules' to manage an economy when fundamental shocks occur.

Stop and think   10.1

What do you think is meant by the 'economic cycle'?

It will be useful to consider government taxation and government expenditure in turn and consider their impacts on businesses and households.

Taxation

Taxation is the major source of government revenue, with a 'tax' being a compulsory charge laid down by government. You must remember that the government is spending your money; it has no money of its own. Apart from government borrowing, it only has the money which it generates from taxation. Don't forget that everyone pays taxes. Even those who do not work pay expenditure taxes (e.g. VAT).

Example

Taxation in various economies

It is often said that the UK is overtaxed. Currently around 37% of all UK national income is taken in various forms of taxation, which actually places the UK as only a middle-ranked country in terms of tax burden. Of the 20 largest world economies, ten have a higher tax burden than the UK. For example, over 50% of national income is taken in tax in Sweden, 49% in Denmark, 42% in Austria, 45% in Belgium, Norway and Finland, though only around 27% in the USA.

Types of taxation

As long ago as the eighteenth century, Adam Smith laid down the rules for a 'good tax' in his so-called 'canons of taxation'. A tax should be:

1 *equitable* (fair): those who can afford to pay more should do so;
2 *economic*: more should be collected in tax than is needed to cover the costs of administration;
3 *transparent*: individuals should know how much tax they are paying;
4 *convenient*: the taxpayer should not find it difficult to pay the tax.

Direct and indirect taxes

Taxes are often grouped under these headings depending on the administrative arrangements for their collection.

● *Direct taxes*. These taxes are paid directly to the Exchequer by the taxpayer, whether by individuals (e.g. Income Tax, Employee's National Insurance, Capital Gains Tax) or by companies (e.g. Corporation Tax, Employer's National Insurance). Most of the revenue from direct taxes comes from taxing the *income* of the individuals and companies.

● *Indirect taxes*. These taxes are paid indirectly to the Exchequer by the taxpayer, e.g. via retailers. Other indirect taxes include a range of excise duties (on oil, tobacco and cars) and import duties. Most of the revenue from indirect taxes comes from taxing the *expenditure* of individuals and companies.

Table 10.1 shows that *direct taxes* contribute some 59% of total tax revenue, when we include employers' and employees' National Insurance Contributions, corporation taxes on company profits and capital gains and inheritance taxes. Indirect taxes contribute some 26% of total tax revenues, with VAT the most important of these, and 'other taxes' (e.g. council tax, business rates, etc.) make up the other 15%.

There is a danger in discussing tax issues to forget that households and businesses are affected by tax in *general* (via the circular flow) and sometimes by taxes in *particular*.

Table 10.1 **Types of tax: % of tax revenue in 2009/10**

Direct taxes	% of total tax revenue
Income Tax	30.3%
National Insurance (Employers + Employees)	19.9%
Corporation Tax	7.5%
Capital Gains, Inheritance Tax	1.0%
Total direct	58.7%
Indirect tax	**% of total tax revenue**
VAT	14.7%
Fuel duties	5.5%
Tobacco	1.8%
Alcohol	1.9%
Other indirect	2.0%
Total indirect	25.9%

Source: Treasury (2010) Budget Report

Some 30 years of VAT in the UK has had different implications for Blackpool Pleasure Beach and United Biscuits, as is indicated in the example below.

Example

VAT, Blackpool Pleasure Beach and United Biscuits

VAT was invented in 1965 by Maurice Laure, a French civil servant, for use in the then European Common Market. The UK adopted the system in 1973. Because VAT is not supposed to be levied on 'essential' products but only on 'luxuries', various businesses have sought to be VAT exempt, sometimes with controversial results (e.g. cakes are VAT exempt, biscuits are not).

In 1974 Blackpool Pleasure Beach brought one of the first claims against Britain's new tax. They said their Big Dipper rollercoaster was a form of transport (VAT exempt) and argued that passengers should therefore be exempt from VAT. Customs and excise didn't agree. United Biscuits got into a wrangle with the authorities when it claimed its Jaffa Cakes snacks were cakes and not biscuits, thereby making them exempt from VAT. After taking the case to a tribunal the company won.

Total revenues since the introduction of VAT in 1973 add up to £826bn. The annual revenue for this tax in 2010 was around £85bn, up from £2.5bn in 1973. At 25% Denmark and Sweden have the highest VAT rates in Europe.

At the end of this section (p. 308) we look in more detail at the advantages and disadvantages of both direct and indirect taxation.

Specific and percentage taxes

Links

Chapter 2 (p. 49) looks at the impact of specific (lump-sum) and percentage taxes on business costs and supply curves.

- *Specific tax.* This is expressed as an *absolute* sum of money per unit of the product and is sometimes called a 'lump-sum' tax. Excise duties are often of this kind, being so many pence per packet of cigarettes or per proof of spirit or per litre of petrol.
- *Percentage tax.* This is levied not on volume but on value; e.g. in the UK in 2011 VAT was 20% of sales price, and corporation tax was 28% of assessable profits for larger companies and 21% of assessable profits for smaller companies. These percentage taxes are sometimes called *ad valorem* (to vary) since the absolute sum of money paid per unit of the product varies with the price.

Progressive and regressive taxes

- *Progressive taxes.* These occur when, as incomes rise, *the proportion of total income paid in tax rises.* Income tax is progressive, partly because of allowances for low-paid workers before any tax is paid, and partly because tax rates rise for higher income groups.
- *Regressive taxes.* These occur when, as incomes rise, *the proportion of total income paid in tax falls.* VAT is regressive, since the same absolute amount is paid by rich and poor alike, which means that for those on higher incomes a lower proportion of higher incomes is paid in VAT and most other indirect taxes.
- *Proportional taxes.* These occur when, as incomes rise, *the proportion of total income paid in tax remains unchanged.*

Those who suggest that more tax revenue should come from indirect taxes on expenditure are, according to this analysis, supporting a more regressive tax regime.

Hypothecated taxes

A recent approach favoured by many as a means of raising the tax take, while retaining public support, involves the idea of *hypothecation*. This is the allocation of monies received from current or additional taxes to specific *spending* outcomes.

Individual taxes

Here we consider some of the different taxes in a little more detail.

Income tax in the UK

Not all income is taxed; everyone is allowed to earn a certain amount before paying tax, which is shown in the tax code. For example, in 2010/11 each single person in the UK under 65 years had a *tax allowance* of £6,475 before tax.

Most workers have their tax paid for them by their employer using PAYE (Pay As You Earn). This conforms to the third and fourth 'canons of taxation', namely that taxes should be *transparent* and *convenient*. Employers have to give the worker a salary advice form showing the amount of tax deducted for the current time period (a week or a month) and the amount of accumulated tax deducted in the current tax year.

Table 10.2 shows how UK income tax rates have been simplified and lowered in the 23 years from 1987/8 to 2010/11.

> **Make a note**
>
> The basic rate of income tax in 2010/11 is 20%, with the previous lower 10% rate having been abolished in 2008, when the basic rate was reduced from 22% to 20%.

Other direct taxes in the UK

- *National Insurance.* A tax on employment, paid by both employees and employers. In 2010/11 this is levied at 0% on employees earning up to £110 per week, rising sharply to 11% on earnings between £110 and £844 per week, but only 1% on additional earnings over £844 per week.
- *Capital Gains Tax.* A tax on the increased value of an asset when it is sold. Capital gains above £10,100 are taxable at a flat rate of 18%.
- *Inheritance Tax.* A tax on inheritance or gifts. In 2010/11 inheritance tax at a rate of 40% is only paid on estates valued at over £325,000.
- *Corporation Tax.* A tax on company profits at 28% for larger firms, but a lower 21% for small firms.

Indirect taxes in the UK

- *Value Added Tax* (VAT). A tax on expenditure on most goods and services (currently 20% in the UK). Some items (e.g. children's clothes) are VAT exempt. VAT is a tax on expenditure levied by all EU countries, though at different rates.

Table 10.2 **UK income tax schedules 1987/8 and 2010/11**

Rate of tax (%)	1987/8 Taxable income (£)	2010/11 Taxable income (£)
20	–	0–37,400
27	0–17,900	–
40	17,901–20,400	37,401–150,000
45	20,401–25,400	–
50	25,401–33,300	Over 150,000
55	33,301–41,200	–
60	over 41,200	–

Source: HM Treasury (2010), *Budget Report 2010*, Press notice 2, London: HMSO. Crown copyright material is reproduced with the permission of the Controller of HMSO and the Queen's Printer for Scotland under the Click-Use Licence

● *Excise duties*. A specific tax of an absolute amount levied at different rates on goods such as tobacco, petrol, alcohol.

Other taxes in the UK

Some UK taxes are difficult to define or put into neat categories, such as the BBC licence; Road Fund Licence; Council Tax; Stamp Duty; Airport Tax; fees paid by local residents to the council for parking; prescription charges.

Stop and think   10.2

1 Use either the W/J diagram or the 45° diagram to show how each of the following might influence the national income:

   (a) a 1% rise in the basic rate of income tax;

   (b) a £1 increase per item in a specific tax (e.g. excise duty).

2 Would either of these extra taxes influence the national income multiplier?

Taxes and economic incentives

There is an ongoing debate as to whether or not taxes are 'excessive' in the UK and whether current tax rates act as a disincentive to UK households and businesses.

Taxes and incentives to work

Many empirical studies have been conducted on tax rates and incentives, with no clear results. However, one widely accepted approach does warn governments against imposing too high an *overall tax rate*.

Laffer curve

Professor Laffer derived a relationship between tax revenue and tax rates of the form shown in Figure 10.1. The curve was the result of econometric techniques, through which a 'least square line' was fitted to past US observations of tax revenue and tax rate. The dotted line indicates the extension of the fitted relationship (continuous) line, as there will tend to be zero tax revenue at both 0% and 100% tax rates. Tax revenue = tax rate × output (income), so that a 0% tax rate yields zero tax revenue, whatever the level of output. A 100% tax rate is assumed to discourage all output, except that for subsistence, again yielding zero tax revenue. Tax revenue must reach a maximum at some intermediate tax rate between these extremes.

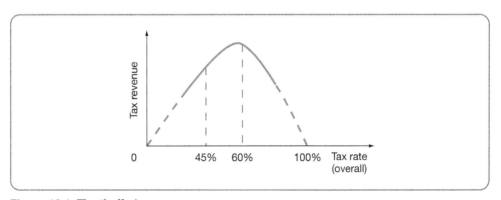

Figure 10.1 The 'Laffer' curve

The London Business School has estimated a Laffer curve for the UK using past data. Tax revenue was found to reach a peak at around a 60% 'composite tax rate', i.e. one which includes both direct and indirect taxes, as well as various social security payments, all expressed as a percentage of GDP. If the composite tax rate rises above 60%, then the disincentive effect on output is so strong (i.e. output falls so much) that tax revenue (tax rate × output) actually falls, despite the higher tax rate.

The Laffer curve in fact begins to flatten out at around a 45% composite tax rate. In other words, as the overall tax rate rises to about 45%, the disincentive effect on output is strong enough to mean that little extra tax revenue results. Econometric studies of this type have given support to those in favour of limiting overall rates of tax. In fact the reduction in the top income tax rate to the then 40% in the UK in 1988/9 was inspired by the Laffer curve.

The focus on tax rates and incentives has also found expression in the debate on the so-called 'flat tax'. The idea of a single, low income tax rate to be paid by all, i.e. a 'flat tax', has been much discussed in recent times. For example, the Adam Smith Institute (ASI) has proposed a 'flat tax rate' of 22% with a personal allowance of £15,000 (three times higher than the current allowance). The justifications put forward by supporters of the flat tax are that the British tax system has become so complex that few can understand it, unintended disincentives to work frequently occur and the UK's failure to follow simpler, lower tax regimes present in the rest of the world is undermining UK international competitiveness.

Direct versus indirect taxes

It might be useful to consider in more detail the advantages and disadvantages of direct and indirect systems of taxation. For convenience we shall compare the systems under four main headings, with indirect taxes considered first in each case.

Macroeconomic management

Indirect taxes can be varied more quickly and easily, taking more immediate effect, than can direct taxes. Since the Finance Act of 1961, the Chancellor of the Exchequer has had the power (via 'the regulator') to vary the rates of indirect taxation at any time between Budgets. Excise and import duties can be varied by up to 10%, and VAT by up to 25% (i.e. between 15% and 25% for a 20% rate of VAT). In contrast direct taxes can only be changed at Budget time. In the case of income tax, any change involves time-consuming revisions to PAYE codings. For these reasons, indirect taxes are usually regarded as a more flexible instrument of macroeconomic policy.

Economic incentives

We have already seen how, in both theory and practice, direct taxes on income affect incentives to work. We found that neither in theory nor in practice need the net effect be one of disincentive. Nevertheless, it is often argued that if the same sum were derived from indirect taxation, then any net disincentive effect that did occur would be that much smaller. In particular, it is often said that indirect taxes are less visible (than direct), being to some extent hidden in the quoted price of the product. However, others suggest that consumers are well aware of the impact of indirect taxes on the price level. Certainly for products with relatively inelastic demands (Chapter 2, p. 49) any higher indirect taxes will be passed on to consumers as higher prices, and will therefore not be less visible than extra direct taxation.

Economic welfare

It is sometimes argued that indirect taxes are, in welfare terms, preferable to direct taxes, as they leave the taxpayer free to make a choice. The individual can, for instance, avoid the tax by choosing not to consume the taxed commodity. Although this 'voluntary' aspect of indirect taxes may apply to a particular individual and a particular tax, it cannot apply to all individuals and all taxes. In other words, indirect taxes cannot be 'voluntary' for the community as a whole. If a chancellor is to raise a given sum through a system of indirect taxes, individual choices not to consume taxed items must, if widespread, be countered either by raising rates of tax or by extending the range of goods and services taxed.

Another argument used to support indirect taxes on welfare grounds is that they can be used to combat 'externalities'. In Chapter 8 we noted that an externality occurs where private and social costs diverge. Where private costs of production are below social costs, an indirect tax could be imposed, or increased, so that price is raised to reflect the true social costs of production. Taxes on alcohol and tobacco could be justified on these grounds. By discriminating between different goods and services, indirect taxes can help reallocate resources in a way that raises economic welfare for society as a whole.

On the other hand, indirect taxes have also been criticised on welfare grounds for being regressive, the element of indirect tax embodied in product prices taking a higher proportion of the income from lower-paid groups. Nor is it easy to correct for this. It would be impossible administratively to place a higher tax on a given item for those with higher incomes, although one could impose indirect taxes mainly on the goods and services consumed by higher-income groups, and perhaps at higher rates.

In terms of economic welfare, as in terms of economic incentives, the picture is again unclear. A case can be made, with some conviction, both for and against direct and indirect taxes in terms of economic welfare.

Administrative costs

Indirect taxes are often easy and cheap to administer. They are paid by manufacturers and traders, which are obviously fewer in number than the total of individuals paying income tax. This makes indirect taxes such as excise and import duties much cheaper to collect than direct taxes, though the difference is less marked for VAT, which requires the authorities to deal with a large number of mainly smaller traders.

Even if indirect taxes do impose smaller administrative costs than direct taxes for a given revenue yield, not too much should be made of this. It is, for instance, always possible to reform the system of PAYE and reduce administrative costs; for example, the computerisation of Inland Revenue operations may, in the long run, significantly reduce the administrative costs associated with the collection of direct taxes.

In summary, there is no clear case for one type of tax system compared to another. The macroeconomic management and administrative cost grounds may appear to favour indirect taxes, though the comparison is only with the current system of direct taxation. That system can, of course, be changed to accommodate criticisms along these lines. On perhaps the more important grounds of economic incentives and economic welfare the case is very mixed, with arguments for and against each type of tax finely balanced.

Government expenditure

Government expenditure was almost 49% of national income in the UK in 1981, but by 2007 it had fallen to around 42% of national income, but had risen sharply to 53% by 2010 as the UK government sought to bail out banks and other companies during the 'credit crunch'. In fact as Case Study 10.1 indicates this need to reduce government expenditure as a proportion of national income is common to many countries which have attempted to avoid the recessionary impacts of falling consumer expenditure associated with the 'credit crunch' by increasing government expenditures or reducing government revenues via taxation.

| Case Study 10.1 | Global budgetary problems and the 'credit crunch' |

The G20 group of major developed economies all face problems of rapidly increasing public sector deficits as they seek to stimulate their economies in response to the 'credit crunch'. As can be seen in the table, the national debt (what the government owes its creditors) of the G20 countries is to rise from 100.6% of G20 GDP in 2009 (it had only been 79% of G20 GDP in 2007) to almost 120% of GDP in 2014 (Table 10.3).

Table 10.3 **Percentage of GDP, forecasts**

Country	Debt 2009	Debt 2014	Budget deficit* 2009	Budget surplus required† in 2014
United States	88.8	112.0	−12.3	4.3
Japan	217.4	239.2	−9.0	9.8
Germany	79.8	91.4	−2.3	2.8
France	77.4	95.5	−5.3	3.1
Britain	68.6	99.7	−10.0	3.4
G20	100.6	119.7	−8.6	4.5

*Before interest payments
†To keep public debt under control
Source: Based on information from IMF

This increase in national debt is, of course, the consequence of increased government spending and/or reduced tax revenues from attempts to stimulate national economies. But it is not just fiscal policy but monetary policy too (see pp. 316–20) which has contributed to the sharp rise in national debt. 'Quantitative easing' in the UK, for example, refers to increases in the money supply, often involving the purchases of government debt such as treasury bills, with cheques drawn on the government itself (see p. 319). This has increased cash and liquidity for the financial institutions and for individuals selling their bills and bonds, but also increased the national debt!

Other increases in the national debt have involved sharply increased expenditures by government departments on a wide range of projects to stimulate their respective economies.

The table also shows the average *budget deficit* (G > T) for the G20 countries, recorded at −8.6% of GDP in 2009, a figure significantly higher than the average −1.1% of GDP recorded as recently as 2007 for the G20. This captures both the sharp rise in government spending on 'bail outs' and other activities to stimulate domestic economies and also the fall in revenues from tax cuts also aimed at stimulating domestic economies. For example, VAT was temporarily cut from 17.5% to 15% in the UK for a 12-month period in 2009/10.

The table also shows the projected *budget surplus* required of the G20 countries by 2014 in order 'to keep public debt under control', defined here as bringing the respective national debts back to a maximum of 60% of GDP by 2014. The size of this task can be gauged by the fact that an average annual *budget surplus* of +4.5% will be required by 2014 to achieve this across the G20 countries, as compared to the average annual *budget deficit* of −8.6% in those countries in 2009. It will be a major challenge for many countries to achieve such a turnaround; for the US it will require the budget deficit of −12.3% in 2009 to be transformed to a budget surplus of +4.3% by 2014, and for Britain it will require the budget deficit of −10.0% in 2009 to be transformed to a budget surplus of +3.4% by 2014.

Whatever governments are in power in the various G20 countries, such a dramatic transformation in their budgetary situations in less than five years will require sharp reductions in public expenditure and/or increases in taxation.

Questions

1 Explain why the national debt of the various G20 countries is so high in 2009, and projected to rise still higher by 2014?

2 Examine the policy measures which must be taken if this growth in national debt is to be reversed by 2014. Pay particular attention to the situation in your home country.

Table 10.4 **UK government expenditure:
% shares by function/programme, 2010/11**

Function/programme	%
Social protection	27.8
Health	17.4
Education and training	12.6
Debt interest	6.2
Defence	5.7
Public order and safety	5.2
Personal social services	4.7
Housing and environment	3.8
Transport	3.3
Industry, agriculture and employment	2.8
Others	10.5
Total	100.0

Source: Adapted from HM Treasury (2010) *Budget in Graphics*,
March. London: HMSO. Crown copyright material is reproduced
with the permission of the Controller of HMSO and the Queen's
Printer for Scotland under the Click-Use Licence

Table 10.4 gives a broad breakdown of the share of various departments and programmes in UK total government spending in 2010/11.

Clearly, Social Security, Health, Education and Training are the key spending areas, taking around 58% of all government expenditure. The impact on business of extra government spending will depend on the sectors in which the money is spent. Obviously, defence contractors will benefit directly from extra spending on the armed services. However, as we noted in Chapter 9 (p. 293), the 'multiplier effect' from the extra government spending will increase output, employment, income and spending indirectly in many sectors of economic activity.

We have already considered (p. 303) the various 'rules' the former Labour government established for broadly controlling the growth of government expenditure over the economic cycle. Given the criticism that is often made of allegedly 'excessive' government spending in the UK, it is interesting to note that the UK is below average on most cross-country indices of government spending.

Example

Government spending in various economies

Although the UK government is sometimes criticised for excessive spending, at 53% of national income, government spending is only slightly more than the 51% average across the EU countries, though significantly more than the 41% of national income recorded for government spending in the US. In fact, in 2010, out of 14 major countries, the UK was only sixth highest in terms of the share of national income given to government expenditure. For all countries the last few years have seen a significant increase in the proportion of national income going to government expenditure as governments have sought to stimulate their economies at a time of global recession.

Case for controlling public expenditure

The arguments used by those in favour of restricting public expenditure include the following.

More freedom and choice

The suggestion here is that excessive government expenditure adversely affects individual freedom and choice.

- First, it is feared that it spoonfeeds individuals, taking away the incentive for personal provision, as with private insurance for sickness or old age.
- Second, that by impeding the market mechanism it may restrict consumer choice. For instance, the state may provide goods and services that are in little demand, while discouraging others (via taxation) that might otherwise have been bought.
- Third, it has been suggested that government provision may encourage an unhelpful separation between payment and cost in the minds of consumers. With government provision, the good or service may be free or subsidised, so that the amount paid by the consumer will understate the true cost (higher taxes etc.) of providing him or her with that good or service, thereby encouraging excessive consumption of the item.

Crowding out the private sector

The previous Conservative government had long believed that (excessive) public expenditure was at the heart of Britain's economic difficulties. It regarded the private sector as the source of wealth creation, part of which was being used to subsidise the public sector. Sir Keith Joseph clarified this view during the 1970s by alleging that 'a wealth-creating sector which accounts for one-third of the national product carries on its back a State-subsidised sector which accounts for two-thirds. The rider is twice as heavy as the horse.'

Bacon and Eltis (1978) attempted to give substance to this view. They suggested that public expenditure growth had led to a transfer of productive resources from the private sector to a public sector producing largely non-marketed output and that this had been a major factor in the UK's poor performance in the post-war period. Bacon and Eltis noted that public sector employment had increased by some 26%, from 5.8 million workers to 7.3 million, between 1960 and 1978, a time when total employment was being squeezed by higher taxes to finance this growth in the public sector – the result being deindustrialisation, low labour productivity, low economic growth and balance of payments problems.

Control of money

Another argument used by those who favour restricting public expenditure is that it must be cut in order to limit the growth of money supply (see p. 316) and to curb inflation. The argument is that a high PSBR (now PSNCR – public sector net cash requirement), following public expenditure growth, must be funded by the issue of Treasury bills and government stock, which increase liquidity in the system and can lead to a multiple expansion of bank deposits (money), with perhaps inflationary consequences.

A related argument is that public expenditure must be restricted, not only to limit the supply of money, but also its 'price' – the rate of interest. The suggestion here is that to sell the extra bills and bonds to fund a budget deficit, interest rates must rise to attract investors. This then puts pressure on private sector borrowing with the rise in interest rates inhibiting private sector investment and investment-led growth. A major policy aim of governments has, therefore, often been to control public sector borrowing.

Incentives to work, save and take risks

There are also worries that increased public spending not only pushes up government borrowing, but also leads to higher taxes, thereby reducing the incentives to work, save and take risks. However, we have already noted that the evidence to support the general proposition that higher taxes undermine the work ethic is largely inconclusive.

Balance of payments stability

A further line of attack has been that the growth of public expenditure may create problems for the balance of payments. The common sense of this argument is that higher public spending raises interest rates and attracts capital inflow, which in turn raise the demand for sterling and therefore the exchange rate. A higher pound then makes exports dearer and imports cheaper so that the balance of payments deteriorates.

The debate on the role of public expenditure continues. However, the UK government, alongside the governments of many countries, has placed great emphasis on containing such expenditure by introducing 'austerity' budgets!

Stop and think   10.3

1 Use either the W/J diagram or the 45° diagram to show how a major reduction in government expenditure might influence the equilibrium level of national income.

2 Can you suggest any other possible consequences from such a reduction in government expenditure?

Fiscal policy and stabilisation

Business cycle

The terms **business cycle** or **trade cycle** are often used to refer to the tendency for economies to move from economic boom into economic recession, or vice versa. Economic historians have claimed to observe a five- to eight-year cycle of economic activity between successive peaks (A,C) or successive troughs (B,D) around a general upward trend (T) of the type shown in Figure 10.2.

From a business perspective it is clearly important to be aware of such a business cycle, since investment in extra capacity in boom year A might be problematic if demand had fallen relative to trend by the time the capacity came on stream in the recession year B.

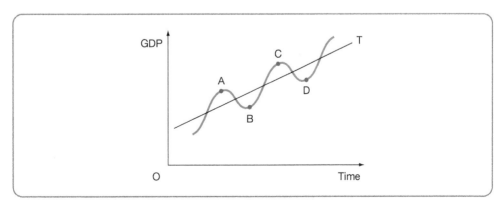

Figure 10.2 Business (trade) cycle

> **Example**
>
> ### Microchip manufacture
>
> In the boom dot.com years of the late 1990s many of the major chip-making firms such as Intel, Samsung, Fujitsu and Siemens invested in extra chip-making plants. Unfortunately, by the time many of these were ready for operation, the dot.com boom had turned to bust and many of these state-of-the-art plants had to be closed when excess chip supply resulted in plunging prices.

From a business perspective, investment might be better timed to take place at or around points B or D in Figure 10.2, depending on the time lags involved. Even better would be a situation in which government fiscal policies had 'smoothed' or stabilised the business cycle around the trend value (T) by making use of 'built-in' stabilisers or by using 'discretionary' fiscal policy. It is to this policy objective that we now turn.

Built-in stabilisation

Some of the tax and spending programmes we have discussed will act as **built-in** (or automatic) **stabilisers**. They do this in at least two ways.

- Bringing about an *automatic* rise in withdrawals and/or fall in injections in times of 'boom'. For example, when the economy is growing rapidly, individual incomes, business incomes and spending on goods and services will all be rising in value, thereby increasing the government's revenue from both direct and indirect taxes. At the same time, unemployment is likely to be falling, reducing the government's spending on social security, unemployment and other benefits.

    This 'automatic' rise in withdrawals and reduction in injections will help to dampen any excessive growth in national income which might otherwise result in rapid inflation and unsustainable 'boom' conditions.

- Bringing about an *automatic* fall in withdrawals and/or rise in injections in times of recession. For example, when the economy is contracting, individual incomes, business incomes and spending on goods and services will all be falling in value, thereby reducing the government's tax revenue from both direct and indirect taxes. At the same time, unemployment is likely to be rising, increasing the government's spending on social security, unemployment and other benefits.

    This 'automatic' fall in withdrawals and rise in injections will help to stimulate the economy and prevent national income from falling as far as it otherwise might have done.

> **Stop and think**   **10.4**
>
> How can the government use fiscal policy to increase the extent of built-in (automatic) stability in the economy?

Discretionary stabilisation

On occasions, governments will intervene in the economy for specific purposes, such as reinforcing the built-in stabilisers already described.

- If an 'inflationary gap' is identified (Chapter 9, p. 298) then the government may seek to reduce G or raise T to eliminate it.

- If a 'deflationary gap' is identified (Chapter 9, p. 299) then the government may seek to raise G or reduce T to close it.

These are examples of *discretionary* fiscal policy, where the government makes a conscious decision to change its spending or taxation policy. As compared to built-in stabilisers, discretionary fiscal stabilisation policy faces a number of difficulties.

Time lags

At least two time lags can be identified.

- *Recognition lag.* It takes time for the government to collect and analyse data, recognise any problem that may exist, and then decide what government spending and taxation decisions to take.
- *Execution lag.* Having made its fiscal policy decisions, it takes time to implement these changes and it also takes time for these changes to have an effect on the economy.

In terms of discretionary fiscal policy these time lags can result in the government reinforcing the business cycle, rather than stabilising it, as indicated in Figure 10.3.

- *The business (trade) cycle* is shown as a continuous line in the diagram, with a complete cycle (peak to peak) lasting four time periods. For the business cycle the relevant variable on the vertical axis is 'Actual output (Y) minus full employment output' (Y_F).
  - Where this is *positive*, as in time periods 1 and 2, we have our familiar 'inflationary gap' (since $Y > Y_F$).
  - Where this is *negative*, as in time periods 3 and 4, we have our familiar 'deflationary gap' (since $Y < Y_F$).
- *Discretionary fiscal policy* is shown as both a coloured continuous line (no time lag) and a dotted line (two-period time lag) in the diagram. For discretionary fiscal policy the relevant variable on the vertical axis is 'Government spending minus tax revenue'.
  - Where the business cycle is experiencing an 'inflationary gap' (time periods 1 and 2), the appropriate discretionary fiscal policy is a *budget surplus* ($G < T$). This is the case with the coloured continuous line.

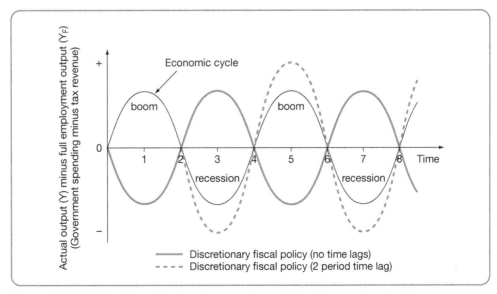

Figure 10.3 Stabilisation of the business cycle and discretionary fiscal policy

– Where the business cycle is experiencing a 'deflationary gap' (time periods 3 and 4), the appropriate discretionary fiscal policy is a *budget deficit* (G > T). This is again the case with the coloured continuous line.

If the timing of the discretionary fiscal policy is correct, as with the coloured continuous line (no time lag), then intervention by the government will help to 'stabilise' the business cycle, with discretionary fiscal policy resulting in a net withdrawal in times of 'boom' and a net injection in times of recession.

However, when the recognition and execution time lags are present, discretionary fiscal policy can actually turn out to be 'destabilising'. This is the case in Figure 10.3 if these time lags cause a *two-time-period delay* in discretionary fiscal policy coming into effect. The dotted line of Figure 10.3 shows government intervention resulting in a budget surplus at times of recession (time periods 3 and 4) and a budget deficit at times of boom (time periods 5 and 6). This is exactly the opposite of what is needed for a discretionary fiscal policy to help stabilise the business cycle.

Stop and think   10.5

Why might an inaccurate estimate of the national income multiplier by government also pose a problem for the use of discretionary fiscal policy?

Although fiscal policy is widely regarded as the most important policy approach in the UK, monetary policy can also have important impacts on national income and therefore on the prospects for businesses and households.

Monetary policy

Monetary policy has been defined as the attempt by government to manipulate the supply of, or demand for, money in order to achieve specific objectives. Since the rate of interest has an important role in determining the demand for money, monetary policy often concentrates on two key variables:

● money supply;
● rate of interest.

Of course, the whole context of monetary policy is under review by all governments after the experiences of financial intermediaries, public and private organisations and individual households following the impacts of the sub-prime market and the global credit crunch! These issues have already been touched upon elsewhere (e.g. Chapter 9, p. 285 and are further reviewed later in this chapter (pp. 344–6).

Money supply

If government is to control the money supply it must know what money is!

Definition of money

This may seem obvious but in a modern economy it is not. Money has been defined as anything that is generally acceptable in exchange for goods and services or in settlement of debts. Taking it further 10.1 looks at the functions which an asset must fulfil if it is to be regarded as 'money'.

There are four key functions which money performs.

1 *To act as a medium of exchange* or means of payment. Money is unique in performing this function, since it is the only asset which is universally acceptable in exchange for goods and services. In the absence of a medium of exchange, trade could only take place if there was a *double coincidence of wants*; in other words, only if two people had mutually acceptable commodities to exchange. (I want yours, you want mine.) Trade of this type takes place on the basis of *barter*.

   Clearly barter would restrict the growth of trade. It would also severely limit the extent to which individuals were able to specialise. By acting as a medium of exchange money therefore promotes specialisation. A person can exchange his/her labour for money, and then use that money to purchase the output produced by others. We have seen in Chapter 3 that specialisation greatly increases the wealth of the community. By acting as a medium of exchange money is therefore fulfilling a crucial function, enhancing trade, specialisation and wealth creation.

2 *To act as a unit of account.* By acting as a medium of exchange, money also provides a means of expressing value. The prices quoted for goods and services reflect their relative value and in this way money acts as a unit of account.

3 *To act as a store of wealth.* Because money can be exchanged immediately for goods and services it is a convenient way of holding wealth until goods and services are required. In this sense money acts as a store of wealth.

4 *To act as a standard for deferred payment.* In the modern world, goods and services are often purchased on credit, with the amount to be repaid being fixed in money terms. It would be impractical to agree repayment in terms of some other commodity; for example, it may not always be easy to predict the future availability or the future requirements for that commodity. It is therefore money which serves as a standard for deferred payments.

In the UK, notes, coins, cheques and credit cards are all used as a means of payment and all help to promote the exchange of goods and services and help to settle debts. However, cheques and credit cards are *not* strictly regarded as part of the money supply. Rather it is the underlying *bank deposit* behind the cheque or credit card which is regarded as part of the money supply. Cheques are simply an instruction to a bank to transfer ownership of the bank deposit, and, of course, a cheque drawn against a non-existent bank deposit will be dishonoured by a bank and the debt will remain; this will also be the case if an attempt is made to settle a transaction by using an invalid credit card.

Therefore a general definition of money in the UK today is notes, coins and bank and building society deposits.

Money and liquidity

One term frequently used in connection with money is *liquidity*. An asset is more liquid the more swiftly and less costly the process of converting the asset into the means of payment. It follows that money is the most liquid asset of all.

Creating money

When we say that banks and other financial institutions 'create money', what we mean is that at any one time these financial institutions only need to keep a small percentage of their deposits to fulfil their commitments to provide cash for their customers; the rest they can lend out as overdrafts or loans. Since deposits taking the form of overdrafts and loans are generally acceptable as a means of payment, they are part of the money supply.

- Each month the salaries of millions of people are paid into their *current accounts* (often called *sight deposits*) for use throughout the month. The banks know that during the month much of this money will lie idle, so they can lend some of the money out to people.

- Each month millions of people pay money into their *deposit accounts* (often called *time deposits*). This money tends to remain with the financial institutions for much longer periods than is the case with current accounts, so an even higher proportion of this money too can be lent out.

The amount of money that a financial institution does need to keep to fulfil its obligations to its customers is often called its 'cash ratio'.

As well as creating money by providing overdrafts and loans, the financial institutions also buy and sell *government securities*, such as Treasury Bills and Gilts (Government bonds). They also buy and sell *private securities* issued by firms, such as shares (equities) and debentures (company bonds). Taking it further 10.2 looks more carefully at these various types of security.

Taking it further   **Various types of bills, bonds and other securities**   10.2

- *Sterling commercial paper.* This term covers various securities (7–364 days) issued by companies seeking to borrow. The company promises to pay back a guaranteed sum in sterling at the specified future date.

- *Certificates of deposit.* A certificate of deposit (CD) is a document certifying that a deposit has been placed with a bank, and that the deposit is repayable with interest after a stated time. The minimum value of the deposit is usually £50,000 and CDs normally mature in twelve months or less, although they have been issued with a five-year maturity.

- *Treasury bills.* Treasury bills are issued by the Bank of England on behalf of the government and normally mature (are repayable) 91 days after issue. These again are a promise to pay a fixed sum of money at a specified future date. The purchaser of the Treasury bill earns a return by 'discounting' it, i.e. by offering to buy it at less than 'face value', the sum which is actually paid back at the future date. The rate of interest the government pays on its short-term borrowing is therefore determined by the price at which Treasury bills are bought at the weekly tender. The higher the bid price, the lower the rate of interest the government pays on its short-term borrowing.

- *Equities.* These are the various types of shares issued by companies.

- *Bonds.* These are longer-term securities (usually three years and upwards) issued by governments and companies seeking to borrow money. They pay an interest payment on the nominal (face) value of the bond. When issued by the government they are often called 'gilts', based on the belief that they are 'gilt-edged' (entirely secure). When issued by private companies they are often called 'debentures'.

By buying and selling these various securities, the financial intermediaries influence the general 'liquidity' of the financial system.

Near money

Figure 10.4 shows how, as well as those assets strictly included in our definition of 'money', a range of assets can be ranked in terms of their 'liquidity', i.e. the relative ease with which they can be converted into cash.

In seeking to influence the 'money supply', the government will be trying to influence not only the amount of 'money' available, strictly defined, but also the availability of many of these 'near money' assets. The more available are those assets at the 'more

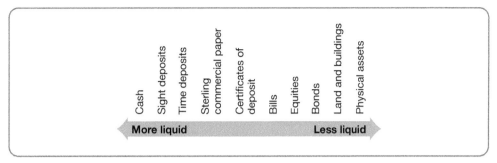

Figure 10.4 **Liquidity spectrum**

liquid' end of the spectrum in Figure 10.4, the more purchasing power will tend to be available in an economy.

Controlling the money supply

- When the government wishes to stimulate the economy, it is likely to seek to *increase* the money supply.
- When the government wishes to dampen down the economy, it is likely to seek to *reduce* the money supply.

The government can influence the supply of money by various techniques, including:

- *Issuing notes and coins.* The government can decide on the value of notes and coins to be issued through the Bank of England and by the Royal Mint.
- *'Open market' and other operations.* Making available more liquid assets in the financial system (e.g. Treasury bills). For example, the Bank of England might be instructed to buy securities in the 'open market' with cheques drawn on the government. This will increase cash and liquidity for the financial institutions and individuals selling their bonds and bills.

Example

Quantitative easing

This is the term used to describe the UK government policy of creating extra money supply to buy back government bonds and other assets held by the various financial institutions in order to increase their liquidity and help restore their capital bases. The UK bought back some £200 billion of such securities in the period 2008–2010, in an attempt to shore up the banking system, increase lending and demand in the UK and avoid a deeper recession. The policy ceased in mid-2010.

Stop and think   10.6

Consider the likely effects of an increase in the money supply on:

(a) the W/J diagram;

(b) the 45° diagram.

Today, less emphasis is placed on controlling the money supply than was the case in the past. Instead, rather more attention is now given to controlling the demand for money using interest rates.

Controlling the rate of interest

There are, in fact, many rates of interest charged by different lenders. For example, a loan for a longer period of time will tend to carry a higher rate of interest, as might a loan to smaller companies or to individuals considered to be 'higher risk' by the lender. However, all these rates of interest tend to move upwards or downwards in line with the monthly rate of interest set by the Bank of England.

Since 1997 the Bank of England has been given independence by the government, and is now responsible for setting the interest rate each month. This is done at a monthly meeting of the nine members of the *Monetary Policy Committee* (MPC) at the Bank of England. The MPC takes into account the 'inflation target' the government has set and projections for future inflation when deciding upon the rate of interest.

Interest rates and the economy

Changing the interest rate affects the economy in a number of ways.

- *Savings.* Higher interest rates encourage saving, since the reward for saving and thereby postponing current consumption has now increased. Lower interest rates discourage saving by making spending for current consumption relatively more attractive.

- *Borrowing.* Higher interest rates discourage borrowing as it has now become more expensive, while lower interest rates encourage borrowing as it has now become cheaper. Borrowing on credit has played an important role in the growth of consumer spending and Chapter 9 (p. 285) showed how relatively small changes in interest rates in the UK result in major changes in the costs of borrowing.

- *Discretionary expenditure.* For many people their mortgage is the most important item of expenditure. To avoid losing their home, people must keep up with the mortgage repayments. Most people are on variable rate mortgages, so that if interest rates rise they must pay back more per month, leaving less income to spend on other things. Similarly, if interest rates fall, there will be increased income left in the family budget to spend on other things.

- *Exchange rate.* Increasing interest rates in the UK tends to make holding sterling deposits in the UK more attractive. As we see below (p. 338), an increased demand for sterling is likely to raise the exchange rate for sterling. Raising the exchange rate will make exports more expensive abroad and imports cheaper in the UK. Lowering interest rates will have the opposite effect, reducing the exchange rate for sterling, thereby making exports cheaper abroad and imports dearer in the UK.

Stop and think   10.7

Can you suggest how a change in the interest rate will affect some businesses more than others?

Links

Later in this chapter (p. 322) we consider the impacts of both fiscal and monetary policy on businesses and households using 'aggregate demand' and 'aggregate supply' analysis.

Direct controls

As well as using fiscal and monetary policy, the government has the ability to change many rules and regulations which influence UK households and businesses. These so-called 'direct controls' were considered in more detail in Chapter 8.

You try 10.1 gives you an opportunity to check your understanding of government policy instruments.

You try   10.1

1 Fill in the grid below with one or more of the letters, each representing a policy instrument.

   (a) Increase tax allowances.
   (b) Reduce interest rates.
   (c) Increase interest rates.
   (d) Reduce the top rate of income tax.
   (e) Help given to firms moving to less developed areas.
   (f) Reduce the basic rate of income tax.
   (g) Increase VAT.
   (h) Reduce VAT.
   (i) Increase excise duties.
   (j) Decrease excise duties.
   (k) Increase restrictions on credit cards.
   (l) Decrease restrictions on credit cards.
   (m) Increase cash base.
   (n) Decrease cash base.

Objective	Fiscal policy	Monetary policy
Increase economic growth		
Reduce inflationary pressures		
Reduce balance of payments deficit		
Reduce unemployment		
Reduce unemployment in the North East		

2 Consider some of the problems that might occur when trying to introduce the policies you identified as helping 'increase economic growth'.

3 Look carefully at the table below, which shows how indirect taxes influence groups of UK households arranged in quintiles (20% groups) from poorest to richest.

Quintile groups of households	Indirect taxes as percentage of disposable income per household		
	VAT	Other indirect taxes	Total indirect taxes
Bottom fifth	12.1	19.2	31.3
Next fifth	8.4	13.3	21.7
Middle fifth	8.0	11.6	19.6
Next fifth	7.4	10.1	17.5
Top fifth	5.9	7.4	13.3

Source: Adapted from ONS (2009) *The Effects of Taxes and Benefits on Household Income*, London: HMSO. Crown copyright material is reproduced with the permission of the Controller of HMSO and the Queen's Printer for Scotland under the Click-Use Licence

Question: What does the table suggest?

Answers can be found on pp. 525–546.

In the definitions we used at the beginning of our sections on both fiscal policy and monetary policy, the phrase 'in order to achieve specific objectives' was used. The rest of this chapter looks at a number of such *objectives*, including unemployment, inflation, economic growth and the balance of payments, paying particular attention to the impact of policies in these areas on businesses and households.

It will be useful at this stage to introduce an approach which develops further our earlier work on finding the equilibrium value of national income. This approach makes use of aggregate demand and aggregate supply curves, rather than the W/J or 45° diagrams used in Chapter 9.

Aggregate demand and aggregate supply analysis

In using these schedules we are seeking to establish linkages between the level of national output (income) and the general level of prices.

Aggregate demand schedule

We have already considered *aggregate expenditure* as consisting of consumption plus injection expenditure, C + I + G + X using the symbols of Chapter 9, p. 283. However, in this analysis we take the *net* contributions to aggregate demand from overseas trade, i.e. exports (injection) *minus* imports (withdrawal).

This gives us our expression for *aggregate demand* (AD).

$$AD = C + I + G + X - M$$

where   C = consumer expenditure
           I = investment expenditure
           G = government expenditure
           X = exports
           M = imports

Aggregate demand and the price level

Another difference from our previous analysis is that we plot the general *price level* on the vertical axis and *national output* on the horizontal axis, as in Figure 10.5. Just as the *firm*

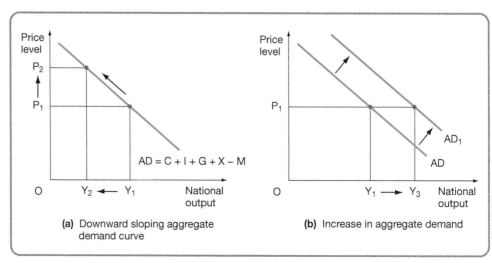

(a) Downward sloping aggregate demand curve

(b) Increase in aggregate demand

Figure 10.5 **Aggregate demand (AD) schedules**

demand curve shows an inverse (negative) relationship between price and demand for its output, the suggestion here is that the *aggregate* demand curve shows a similar inverse relationship between the average level of prices and aggregate demand in the economy.

In Figure 10.5(a) we can see that a rise in the average price level from P_1 to P_2 reduces AD from Y_1 to Y_2. For example, a higher price level reduces the real value of money holdings which (via the 'real balance' effect, p. 287) is likely to cut consumer spending (C), while a higher price level is also likely to result in interest rates being raised to curb inflationary pressures, with higher interest rates then discouraging both consumption (C) and investment (I) expenditures. As a result, as the average price level rises from P_1 to P_2, aggregate demand falls from Y_1 to Y_2.

In Figure 10.5(b) a rise in any one or more of the components of aggregate demand C, I, G or (X − M) will shift the AD curve rightwards and upwards to AD_1. Aggregate demand is now higher (Y_3) at any given price level (P_1).

The impact of changes in aggregate demand on equilibrium national output and inflation are considered further after we have introduced the aggregate supply curve (AS).

Aggregate supply schedule

We have previously noted a direct (positive) relationship between price and *firm* supply (e.g. Chapter 1) with a higher price resulting in an expansion of supply. The suggestion here is that the aggregate supply (AS) curve shows a similar direct relationship between the average level of prices and *aggregate* supply in the economy.

However, for aggregate supply we often make a distinction between the *short-run* and *long-run* time periods. In the short run at least one factor of production is fixed, whereas in the long run all factors can be varied.

Short-run aggregate supply

Figure 10.6(a) shows the upward sloping short-run aggregate supply curve (AS). It assumes that some input costs, particularly money wages, remain relatively fixed as the general price level changes. It then follows that an increase in the general price level from P_1 to P_2, while input costs remain relatively fixed, increases the profitability of production and induces firms to expand output, raising aggregate supply from Y_1 to Y_2.

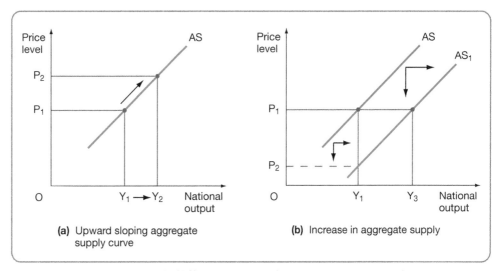

(a) Upward sloping aggregate
supply curve

(b) Increase in aggregate supply

Figure 10.6 Aggregate supply (AS) schedules in the short-run time period

There are two explanations as to why an important input cost, namely wages, may remain constant even though prices have risen.

- First, many employees are hired under fixed-wage contracts. Once these contracts are agreed it is the firm that determines (within reason) the number of labour hours actually worked. If prices rise, the negotiated *real wage* (i.e. money wage divided by prices) will fall and firms will want to hire more labour time and raise output.

- Second, workers may not immediately be aware of price level changes, i.e. they may suffer from 'money illusion'. If workers' expectations lag behind actual price level rises, then workers will not be aware that their real wages have fallen and will not adjust their money wage demands appropriately.

Both these reasons imply that as the general price level rises, real wages will fall, reducing costs of production and raising profitability, thereby encouraging firms to raise output.

In Figure 10.6(b) a rise in the productivity of any factor input or fall in its cost will shift the AS curve rightwards and downwards to AS_1. Aggregate supply is now higher (Y_3) at any given price level (P_1). Put another way, any given output (Y_1) can now be supplied at a lower price level (P_2).

Long-run aggregate supply

In the long run it is often assumed that factor markets are more flexible and better informed so that input prices (e.g. money wages) fully adjust to changes in the general price level and vice versa. If this is the case, then we have the *vertical* long-run aggregate supply (AS) curve in Figure 10.7.

Make a note

Flexible wage contracts and fuller information

Workers in the long run can gather full information on price level changes and can renegotiate wage contracts in line with higher or lower prices. This time, any given percentage increase in the general price level from P_1 to P_2 is matched by increases in input costs. For example, if general prices rise by 5% then wages rise by 5% so that the 'real wage' does not fall. In this situation there is no increase in the profitability of production when prices rise from P_1 to P_2, so that long-run aggregate supply remains unchanged at Y_1.

Make a note

Of course, a short-run aggregate supply curve might be vertical if no 'money illusion' exists. Alternatively, a long-run aggregate supply curve could itself slope upwards from left to right if 'money illusion' persists into the long-run time period.

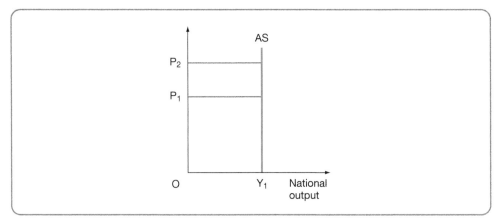

Figure 10.7 Aggregate supply (AS) schedule in the long-run time period (or short-run time period if input costs fully reflect any changes in prices)

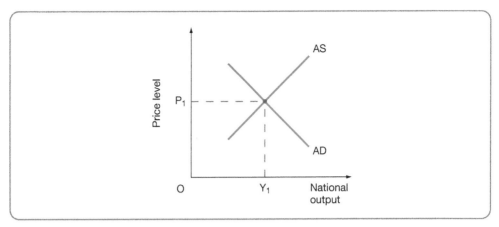

Figure 10.8 **Equilibrium values for the price level and national output**

AD/AS and equilibrium national output

It will be useful at this stage to look at how AD and AS schedules can be used to find the equilibrium levels for the general price level and for national output.

We initially assume that wages and other input costs do not fully adjust to price level changes to that the aggregate supply (AS) curve slopes upwards from left to right and is not vertical.

Only where AD and AS *intersect* at a general price level of P_1 and national output Y_1 in Figure 10.8 do we have an equilibrium outcome for the economy. Any other combination of price level and national output is unsustainable, with an excess of either aggregate demand or aggregate supply.

For example, for price levels *above* P_1, AS exceeds AD, putting downward pressure on prices and national output. As the general price level falls, aggregate demand (AD) expands (positive 'real balance effect', via increase in real value of wealth holdings raising C and likely reductions in interest rates, raising C and I etc.) and aggregate supply (AS) contracts (profitability is squeezed as prices fall faster than the less flexible input costs for producers). Only at P_1/Y_1 do we have an equilibrium outcome.

> *Stop and think*   *10.8*
>
> Can you explain why price levels *below* P_1 are not sustainable in Figure 10.8?

As we consider the various policy issues involving inflation, unemployment, economic growth, the balance of payments and exchange rates, we shall use aggregate demand and aggregate supply analysis wherever appropriate.

Inflation

Inflation is a term often applied to a situation in which there is a persistent tendency for the general level of prices to rise. The 'rate of inflation' over the past 12 months is, in effect, telling us how much extra money we would need now in order to be able to purchase the same 'basket' of goods and services as we did 12 months ago.

Measuring inflation

A number of measures have been used to calculate the rate of inflation in the UK.

- The **Retail Price Index** (**RPI**). This has been the main official measure in the UK, showing the change from month to month in the cost of a representative 'basket' of goods and services bought by a typical household. The rate of inflation measured using the RPI is often referred to as the *headline* rate of inflation. In January 2010 the RPI stood at 217.9 which means that average prices have risen by 117.9% between January 1987 and January 2010. As the index is an average, this figure conceals the fact that some prices have increased more rapidly (alcohol and tobacco 184.1%, rent 206.2%, water and other charges 220.6%) while other prices have actually fallen (telephone/telemessages 13.2%, women's outerwear 50.2%, CDs and tapes 9.4%).

  Once the RPI has been constructed, the rate of inflation can then be calculated, with the most usual measure being the 12-monthly change in the RPI. For example, the RPI stood at 210.1 in January 2009. In January 2010 it stood at 217.9 and therefore the annual rate of inflation over the period to January 2010 was:

$$\frac{217.9 - 210.1}{210.1} \times 100\% = 3.7\%$$

- **RPIX**. For policy makers in the UK, however, the RPI has been superseded by the RPIX (the RPI excluding mortgage interest payments). The RPIX is referred to as measuring 'underlying' inflation and this was (until 2003 – see below) the subject of the government's 2.5% inflation target. Excluding mortgage interest rates from the RPI eliminates a rather perverse effect, namely that raising the interest rate to moderate inflationary pressure will actually increase the RPI measure of inflation!

- **RPIY**. However, both the RPI and the RPIX are influenced by increases in indirect taxes and in the council tax. If these taxes increase, for example a rise in excise duty on cigarettes to discourage smoking, then the RPIX measure of inflation will increase without any increase in inflationary pressure in the economy. The Bank of England publishes the RPIY (RPIX minus VAT, local authority taxes and excise duty) to eliminate this effect.

- **Consumer Price Index** (**CPI**). This was adopted in December 2003 as the official measure of inflation in the UK and is based on **Harmonised Index of Consumer Prices** (**HICP**), the official measure in the EU. The European Central Bank aims to keep EU inflation below 2% as measured by the HICP, and 2% is now also the target for UK inflation using the CPI.

Taking it further 10.3 considers the RPI in more detail.

Taking it further **The Retail Price Index (RPI)**   10.3

The RPI measures the change from month to month in the cost of a representative 'basket' of goods and services of the type bought by a typical household.

A number of stages are involved in the calculation of the RPI. The first stage is to select the items to be included in the index and to weight these items according to their relative importance in the average family budget. Obviously, items on which a family spends a large proportion of its income are given heavier weights than those items on which the family spends relatively little. For example, in 2010 the weight given to tea in the index was 1, whereas that for electricity was 14 (out of a total 'all items weight' of 1,000). The weights used are changed annually to reflect the changes in the composition of family expenditure.

Taking it further 10.3 continued

The weights used for groups of items are shown in Table 10.5. It can be seen that food has been replaced as the largest item by housing (rent, mortgage interest, rates and council tax, water charges, repairs and dwelling insurance). This is part of a longer-run trend associated with differing income elasticities of demand for the items in the 'basket'. Note also the fall in the weight of tobacco, clothing and footwear, and alcoholic drink.

Table 10.5 **General index of retail prices: group weights**

	1987	2010
Food	167	112
Catering	46	47
Alcoholic drink	76	64
Tobacco	38	27
Housing	157	237
Fuel and light	61	40
Household goods	73	67
Household services	44	59
Clothing and footwear	74	40
Personal goods and services	40	41
Motoring expenditure	127	144
Fares and other travel costs	22	20
Leisure goods	47	37
Leisure services	30	65

Source: Gooding, P. (2010) Consumer Prices Index and Retail Prices Index, 2010 Basket of Goods and Services, ONS 15 March, Table 2. Crown copyright material is reproduced with the permission of the Controller of HMSO and the Queen's Printer for Scotland under the Click-Use Licence.

The second stage in deriving the RPI involves collecting the price data. For most items, prices are collected on a specific day each month, usually the Tuesday nearest the middle of the month. Prices are obtained from a sample of retail outlets in some 180 different areas. Care is taken to make sure a representative range of retail outlets, small retailers, supermarkets, department stores, etc. are surveyed. In all, around 150,000 price quotations are collected each month. An average price is then calculated for each item in the index.

The final stage is to calculate the RPI from all these data. All index numbers must relate to some base period or reference date. In the case of the RPI the base period is January 1987 = 100.

CPI and RPI

It is worth noting that the CPI and the RPI are different in a number of ways.

- The RPI excludes the richest 4% of households and the poorest pensioner householders when calculating the weights to be used in the index, believing these patterns of expenditure to be 'unrepresentative'. However, the CPI includes everyone.
- The basket of goods also differs mainly in its treatment of housing and related costs. A number of items included in the RPI are excluded from the CPI, such as council tax, mortgage interest payments, house depreciation and buildings insurance.

The CPI measure of inflation for the UK has systematically been below that of both the RPI and RPIX. For example, between January 2009 and January 2010 the CPI gave an inflation rate in the UK of only 3.5% compared to around 3.7% using RPI and 4.6% using RPIX.

Businesses have expressed some concern that the lower recorded figure for inflation using the CPI might encourage the UK Chancellor to raise VAT and other taxes on goods and services without breaching the inflation target! However, when the government changed from RIPX to CPI in December 2003 it also reduced the inflation target under the new index from 2.5% to 2%.

> **Make a note**
>
> If inflation is a period of rising prices, people assume that *deflation* is a period of falling prices. This is actually incorrect. Deflation is usually used to refer to an economy which is slowing down, in which output is falling and unemployment rising. Prices might or might not fall in a situation of 'deflation'. *Disinflation* is technically the correct word to use for falling prices.

Governments are anxious to curb the rate of inflation because of the 'costs' associated with a high inflation rate.

Costs of inflation

- 'Shoe leather costs' whereby individuals and businesses make more frequent trips to banks etc. since holding cash is more expensive (e.g. higher opportunity cost in terms of interest forgone).
- 'Menu costs' whereby businesses have to change price tags, cash tills, vending machines and price lists more frequently.
- 'Decision-taking costs' whereby future contracts become less certain, with businesses now requiring a higher future return (i.e. higher risk premium) to cover increased future uncertainties from inflation.
- 'Inflation illusion' whereby businesses lose customers who think that prices have risen excessively when in fact money incomes have risen even more rapidly so that real incomes have increased. By cutting back on consumer spending in the (mistaken) belief that prices have risen too rapidly, aggregate demand may fall and an economic slowdown occur.
- 'Redistribution costs' whereby businesses on fixed contracts or individuals on fixed money incomes lose out. Also, creditors lose since the real value of repayments to the lender is reduced in the future.
- 'Fiscal drag' whereby if the government fails to increase tax allowance in line with inflation, then even with tax rates unchanged more tax is paid by businesses (e.g. corporation tax) and individuals (e.g. income tax) than before. The extra withdrawals from the circular flow may then discourage economic activity.

Benefits of inflation

Of course, there are also beneficiaries from inflation.

- Businesses will find it easier to pass on cost increases (e.g. higher wages) as price increases during times of modest inflation.
- Businesses and individuals who owe money (i.e. are debtors) will gain since inflation reduces the real value of their debt.

While there may be benefits from modest inflation, few would argue that there are any benefits from periods of excessive inflation. Case Study 10.2 uses the experience of Germany to give a useful insight into the costs of accelerating rates of inflation.

Case Study 10.2   German hyperinflation

When people discuss inflation and its problems they often examine inflation in its more 'moderate' forms. However, if inflation gets out of hand, then it can take on the extreme form sometimes described as 'hyperinflation'. While this word does not have a specific definition, it tends to be used for extreme situations where, say, prices are rising in double-digit figures on a daily or weekly basis. The example of Germany in the early years of the 1920s is often used as an example.

To illustrate the German experience we can look at changes in the price of a postage stamp in these years, shown in the table opposite.

Many stories come from this period in Germany to illustrate the problems of hyperinflation. A famous one tells of a man who filled up his wheelbarrow with deutschmarks to go the shops, only to be mugged en route to his destination; the robber tipped out the notes and stole the wheelbarrow. Another refers to the Berlin Symphony Orchestra which walked out halfway through an afternoon performance because they had just been paid, knowing that if they waited to the end of the performance their wages would be able to buy so much less. Yet another refers to coffee drinkers in Berlin's cafés who insisted on paying before they drank their cup of coffee, aware that one hour later they might be unable to afford it. It doesn't take very much imagination to realise that everyday life would simply break down if faced by such dramatic falls in the value of money.

Historically, annual price increases of less than 5% have not been considered too much of a problem, though lower figures than this have become the stated aim of many advanced industrialised economies. For example, the UK government has for many years instructed the Bank of England to keep inflation (CPI) below 2.0% per annum and the European Central Bank aims to keep its official measure of inflation (HICP) below 2% per annum.

The price of a postage stamp in Germany, 1921 to 1923

	Deutschmarks
1 April 1921	0.60
1 Jan 1922	2
1 Jul	3
1 Oct	6
15 Nov	12
15 Dec	25
15 Jan 1923	50
1 Mar	100
1 July	300
1 Aug	1,000
24 Aug	20,000
1 Sep	75,000
20 Sep	250,000
1 Oct	2,000,000
10 Oct	5,000,000
20 Oct	10,000,000
1 Nov	100,000,000
5 Nov	1,000,000,000
12 Nov	10,000,000,000
20 Nov	20,000,000,000
26 Nov	80,000,000,000
1 Dec	100,000,000,000 or 0.10 new marks

Questions

1 Why do some suggest that it is useful for us to carefully consider historical cases of hyperinflation, such as that in Germany, even though hyperinflation rarely occurs?

2 How might a government seek to bring a situation of hyperinflation under control?

Types of inflation

Various types of inflation are often discussed, in particular 'demand-pull' and 'cost-push' inflation, though in practice inflation may involve elements of both types. We can use our earlier aggregate demand and aggregate supply analysis to consider these two types of inflation.

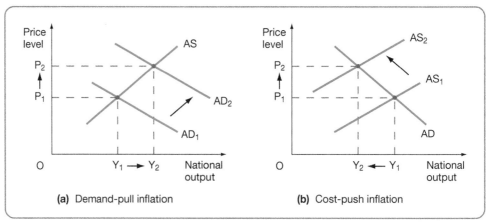

Figure 10.9 **Demand-pull and cost-push inflation**

Demand-pull inflation

Demand-pull inflation is seen as being caused mainly by an increase in the components of aggregate demand (e.g. consumption, investment, public expenditure, exports). A rise in any of these components will shift aggregate demand upwards and to the right from AD_1 to AD_2 in Figure 10.9(a). This raises the average level of prices from P_1 to P_2 and raises national output from Y_1 to Y_2. The rise in aggregate demand results in many more consumers buying products, but a rise in aggregate output to Y_2 requires a higher price to cover the extra production costs (marginal and average) incurred. With demand-pull inflation we move along the aggregate supply curve to a point where both output and price levels are higher.

Cost-push inflation

Cost-push inflation is seen as being caused mainly by an increase in the costs of production, which occurs independently of the level of aggregate demand. Firms then pass on these higher costs to consumers in the form of higher prices. The rise in costs reduces profit margins and results in some firms becoming insolvent so that they exit the market. As a result, the aggregate supply curve shifts upwards and to the left from AS_1 to AS_2 in Figure 10.9(b), with less output supplied at any given price. This raises the average level of prices from P_1 to P_2 but reduces national output from Y_1 to Y_2.

With cost-push inflation we move along the aggregate demand curve to a point where output is lower and price levels are higher.

Make a note

The analysis has assumed throughout that prices adjust more rapidly than input costs, so that there is some profit incentive for higher prices to result in extra output. In other words, the AS curves slope upwards from left to right in our diagrams.

Employment and unemployment

We have already considered government policy affecting unemployment and inflation in our discussion of inflationary and deflationary gaps (Chapter 9, pp. 297–9). Here we consider various aspects of employment and unemployment in rather more detail.

Output and employment

As national output/income rises, so too will *employment* since, for a given level of technology, more labour input will be needed to produce more output. It therefore follows that a rise in national output (income) can be expected to result in a rise in employment. In 2010 employment in the UK was at an all-time high of 29.6 million people. Of course, as employment rises, unemployment will usually fall.

While *unemployment* in the UK reached over 3 million people in the mid-1980s, some 11% of the workforce, in 2010 the unemployment rate has fallen to around 5% of the workforce, well below the EU average of over 10% of the workforce unemployed.

Jobless growth

Nevertheless, many economists have been expressing concern in recent years at what they fear may be 'jobless growth'. In other words, a situation where a rise in national output does not seem to be associated with higher levels of employment (and therefore falling levels of unemployment), as was previously the case.

A number of possible explanations have been suggested.

Links

We consider issues of outsourcing and multinational value chains in more detail in Chapter 14, pp. 496–9.

- New technologies have raised the productivity of labour significantly in many activities, so that fewer workers are required for even higher levels of output. This is often referred to as 'technological unemployment' (see p. 331).
- Outsourcing of jobs (see p. 496) by multinational companies relocating labour intensive processes to lower wage economies. Employment may be growing worldwide but not in the high-wage, developed economies as 'footloose' multinationals reconfigure their value chains.

Measuring unemployment

There are two main methods for counting the unemployed in the UK, the first of which is now the official measure of UK unemployment.

- *Survey method.* The UK's quarterly Labour Force Survey (LFS) uses the International Labour Office (ILO) definition of unemployment: people without a job who were available to start work within the next two weeks and who had either looked for work within the four weeks prior to interview or who were waiting to start a job. The LFS samples around 61,000 households in any three-month period and interviews are taken from approximately 120,000 people aged 16 and over.
- *Claimant count.* A monthly count by the Benefits Agency of the number of people claiming unemployment-related benefits.

Many regard the survey method as the more accurate; for example, women and others who are actively seeking work but who may not qualify for benefit will not appear in the claimant count.

Types of unemployment

The various types of unemployment are outlined in Table 10.6. Frictional, structural and regional unemployment are clearly defined but we might usefully consider the other types of unemployment in a little more detail.

Technological unemployment

New technologies can both create and destroy jobs. Where the new technologies involve process innovation then labour is often replaced by capital equipment in the production

Table 10.6 **Types of unemployment**

Term	Definition
Frictional (search) unemployment	There is always this type of unemployment as some workers will always be in the process of changing jobs
Structural unemployment	This results from longer-term changes in the demand for, and supply of, labour in specific industries as the structure of the economy changes (e.g. decline in shipbuilding and in textiles in the UK)
Regional unemployment	This results from changes in demand for the outputs of industries which tend to be located in specific regions of a country, e.g. shipbuilding in Clydeside (Scotland) and Tyneside (NE England)
Technological unemployment	Technological changes may lead to significant changes in labour and capital productivity, resulting in job losses
Real wage unemployment	This results from rigidities in the labour market which prevents the real wage from falling to a level that would 'clear' the market
Demand deficient unemployment	Where the major cause is excess supply (i.e. lack of demand) in the product market: often associated with economic recessions
Natural rate of unemployment	Defined as the rate of unemployment at which there is no excess or deficiency of demand for labour

process and the term 'technological unemployment' is often used. For example, a US Internet banking company has introduced 'smart' technologies into every aspect of its operations, so that its $2.4bn of deposits are now managed by just 180 people, compared to the 2,000 people required to manage deposits of this size in less technologically advanced banks.

However, the new technologies may lower product prices and raise product quality, thereby increasing product demand and creating new jobs, even if these are different from the original jobs displaced. The 'employment multiplier' effect of the initial investment in new technologies (see p. 297) will further support this outcome. The *net* effect may be positive or negative for jobs.

Technological unemployment may, however, be about to enter a new phase! There is increasing concern that new technologies are increasing productivity at ever-accelerating rates in both industrial and service sectors, so much so that job destruction is outweighing job creation. Advocates of this concern point to the astonishing growth in US productivity over the past decade, accompanied by increasing, not falling, unemployment. However, we return to this issue in more detail in Case Study 10.3 (p. 335) and in Chapter 11 (pp. 374–6).

> Quote

Greatly increased productivity has been at the expense of more workers being marginalized into part-time employment or given notice to quit. A shrinking workforce, however, means diminishing income, reduced consumer demand and an economy unable to grow.

(J. Rifkin, 2004)

Real wage unemployment

Real wage unemployment is sometimes called 'classical unemployment', as shown in Figure 10.10.

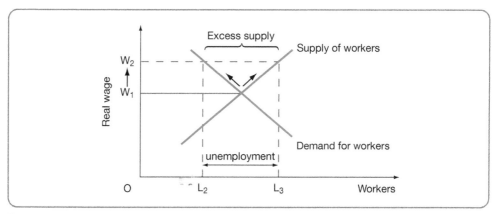

Figure 10.10 **Real wage ('classical') unemployment**

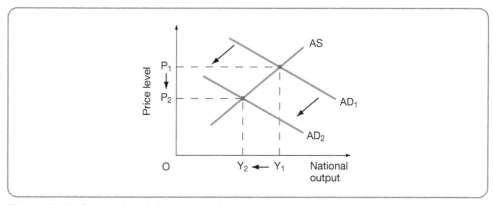

Figure 10.11 **Demand-deficient unemployment**

Only at the real wage rate W_1 does the supply of labour exactly match the demand for labour (i.e. the market clears). If the real wage is too high (W_2), then more workers will offer themselves for work (L_3) but employers will only be willing to have fewer workers (L_2) at this higher real wage. The result is excess supply of workers ($L_3 - L_2$), i.e. unemployment caused by a failure of the labour market to reach the 'market clearing' real wage W_1.

Demand deficient unemployment

In Figure 10.11 a decrease in aggregate demand resulting from a fall in C, I, G or (X − M) will shift the aggregate demand curve downwards from AD_1 to AD_2. This will reduce the equilibrium level of national output from Y_1 to Y_2 and with it the level of employment (i.e. unemployment will result).

Natural rate of unemployment

Taking it further 10.4 uses some rather more technical analysis to investigate the so-called 'natural rate of unemployment'.

Taking it further **Natural rate of unemployment (NRU)**   *10.4*

The labour market diagram shown in Figure 10.12 can be used to illustrate the idea of the 'natural rate of unemployment' (NRU), which was introduced by Milton Friedman. Here labour demand, L^D, reflects the *marginal revenue product* (MRP) of workers, i.e. the extra revenue earned from employing the

Taking it further 10.4 continued

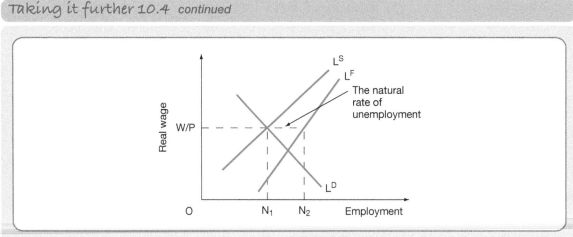

Figure 10.12 Finding the natural rate of unemployment (NRU)

last worker (see Chapter 7, p. 203). This is downward sloping, in line with the assumption of a diminishing *marginal physical product* (MPP) for workers.

- *Labour supply*, L^S, represents all those workers willing and able (i.e. they have the right skills and are in the right location) to accept jobs at a given real wage.
- *The labour force*, L^F, shows the total number of workers who consider themselves to be members of the labour force at any given real wage; of course, not all of these are willing or able to accept job offers, perhaps because they are still searching for a better offer or because they have not yet acquired the appropriate skills or are not in an appropriate location.

At the equilibrium real wage (W/P) in Figure 10.12, N_1 workers are willing and able to accept job offers whereas N_2 workers consider themselves to be members of the labour force. That part of the labour force unwilling or unable to accept job offers at the equilibrium real wage ($N_2 - N_1$) is defined as being the *natural rate of unemployment* (NRU). In terms of our earlier classification of the unemployed the NRU can be regarded as including the frictionally, structurally and regionally unemployed.

It can be seen that anything that *reduces the labour supply* (the numbers willing and able to accept a job at a given real wage) will, other things being equal, cause the NRU to increase. Possible factors might include an increase in the level or availability of unemployment benefits, thereby encouraging unemployed members of the labour force to engage in more prolonged search activity. An increase in trade union power might also reduce the numbers willing and able to accept a job at a given real wage, especially if the trade union is able to restrict the effective labour supply as part of a strategy for raising wages. A reduced labour supply might also result from increased technological change or increased global competition, both of which change the nature of the labour market skills required for employment. Higher taxes on earned income are also likely to reduce the labour supply at any given real wage.

Similarly, anything that *reduces the labour demand* will, other things equal, cause the NRU to increase. A fall in the marginal revenue product of labour, via a fall in marginal physical productivity or in the product price, might be expected to reduce labour demand. Many economists believe that the two sharp oil price increases in the 1970s had this effect, with the resulting fall in aggregate demand causing firms to cut back on capital spending, reducing the overall capital stock and hence the marginal physical productivity of labour.

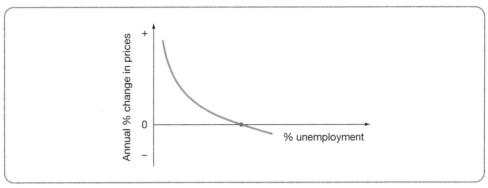

Figure 10.13 Phillips curve suggesting that higher levels of demand (lower % unemployment) result in higher rates of wage and price inflation

Unemployment and inflation

It is often suggested that if employment rises too high (i.e. unemployment falls too low) then inflationary pressures will build up in the economy. This suggestion underpins the so-called 'Phillips curve'.

Phillips curve

The **Phillips curve** (Figure 10.13) is based on finding a 'line of best fit' for UK time series data relating unemployment to inflation over almost 100 years (1861–1957). It suggested that lower levels of unemployment will result in higher *wage inflation* as a result of higher demand for labour, which in turn will result in higher *price inflation*. The Phillips curve has often been seen as supporting a 'demand-pull' view of inflation (see p. 330). It suggests that we can only have less wage and price inflation by accepting a lower level of demand and therefore more unemployment.

This simple statistical 'trade-off' between unemployment and inflation was seen to break down in the 1960s. From that time onwards, variable and often higher levels of inflation seemed to be associated with any given level of unemployment.

One of the reasons suggested for this breakdown in the Phillips curve is the growing importance of 'cost-push' inflation (see p. 330). Increases in the costs of raw materials and components or in wage rates (e.g. trade union pressures) may push costs and prices up irrespective of the pressure of demand.

Case Study 10.3 looks at links between productivity, employment and unemployment from a global perspective.

Check the net

The International Labour Organization's Economic and Labour Market Analysis is available at:

www.ilo.org/public/english/employment/strat/global.htm

Case Study 10.3   Productivity, employment and unemployment

Like physical fitness or a healthy diet, productivity is a worthy goal that can require an unappetising change in habits. Producing more by working less is the key to rising living standards, but in the short term there is a tension between efficiency and jobs. America and Europe have managed this trade-off rather differently. America has gone on a diet: it has squeezed extra output from a smaller workforce and suffered a big rise in unemployment as a consequence. Europe, meanwhile, is hoping to burn off the calories in the future. It has opted to contain job losses at the cost of lower productivity. That probably means America's recovery will be swifter. Further out, productivity trends in both continents are likely to be uniformly sluggish.

Case Study 10.3 *continued*

Analysis by the conference board, a research firm, shows just how different the recession was on either side of the Atlantic. America's economy shrank by around 2.5% in 2009 but hours worked fell by 5.1%, over twice that rate, so productivity (GDP per hour) rose by 2.5%. The average drop in GDP in 2009 in the 15 countries that made up the European Union before its expansion in 2004 was larger, at 4.2%. But hours worked fell less sharply than in America and, as a result, EU productivity fell by only 1.1% (see Table 10.7). Workers that held on to jobs in America and Europe had their hours cut by similar amounts. The reason total hours worked fell by more in America was that there were more job losses there: employment fell by 3.6% in 2009 in the US compared with a 1.9% fall in the EU.

Table 10.7 **GDP and productivity, % change 2009**

	United States	EU-15
Hours worked	−5.1	−3.1
GDP per hour	2.5	−1.1
GDP	−2.5	−4.2
Employment	−3.6	−1.9

What accounts for this stark contrast? In fact, much of the productivity growth gap is explained by different labour regulations. America's more flexible jobs market makes it far easier and cheaper to lay off workers. In many parts of Europe, by contrast, firing workers is costly and unemployment benefits are generous. Firms think twice about firing, and governments are keener to provide in-work subsidies if it means avoiding payouts to the newly jobless. Unemployment has risen most where workers are easiest to offload, as in Ireland and Spain.

American workers who can so easily be laid off may not be hired back as quickly. Some fear a repeat of the 'jobless recovery' after the 2001 recession when increasing demand was met by rising productivity. That surge in productivity was in part a result of an earlier splurge in capital spending on information technology. Though IT spending had collapsed in 2000, firms were still finding new ways to apply the computing power they had invested in so heavily. It will be harder this time since much of the capital accumulated during the

last boom was in housing, there is not the same scope for a similar burst of 'delayed' productivity.

Even if productivity growth does tail off, it may still be strong enough to match sluggish demand. And if spending is more robust, businesses will first choose to offer existing part-time workers longer hours. The Federal Reserve observed in March 2010 that although the economy was stronger, firms were still reluctant to hire.

In Europe the shock of recession is likely to persist for even longer. Falling productivity pushes up unit wage costs, hurting profits and cash flow. Firms cannot bear that forever. Long hiring freezes seem likely and some businesses will be forced into lay-offs. Aggregate demand is likely to stay feeble. Weak profits will hurt investment, and consumers will not spend freely if they believe jobs will be shed. Few scale economies exist across Europe because of continued formal and informal national regulations on retailing, transport, financial and business services.

Table 10.8 **Slower growers**

Country	1998–2008	2009–2019
World	3.0	2.6
US	2.1	1.5
Japan	1.8	1.1
Britain	1.8	1.4
Germany	1.5	1.5
France	1.4	1.3
Italy	0.4	0.5

The drive for more output from fewer workers seems a threat when jobs are scarce. But over time productivity is essential to improving living standards; indeed, as the share of working-age adults in the population shrinks, there will be a greater reliance on productivity to drive GDP growth. That makes it all the more worrying that analysts have become gloomier about medium-term prospects. America's productivity will grow by just 1.5% a year in the next decade, according to new forecasts by Dale Jorgensen of Harvard University and Khuong Vu of the National University of Singapore. Much of the expected slowdown reflects changes in technology, says Mr Jorgenson. The burst of strong growth in American productivity after 1995 was spurred by advances in the semi-conductor industry, which led to sharp falls in the price of computing power. The technology is still improving but at a slower pace, and productivity trends in the US will reflect that.

Source: Productivity growth, 'slash and earn', www.economist.com, © The Economist Newspaper Ltd, London (18/03/2010)

Questions

1 Identify and explain the differences in the relationship between productivity and employment observed in the US and the UK in the case study.

2 What implications do these observations have for policy makers in the US and UK respectively?

Balance of payments

The balance of payments situation for a country will both influence the exchange rate for its currency and in turn be influenced by that exchange rate.

As well as a high level of employment (low unemployment) and low inflation, government policy will seek to contain within reasonable limits any deficit on the balance of payments and may even seek a surplus.

The UK balance of payments is often broken down into the current account, capital account and financial account.

Current account

This consists of two main sub-accounts, the 'balance on goods' (formerly 'visible trade balance') and the 'balance on services' (formerly 'invisible trade balance'). Exports are given a positive sign, imports a negative sign: when exports exceed imports, we speak of a 'surplus' and when imports exceed exports, a 'deficit'.

- **Balance on goods** is split into oil goods and non-oil goods.
- **Balance on services** includes shipping, insurance, finance etc.

The current account is completed by adding two further items: the 'investment income balance' (i.e. net income from interest, profits and dividends) and the 'transfer balance' (i.e. net value of government transfers to institutions such as the EU, World Bank etc.). Table 10.9 presents the components of the UK current account over the past ten years.

Capital account

This records the flow of money into the country (positive sign) and out of the country (negative sign) resulting from the purchase or sale of fixed assets (e.g. land) and selected capital transfers.

Financial account

This records the flows of money into the country (positive sign) and out of the country (negative sign) resulting from investment-related or other financial activity.

- Direct investment usually involves physical assets of a company (e.g. plant, equipment).
- Portfolio investment involves paper assets (e.g. shares, bonds).
- 'Other financial flows' may involve the movement of deposits between countries.

If the net value of the items mentioned in the three accounts so far are negative, we speak of a *balance of payments deficit*; if positive, of a *balance of payments surplus*.

Table 10.9 Components of UK current account, 1999–2009 (£m)

Year	Trade in goods and services					Investment income[1] balance	Transfer balance	Current balance
	Balance on goods			Balance on services	Balance on services			
	Total	Oil	Non-Oil					
1999	−29,051	+4,448	−33,499	+15,562	−13,489	−1,043	−7,322	−21,854
2000	−32,976	+6,536	−39,512	+15,002	−17,974	+1,962	−9,775	−25,787
2001	−41,212	+5,290	−46,502	+17,200	−24,012	+9,425	−6,515	−21,102
2002	−47,705	+5,108	−52,813	+19,632	−28,073	+18,286	−8,870	−18,657
2003	−48,607	+3,376	−51,983	+22,612	−25,995	+17,523	−9,835	−18,307
2004	−60,900	+893	−61,793	+28,414	−32,486	+17,845	−10,276	−24,917
2005	−68,589	−2,195	−66,394	+25,742	−42,847	+21,855	−11,849	−32,841
2006	−76,312	−2,794	−73,518	+34,782	−41,530	+9,573	−11,885	−43,842
2007	−89,754	−4,031	−85,723	+44,807	−44,947	+20,775	−13,538	−37,710
2008	−93,381	−5,860	−87,513	+55,142	−38,239	+30,293	−14,029	−21,975
2009	−81,790	−3,237	−78,553	+49,313	−32,477	+28,656	−14,614	−18,435

[1]This total includes both 'compensation to employees' and 'investment income' but in statistical terms it is nearly all investment income.

Source: Adapted from *UK Balance of Payments: The Pink Book*, ONS (2009) and *Statistical Bulletin*, HMSO (2010), 30 March. Crown copyright material is reproduced with the permission of the Controller of HMSO and the Queen's Printer for Scotland under the Click-Use Licence

Balancing item

The overall accounts are constructed so that they *must* balance (accounting identity), with this balance achieved by either drawing on reserves (if deficit) or adding to reserves (if surplus). The 'balancing item' represents these values, which are required to maintain the accounting identity.

Exchange rate

This can be quoted as the number of units of the *foreign currency* that is needed to purchase one unit of the domestic currency: e.g. £1 = €1.50. Alternatively, it can be quoted as the number of units of the *domestic currency* needed to purchase one unit of the foreign currency: e.g. €1 = £0.666.

The exchange rate is a key 'price' affecting the competitiveness of UK exporters and UK producers of import substitutes.

- *A fall (depreciation) in the sterling exchange rate* makes UK exports cheaper abroad (in the foreign currency) and imports into the UK dearer at home (in £ sterling).
- *A rise (appreciation) in the sterling exchange rate* makes UK exports dearer abroad (in the foreign currency) and imports into the UK cheaper at home (in £ sterling).

We can illustrate the former using the £ : $ exchange rate. In recent times sterling has fallen (depreciated) significantly in value against the US dollar.

Example: £1 = $1.8 (August 2008)
            £1 = $1.5 (August 2010)

As a result, a £100 export from the UK costing $180 in the USA in 2008 costs $150 in 2010. Similarly, an import from the USA costing $150 would sell for £100 in the UK in 2008 but £120 in 2010.

The change in value of UK exports and UK imports after a change in the exchange rate will depend crucially on the **price elasticity of demand (PED)** for both exports and imports. The more elastic the demand for exports and imports, the greater the impact on the balance of payments of any change in the exchange rate, and vice versa.

Types of exchange rate

- *Nominal exchange rate*. This is the rate at which one currency is quoted against any other currency. The nominal exchange rate is therefore a *bilateral* (two country) exchange rate.

- *Effective exchange rate* (EER). This is a measure which takes into account the fact that sterling varies in value by different amounts against other currencies. It is calculated as a *weighted average* of the bilateral rates against all other currencies, and is expressed as an index number relative to the base year. The EER is therefore a *multilateral* (many country) exchange rate, expressed as an index number.

- *Real exchange rate (RER)* is designed to measure the rate at which home products exchange for products from other countries, rather than the rate at which the currencies themselves are traded. It is thus a measure of competitiveness. When we consider *multilateral* UK trade, it is defined as:

$$RER = EER \times P(UK)/P(F)$$

In other words, the real exchange rate for the UK (RER) is equal to the effective exchange rate (EER) multiplied by the ratio of home price, P(UK), to foreign price, P(F), of products.

  – If UK prices rise relative to foreign prices, the real exchange rate (RER) will rise, unless the sterling effective exchange rate (EER) falls sufficiently to offset this impact.

  – Similarly, if the sterling effective exchange rate (EER) rises, the real exchange rate will rise, unless UK prices fall sufficiently relative to foreign prices.

Table 10.10 outlines the nominal rate of exchange for sterling against other currencies and the overall sterling effective exchange rate (EER) against a 'basket' of other currencies.

Notice the rapid *appreciation* in the nominal exchange rate of sterling against the US dollar between 2001 and 2007 (i.e. the US dollar has *depreciated* significantly against sterling). However, sterling has *depreciated* in value against both the US dollar and the euro in the last few years.

> Stop and think   10.9
>
> How are the changes in the sterling exchange rate over the last few years shown in Table 10.10 likely to affect the UK balance of payments? See also Case Study 10.4.

Links

See Chapter 14 (p. 498) for an assessment of the role of exchange rates in determining international competitiveness.

The impact of exchange rate changes are considered in many chapters of this book, since they clearly have an important impact on the competitiveness of exports in foreign markets and of imports in domestic markets.

We now turn to an important issue in the UK, namely whether or not to join the single currency.

Table 10.10 Sterling nominal exchange rates, 1997–2009

Year	US dollar	French franc	Japanese yen	German mark	Sterling effective exchange rate (2005 = 100)	Euro
1997	1.64	9.56	198.12	2.84	96.37	–
1998	1.66	9.77	216.75	2.91	100.00	–
1999	1.62	9.97	183.94	2.97	99.37	1.52
2000	1.52	10.77	163.27	3.21	101.15	1.64
2001	1.44	10.55	174.84	3.15	99.49	1.61
2002	1.50	–	187.87	–	100.56	1.59
2003	1.64	–	189.32	–	96.88	1.45
2004	1.83	–	198.10	–	101.60	1.47
2005	1.82	–	200.16	–	100.43	1.46
2006	1.84	–	214.33	–	101.22	1.47
2007	2.00	–	235.71	–	103.59	1.46
2008	1.85	–	192.36	–	90.78	1.26
2009	1.57	–	146.47	–	80.13	1.12
2010 (March)	1.51	–	136.62	–	77.21	1.11

Notes: Figures have been rounded to 2 decimal places. The annual sterling effective exchange rate figures were calculated by averaging the daily values sourced from the Bank of England's Interactive Database.

Source: Based on information from Bank of England (2010) *Statistics Interactive Database*: Interest and exchange rates, 3 April. Reprinted with permission

---

Case Study 10.4   **Weak pound boosts UK shares**

Shares in HSBC, BP and Vodafone – as well as other London-listed companies that generate a large proportion of their earnings outside the UK – have risen as sterling has weakened. Equity strategists at asset management firms say they are rebalancing their UK portfolios, and issuing new share purchasing recommendations, following the pound's continued weakness in the currency market – which in March 2010 reduced the sterling/dollar exchange rate below $1.50.

Sterling weakness tends to help investors with holdings in FTSE 100-listed companies as about 70% of the index's earnings come from outside the UK, according to Goldman Sachs. It can also benefit smaller exporters in the FTSE 250, which are likely to receive a 'competitive boost' from a falling pound. Goldman's strategists are therefore encouraging investors to take long positions in UK companies with exposure to foreign markets and short-sell or avoid UK companies whose fortunes are tied more directly to the domestic economy.

Stocks on the bank's buy list include: Unilever and Diageo, the food and beverage groups that both trade on 15 times next year's earnings;

AstraZeneca, trading on seven times 2010 earnings; Pearson, parent company of the *Financial Times*; Imperial Tobacco and Royal Dutch Shell.

Stocks deemed unlikely to benefit from weaker sterling are Balfour Beatty, Carillion, British Land, Hammerson, Premier Foods, Green King, Ladbrokes and Marks and Spencer. As these companies' fortunes depend more on the UK economy, their share prices have been more closely correlated to movements in sterling.

The pound in March 2010 has fallen 29% against the US dollar since hitting its last high in November 2007, and it is also down 27% against the euro since its high in January 2007.

Source: from Weak pound boost UK shares, *Financial Times*, 06/03/2010 (Kelleher, E.), © The Financial Times Ltd

Questions

1 How might expectations of future exchange rate movements for sterling influence investor decisions?

2 Explain the role of the exchange rate in such investor decisions. What other factors might influence such investor decisions?

Single currency (euro)

Eleven countries formally replaced their national currencies with the euro on 1 January 1999, with Greece becoming the twelfth member of this eurozone in 2001.

Advantages of a single currency

- *Lower costs of exchange*: importers no longer have to obtain foreign currency to pay exporters from the eurozone.
- *Reduced exchange rate uncertainty*: all members face fixed exchange rates within the eurozone.
- *Eliminates competitive depreciations/devaluations*: historically countries have tried to match any fall in the exchange rates of rival countries, with such 'competitive depreciations' creating uncertainty and discouraging trade.
- *Prevents speculative attacks*: speculators can sometimes force individual currencies to depreciate/devalue their currency by selling large amounts of that currency. The euro, being supported by all member countries, is much better equipped to resist such speculative attacks.

Disadvantages of a single currency

- *Loss of independent exchange rate policy*: governments can no longer seek to remedy a balance of payment deficit with a member of the eurozone by lowering their exchange rate, thereby making exports cheaper in that country and imports dearer from that country.
- *Loss of independent monetary policy*: the eurozone has a European Central Bank which determines the money supply and interest rate policy for all member countries.

Stop and think   10.10

1 How is a fall in the exchange rate of sterling likely to affect the equilibrium values for price level and national output in the aggregate demand and aggregate supply analysis?

2 Now repeat your analysis for a rise in the exchange rate of sterling.

Case Study 10.5 looks at a less official mechanism for expressing relative exchange rates.

Case Study 10.5   Exchange rates and burgers

There is a widely recognised theory that, in the long run, exchange rates will move towards levels at which a given 'basket' of goods and services will cost the same in different countries using the local currency. In other words, a global currency such as the dollar should, when converted into a local currency, buy the same goods and services wherever these are sold.

On that basis *The Economist* has for many years presented the so-called 'Big Mac' Index, showing how the price of a McDonald's burger varies in different countries, after exchanging the dollar into the currency of that country (Table 10.11). For example, the 'Big Mac' only costs the equivalent of $1.83 in China, using the yuan/dollar exchange rate in March 2010. Yet the same 'Big Mac' costs $3.58 in America in March 2010. This suggests that the Chinese currency, the yuan, is *undervalued* by 49% against the US dollar. In other words, if 1 yuan exchanged for 49% more US dollars *than was the case in March 2010*, then the 'Big Mac' would have had the same dollar-equivalent price in both countries.

Case Study 10.5 *continued*

Table 10.11 **The 'Big Mac' Index* and the price of a 'Big Mac' (March 2010)**

Country/ Area	McDonald's 'Big Mac' Index	Price of 'Big Mac' ($)
USA	0%	3.58
Britain	−3%	3.48
China	−49%	1.83
Euro area	+28%	4.62
Switzerland	+72%	6.16

* % refers to under (−) or over (+) valuation of each national currency against the US dollar

Source: Based on information from The Economist (2010) 17 March

While on the 'Big Mac' Index the Chinese currency would seem undervalued, the euro would seem *overvalued*. The average price of a 'Big Mac' in the 'euro area' in March 2010 was $4.62, using the euro: dollar exchange rate of that date. This suggests that the euro is around 28% *overvalued* against the dollar, given the $3.58 price of the 'Big Mac' in the USA. This time, 1 euro would need to exchange against 28% fewer US dollars than was the case in March 2010 for the 'Big Mac' to have had the same dollar-equivalent price in both countries.

Source: Based on information from The Economist (2010) 17 March

Questions

1 Why is the 'Big Mac' used as the basis for an index?

2 What do you notice from Table 10.11?

3 What use might Table 10.11 be to businesses, individuals and governments?

4 What criticisms might be made of such indices?

Economic growth

Economic growth is usually defined as the rate of change of national output (income). When this is negative, we often use the term *economic recession*, although strictly speaking we should only use this term when national output has fallen in value over two successive quarters. Economic growth is usually expressed in 'real' terms, i.e. after taking inflation into account.

Governments rarely announce growth targets. However, historically GDP has grown in the UK at an average rate of just over 2% per annum (in real terms) over the past 50 or so years.

In terms of the *production possibility frontier* of Chapter 1 (Figure 1.1, p. 4), economic growth can involve either:

● a move from a point inside the frontier towards a point nearer to or actually on an unchanged frontier; or

● a move from a point inside or on an existing frontier to a point previously outside the frontier, as a result of an outward shift in the frontier itself.

In the first case, recorded economic growth involves a fuller use of existing productive resources. For example, higher aggregate demand may have contributed to such economic growth, allowing a fuller use of existing productive capacity.

In the second case, recorded economic growth involves some increase in the productive capacity of the economy as a whole. While higher aggregate demand may also have played a part in such growth, there would seem also to have been an improvement in the 'supply side' of the economy. It is to this issue that we now turn.

Supply-side policies

Some people have suggested that the UK experienced a supply-side 'revolution' since the 1980s, which included a wide range of policies which sought to raise the productivity of both labour and capital.

Such 'supply side' policies have included, among others:

- assistance with investment;
- trade union reform;
- deregulation/privatisation;
- making more training grants available;
- increasing the number of people at universities;
- helping people to set up new firms;
- income tax cuts to increase incentives to work;
- cuts in welfare payments to encourage people to return to work;
- a government commitment to keep inflation low in order to aid investment plans;
- cutting government expenditure in order to release resources to the private sector;
- abolishing exchange controls in order to allow capital to move freely.

Any increase in labour or capital productivity resulting from these supply-side policies would then shift outwards the production possibility frontier of Chapter 1. Successful supply-side policies would also increase the aggregate supply curve in Figure 10.14, shifting it downwards and to the right from AS_1 to AS_2. The result is shown as raising the equilibrium level of national output (e.g. GDP) from Y_1 to Y_2 and reducing the average price level from P_1 to P_2.

Stop and think   10.11

Can you use the aggregate demand and aggregate supply schedules to show how coupling supply-side policies with increases in aggregate demand might help to achieve non-inflationary growth?

Many of these supply-side policy issues are considered elsewhere in the book, especially in Chapter 7 on labour and other factor markets. However, here we further review the key role of the financial market institutions and instruments in supply side policies and in

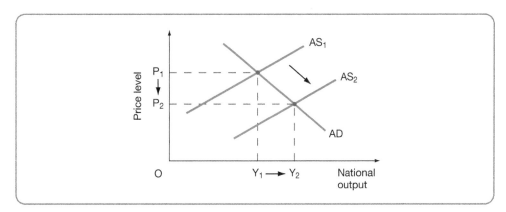

Figure 10.14 **Supply-side policies**

the so-called 'credit crunch', identifying changes underway as a result of deficiencies widely recognised in the construction and operation of these financial markets and instruments.

Financial intermediation: post credit crunch

Firms can raise short- and long-term loans on international as well as domestic financial markets. The term 'money markets' is usually applied to the buying and selling of short-term (less than one year to maturity) debt instruments, whereas the term 'bond markets' refers to trading longer-term (more than one year to maturity) debt instruments.

Here we select a number of important international financial markets by way of illustration. In doing so we examine the sources and impacts of the so-called 'credit crunch' and the new financial derivatives and instruments which have been widely traded across the world, and which underpin many of the contemporary issues that have arisen within global finance and trade. In fact, given the current volatility in international financial markets, it may be helpful to begin with the market in a wide range of *structured investment vehicles* (SIVs) and the origins of that market.

Structured investment vehicles (SIV) market

These are the financial instruments that have emerged in recent years and which consist of not one, but a *variety* of securities, some of which involve mortgage debt (see Figure 10.15). Before reviewing the contribution of SIVs to current international financial developments, it will help to consider the so-called *sub-prime* market, and the impacts this has had on the value of SIVs, many of which involve a mortgage-backed 'slice' of their overall portfolio.

Sub-prime market

The term 'sub-prime' is widely used to refer to excessive lending for mortgage purposes in the US to low-income borrowers at high risk. Case Study 9.4 (p. 285) has already reviewed the origins of the sub-prime market, particularly the high-risk lending to borrowers in the US housing market in 2006/7.

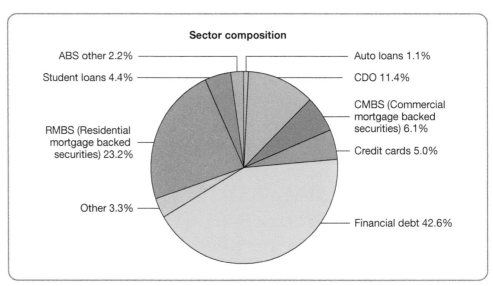

Figure 10.15 Structured investment vehicle (SIV)

Source: from SIV managers dig out their manuals, *Financial Times*, 30/08/2007 (Davies, P.), © The Financial Times Ltd

Taking it further 10.5 takes a closer look at what exactly constitutes an SIV.

Taking it further   Structured investment vehicle (SIV)   *10.5*

1 A **structured investment vehicle (SIV)** exists to help those acquiring it make a profit from the difference between the low cost of short-term debt funding and the higher returns, or yields, of longer term debt investments.

2 A SIV consists of a pool of debts of financial companies, such as banks and insurers, including asset-backed securities, or bonds, backed by mortgages, loans or other debt (see Figure 10.15).

3 The SIV funds these more profitable longer term investments by issuing debt itself. A small portion of this debt (between 5% and 12%) is longer term and carries the first risk of losses if assets in the pool of investments start to go bad. This debt is also the last to be repaid, but it shares some of the profits made by the vehicle. This is the *junior debt*, otherwise known as the *capital notes*.

4 The lion's share of debt issued by the SIV is very low cost short-term commercial paper, which has a life span of days or weeks, and medium-term notes, which have a life span of three to six months. This is the *senior debt*.

Problems in this market for SIVs and associated financial instruments such as **collateralised debt obligations (CDOs)** have played a key role in the events unfolding globally over recent years. Collateralised debt obligations (CDOs) are themselves bundles of other securities and have been traded on international financial markets singly, or as part of broader SIVs. The linkage of slices of these securities to the falling value of mortgages and to other assets of diminishing value, has been a major element in the declining portfolio and capital values of many international organisations.

Clearly attempts are being made to establish improved financial regulations and supervision, a stronger capital basis for financial institutions and better approaches to risk management, as Case Study 10.6 indicates.

Case Study 10.6   Risk needs a human touch   **FT**

In extraordinary and treacherous conditions, aircraft passengers would almost certainly prefer a human pilot to be at the controls than the autopilot – and for good reasons. No matter how powerful and sophisticated our computers are, there are always subtleties and nuances of experience that we cannot yet program them to judge. A computer would never have pulled off the emergency landing such as the one that occurred on New York's Hudson river in January 2009.

Investigators into the global financial crash landing are already producing remedies even as the disaster continues. A major realisation has been that banks and their supervisors trusted too much in the risk management autopilot. Lord Turner, chairman of the UK's Financial Services Authority, has highlighted attempts by the Basel Committee to overhaul the use of 'value at risk' (VaR) models, which predict how much a bank can lose on a given day. These models have allowed the systematic underestimation of risk, which in turn has meant that only very small capital cushions were required in banks' trading operations. VaR models used unduly short historical data sets to predict future developments and discounted the worth of incorporating rare, but extremely painful outcomes. VaR, he said, 'fails to allow for the fact that historically low volatility may actually be an indication of irrationally low risk-aversion and therefore increased systemic risk'. Lord Turner gave an example of a bank whose trading assets made up 57% of its total book, but which set its market risk capital requirement at just 0.1% of trading assets. This is extreme, but others in the sample chose 0.4% and 1.1% – better, but hardly a paradigm of prudence.

The Basel Committee, unsurprisingly, wants to raise these capital charges as swiftly and comprehensively as possible. The key driver for its action is the mind-boggling losses suffered in 2008 in the trading books of banks such as UBS, Merrill Lynch and Citigroup. Institutions exploited the low capital demands of VaR models to keep very large and long-term complex structured bond positions in a book really meant only for temporary asset positions.

The Basel Committee is cracking down hard on this area and their changes look likely to handicap seriously the potential for any recovery in securitisation. It will prohibit banks from recognising any capital benefits from securitisations, even as hedging tools. This is because the Committee believes that 'the state of risk modelling in this area is not sufficiently reliable as to warrant recognising hedging or diversification benefits attributable to securitisation positions'.

For the most part, banks seem only too willing to accept these changes. Many bankers with global responsibility for credit trading are seeking different kinds of risk manager in their businesses. The new risk manager's human judgement would be the final arbiter rather than the strict letter of the VaR law, which could only act as a guide. Most important would be 'intent'. People in risk management should not be allowed to work for themselves, embattled and concerned mainly with their own job security. 'They need to be close to the action, but not so close that they lose their perspective. In volatile, liquidity-strained times, traders need to be given more freedom around risk limits, but everyone needs to have a rounded view, across asset classes, markets and the full trading room. What is needed, it is suggested, is a greater spirit of collectivism – an attitude of solving for the greater good.

Fine words, but markets are social phenomena riddled with dysfunction. They pursue bad leads and develop sustained distortions. As the lending drought shows, there are conflicts between what is rational for the individual and what is rational for the whole. And as investors have felt repeatedly in this crisis, markets can stay insane longer than they can stay solvent.

But the biggest difficulty and the reason VaR dominates is the business case. It is very difficult to turn human, qualitative judgement into numbers in the boardroom. Banks more than most demand quantitative assessment and as long as bonuses need to be calculated, this will not change.

Source: from Risk needs a human touch but models hold the whip hand, *Financial Times*, 23/01/2009 (Davies, P.), © The Financial Times Ltd

Question

Consider the advantages and disadvantages of the use of automated risk management models.

Sovereign wealth funds (SWFs) and sovereign debt

A new emphasis in financial risk management is being placed on *sovereign debt ratings*, linked closely to the growth of *sovereign wealth funds* (SWFs). These are government owned investment vehicles managed separately from the official reserves of the country. They have usually been accumulated by those governments as the result of high global commodity prices for their exports. High energy (e.g. oil), food and other primary product prices over recent years have meant that an estimated $5,000bn is now available for potential investment by countries such as the United Arab Emirates, Saudi Arabia, Dubai, Kuwait, China, Norway, the Russian Federation and Singapore, among others. The SWFs will often be invested in projects with higher risks but higher expected future returns. Professional portfolio management techniques are often adopted with a view to generating a sustainable future income stream via investments in bonds, equities and other assets. In 2009 Barclays Bank raised $7bn of funds from this source rather than accept UK government funding to help it cope with the liquidity crisis of the 'credit crunch'. In 2010 there were 70 SWFs in 44 countries with assets ranging in value from $20 million (Sao Tome and Principe) to more than $500bn in the United Arab Emirates.

| Case Study 10.7 | Sovereign debt ratings |

There has been much criticism of the credit rating agencies as regards their giving high (triple A) ratings to financial institutions found to be anything but credit worthy as events in the sub-prime market unfolded. Investors who subsequently lost huge amounts of money complained that they had been misled by the AAA ratings that the agencies had handed out on complex packages of mortgage-related debt. The critics further argue that there is a clear conflict of interest when the credit rating agencies are themselves paid by the issuers to assess their bonds and other debt instruments.

Investor attention has now shifted to sovereign debt risk and the three big agencies (Fitch, Moody's and Standard & Poor's) again find themselves at the centre of attention. Sovereign debt upgrades actually exceeded downgrades in every year between 1999 and 2007, but that has changed as a result of the financial crisis and over the period 2008–10 sovereign debt downgrades exceeded upgrades by a ratio of 7:1, the exact reverse of previous experiences.

The workings of the financial system make these ratings even more important; for example should any EU country be downgraded below A−, then that country's bonds become ineligible for use as collateral by the European Central Bank under the tighter ECB rules from the end of 2010. This concern was a key factor in persuading the Greek government to accept austerity measures as a condition for the huge €110 billion support for its currency from the EU and IMF in 2010. Without such support a downgrade would have been inevitable. Politicians also place great emphasis on such ratings. Tim Geithner, the US Treasury Secretary, claims that America will 'never' lose its AAA mark. Political parties in Britain have also promised to defend its AAA rating.

Over the long term the ratings of most developed nations have been remarkably stable. No country rated AAA, AA or A by S&P has gone on to default within a subsequent 15-year period. Indeed, nearly 98% of countries ranked AAA were either at that rating, or the AA level, 15 years later. That stable record may not persist. Investors have been buying government debt for years in the belief it is 'risk-free', almost regardless of the economic fundamentals. But if they lose faith in a government's policies, the situation can change very quickly. Such concerns are especially true since sovereign debt has increased from 62% of World GDP in 2006 to over 85% in 2010.

Some, however, argue that governments and investors place too much importance on credit rating. Canada lost its AAA rating in the 1990s, but then regained it during the past decade, while Japan managed to keep borrowing at a cheap rate, despite losing its triple AAA rating.

The agencies are well aware that ratings changes are highly sensitive. Decisions are therefore made by committee, rather than by an individual, to reduce the scope for outside pressure. Consensus is generally sought before a downgrade is made. The agencies also seek to protect themselves from criticism by being as transparent as possible.

A number of factors help determine whether a country's AAA status can be maintained, including economic and institutional strength, the government's finances and susceptibility to specific shocks. Others argue that the key ratio is not debt-to-GDP but interest payments as a proportion of government revenues. Once that gets beyond 10%, a government may face difficulties.

That does not mean a downgrade is inevitable, however. If the government is implementing a credible plan to cut its deficit, then it may maintain its AAA status. Agencies may also have to make qualitative judgements about a range of other factors, e.g. the willingness of Eurozone countries to bail out countries such as Greece when they enter financial difficulties.

Source: Based on information from *The Economist* (2010) 6 March, p. 88

Questions

1 Why are countries concerned about their sovereign debt ratings?

2 What factors will help a country maintain a high debt rating (e.g. AAA)?

3 Why is there greater volatility in these ratings than was previously the case?

You try 10.2 gives you an opportunity to check your understanding of policy instruments and approaches to unemployment, inflation and the balance of payments.

You try   10.2

1 In this question you'll see a description of a particular type of policy instrument
   used by government in an attempt to tackle unemployment. Try to match the lettered
   description with the numbered type of unemployment that is likely to be the focus of
   each policy.

Description

(a) The government increases the number of job centres and uses more advanced
    computers to improve the information database.

(b) A new skills training initiative is aimed at increasing the ability of those out of work
    to take the jobs on offer in a rapidly changing environment.

(c) To offset the downswing in the business cycle, the government announces a major
    increase in public expenditure.

(d) A programme to support small business start-ups is launched on Tyneside after the
    recent announcement of further closures in the shipbuilding industry.

(e) The government puts pressure on trade unions to make pay claims which are below
    the increase in productivity over the past year.

Terms

(i)   Demand deficient unemployment

(ii) Structural unemployment

(iii) Regional unemployment

(iv) Frictional unemployment

(v)   Real wage unemployment

(vi) Technological unemployment

2 **True or False**

(a) A fall in the rate of inflation means that the average price level is
    now lower.   True/False

(b) A rise in the rate of inflation means that the percentage rise in average
    prices is higher than previously.   True/False

(c) One of the costs of inflation is that those on variable incomes do
    better than those on fixed incomes.   True/False

(d) If a rise in raw material costs feeds through to higher prices we use
    the term 'cost-push' inflation.   True/False

(e) The Phillips curve suggests that higher levels of unemployment
    lead to higher levels of inflation.   True/False

3 Inflation can be measured using different indices.

   RPI = Retail Price Index
   RPIX = RPI excluding mortgage interest payments
   RPIY = RPI excluding mortgage interest payment and indirect taxes

   For each of the following situations identify which of the above measures of inflation
   would show the largest increase.

(a) Over the past year the cost of a basket of products purchased by a typical house-
    hold rises by 5%, mortgage interest payments by 6% and indirect taxes by 7%.

(b) Over the past year the cost of a basket of products purchased by a typical house-
    hold rises by 4%, mortgage interest rates by 2% and indirect taxes by 1%.

You try 10.2 *continued*

(c) Over the past year the cost of a basket of products purchased by a typical household rises by 3%, mortgage interest rates by 2% and indirect taxes by 5%.

4 In this question you'll see a description of a particular type of transaction in the balance of payments of the UK. Try to match that description with its correct term from the balance of payments accounts.

Description

(a) A UK resident purchases shares in a US firm.

(b) A UK firm exports farm machinery to Poland.

(c) A French multimillionaire purchases a fixed asset (land) in the UK.

(d) BP (UK) makes a major sale of oil to Germany.

(e) The UK pays for a major deficit with the USA by running down its gold and foreign exchange reserves.

(f) A Japanese multinational purchases a car component factory in the North East of England.

(g) Virgin Atlantic receives more income from US passengers on its routes.

Terms

(i)   Current account: balance on oil goods

(ii) Current account: balance on non-oil goods

(iii) Current account: balance on services

(iv) Capital account

(v) Financial account: direct investment

(vi) Financial account: portfolio investment

(vii) Financial account: reserves

Answers can be found on pp. 525–546.

Recap

- Fiscal policy involves changes in government expenditure and/or taxation.

- Fiscal policy can be 'automatic', involving 'built-in stabilisers', or discretionary.

- Direct taxes tend to be more progressive than indirect taxes but a fuller comparison involves issues of macroeconomic management, economic incentives, economic welfare and administration.

- The UK government has a 'golden rule' whereby over the economic cycle the government will only borrow to invest and not to fund current expenditure.

- Monetary policy involves influencing the money supply and/or the rate of interest.

- As well as cash, there are a range of 'near money' assets of varying degrees of liquidity.

- Unemployment and inflation are important policy issues in their own right, but have been linked together in the Phillips curve.

- Various types of unemployment can be distinguished – frictional, structural, regional, technological, demand deficient, real wage and 'natural'.

- Inflation can be measured using various indices, such as RPI, RPIX, RPIY and now the Consumer Price Index (CPI).
- The balance of payments can be split into various components, including current and capital accounts, each of which can be broken down still further.
- The exchange rate has a key impact on the price of exports and imports.
- The euro has various advantages and disadvantages.

Key terms

Aggregate demand The total demand in the economy, usually expressed as $C + I + G + (X - M)$.

Aggregate supply The total output in the economy. In the short run a rise in the average price level is usually assumed to exceed rises in input costs, raising profitability and providing an incentive for an expansion in aggregate supply.

Appreciation A rise in the exchange rate of one currency against another. Often used in the context of floating exchange rates.

Balance on goods Net value of trade in tangible goods (exports +, imports −). Previously known as the 'visible trade balance'.

Balance on services Net value of trade in services (exports +, imports −). Previously known as the 'invisible trade balance'.

Balanced budget When tax revenue equals public expenditure.

Budget deficit When tax revenue falls short of public expenditure.

Budget surplus When tax revenue is greater than public expenditure.

Built-in stabilsers Result in a *net* increase in withdrawals in 'boom' conditions and a *net* increase in injections during recession.

Business cycle The tendency for economies to move from economic boom into economic recession and vice versa.

Capital account Records the flows of money into the country (positive sign) and out of the country (negative sign) resulting from the purchase or sale of fixed assets (e.g. land) and selected capital transfers.

Collateral Debt Obligation (CDO) Bundle of securities the value of at least part of which is linked to the value of mortgages.

Consumer Price Index (CPI) Since December 2003 this has replaced RPIX as the official measure of inflation in the UK.

Cost-push inflation Inflation seen as being caused mainly by an increase in the costs of production, which firms pass on as higher prices.

Current account Consists of two main sub-accounts, the 'balance on goods' (formerly 'visible trade balance') and the 'balance on services' (formerly 'invisible trade balance').

Demand-pull inflation Inflation seen as being caused mainly by an increase in the components of aggregate demand.

Depreciation A fall in the exchange rate of one currency against another. Often used in the context of floating exchange rates.

Direct investment Involves physical assets of a company (e.g. plant and equipment).

Economic growth The rate of change of national income, usually over a period of time.

Eurozone The grouping of countries with the euro as their common currency.

Financial account Records the flows of money into the country (+) and out of the country (−) from investment-related (direct and portfolio) or other financial activity (e.g. movement of deposits between countries).

Fiscal drag The tendency for the tax-take to rise as a result of a rise in money incomes.

'Golden rule' Over the economic cycle the government will only borrow to invest and not to fund current expenditure.

Harmonised Index of Consumer Prices (HICP) Uses a different 'basket' of goods to the RPI. Now the UK as well as the EU 'official' inflation measure.

Inflation Average level of prices in the economy rises. Different measures exist (RPI, RPIX, RPIY etc.).

Natural rate of unemployment The rate of unemployment at which there is no excess or deficiency of demand for labour.

Other financial flows Records the movement of deposits between countries. Part of the 'financial account' of the balance of payments.

Phillips curve A curve showing the relationship between (price) inflation and unemployment. The original Phillips curve plotted wage inflation against unemployment in the UK over the years 1861–1957.

Portfolio investment Involves investment in paper assets (e.g. shares, bonds).

Price elasticity of demand (PED) A measure of the responsiveness of demand to a change in the price of the product itself.

Public sector borrowing requirement The borrowing required by government as a result of public expenditure exceeding tax revenue.

Public sector net cash requirement (PSNCR) Now used instead of the 'Public Sector Borrowing Requirement' (PSBR).

Reserves Part of the 'financial account' of the balance of payments. Reserves may be run down in times of overall deficit, and added to in time of surplus. They help to preserve the balance of payments accounting identity (i.e. defined so that they must balance overall).

Retail Price Index (RPI) Shows the change from month to month in the cost of a representative 'basket' of goods and services bought by a typical household.

RPIX Retail Price Index (RPI) excluding mortgage interest payments.

RPIY Retail Price Index excluding mortgage interest payments and indirect taxes.

Stagflation Where real GDP falls but the price level rises.

Structured Investment Vehicle (SIV) A pool of debt obligations which include CDO's.

Trade cycle *see* 'Business cycle'.

Unemployment The number of people actively looking for work who are currently out of a job.

Chapter 11

Political, legal, ecological and technological environment

Introduction

In this chapter we concentrate on the political, legal, ecological and technological environments which may play key roles in shaping the opportunities and threats faced by the organisation. Various acronyms (letter arrangements) are widely used to identify such features of the external environment in which the organisation finds itself. PEST is one (Political, Economic, Socio-cultural and Technological), PESTLE is another, with Legal and Ecological/Environmental added on to PEST. The economic environment has already been considered in detail from a micro perspective in Chapters 1 to 8 and from a macro perspective in Chapters 9 and 10 and the Socio-cultural environment is examined further in Chapter 13.

While the focus of this chapter is the 'external environment' in which the organisation must operate, the strengths and weaknesses inherent in the organisation (i.e. the 'internal environment') will of necessity by touched upon at times. However, a more detailed assessment of the strategic interface between internal and external environments is left to Chapter 14.

What you'll learn

By the end of this chapter you should be able to:

- examine the various ways in which political factors influence business and organisational decision making
- assess the impacts of legal and regulatory frameworks on businesses and organisations
- evaluate the relevance of 'sustainability' and other ecological issues to decision making within businesses
- discuss the opportunities and threats from a rapidly changing technological environment.

Political environment

Most organisations operate within a *nation state* (e.g. UK) and many also operate within *supra-national bodies* which comprise collections of nation states (e.g. EU). Decisions within both types of political entity can have major impacts on the prospects for business organisations achieving the objectives they have set themselves. We review the various types of political risk and some of the techniques that might be used to counter these risks.

Types of political risk

Two broad categories of political risk are often identified, namely 'macropolitical' and 'micropolitical'.

Macropolitical risks

Macropolitical risks potentially affect *all* firms in a country, as in the case of war, a sudden change of government, the onset of national economic recession, and so on. Such risks may even result in governments seizing the assets of the firm without compensation. However, macropolitical risks more usually take the form of the 'threat' of adverse economic circumstances in a country, for example economic recession with less aggregate demand for a broad range of products. Similarly, higher general levels of inflation or taxation might adversely affect all firms, as might security risks related to terrorism etc.

Example

> In 2010 new data suggested that the Greek government debt had risen dramatically to over 124% of its GDP (national income), more than twice the permitted maximum (60%) of GDP for Eurozone countries. This forced the Greek government, under pressure from other EU countries, to introduce sharp rises in taxes and cuts in government spending to fulfil the Eurozone rules and restore investor confidence, thereby cutting consumer spending on the output of all firms in Greece.

> Stop and think   11.1
> Can you use the materials of Chapters 9 and 10 to assess the possible macroeconomic effects of these developments for the Greek economy? Can you provide other examples of macropolitical risk?

Micropolitical risks

Micropolitical risks only affect *specific* firms, industries or types of venture. Such risks may take the form of new regulations or taxes imposed on specific types of businesses in the country.

Example

> An example of micropolitical risk emerged in January 2010 when President Obama announced a new tax on large US banks and insurance companies with assets over $50 billion. The 'Financial Crisis Responsibility Fee' will last a minimum of ten years and will take 0.15% of their 'eligible liabilities' in each year in order to recompense the US taxpayer for funding the 'bail-out' of these companies.

> *Stop and think*   11.2
>
> Can you provide other examples of micropolitical risk?

The 'risk' element of political decision making need not always be adverse, nor need it always fit neatly into the micro and macro political categories outlined above, as Case Study 11.1 indicates.

Case Study 11.1   The politics of rum: Sir Henry's legacy

A recent deal between Diageo, the world's largest drinks company, and the government of the United States Virgin Islands (USVI) is being seen by some as a shrewd deal and by others as Caribbean piracy. A bitter dispute broke out in 2010 between Puerto Rico and the USVI, both of which are US territories in which the production of rum is a major economic activity. The dispute involves the use of tax revenues on rum produced in these territories but sold in the USA; currently some 98% of the tax revenues collected in the US on sales of their rum are given back to them. In fact, the federal government in Washington DC returns $13.25 of every $13.50 it collects per proof-gallon of rum to Puerto Rico and the USVI. Puerto Rico currently receives 84% of the total tax rebate on rum as most of the rum is produced there, and it uses over 90% of those funds for infrastructure, land conservation, health services and other economic and social supports; it returns no more than 10% of its tax rebate to the rum industry in its territory.

However, the deal struck with the USVI provides Diageo with nearly $3 billion in tax breaks over the next 30 years – including marketing subsidies, a 90% reduction in corporate-income taxes, exemption from property taxes and a new distillery and warehouses to be paid for by the USVI, all to produce Captain Morgan, a swiftly growing brand of spiced rum.

The money for this exceptionally generous deal comes from the excise-tax rebates, but the problem is that much of Captain Morgan rum is currently produced in the Serralles distillery in Ponce, Puerto Rico, and Diageo has announced its intention to switch production to St. Croix in the USVI in 2011.

Donna Christensen and Pedro Pierluisi, the (non-voting) congressional representatives from the USVI and Puerto Rico respectively, have introduced warring bills on Capitol Hill. Ms Christensen's bill would make permanent the remittance from the federal rum tax – as things stand, Congress must vote every two years to keep it at $13.25 a gallon, otherwise it falls to $10.50. Mr Pierluisi's bill, on the other hand, would cap the proportion of funds that can be returned to rum producers at 10%.

Mr deJongh, the governor of the USVI, and Diageo point out that the company was considering moving production out of the United States altogether; this deal keeps it in the country, though admittedly at the cost of jobs in Puerto Rico.

Source: Based on information from *The Economist* (2010) 2 January, p. 33

Questions

1 Identify and explain the micropolitical risks for companies in Puerto Rico, the US Virgin Islands (USVI) and elsewhere?

2 Identify and explain the possible macropolitical risks, for Puerto Rico, the US Virgin Islands and the US itself?

It may be useful to disaggregate the types of political risk further, as indicated for macropolitical risks in Table 11.1.

Table 11.1 **Types of macropolitical risk and their impacts on firms**

Type	Impact on firms
Expropriation	Loss of sales
Confiscation	Loss of assets
	Loss of future profits
Campaigns against foreign goods	Loss of sales
	Increased cost of public relations campaigns to improve public image
Mandatory labour benefits legislation	Increased operating costs
Kidnappings, terrorist threats and other forms of violence	Disrupted production
	Increased security costs
	Increased managerial costs
	Lower productivity
Civil wars	Destruction of property
	Lost sales
	Disruption of production
	Increased security costs
	Lower productivity
Inflation	Higher operating costs
Currency devaluations/depreciation	Reduced value of repatriated earnings
Currency revaluations/appreciation	Less competitive in overseas markets and in competing against imports in home market
Increased taxation	Lower after-tax profits
Global recession: 'credit crunch'	Wide range of adverse impacts at national, sectoral and firm specific levels

Make a note

When we reviewed the 'credit crunch' and its contribution to global recession in Chapter 10, our analysis suggested both *macropolitical* and *micropolitical* risks. It is estimated that the public finances of the G20 countries will bear much of the strain of this recession, with national debt projected to rise from the current and high 79% of GDP to almost 120% of GDP by 2014. As regards the resulting *macropolitical risk*, studies have estimated that even seven years after the deepest point of previous banking-related recessions, an economy's level of output would still be 10% below what it would have been without such a banking crisis (*World Economic Outlook*, 2009). Indeed Goldman Sachs estimated that between January 2008 and April 2009, the global financial crisis eroded $30 trillion off the value of global shares and $11 trillion off the value of global homes; altogether a loss of around 75% of World Global GDP. As regards the *micropolitical risk*, the banks and other financial institutions holding securitised assets, such as collateralised debt obligations (CDOs) have been the most vulnerable to the 'credit crunch'. Banks suffered 30% of all 'sub-prime' losses, having kept such securities on their balance sheets for 'leverage' purposes (i.e. to borrow against them).

Responding to political risk

A common criticism of political risk analysis is that it usually takes place too late, when projects are already under way. More management time and effort is now being directed towards appraising political risk at the initiation stage of projects as companies become more aware of the importance of political risk to their future operations. For example, organisations seeking to internationalise typically investigate the following factors in countries which

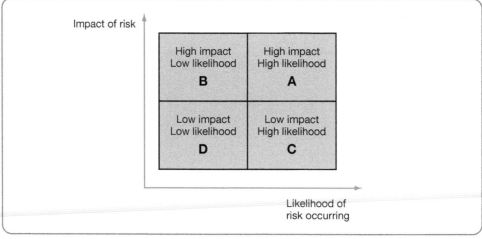

Figure 11.1 **Prioritising (political) risk**

might become the focus of fdi activity: the system of government, foreign capital controls, industrial regulations, history of civil unrest, diplomatic tensions and so on.

Assessing political risk factors

Managers or their representatives may well visit the countries under investigation, as well as using information and data sources from libraries, the Internet, industry associations, government agencies, banks and insurers. Country-risk reports are also available from risk assessment companies and specialists in particular business activities, often consisting of a country profile and macro-level market/non-market risk assessment. However, such analyses may not include the fine detail that might be vital for particular ventures, and at best provide only an indication of the socio-political background.

Prioritising political risk factors

Once identified and assessed, such political risks can be *prioritised*, as in Figure 11.1. The 'gross risks' (expected values) associated with the various political factors or events are sometimes placed by businesses in a two-by-two diagram, giving four 'boxes'. Box A shows risks (high impact/high likelihood) requiring *immediate action*, resulting in attempts by the firm to reduce either the probability of their occurrence or the adverse impacts should they occur. Perhaps it would also be sensible to have in place contingency plans to cover some of the risks in boxes B and C, but those in D would be of lesser concern.

   Taking it further 11.1 looks at ways in which a *quantitative value* might be placed on those political risks regarded as high priority.

Taking it further **Expected value and political risk**   11.1

It is not only the *probability* of a particular political risk factor occurring but the magnitude of its potential *impact* on the objectives of the company which must also be taken into account. It is worth remembering that the expected value of an event is the sum of the probability of each possible outcome multiplied by the value (impact) of each outcome.

$$EV = \sum_{i=1}^{n} p_i x_i$$

where p_i = probability of outcome i (as a decimal)
        x_i = value of outcome i
        n = number of possible outcomes

Taking it further 11.1 *continued*

So if the firm estimated a 60% probability of a 'strike' type of labour dispute occurring so that profits are £20m and a 40% probability of a 'work to rule' occurring so that profits are £40m, the expected value (EV) should a labour dispute occur would be:

$$EV(£m) = (0.60 \times 20) + (0.40 \times 40)$$

$$= \underline{£28m}$$

A change in the firm's assessment of the probabilities of these events occurring or the value of their impacts should they occur would, of course, influence the expected value calculation.

Improving relative bargaining power

In an attempt to overcome political risk, some firms may seek to develop a stronger bargaining position in the country within which they are operating. For example, a firm might attempt to create a situation in which the government of the country loses more than it gains by taking action against the interests of the company. This could be the case when the firm has technical knowledge that will be lost to the country if the company moves elsewhere (with significant job losses) to avoid new regulations. Such bargaining power may be improved if the firm is as fully integrated as possible with the local economy, so that it becomes part of the country's infrastructure. Techniques here may include: developing good relations with the host government and other local political groups; producing as much of the product locally as is possible; creating joint ventures and hiring local people to manage and run the operation; carrying out extensive local research and development; developing good employee relations with the local labour force. These techniques raise the 'costs' to the host country economy of unwelcome interference in the firm's activities.

> Stop and think   11.3
>
> Can you give any examples of companies seeking to reduce political risk in this way?

Restricting exposure to government influence

The firm may seek to limit, in advance, the 'costs' to the business should the host government interfere in its activities. Such techniques may include doing as little local manufacturing as possible, locating all research and development outside the country, hiring only those local personnel who are essential, manufacturing the same product in many other different countries, and so on.

Case Study 11.2 looks at the suggestion that there is increased political risk for those doing business in Russia.

Case Study 11.2   Political risk for business in Russia

In recent years BP and other major energy companies with oil fields and other assets in Russia have come under increasing political and business pressure to relinquish control of such assets to Russian owned companies, such as Gazprom. The origins of such pressures are seen, by many observers, as having their roots in the ways in which privatisation of state assets took place in the early 1990s. In particular, a small group of businessmen (the so-called 'oligarchs') and their companies gained control of

Case Study 11.2 *continued*

huge amounts of previously Russian state industries at what many saw as 'knock-down' prices. These men did not, however, become billionaires by violence or mafia-style tactics, but by using their political influence more effectively than others during Russia's free-for-all transition to capitalism.

One such oligarch was Mikhail Khodorkovsky who, in 1996, became chairman of Yukos, then Russia's second largest oil company (now the largest) with $170bn in oil reserves. Khodorkovsky went on to gain control of massive mineral and timber interests, and was named in 2002 by *Forbes* as Russia's richest man. Amy Chua [*World on Fire*, Heinemann, 2003] stresses that it was political influence, starting with communist linkages before 1990 and continuing with close government linkages after communism that was the platform for the concentration of wealth in Khodorkovsky's hands.

How things can change! Political intrigue would seem to have been the root cause of his fall. President Putin, having been helped to power by the oligarchs, has now turned on many of them, especially those (like Khodorkovsky) who have financed and supported his political opponents. In October 2003 Mr Khodorkovsky was arrested for alleged fraud and tax evasion and was subsequently jailed, the assets of Yukos sold to other Russian companies at 'knock-down' prices and Yukos eventually disbanded. At the time of Mr Khodorkovsky's arrest, shares not only in Yukos but in the whole Russian stock market plunged (over 25% lost in three weeks), as did the share price of Exxon, BP and other major international oil companies with interests in Russia. Financial assets were also withdrawn from Russia as Russian and overseas investors (individuals and governments) withdrew over $50bn in the following few months, worried that Russia was no longer a safe place to hold assets.

There is a general concern for those with an interest in Russian business that the Yukos affair is 'a sign that the state is not willing to see business as a partner but only as a subordinate', said Vladimir Ryzhkov, of the Russian Duma (Parliament). In more recent times Russia has used its control of huge energy reserves and its monopoly control over supplies of power to put political pressure on former states such as Ukraine and Georgia, among others.

Questions

1 What types of political risk have been increased by the Yukos situation?

2 How might this, and similar situations have adverse effects on Russian and international business?

3 How might such businesses respond to this increased political risk?

To minimise political risk the company must be fully aware of present developments in the countries in which it operates, and of likely future developments. For example, MNEs operating in Japan might usefully review the findings of a major report by the *Invest Japan Forum* in December 2002 which identified specific problems in the Japanese business practice and culture which have contributed to the so-called 'lost decade' of effectively zero growth for Japan. The report describes Japan as 'closed' and blames 'problems within the country that are structural and also issues which are rooted in mental attitude'. The main proposals of the report are outlined below. What is important to note here is that many of the proposals involve recommendations to the *Japanese government* to implement and support various changes. An MNE with Japanese interest will need to assess the political likelihood of these changes being made and any impacts which might then result. The report suggested:

● Sweeping changes to the Law on Special Measures for Industrialisation and commercial code to make cross-border M&A activity far easier.

● Changes to tax laws in line with demands from Japanese industry. Particularly looking for tax breaks for R&D activity.

- Greater transparency for financial markets. The report proposes setting up an independent oversight authority along the lines of the US Securities and Exchange Commission.
- A forced change in the mentality of bureaucrats, reminding them they are public servants and placing a new emphasis on making them 'user friendly'.
- Creating a more outward-looking attitude in Japanese industry by introducing foreign language teaching at younger levels.
- Central government to use plain speech in explaining itself.

Before leaving the idea of political risk and its impacts, we might note an *indirect* way of assessing the market's perception of the degree of political risk in a government. This involves checking the *credit rating* given to the bonds (IOUs) issued by that government. *Taking it further* 11.2 considers such credit rating further, with any perception of an increased risk that a government might find it difficult to repay its loans to its creditors resulting in a downgrading of its bond rating.

Taking it further **Assessing risk via bond ratings**   11.2

Before issuing bonds in the public markets, an issuer will often seek a rating from one or more private credit ratings agencies. The selected agencies investigate the issuer's ability to pay interest on the bonds and to repay the full initial loan when the bonds 'mature' (fall due for repayment). The credit agencies look in particular at such matters as financial strength, the intended use of the funds, the political and regulatory environment in which the issuer is operating and any potential economic changes in that environment. After conducting these investigations, the agency will make its estimate of the 'default risk', i.e. the likelihood that the issuer will fail to service the bonds as required. The expense involved in making this rating is normally paid for by the issuer, although in some cases an agency will issue such ratings on its own initiative.

The well-known companies, *Moody's Investors Service* and *Standard & Poor's*, both based in New York, dominate the ratings industry. Two smaller firms, *Fitch IBCA* and *Duff & Phelps Credit Rating Co.*, also issue ratings for many types of bonds internationally. The firms' ratings of a particular issue are not always in agreement, as each uses a different methodology. Table 11.2 interprets the default ratings of the four international firms.

There are also many other ratings agencies that operate in a single country, and several that specialise in a particular industry, such as banking. A downgrading of the credit ratings of either private company or government bonds can have serious implications for the issuer. Lenders will insist on higher interest rates on any future loans to that company or government in order to cover the increased risks of making such loans.

This can be important for both individual businesses and for the macroenvironment in which they operate since higher interest rates are likely to depress aggregate demand (both consumption and investment) in the country and increase the prospects of economic recession.

Table 11.2 **What bond ratings mean**

	Moody's	Standard & Poor's	Fitch IBCA	Duff & Phelps
Highest credit quality; issuer has strong ability to meet obligations	Aaa	AAA	AAA	AAA
Very high credit quality; low risk of default	Aa1 Aa2 Aa3	AA+ AA AA−	AA	AA+ AA AA−

(continued)

▶

Taking it further 11.2 *continued*

Table 11.2 (continued)

	Moody's	Standard & Poor's	Fitch IBCA	Duff & Phelps
High credit quality, but more vulnerable to changes in economy or business	A1 A2 A3	AA+ AA AA−	AA	AA+ AA AA−
Adequate credit quality for now, but more likely to be impaired if conditions worse	Baa1 Baa2 Baa3	BBB+ BBB BBB−	BBB	BBB+ BBB BBB−
Below investment grade, but good chance that issuer can meet commitments	Ba1 Ba2 Ba3	BB+ BB BB−	BB	BB+ BB BB−
Significant credit risk, but issuer is presently able to meet obligations	B1 B2 B3	B+ B B−	B	B+ B B−
High default risk	Caa1 Caa2 Caa3	CCC+ CCC CCC−	CCC CC C	CCC
Issuer failed to meet scheduled interest or principal payments	C	D	DDD DD D	DD

Sovereign risk

Arguably a new kind of risk, namely *sovereign risk*, has become a feature of international business debate. The so called 'PIIGS' economies (Portugal, Italy, Ireland, Greece and Spain) have been the focus of much concern in Europe with their excessive public debt: GDP ratios. Indeed Standard and Poor (S&P) had, during 2009, downgraded several nations from their usual AAA rating, namely Greece to A−, Portugal to A+ and Spain to AA+, and had threatened to do the same to Ireland. However, in the February 2010 meeting of the G20 at Davos, Switzerland, Moody's Investment Service and other ratings agencies had suggested that the sovereign credit rating of the US and UK might also come under similar pressure if the markets became still less convinced of effective action by the respective governments in reducing their high debt:GDP ratios in the coming years!

Stop and think   11.4

Can you give examples of the ways in which a downgrade of the credit rating of the US or UK would influence the respective economies and their international business prospects?

Legal environment

Legal systems have a major impact on the ways in which national and international business is conducted. In this section we consider the relevance of the legal environment to business, noting that in practice it is often difficult to separate political and legal environments, with the latter heavily influenced by the former. Nor can we only concentrate on national laws. With the growth of supra-national bodies (e.g. EU) and other global institutions, laws and regulations devised outside the UK can have a major influence on UK business activity.

Types of legal system

The different types of legal system can generally be divided into the following categories: common law; statute law; code law; religious law; bureaucratic law. These categories need not be mutually exclusive: for example, common law can coexist with various types of code law, e.g. civil law.

- *Common law*. This is the foundation of the legal system in the UK and its former colonies, including the US, Canada, Australia, India, New Zealand and much of the Caribbean. Common law is essentially unwritten, has developed over long periods of time and is largely founded on the decisions reached by judges over the years on different cases. When a judge makes a particular decision, then a *legal precedent* is established.

- *Statute law*. Common law countries depend not only on case law but also on statutory law, i.e. legislation, laws passed by government. In the UK this involves Acts of Parliament which are first published as 'bills' to be debated in the House of Commons and House of Lords.

- *Code law*. This is the world's most common system. It is an explicit codification in written terms of what is and what is not permissible. Such laws can be written down in criminal, civil and/or commercial codes which are then used to determine the outcome of all legal matters. When a legal issue is in dispute it can then be resolved by reference to the relevant code. Most continental European countries, together with their former colonies, follow this type of legal system.

- *Religious law*. Religious law is based on rules related to the faith and practice of a particular religion. A country that works in this way is called a *theocracy*. Iran is one such example. Here a group of mullahs (holy men) determine what is legal or illegal depending on their interpretation of the Koran, the holy book of Islam.

- *Bureaucratic law*. This occurs in dictatorships and communist countries when bureaucrats largely determine what the laws are, even if these are contrary to the historical laws of the land. MNEs operating in such countries have often found it difficult to manage their affairs as there tends to be a lack of consistency, predictability and appeals procedures.

Effects of laws on business

National laws affect national and international business in a variety of ways. There may be legal rules relating to specific aspects of business operations such as the ways in which financial accounts are prepared and disclosed. National laws may also affect aspects of the companies' internal organisation such as its human resource management and health and safety policies. These might include factors such as the provision of maternity and paternity leave, payment of a statutory minimum wage, physical working conditions, protection of employees against hazards at work and pollution, pension and medical provisions and childcare facilities.

Of course, the nature of these rules and regulations may, to some extent, reflect the national government's stance towards trade and industrial policies. Some governments positively encourage inward investment while others may create a whole web of red tape to discourage imports or inward investment, especially where the national interest is deemed 'at risk'.

Example

US takeovers by foreign state-owned companies will now face heightened scrutiny by the inter-agency panel that investigates deals on national security grounds. The Foreign Investment and National Security Act, signed into law in July 2007 by the then President George W. Bush. It requires the Committee on Foreign Investment (Cfius) to conduct a full 90-day investigation of takeovers by government-owned companies, unless the treasury secretary, or another cabinet-level official or deputy, determines they would not impair US national security.

Certainly businesses which operate internationally should be aware of national regulations in the following areas.

- *Trade restrictions.* Law and various types of regulations may be imposed to restrict trade, even to the extent of imposing sanctions or embargoes on trade with particular countries. Sanctions can take many forms, such as restricting access to high-technology goods, withdrawing preferential tariff treatment, boycotting the country's goods or denying new loans.

- *Foreign ownership restrictions.* Many governments may limit the foreign ownership of firms for economic or political reasons. This may sometimes be applied to particular industrial sectors, such as air transportation, financial services or telecommunications.

Check the net

The Business Bureau provides information on legal issues facing business:

www.businessbureau-uk.co.uk

- *Environmental restrictions.* Sometimes domestic laws in a country can indirectly affect the competitiveness of international firms which operate there. For example, the extensive legislation involving the environmental packaging of goods in Germany means higher costs if products are to meet these environmental restrictions.

- *Exit restrictions.* International businesses also need to take account of the costs of exiting a country, should they need to. Many countries impose legal restraints on the closing of plants in order to protect the rights of employees.

Businesses which operate internationally should also be aware of the differences between different international jurisdictions on both the damages available to winning a successful case and the costs of conducting such a case.

Example

The 'price of justice' varies considerably between national jurisdictions. The estimated cost of a contested libel case varies substantially, according to a 2009 Oxford University study. England costs £4.25m, Ireland £0.87m, France £0.05m and Sweden only £0.02m. Clearly an individual or company which might be the subject of such an action might seek to deter the complainant by contesting the action in the UK, where the cost to the complainant would be so much higher for even bringing the case.

EU laws and regulations

European Union laws are adopted after passing through various EU bodies, as indicated in Figure 11.2. For example, most laws involving business issues are initiated by proposals

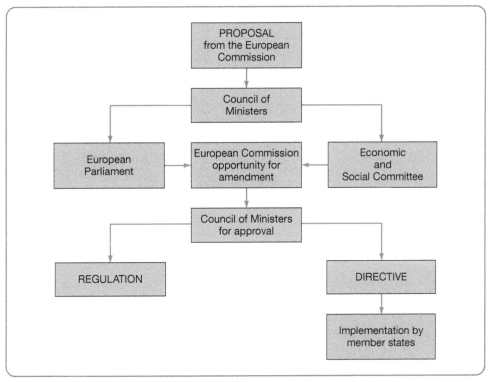

Figure 11.2 **The consultation procedure for law-making in the EU**

from the *European Commission*. These proposals are then passed to the *Council of Ministers* for comment, amendment and ultimately approval. However, the *European Parliament* has the power to reject new legislation coming before it.

Within the framework outlined in Figure 11.2, European Union law takes three main forms:

- **Regulations.** These are applied directly without the need for national measures to implement them.
- **Directives.** These bind members of the EU with respect to objectives but allow individual countries to decide the form and means of implementation; most legislation with respect to banking and finance takes the form of Directives.
- **Decisions.** These are binding in all aspects according to whether they are addressed to member states, to institutions or to individuals.
- *Recommendations and opinions.* These are not binding.

In 2009 alone approximately 240 Regulations, 16 Directives and 131 Decisions were adopted.

As we note in Chapter 13, not only is the EU a major destination for UK exports (around 60% of total goods exports) and a major source of UK imports (around 54% of total goods imports), it is also the location in which many subsidiary companies of UK-owned multinationals operate. Indeed EU laws and regulations often take precedence over UK laws and regulations. For all these reasons the content of EU law is of vital importance to UK individuals and businesses.

Case Study 11.3 looks at the impact of EU law (in the form of Regulations) on individuals and businesses in the particular context of milk production and sales.

Case Study 11.3   Milk regulations

The impact of EU regulations on international business is usefully illustrated by the 2008 changes in the definition of 'milk'. Until 1 January 2008 the only three categories available for use by EU producers were whole or 'full fat milk' (3.5% fat or above), 'semi-skimmed milk' (1.5% to 1.8% fat) and 'skimmed milk' (less than 0.5% fat). Since 1 January 2008, however, two further categories have become available to milk producers and can adopt the 'milk' label, namely '2% fat milk' and '1% fat milk'.

Dairy experts and health chiefs believe that using 5 rather than 3 categories for 'milk' will encourage greater *overall* consumption of milk as well as encouraging consumers to switch to milk products with lower fat content than they currently purchase. Some 64% of total milk consumption in the EU, prior to the new regulations, was semi-skimmed milk, 25% whole or full fat milk and only 11% skimmed milk. Overall milk consumption had fallen from four pints per person to three pint per person over the past decade.

Having a wider range of categories of 'milk' will encourage greater switching, according to research (e.g. the Dairy Council of the UK), since consumers can more easily adapt to the smaller change in taste when a milk with only marginally less fat content is consumed. For example adults who prefer whole or full fat milk will more readily switch to '2% fat

milk' than to the 1.5% to 1.8% 'semi-skimmed milk', or from 'semi-skimmed milk' to '1% fat milk' than to the 0.5% (or less) 'skimmed milk'.

Food manufacturers are expected to make increased use of these new and lower food fat milk and cheese products in sauces, ready meals and dairy-based desserts without losing consumer commitment to their products.

A recent scientific report in the UK for the 'Foresight Programme' on health futures, suggested that unless diet is changed substantially, almost half of UK adults and a quarter of UK children will be dangerously overweight by 2050, costing £45 billion a year in health care costs, with £7 billion per annum needed to pay for the treatment of type 2 diabetes, strokes, high blood pressure, cancer and heart disease linked to diet, and £38 billion per annum needed to cover the cost of related absenteeism or of benefits paid to the unemployed or disabled.

Questions

1 Why might the regulatory change allowing the use of extra categories of 'milk' products increase overall (EU) milk consumption?

2 Why might any such increase in EU milk consumption benefit the health of individuals?

3 What other implications might follow from this regulatory change?

Intellectual property rights (IPRs)

Links

You can find more detail on the EU in other chapters of this book, e.g. Chapter 8 (pp. 252–5), Chapter 13 (pp. 451–4).

Most advanced industrialised economies are progressively becoming 'knowledge based', so that questions of intellectual property rights (IPRs) are becoming ever more important. The value of intellectual property can quickly be destroyed unless companies enforce their rights in this area. Intellectual property rights can take various forms, with patents, trademarks and copyrights being particularly important.

Patents

Patent law confers ownership rights on the *inventor*. To qualify as the subject matter of a patent the invention must be novel, involve an inventive step and be capable of industrial application. 'Novel' seeks to exclude granting monopoly ownership rights to something that already exists; 'inventive' seeks to establish that a step has been taken which would not be obvious to experts in the field; 'industrial application' seeks to avoid the restrictions which would result from ideas and principles being patentable, instead limiting such protection to specific applications of these ideas. Patents depend upon registration for their validity.

Case Study 11.4 suggests that in a global economy there is a growing international awareness of the need to protect intellectual property rights, here patents, if inward foreign direct investment is to continue to grow.

| Case Study 11.4 | Kettle company wins damages in China | |

Foreign companies are increasingly able to protect their intellectual property rights through China's legal system, according to the world's largest maker of electric kettle components after a court ordered two Chinese rivals to pay it damages. Strix, founded on the Isle of Man in 1951, which now provides thermostatic controls for two-thirds of the world's kettles, had accused two Chinese companies of copying its patented technology, which automatically switches off electric kettles after the water has reached boiling point. The Beijing Intermediate People's Court has ordered Zhejiang Jiatai Electrical Appliance Manufacturing and Leqing Fada Electrical Appliance to pay damages of Rmb7.1m ($1.04m) and Rmb2m respectively. Paul Huggey, Strix chief executive, told the *Financial Times* that the outcome was 'unprecedented' in China's small appliances industry, which is concentrated in southern Guangdong province near Hong Kong.

'We have increasing faith in China's legal system,' said Mr Hussey, whose company's manufacturing operations are based in Guangzhou, Guangdong's provincial capital. 'Knowing that the courts will listen to [intellectual property cases] in an open and honest manner is a huge step forward.'

Strix was further emboldened by the fact the award was accompanied by a 'cease-and-desist' instruction to the two defendants. The court had also issued a 'property preservation' order, freezing the 'copyists' bank accounts when Strix first brought its case in late 2008. Mr Hussey said that the initial order was a testament to the strength of the case Strix had painstakingly built against the alleged infringers.

'Our frustration with these companies had been growing for some time,' Mr Hussey said. 'They were making inroads in a business they had no business being in.'

Strix also made a deliberate decision to pursue legal action in Beijing, China's capital. While its manufacturing operations are in Guangzhou those of Zhejiang Jiatai's are in an eastern province near Shanghai. The Beijing Intermediate People's Court therefore offered a neutral venue with nationwide authority. To bring its lawsuit in Beijing, the Isle of Man company had to prove that the kettles that infringed Strix's patent, and which were being sold across the country, were also available in the capital.

Strix employs 700 people at this Guangzhou manufacturing headquarters, which opened in 1997. From there, the company can serve the world's leading appliance brands and their contract manufacturers, most of which are less than a two-hour drive away. A smaller Strix team of about 40 people continues to operate on the Isle of Man, a UK dependency in the middle of the Irish Sea. Strix produces a crucial 'blade' component consisting of a sensitive metal alloy that ensures electric kettles do not overheat.

Source: from Kettle company wins damages in China, Financial Times, 01/02/2010 (Mitchell, T.), © The Financial Times Ltd

Questions

1 Why is this legal ruling by the Beijing court seen as important by many non-Chinese companies?

2 Why did Strix seek to have the case heard in Beijing?

Trademarks

Trademarks have been defined as '. . . any sign capable of being represented graphically which is capable of distinguishing goods or services of one undertaking from those of other undertakings' (*UK Trade Marks Act 1994*). This is sometimes referred to as the 'product differentiation' function. Such trademarks require less intellectual activity than patents or copyright to be deemed protectable, with the focus instead being on the commercial activity associated with such trademarks. As with patents, trademarks depend on registration for their validity, which gives the holder the exclusive right to *use* the mark in the UK for 10 years, subject to further renewals in periods of 10 years. Infringement occurs where others use the trademark without permission.

To simplify global protection of trademarks the *World Intellectual Property Organization* (WIPO) allows trademark owners to seek protection in up to 74 countries with one application. Established as far back as 1891 in Madrid, WIPO originally comprised mainly French-speaking nations but the 1996 *Madrid Protocol* made English a second working language. The US, the country with the largest trademark activity, joined WIPO in 2003 and by 2010 over 506,000 international trademarks were registered. The decision by WIPO in 2004 to make Spanish a third working language has increased still further both the number of countries covered by the international trademark agreement and the number of international trademarks registered.

WIPO defines a trademark as:

- any sign that serves, in trade, to differentiate the goods and services of one person or company from those of another;
- consisting of a word, figures, label, sound, in three dimensions;
- that which identifies the products of that person or company so that it is not confused with others.

Copyrights

Copyright law prevents the copying of forms of work (e.g. an article, book, play, poem, music score etc.) rather than the ideas contained within these forms. However, sometimes the copyright can be extended to the 'structure' underpinning the form actually used (e.g. the plot of a book as well as the book itself).

Copyright (unlike patents and trademarks) applies automatically and does not require registration. For copyright to apply there must be three key conditions.

(i) *A recorded work which is 'original'*, in the sense that the work is different from that of its contemporaries.

(ii) *Of an appropriate description*, i.e. literacy, dramatic, music, artistic, sound recordings, films and broadcasts all qualify. Even business letters can receive protection as 'literacy works'.

(iii) *Being sufficiently connected to the country in question*, since copyright is essentially national in character, at least in the first instance. So in the case of the UK, the author (or work) must be connected to the UK by nationality, domicile, source of publication or some other acceptable way.

The period of copyright extends to the life of the author plus 70 years. Copyright protection is not absolute: for example, limited copying of copyright material is permitted for purposes of research or fair journalistic reporting. Breaching copyright beyond any existing provision can result in an injunction to desist and/or the award of damages.

Copyright is different to the other types of IPR as it is an unregistered right (in the UK). Copyright comes into effect immediately as soon as something is put onto paper, film, the Internet etc. The UK Patent Office recommends marking your work with the copyright symbol, ©, followed by your name and the date. This is a warning to others who may consider copying your ideas. However, in the UK this is not legally necessary.

Case Study 11.5 examines the way in which copyright law has changed from the original intention of this type of protection of intellectual property rights.

Case Study 11.5   Copyright and wrong

When the British parliament decided, in 1709, to create a law that would protect books from piracy the London-based publishers and booksellers who had been pushing for such protection were overjoyed. When Queen Anne gave her assent on 10 April the following year – to 'An act for the encouragement of learning' they were less enthused. Parliament had given them rights, but it had set a time limit on them: 21 years for books already in print and 14 years for new ones, with an additional 14 years if the author was still alive when the first term ran out. After that, the material would enter the public domain so that anyone could reproduce it. The lawmakers intended thus to balance the incentive to create with the interest that society has in free access to knowledge and art. The Statute of Anne thus helped nurture and channel the spate of inventiveness that Enlightenment society and its successors have since enjoyed.

Over the past 50 years, however, that balance has shifted. Largely thanks to the entertainment industry's lawyers and lobbyists, copyright's scope and duration have vastly increased. In America, copyright holders get 95 years' protection as a result of an extension granted in 1998, derided by critics as the 'Mickey Mouse Protection Act'. They are now calling for even greater protection, and there have been efforts to introduce similar terms in Europe. Such arguments should be resisted: it is time to tip the balance back.

Annie get your gun

Lengthy protection, it is argued, increases the incentive to create. Digital technology seems to strengthen the arguments: by making copying easier, it seems to demand greater protection in return. The idea of extending copyright also has a moral appeal. Intellectual property can seem very like real property, especially when it is yours, and not some faceless corporations. As a result people feel that once they own it – especially if they have made it – they should go on owning it, much as they would a house that they could pass on to their descendants. On this reading, protection should be perpetual. Ratcheting up the time limit on a regular basis becomes a reasonable way of approximating that perpetuity.

The notion that lengthening copyright increases creativity is questionable, however. Authors and artists do not generally consult the statutes book before deciding whether or not to pick up pen or paintbrush. And overlong copyrights often limit, rather than encourage, a work's dissemination, impact and influence. It can be difficult to locate copyright holders to obtain the rights to re-use old material. As a result, much content ends up in legal limbo (and in the case of old movies and sound recordings, is left to deteriorate – copying them in order to preserve them may constitute an act of infringement). The penalties even for inadvertent infringement are so punishing that creators routinely have to self-censor their work. Nor does the advent of digital technology strengthen the case for extending the period of protection. Copyright protection is needed partly to cover the costs of creating and distributing works in physical form. Digital technology slashes such costs and thus reduces the argument for protection.

The moral case, although easy to sympathise with, is a way of trying to have one's cake and eat it. Copyright was originally the grant of a temporary government-supported monopoly on copying a work, not a property right. From 1710 onwards, it has involved a deal in which the creator or publisher gives up any natural and perpetual claim in order to have the state protect an artificial and limited one. So it remains.

The question is how such a deal can be made equitably. At the moment, the terms of trade favour publishers too much. A return to the 28-year copyrights of the Statute of Anne would be in many ways arbitrary, but not unreasonable. If there is a case for longer terms, they should be on a renewal basis, so that content is not locked up automatically. The value society places on creativity means that fair use needs to be expanded and inadvertent infringement should be minimally penalised. None of this should get in the way of the enforcement of copyright, which remains a vital tool in the encouragement of learning. But tools are not ends in themselves.

Source: Adapted from Protecting creativity, 'copyright and wrong', www.economist.com, © The Economist Newspaper Ltd, London (08/04/2010)

Questions

1 What was the original intention of copyright protection?

2 To what extent has the situation changed and what advantages and disadvantages follow from these changes?

Table 11.3 **Examples of works protected by copyright**

1 Original literary works, e.g. novels, articles in newspapers

2 Original musical works

3 Original artistic work, e.g. paintings, drawings, photographs, diagrams, logos

4 Original dramatic works; these include dance or mime

5 Published editions of works

6 Films, videos and DVDs

7 Broadcasts and cable programmes

8 Sound recordings, based on any medium

9 Any original work displayed over the Internet

Source: Adapted from the UK Patent Office website (see **www.patent.gov.uk**). Crown copyright material is reproduced with the permission of the Controller of HMSO under the Click-Use Licence

---

Stop and think 11.5

Can you give any recent examples involving patents, trademarks or copyright?

Table 11.3 provides some examples of the types of works protected by copyright.

Trade-related aspects of intellectual property rights (TRIPS)

The WTO Agreement on *Trade-Related Aspects of Intellectual Property Rights*, the so-called TRIPS Agreement, is based on a recognition that increasingly the value of goods and services entering into international trade resides in the know-how and creativity incorporated into them. The TRIPS Agreement provides for minimum international standards of protection for such know-how and creativity in the areas of copyright and related rights, trademarks, geographical indications, industrial designs, patents, layout-designs of integrated circuits and undisclosed information. It also contains provisions aimed at the effective enforcement of such intellectual property rights, and provides for multilateral dispute settlement. It gives all WTO members transitional periods so that they can meet their obligations under it. Developed-country members have had to comply with all of the provisions of the Agreement since 1 January 1996. For developing countries and certain transition economies, the general transitional period ended on 1 January 2000. For the least-developed countries, the transitional period was 11 years and ended on 1 January 2006.

Check the net

The UK government site relating to intellectual property rights is **www.patent.gov.uk**

The US Patent and Trademark Office website is **www.uspto.gov**

The World Intellectual Property Organization (WIPO) site is **www.wipo.int**

You try 11.1 involves materials on both the political and legal environments.

You try 11.1

1 Read the text below and answer the question which follows.

Chinese government and EU milk products

In late 2007, EU producers and consumers of milk products become only too well aware of how political decisions in one part of the world can, with interconnected global markets, transmit market 'shocks' to all corners of the world. A drive by the Chinese government to provide all Chinese children with half a litre of milk a day caused demand for milk to increase dramatically by around 25% a year, with around one-third of all the worldwide production of milk now exported to China. Prices of a litre of milk in EU rose by over 25% in one week

You try 11.1 *continued*

alone in August 2007, with substantial price increases in dairy-based products such as cheese, butter and yogurt following closely behind. For example, Kraft raised prices of its cheese based products by 12% in 2007, linking the price rise explicitly to higher milk costs.

However, others blame over regulation in the EU rather than globalisation, for milk-based inflation. They argue that it is the excessive milk quotas imposed by the EU in 1984 and due to last until 2015 that has prevented the supply side of the EU market for milk from adjusting to this surge of Chinese demand. Even so some market adjustment is taking place, if only slowly. For example, EU dairy farmers are breeding high-performance milk cows and selling these to Chinese farmers, who have little or no tradition of dairy farming. Increased Chinese production of milk is also being helped by Chinese government subsidies for farmers who switch to dairy farming.

Question: What aspects of political risk are involved here and how might those political risks have been taken into account?

2 Which of the following scenarios would be given the highest priority in political risk assessment?

(a) High impact, low likelihood

(b) Low impact, high likelihood

(c) Low impact, low likelihood

(d) High impact, high likelihood

(e) Low expected value for the possible event.

3 Which *three* of the following approaches may be adopted by an international business attempting to reduce the political risks from operating in a host country?

(a) Avoid using local labour or developing skills in local labour markets.

(b) Improve the relative bargaining power of an international business vis-à-vis the host country.

(c) Ensure that any technology the international business owns is available to the host country whether or not the business operates there.

(d) Use protective and defensive techniques to limit the 'costs' to the international business should the host country interfere in its activities.

(e) Use integrative techniques to ensure that the international business becomes part of the host country's infrastructure.

4 Which *one* of the following confers ownership rights on the inventor?

(a) Trademarks

(b) Patents

(c) Copyrights

(d) Litigation

(e) Arbitration

5 Match each of the *lettered* descriptions with the correct *numbered* term.

Descriptions

(a) Where subsequent judicial decisions are directly influenced by earlier decisions.

(b) Risks associated with events such as war which affect all the firms in a country.

(c) Describes the type of legal system which often occurs in dictatorships and communist countries.

(d) The world's most common system and explicitly states what is and is not permissible.

> **You try 11.1** *continued*
>
> (e) Risks associated with the prospect of company specific taxes being imposed.
>
> (f) Where 'fatwas' and other decrees from mullahs determine what is lawful.
>
> *Terms*
>
> (i) Micropolitical
>
> (ii) Common law
>
> (iii) Religious law
>
> (iv) Bureaucratic law
>
> (v) Macropolitical
>
> (vi) Code law
>
> *Answers can be found on pp. 525–546.*

Ecological environment

We noted in Chapter 4 (pp. 124–6) that firms which actively support 'green' policies need not necessarily do so at the expense of profit. Here we look in rather more detail at the reasons why businesses may have a strong interest in taking into account the ecological environment in which they operate.

The last section pointed out *legal* reasons for complying with legal regulations, many of which are intended to improve social and environmental conditions for citizens. But what *voluntary* reasons might encourage a firm to move in the direction of environmental awareness?

Environmental awareness in a global economy

In today's global economy a number of driving forces are arguably raising environmental concerns to the forefront of *corporate* policy debate.

● *Environmentally conscious consumers.* Consumer awareness of environmental issues is creating a market for 'green products'. Patagonia, a California-based producer of recreational clothing, has developed a loyal base of high-income customers partly because its brand identity includes a commitment to conservation. A similar successful approach has been used by the Body Shop. Consumers have long claimed to be more virtuous than they are. Retailers called it the '30:3 phenomenon' – 30% of purchasers told pollsters that they thought about workers' rights, animal welfare and the state of the planet when they decided what to buy, but sales figures showed that only 3% of them acted on those thoughts. Now, however, retailers are behaving as if consumers mean it. It was reported in 2009 that annual sales of Fairtrade food and drink in Britain had reached over £380 million, having grown at over 40% per year over the past decade. A Mori poll found that two-thirds of UK consumers claimed to be 'green' or ethical and actively look to purchase products with an environmental/ethical association. In the UK, J. Sainsbury is selling only bananas with the Fairtrade label, which guarantees a decent income to the grower. Marks and Spencer is stocking only Fairtrade coffee and tea and is buying a third of the world's supply of Fairtrade cotton. In the US, Dunkin' Donuts has decided to sell only Fairtrade espresso coffee in its North American and European outlets. Wal-Mart has devoted itself to a range of 'sustainability' projects.

It has been suggested that three key conditions are required for success with *'environmental product differentiation'*, i.e. segmenting the market so that consumers will pay higher prices for overtly 'environmentally friendly' products.

- First, the company must have identified a distinctive market segment consisting of consumers who really are willing to pay more for environmentally friendly products.
- Second, the branding/corporate image must clearly and credibly convey the environmental benefits related to the products.
- Third, the company must be able to protect itself from imitations for long enough to profit from its 'investment' in the previous two conditions.

Stop and think   11.6
Can you give any examples of 'environmental product differentiation'?

- *Environmentally and cost-conscious producers.* Producers are increasingly aware that adherence to high environmental standards need not be at the expense of their cost base. In other words, they can be environmentally friendly at the same time as reducing (rather than raising) their cost base.
- *Environmentally and credit-risk-conscious producers.* International businesses are increasingly aware that failure to manage environmental risk factors effectively can lead to adverse publicity, lost revenue and profit and perhaps even more seriously a reduction in their official credit rating, making it more difficult and costly (e.g. higher interest rates) to finance future investment plans.
- *Environmentally conscious governments.* Businesses have a further reason for considering the environmental impacts of their activities, namely the scrutiny of host governments. Where production of a product causes environmental damage, it is likely that this will result in the imposition of taxes or regulations by government.

Environmental sustainability

'Sustainable' and 'sustainability' are now key trigger words in the world of advertising for positive, emotive images associated with words such as 'green', 'wholesome', 'goodness', 'justice', 'environment', among others. They are used sophisticatedly to sell cars, nappies, holidays and even lifestyles. Sustainability sells – how has this come about and what exactly are we being encouraged to buy?

As long ago as 1987, a United Nations report entitled *Our Common Future* provided the most widely used definition of sustainable development: 'development which meets the needs of the present without compromising the ability of future generations to meet their own needs'. Of course, there have been many different views as to how this definition should affect individual, corporate and government actions, though one theme that has been constant in most views is that of 'intergenerational equity'.

- *Intergenerational equity*: where the development process seeks to minimise any adverse impacts on future generations. These clearly include avoiding adverse environmental impacts such as excessive resource depletion today reducing the stock of resources available for future use, or levels of pollution emission and waste disposal today beyond the ability of the environment to absorb them, thereby imposing long-term damage on future generations.

Check the net

The issue of sustainability can be considered at:
www.sustainability.co.uk
The National Environment Trust is at
www.pewtrusts.org
Visit The Body Shop website for material on human rights and environmental issues:
www.bodyshop.co.uk
Pressure group websites include:
www.foe.co.uk
www.greenpeace.org.uk
www.panda.org

A recent census in China has identified significant levels of pollution and has influenced government policy in the direction of pollution reduction, as Case Study 11.6 indicates.

Case Study 11.6   Beijing census exposes high levels of pollution

The high levels of pollution reported in China in 2010 in its first national census of pollution has revealed such an environmental problem that the government has proposed a new tax on its sources, according to reports. The level of water pollution countrywide was found to be more than twice government estimates. Farms are revealed by the report to be the biggest single source of the main water pollutants. In 2007, the year covered by the census, more than 209bn tonnes of waste water were also discharged. Preventing and controlling agricultural pollution would be a higher priority in future, said Zhang Lijun, vice minister of environmental protection, announcing the results of the census in February 2010.

The census found more than 63.7 trillion cubic metres of 'waste gases' were emitted that year. These included emissions of 23m tonnes of sulphur dioxide, which causes acid rain and is commonly the result of burning coal in power stations without 'scrubbers' to remove it. Wen Jiabao, the Chinese premier, admitted last month that the country's pollution was 'grim'. Beijing is understood to be concerned that high levels of pollution and other forms of environmental degradation could provoke social unrest.

The census will be used to inform policy. The data were much more comprehensive and broken down into much more detail than any information on pollutants China has published previously. But green campaigners complained the data gathered were not published in full.

The census took two years, as about 6m sources of pollution – factories, farms, residential sources and others – had to be examined. Mr Zhang said 'The census of pollution sources for the first time in the country is a significant survey on the national situation. Its operations went smoothly and its main tasks were basically completed.' Mr Zhang painted a relatively optimistic picture, forecasting pollution would soon peak, and that the government could take a more targeted approaches to combat pollution in future. He said discharges of industrial pollution were concentrated in very few industries and regions. There were 'no major surprises'.

China's State Council ordered the census in 2006 which involved more than 570,000 people countrywide.

Source: from Beijing considers pollution tax, *Financial Times*, 10/02/2010 (Harvey, F.), © The Financial Times Ltd

Questions

1 How might the results of this census influence Chinese business activity?

2 How might the results of this census influence international business activity?

Sustainability is clearly high on the agenda of governments, including the issue of reducing the 'carbon footprint' and lessening the impacts of global warming. However, Case Study 11.7 suggests that some of the claims made for sustainable policies and products may not always be well founded!

Case Study 11.7   Biofuels subsidies criticised

Governments need to scrap subsidies for biofuels as the current rush to support alternative energy sources will lead to surging food prices and the potential destruction of natural habitats, the Organization for Economic Co-operation and Development warned in September 2007. The OECD report argued that politicians are rigging the market in favour of an untried technology that will have only limited impact on climate change.

'The current push to expand the use of biofuels is creating unsustainable tensions that will disrupt markets without generating significant environmental benefits,' say the authors of the study. The survey says biofuels would cut energy-related emissions by 3% at most. This benefit would come at a huge cost, which would swiftly make them unpopular among taxpayers.

The study estimates the USA alone spends $7bn (£3.4bn) a year helping make ethanol, with each tonne of carbon dioxide avoided costing more than $500. In the European Union, it can be almost 10 times that. It says biofuels could lead to some damage to the environment. 'As long as environmental values are not adequately priced in the market, there will be powerful incentives to replace natural ecosystems such as forests, wetlands and pasture with dedicated bio-energy crops,' it says.

The report recommends governments phase out biofuel subsidies, using 'technology-neutral' carbon taxes to allow the market to find the most efficient ways of reducing greenhouse gases. The survey puts a question mark over the EU's plans to derive 10% of transport fuel from plants by 2020. It says money saved from phasing out

subsidies should fund research into so-called second-generation fuels, which are being developed to use waste products and so emit less CO_2 when they are made.

Adrian Bebb, biofuels campaigner with Friends of the Earth, said, 'The OECD is right to warn against throwing ourselves head-first down the agro fuels path'. Wheat costs actually doubled in 2007, not only because of a poor harvest but also because farmland previously used for cereals had been converted to growing biofuel energy crops such as rapeseed – the increased demand for biofuels having raised the price of such crops.

Source: adapted from OECD slams biofuels subsidies for sparking food inflation price, *Financial Times*, 11/09/2010 (Bounds, A.), © The Financial Times Ltd

Question

Why might subsidising biofuels actually damage the environment?

Hardly surprisingly, in view of the above, business is increasingly attracted to 'green marketing'.

Green marketing

An important issue in today's business environment is that a firm must be seen to be 'green' among the local community, customers, potential customers and all stakeholders in the business. The following green marketing strategies have been suggested in order to get this message across.

1 Adopt a thorough approach to corporate greening. This includes all functions of the business. Everything from being energy efficient to introducing environmentally friendly fuel.

2 Appoint a highly visible Chief Executive Officer (CEO) with environmental leanings and make him/her the centrepiece of your corporate social image, e.g. the late Anita Roddick of The Body Shop.

3 Be transparent. Allow stakeholders access to information so that they know exactly what are the level of potential health risks associated with various projects.

4 Work cooperatively with third parties, such as government agencies and environmental pressure groups.

5 Vigorously communicate your company's commitment to accountability and continuous improvement. This can include 'cause-related marketing'. For example, the UK supermarket giant Tesco works with a different charity every year.

6 Act now. Do not wait to get the green message across.

'Green marketing' has already been seen to strike a chord with consumer groups. For example, in Chapter 4 (pp. 124–6) we noted that companies adopting a more explicitly ethical stance had outperformed other companies in terms of various stock market indices.

However, for 'green marketing' to be ultimately successful the company must actually embody the image it portrays. BP has sought to rebrand itself as 'Beyond Petroleum' rather than 'British Petroleum', recognising that too close an association with fuels implicated in global warming is not to its advantage! However, despite the careful attempts to associate BP with a 'green' agenda, BP Amoco was fined £60,000 in 2002 (the highest recorded fine in the UK) for pollution from a petrol station, after leaking petrol endangered drinking water in Luton and in the same year the Norwegian Petroleum Directorate issued a severe reprimand to BP citing 'many violations of health, environmental and safety standards'. In a further blow, one of the UK's leading ethical investment funds, Henderson Global Investors, announced that it was selling millions of pounds of BP shares because it could no longer assure its investors of the company's commitment to worker safety and to the environment, an image problem further aggravated for BP in 2006 with a major explosion in its oil-refining facility in Texas, for which it received a major fine for negligence.

Stop and think 11.7

Select a company from *one* of the following industries:

1 Chemicals
2 Cosmetics
3 Furniture retailing.

Conduct your own research to find out the extent to which they are involved in green marketing. Make your own recommendations as to how your chosen firm can develop/improve its green marketing.

Technological environment

Technological change can have important effects on the decisions taken by businesses. Technological change can involve new processes of production, i.e. new ways of doing things which raise the productivity of factor inputs, as with the use of robotics in car assembly techniques which has dramatically raised output per assembly line worker. Around 80% of technological change has been *process innovation*. However, technological change can also be embodied in new products (goods or services) which were not previously available. Online banking and many new financial services are the direct result of advances in microprocessor-based technologies. Less than 20% of technological change has involved such *product innovation*.

Taking it further 11.3 examines the key issue as to whether new technologies create jobs or destroy jobs! As we shall see, the outcome will depend on some of the economic principles we introduced in Chapters 1–3.

Taking it further Creating or destroying jobs 11.3

New technologies have substantially raised output per unit of labour input (labour productivity) and per unit of factor input, both labour and capital (total factor productivity). There has been much concern that the impact of these productivity gains has been to reduce jobs, i.e. to create technological unemployment. We now consider the principles which will, in fact, determine whether or not jobs will be lost (or gained) as a result of technological change.

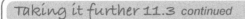

Taking it further 11.3 continued

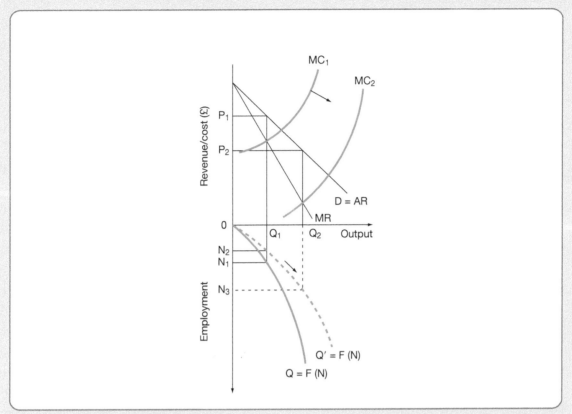

Figure 11.3 **Technical change and the level of employment**

Higher output per unit of factor input reduces costs of production, provided only that wage rates and other factor price increases do not absorb the whole of any productivity gain. Computer-controlled machine tools are a case in point. Data from Renault show that the use of DNC machine tools resulted in machining costs one-third less than those of general-purpose machine tools at the same level of output. Lower costs will cause the profit-maximising firm to lower price and raise output under most market forms, as in Figure 11.3. A downward shift of the average cost curve, via the new technologies, lowers the marginal cost curve from MC_1 to MC_2. The profit-maximising price/output combination (MC = MR) now changes from P_1/Q_1 to P_2/Q_2. Price has fallen, output has risen.

The dual effect on employment of higher output per unit of labour (and capital) input can usefully be illustrated from Figure 11.3. The curve Q = F(N) is the familiar production function of economic theory, showing how output (Q) varies with labour input (N), capital and other factors assumed constant. On the one hand the higher labour productivity from technical change shifts the production function outwards to the dashed line Q' = F(N). The original output Q_1 can now be produced with less labour, i.e. with only N_2 labour input instead of N_1 as previously. On the other hand, the cost and price reduction has so raised demand that more output is required. We now move along the new production function Q' until we reach Q_2 output, which requires N_3 labour input. In our example the reduction in labour required per unit output has been more than compensated for by the expansion of output, via lower prices, so that employment has, in fact, risen from N_1 to N_3.

This analysis highlights a number of points on which the final employment outcome for a firm adopting the new techniques will depend:

1 The relationship between new technology and labour productivity, i.e. the extent to which the production function Q shifts outwards.

Taking it further 11.3 continued

2 The relationship between labour productivity and cost, i.e. the extent to which the marginal cost curve shifts downwards.

3 The relationship between cost and price, i.e. the extent to which cost reductions are passed on to consumers as lower prices.

4 The relationship between lower price and higher demand, i.e. the price elasticity of the demand curve (*see* Chapter 2, pp. 40–47).

Suppose, for instance, that the new process halved labour input per unit output! If this increase in labour productivity (1 above), reduces cost (2 above), and price (3 above), and output doubled (4 above), then the same total labour input would be required. If output more than doubled, then more labour would be employed. The magnitude of the four relationships above will determine whether the firm offers the same, more, or less employment after technical change in the production process.

Technological advance can occur in all sectors, as for example in the agricultural sector of India considered in *You try* 11.2, Question 1 (p. 377). However, here we concentrate on technological change involving information and communication technologies.

Information and communication technologies

Many technological advances involve information and communication techniques (ICT) of one type or another. One of the major growth areas in recent years has been the development of mobile applications, a market dominated by Apple, especially after it established its App Store, from which more than three billion apps were downloaded to iPhones in the first 18 months after its opening. Gartner, the research consultancy firm, predicts that spending on handset apps – including games, maps and office tools – will exceed £4 billion pounds in 2010 as the volume of app downloads rises to around £5 billion.

Case Study 11.8 examines the impact of the opening of the App Store on one game supplier.

Case Study 11.8   **Games guru puts his finger on chart success**   **FT**

Inside the San Francisco offices of iPhone app-maker Ngmoco, across from the Giants' baseball stadium, the forces of modern games are colliding. Chief executive Neil Young left Electronic Arts, one of the two leading electronic gaming companies, to start Ngmoco last year to take advantage of big developments in the industry.

First, games that did not require a lot of time or processing power, such as the role-playing games *Mobsters* and *Mafia Wars*, had started to spread on MySpace and Facebook. Social games have a financial advantage over console games, where Electronic Arts and Activision are strongest, because they require much less up-front investment

and because they can be improved daily in response to how they are played. Distribution costs can be as little as zero, if friends convince other friends to play.

Second, in 2008 Apple announced that it would open its App Store to outsiders, putting pretty well any developer with a great product a few finger-taps away from millions of iPhone users. 'It felt like one of those inflection moments. This felt like one of the biggest,' Mr Young said, and in March he started assembling a cadre of like-minded industry veterans and venture funding. In the year-and-a-half since, the company – which has fewer than 40 employees – has landed six games in

Case Study 11.8 *continued*

Apples' top Ten charts, notching up more than 10m downloads.

One of the guiding principles that Ngmoco espouses is to combine games with a heavy social component, so that people interact while playing and thus recruit additional players. Another is that games should be free to play, but that spending money inside them should make them more enjoyable. Ngmoco's *Eliminate* did that so well that it became the first game to make the separate Top Ten charts for free games and also for top-grossing games.

In June Ngmoco became the latest gamemaker to deploy a social network for its games and those of partners, so that the players who know each other from one imagined world can find each other in another, while the company cross-promotes its wares. But all of that is so far only on the iPhone, and that is not where Ngmoco is going to stay. 'The web is the central platform,' said Clive Downie, marketing vice-president. 'The question is how we make games on other devices that utilise the web as well.'

Source: from Games guru puts his finger on chart success, *Financial Times*, 22/12/2009 (Menn, J.), © The Financial Times Ltd

Questions

1 Identify the technological and other factors helping Ngmoco to achieve its success.

2 Examine the opportunities and threats Ngmoco might face in the future.

Other mobile phone operators are seeking to challenge the success of Apple in the apps market. Orange, Telefonica, AT&T and nine other major companies are seeking to build an open technology platform which they can use to deliver their applications to all mobile phone users, rather than to users of Apple's iPhone and rivals such as Blackberry and Google.

Technological change often blurs industry/sector boundaries. For example, mobile phones, personal computers and e-readers are becoming interchangeable, with most of Apple's 140,000 apps being compatible with the new iPad, Apple's tablet computer.

You try 11.2 gives you the opportunities to review some of the materials on the ecological and technological environments.

You try   11.2

1 Read the text below which reviews a major technological advance in the agricultural production of a feedstock in India.

New technology helps Indian farmers   **FT**

In the semi-arid farmlands east of Mumbai is a small ethanol plant that, in a modest way, represents a global first. Controlled by the local farmers in the Baramati district, the factory, Harneshwar Agro Products Power & Yeast (India), or 'Happy India', uses a large rock-like vegetable known as tropical sugar beet for its feedstock.

Developed more than a decade ago by Swiss-based Syngenta, the world's largest agro-chemicals groups, the crop – which is only now entering commercial production for the first time at this plant – produces as much sugar as conventional sugar cane in half the time with one-third of the water. 'It frees more land for food production without reducing sugar output,' says global head of biofuels development at Syngenta international, Dilip Gokhale.

The initiative is part of a push by global agribusiness groups such as Syngenta and US-based Monsanto to position themselves in the Indian agricultural market, potentially one of the world's largest. Syngenta's Indian unit reported sales of Rs 8.9bn ($214m) in 2006, up about 9% on a year earlier and comprising nearly 20% of its total sales for the Asia-Pacific region of $1.1bn.

You try 11.2 continued

With 65% of India's 1.1bn people living in rural areas, agriculture is one of the country's most important sectors. But it is only growing at a rate of about 2% a year because of chronically outdated methods and an inefficient supply chain. 'Turning agriculture into an organised business – with the farmer as the entrepreneur – should be the key to the second green revolution,' Surabhi Mittal, of the Indian Council for Research on International Economic Relations, wrote in a paper.

Mr Gokhale first saw the potential of sugar beets in 1995 in Europe, where they are grown for only six months of the year. The conventional wisdom was that sugar beets were for temperate climates and sugar cane was for the tropics. When he suggested introducing it to India, he remembers being told 'don't waste your time, this has been tried many times before and it doesn't work.'

Mr Gokhale selected 10 varieties and painstakingly tested them over 10 years in Baramati, elsewhere in India and around the world, eventually developing a strain resistant to very hot and dry conditions.

BS Charaware, a farmer in the Baramati area and the chairman of Happy India, worked with Syngenta to persuade 12,300 local farmers to fund the ethanol project in exchange for shares and a place to process their new beet crops.

Large-scale adoption of the new beets will take time. The crop requires more work – it must be harvested every six months and needs more management for pests and other factors. Still, the beets are slowly catching on with more adventurous farmers. As more of them successfully cultivate the crop, Mr Gokhale hopes others will follow. 'Seeing is believing,' he says.

Source: from Sugar beet sweetens India's output prospects, *Financial Times*, 20/08/2007 (Leahy, J.), © The Financial Times Ltd

Questions:

(a) What are the benefits to Indian farmers of this technological advance?

(b) What are the benefits to Syngenta of this technological advance?

2 Which *three* of the following conditions will help firms to segment the market so that consumers will pay higher prices for overtly 'environmentally friendly' products?

(a) Consumers are indifferent to environmental issues.

(b) The company must have identified a distinctive market segment consisting of consumers who really are willing to pay more for environmentally friendly products.

(c) The branding/corporate image must clearly and credibly convey the environmental benefits related to the products.

(d) The company must be able to protect itself from imitations for long enough to profit from its 'investment' in environmentally friendly products.

(e) Studies suggest a lack of consumer willingness to pay for environmental characteristics of products.

Answers can be found on pp. 525–546.

Recap

- 'Macropolitical' risks affect all firms in a country whereas 'micropolitical' risks are more narrowly focused.

- Political risks can be assessed and prioritised. High impact and high probability risks will be given precedence.

- Firms can seek to improve their bargaining power with governments by seeking to embed themselves in the host country and raise the 'costs' of any unwelcome interference.

- Alternatively, firms can minimise their active engagement with the host country, limiting in advance any 'costs' of interference.

- Legal systems can have important impacts on international businesses. EU Directives, for example, can cause major changes in business practices.

- Environmental 'friendliness' can be a positive strategy for businesses, in their own self-interest.

- Technological change, whether in process or product, creates both opportunities and threats.

Key terms

Bureaucratic law Where those who are involved in its administration have an important influence on its interpretation.

Code law Explicit set of written rules.

Common law Unwritten, based largely on precedent.

Decisions Binding on all members of the EU.

Directives EU objectives are established but the means to achieve them left in the hands of individual nations.

Expected value The probability of each outcome multiplied by the value (impact) of each outcome and summed over all outcomes.

Intellectual property rights (IPRs) Patents, trademarks and copyright protecting knowledge in its various forms.

Macropolitical risk Affects all firms and most or all activities.

Micropolitical risk Only affects specific firms or activities.

Regulations Applied in EU without the need for national measures.

Religious law Based on religious principles.

Statute law Legislation passed by governments.

Sustainability Whereby what is inherited in environmental terms is passed on, intact, to future generations.

Functions of management: domestic business environment

Introduction

In this chapter we review some important management functions, namely the marketing, human resource and management accounting functions of firms operating within the domestic business environment. Chapter 13 extends the discussion of these three key functional areas for management into situations in which multinational firms are operating across international borders.

What you'll learn

By the end of this chapter you should be able to:

- review the principal activities involved in domestic marketing
- examine the key elements in the 'marketing mix', including product, price, promotion and place
- explain why it is so important to manage people efficiently
- assess the HRM function and the effectiveness of various HRM approaches within domestic companies
- understand the benefits and limitations of accounting data for management, including the use of ratio analysis and estimates of break-even output.

Chapter 13 looks in more detail at various *international* aspects of these functional areas of management as well as considering the broader international business environment.

Marketing

Marketing is an integrated activity that takes place throughout the organisation and seeks to align customer needs with the capabilities and goals of the organisation. Market analysis, market planning and management and the so-called 'marketing mix' are important activities for the marketer.

Market analysis

Market analysis can itself be broken down into at least three elements.

1 *Environmental analysis.* This may involve scanning the environment for risks and opportunities, and seeking to identify factors outside the firm's control. Once the environment has been scanned, the organisation must develop a marketing strategy or focus to give a sense of direction for marketing activity. Market segmentation, market research and market planning and management are key elements in devising such a strategy.

2 *Buyer behaviour.* Firms need to have a profile of their existing and potential customer base, and to know how and why their customers purchase. Marketing seeks to identify the buyers, their potential motivation for purchase, their educational levels, income, class, age and many other factors which might influence the decision to purchase.

3 *Market research.* This is the process by which much of the information about the firm's customers and its environment is collected. Without such market research, organisations would have to make guesses about their customers. Such research may involve using data which already exist (secondary data) or using surveys and other methods to collect entirely new data (primary data).

It may be useful to consider each of these elements in turn.

Environmental analysis

PEST, PESTLE, SWOT and other techniques of assessing the external and internal environment in which the firm operates are considered in Chapters 11 and 14 and make an important contribution to environmental analysis.

Buyer behaviour

Major decisions need to be taken as to which *market segments* to target. A market segment is a group of potential customers who have certain characteristics in common, for example being within a certain age range, income range or occupational profile (see Taking it further 12.1). Some of these market segments may be identified as more likely to purchase that product than others. When these segments have been identified, the organisation needs to decide whether one segment or a number of segments are to be targeted. Once that strategic decision is made, then the product can be positioned to meet the particular needs or wants which characterise that segment. The task here is to ensure that the product has a particular set of characteristics which make it competitive with other products in the market.

Taking it further **Market segmentation**   12.1

Producers tend to define markets broadly, but within these markets are groups of people who have more specific requirements. Market segmentation is the process by which a total market is broken down into separate groups of customers having identifiably different product needs, using characteristics such as income, age, ethnicity and so on.

Occupational profile

There are many different methods of segmenting a market. One widely used technique is to classify people according to the occupation of the head of the household as shown in Table 12.1, since market research suggests that consumer buying behaviour changes as individuals move from one such group or 'class' to another. Interestingly, BSkyB reported that the 'old' analogue TV system attracted 46% of ABC_1 users, whereas the 'new' digital TV system was attracting 52% of ABC_1 users. The suggestion here was that digital TV appealed to a more 'up-market' audience because it allowed users to access home shopping and other interactive services as well as the Internet.

Table 12.1 **Occupation of head of household**

Group	Description	% of population
A	Higher managerial and professional	3
B	Middle management	11
C_1	Supervisory and clerical	22
C_2	Skilled manual	32
D	Semi-skilled and manual workers	23
E	Pensioners, unemployed	9

VALS framework

Originally developed by Arnold Mitchell in the USA in the 1960s, this framework has been much refined and is increasingly used by national and international marketers. It focuses on psychological, demographic and lifestyle factors to segment consumer groups. The latest version of VALS segments the English-speaking population aged 18 or older into eight consumer groups.

- *Innovators* – high esteem, take charge, sophisticated, curious. Purchases reflect cultivated tastes for up-market, niche products and services.
- *Thinkers* – motivated by ideas, mature, well educated and reflective. Purchases favour durability, functionality and value.
- *Believers* – strongly traditional and respect authority. Choose familiar products and established brands.
- *Achievers* – goal-oriented lifestyles centred on family and career. Purchase premium products that demonstrates success to their peers.
- *Strivers* – trendy and fun-loving. Purchase stylish products that emulate the purchasers of higher income groups.
- *Experiencers* – unconventional, active and impulsive. Purchase fashionable products and those related to socialising and entertainment.
- *Makers* – practical, responsible and self-sufficient. Purchase basic products, reflecting value rather than luxury.
- *Survivors* – lead narrowly focused lives with few resources, seek safety and security. Purchase low-cost, well-known brands (i.e. exhibit brand loyalty) and seek out available discounted products.

Segmentation has allowed the growth of small specialist or 'niche' markets. As people have become more affluent, they have been prepared to pay the higher price for a product that meets their precise requirements. The growth of niche markets has also been important in supporting the existence of small firms. In many cases the large firm has found many of these segments to be too small to service profitably.

Example

Shampoo and market segmentation

Shampoo was once considered one market, but new product development, branding and packaging have segmented this in many ways. Shampoo products may be seen to be segmented into medicated hair products (Head & Shoulders), two-in-one (Wash & Go), children's shampoos (L'Oreal Kids), 'balanced' shampoos (Organics, Fructis) and environmentally sensitive shampoos (The Body Shop range). Such strategies permit manufacturers such as Unilever and Procter & Gamble to place a premium price on many of their shampoo products. These forms of lifestyle segmentation are now used by many firms in preference to the social class distinctions of the previous four decades.

However, it may be unwise to assume that past methods of market segmentation will be valid in the future.

The 'no brow' consumer

While marketers spend a lot of time trying to understand how consumers' age, income and lifestyle affect their choice of brands, recent research suggests brand owners could have a new challenge on their hands: a type of consumer who does not fit the traditional socioeconomic or demographic criteria. This consumer has been dubbed 'no-brow'.

The 'no-brow' consumer is a term used to describe an attitude towards brands and consumerism that prevails among those traditionally categorised as BC_1 – so-called 'middle Englanders' – who make up the UK population's largest group by disposable income. Recent research findings suggest that BC_1 consumers feel increasingly frustrated with the homogeneous nature of the mass market, and are losing their loyalty to traditional brands. As a result, they are engaged by so-called upmarket or high-brow brands but are just as willing to buy cheaper, low-brow brands. They regularly mix and match a wide variety of high- and low-status brands to satisfy their preoccupations with individualism and self-expression.

One reason for the rise of the 'no brow' is the blurring of the line between traditional definitions of 'mass market' and 'premium'. This has been driven by a number of mass market brands assuming a premium positioning, such as Tesco with the launch of its Tesco Finest range and the so-called 'democratisation' of premium, luxury brands such as Hackett, the British men's wear label, Ralph Lauren and Burberry, which are now seen by ordinary consumers as attainable.

All this leaves the brand owner struggling to define a target market and battling against declining consumer loyalty as consumers buy into a broader, more eclectic mix of high- and low-brow brands. Recent findings suggest, increasingly, the no-brow consumer does not want to buy something that has already been packaged. This extends beyond fashion and into interiors, food and even travel, where a growing number of people fly budget airlines but check into five-star hotels at their destination.

IKEA, Nissan and John Lewis, the department store chain, are among brands that, either deliberately or otherwise, are close to the no-brow mindset, with market research suggesting that no-brow consumers value them for providing flexibility instead of a bespoke product or service; for providing both emotional and rational reasons to buy; and for brand values such as consistency, authenticity and integrity.

Market research

Market research can be divided into two types:

- *desk research* which means using information which has already been gathered for another purpose (secondary data), and
- *field research*, which involves obtaining information specifically directed towards a particular marketing issue and which is usually original (primary data).

Desk research

There are numerous sources of secondary information (desk research) available to the marketer.

- *National publications.* In the UK the Office for National Statistics (ONS) publishes detailed annual (sometimes monthly or quarterly) data on most types of economic and socio-economic indicator. Similar information is available in most advanced industrialised economies.
- *National trade associations and Chambers of Commerce (or equivalents).* These business agencies in the various countries can be invaluable in providing up-to-date market information.
- *Trade journals.* These often provide up-to-the-minute profiles of various aspects of industries, countries or specific market sectors.
- *Financial press.* The various FT indices and ratios (and their equivalents elsewhere) provide an invaluable source of up-to-date information on firms and industrial sectors.
- *Internet.* Finally, of course, there is the Internet, though information found here is only as good as the researcher who is using it. Remember that many of the Web pages are commercially based, and companies will not reveal any secrets that they feel might be useful to their competitors.

The major problems with secondary data are that it is available to competitors, it may be of limited value in terms of comparability between countries, and there may be large gaps in statistical coverage in certain countries. However, it is quick, easy to access, and may save valuable time as compared to field research.

Field research

Primary data may be obtained from a variety of sources. The main advantage of field research is that it is customised to the firm and is unavailable to competitors. However, it is expensive and time-consuming and may present particular problems, such as collecting data in some national cultures which have little experience of using scientifically based research methods. Survey methods that assume a high level of literacy, certain education levels, access to telephones or a willingness to respond by those surveyed may need to be reassessed in some international situations.

- *Research agencies.* In most countries there are many enterprises that are specialists in research. Companies can specify the type of data they are interested in and the agency will carry out the research on their behalf.
- *Company networks/personnel.* Original data may be obtained from company networks (e.g. suppliers who also work for rival firms). Sometimes members of a company are sent to investigate the nature of specified markets through 'shopping trips' which, while not rigorously scientific, can help the organisation 'get a feel' for the types of markets they may enter.

Check the net

The Market Research Association can be found at: www.mra.org.uk

and the Market Research Society at: www.marketresearch.org.uk

Case Study 12.1 reviews some of the benefits from data collection and data analysis in market research.

Case Study 12.1   A better burger thanks to data crunching

HG Wells foresaw a time when what he called 'statistical thinking' would play a key role in the running of society. Those who think of statistics as a way of keeping tabs on Albanian coal output will see this as one of his less inspirational predictions. But for anyone who believes in the power of data to create a better world where evidence reigns supreme, the good news is that the future is already here. Or at least the foundations are, in the form of data mining: the extraction of insight from data gathering during the operation of everything from airlines and bookstores to supermarkets and schools.

This was all but impossible before machine-readable records and computing power to crunch the stuff. But now we have both, and it is starting to transform our lives, as Yale Law School econometrician Ian Ayres suggests in his book *Super Crunchers* (2007). Two statistical techniques lie at the heart of the revolution: regression and randomisation. The use of regression analysis uncovers connections between say, the chances of people defaulting on their mortgage and factors influencing that risk, such as age, income and type of work.

Airlines, supermarkets, car hire companies and even dating agencies all run computerised 'regression analysis' on their raw data to identify the key factors behind everything from sales of dog food to success in love. The effects can be felt by consumers, says Ayres, in subtle changes in the way they are treated. For example, when airlines cancel flights, some no longer woo faithful frequent fliers, but focus instead on the customers that regression analysis reveals are most likely never to fly with the airline again. Similarly, credit card users wanting to close accounts are assessed using regression methods – only those predicted to be profitable get the sweet-talk.

To reveal the influence of a single factor – say, some new education policy – in the presence of lots of extraneous effects, data miners turn to *randomisation*. People are randomly allocated to two groups: those who will and those who won't be exposed to the new policy. Differences between the two groups can then be put down to the effect on the policy change, as all the other factors have been evenly distributed between them. Medical scientists have used the technique for decades to identify life-saving new therapies, via patients recruited into randomised controlled trials (RCTs). Now its power is being seized on by business. Ads, mail-shot campaigns, even book titles, are tested before launch in colossal RCTs involving hundreds of thousands of people. National policy programmes are starting to be based on RCT results. Ayres cites Mexico's Progresa programme, which targets grants and nutritional supplements on families whose kids stay at school.

Ayres balances his infectious enthusiasm with tales of where data mining can and has gone wrong. Correlation is not causation and 'garbage in' still means 'garbage out' – as demonstrated by the salutary story of how honest mistakes led to a spurious correlation between wider gun ownership and lower crime rates – and to several US states changing their law in line with the 'evidence'.

As Ayres points out, some people have a visceral loathing of the suggestion that the quality of a wine, a movie script or a relationship can be reduced to mere numbers. Yet those seeking a better world, or just a better burger, may have to get used to the idea that, to paraphrase Churchill on democracy, data mining is the worst possible basis for big decisions – apart from all the others.

Source: R. Matthews (2007) from A better burger thanks to data crunching, *Financial Times*, 6 September

Question

What does this case study suggest are the benefits of a quantitative approach to market research?

Planning and management

These various marketing activities need to be integrated throughout the organisation, and this can only be done through careful planning and managing of the whole process.

- *Planning* is the process of assessing market opportunities and matching them with the resources and capabilities of the organisation in order to achieve its objectives. However, planning is not just a one-off exercise. It needs to be integrated into the ever-shifting environment of the firm so that new issues are constantly addressed and met. Forecasts made at this stage will have a major effect on production, financial decisions, research and development and human resource planning.

- *Managing* the process can involve many aspects. For example, in order for the planning to be ongoing, the whole process needs to be monitored to ensure that customer needs are being met effectively. This may involve measuring the outcomes of marketing strategies against objectives that may have been set at the strategic stage, for example checking whether specific targets have been met for individual products. Customer surveys may also be used to audit the quality of the services delivered. Whatever the method, it is important that monitoring is built into the plan, so that major or minor adjustments can be made. Managing may also involve *organising* the marketing function, for example allocating different tasks to different individuals or different departments.

> **Check the net**
>
> Information on market issues including objectives, planning and management can be found at:
>
> www.brandrepublic.com
>
> www.keynote.co.uk
>
> www.euromonitor.com
>
> www.bized.co.uk

Marketing mix

Refining the marketing strategy and making it operational invariably involves considering the 4 Ps of the so-called 'marketing mix', i.e. product, price, promotion and place. For example, marketing strategy involving the 4 Ps may involve attempts to use or modify the various stages of the 'product life cycle' (Chapter 4, p. 135), i.e. the so-called introduction, growth, maturity and decline stages. Table 12.2 outlines some possible marketing mix responses to the product life cycle.

We might now consider each of the 4 Ps in rather more detail.

Table 12.2 **Marketing responses to the product life cycle**

	Introduction	Growth	Maturity	Decline
Marketing emphasis	Create product awareness Encourage product trial	Establish high market share	Fight off competition Generate profits	Minimise marketing expenditure
Product strategy	Introduce basic products	Improve features of basic products	Design product version of different segments	Rationalise the product range
Pricing strategy	**Price skimming** or price penetration	Reduce prices enough to expand the market and establish market share	Match or beat the competition	Reduce prices further
Promotional strategy	Advertising and sales promotion to end-users and dealers	Mass media advertising to establish brand image	Emphasise brand strengths to different segments	Minimal level to retain loyal customers
Distribution strategy (place)	Build selective distribution	Increase the number of outlets	Maintain intensive distribution	Rationalise outlets to minimise distribution costs

Product

This is the starting point of the marketing mix, since decisions involving price, promotion and place are usually based on the characteristics of a product which already exists.

Standardised or differentiated product

We have already noted in Chapter 2 the cost benefits from large-scale production of a *standardised product*. These 'economies of scale' can reduce average costs in non-technical areas such as promotion, distribution and administration as well as in the more technical areas of production. They can be significant when the domestic market is the main concern and still more so when we consider the still larger international market in Chapter 13.

Of course, there are also arguments in favour of a more *differentiated product*, as when consumer responses in different market segments vary significantly. For example, high income groups (Groups A, B and C_1 in Table 12.1) may attach greater importance to certain product characteristics than lower income groups (e.g. C_2, D and E) and may be willing to pay a price premium for these characteristics.

Example

Product differentiation in disposable nappies

The disposable nappy is a well-known product, yet producers are constantly seeking ways of updating the design of disposable nappies, with higher prices often associated with the updated and redesigned version of this (mature) product. The point here is that the 'update' helps retain existing customer loyalty, helps attract new customers and may also give some latitude for price variation (increase). Procter & Gamble, the makers of Pampers Baby-Dry and Pampers Premium disposable nappies, have continuously sought to upgrade and differentiate products such as these in order to maintain the 'mature phase' for as long as possible, i.e. to use updating investments as a means of delaying the onset of the 'decline phase'.

Table 12.3 outlines some factors the firm must take into account when making the decision as to product standardisation or product differentiation.

Branding

Links

Chapter 13 (p. 446) extends the list of factors in this table when 'product' is considered within the *international marketing mix*.

Establishing product characteristics which are different from those of the firm's main competitors may be important in helping the firm establish a brand image. Of course, brand image may depend not so much on *actual* product differences but on consumer *perceptions* of product differences, created and reinforced by extensive advertising.

Certainly the potential benefits of brand image may influence the product characteristics sought at the introduction stage of the product life cycle or the modifications considered during the growth or maturity stages of that life cycle. For example, a product may

Table 12.3 **Factors supporting product standardisation or product differentiation**

Factors supporting standardisation	Factors supporting product differentiation
Rapid technological change, reducing product life cycles (places a premium on rapid global penetration)	Slow technological change, lengthening product life cycles
Substantial scale economies	Few scale economies
Strong and favourable brand image	Weak and/or unfavourable brand image
Homogeneous consumer preferences (within a given group, e.g. high income, and/or between groups)	Heterogeneous consumer preferences (within a given group, e.g. high income, and/or between groups)

be modified in order to reposition it and/or extend the reach of the brand at the maturity stage of the product life cycle. Such 'brand extension strategies' often appeal to larger companies who are well aware of the value to sales and profits resulting from past investment in brands.

> **Example**
>
> ### Brand value
>
> Calculations of brand value involve comparing the prices of similar generic (own-brand) products with the higher price of the branded product. Data from *Interbrand* in 2008 ranked the top five global brands and their associated brand values as follows:
>
> | | |
> |---|---|
> | Coca-Cola | $65.3bn |
> | Microsoft | $58.7bn |
> | IBM | $57.1bn |
> | General Electric | $51.6bn |
> | Nokia | $33.7bn |

Successful branding can help increase consumer demand (shift the demand curve to the right) and may also make demand less price elastic (see Chapter 2, p. 40). For example, in 2010 Topshop yet again outperformed its major rivals in clothing and fashion. Some analysts say that the Topshop brand success has been achieved by imitating designer clothes on the 'catwalks' of the world's top fashion shows, but selling those imitations at a much lower price and very quickly after they have been introduced. The emphasis on accessible design by Topshop has also drawn in older shoppers, widening the store's appeal from teens to women in their 40s. Links with young British designers have won over fashion magazines and allowed Topshop to stand out from rivals. Signing Kate Moss and using her to celebrity-brand a clothing range has been hugely successful. The *Los Angeles Times* called the store a 'laboratory for trends' and there's no doubt that Topshop's links with young British design talent has given it a reflected 'glow'. Other early innovations were Style Advisors which borrowed the personal shopping service usually reserved for expensive department stores, and a successful e-commerce site. Through its sponsorship of the London Fashion Week Topshop has also won over influential fashion publications.

Price

In terms of the product life cycle, different pricing strategies are often associated with different stages of the life cycle. For example, in the *introduction* and *growth* stages two pricing approaches are often used.

Penetration pricing

Penetration pricing occurs where the price for a new product may even be set below average cost in order to capture market share. The expectation is that prices can be raised and profit margins restored later on in the growth/maturity stages, helped by the fact that average costs may themselves be falling in those stages via the various economies of scale.

> **Example**
>
> ### Freeview captures market share
>
> 'Freeview', the successor to ITV Digital, was the first to provide 'free' access to 25 channels for the cost of a once-for-all purchase of a £100 set-top decoder, rather than expensive and recurrent subscription charges. Over 500,000 decoders were sold in the first three months of operation in 2003.

'Price-skimming'

Here a high price is set for a new product in the *introduction yearly growth* stages which 'skims off' a small but lucrative part of the market. Producers of fashion products, which have a short life and high innovative value as long as only a few people own them, often adopt a skimming strategy. Companies such as IBM, Polaroid and Bosch have operated such price-skimming systems over time. Bosch used a successful skimming policy, supported by patents, in its launch of fuel injection and antilock braking systems.

> **Example**
>
> ### Price-skimming in soap-capsules
>
> Both Unilever and Procter & Gamble launched liquid soap-capsules in 2001, i.e. capsules of pre-measured doses of liquid detergent which could be placed into washing machines, to save people the bother of working out how much soap to use per wash. As a 'premium priced' product, the capsules were seen by the two companies as offering good price-skimming opportunities.

Other pricing approaches

In the *mature* stage of product life cycles a wide variety of pricing strategies may suggest themselves, depending on firm objectives and market characteristics. Many of these pricing strategies have already been covered in other chapters of this book.

- *Price elasticity of demand* (Chapter 2, p. 40). If demand for the product is relatively inelastic, a price increase will raise revenue. However, if demand for the product is relatively inelastic then a price reduction will raise revenue.
- *Prestige pricing* (Chapter 2, p. 60). Prestige pricing is where higher prices are associated with higher quality ('Veblen effect').
- *Firm objective* (Chapter 4, p. 121). The more interested the firm is in profit rather than revenue or market share objectives, the higher price the firm is likely to set.
- *Competitor pricing* (Chapter 6, p. 194). As, for example, where the firm follows the prices set by the market leader or engages in price warfare under oligopoly market structures.
- *Price discrimination* (Chapter 6, p. 196). Price discrimination occurs where demand for a given product can be broken down into market segments, some being more price sensitive than others, then revenue and profits can be increased by charging a different price in each market segment.

> **Make a note**
>
> ### More pricing terminology
>
> Some other pricing terms and approaches include:
>
> **Loss leader (bait) pricing** where a limited number of products are priced at or below cost to entice customers who may then pay full price on other purchases (e.g. for selected products in supermarkets).
>
> **Clearance pricing** where rock-bottom prices are charged to clear stock and make resources available for alternative uses.
>
> **Parallel pricing** where several firms change prices in the same direction and by broadly the same amount.
>
> **Product line pricing** where the pricing of one item is related to that of complementary items, with a view to maximising the return on the whole product line. For example, the price of a 'core' product might be set at a low level to encourage sales and then the 'accessories' priced at high levels.

Promotion

Promotion is necessary to make consumers aware of what a firm has to offer. The major elements of promotion include advertising, sales promotion, personal selling, public relations and so on.

Advertising

General advertising

This may be used to increase consumer awareness of the product, consolidating the commitment of existing customers and attracting new customers. Where successful, advertising will help *shift* the demand curve for the product outwards, increasing market share. At the same time successful advertising may cause the demand curve to *pivot* and become steeper (i.e. less price elastic). Both outcomes may provide the firm with opportunities to raise revenue and profit.

Stop and think   12.1

If general advertising causes the demand curve for the product to become less elastic (steeper), how might the firm benefit?

Comparative advertising

This appears to be increasingly common in the UK. Recent legislation means it is now legal for a firm to name a competitor in their advertising and compare service/pricing. However, any statement made should be true and not mislead the customer. A recent example of comparative advertising is the campaign conducted by easyJet versus British Airways, whereby easyJet has pointed to many customer advantages of using its services compared to those of BA. This type of advertising has proved popular for potential customers of car insurance, telephone user charges, bank accounts, loans etc. because it has provided transparency and given customers the ability to compare rates, saving customers time and energy searching for the information themselves. However, if a firm continuously compares itself with a competitor, customers may begin to wonder why this is the case.

Sales promotion

This involves short-term product-focused activities, such as encouraging trial purchases with the hope that these result in repeat business. More is now spent in the UK on sales promotion than general advertising. 'Push' and 'pull' tactics are often employed.

- 'Push' tactics focus on the producer offering incentives to key players in each distributional 'channel' to promote their products (e.g. the firm may offer incentives to wholesalers so that they 'push' the firm's products to retailers etc.). Offering higher discounts to those who stock and display your product is a typical 'push' tactic. Providing point-of-sale materials such as display cabinets and refrigerated units may also prove helpful, as might good after-sales support services.

- 'Pull' tactics focus on the final consumer, the idea being to stimulate consumer demands which will then stimulate ('pull') retailers/wholesalers into stocking the firm's products. Advertising may itself be a 'pull' tactic to support sales promotion. Of course, the adverts must be socially and culturally appropriate to the contemporary market.

Example

Goodbye to the man in black

Cadbury was taken over by Kraft in 2010 but had already decided to kill off the 'man in black' campaign which emphasised a 'James Bond' type figure daringly overcoming major obstacles to present a gift of Cadbury Milk Tray chocolates after a 35-year run. Changing social relationships mean that this advert, developed in the 1960s, had proved less effective now that relationships between men and women are more informal and less courtly and now that calorie-lite health and fitness attributes are more closely associated with male to female gift giving.

Personal selling and public relations (PR)

Personal selling is very much based on relationship building and networking. Personal selling is usually divided between soft and hard selling. 'Soft selling' is not based on pressure tactics and is usually conducted over a long period of time. 'Hard selling' is the opposite in that sales people are heavily motivated by commission and may resort to pressure tactics in order to reach sales targets. *Public relations* (PR) is less focused than personal selling, and involves developing an ambiance or context conducive to sales over an extended period of time. PR is also favoured by companies seeking to sell products facing advertising restrictions, as, for example, tobacco-related products.

Example

Personal selling

M&S Direct communicates with its customers on Facebook, where it has more than 100,000 customers logged on its site. It also encourages shoppers to contribute public reviews of products on its own website.

Stop and think   12.2

You might consider some of the implications of the Internet data shown in the note below for promotional activity.

Place

Distributional and logistical issues may be involved here. Producers must select an appropriate distributional channel for their product, such as producer to wholesaler/retailer, direct selling to customers (missing out intermediates), Internet selling and so on. A choice of transport system will often be involved for tangible products both for inputs and outputs.

Make a note

Key internet trends

- Britons are the most active Web users in Europe and spent an average 39 minutes each online every day in 2010, up from 14 minutes in 2002.
- Three-quarters of 11-year-olds have their own TV, games console and mobile phone.
- Two-thirds of children do not believe they could easily live without a mobile phone and the internet.
- Some 22% of UK households have a digital video recorder and 84% use it to fast-forward through advertisements.

- Some 20% of over-65s use the Web. They surf for 44 hours every month, more than any other age group. One-quarter of UK Web users are over 50.
- Two-thirds of phone owners use its alarm function instead of a clock.

Types of distribution channel

'Distributional channel' refers to the route the product takes from producer to the final consumer. Such channels must fulfil a number of functions, including the physical movement of the products and their presentation to the customer.

Factors influencing the choice of distributional channel include the following.

- *Customer characteristics*. Wherever possible, marketers will put the customer at the centre of this choice. What is the number and geographical location of customers, how often do they purchase, where do they expect to find the products (goods or services) in question? For example, if the majority of customers are clustered in a small number of large cities and expect to purchase the product in large retail environments in which rival or complementary products are displayed, then producer to retailer/wholesaler channels are likely to be selected.
- *Product characteristics*. For example, 'perishable' products such as fruit, vegetables and even daily newspapers must select distributional channels which minimise time-to-customer. Products with a high ratio of value to weight/volume (i.e. 'high value density') lend themselves to direct selling. Dangerous or very valuable products will require distributional channels which can guarantee safety and security.
- *Channel characteristics*. The lowest-cost route to customers may influence channel choice, as may the channel already selected by competitors. Increasingly, companies are looking at targeting customers directly. Through bypassing intermediaries, producers gain greater control of channel management and obtain more insight into customer characteristics.

Example

e-commerce distributional channels

Producers may use e-commerce to sell directly (online) to retailers or to customers. The ability to sell direct online has helped to generate hundreds of new companies, such as 'Amazon.com' (books) and 'Lastminute.com' (travel, entertainment). Many of these firms are able to offer highly competitive prices because by selling direct, the channel of distribution is shortened, thereby saving money which can then be passed on to the customer as lower prices. In 2010, £42bn was spent on internet purchases in the UK, a 40% increase on 2005 internet purchases.

Case Study 12.2 provides a useful illustration of the increasing importance of online channels.

Case Study 12.2   **Asos aims to wrest the web crown from Next**   **FT**

Asos, the pioneering online fashion retailer, has a loyal following and big ambitions. The cover of Asos' annual report features a banner with the message: 'Winning the online fashion race'. Asos is the UK's second most popular fashion retail website, having trailed Next, the fashion and homeware group, for the past three years, according to Experian Hitwise. Sitting in the company's art deco

Case Study 12.2 *continued*

headquarters in north London, Mr Robertson, the CEO of Asos, exuded confidence and an air of restless ambition. He has taken the company from its first incarnation, As Seen on Screen, selling discount imitations of celebrity outfits online, to a broader proposition as a pioneering fashion e-tailor, offering 870 brands – including Gap, Chloe and DKNY – to 16–34 year-olds.

Boosted by early popularity with fashion magazines such as More, which named Asos 'most addictive online shopping site' in 2006, the company's success rests on two trends: the vogue for fast fashion, where catwalk looks are swiftly and cheaply recreated for the non-couture shopper, and the growth of e-commerce.

Deloitte estimates online shopping will be worth £25bn in the UK in 2010, compared with less than £9bn in 2005. Asos sales have risen from £250,000 in 2001 to £234m with pre-tax profit of £20m in 2010. The retailer has moved warehouses five times in seven years to cope with its growth. In 2008, it was AIM company of the year, and at the end of 2009, it held net cash of £13.6m.

But when Mr Robertson announced in January that sales had risen 38% in 42 weeks – a figure any rival would envy – Asos's share price fell. Growth in the first half had been even higher, at 47%, and investors whispered that the remarkable ascent appeared to be tapering off.

Asos faces increasingly aggressive competition. High-street clothing retailers, many of whose web offerings were once bland, tricky to use or non-existent, have begun to replicate the online techniques Asos helped pioneer, from catwalk videos to zoom functions, stronger search and user reviews.

'Some of the growth the pure play fashion retailers enjoyed was from relatively low-hanging fruit, because the high-street retailers were quite late to embrace the internet,' Richard Hyman, strategic retail advisor at Deloitte, says. 'As the embryonic market for online fashion develops, progress inevitably becomes more difficult.' Mr Robertson believes constant innovation is vital. Asos is leading the charge in using social networking to fuel sales, while Asos Premier, a delivery loyalty scheme similar to Amazon's prime service, could help protect market share. Customers pay an annual fee of £24.95 to gain unlimited next day delivery, encouraging them to increase the frequency of orders while giving them a loyalty incentive.

Source: from Asos founder turns to online homeware, *Financial Times*, 28/06/2010 (Kuchler, H), © The Financial Times Ltd.

Questions

1 What marketing principles have been exploited by Asos to help it achieve success?

2 What challenges does Asos face if it is to maintain that success?

You try 12.1 gives you the opportunity to self-check some of your work on marketing.

Links

For more on the international marketing mix, see Chapter 13, pp. 441–8.

You try   12.1

1 Choose a popular food product and examine the *marketing mix* used in recent years for that product.

2 Select a major household product (e.g. TV, washing machine, refrigerator etc.). Use all the *secondary* sources of information available to you to find out more about that product. List the sources involved.

3 Decide upon a well-known branded product. Suggest how you might go about estimating the *brand value* associated with that product.

4 For the product used in Question 3, examine the channels of distribution used in reaching the market. Can you explain why those channels are used and any other options that might exist?

Answers can be found on pp. 525–546.

Human resource management

Human resource management (HRM) involves a wide range of activities that deal with the human side of an organisation. Until the early 1980s the title more commonly associated with these activities was 'personnel management', then taken to refer mainly to practical aspects such as recruitment, staff appraisal, training and job evaluation. What perhaps distinguishes HRM from personnel management is the more *strategic* emphasis now given to this role.

> **Quote**
>
> *HRM can be regarded as ... a strategic and coherent approach to the management of an organisation's most valued assets – the people working there who individually and collectively contribute to the achievement of its goals.*
>
> (Armstrong, 2009)

HRM is widely seen as having a strategic dimension and involving the total deployment of all the human resources available to the firm, including the integration of personnel and other HRM considerations into the firm's overall corporate planning and strategy formulation procedures. It is seen as proactive, seeking to continuously discover new ways of utilising the labour force in a more productive manner with the intention of giving the business a competitive edge.

Harvard model

In an attempt to investigate HRM issues at the strategic level, a model of human resource management was developed by Beer *et al.* (1984) at Harvard University. According to this Harvard model, HRM strategies should develop from an in-depth analysis of:

(a) the demands of the various stakeholders in a business (e.g. shareholders, the employees, the government etc.) and

(b) a number of situational factors (e.g. the state of the labour market, the skills and motivation of the workforce, management styles etc.)

According to the Harvard researchers, both stakeholder expectations and situational factors need to be considered when formulating human resource strategies and the effectiveness of the outcomes should be evaluated under four headings:

1 Commitment (i.e. employees' loyalty).

2 Competence (i.e. employees' skills).

3 Congruence (i.e. shared vision of workers and management).

4 Cost efficiencies (i.e. operational efficiency).

The Harvard model suggests that human resource policies should be directed towards raising attainment levels for each of these four categories; for example, competence could be increased through the provision of extra training, adjustments to recruitment policy, different incentivisation schemes and so on.

Hendry and Pettigrew (1990) offer an adaptation of the Harvard model (Figure 12.1) that attempts to integrate HRM issues with a still broader range of external societal influences (such as socio-economic, technical, political, legal and competitive issues) which may vary considerably in different countries. These 'outer context' issues will influence HRM strategies and practices, as will a variety of 'inner context' and business strategic issues.

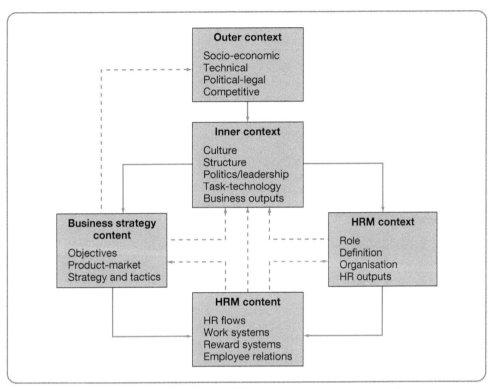

Figure 12.1 **Model of strategic change and human resource management**

Case Study 12.3 reviews the strategic nature of the HRM function using the Royal Bank of Scotland as a context for the discussion.

Case Study 12.3   HRM and Royal Bank of Scotland

RBS has been much in the news in recent times, especially as regards the adverse effects of the 'credit crunch' on its business activities! These included a large 'bail out' by the UK government to such an extent that 84% of RBS is now government owned. Here we evaluate the impact of both external and internal factors on HRM policies in RBS, both in shorter- and longer-term time periods.

A thorough understanding of the components of the external environment and their dynamic nature is crucial if an organisation such as Royal Bank of Scotland (RBS) is to achieve long-term success, as has been well illustrated by the seismic impacts of the 'credit crunch' on RBS and other financial institutions. Before that overwhelming event the emphasis in RBS had been on devising HRM strategies to respond to the prevailing belief that the most important characteristic of today's business environment – and therefore the yardstick against which management techniques must be measured – is increasing competition within both the domestic and international financial market. Increasing levels of competition within the financial services industry compel organisations in this sector to strive to improve productivity, with a key way of achieving this improvement being to manage human resources more effectively. The HRM department of RBS sought to achieve this by empowering employees (i.e. allowing workers to have more influence over job-related decisions thereby increasing staff involvement), encouraging teamwork (in order to improve quality and efficiency) and introducing clear and consistently applied communication and assessment mechanisms (to enhance staff performance and increase awareness).

By introducing these initiatives into the workforce RBS has been seeking to encourage employee involvement, thereby maximising the contribution made by employees. The direct effect of involvement in the organisation is expected to be an increase in the individual employee's commitment to the workplace or the job (one of the four important categories under the Harvard model), reflected in increased productivity, lower labour turnover and reduced absenteeism. Of course, RBS recognised that this empowerment of employees may also call for new skills on the part of both the managers and employees and it will be the role of the HRM function to try to successfully implement these changes, with the HRM department involved in designing policies and procedures to encourage employee involvement in line with the overall strategic plan of RBS. For example, managers may need training in the techniques of participative management if they have been used to a control management style, and employees may require confidence-building sessions and training in decision making. This departure from a control culture which focuses upon close supervision can also have an impact on organisational structures; for example, the tall hierarchies with numerous reporting levels traditionally associated with companies like RBS, may need to be replaced by the more modern, flatter structures which better facilitate empowerment. However, the huge fines imposed in 2010 on RBS (see Case Study 8.6, p. 251) for key employees illegally sharing sensitive price data with external clients, is likely to restrict any attempts to move too far away from the earlier control culture.

A further component of the external environment that RBS needs to consider involves the workforce and the changes that are occurring within it. For example, the British labour force has increased by 1.8m people between 1995 and 2010 (i.e. from 27.8 to 29.6m), with an estimated 1.4m of this increase being women so that by 2010 women represented 46% of the entire British labour force. These statistics arguably highlight the importance to the HRM department of RBS of effectively utilising programmes for managing diversity among its workforce, whereby women and other minority employees receive support, recognition and the same opportunities as non-minority workers. The increasing proportion of women in the workforce may be attributed in part to socio-economic influences such as the social acceptability of women in employment and the growing availability of part-time work. These factors may oblige RBS to adopt more open approaches to recruitment and to consider the necessity of providing more extensive training. It will be the role of the HRM department to proactively implement strategies to successfully manage diversity among the workforce. This may involve addressing stereotypes to ensure that a job does not become 'sex-typed' (i.e. deemed appropriate only for one gender) and developing gender-neutral job titles to encourage both male and female applicants. The HRM department might, for example, suggest that RBS becomes involved in government-supported national projects, specifically aimed at increasing the proportion of women in management.

The HRM department of RBS must also undertake a thorough analysis of the internal environment in order for the organisation to retain its competitive edge. These internal influences may include: the company's strategy, objectives and values; the leadership styles and goals of top management; the organisational structure, size and culture; and the nature of the business.

An organisation's vision or mission statement is a brief explanation of its fundamental purpose and objectives and what it is striving to achieve. For example, the mission statement of RBS includes: 'to provide financial services of the highest quality'. Organisations then develop objectives and strategies in an attempt to provide more focus and guidance for employees in seeking to achieve the company's mission. The role of the HRM department here will be to support the process of sharing an understanding about what needs to be achieved, and then managing and developing people in a way which will facilitate the achievement of these objectives. For example, in common with other companies in the financial services sector, RBS has been seeking to change from a culture that rewards performance using a 'slow' incremental pay system, into one that more closely relates pay to personal performance and achievement. The HRM department has therefore been involved in introducing new performance appraisal systems and incentive

Case Study 12.3 *continued*

schemes in an attempt to help the company achieve its long-term strategic objectives. By introducing more beneficial bonus and profit sharing schemes, whereby pay is more closely related to individual and corporate performance, employees will arguably become more motivated to contribute to the achievement of the overall goals of the RBS.

However, the reward policies of RBS are also being influenced by internal and external criticism of excessive bonus payments to bankers and others seen as leading to the excessive risk taking and bank failures. As we have already noted in Case Study 4.2 (p. 117), the HRM department of RBS has devised new reward mechanisms which explicitly link pay to more challenging profit targets.

A further internal factor that will influence the HRM function is the merger of RBS with the Dutch bank ABN Amro in 2007, with RBS heading a consortium including Santander, the Spanish Bank. While such mergers may be of potential benefit to many employees by creating new opportunities and offering enhanced career prospects in the new, larger business, they also place greater emphasis on the HRM function of the company, perhaps involving an expansion of the existing department and its operations into cross-cultural and international aspects of HRM operations (see Chapter 13, p. 435). It will certainly be necessary to review the current HRM practices of the new and enlarged business and perhaps revise these in order to bring them into line with the objectives of RBS. As well as increasing the activity of the HRM department in areas such as recruitment, selection, training and development, this expansion will inevitably also require the clear communication of RBS's culture, values and strategy across a wider and more disparate cohort of employees. It is essential that the HRM functions of both businesses be closely integrated so that there is a well-defined, common goal for the new, expanded business.

Of course, internal HRM goals and strategies must be constantly reviewed when external realities change. The emphasis in 2010 for RBS is in managing 'downsizing', as for example with the European Commission forcing RBS to sell 318 branches to stimulate competition in 2010, given the perceived monopoly 'dangers' from the UK government holding an 87% stake in RBS. Another emphasis involves changing HRM strategies in response to a realisation that arguably reward structures have moved too far in incentivising a short-term outlook by RBS managers as opposed to the longer-term outlook required for a sustainable business in the financial services sector.

Questions

1 Can you identify HRM policies for RBS which might support the four outcomes identified in the Harvard model, namely commitment, competence, congruence and cost efficiencies?

2 Examine the ways in which the 'credit crunch' might impact specific HRM policies within RBS.

HRM and line management

A *line manager* is the person with direct responsibility for employees and their work. Although the job specification of line managers is likely to focus on task completion of employees within designated functional areas (marketing, administration etc.) they will invariably acquire responsibilities for the personal development of employees, not least when involved in staff appraisal. Line managers seem increasingly to be involved in training and recruitment issues within the modern organisation.

In practice, only those at the highest levels of responsibility for the HRM function within an organisation will be involved in board-level meetings where strategic options are discussed. Nevertheless, those involved in the HRM function at *all* levels are expected to subscribe to the view that competitive advantages for an organisation can best be developed by maximising the potential of its employees.

HRM responsibilities

Despite the concern to avoid excessively task-specific responsibilities, HRM specialists are invariably deployed on certain functional activities within organisations, including the following:

- recruitment and selection
- training and development
- human resource planning
- provision of contracts
- provision of fair treatment
- provision of equal opportunities
- assessing performance of employees
- employee counselling and welfare

- payment and reward of employees
- health and safety
- disciplining individuals
- dealing with grievances
- dismissal
- redundancy
- negotiation
- encouraging involvement.

In undertaking these tasks the HRM specialist will, in effect, be seeking to put into practice well-established principles involving managing people effectively. *Taking it further* 12.2 outlines some of these principles in the particular context of motivation.

Taking it further Motivation theory and HRM   12.2

The human relations approach to management relied heavily on the work of Elton Mayo, who undertook work on the link between productivity and working conditions. He found that productivity rose even when working conditions deteriorated. Mayo conducted a whole series of experiments at the Hawthorne Plant of General Electric between 1927 and 1932. His conclusions were as follows.

- *Work pacing*. The pace at which people produce is one set informally by the work group.
- *Recognition*. Acknowledgement of an employee's contribution by those in authority tends to increase output, as do other forms of social approval.
- *Social interaction*. The opportunities provided by the working situation for social interaction between fellow workers, especially if they could select for interaction those with whom they were compatible, enhanced job satisfaction and sometimes influenced output.
- *The Hawthorne effect*. Regardless of what changes were made to the way the employees were treated, productivity went up as they seemed to enjoy the novelty of the situation and the extra attention – the so-called 'Hawthorne effect'.
- *Grievances*. Employees responded well to having someone to whom to let off steam by talking through problems they were having.
- *Conforming*. The pressure from workmates in the group was far more influential on behaviour than any incentive from management.

The importance of this work was to show the effect of work groups and social context on behaviour. It also helped to generate new ideas about the nature of supervision to include better communication and better management of people. It was perhaps most important in recognising the critical nature of informal processes at work as well as the rational, scientific procedures that management prescribes, the latter being the conclusions from earlier work by F. W. Taylor.

Maslow and 'hierarchy of needs'

Maslow argued that workers have a **'hierarchy of needs'** (Figure 12.2). The first three needs, physiological, safety and social needs, are identified as *lower-order* needs and are satisfied from the *context* within

Taking it further 12.2 *continued*

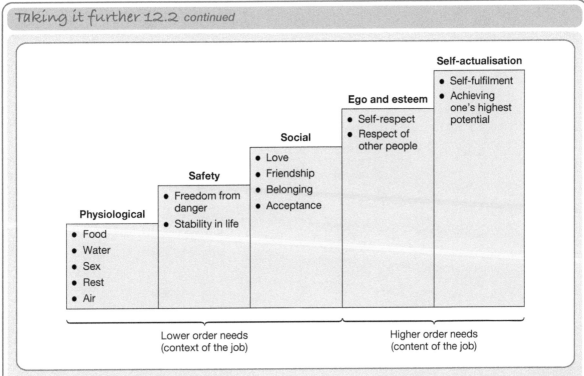

Figure 12.2 Maslow's 'hierarchy of needs'

Source: Maslow *et al.* (1987)

which the job is undertaken. Self-esteem and self-actualisation are identified as *higher-order needs* and are met through the *content* of the job.

Maslow went further. He argued that at any one time one need is dominant and acts as a motivator. However, once that need is satisfied it will no longer motivate, but be replaced by the next higher-level need.

The implications of this theory for managers including their having to try to satisfy their workers' needs both in terms of the organisational context in which work takes place and what the worker is required to do. Some examples of how this might be achieved include:

- *physiological* – pay, rest periods, holidays;
- *safety* – health and safety measures, employment security, pensions;
- *social* – formal and informal groups, social events, sports clubs;
- *self-esteem* – power, titles, status symbols, promotion.

Herzberg and the 'two factor theory'

Herzberg's 'two factor theory' was based on a survey of what made managers feel good or bad about their job. He discovered that the factors which created dissatisfaction about the job related to the context within which the job was done. He termed these factors 'hygiene factors', as indicated in Figure 12.3.

However, ensuring that these factors were met while helping avoid dissatisfaction did not result in positive satisfaction.

The factors contributing to positive job satisfaction related more to the content of the job. The presence of each of these factors (motivators) was capable of causing high levels of satisfaction.

The implications for the practising human resource manager were twofold. First, to ensure that the hygiene factors are met adequately to avoid dissatisfaction, but not to expect these to motivate employees. Second, to ensure that the motivators are met to create positive job satisfaction.

Taking it further 12.2 *continued*

Hygiene factors (avoid dissatisfaction)

    Company policy
    Supervision
    Working conditions
    Salary
    Relationship with peers
    Personal life
    Relationship with subordinates
    Status
    Security

Motivators (create satisfaction)

    Achievement
    Recognition
    Work itself
    Responsibility
    Advancement
    Growth

Figure 12.3 Herzberg's theory of motivation

Stop and think   12.3

Can you suggest any other ways in which motivational theory might be of practical use to the HRM specialist?

Links

For more on HRM in an international context see Chapter 13, pp. 434–6.

Case Study 12.4 reviews new and emerging HRM approaches to support flexible working in a range of domestic (UK) companies.

| Case Study 12.4 | HRM and flexible working | |

KPMG is examining new approaches, after the success of its 'Flexible Futures' programme in signing up employees for sabbaticals or reduced weeks. Roughly 85% of the 10,000 UK staff and 95% of partners, volunteered at the start of last year. Approximately 800 people moved temporarily to four-day weeks, with the heaviest use of the programme in May and June 2009. The firm saved £4m in 2009, or the equivalent of 100 full-time jobs, says Michelle Quest, UK head of people. When the programme was relaunched for 2010 71% volunteered. 'One of the softer benefits is moving the whole idea of flexible working up the agenda for everybody,' says Ms Quest. The firm is now considering more active promotion of job

sharing, because this type of arrangement provides all-week cover for clients.

The business benefits of alternative working patterns are increasingly well documented by both large and small employers. A survey of small firms by the British Chambers of Commerce found most of those that had introduced flexible working reported a positive effect on employee relations, retention and productivity. Benefits also include extended customer service cover, more efficient use of office space, reduced absenteeism and access to new employees who need such flexibility to work.

Many employers still see flexible working as an employee benefit – and therefore a cost – rather than a tool to improve the business. They remain nervous about allowing staff greater flexibility, and managers fear losing control of employees if they work from home or on the move. Yet nearly 60% of people who work from home at least some of the time say they are definitely more productive than in their workplace, and more than 20% say they are probably more productive, according to a recent online survey. The main reasons are being able to work uninterrupted, saving time on commuting and being able to fit work around other commitments. Twelve per cent say their output at home is at least 50% higher. 'In a time of unsteady recovery from recession, employers from all sectors must look for continued improvements in efficiency,' says Peter Thomson, director of research at the Telework Association, which conducted the survey. 'Ultimately, the organisations that do not adopt new ways of working, including home working, will lose not just good people, but also high performers. Those that do allow people to work at home will reap the benefits of substantial increases in output.'

UK government policy has focused on extending parents' and carers' right to request flexible working. However, some large and small employers offer flexibility to all their employees, arguing this is more productive and less divisive.

At Centrica, owner of British Gas, roughly 60% of employees work a variety of non-standard arrangements, most of them informal. Research by Cranfield School of Management found that Centrica employees working flexibly scored significantly higher than non-flexible workers on job satisfaction and fulfilment, commitment to the company and empowerment.

At the other end of the scale in terms of size is Clock, a digital agency in Hertfordshire employing about 30 people, mostly men. Syd Nadim, chief executive, offers flexibility to attract and keep skilled web designers and developers. Managers set staff objectives and give them leeway to meet these as they think best. Flexible start and finish times mean the agency's office is staffed from 8am to 9pm, while employees are also available to clients on their mobile phones. 'We're successful and we're making money while creating an environment for people to enjoy their lives,' says Mr Nadim.

Source: from A different way of working, *Financial Times*, 23/03/2010 (Maitland, A.), © The Financial Times Ltd

Questions

1 Why are HRM policies becoming more supportive of flexible working?

2 To what extent are the motivational theories of HRM (*Taking it further* 12.2) relevant to this Case Study?

You try 12.2 provides some self-check questions on the HRM function.

You try   12.2

1 Examine three advertisements for jobs in personal management/human resource management. Make a list of the range of activities described in those job advertisements. Are there any differences in approach and duties shown by those advertising for human resource managers and those advertising for personnel managers?

2 Try out the websites given below and find out more about issues of concern to those involved in human resource management in the UK.

www.berr.gov.uk: The Department for Business, Enterprise and Regulatory Reform (many useful publications, discussion documents and booklets can be found on this site).

www.direct.gov.uk: The government (useful information site, especially for the text of legislation).

www.tuc.org.uk: The Trades Union Congress (this gives the TUC's views on many current HRM issues and new legislation in Britain).

You try 12.2 *continued*

www.cipd.co.uk: The Chartered Institute of Personnel and Development (the website for the professional body that represents personnel and development professionals in the UK).

www.incomesdata.co.uk: Incomes Data Services Limited (some very useful articles on a range of HRM topics, including a section on management pay and remuneration, plus lists of context for IDS publications).

www.peoplemanagement.co.uk: *People Management* (journal produced on behalf of the CIPD with topical articles relating to personnel management issues).

3 David works for a medium-sized company in the human resources department. His view is that:

'The human resource is the chief asset of the company. It is also the major cost, taking up over 70% of the business's costs in any one time period. It is therefore essential to gain the maximum possible return from this expenditure. People need to be motivated if they are to be made best use of. Anything which adds to the productivity of individual employees should be seen as an essential ingredient of human resource policy.'

Sarah also works for a medium-sized company in the human resources department. She agrees with John that the human resource is the key resource. She says:

'Human resources should be seen as an asset by the organisation. The organisation needs to look at how it can best meet the needs of this asset in order to help people to develop themselves to the full. By involving people in decision making, it is possible to enable them to help the organisation to develop while meeting their own development needs.'

Questions

(a) Are David and Sarah saying the same thing or can you see a difference in their approach?

(b) How might the views of these two individuals influence the sorts of activities they would undertake in human resource management?

(c) Can you give any specific examples of actions that David might take which would be different to the actions that Sarah would take?

Answers can be found on pp. 525–546.

Accounting and management

Accounting has been defined as: the process of identifying, measuring and communicating economic information about an organisation or other entity, in order to permit informed judgements by users of the information. It can be divided into two types, financial accounting and management accounting.

- **Financial accounting.** This is concerned with the production of the principal accounting statements that provide stakeholders in the business (management, employees, shareholders, creditors, consumers and government) with an accurate view of the firm's financial position. It uses *historic data* and is predominantly backward looking in that it summarises what has happened in the previous accounting period. The principal output would include profit and loss accounts, balance sheets and cash flow statements.

- **Management accounting.** This generates information for internal use to aid the analysis, planning and control of the firm's activities. Management accountants are principally *forward looking*, acting as 'information providers' to senior management. This information might be in the form of financial forecasts, budgets, contribution statements and break-even charts.

Together the two types of accounting provide insights for stakeholders into the success or failure of *past* decisions and operations and help management be better aware of the *future* opportunities and difficulties likely to be encountered.

Make a note

All businesses have a legal obligation to produce a set of accounts even if it is only for tax purposes. Private limited companies and PLCs must file a set of accounts each year with the Registrar of Companies, which is then available for public scrutiny. See Black, G. (2007) for more detail on the content of this section.

Accounting concepts and conventions

Concepts

There are four fundamental concepts that underlie the production of a set of accounts.

- *Going concern* – assumes the business will continue to trade 'for the foreseeable future'.
- *Accruals or matching principle* – relates revenues and costs to the period in which they occur.
- *Prudence or conservatism* – avoids an over-optimistic view of the performance of the business; the accountant recognises revenue only when it is realised in an acceptable form but provides for all expenses and losses as soon as they are known.
- *Consistency* – maintains the same approach to asset valuation and the allocation of costs so that comparisons can be made over time.

Conventions

Many accounting conventions have been adopted over time as tried and tested general rules. Here are five key accounting conventions.

- *Objectivity* – accounts are based on measurable facts that can be verified.
- *Separate entity* – the company is recognised as a legal person in its own right, entirely separate from its managers and owners.
- *Money measurement* – all assets and liabilities are expressed in money terms.
- *Historic cost* – all valuations are based on the original cost rather than current worth. Where items fall in value through use, they are depreciated or written down in value. This gives the company an objective valuation of its assets.
- *Double entry* – all transactions involve two sides: giving and receiving. This is acknowledged in the double-entry system of bookkeeping where the source of funds is balanced by the use made of them.

Legal requirements

The *Companies Acts of 1985 and 1989* contain regulations which limited companies must follow in the preparation of their published financial information statements. The main points are:

- Public limited companies and some larger private limited companies must have their accounts independently audited and confirmed by the auditors that they represent a 'true and fair view'.

● A set of accounts must be sent to shareholders and also made available for public scrutiny at Companies House.

The concepts, conventions and legal requirements which shape the presentation of the accounts have become a matter of intense debate following recent corporate 'scandals'. The attempts to harmonise accounting standards between countries has also become a key issue for businesses.

Accounting standards

The International Accounting Standards Board is seeking a global convergence on an agreed standard for accounting for pensions – and is modelling its proposals largely on rules recently introduced in the UK. Sir David Tweedie, IASB chairman, wrote FRS 17, as the UK rule is known, when he was head of the UK Accounting Standards Board and some companies have blamed it for forcing the closure of their relatively generous defined benefit pension schemes. Like the IASB's standard on financial instruments, the new rule on pensions puts a heavy emphasis on 'fair value' accounting. Under FRS 17, the measurement of the assets in a defined benefit pension scheme should reflect their fair or market value. FRS 17 also tells accountants how to arrive at the present value for future liabilities; it adds them up and discounts back at an interest rate equal to that on AA-rated corporate bonds. Credit ratings agencies are responding to FRS 17 by downgrading the debt of companies such as BAE Systems, the defence group, where they have concerns about pension deficits. Many UK employers, however, argue that FRS 17 is misleading: although a pension shortfall is presented as a liability, it is not one about to come due in full any time soon.

Make a note

More than 110 countries, including most of Europe and Asia, use the International Financial Reporting Standards drawn up by the IASB. US companies continue to report under Generally Accepted Accounting Principles while its regulators consider whether to endorse IFRS.

The *annual report* of a public limited company (PLC) will include the following components:

● *Chairman's statement* – a general review of the past period of trading, comments on market conditions and an assessment of future prospects.

● *The Directors' Report* – a more detailed report on the company's activities and policies.

● *A profit and loss account, balance sheet* and *cash flow statement.*

● *Notes to the accounts* – further explanation of the figures in the main financial statements.

● *Auditor's report* – an inspection of the accounts on behalf of the shareholders to ensure truth and fairness.

Stop and think   12.4

Can you suggest who might benefit from the annual report?

Case Study 12.5 suggests, however, that current accounting rules are far from adequate to cover misinformation to stakeholders with damaging results.

Case Study 12.5   Fooled again

In the wake of revelations on how Lehman flattered its balance sheet, questions are arising about how such techniques became possible and what can be done to curb them. On 18 March 2008, Erin Callan, Lehman Brothers' chief financial officer, told a conference call that the bank was 'trying to give the group a great amount of transparency on the balance sheet' by providing more details. Analysts on the line even thanked her for it. But what Ms Callan did not tell them is that Lehman had shifted $49bn (€36bn, £32bn) off its balance sheet in the quarter just ended, using a process it nicknamed Repo 105. That was expressly to help bring down the bank's reported leverage – or the ratio of assets to equity – the very reduction of which she was promoting to the analysts.

That and other similar deals came to light in March 2010 in a 2,200 page report by Anton Valukas, the bankruptcy court-appointed examiner. With little or no economic rationale they are simply a form of the age-old accounting wheeze of window-dressing the books to look better temporarily. What has grabbed attention two years on is the matter-of-fact way the arrangements were discussed inside the bank by senior executives and were accepted by its counterparties – other financial groups with which Lehman did business before its collapse that September.

Yet even inside Lehman, not everyone saw the mechanism in so benign a way. Bart McDade, who became chief operating officer in June 2008, called Repo 105 'another drug we [are] on' in an e-mail, and planned to slash its use, amid howls of protest from some departments. Martin Kelly, global financial controller, warned his bosses about the 'headline risk' to Lehman's reputation if the deals were to become public.

The process even cost the bank money. As one e-mail from another staffer put it: 'everyone knows 105 is an off-balance sheet mechanism so counterparties are looking for ridiculous levels [of prices] to take them.' But the pressure to do more of the deals grew in 2008, as did the outside world's obsession with the bank's precarious finances, particularly its leverage. Internal e-mails exhorted managers to work harder to get assets off the books.

Among the questions the Valukas report raises about the appropriateness of the accounting – and the auditing conducted by Ernst & Young – lies a bigger issue: how did this sort of financial engineering come to be considered a legitimate business tool and what, if anything, can be done about it?

Window-dressing the accounts is not new and can take many forms. In manufacturing companies, for example, a manager might engage in 'channel stuffing' – shifting products just before quarter-end, even if they have not been expressly ordered – to help meet targets and boost reported revenues.

Sean FitzPatrick resigned in 2010 as chairman of Dublin-based Anglo Irish Bank following the revelation that he had for years concealed personal loans worth up to €87m ($119m, £77m). He did so by transferring them to another bank just before his bank's year-end, then returning them after the balance sheet date.

Two years before Mr Fitzpatrick's departure, the US Securities and Exchange Commission forced a group of Puerto Rican banks to restate their accounts following its investigation into several misdemeanours, including managing earnings through a series of simultaneous purchase and sale transactions with other banks.

The practice is hardly recent: in 1973, the UK's London and County Securities collapsed after a government-initiated credit squeeze helped fulfil widespread market suspicions about its rocky finances. On unpicking L&Cs accounts, the liquidators found, among many sharp practices, a window-dressing system involving a ring of banks that deposited funds with each other just before year-end to boost their reported liquidity.

How Repo worked

Banks use repurchase agreements, known as repos, all the time for short-term financing. One borrows cash and gives the other securities, such as government bonds, as collateral. Both agree to unwind the arrangement on a set date. The deals, which usually run only for days or weeks, are accounted for as financings, and remain on the books with banks recording an asset – the cash – and a matching liability in the promise to buy back the collateral.

Lehman's 105 was different – instead of handing over securities equivalent to the cash it received, the bank gave more than was necessary.

The point was to exploit a loophole allowing such over-collateralised deals to be accounted for as true sales. Lehman then reported its obligation to repurchase the securities at a fraction of the full cost, and used the cash it had received to pay off its liability, thereby 'shrinking' its balance sheet.

Use of Repo 105 peaked sharply at the end of each accounting quarter – more so in 2008 as pressure grew on Lehman to reduce its leverage – and fell just as dramatically soon after the new accounting period began, as deals were unwound.

Source: from Fooled again, *Financial Times*, 19/03/2010 (Hughes, J.), © The Financial Times Ltd

Questions

1 What do you understand by 'off balance sheet' accounting?

2 How did such practices contribute to the collapse of Lehman Brothers?

Here we consider the various accounts included within the annual report.

Profit and loss (P&L) account

The P&L account summarises the income and expenditure of a specified period, showing whether the organisation has made a profit or loss. Careful examination can reveal how effectively the business is coping with the market and any changes in it. Examining the P&L over several years will help identify the trend for sales, costs and profitability.

The P&L account is in three parts.

1 The trading account

The trading account shows whether or not the firm is making a gross profit from its core activities. It includes the revenue from sales (also referred to as turnover) minus the direct cost of production (the cost of goods sold). In order to conform to the 'matching principle' only the cost of those goods actually sold must be included. To achieve this the following formula is used:

Opening stock

+ Purchases

− Closing stock

= Cost of goods sold

This takes account of the stock brought forward from the previous year and available for sale, and the stock left unsold at the end of the year.

The format for the trading account is:

	£m
Sales turnover	180
Less cost of goods sold	90
Gross profit	90

If cost of goods sold exceeds turnover a 'gross loss' is made.

2 The profit and loss account

The second of these three parts has the name of the whole account. It shows whether the firm makes an operating profit, when all other expenses are deducted from the gross profit, such as administration, selling costs and depreciation. This is a useful indicator of the trading performance of the business. To this figure must be added any non-operating revenue, which then gives us the *profit before interest and tax (PBIT)*. Interest payable is then deducted to give the *profit liable to tax*. Interest is dealt with as a separate item, as it reflects how the company is financed rather than how it carries on its core business.

The format for the profit and loss account is:

	£m
Gross profit	60
Less expenses	25
Operating profit	35
Add non-operating income	10
Profit before interest and tax (PBIT)	45
Less interest	4
Profit before tax	41

3 The appropriation account

The appropriation account explains how the profit after tax is used. The after-tax profit could be used to pay dividends to shareholders or to keep as retained or undistributed profits (reserves) for future use in the business. Shareholders generally expect dividends to rise in line with any improvement in the performance of the business. Management, however, may want to retain profit to help expand the business.

The format for the appropriation account is:

	£m
Profit before tax	60
Tax	22
Profit after tax	38
Dividends	14
Retained profit	24

Balance sheet

The balance sheet is a financial snapshot of the business on a particular date. It illustrates an organisation's resources in terms of what it owns (*assets*) and what it owes (*liabilities*). The balance sheet is important because it illustrates the financial health of the business. It shows whether the business can meet its short- and long-term debts and by allowing comparisons to be made with earlier balance sheets, it also reveals any changes taking place in the business.

The double entry system

Double entry bookkeeping is a system of accounting that recognises that all transactions have a dual nature, a giving and a receiving. Each event is recorded in two accounts as a *debit* in one and a *credit* in another. For example, £2,000 spent on materials will reduce cash by £2,000 but increase stock by £2,000, leaving the balance sheet in balance.

Assets and liabilities

Assets are the items that the business 'owns'. They can be classified according to how long the business expects to use them.

- *Fixed assets*: assets that are to be used for more than a year, for example machinery, vehicles and buildings.
- *Current assets*: short-term assets whose value changes frequently during the year, for example stock, debtors and cash.

Liabilities are the amounts that the business owes and can be classified as follows.

- *Current liabilities*: those debts that have to be paid within 12 months and may consist typically of creditors, overdrafts, declared dividends and tax due.
- *Long-term liabilities*: money owed by the firm that has more than a year to maturity, such as bank loans and debentures.
- *Shareholders funds*: money or resources invested by the shareholders for long-term use by the business, such as share capital and retained profit.

Use of funds

The *top half* of a vertical balance sheet displays the assets that a business owns less its current liabilities at the bottom. It is normally set out in a two-column format, so that individual items can be shown on the left, leaving the main totals to be seen clearly on the right (values in brackets are to be deducted).

Balance sheet as at 31/12/2010

	£m	£m
Fixed assets		
Land 1 buildings	50	
Machinery 1 vehicles	4	54
Current assets		
Stock	26	
Debtors	6	
Cash	4	
	36	
Less: Current liabilities	(26)	
Net current assets (working capital)		10
Assets employed		64

Source of funds

For a limited company, assets employed are matched by share capital, reserves and possibly long-term loans.

Financed by:	£m	£m
Shareholders' funds		
Ordinary share capital	18	
Retained profit	9	27
Long-term liabilities		
Bank loan	6	
Mortgage	8	14
Capital employed		41

The balance between permanent capital provided by shareholders and borrowed funds ('gearing') is important. Too much borrowing places an interest burden on the business that legally must be met.

Working capital

Working capital is defined as current assets minus current liabilities. It is vitally important as many businesses fail not because they are unprofitable but because they lack sufficient liquid assets to pay their short-term debts. Small companies are often affected when they expand too quickly. Cash is needed immediately to pay for extra materials and labour but problems arise when the increased sales are on credit. This situation forces the business to increase overdrafts or loans. This raises the firm's costs and places it at risk from a rise in interest rates.

The cash flow statement

Even profitable businesses can fail due to their inability to find enough cash to pay their creditors, so a third statement is produced which concentrates on changes in the *liquidity* of the company during the financial period. Liquidity is the ability of a company to access enough cash and bank resources to meet liabilities as they fall due, and the statement focuses on the overall change in cash balances during the financial period. The cash flow statement usually breaks down information into cash flows from operating activities (e.g. trading), investing activities (e.g. buying and selling fixed assets) and financing activities (e.g. issue of shares, raising or repaying loans).

Ratio analysis

This involves the examination of accounting data to gain understanding of the financial performance of a company. It is useful to all stakeholders as it provides insights into the performance, financial liquidity and shareholder returns of the business over time.

The construction of several simple ratios from the information contained within the balance sheet can give a clear assessment of the company's performance by making the following comparisons:

- with its own performance in previous time periods;
- with that of other companies in the same sector; and/or
- with accepted standards of performance, i.e. with particular values ('norms') for each ratio.

For illustration we present the most recent outcomes for the supermarket (major food retailing) sector in the UK for these various ratios.

Profitability ratios

Profitability ratios measure the relationship between profit in its various forms and sales, assets and capital employed.

- *Gross profit margin* – this ratio examines the relationship between profit (before overheads are taken into account) and sales.

$$\text{Gross profit margin} = \frac{\text{Gross profit}}{\text{Sales}} \times 100\%$$

A gross profit margin of 4% is typical for UK supermarkets.

- *ROCE (Return On Capital Employed)* – this is the most important ratio as it measures the efficiency with which the business generates profits from the capital invested in it.

$$\text{ROCE} = \frac{\text{Operating profit}}{\text{Capital employed}} \times 100\%$$

ROCE ratio is a healthy 10% for UK supermarkets.

These profitability ratios provide a picture of the profitability and efficiency of the business.

Activity ratios

Activity ratios measure how well a firm manages it resources.

- *Stock turnover* – this measures how long it takes for a firm to sell and replace its stock. Each time the stock is sold it generates more profit so the aim is to turn the stock over as quickly as possible. The ratio can be expressed as a number of days or as a number of times per year.

$$\text{Stock turnover} = \frac{\text{Stock}}{\text{Sales}} \times 365 \text{ days}$$

This ratio will vary widely according to the sector of economic activity. The stock turnover ratio is less than 4% for UK supermarkets, suggesting that their stock is sold entirely every 14 days.

- *Debtor turnover* – this measures how quickly debtors are paying their bills, i.e. the average collection period.

$$\text{Debtor turnover} = \frac{\text{Debtors}}{\text{Sales}} \times 365 \text{ days}$$

Supermarkets have hardly any debtors since goods are paid for on a cash-and-carry basis, giving a debtors turnover ratio of below 2%.

Liquidity ratios

Liquidity ratios provide a measure of risk, as they are concerned with the short-term financial health of the business. Too little working capital and the business will not be able to meet its debts. However, too much working capital represents an inefficient use of resources.

- *Current ratio*: measures how well short-term assets cover current liabilities. For most businesses a ratio between 1.5 and 2 is ideal.

$$\text{Current ratio} = \frac{\text{Current assets}}{\text{Current liabilities}}$$
$$= \frac{\text{Stocks + Debtors + Cash}}{\text{Overdraft + Creditors + Taxation + Dividends}}$$

A ratio of more than 1.5 is not necessarily a sign of strength, since it may mean excessive stocks or debtors, or an uneconomic use of liquid funds. Food retailers are unusual in that their rapid turnovers, together with the cash-and-carry nature of their business, will give relatively low 'stock' and 'debtor' items respectively. In this way 'current assets' will be small and so a very low current ratio is to be expected, often around 0.5, and must be viewed in this context.

- *Quick assets ratio* (*acid test ratio*). This is a more stringent test of liquidity as it only takes account of current assets that can easily be turned into liquid funds (cash and debtors).

$$\text{Quick assets ratio} = \frac{\text{Current assets} - \text{Stock}}{\text{Current liabilities}}$$

Most firms seek a value of at least 1, though again traders with a rapid turnover of cash sales will have a lower level of current assets and therefore a very low ratio of 0.3 has been recorded for UK supermarkets.

Gearing ratio

The gearing ratio focuses on the long-term financial health of the business by showing how reliant it is on borrowings. Highly geared companies have a large interest burden that might prove difficult to sustain in an economic downturn.

$$\text{Gearing ratio} = \frac{\text{Long-term loans}}{\text{Capital employed}} \times 100\%$$

A gearing ratio of around 33% is typical in the supermarket sector, with a percentage above this reflecting a highly geared company.

Shareholder ratios

Shareholder ratios reflect the returns on investments.

● *Earnings per share* (EPS): a good indicator of management's use of the investors' capital as it measures the profit performance over time.

$$\text{EPS} = \frac{\text{Net profit after tax}}{\text{Number of ordinary shares}}$$

Supermarkets had average earnings of around 19 pence per share in 2010/11, with the average share price then around 331 pence. The more highly regarded the company, the higher its P/E ratio, suggesting that the market anticipates a sustained earnings performance over a lengthy period.

● *The price/earnings ratio* (P/E ratio). This is an indicator of investor confidence as it shows the relationship between earnings and the current market price of the share.

$$\text{P/E ratio} = \frac{\text{Share price}}{\text{Earnings per share (pence)}}$$

The P/E ratio has an average for UK supermarkets of around 22.

● *Dividend yield*. This is the annual dividend expressed as a percentage of the current market price for shares and shows the return that a new investor could expect. It is easy to compare this ratio to other forms of investment, such as savings accounts.

$$\text{Dividend yield} = \frac{\text{Dividends per share}}{\text{Market price per share}} \times 100\%$$

The average supermarket dividend yield is around 2.5%.

Shareholders want to see two trends, an increasing return on investment in the form of improved dividends and an increase in the capital value of the investment in the form of a rising share price.

Ratio analysis can provide useful information to all the firm's stakeholders, making possible comparisons with other firms in the same sector of economic activity. However, as we have noted, care must be taken in interpreting the results.

Break-even analysis is another useful source of information for management and stakeholders in general.

Break-even analysis

The idea here is to find that level of output which the firm must achieve if it is to 'break even', i.e. to cover all its costs. The usual assumption is that all relationships are straight line (linear).

Check that you are familiar with the following definitions of revenue, cost and profit. As we shall see, these definitions are widely used in break-even analysis.

$$\textbf{Total revenue} = \textbf{Price} \times \textbf{Quantity sold}$$
$$\text{i.e}\quad TR = P \times Q$$

$$\text{Average revenue} = \text{Revenue per unit sold}$$

$$\text{i.e} \quad AR = \frac{TR}{Q} = P$$

$$\text{Total cost} = \text{Total fixed cost} + \text{Total variable cost}$$

$$\text{i.e.} \quad TC = TFC + TVC$$

$$\text{Total profit} = \text{Total revenue} - \text{Total cost}$$

$$\text{i.e} \quad TP = TR - TC$$

At the break-even level of output, total revenue exactly equals total cost so that total profit is zero.

At break-even output

$$TR = TC$$

$$\text{i.e.} \ TR = TFC + TVC$$

$$\text{and } TP = TR - TC = 0$$

Types of cost

- **Fixed costs.** These are costs that *do not* vary with output, and are sometimes called 'overheads'. Costs such as business rates, lighting, heating are often regarded as fixed costs. Fixed costs are incurred before production begins and are unchanged thereafter.
- **Variable costs.** These are costs that *do* vary with output, and are sometimes called 'running costs'. Costs such as wages, raw materials, energy are often regarded as variable costs.

Costs and linearity

The linearity (straight line) assumption underlying break-even analysis is reflected in the cost lines of Figure 12.4(a).

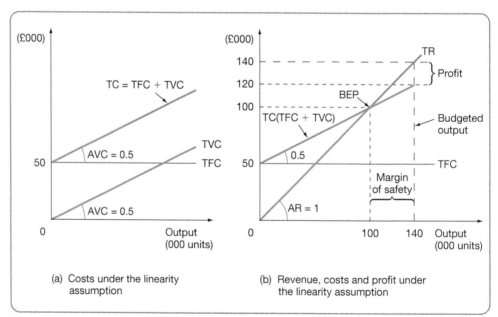

(a) Costs under the linearity assumption

(b) Revenue, costs and profit under the linearity assumption

Figure 12.4 **Aspects of break-even analysis**

In this example the firm has:

$$\text{Total fixed costs (TFC)} = £50,000$$
$$\text{Average variable costs (AVC)} = £0.50 \text{ per unit}$$

Notice that both TFC and TVC are represented by straight lines with *constant* slopes or gradients.

- slope of TFC = zero
- slope of TVC = AVC = 0.50

You should be familiar with the fact that we obtain the TC line by summing vertically the TFC and TVC lines. The slope of TC will be the same as that for TVC, i.e. 0.5.

NB. Since AVC is constant at £0.5 per unit, *marginal cost* (MC) = AVC in this case. In other words, each extra (marginal) unit adds £0.5 to total cost, which is the same as the £0.5 AVC per unit.

Revenue and linearity

Figure 12.4(b) reproduces the cost lines of Figure 12.4(a), together with a total revenue (TR) line drawn on the assumption that the firm can sell each unit at a price (AR) of £1.

Of course, the TR then has a slope (=AR) of 1 and an intercept of zero (since zero output means zero revenue).

NB. Since price (AR) is constant at £1 per unit, *marginal revenue* (MR) = AR in this case. In other words, each extra (marginal) unit adds £1 to total revenue, which is the same as the £1 AR per unit.

Break-even point (BEP)

The break-even point (BEP) is often defined as that level of output for which all costs are covered;

$$\text{i.e. where TR = TC so that TP = zero.}$$

In Figure 12.4(b) we can see that BEP occurs at an output of 100,000 units.
Clearly we can solve for BEP either:

(a) using graphical analysis;

(b) using simple algebra.

Check

$$TR = P \times Q = £1 \times 100,000 = £100,000$$
$$TC = TFC + TVC$$
$$\underline{TFC = £50,000}$$

$$TVC = AVC \times Q$$
$$TVC = £0.5 \times 100,000$$
$$\underline{TVC = £50,000}$$
$$\underline{\text{i.e. } TC = £50,000 + £50,000 = £100,000}$$

$$TC = TR - TC$$
$$\text{i.e. } TP = £100,000 - £100,000$$
$$\underline{TP = £0}$$

Even if we use graphical analysis, simple algebra can be a useful check on our solution. The following expressions will help our calculations of BEP.

Contribution per unit

This tells the firm what each unit of output is contributing (over and above the variable costs of its production) to the fixed costs already incurred.

$$\text{Contribution per unit } (C/U) = \text{Price (AR)} - \text{AVC}$$

We can now express the break-even point (BEP) as:

$$\text{BEP} = \frac{\text{Total fixed costs}}{\text{Contribution per unit}}$$

In our example:

$$C/U = £1 - £0.5$$
$$C/U = £0.5$$
$$\text{BEP} = \frac{\text{TFC}}{C/U} = \frac{£50,000}{£0.5} = 100,000 \text{ units}$$

In other words, the firm must produce 100,000 units if it is to earn sufficient revenue over and above its variable costs to cover the £50,000 of fixed costs already incurred.

Budgeted output

Budgeted output is the level of output the firm intends (budgets) to produce. One would normally expect the budgeted output to be *greater than* the BEP.

Suppose the budgeted output in Figure 12.4(b) is 140,000 units. At this budgeted output:

$$\text{TR} = \text{P} \times \text{Q} = £1 \times 140,000 = £140,000$$
$$\text{TC} = \text{TFC} + \text{TVC}$$
$$= £50,000 + (140,000 \times £0.5)$$
$$= £50,000 + £70,000 = £120,000$$
$$\text{TP} = \text{TR} - \text{TC}$$
$$\text{TP} = £140,000 - £120,000$$
$$\underline{\text{TP} = £20,000 \text{ at budgeted output}}$$

In other words, at a budgeted output of 140,000 units, the firm can expect to earn a total profit (TP) of £20,000, as can be seen in Figure 12.4(b).

Margin of safety

The firm will usually seek to operate with some **margin of safety,** here defined as the difference between budgeted (intended) output and the break-even output.

$$\text{Margin of safety} = \text{Budged output} - \text{Break-even output}$$

In Figure 12.4(b):

$$\text{Margin of safety} = 140,000 - 100,000$$
$$\underline{\text{Margin of safety} = 40,000 \text{ units}}$$

The margin of safety is often expressed as a *percentage of the budgeted output.*

$$\text{Margin of safety (\%)} = \frac{\text{Budgeted output} - \text{BEP}}{\text{Budgeted output}} \times 100$$
$$\text{i.e. Margin of safety} = \frac{40,000}{140,000} \times 100$$
$$\underline{\text{Margin of safety} = 28.6\%}$$

This tells us that the output of the firm can fall by as much as 28.6% *below* its budgeted output and still break even or better.

In other words, the margin of safety is a useful measure of *risk*. The larger the margin of safety, the lower the risk of indebtedness should unexpected events cause the firm to fall short of the budgeted output.

You try 12.3 gives you an opportunity to check some of these aspects of accounting and management.

You try   12.3

1 If the current assets exceed the current liabilities, we can definitely say that:
   (a) the business has made a profit
   (b) fixed assets are greater than current assets
   (c) the current ratio is over 1:1
   (d) the acid test ratio is over 1:1.

2 A limited company has a very low gearing level. Which of the following statements best describes that company?
   (a) It has few borrowings.
   (b) It is a very risky company.
   (c) It has high borrowings.
   (d) It has very high fixed assets.

3 If a company's shares are stated to have a P/E ratio of 15 times, which of the following statements is certain about that company?
   (a) The share price is fifteen times the dividend per share.
   (b) The dividend is fifteen times the profits per share after tax.
   (c) The dividend is fifteen times the profits per share before tax.
   (d) The share price is fifteen times the earnings per share.

4 A company's sales total £600,000, its debtors £40,000 and its creditors £60,000. Which one of the following is correct?
   (a) Debtors' collection period is 36.5 days and its creditor payment period is 24.3 days.
   (b) Debtors' collection period is 24.3 days and its creditor payment period is 36.5 days.
   (c) Debtors' collection period is 73 days and its creditor payment period is 36.5 days.
   (d) Debtors' collection period is 46.6 days and its creditor payment period is 73 days.

5 Which of the following most accurately describes a profit and loss account?
   (a) All income less all expenses.
   (b) All cash received less all cash paid.
   (c) All assets less all liabilities.
   (d) All income less all cash paid.

6 A company sells a product which has a variable cost of £3 a unit. Fixed costs are £10,000. It has been estimated that if the price is set at £5 a unit, the sales volume will be 10,000 units; whereas if the price is reduced to £4 a unit, the sales volume will rise to 15,000.
   (a) Draw a break-even chart covering each of the possible sales prices, and state the budgeted profits, the break-even points and the margins of safety.
   (b) Compare the two possible situations. Consider the assumptions and limitations of your analysis.

Answers can be found on pp. 525–546.

Recap

- The 'marketing mix' involves price, product, promotion and place.
- Field and desk research, using primary and secondary data, are key elements in market research.
- Segmentation of markets into groups with similar characteristics helps marketers better understand buyer behaviour.
- HRM specialists have an important strategic role within the business as well as personnel-related responsibilities.
- HRM specialists can more effectively influence productivity and job satisfaction within an organisation by being aware of the various theories of motivation.
- All limited companies in the UK have to publish financial information.
- All PLCs have to appoint an independent auditor to report to the shareholders on the truth and fairness of the financial statements.
- The majority of the financial information contained within the annual report is required by either legislation (the Companies Act), Stock Exchange regulations or accounting standards.
- Important financial statements include the balance sheet, the profit and loss account and the cash flow statement which provide still further information via various accounting ratios.
- Break-even analysis gives the firm and investors some idea of the level of risk associated with the firm's operations.

Key terms

Break-even point That output at which all costs are covered.

Desk research The collection of secondary data.

Gearing ratio Reflects the financial risk to which the company is subject. It is the ratio of external borrowing to total capital employed.

'Hierarchy of needs' Maslow's theory of motivation suggesting 'lower' and 'higher' order needs.

Liquidity ratios Give an indication of the availability of cash or readily marketable assets to meet current (short-term) liabilities. Include current ratio and quick assets (acid test) ratio.

Margin of safety The difference between budgeted (intended) output and the break-even point. Serves as an indicator of risk.

Market segmentation Groups of consumers with similar characteristics. Occupational classifications (A, B, C_1, C_2, D and E) are widely used.

Marketing mix The marketing tools that an organisation can use to influence demand (product, price, promotion and place).

Penetration pricing Low price to secure market share.

Prestige pricing High price associated with high quality.

Price discrimination Charging different prices for an identical product to different markets.

Price skimming High price to 'cream off' those committed to purchasing the product.

Primary data New data collected for a specific project.

Product life cycle A model for describing the common patterns of sales growth and decline over the lifetime of a product.

Product line pricing Prices are set for each item with the whole of the product line in mind.

Profitability ratios Include profit margin and return on assets ratios (also known as the return on capital employed ROCE).

Secondary data Data which already exists in published form.

International business environment

Introduction

How do businesses seek to internationalise their operations and why do so many businesses fail when entering a new international market? Even though many firms opt for an alliance with a foreign partner when entering an international market, many such alliances still fail. Reasons for such high failure rates can largely be attributed to a lack of understanding of the international business environment and the factors that affect how an international company operates.

This chapter takes forward the discussions in Chapter 12, paying particular attention to the *international* business environment, along with how functional areas of management such as marketing and HRM may need to adapt to an international setting. It reviews the increasingly important contribution of the multinational enterprise (MNE) to international business activity and takes an in-depth look at the three major trading regions vital to international business, namely the European Union, North America and the Pacific Rim. Within this so-called 'triad' particular attention is paid to the rapidly developing Chinese economy. Many economists predict that China will eventually become the world's largest economic market, although the country remains an extremely complex international environment, with relatively few foreign companies operating in China experiencing short-term success. Reasons for this will be considered, as well as possible success factors identified. After assessing the role of the World Trade Organization and other major international institutions in supporting international business, the chapter concludes by reviewing the case of those who advocate free trade in international business and those who advocate protectionism.

Although this and other chapters incorporate a 'globalised' perspective, a more detailed consideration of the characteristics associated with globalisation is undertaken in Chapter 14 (pp. 490–504).

What you'll learn

By the end of this chapter you should be able to:

● explain the problems companies face when entering a new international market

● understand how marketing, HRM and other management functions must be adjusted to the international business environment if overseas business activities are to be successful

What you'll learn continued

- review the characteristics of the multinational enterprise, its relevance to international business and its approaches to international HRM and international marketing
- examine the importance to international business of the so-called 'triad' consisting of the EU, North America and Pacific Rim regions
- show an understanding of why China is considered a future economic world leader
- identify the arguments involved in the free trade versus protectionism debate and be aware of the role of the key international institutions in promoting international trade and investment.

The internationalisation process

In today's highly competitive markets, many companies see internationalisation as a natural progression from producing solely for the domestic market. There are a number of reasons why firms internationalise. It may be that the domestic market is saturated, or that production (and sales) needs to expand beyond the domestic market in order to achieve lower average costs, or that overseas governments offer attractive incentives for the firm to invest abroad. Figure 13.1 indicates some of the reasons for internationalisation.

The difficult question many companies face is not whether to internationalise, but *how* to internationalise. The options regarding the choice of method for internationalisation are reviewed in Table 13.1.

- After moving beyond domestic marketing, the next stage towards internationalisation is often rather limited, involving a search for information with a possible view to exporting.
- After this 'pre-export' stage the firm may start exporting via an independent agent. Such 'indirect exporting' often involves the agent (e.g. export house, confirming house or buying house) taking responsibility for the physical distribution of products and even for setting up the sales and distribution channels in the foreign market.

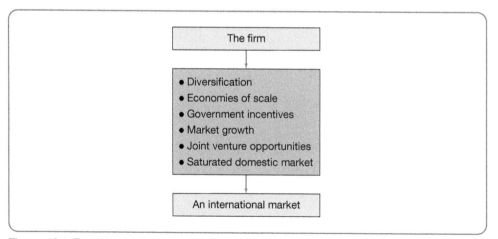

Figure 13.1 Reasons firms internationalise

Table 13.1 **Stages in the internationalisation process**

Stage	Description
Stage 1: Domestic marketing	The firm is only involved in the domestic market and does not export at all
Stage 2: Pre-export	The firm searches for information with a possible view to exporting
Stage 3: Indirect or direct exporting	The firm starts exporting on a small basis, to geographically adjacent and culturally similar countries. Likely mode of entry involves indirect (using an agency) exporting or direct exporting
Stage 4: Active involvement	There is a systematic effort to increase sales through exporting to multiple countries. Likely mode of entry involves joint ventures, licensing or franchising
Stage 5: Committed involvement	The firms depends heavily on foreign markets. Likely mode of entry involves foreign direct investment (fdi)

- As the firm gains more experience and makes a more long-term commitment to exporting, it may seek to control the export process itself, distributing and selling its own products to the foreign market, i.e. by 'direct' exporting.

- More active involvement might include establishing joint ventures or engaging in licensing or franchising arrangements overseas, especially when more than one country is involved.

- Finally, the firm may reach a point where it sees it as appropriate to commit itself still further by establishing production facilities in one or more foreign country, i.e. becoming a multinational enterprise (MNE).

The internationalisation process very often begins with a firm becoming involved with an international market it readily understands. The level of understanding attributed to an international market can be based on language, a familiarity with the social and lifestyle patterns of behaviour (culture), knowledge of the economy and of the legal and institutional frameworks within the country. The importance of having a network of contacts can also influence the internationalisation process. For example, a firm that already has established suppliers in Taiwan may use this long-term relationship to support possible market entry into that country. The suppliers can advise on market entry procedures, government contacts and the nature of the market. Having a network of close relationships within a country can be the difference between entering or passing over a particular international market.

Example

UK firms prefer Dublin

Many UK companies prefer entering the Republic of Ireland at an early stage in the internationalisation process. Dublin, in particular, is a thriving business centre that shares many similarities with British cities. Close geographical proximity and language and cultural affinity make it an attractive proposition for UK firms making that first step towards internationalisation.

Methods of internationalisation

We touched on some of these methods in the context of firm growth in Chapter 5. However, the focus here is on their role in the internationalisation process. The various

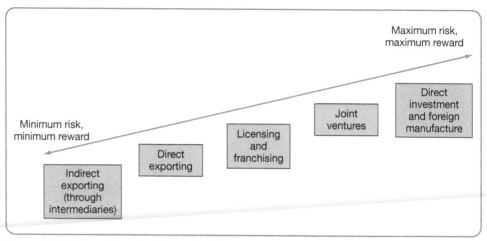

Figure 13.2 **Internationalisation methods**

market entry options open to firms considering internationalisation are now considered. We note that each carries a varying degree of risk, as indicated in Figure 13.2. Indirect exporting carries the least risk, in that it requires little commitment and resources, while foreign direct investment implies a long-term commitment and can be hugely expensive. However, rewards to firms are often directly related to the degree of risk, with the lowest returns from indirect exporting and the highest returns from fdi.

Indirect exporting

Indirect exporting happens when a firm does not itself undertake any special international activity but rather operates through intermediaries. Under this approach the exporting function is outsourced to other parties which may prepare the export documentation, take responsibility for the physical distribution of goods and even set up the sales and distribution channels in the foreign market. The role of the intermediary may be played by export houses, confirming houses and buying houses.

- *Export house* buys products from a domestic firm and sells them abroad on its own account.
- *Confirming house* acts for foreign buyers and is paid on a commission basis. Brings sellers and buyers into direct contact (unlike export house) and guaranteed payment will be made to exporter by end user.
- *Buying house* performs similar functions to those of the confirming house but is more active in seeking out sellers to match the buyer's particular needs.

Direct exporting

Direct exporting would typically involve a firm in distributing and selling its own products to the foreign market. This would generally mean a longer-term commitment to a particular foreign market, with the firm choosing local agents and distributors specific to that market. In-house expertise would need to be developed to keep up these contacts, to conduct market research, prepare the necessary documentation and establish local pricing policies. The advantages of such an approach are that it:

- allows the exporter to closely monitor developments and competition in the host market;
- promotes interaction between producer and end-user;

- involves long-term commitments, such as providing after-sales services to encourage repeat purchases.

Franchising

McDonald's and Burger King are perhaps the two best-known examples of international franchises. However, franchising is a very popular method of market entry and is not limited to the fast food industry. Examples include cleaning (Chem-Dry), clothing (Benetton) and childcare (Tiny Tots).

In international franchising, a supplier (*franchiser*) permits a dealer (*franchisee*) the right to market its products and services in that country in exchange for a financial commitment. This commitment usually involves a fee upfront and royalties based on product sales.

- *Advantages for the franchisee* are that they are buying into an existing brand and should receive full support from the franchiser in terms of marketing, training and starting up. When customers walk into a McDonald's restaurant; they know exactly what to expect. This is one advantage of global branding.
- *Disadvantages for the franchisee* include restrictions on what they can and can't do. For example, McDonald's have very strict regulations concerning marketing, pricing, training etc. A franchisee cannot simply change the staff uniform, alter prices or vary opening hours as the company operates a standardised approach to doing business.
- *Advantages for the franchiser* are that overseas expansion can be much less expensive and that any local adaptations can (with agreement) be made by those well acquainted with cultural issues in that country.
- *Disadvantages for the franchiser* include possible conflict with the franchisee for not following regulations and agreements as well as a threat that the franchisee may opt to 'go it alone' in the future and thus become a direct competitor.

Licensing

This allows one company (the *licensee*) to use the property of some other company (*the licensor*). Very often this relates to intellectual property, e.g. trademarks, patents and copyright (see Chapter 11, p. 364). For example, a medium-sized UK stationery company may decide it wishes to produce a range of stationery based on Walt Disney characters. In order to do this, the company would need to approach Disney and discuss the possibility of gaining a licence to sell Disney branded goods in the UK. The licensee (in this case the UK stationery company) pays a fee to Disney in exchange for the rights to use their brand name/logo.

An advantage of licensing to licensors is that they do not have to make a substantial investment in order to gain a presence in overseas markets and they need not acquire the local knowledge which may be so important for success in such markets. Licensing is also an effective way of increasing levels of brand awareness. However, a licensor can be damaged if a licensee produces products of an inferior standard. Licensing is very common in the film and music industry. Products include calendars, videos, books, posters and clothing.

Joint venture

Narrowly defined, a joint venture occurs when two or more firms pool a portion of their resources within a common legal organisation. A joint venture is popular for firms entering an international market at a large cultural distance (p. 427) from the home market. For example, many Western firms opt for a joint venture when entering China and

Taiwan, simply because of major cultural differences, including language, social relationships, style of management and political environment. A joint venture takes place because both firms believe that their partner has something to offer. In the case of a Western firm entering Taiwan, the Western firm is getting access to new markets, a partner with local language and cultural knowledge and an already established network of contacts. It is likely that the Taiwanese firm is in turn expecting to gain access to new technology, to marketing expertise and above all to extra finance from their Western partner. Nevertheless, international joint ventures tend to experience high failure rates.

Two particular types of international joint venture are considered below.

- *Equity joint venture* (EJV). This remains a popular method of market entry for foreign companies with the equity stake by the foreign partner usually not lower than 25% of voting shares. The equity joint venture requires investment from all of the parties who jointly operate it, share the risks of it in accordance with their different proportions of investment, and are jointly held responsible for the profits and losses of it. For companies looking to access a large share of the Chinese market, the establishment of multiple equity joint ventures provides a means for obtaining the connections necessary for doing business in China.

- *Co-operative joint venture* (CJV). This differs from an equity joint venture in that it usually has a profit sharing mechanism rather than equity ownership by each company. Reasons for choosing a cooperative joint venture may include less need to formally value capital contributions, greater flexibility in relation to profit sharing and fewer restrictions on management structure.

Of course, there is a risk that the extent to which each partner relies on the other's skills can change over time, sometimes to such an extent that there may no longer be a need for the international joint venture to continue. Studies have found that, at the time many international joint ventures were formed, each partner admitted that they could not have carried out the task without their partner's help, but that within a short space of time the partners learned so much from each other that they no longer felt the need for shared management. However, international joint ventures can also lead to increased trust and commitment. In Chinese culture, personal trust develops over time and involves 'getting to know' a partner. Past experience between partners is extremely important because it can help develop close long-term relationships built on trust and commitment, which can then lead on to even closer collaboration in the future.

> **Links**
>
> Examples and discussions of strategic joint ventures are presented in Chapter 14 (pp. 501–504).

Foreign direct investment (fdi)

Foreign direct investment (fdi) is a high-risk strategy whereby a firm sets up its own facilities in an international market. Some of the problems of joint ventures (especially those involving decision making and culture clashes) can be avoided by wholly owning the foreign subsidiaries. This can be achieved through acquisition of an existing firm or through establishing an entirely new foreign operation ('**greenfield' investment**).

Acquisition of an existing foreign company has a number of advantages compared to 'greenfield' investment; for example, it allows a more rapid market entry, so that there is a quicker return on capital and a ready access to knowledge of the local market. Because of its rapidity such acquisition can pre-empt a rival's entry into the same market. Further, many of the problems associated with setting up a 'greenfield' site in a foreign country (such as cultural, legal and management issues) can be avoided. By involving a change in ownership, acquisition also avoids costly competitive reactions from the acquired firm.

> **Links**
>
> Strategic aspects of mergers and acquisitions policies are considered in more detail on pp. 492–504.

Case Study 13.1 reviews some of the issues involved in the internationalisation process using the example of Portugal.

Case Study 13.1   Internationalisation of Portuguese firms

An important recent development has been the strong surge in Portuguese investment abroad. During the 1990s and the early years of the new millennium Portugal's outward foreign direct investment multiplied at an impressive rate. By 2010 Portugal was among the leading 15 countries that invest overseas, with most of the fdi taking the form of cross-border acquisitions or partnerships. Internationalisation efforts have followed a distinct pattern in terms of their economic geography. Typically the first moves were made into the neighbouring economy, Spain. An example of this 'toe in the water' stage was the acquisition by Cimpor, the leading Portuguese cement maker, of Corporación Noroeste, a Spanish cement maker based in Galicia. The next move was for Portuguese firms as diverse as Cenoura, Petrogal, Transportes Luis Simões and Caixa Geral de Depósitos to penetrate the wider Spanish market. A survey conducted among Portuguese companies found that the priority markets for internationalisation were Spain (69.9%), the former Portuguese African colonies or PALOPs (47.3%), the rest of the EU (38.7%) and Brazil (35.5%).

A clear pattern and trajectory is discernible in Portugal's internationalisation efforts. Typically the first moves, as indicated above, are made into the neighbouring economy. As a result of these rapidly expanding two-way flows, an EU regional bloc based in the Iberian peninsula came into existence during the 1990s as a buoyant new trading area. Using Spain as a springboard, the next natural step was into North Africa and the countries that were formerly Portugal's African colonies (PALOPs). The latter were attractive because they were undertaking privatisation programmes, while Brazil became a focal point for economic relations with Mercosur. The most recent stage has involved investments in the more advanced EU economies. In some cases, a presence has also been established in Eastern Europe, notably Poland, Hungary and Russia.

The Portuguese expansion strategy is driven by the need to stay competitive in order to survive by 'growing' the size of domestic firms via international involvement. The problem of scale is important. Given the country's dimensions, large nationally based groups are inevitably thin on the ground. World-ranking tables, for instance, placed Portugal's largest bank, CGD, in 146th place. In such circumstances, there exists an ever-present danger that Portuguese firms will fall prey to foreign, perhaps Spanish, transnationals.

Questions

1 What does the Portuguese experience suggest about the internationalisation process?

2 What policies might be used to encourage further internationalisation by Portuguese firms?

Portugal is increasingly being challenged by Eastern Europe as an attractive location for MNE investment in motor vehicles and many other manufacturing activities. Indeed, many former Eastern bloc countries, especially the Czech Republic and Hungary, are attracting a higher proportion of EU-based inward investment. These countries are geographically well situated, have good language skills (English and other north European languages, including Russian) relevant to growing EU markets, and are now inside the enlarged EU. Wage rates per unit output are estimated at some 50% lower in the Czech Republic than in Portugal for many manufacturing activities.

You try 13.1 gives you the opportunity to further investigate the internationalisation process.

You try   13.1

1 Case Study: Wilona Training Ltd

Peter Williams and David Wong founded Wilona Training Ltd in 2001 in Liverpool, England. Given their wealth of experience as training managers, both men felt it was time to establish their own company. With the UK being an extremely competitive market, and with many of

You try 13.1 continued

the leading training organisations being located in the Liverpool area, they decided to target small and medium-sized enterprises (SMEs).

Although they had no formal management qualifications, both men gained much of their experience through working for two of the UK's leading blue chip companies. Their specialised training topics included sales techniques, business negotiation skills, communication skills and effective presentations. With the help of a £50,000 business start-up loan, David and Peter were soon concentrating on winning business and making money.

Both men demonstrated a flair for selling their services and soon began to bring in some lucrative contracts from small and medium companies in the Liverpool area. As was to be expected, in their first year of business Wilona found it difficult to win clients, making a small profit. But by the second year they had achieved impressive sales turnover of £130,000 and were beginning to make profits. Wilona had established a reputation for providing excellent service at competitive prices. Although the company did very little in the way of marketing, positive word of mouth communication meant new clients were requesting their services on a regular basis.

Problems for Wilona began to emerge, however, in 2004. Sales and profits were down. Further declines followed in 2005. Peter and David responded by selling even harder than before, and by placing advertisements in the local newspaper. This did not immediately help Wilona profits. They had to cut their prices because of the increasingly competitive marketplace. Wilona found it was not able to compete with the resources and competitive pricing strategies of the larger training providers.

Currently, Wilona Training Ltd is surviving, but the long-term prospects do not look good. Therefore, Peter and David have decided to look at the possibility of entering neighbouring Ireland. Northern Ireland appears to hold a number of opportunities for Wilona. In order to assess the possibility of entering the Irish market, Peter and David have decided to employ the services of an international marketing consultant in the hope that the company can begin to be profitable once again.

Questions

As an international marketing consultant, you are required to find answers to the following questions:

(1) Explain the reasons why Northern Ireland may prove a suitable international market for Wilona.

(2) Discuss possible market entry options for Wilona.

(3) Given Wilona's poor financial position, where can the company go for support and advice on entering the Irish market?

2 Case Study: Havering Promotional Products (HPP)

Established in the late 1960s, HPP specialises in the manufacture and supply of business and advertising gifts. Based in the London Borough of Havering, the company employs a total of 100 people. Products include pens, desk accessories, mugs and key rings, which are printed with the client's name and are designed as give-aways to customers.

The business and promotional gifts market has become increasingly competitive recently. This is due to low barriers of entry, an increase in the number of competitors and the domestic market reaching a maturity stage.

Having experienced 15 years of continuous sales and profit growth, HPP's management was concerned to find that the sales performance had become static, and that in the past year had actually declined. This was disappointing, as part of the firm's long-term corporate strategy is to increase year-on-year profits by several per cent, thus achieving economies of scale. As 100% of HPP's business was within the UK, the firm finally took

You try 13.1 continued

the decision to look at international markets. With no previous experience of operating in an international environment, the responsibility for handling this was given to the Assistant Marketing Manager, who was one of the few within the company with any language ability.

A market research agency was appointed to find out why the firm's brand image and performance were so disappointing in the UK and to analyse possible international markets the firm could enter. The research findings suggested the following:

1 Although the firm is well known in the industry, it is seen as old fashioned, and has been quoted as the 'Marks & Spencer' of the promotional gifts market.

2 The firm does not come across as having a particular strong brand identity.

3 The promotional gifts market in the UK is almost stagnant.

4 Prices of HPP are perceived to be higher than the industry norms. Many people quoted the biggest firms in the market – 'Gifts for All' and 'STW Promotional Gifts' – as being considerably cheaper for similar products.

5 HPP is seen as having a strong London base with only a limited ability to service clients outside this area.

6 There appear to be international market opportunities in Eastern Europe and China within the promotional gifts industry. This is largely due to the increasing amount of foreign direct investment from overseas into these countries.

When respondents were asked how likely it was that they would do business with HPP over the next 12 months, the mean (average) pattern of responses suggested that this would be 'fairly unlikely'. The conclusion also highlighted that a small number of respondents even believed the company to have gone out of business within the preceding six months!

The board of directors all agreed that the report should be taken seriously and recommended that a marketing consultant be employed to make recommendations on future strategy.

Questions

(1) Explain why HPP should internationalise. Use case examples of other companies wherever possible.

(2) Discuss the range of international market entry methods that are available to HPP.

(3) Think of an example of a successful joint venture in an international market. Investigate the background to the joint venture, and then analyse the benefits both parties to the venture have derived, as well as any possible areas of conflict.

Answers can be found on pp. 525–546.

International business environment

There are a number of elements of the international business environment that can also influence the internationalisation process. These are outlined in Figure 13.3.

We have already considered many of these elements in Chapter 12, though mainly from a *domestic* point of view. However, a company operating in an international market is likely to experience these environmental issues from a different perspective as compared to its domestic market. Here we briefly highlight some of the key external environmental questions which firms need to consider when entering international markets.

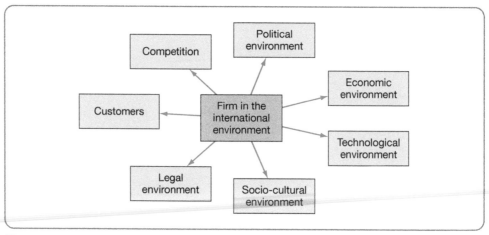

Figure 13.3 **International environment**

Questions for firms entering international markets

The following are just some of the questions which a firm seeking to enter a particular overseas market might ask.

Economic environment

- What is the current rate of unemployment?
- Are there enough suitably qualified potential employees living in the area?
- How will inflation affect pricing?
- What is the current level of interest rates?
- Can the economic climate be described as stable?

Political/legal environment

- What is the legislation concerning working hours?
- How important is the contract?
- Is the country's legal system fully developed?
- Is there any new legislation pending that will have a serious impact on how we run our business?

Socio-cultural environment

- What are local tastes towards our product?
- Will the name be accepted locally?
- Does our product go against any religious values?
- Do we need to make changes in order to appeal to different sub-cultures?

Technological environment

- What is the figure for Internet access per head of the population?
- Is broadband capability available to subscribers?
- What percentage of the population has the necessary buying power to buy certain technological products?
- Does the culture embrace advancement in technology?

Competition

- What is the nature of the current market? For example, is it highly fragmented or oligopolistic?
- Who are our main competitors (both local firms and multinational)?
- How will they react to our entering the market?
- How can we compete against existing competitors in the marketplace?

Customers

- Are customer needs overseas likely to be different to those in our domestic market?
- How will we segment the market?
- Who is our main target audience?
- How will our product be positioned in the marketplace?
- Where are our customers likely to be located?
- What routes (channels) will we use in trying to reach our customers?

It may be useful, when considering the internationalisation process, to look in a little more detail at some of these questions.

Cultural and ethical issues

While there are many definitions of 'culture', most agree that it refers to ways in which people structure, share and transmit values and information within a particular society. According to Hall (1960), cultures differ widely in the extent to which unspoken, unformulated and inexplicit rules govern how information is handled and how people interact and relate to each other. In 'high context' cultures, much of human behaviour is covert or implicit, whereas in 'low context' cultures much is overt or explicit. For Hall, the high context cultures include countries or regions such as Japan, China, the Middle East, South America and the southern European countries. Most Western countries (including the US) are regarded as low context cultures.

High and low context cultures

High-context cultures

- Much information transmitted by the physical context (i.e. non-verbal means, e.g. body language) or internalised within people.
- Strong bonds and high involvement between people (more group oriented than individualistic).
- Greater distinctions between insiders and outsiders.
- Cultural patterns long lived and slow to change.
- Punctuality and schedules have low priority.

Low-context cultures

- Much information transmitted by explicit, coded messages (less via non-verbal means, e.g. body language).
- Fragile bonds and low involvement between people (more individualistic than group oriented).
- Fewer distinctions made between insiders and outsiders.
- Change easy and rapid.
- Punctuality and schedules important.

China is particularly high context in cultural terms, for example it is regarded as impolite to deny anything. Hence instead of saying 'no', other phrases are used to describe an inconvenience which imply that the answer is no. While Chinese often use high context patterns, Westerners are more inclined to use low context patterns. German culture is traditionally associated with being low context, for example being very 'frank' in their spoken communication.

Being aware of such cultural aspects is vitally important to international business. Recently a well-used TV advert for HSBC stresses its credentials for international business by its awareness of cultural differences worldwide. It shows an Englishman eating platefuls of unappetising snake fish dishes in Hong Kong in an attempt to please Chinese businessmen, unaware that a clean plate implies that the host has provided insufficient food for the guest. Both parties are bemused – the Englishman longing to receive no more food, the Chinese businessman longing for the Englishman to leave some food to indicate sufficiency and thereby acknowledge the host's generosity. HSBC trumpets its global banking reach as making it well positioned to advise potential business partners on cultural differences as an aid to international deal making.

Check the net

For aspects of Asian culture check:

www.apmforum.com

http://english.china.com

www.japanecho.com

Hofstede's cultural dimensions

Hofstede (1980) has researched the nature and extent of cultural differences and identified different 'dimensions of culture' (Figure 13.4).

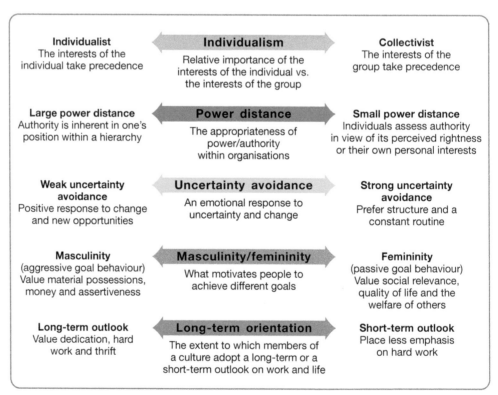

Figure 13.4 Hofstede's five dimensions of culture

Source: Adapted from Griffin, Ricky Y. and Pustay, Michael, *International Business*, 6th Edition, copyright 2010, p. 104, Fig. 4.3. Adapted by permission of Pearson Education, Inc., Upper Saddle River, NJ.

Hofstede has shown that certain management practices can be compatible, and others incompatible, with the culture of a society, as expressed via these different 'dimensions'. He further suggested that cultural incompatibility undermines the successful transfer of managerial practices from developed countries to developing countries.

Ethical issues

We have already touched on the importance of ethical issues in Chapter 4. No longer can international companies run their overseas businesses however they want. Key ethical issues such as employing child labour and gift-giving can, if breached, result in great damage to a firm. Since the world is now so interconnected, customers are better informed about such practices, and often express concerns about firms that do not appear to be employing ethical standards.

Ethics refers to what is acceptable in a particular society. However, ethical issues are often complex since the international business environment is made up of different cultural values and it is these values that determine what is regarded as ethical or unethical. For example, in some societies gift-giving and using relationships to generate results is perfectly acceptable, though in many of the world's developed countries such practices are regarded as unethical.

Example

Tesco introduces ethical advisers

Tesco, the UK's leading supermarket chain, has in the past received negative publicity as a result of a TV documentary about the conditions for workers growing foodstuffs, such as mange tout in Africa, exported to the supermarket chain. It has therefore established its own code of conduct and set up a 70-strong team of ethical advisers to help monitor the goods it sells in its stores. The advisers check foodstuffs and other products the chain sells so that its new code of conduct, designed to ensure that its Third World suppliers do not exploit child or forced labour, is adhered to.

Microenvironment

Figure 13.5 identifies some of the more local influences on the firm's attempt to internationalise, which are sometimes described as being part of the firm's *microenvironment*.

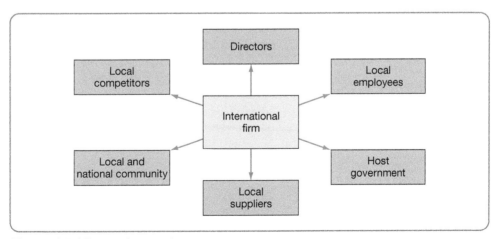

Figure 13.5 **Microenvironment**

Directors

When entering an international market, it is important that the board of directors is fully behind the strategy. Entering a new market is a high-risk strategy that can only work if the entire company's management is fully behind the project. For example, entering a complex market such as China can take many years before a Western firm begins to generate profit. This can test the patience of many a director!

Local employees

If entering an international market involves setting up production facilities, it is important that a firm considers the number of potential employees living locally who will be able and willing to work for the company. If there is a severe lack of appropriately skilled staff, then arrangements need to be made to develop training programmes in order to overcome these.

Local suppliers

These provide the firm with the intermediate inputs (e.g. components, raw materials etc.) which allow the production of the final products for customers. It is important to identify suitable suppliers in the overseas economy, as choosing unreliable partners can damage a channel of distribution, ultimately affecting a firm's competitiveness in an international market. If a firm is planning on selling existing products to new markets, it is likely that it will review the ability of existing suppliers to meet the demand from new market entry. However, if the strategy is one of diversification (new product, new market), then new supplier(s) will need to be found. The relationship between a firm and its supplier is very much built on trust and adaptation. In Japanese business markets it is not unusual for a firm to continue to use the same suppliers for decades.

Local and host national community

Setting up production facilities in a new international market requires strong support from the local and host national community. This is true not only in terms of people willing to work for the company, but also in community support for the firm through demonstrating a willingness to buy its products. Toyota has a large manufacturing plant in Derbyshire, UK, and makes every effort to show its commitment to the community by employing local staff and working with the local community by supporting local projects. It has also reoriented its supply chain to include more local and UK component suppliers.

Local competitors

These can be a direct threat to an international firm. Sometimes it can be difficult to win customers from local companies quite simply because local people may work for them so that they have high levels of customer loyalty. In order to gain customers from local competitors international firms may need to use sales promotion activities (e.g. introductory special offers) or product differentiation strategies (e.g. highlighting important differences between their products and local products). The intention behind both approaches is to persuade local consumers that this new product adds value as compared to existing products.

Host government

International firms need to be aware of the impact of government at both national and local levels on their operations. At the national level, central government may offer tax and other incentives to firms to encourage market entry. However, central government can also hinder international market entry by increasing import tariffs for certain foreign products. At the national and local level, governments and authorities may aim to protect local firms by developing a range of restrictions and 'red tape' (bureaucracy) for foreign investors.

Multinational enterprise (MNE)

Put simply, a **multinational enterprise** (sometimes called a **transnational**) is a company that has headquarters in one country but operations in other countries. It is not always obvious that a firm is a multinational. The growth in alliances, joint ventures and mergers and acquisitions means that consumers tend to recognise the brand, rather than know who the parent company is. Who, for example, now owns Jaguar or Land Rover? The answer in this case is Ford.

> *Stop and think*   13.1
>
> Can you think of brands for three different types of product and identify the multinational company which owns those brands in each case?

Links

Chapter 14 (pp. 493–9) looks in more detail at the strategies for global production adopted by MNEs.

Dunning (1993) defines the multinational as a firm 'that engages in foreign direct investment and owns or controls value-adding activities in more than one country'. Typically the multinational would not just own value-adding activities, but might buy resources and create goods and/or services in a variety of countries. While the central strategic planning takes place at headquarters, considerable latitude will usually be given to affiliates (subsidiaries) to enable them to operate in harmony with their local environments.

Ranking multinationals

From a statistical point of view, there are two main methods of ranking the world's top multinationals: first, ranking them according to the amount of foreign assets they control and second, ranking them in terms of a '**transnationality index**'.

- *Foreign assets.* Table 13.2 ranks the top ten multinationals according to the *value of foreign assets* they control and we can see that three of the top ten are from the USA, three from the UK, two from France and one from both Germany and Japan. They are primarily based in the petroleum, electronics/computing, utilities and motor vehicle sectors.

- *Transnationality index.* However, Table 13.2 also provides each company's transnationality index and its transnationality ranking. The *transnationality index* takes a more comprehensive view of a company's global activity and is calculated as the average of the following three ratios:
  - foreign assets/total assets;
  - foreign sales/total sales;
  - foreign employment/total employment.

For example, we can see that the largest multinational company is General Electric in terms of the foreign assets it owns. However, its transnationality index of 52% means that it is only ranked 76th in terms of this criterion. The reason for this is that even though it has large investments overseas in absolute value, in *percentage* terms most of its assets, sales and employment are still located in the USA. This is in contrast with British

Table 13.2 World's top ten non-financial multinationals ranked by foreign assets, 2008

		Rankings			
Foreign assets	Trans-nationality index	Company	Country	Industry	Trans-nationality index (%)
1	76	General Electric	USA	Electrical/electronic	52
2	6	Vodafone	UK	Telecommunications	89
3	35	Royal Dutch/Shell	UK/Neth	Petroleum	73
4	23	British Petroleum	UK	Petroleum	81
5	41	ExxonMobil	USA	Petroleum	68
6	75	Toyota Motor	Japan	Motor vehicles	53
7	26	Total	France	Petroleum	75
8	94	Electricité de France	France	Electricity/gas/water	35
9	78	Ford Motor Co.	USA	Motor vehicles	56
10	69	E.ON AG	Germany	Electricity/gas/water-	55

Source: Based on UNCTAD (2009) *World Investment Report*, Table Annex A1.10.

Petroleum, where 81% of its overall activity in terms of the three ratios is based abroad, and Vodafone where this figure rises as high as 89%.

If we wanted to find the companies which operate mostly outside their home country, we would have to look at the ten top multinationals in terms of the transnationality index only. These are shown in Table 13.3 and here we see the dominance of EU companies in sectors such as food/beverages, pharmaceuticals/chemicals, electrics/electronics, media and business services. The companies with the highest transnationality index are often from the smaller countries in terms of population as a more restricted domestic market creates incentives to operate abroad if they are to maximise their growth in terms of revenue or profits.

Table 13.3 World's top ten non-financial multinationals ranked by transnationality index, 2008

		Rankings			
Trans-nationality index	Foreign assets	Company	Country	Industry	Trans-nationality index (%)
1	42	Xstrata plc	UK	Mining/quarrying	94
2	63	Linde AG	Germany	Chemicals	90
3	11	ArcelorMittal	Luxembourg	Metals	89
4	90	Pernod Ricard SA	France	Food/beverages/tobacco	89
5	67	WPP Group plc	UK	Other business services	88
6	2	Vodafone	UK	Telecommunications	87
7	28	Nestle	Switzerland	Food and beverages	87
8	97	AkzoNobel	Netherlands	Pharmaceuticals	85
9	48	Nokia	Finland	Telecommunications	84
10	100	Thomson Reuters	Canada	Other business services	84

Source: Based on UNCTAD (2009) *World Investment Report*, Table, Annex A1.9.

Technical definitions of multinationals, however, fail to convey the true scope and diversity of global business, which covers everything from the thousands of medium-sized firms which have overseas operations to the truly gigantic multinationals like IBM, General Motors and Ford. Some multinationals are *vertically integrated*, with different stages of the same productive process taking place in different countries (e.g. British Petroleum). Others are *horizontally integrated*, performing the same basic production operations in each of the countries in which they operate (e.g. Marks & Spencer). Many multinationals are household names, marketing global brands (e.g. Rothmans International, IBM, British Airways). Others are holding companies for a portfolio of international companies (e.g. Diageo) or specialise in capital goods that have little name-recognition in the high street (e.g. BTR, Hawker Siddley, GKN).

How important are the multinationals?

In 2009 the United Nations Division on Transnational Corporations and Investment estimated that there are almost 82,000 multinationals, collectively controlling a total of over 810,000 foreign affiliates (subsidiaries) and employing over 77m people worldwide. Table 13.4 provides an overview of multinational activity. It shows that in 2008 the sales of multinationals' foreign affiliates (subsidiaries) exceeded the total global export of goods and services, and amounted to 50% of world gross domestic product (GDP). It also shows that foreign direct investment has grown much faster than the rate of growth of exports for much of that period.

Although not shown in Table 13.4, the gross output of the world's largest 100 MNEs alone was $6.1 trillion (i.e. $6,100bn) in 2008, accounting for around 16% of world GDP and providing employment for over 15m persons, i.e. around 12% of world employment. Ranked by either turnover or GDP, half of the world's largest economic 'units' are multinationals, rather than countries. Only 14 nation states have a GDP that exceeds the turnover of Exxon, Ford or General Motors.

Historically, the bulk of multinational activity has been concentrated in the developed world. Indeed, as recently as the mid-1980s, half of all multinational production took place in only five countries – the United States, Canada, the UK, Germany and the Netherlands. This pattern is now changing rapidly. The rapid industrialisation and economic growth in the newly industrialising nations of the world has led to a sharp increase in multinational investment in Asia and (to a lesser extent) Latin America. Some of these countries, notably the 'four tigers' (Taiwan, South Korea, Hong Kong and Singapore), now have per capita GDP levels which exceed those of most European nations and their indigenous companies are now beginning to establish production facilities in the 'old world'.

Table 13.4 **Multinational activity in a global context**

| | 2008 ($bn) | Average annual growth rates (%) | | | | | |
		1991–1995	1996–2000	2005	2006	2007	2008
FDI outflows	1,858	16.5	35.6	−5.4	58.9	53.7	−13.5
FDI outward stock	16,206	10.6	16.9	5.1	22.2	25.3	−0.1
Sales of foreign affiliates	30,311	8.8	8.1	5.4	18.9	23.6	−4.6
World GDP at current prices	60,780	5.9	1.3	8.4	8.2	12.5	10.3
World gross fixed capital formation	13,824	5.4	1.1	11.8	10.9	13.8	11.5
Exports of goods and non-factor services	19,990	7.9	3.7	13.8	15.0	16.3	15.4

Source: Based on UNCTAD (2009) *World Investment Report*, Table 1.6.

Make a note

The so-called 'triad' of North America, the European Union and the Pacific Rim economies of East and South East Asia account for approximately 80% of the world's exports and 84% of world manufacturing output and almost all multinational activity. We consider these three key regions for international business separately at the end of the chapter.

International human resource management (IHRM)

When conducting international business, firms will also need to integrate the domestic HRM approaches considered in Chapter 12 (p. 394) into their international operations. How they do this will depend on the approach they adopt as regards HRM policies.

Approaches to IHRM

Four approaches have been identified to describe the ways in which MNEs might conduct their international HRM policies.

- *The ethnocentric approach.* In the ethnocentric approach, all key positions in the host country subsidiary are filled by nationals of the parent company. This approach offers the most direct control by the parent company over the host country subsidiary, and is often adopted when there is felt to be a need to maintain good communications between the headquarters of the MNE and the subsidiary. This ethnocentric approach is often followed in the early stages of internationalisation when the MNE is seeking to establish a new business or product in another country.

- *The polycentric approach.* Here, host country nationals are recruited to manage the subsidiaries in their own country. This allows the MNE to take a lower profile in sensitive economic and political situations and helps to avoid intercultural management problems.

- *The geocentric approach.* This approach utilises the best people for all the key jobs throughout the organisation, whatever their nationality or whatever the geographical location of the post to be filled. In this way an international executive team can be developed.

- *The regiocentric approach.* Here the MNE divides its operations into geographic regions and moves staff *within* particular regions, e.g. Europe, America, Asia rather than between regions.

Choices between these different approaches will depend on the culture, philosophy and the local conditions in which the firm operates. Some international companies may adopt an ethnocentric approach in some countries and a polycentric approach in others. However, a key element in this choice will involve the question as to how an international firm can manage a dispersed and diverse workforce responsively and effectively, retaining a measure of overall cohesion while being sensitive to local conditions.

Stop and think   13.2

Choose a company that follows an ethnocentric approach. Analyse the appropriateness of this method, making suggestions as to why you agree or disagree with their chosen management orientation.

Case Study 13.2 looks further at IHRM issues using Hofstede's cultural dimensions (p. 428) to inform the running of overseas subsidiaries.

Case Study 13.2   IHRM and cultural characteristics

While the global nature of multinational activity may call for increased consistency, the variety of cultural environments in which the MNE operates may call for differentiation. Workplace values and behaviours are widely regarded as being influenced by national as well as corporate cultural characteristics. As Laurent (1986) claims,

> 'if we accept the view that human resource management (HRM) approaches are cultural artefacts reflecting the basic assumptions and values of the national culture in which organisations are embedded, international HRM becomes one of the most challenging corporate tasks in multinational organisations'.

Greece is clustered in the 'Mediterranean culture' sector of managerial models, with native managers assumed to be less individualistic and more comfortable with highly bureaucratic organisational structures in order to achieve their objectives. In Hofstede's terms Greece is characterised by large power distance and strong uncertainty avoidance (see Figure 13.4, p. 428). Since the early 1960s, Greece has been the host country for many foreign firms, initially in manufacturing and more recently in services.

It is broadly accepted that management practices which reinforce national cultural values are more likely to yield better outcomes in terms of performance, with a mismatch between work unit management practices and national culture likely to reduce performance (Newman and Nollen, 1996). The suggestion here is that multinational firms, which have established their affiliates in Greece, will be more efficient if their management practices are better adapted to the national culture of Greece. Theory suggests that this adaptation will be better achieved where the national culture

of the home country of the MNE is close to that of Greece. In other words, MNEs from collectivist, large power distance and strong uncertainty avoidance countries will be at a *small cultural distance* from Greece and will better integrate into the organisational culture of the Greek affiliate. The following hypothesis is therefore suggested by Kessapidou and Varsakelis (2000).

Hypothesis: MNEs from home countries at a *large cultural distance* from Greece will prefer to employ local managers and permit more decentralised IHRM practices.

This hypothesis would then predict that MNEs from home countries with national cultural characteristics of the individualist, small power distance and weak uncertainty avoidance variety (i.e. the opposites to Greece) will prefer to employ local managers and permit more decentralised IHRM practices.

In their analysis of the operations of 485 foreign affiliates in Greece over the years 1994–96, Kessapidou and Varsakelis found considerable evidence to support this hypothesis. MNEs from home countries at a large cultural distance from Greece (e.g. UK, Netherlands, US with cultural distance factors 4.27, 4.03 and 3.47 respectively) were much more likely to employ local managers and adopt a decentralised approach to IHRM than countries at a small cultural distance from Greece (e.g. Italy, France and Spain with cultural distance factors 1.46, 0.99 and 0.58 respectively).

Source: Adapted from Kessapidou, S. and Varsakelis, N. (2000)

Question

What relevance does this case study have for IHRM aspects of multinational firm activity?

Organisational culture and IHRM

The issue of organisational 'culture' is touched on in a recent book, *Who Says Elephants Can't Dance* by Louis Gerstner, the managing director of IBM, who places particular emphasis on organisational culture in IHRM issues and ultimately in business success. Faced with huge losses in the early 1990s, Gerstner embarked on a challenging strategy to change IBM from a (*multidomestic*) company selling IBM products only via national sub-sidiaries (e.g. IBM France) to a *global company* selling solutions to problems and packaging the most appropriate products and services (even if some are non-IBM) to meet the individual needs of customers. To meet this need for 'culture change' at IBM a whole raft of IHRM practices were established. For example, IBM established incentive systems for its employees whereby their bonuses depended less on selling IBM products and more on meeting goals within the customer service sphere. Again, education and training packages were designed to give IBM sales personnel expertise across a wide range of computer functions so that they would be able to devise multi-functional solutions incorporating hardware and software elements.

Developing cross-cultural awareness

Taking the issue of national cultural attributes in IHRM issues further can be important for the organisation, as suggested in a recent report by *ER Consultants* at Cambridge. Cross-cultural awareness at an individual level may be developed through formal systems such as induction training and team building or informally in a discussion over lunch or through a mentoring relationship. Running training sessions on cross-cultural differences for delegates from different countries can also be effective. Some of the key issues include the openness of communication, style of management and, above all, how to motivate people in different parts of the world so that they felt part of the same organisation.

At an organisational level there are a number of cultural factors which are integral to the structures of organisations that can effect the perception of information and communication. These can be mapped on a number of different dimensions, but perhaps the most well known and important are the dimensions developed by Geert Hofstede. As already noted (p. 428) one of the dimensions he identified was that between Individualism and Collectivism, which refers to the extent to which people prefer to take care of themselves and their immediate families, remaining emotionally independent from groups and organisations. For example, he placed the US, Australia and England towards the 'Individualist' end of the spectrum but Columbia, Venezuela and Equador towards the 'Collectivist' end of the spectrum.

Within a highly individualistic country, autonomy is more important than in highly collectivist countries where security is more important. In individualist countries, specific friendships are more important than being part of an 'in group'. The different dimensions have a number of practical implications in areas ranging from understanding the structure of organisations and how to get things to happen through to implementing processes that will be effective across different cultures, e.g. competency frameworks, surveys etc.

It can be useful to be aware of cross-cultural behaviour patterns. How do you say to someone at work that:

- Their lack of eye contact is making you suspicious of them (English perception of Asian behaviour).
- They should say hello to each individual person in the office, not everyone at once because it is rude (French perception of English behaviour).
- A weak handshake is a sign of a weak character (American perception of English behaviour).
- You can actually mean no (Japanese understanding of language).

The essence of good cross-cultural communication is to ensure that such differences are not viewed as negative behaviours. It is only by raising awareness of these differences explicitly that we can begin to tackle such misunderstandings.

International marketing

This is concerned with marketing arising in the course of managing the firm's international operations and takes further the marketing strategies already discussed in a more domestic context in Chapter 12 (p. 38). Challenges in international marketing include: unstable governments, difficulty in combating intellectual property right infringements, corruption, foreign exchange problems, tariffs and trade barriers and understanding cultural differences.

Many brand names do not travel well. There are many examples of companies that have adopted a standardised approach to their branding, but have not researched the implications of translation when launching a brand into another country. For example, Coca-Cola when they first launched in China realised the name translated as 'bite the wax tadpole'. Fortunately, Esteé Lauder was quick to notice their proposed export of Country Mist makeup to Germany could experience problems. This is because 'mist' in Germany is slang for 'manure'. Subsequently the product became Country Moist in Germany.

Very often brand names are changed in order to follow a standardisation strategy. For example, in the UK the following products have changed names to fall in line with the same product in other countries: Starburst (formerly Opal Fruits), Cif (formerly Jif) and Snickers (formerly Marathon). Mars (the manufacturers of Snickers and Starburst) decided the sweets should be called the same name in the UK as they are in the rest of the world. Reasons for having one universal brand name can be attributed to cost savings by producing a single global advertising and marketing campaign for all countries. Also, with increased travel, consumers are able to recognise a brand abroad. Usually companies adopt expensive advertising campaigns advising of the name change. This needs to be done in a positive way to ensure the brand image maintains its current position in the mind of the consumer.

Steps in international marketing

We now consider each of the following steps in international marketing.

1 Examine the international environment.

2 Should we go international?

3 Which markets to enter?

4 How to enter?

5 Type of marketing programme?

Examine the international environment

Before entering a new marketplace extensive research needs to be carried out on the international environmental issues facing the company. For example, the number of competitors, state of the economy, is there a market for our product or services? What do potential customers think about us? A firm may produce a short list of potential international markets. The factors for selecting an international market are many, but ultimately depend on the potential demand from consumers and the extent of the competition.

The approach to market research in a national (UK) setting has already been considered in Chapter 12 (p. 381). Key factors in undertaking international market research include:

1 Understand the macro-environment (e.g. GNP, demographic changes, inflation, exchange rates etc.).

Check the net

Material on global marketing and segmentation strategies can be obtained from:
www.marketingweek.co.uk
www.globalweb.co.uk

2 Understand the micro-environment (e.g. firm sizes, productivities, cost structures, competitor reactions, consumer behaviour, distribution channels available etc.).

3 Understand cultural differences.

4 Determine who is going to undertake the research.

Should we go international?

If the firm does decide to go international it may be because of any one or more of the following factors.

● *Increasing the size of the market.* Developing new markets abroad may permit the firm to fully exploit scale economies, particularly important when these are substantial for that product. In some cases the minimum efficient size for a firm's production may be greater than the total sales potential of the domestic market. In this case the firm's average costs can only be reduced to their lowest level by finding extra sales in overseas markets.

● *Extending the product life cycle.* Finding new markets abroad may help extend the maturity stage of the product life cycle. This can be particularly important when domestic markets have reached 'saturation point' for a product.

● *Supporting international specialisation.* In an attempt to reduce overall production costs, separate elements of an overall product may be produced in large scale in different geographical locations worldwide. For example, labour-intensive components will often be produced in low-cost labour locations, whereas capital-intensive components are more likely to be produced in high technology locations. The final product, once assembled, must by definition be marketed internationally to achieve the huge sales volumes which are a prerequisite for international specialisation.

● *Helping reduce investment pay-back periods.* Finding overseas markets helps achieve high-volume sales early in the product life cycle, thereby reducing the pay-back period needed to return the initial capital outlay and making many investment projects more attractive. This may help to compensate for modern trends towards shorter product life cycles which are tending to inhibit investment expenditure.

● *Reducing stock-holding costs.* Overseas markets may provide new sales outlets for surplus stocks (inventories), thereby reducing warehousing and other stock-holding costs.

Which markets to enter and what market entry method to adopt?

A decision must eventually be made as to which market(s) to enter. A company will hope the extensive research will indicate in which overseas market they are most likely to achieve their objectives through internationalisation. We have already noted the attraction of entering countries at close geographical and cultural proximity to the country in which the firm has begun operations.

As already discussed earlier (pp. 419–423) the type of market entry method selected will depend in part on the risk–reward perception that the firm has of the different methods of internationalisation. It also depends on the stage the firm has already reached in the internationalisation process (Table 13.1, p. 419). Many firms often prefer to adopt an exporting method as the lowest-risk entry strategy, but also because it may be appropriate when first entering a complex market. The relative merits of the more committed international market entry methods such as licensing, franchising, joint ventures and foreign direct investment must obviously be assessed here.

Type of marketing programme?

A firm may need to rethink its marketing strategy when entering an international market. The product may be positioned differently in the international market, requiring a different approach to promotional activity. For example, the Belgian beer Stella Artois is positioned as a premium-priced lager in the UK, while in Belgium it is marketed as a cheaper alcoholic beverage. There may be stricter legislation in the international market concerning advertising. In fact, the firm will need to revisit any marketing approach it has adopted in the domestic market and consider an appropriate *international marketing mix*. After reviewing the international marketing situation facing IKEA, we return to the possible components of the international marketing mix in the next section.

Case Study 13.3 provides a useful example of international marketing issues using IKEA.

Case Study 13.3   'IKEA – flat pack success!'

IKEA continues to be a global phenomenon. Ingvar Kamprad founded IKEA in 1943. Today, Inter IKEA Systems B.V. is now the owner and franchiser of the IKEA concept. All IKEA stores operate on a franchise basis. IKEA of Sweden AB is responsible for the IKEA product range; making sure all IKEA products are endorsed 'Design and Quality, IKEA of Sweden'. The IKEA Group is owned by a charitable foundation in the Netherlands.

IKEA introduced its first store in the UK in 1987. Competition comes from MFI, Texas, B&Q and small and medium-sized mail-order firms. IKEA's competitors vary from country to country, although no other furniture company in the UK operates with the same global success.

In 2009 IKEA had 301 stores in 37 countries. The IKEA Group itself owns 267 stores in 25 countries while the rest are owned and run by franchises. The company employs 123,000 people worldwide and has 1,220 suppliers in 55 countries which help supply its range of 9,500 products. Its sales for the financial year 2009 totalled €21.5bn (£13.7bn). A breakdown of some basic facts about IKEA can be seen in Table 13.5.

Table 13.5 Distribution of IKEA sales, purchasing and workforce, 2009 (%)

	Sales (%)	Purchasing (%)	Workforce (%)
Europe	80	67	81
North America	15	3	13
Asia/Australia	5	30	6

Source: www.ikea.com, © Inter Ikea Systems BV

IKEA generates over 75% of its turnover from international business. However, the firm does as little as possible to tailor its ranges to local tastes, preferring to opt for a standardisation approach. IKEA in Beijing, China, has the same concept, branding, and many product ranges as IKEA Lakeside (UK). To many customers, part of IKEA's appeal is its Swedishness.

As can be seen, IKEA sales to Europe comprise 80% of its total sales and 81% of its workforce are based in Europe. However, nearly a third of the purchasing from suppliers takes place in Asia/Australia. The company has 31 Trading Service Offices in 26 countries dealing with purchasing and whose job it is to monitor production quality and test any new ideas from the suppliers.

IKEA is renowned for its innovative Swedish-designed furniture. The profile of its 9,500-product range is well-designed, high quality at low prices. The firm's mission is 'we shall offer a wide range of well-designed, functional home furnishing products at prices so low that as many people as possible will be able to afford them'. IKEA provides a comfortable environment for its customers, with mock room settings so that they can see products in context. These include books in bookcases, lamps on tables and fake fruit in fruit bowls! Many IKEA stores offer a home decoration service if customers wish to furnish an entire room or home, and a kitchen planning service. Using computer simulations, specially trained kitchen planners can help plan and choose a person's ideal kitchen. The company provides free pencils and tape measures for making notes and checking dimensions. Amenities include a restaurant, Swedish food shop, children's play area and hotdog stall. Customers are able to self-select the products they want from pallets in the company's warehouse, and then take these to the checkout for payment.

A strong selling point to many people is the fact most of the products are flat packed, making it easier for the buyer to transport. By providing products in this format, IKEA is able to reduce its costs in relation to manufacturing and distribution. The company provides home delivery for larger items, although this is not included in the product price. Items are easy to assemble, and the tools required for assembly are sold with the furniture. IKEA produces a catalogue of its product range, which is available in store free of charge. In January 2009 the UK's first BoKlok flatpack home was unveiled in Gateshead with prices starting at £132,500. These were energy efficient 'flatpack' wood framed homes of Scandinavian design which IKEA developed in conjunction with the Swedish construction company, Skanska. The first BoKlok town houses were launched in Germany in April 2010 at prices starting at €99,500. In the same year some 4,000 BoKlok houses had already been built in Sweden, Norway, Denmark, Finland and the UK.

The company is mainly a business-to-consumer (B2C) organisation and therefore offers no trade discount for organisational purchasers. In order to portray a customer-orientated approach, all employees wear staff uniform, and certain stores in the UK are now open until 10 pm weekdays to meet consumer demand for late-night shopping. This is promoted locally with outdoor advertising, while TV advertising continues to promote brand awareness. Stores are large, warehouse-style complexes located out of town. An example in the UK is the store based at Lakeside Retail Park in Essex.

The company has ongoing environmental action plans, as indicated in its yearly Social and Environmental Responsibilities Report. These reports tend to concentrate on environmental improvements within five areas: products and materials, forestry, environmental work at suppliers, goods transport and environmental work at the stores. A Waste Management Manual for the IKEA Group is established. It means that all stores must, as a minimum requirement, sort the five most common fractions of their waste. This ensures that 75% of a store's waste is reused, recycled or used for energy production. In 2008, for example, the proportion of renewable materials used in the production of its products rose to 72%, with a target of 75% by the end of 2009. Similarly, the percentage of waste recycled, reclaimed or used in energy production in its stores and distribution centres reached 85% in 2008. It also has IWAY, which is the 'IKEA way' of purchasing home furnishing products from suppliers and is based on a code of conduct which incorporates international conventions on relationships between IKEA and its suppliers. For example, in 2008 IKEA terminated the contracts of 48 suppliers for failure to comply with its standards etc.

In order to avoid contributing to the devastation of intact natural forests in need of protection, trees from these forests are not used for the manufacture of its solid wood products. Each store has its own environmental coordinator whose job includes organising and carrying out environmental training for the store's co-workers. The aim of this training is to give people an insight into, an understanding of, and information about the environment in general and environmental work within the IKEA Group. Also included in the Environmental Action Plans is making the stores' energy consumption as efficient as possible. Methods used are energy-efficient lighting, tests with alternative energy systems such as solar power, geothermal energy and energy from underground aquifers. Up to 90% of the waste from IKEA stores worldwide goes to specialist companies for recycling, which is currently being introduced as a comprehensive waste-sorting programme.

IKEA works closely with both suppliers and packaging manufacturers to develop sensible packaging that offers effective, environmentally friendly solutions. The aim is to use a single material to make recycling easier. Most IKEA packaging consists of what is probably the most environmentally friendly material of them all, corrugated cardboard with a high content of recycled material. By measuring and monitoring the environmental impact of its transport activities, IKEA hopes to be able to improve the systems it uses to assess the environmental work of the freight companies it works with. This will encourage distributors to continue with their own environmental

Case Study 13.3 *continued*

improvement initiatives, at the same time as it makes it easier for IKEA to select the right freight company. IKEA decided in 2007 to switch its entire UK company car fleet to hybrid vehicles as soon as possible by replacing its Skoda cars with Honda Civic Hybrids. By 2010 all IKEA company cars were to meet the EU carbon dioxide emissions target of 120 grams of carbon dioxide per kilometre driven.

In 2010 approximately 1,450 IKEA suppliers in 55 countries manufacture the products that are marketed and sold in the IKEA catalogues and via the IKEA stores. A large proportion of IKEA products come from suppliers in countries where environmental work is, on the whole, well developed, but the firm also purchases products from countries where environmental work is less developed.

IKEA currently employs the advertising agency St Luke's for its UK advertising campaigns. Until 1995 IKEA was promoted through tactical campaigns in the UK, which focused on price and range. St Luke's won the highly competitive pitch for this project on the premise that further growth for IKEA in the UK could not be achieved without tackling the British preference for traditional furniture. By breaking this taboo area for advertisers, with the 'Chuck out the Chintz' campaign, the agency fuelled a cultural shift in favour of more modern tastes. The chintz campaign generated an unusual amount of media attention in the months following its launch. Shortly after this campaign came an even more irreverent and tongue-in-cheek series of ads, highlighting the correlation between people's taste in furniture and their habits or lifestyles. Based on genuine market research, the furniture findings campaign went out on posters and TV nationally and stimulated a media debate about contemporary tastes in the UK. Likewise, in an attempt to encourage IKEA customers to be more individualistic and to use more bold colours, St Luke's designed a 'be brave, not beige' campaign in 2009.

Like all multinationals, IKEA does not always receive positive promotion. For example, IKEA has a complicated corporate structure whereby profits can be channelled through a non-profit foundation, the INGKA Foundation, which can tend to reduce IKEA's tax burden. In 2007 the Berne declaration, a non-profit organisation that promotes corporate responsibility, formally criticised IKEA for its tax-avoidance strategies. In addition, IKEA still refused in 2010 to sign up to the industry standard international 'Rugmark' which guarantees that child labour has not been used in the manufacture of its products. This policy continues even though over a decade previously the company was criticised in a TV documentary for continuing to exploit child labour in the Philippines and Vietnam.

Source: Adapted from **www.ikea.com**, © Inter Ikea Systems BV. Reprinted with permission

Questions

1 Conduct an environmental analysis of the company.

2 Discuss a suitable market entry method for IKEA entering South Korea.

3 Select one of IKEA's main competitors and discuss what steps they can take in order to try to compete with IKEA.

International marketing mix

In order for a firm to compete successfully in an international market we have noted that it will need to consider the extent to which the *domestic marketing mix* needs to be adapted. We now consider each of the four 'Ps' in turn from a more international perspective.

Promotion

International marketing communications (IMC) is a broad term often used in this context and consists of advertising, personal selling, direct marketing, trade shows, public relations and sales promotion. Certainly advertising tends to be the favoured method for international marketers in consumer marketing, while personal selling is widely used by international business-to-business marketers as the main form of communication. However, the promotional elements selected will depend on the international target market.

● *What is the technological infrastructure of the country?* This will influence the prospects for reaching the final consumer. For example, in most industrialised countries over 90% of households own a TV, but this is often only a minority in the developing countries. If using direct selling by telesales, what proportion of the target market in that country possesses a telephone? If planning a poster campaign, what are the panel sizes available in different countries? Panel sizes are different, for example, in France and the UK, which can be important given the high costs of preparing and printing panels of varying sizes.

● *What appeals culturally in the advertisement?* English advertisements quite frequently use humour, French ones use erotic imagery, while in Germany the advertisements tend to be very factual. Great attention therefore needs to be paid to style and content in terms of the cultural impact of the campaign. If using direct selling, what type of sales force will be acceptable? For example, should we use local salespeople, an expatriate sales force or nationals from third countries?

Example

Culture, humour and advertising strategy

Many pan-European advertising campaigns have failed to deliver because of lack of research into how cultural differences may impact the viewer's response to the advertising. For example, an advert for slimming pills showing an overweight person on the left, pointing to slimming pills in the middle, pointing to a slim person on the right is appropriate if the advert runs in a country where the population reads from left to right. However, if the advert were to go out in Japan (where the population read from right to left), this would translate as: eat slimming pills to gain weight!

It is worth remembering that different cultures have different types of humour. Something that may appear humorous to a UK audience may not necessarily have the same affect in Germany. Also, special attention needs to be paid to the use of celebrities in advertising. First, for the purpose of a pan-European campaign, the celebrity should be known throughout Europe. Second, they should carry a positive reputation, encouraging people to buy the product. Third, ideally there should be a certain amount of synergy between the celebrity and the product, e.g. David Beckham advertising Adidas sports wear. David Beckham is certainly well known throughout Europe, and now in the USA with his 2007 move from Real Madrid.

Stop and think   13.3

Find your own example of a product that has not travelled well when entering a new market. Discuss what steps the firm could have taken in order to overcome the problem of cultural differences.

● *What are the regulations on advertising in this particular country?* The UK, Belgium, the Netherlands and Denmark ban TV commercials for tobacco products but allow press adverts. In the UK any advertisement for tobacco products must carry a health warning.

Sweden bans the advertising of 'junk food' to children whereas the UK does not, despite the Food Commission in the UK reporting that during 39 hours of TV viewing for children, there were some 18 adverts per hour, almost half of which involved food items high in sugar, salt and saturated fat. Are there any legal restrictions on the use of direct marketing (such as the use of information stored on computer databases)? Are there any legal restrictions on sales promotions? (Some countries do not allow certain types of free offers to be made; for example, money-off coupons are not allowed in Norway.) Are there any restrictions on comparative advertising?

Example

Comparative advertising in the Thai shampoo market

Unilever and Procter & Gamble are taking their global battle against dandruff to the Thai courts. The global giants, responsible for the majority of leading brands found in supermarkets, have been questioning the effectiveness of each other's product in a country where direct comparative advertising is rarely used. Unilever sought an emergency court injunction to stop P&G broadcasting a Head & Shoulders advertisement that the Anglo-Dutch company says 'intends to attack' Clinic Clear, the leading brand in Thailand's Bt2bn (US$49m) anti-dandruff shampoo market. Unilever also wants Bt471m from P&G for damage to Clinic Clear's reputation. P&G countered with a lawsuit this week demanding Bt750m in damages for a subsequent Unilever advertisement that claimed Clinic Clear is 'three times more effective' than Head & Shoulders. Orapin Milindasuta, managing director of P&G Thailand, said in a statement that she was 'appalled by the directness and viciousness' of Unilever's offensive against Head & Shoulders. But Chutharat Thanapaisarnkit, managing director of Ogilvy Public Relations, said Unilever had no choice but to 'protect the brand' after P&G's 'aggressive' campaign. 'We claim an eye for an eye,' Ms Chutharat said.

- *What are the different media habits of the country?* For example, the current circulation figures per 1,000 of population of women's weekly magazines is around 29 in Germany, compared to 15 for the UK and 5 for Spain. Similar figures for TV guides are 37 for Germany, 10 for the UK and 7 for Spain.

- *What type of packaging do we use to retain the brand image yet meet country requirements* (e.g. ecological requirements demanded in Germany)? Do we need special types of labels? How much information needs to be presented about the content of the product?

We can see from these questions that international promotion is not an easy proposition. It requires an intimate knowledge of the market in each country. Indeed it is quite likely that relationship marketing and personal selling are more important in collectivist societies such as Japan and China, since there is greater emphasis on networking and long-term relationships. Public relations (PR), on the other hand, can help to overcome advertising difficulties. PR is a favoured form of promotion for tobacco companies in many countries, in order to overcome the tight restrictions regarding the advertising of cigarettes. Personal selling may be used to help overcome direct marketing problems; for example, it may be difficult to gather effective data for direct marketing in some countries as government legislation restricts access to such data. Case Study 13.4 provides some useful insights into promotional, branding and other aspects of the international marketing mix in an Indian context.

Case Study 13.4   Perils of blundering into India's cultural minefield

Montblanc's Rs 1.1m, 18-carat gold-and-silver Mahatma Gandhi fountain pen was conceived as a way to raise the brand's connection to India as the country's fast-growing luxury market expands. Instead, the company's commemoration of the man Indians revere as Father of the Nation ended when it was forced in February 2010 to make a humiliating court apology and suspend sales of the hand-crafted writing instruments in India.

The fiasco was a stark warning of the potential perils of marketing luxury in India, a country still divided between the values of the austerity that defined its anti-colonial struggle and socialist-oriented, early independence years and its elite's pursuit of the good life, as part of economic liberalisation.

'You have to be careful in terms of how you try to associate yourself with India, with Indian figures and Indian customs,' says Radha Chada, author of *The Cult of the Luxury Brand: Inside Asia's Love Affair with Luxury*. 'You have to be sensitive about the local culture.'

Montblanc, which has also made a serious pitch to break into the high-end watch industry, opened its first store in India in 1997 and now has 16 outlets, including a jewellery store in Mumbai. It launched its Mahatma Gandhi limited edition pen last September, just before the national holiday honouring the independence leader's birthday.

The first limited edition fountain pen designed specifically for India was unveiled in a blaze of publicity, with full-page advertisements in glossy magazines and massive billboards.

In designing the pen, Montblanc tried to pay homage to the symbolic vocabulary, including the austere asceticism, that Gandhi used in his successful efforts to mobilise the Indian public against British colonial rule in the first half of the twentieth century.

Throughout the independence struggle, he was obsessive about hand-spinning thread – an activity he both engaged in regularly and actively promoted as a powerful assertion of self-reliance among Indians previously dependent on imported English cloth. Gandhi encouraged Indians to burn their imported clothes in favour of rough, homespun cotton.

For its 241 limited edition Gandhi pens – which boasted an 18-carat solid gold, rhodium-plated nib engraved with Gandhi's image and a saffron-coloured mandarin garnet on the clip, Montblanc had the sterling silver cap-and-cone shaped like 'roughly-wound yarn on a spindle', while the white lacquered surface was textured to evoke hand-made cotton fabric, with six metres of gold wire woven around it.

Yet to many Indians, the use of gold and silver to evoke humble homespun cloth, widely known as *khadi*, for a Rs 1.1m pen seemed absurd, especially given Gandhi's asceticism and renunciation of material possessions.

'The contradiction came in using a figure who embodied frugal living and making it stand for exactly the opposite,' says Ms Chadha, who has a luxury strategy consultancy. 'That is where the extreme tension came.' The *Economic Times*, India's biggest business daily, scoffed at 'the irony of designing a writing implement that costs as much as an apartment and naming it after a legendary byword for simplicity'.

But Montblanc's problems were not simply a question of taste. India's Emblems and Names (Prevention of Improper Use) Act, 1950 bans the use of the name or pictorial representations of several figures – including Gandhi, and the first post-independence Prime Minister Jawaharlal Nehru – without permission of the central government.

The Centre for Consumer Education in the southern state of Kerala filed a case in the Kerala High Court, accusing Montblanc of violating the emblems act. In February 2010 Montblanc and its Indian distributor offered the court an unconditional apology and suspended sales of the pens in India.

Source: from Perils of blundering into India's Cultural minefield, *Financial Times*, 19/03/2010 (Kazmin, A.), © The Financial Times Ltd.

Questions

1 What cultural marketing issues are raised by this case study?

2 How might Montblanc more effectively market its luxury fountain pen in India?

Price

The price element of the marketing mix was covered in Chapter 12, p. 388. However, these pricing strategies may need to be adapted to the international market. For example, the Belgium lager Stella Artois is positioned as a low-price value brand in Belgium, but a high-price premium brand in the UK.

Price in any marketing context is governed by competition, production costs and company objectives. International pricing decisions will reflect these aspects and will also need to take into account market differences between countries, exchange rates, difficulties of invoicing and collecting payment across borders, the effects of tariffs and purchase taxes on competitiveness, governmental regulations of the host country and the long-term strategic plan of the company in the different markets in which it operates.

Listed below are some of the major issues faced by those setting prices in different countries.

- **Market differences.** Clearly, some overseas markets are more attractive for a particular product than others in terms of population size, standard of living (e.g. real GNP per head), age profile, purchasing patterns etc.
  - *High income markets.* Clearly, international markets with a higher real income per head have a greater 'willingness to pay' and therefore the firm may seek a higher price in such markets.
  - *Low competition markets.* Some international markets have fewer local competitors providing substitute products. The firm may seek a higher price in such markets.
  - *Separated international markets with different price elasticities.* Of particular interest in terms of international price setting is the possibility and profitability of setting different prices in different geographical markets. When the same product is priced higher in one (international) market than another, this is termed *price discrimination*.
  - For this to be *possible*, there must be barriers preventing resale in another country at the higher price (transport costs, tariff barriers etc.).
- **Longer channels of distribution.** Costs of transporting products and associated insurance are just two factors that help to contribute to the final price of a product. In reality, the longer the channel of distribution, the higher the price likely to be charged for a traded product. Imported products tend to be more expensive than locally made products partly because they pass through a larger number of intermediaries. Many firms are now looking at shortening the channel of distribution by using the Internet to target customers, with any savings made passed on to the customer as a lower price.
- **High proportion of target audience in country.** The target audience has a direct impact on pricing. If the country has a high proportion of the target audience in its population, then the firm may be able to charge a higher price.
- **Exchange rates.** When exchange rates fluctuate this can change the potential profitability of international contracts. For example, marketers must be alert as to any potential movements in the exchange rate between the date of quotation/invoicing and the date of payment so that the profit margin is not eroded. Price may have to be adjusted to cover adverse exchange rate movements. To reduce the impact of such problems currencies may be purchased on futures markets, or products may be priced in 'harder', more stable currencies. Of course, when both parties have a single currency, such as the euro, these problems will be avoided.
- **Cross-border payments.** In contracts for internationally traded products it is important to specify exactly what a price covers. For example, does it cover cost, insurance and freight?
- **Tariffs and other taxes.** Increases in *tariffs* (purchase taxes) on overseas sales can force a firm to raise the quoted price of its exports in order to retain its profit margin.

Whether it will be able to pass these taxes on to the consumer as a higher price will, of course, depend on the price elasticity of demand for the product. The *less* price elastic the demand, the more of any tax increase can be passed on to the overseas consumer (see Chapter 2, p. 50). Tariffs and taxes can have other impacts on trade issues. In an attempt to avoid such tariffs (and sometimes to overcome currency problems) there has been a growth in *countertrade*, namely the barter of goods and services between countries. Some 5% of all international trade has been estimated as being of this type. Further, any increases (or differences between countries) in *profit-related taxes* (e.g. corporation tax) can result in MNEs adopting a policy of 'transfer pricing'. Here firms sell products on to subsidiaries within another country at prices which bear little relation to the true costs incurred at that stage of the overall production process.

- **Government regulations**. As well as taxes, overseas governments may influence the firm's price-setting policies by regulations, perhaps setting maximum or minimum prices of products or minimum quality standards for particular products.

- **Strategic objectives**. Overseas price setting may, of course, be influenced by the strategic objectives of the firm. For example, where market share or revenue maximisation is a primary objective then prices will tend to be lower (e.g. penetration pricing) than they might be under, say, a profit-maximising objective.

Product

A key issue in marketing is the extent to which a standard or differentiated product should be provided.

Standardised or differentiated?

There are good business reasons for trying to make a *standard product* acceptable to as many customers as possible – for example, it can help reduce average costs in design, production, promotion and distribution. Theodore Levitt of the Harvard Business School contends that tastes and preferences in many cultures are becoming more homogeneous due to the increased frequency of world travel and improved worldwide telecommunications. He claims that when marketers appreciate the fact that consumers share basic interests they can market the same product worldwide and achieve economies of scale. A global marketing strategy is one that maintains a single marketing plan across all countries and yields global name recognition. Coca-Cola and McDonald's are examples of companies that use a global approach to market their products in different countries.

As sports enthusiasts will be aware, the 'Beckham brand' is of huge value in marketing terms and has itself become the focus of repositioning and brand extension strategies. For example, in July 2003 plans were announced to turn the entire Beckham family from a primarily UK brand into a global brand. The Beckhams formed a 'joint venture' with Simon Fuller, creator of Pop Idol, who created opportunities for the Beckham brand extending from product endorsement to television shows, mobile phone video clips to fashion boutiques, with the ultimate aim of establishing the couple in Hollywood. 'The Beckham brand is about aspiration and family values, the couple who came from nothing to achieve their dreams,' said Mr Fuller.

Even when arguments for standardisation are strong, those who follow this path may still make subtle variations – for example, McDonald's uses chilli sauce in Mexico instead of ketchup, while in India it serves the 'Maharaja Mac' which features two mutton patties. The motto 'Think global, and act local' symbolises a patterned standardisation strategy which involves developing global product-related marketing strategies while allowing for a degree of adaptation to local market conditions. Some product types would appear more suitable for standardisation than others. Office and industrial equipment, toys, computer games, sporting goods, soft drinks are usually standardised across national borders.

On the other hand, arguments can also be advanced in favour of *product differentiation*. Where international market segments differ from one another, even when some group characteristics are held in common, then a more differentiated product strategy may be advisable. For example, if high income households in Spain display different wants and needs from high income households in Germany, then products may have to be adapted in an attempt to sell to both groups of consumers simultaneously. Where products are highly culturally conditioned (as with many types of food, some types of drink, clothing etc.), differentiated products and marketing strategies are commonplace.

As most companies are looking for some standardisation, they will often use a *modular product design* that allows the company to adapt to local needs while still achieving economies of scale. Carmakers are beginning to adopt this form of production, with a basic body shape forming the shell around which different features are built (e.g. windscreen designs, sun roofs etc.).

Place

Again, at the international level new aspects need to be considered as regards 'place', e.g. the distributional channel selected. Four main types of channel are commonly identified.

● *Direct system*: no intermediaries involved, with orders sent directly from a factory or warehouse in the home country to the overseas purchaser.
● *Transit system*: exports sent to a transit (or 'satellite') warehouse/depot in another country. This then acts as a 'break bulk' point, with some items despatched in bulk over long distances and others in smaller units to more local destinations.
● *Classical system*: here each foreign country has its own separate warehouse/depot. Exports are sent to these and then distributed within that national market. Such warehouses/depots both 'break bulk' and perform a stockholding function, with nationals of that country being served by locally held inventories.
● *Multicountry system*: as for the classical system, except that the separate warehouses/depots may serve several adjoining countries rather than one country only.

Choice of distributional channel

In practice, a few key factors will determine the choice of distributional channel:

● *foreign customer base*: the direct system is more likely to be used where a small number of large overseas purchasers are involved;
● *export volumes*: the use of 'break-bulk' or stockholding warehouses/depots will only be economically viable when export volumes exceed certain 'threshold' levels;
● *value density of product*: those products with a high ratio of value to weight/volume (i.e. high value density) are more suited to direct systems since they can more easily absorb the higher associated transport costs;
● *order lead times*: where direct systems are inappropriate (e.g. low value density) yet customers required rapid and reliable delivery, stock may have to be held locally (i.e. classical or multi-country systems).

Recent evidence suggests a rise in *direct, transit* and *multicountry systems*. The rise of e-commerce is increasing direct systems use with international and personalised delivery via parcel networks (e.g. 'just for you', J4U delivery). Transit and multi-country systems have also been increasing, with many MNEs consolidating warehousing in a few large 'pan-European' distribution centres. Sony, Rank Xerox, Philips, Kellogg's, Nike and IBM have moved in this direction and away from the classical system previously adopted. Some of these choices of distribution channels may be influenced by opportunities for 'economies of scope'.

You try 13.2 provides an opportunity for you to check your understanding of various aspects of international marketing.

You try   13.2

1   Here you'll see a description of a particular situation. Try to match the *lettered* description with its correct *numbered* term.

Descriptions

(a) Benefits include the use of a tried-and-tested business idea.

(b) A firm (the rider) with a compatible product pays another firm (the carrier) to use its distribution.

(c) When a firm distributes and sells its own products to an overseas market.

(d) When each partner brings a specific competency to a joint venture.

(e) When a firm uses a 'confirming house' to bring it into contact with foreign buyers.

Terms

(i)   Direct exporting

(ii) Indirect exporting

(iii) 'Piggy backing'

(iv) Franchising

(v)   Specialised joint venture

(vi) Shared value-added joint venture

2   Read the following text and answer the questions which follow.

Japanese companies struggle in Mexico

Panasonic, the Japanese consumer electronics manufacturer, has erected a series of assembly plants in Tijuana, Mexico that employ nearly 3,000 people and turn out between 10,000 and 11,000 television sets every day. However, the recent removal of attractive tariff exemptions that had previously led to Panasonic locating its factories in Mexico will cost the company over £2m each year. Nevertheless, Japanese companies intend to stay in Mexico. Its low wage costs – less than half those of cities only 30 minutes drive away in California – yet broadly comparable productivity figures make it an attractive location for manufacturing.

Questions

(a) What are the implications of situations like this for multinational firm activities?

(b) What impacts might you expect in the advanced industrialised economies?

3   Which *two* of the following might explain the progressive decrease in share of textiles in UK output and employment?

(a) Low wage competition from countries with an even lower level of productivity per person employed in the textile industries.

(b) Improvements in UK design inputs into textile products.

(c) Low wage competition from countries with an equivalent level of productivity per person employed in the textile industries.

(d) The progressive decline in the primary sector in the UK.

(e) The relatively low income elasticity of demand for textile products over prolonged periods in which real incomes have increased substantially.

4 You are managing director of a US multinational manufacturing microwave ovens. You must choose between four otherwise equally appropriate geographical locations for setting up a new factory to assemble these microwave ovens, for which 50% of all components are imported and 90% of all finished products are exported.

Rank the attractiveness of these four countries for industrial location in terms of their macroeconomic environments (1 – most attractive) on the basis of the following data. All figures refer to average annual percentage changes recorded over the past five years.

UK

Manufacturing productivity	+2%
Wage costs	+3%
Exchange rate	+4%
Manufacturing employment	−3%

Netherlands

Manufacturing productivity	+5%
Wage costs	+3%
Exchange rate	−2%
Manufacturing employment	+1%

France

Manufacturing productivity	+4%
Wage costs	+4%
Exchange rate	−2%
Manufacturing employment	−2%

Denmark

Manufacturing productivity	+5%
Wage costs	+2%
Exchange rate	−4%
Manufacturing employment	+2%

5 **Case Study: Star Toy Co.**

Star Toy Co., based in Hong Kong, makes a range of high-quality electronic products for the toy market. Founded in 1990, the company has a reputation for producing innovative electronic toys tailored towards the premium end of the market. It has a relatively small but highly skilled workforce, and a small management team.

Most of the products are sold locally within Hong Kong and Southern China, but it also has a small export trade to neighbouring countries – Malaysia, South Korea and Australia. Star Toys is able to maintain relatively low labour costs. This puts it in a competitive position compared to Western manufacturers. However, the rise in competition from Chinese manufacturers has meant that the company has found itself in an increasingly difficult trading environment.

You try 13.2 *continued*

In recent years, the company has seen export sales continue to decline. Its exports have fallen largely as a result of the increased competition from Chinese firms. Seeing this decline, the owners are considering entering the USA and Europe. In the early 2000s Star Toy Co. found itself being propositioned by numerous agents from Europe and the USA, captivated by the quality and innovation of its products, with promises of huge, lucrative export earnings. It all seemed very attractive.

However, the owners resisted all attempts by foreign agents to represent their business in the USA and Europe until, one day, they received an enquiry from a major UK-based toy retailer which had the potential to become a major lucrative buyer. At this point, not immediately responding to the enquiry, the owners realised the potential of the company and so decided to explore the possibility of wider overseas representation, particularly in the potentially hugely profitable markets of Europe and the USA. To this end, they hired a British-based consultant to advise them.

Questions

(a) If the company decides to enter the European market, to what extent do you think it will have to adapt/standardise the marketing mix?

(b) Discuss possible communication tools the company could use in the UK toy market. Justify your answer.

(c) Discuss a possible target audience for the US market.

(d) What are some of the business-related issues the firm needs to address if it decides to enter the UK market?

6 **Case Study: China's wary shoppers set store by Western brands**

Eastern and western commerce are mingling again in Urumqi, once a pit-stop on the old Silk Road, at a Carrefour hypermarket next door to the most famous mosque in this heavily Muslim area of western China. Shortly after Friday prayers, the store is thronging with shoppers, recent converts to the French retailer. 'It is certainly a bit more expensive here,' says Kurban Wahab, picking through racks of lamb with a metal stick to check for the best cut. 'But here I know what I am getting is fresh and has been checked by inspectors.'

Safety scandals involving Chinese goods have sent a wave of panic through multinational companies that outsource production to China. But for international retailers looking to expand there, the safety concerns are an enormous opportunity as they seek to target newly affluent Chinese who are increasingly worried about the quality of the produce they consume. 'The food scares over the past few years have been great news for branded goods and retailers,' says Zhang Bing at the Shanghai office of consultants AT Kearney.

Carrefour and Wal-Mart are both expanding aggressively into China, which they hope could become a mainstay of their businesses in the future. Carrefour has 101 hypermarkets in 37 cities, while Wal-Mart has 86 and is in the process of acquiring up to 100 stores belonging to the Trust-Mart chain. Yet as the retailers move inland from China's coastal areas in search of new customers, they are facing huge challenges in ensuring the quality of their products because of primitive logistics infrastructure.

Nowhere is this more apparent than in Urumqi, a city of 2m near the border with Kazakhstan and by far the most remote outpost of Carrefour's China operations. Executives from the French group say it takes seven days for a truck to arrive from Beijing, which is nearly 2,000 miles away. Eric Legros, chief executive of Carrefour in China, insists [the store] uses only food producers that have passed the group's quality tests but the precarious transport system is evident at the supply entrance to the Urumqi store, where a flatbed truck arrives with fruit held in place only by old blankets. According to AT Kearney, there are only 30,000 refrigerated trucks in the whole of China, a country with a similar area to the US and with four times the population. In the US there are 280,000 such trucks, an essential part of the system of keeping food fresh over long distances.

You try 13.2 continued

'The logistics costs are much higher when you have stores in cities so far inland be-cause the infrastructure is weaker,' says Hyang Guoziong, a professor at Renmin University in Beijing. 'It will take them a number of years before they can be profitable.' Retailers also have to cater for very different tastes around the country. Carrefour has three stores in Urumqi, two of which are in neighbourhoods populated mostly by Han Chinese, the country's dominant ethnic group. Their favourite items are similar to those of shoppers in Shanghai and Beijing.

However, the hypermarket beside the Erdaqiao mosque is in an area dominated by ethnic Uighurs and other Muslim minorities from western China, so the shelves carry rows of dried apricots, almonds, saffron and different varieties of raisins. Women in bright headscarves queue for bags of dried lavender. The lamb and beef is halal; fresh pork – the most popular meat in China – is nowhere to be seen.

Carrefour's aggressive expansion into such remote parts of China has been helped by the decentralised model it has adopted, which gives individual store managers flexibility to adapt to different consumer tastes. However, such autonomy has also led to some breaches of quality standards. The group received a fine in 2006 after one store was found to be selling pork past its sell-by date, while another was sued for selling fake Louis Vuitton handbags. In 2007 eight officials involved in meat purchasing were detained by police over allegations of accepting bribes. 'The Carrefour system allows them to be much more flexible, but the downside is that it opens up a lot more space for corruption,' says Paul French, a retail industry consultant in Shanghai.

However, even though such problems have been widely aired in local media, which like to analyse the missteps of multinationals, the French group still enjoys a reputation for good quality among its customers in Urumqi. 'When you buy beef at some of the shops around here, they sometimes try to sell you horse meat or even camel and they cheat you on the scales,' says Zhang Li, a housewife. 'Here at least I know exactly what I am getting.'

Source: from China's wary shoppers set store by Western brands, *Financial Times*, 04/09/2010 (Dyer, G.), © The Financial Times Ltd

Questions

(a) What indications of brand value are suggested in this study?

(b) What does the study contribute to the market segmentation and product differentiation debate?

Answers can be found on pp. 525–546.

It may be useful, in the context of reviewing the international business environment, to examine in rather more detail the three members of the so-called 'triad', namely the EU, North America and the Pacific Rim countries (especially China).

European Union (EU)

The European Union is part of the so-called 'triad' of the global economy. It accounts for some 35% of world exports by value and contributes around 28% of world manufacturing output by value. It is clearly important that international business be aware of the market opportunities (and threats) created by the EU. This is certainly true for UK-based MNEs, since around 60% of UK goods are exported to the EU countries and around 54% of UK goods are imported from the EU countries.

Origins of the EU

The European Union has been in existence in various forms for around 50 years, arguably beginning with the formation of the European Economic Community (EEC) on 1 January 1958 after the signing of the Treaty of Rome. This sought to establish a 'common market' by eliminating all restrictions on the free movements of goods, capital and persons between member countries. By dismantling tariff barriers on industrial trade between members and by imposing a common tariff against non-members, the EEC was to become a protected free-trade area or 'customs union'. The formation of a customs union was to be the first step in the creation of an 'economic union' with national economic policies harmonised across the member countries.

Links

The institutions involved in EU decision making are reviewed in Chapter 12.

The original 'Six' became 'Nine' in 1973 with the accession of the UK, Eire and Denmark, and 'Ten' in 1981 with the entry of Greece. The accession of Spain and Portugal on 1 January 1986 increased the number of member countries to 12. In January 1995 the 12 became 15, as Austria, Finland and Sweden joined. The enlargement of the EU to 25 countries in 2004 meant that a further 75m people were added, together with another 30m in 2007 when Bulgaria and Romania joined.

Single European Act (SEA)

The *Single European Act* came into force in July 1987. The objective was not simply to create an internal market by removing frontier controls but to remove all barriers to the movement of goods, people and capital. Achieving a single European market has meant, among other things, work on standards, procurement, qualifications, banking, capital movements and exchange regulations, tax 'approximation', communication standards and transport.

Maastricht Treaty

The Treaty on European Union which was signed at Maastricht on 7 February 1992 represented one of the most fundamental changes to have occurred in the EU since its foundation. Although, legally speaking, merely an extension and amendment to the Treaty of Rome, Maastricht represented a major step for the member states. For the first time, many of the political and social imperatives of the Community have been explicitly agreed and delineated. Maastricht takes the EU beyond a 'merely' economic institution and takes it towards the full potential, economic and social union foreseen by many of its founders. Some of its major objectives are as follows:

1 to create economic and social progress through an 'area without internal frontiers' and through economic and monetary union (EMU);

2 to develop a common foreign, security and defence policy which 'might lead to common defence';

3 to introduce a 'citizenship of the Union'.

Characteristics of the EU

Country-specific data

Table 13.6 presents some of the important characteristics of the 27 member countries. It shows how diverse they are in terms of population, industrial structure, standard of living, unemployment level and inflation rate. In terms of population the UK is the third largest member, with a smaller proportion engaged in agriculture than in most other EU countries but the sixth largest proportion in services. In overall wealth, however, the UK drops down the rankings. It has the second largest GDP in absolute terms, but comes sixth in terms of GDP per capita, some 16% above the EU (15) average. Table 13.6 presents average data for the EU (12), EU (15) and EU (27), reflecting the countries included at different stages in EU enlargement.

Table 13.6 The 27 in the year 2009: some comparative statistics

Member country	Population (m)	Agriculture (%)	Industry (%)	Services (%)	GDP €(bn)	GDP per capita €(000)s	GDP (%)	Population (%)	Index of GDP per capita	Unemployment (%)	Inflation (%)
		Shares of GDP					Share of EU				
Austria	8.4	3	29	68	281.1	33.5	2.3	1.7	139.6	6.0	1.3
Belgium	10.8	1	26	73	345.5	32.1	2.9	2.2	133.8	9.9	1.3
France	64.8	2	21	77	1,992.0	30.8	16.5	12.9	128.3	10.2	1.1
Finland	5.4	3	33	64	180.1	30.7	1.5	1.0	127.9	10.2	1.6
Germany	81.9	1	30	69	2,436.0	29.8	20.2	16.3	124.2	9.2	0.6
Greece	11.3	4	20	76	243.0	21.4	2.0	2.2	89.2	10.2	1.4
Ireland	4.5	2	34	64	160.5	35.9	1.3	0.9	149.6	14.0	−0.8
Italy	60.4	2	27	71	1,573.0	26.0	13.1	12.0	108.3	8.7	1.8
Luxembourg	0.5	1	16	83	39.1	79.8	0.3	0.1	332.5	7.3	1.7
The Netherlands	16.6	2	25	73	581.8	35.1	4.8	3.3	146.3	5.4	1.2
Portugal	10.7	3	25	72	164.1	15.4	1.4	2.1	64.2	10.7	1.1
Spain	46.6	3	30	66	1,046.0	22.5	8.7	9.3	93.8	20.0	0.8
EU12	**321.9**	**2**	**26**	**72**	**9,042.1**	**28.1**	**75.1**	**64.1**	**117.1**	**10.7**	**1.1**
Bulgaria	7.6	7	31	62	33.6	4.4	2.8	0.2	1.8	8.0	1.3
Cyprus	0.8	2	19	79	17.8	22.1	0.1	0.2	92.1	6.6	3.3
Czech Rep.	10.5	2	39	59	140.9	13.4	1.2	2.1	55.8	7.9	1.4
Denmark	5.5	1	20	79	230.4	41.7	1.9	1.1	173.8	15.2	1.6
Estonia	1.3	3	26	71	13.4	10.1	0.1	0.3	42.1	20.0	0.8
Hungary	10.1	4	30	66	98.1	10.0	0.8	2.1	41.7	11.3	4.2
Latvia	2.2	3	26	71	16.7	7.5	0.1	0.5	31.3	19.9	−3.7
Lithuania	3.5	4	33	63	24.7	7.4	0.2	0.7	30.8	17.6	−1.2
Malta	0.4	2	19	79	5.8	13.9	0.05	0.1	57.9	7.4	1.6
Poland	38.1	4	31	65	327.0	8.5	2.7	7.6	35.4	9.9	2.0
Romania	21.4	7	37	56	122.9	5.7	1.0	4.3	23.8	8.7	3.6
Slovakia	5.4	4	39	57	69.5	12.8	0.6	1.1	53.3	12.8	2.4
Slovenia	2.0	2	31	65	36.3	17.9	0.3	0.4	74.6	8.3	3.9
Sweden	9.3	1	28	71	312.6	33.7	2.6	1.9	140.4	10.2	−1.0
UK	62.2	1	23	76	2,062.0	38.6	16.5	12.4	134.6	5.3	2.4
EU27	**501.9**	**2**	**27**	**71**	**12,048**	**24.0**	**100.0**	**100.0**	**100.0**	**10.3**	**1.2**
EU15	**398.7**	**2**	**26**	**72**	**11,420**	**27.9**	**94.8**	**79.4**	**116.3**	**6.0**	**1.1**

Notes: 1 Figures may be rounded and not add up to 100
2 'Total EU' percentages for agriculture, industry and services are weighted averages.

Source: Adapted from European Commission (2010) *Statistical Annex of European Economy*, Spring; World Bank (2009) *World Development Indicators*, and previous editions; and OECD (2006) *Factbook, 2009*

EU enlargement

In October 2002, the EU Commission approved the most ambitious expansion plans in its history when ten countries were told that they had met the 'Copenhagen criteria' for membership. The criteria include such aspects as institutional stability, democracy, functioning market economies, and adherence to the aims of political, economic and monetary union. These ten countries were deemed to be ready to join in the EU in 2004, while a further two – Bulgaria and Romania – joined in 2007. Table 13.6 also provides some economic data on these countries.

Establishing the EU27 has not been easy and even the optimists believe it will take a decade to fully absorb the 12 new nations, whose per capita income is less than 40% of the EU15 average. Demands for larger subsidies for farming from the new entrants will become an inevitable problem; e.g. in Poland, 25% of the population gain some income from farming. Others argue that most of the gains will go to countries such as Germany, Austria and Italy which are physically closer to the new entrants.

North America

North America is also one of the 'triad' of regions seen as underpinning the global economy. The USA accounts for some 19% of world exports by value and contributes about 27% of world manufacturing output by value. When we consider North America (USA and Canada) and the North American Free Trade Association (USA, Canada and Mexico), those contributions to the global economy grow still larger.

Although the United States is less dependent in trade terms on the global economy than many believe, its influence is felt everywhere. The USA has a population of over 290m people, which is smaller than the EU's single market, but has a huge land area (over 9m square kilometres) which is very resource rich with plentiful supplies of water, timber, coal, iron ore, petrol, gas, copper, bauxite, lead, silver, zinc, mercury and phosphates, among others.

The North American Free Trade Association (NAFTA)

NAFTA is a free trade association formed between the United States, Canada and Mexico on 1 January 1994. The main purpose of the agreement was to reduce tariffs and increase international competitiveness, as indicated by the goals of the NAFTA agreement:

1 To strengthen bonds of friendship and cooperation.
2 As a catalyst to international cooperation.
3 To create, expand and secure future markets.
4 To establish fair rules of trade.
5 To ensure a predictable framework for business planning.
6 To enhance firms' competitiveness in foreign markets.
7 To foster creativity and innovation.
8 To create new employment opportunities.
9 To promote development.
10 To strengthen environmental regulations.

NAFTA has been particularly successful for Mexico which is now the second largest trading partner of the USA. The impact of the USA on the international business environment is impossible to capture in terms of a few summary statistics. Its political, military, economic and socio-cultural influence is felt throughout the globe. One example of such pervasive influence we might usefully consider involves the US currency.

The USA and the dollar

The US dollar has dominated international currency markets for more than 50 years. Although currencies such as the euro are increasing in importance, the bilateral exchange rate that most countries pay particular attention to is between their own currency and the US dollar. For example, even though we noted above that the UK now has the majority of its trade with the EU, the £:$ exchange rate is still hugely important. Investment bank Morgan Stanley calculated that an 8% fall in the dollar against sterling removes £1.2bn from UK dividend payments. This is via the decline in profits of UK firms as exports to the US become more expensive and imports dearer. In fact the dollar had fallen by over 37% against the £ between 2003 and late 2007, and by almost 30% against the euro over the same period. The UK and eurozone countries have therefore been disadvantaged in their trade with the USA. However sterling has reversed this trend since late 2007 (see Case Study 10.4, p. 340) with sterling falling 29% against the US dollar since hitting its peak in November 2007 and falling 27% against the euro.

China has pegged its own currency, the Renminbi, against the dollar, so that it too had fallen against the £ and euro, giving the already competitive Chinese exports to the UK and EU a still further boost, although the strengthening of the dollar since late 2007, against sterling especially, has made Chinese exports somewhat more expensive over the past few years.

The USA and bilateral trade treaties

Links

The WTO multilateral principles are examined on p. 459.

One of the concerns of those supporting global free trade has been the growing importance of *bilateral* trade treaties, especially those agreed between the US and individual countries. As we note below, these treaties give preferential access to US producers rather than equal treatment to all producers, as intended by multilateral bodies such as the World Trade Organization (WTO).

East and South East Asia

Here we consider the 'Pacific rim' countries of East and South East Asia, which also form part of the 'triad' of the global economy (together with Europe and North America). East and South East Asia account for some 28% of world exports by value and contribute around 32% of world manufacturing output by value. However, we shall concentrate on the rapid rise of the Chinese economy within this broader region.

The Chinese economy

China is fast becoming an economic giant, not only in Asia, but also on the world stage. Between 1978 and 2010, China's GDP registered an average annual growth rate of 9.8%, with the per capita GDP growth rate at 8.4% per annum. If it maintains this growth rate, many economists believe it will become the world's largest economy by the year 2020 in terms of absolute value of GDP, though not in terms of GDP per head. For the last two centuries one country has emerged as the dominant economic power. The nineteenth century belonged to the UK, the twentieth century to the US and it looks like the twenty-first century will belong to China.

In 2010, China contributed almost 1% to global GDP growth, almost one-third of the total. Various authors have attributed China's rapid economic development to the trans-

Check the net

www.cbbc.org provides information on doing business in China.

formation from a centrally planned economy towards a market system and the opening of the economy through the 'Open Door Policy'. Since the open door policy was installed during the late 1970s, China has become a highly attractive market for foreign companies. There has also been significant growth in foreign trade.

It can be difficult for a foreign firm to keep track of the constantly changing political and legal factors in China, which has been described as a planned economy characterised by a weak capital market structure, institutional instability and poorly specified property rights. The latter is a major issue for foreign firms entering China. Developing a global brand involves huge investment. Poor enforcement of intellectual property rights (IPR) not only results in companies losing sales to cheaper imitations, but it can also damage the product's brand equity and image: fake products and trademark violations are rife in China. However, since China's accession to the WTO the Chinese government has cracked down hard on IPR infringement.

Case Study 13.5 provides further evidence of moves to improve IPR and quality control standards in China to support international business activity.

Case Study 13.5   **China groups eye production in India**

A group of Chinese handset makers is to consider manufacturing in India in an attempt to be recognised as legitimate suppliers in their most important export market. The decision also reflects the effects on business of India's uneasy relationship with its eastern neighbour. The Shenzhen Mobile Communication Association took a dozen of its members to visit India in February 2010 to negotiate related ventures. 'The goal is to set up several production or assembly lines with a total capacity of up to 10m units,' Tang Ruijin, executive president, said. The manufacturers hope production in India will help them gain political capital in the country and recognition in India as legitimate suppliers, and comes after India last year started to crack down on Chinese-made grey market handsets.

Many of them lack legitimate identification numbers relevant for security purposes or product-quality certification. In 2009 global handset volumes reached 1.14bn units, with China's 'bandit' handsets, or cheap copies of popular branded models, accounting for 20% of the global market.

According to BDA, a Beijing-based telecoms consultancy, Chinese grey market handset makers shipped about 235m units in 2009, 140m for export. In 2010 their exports could rise to 211m units. India has been their biggest export market. India is one of the world's fastest-growing mobile markets, with mobile penetration of slightly more than 40%, according to Strategy Analytics.

Grey market handsets are devices lacking some or all measure of legitimacy such as licences, product certification, intellectual property or security IDs. They include outright counterfeits, unbranded phones and nascent brands. 'Chinese handsets had grabbed up to 40% of the Indian market last year,

but we are being locked out of the market now,' said Mr Tang. 'We must be seen as producing Indian handsets, with Shenzhen manufacturing know-how.'

That strategy follows a high-profile pledge by Huawei, the world's second largest telecoms equivalent vendor, in 2010 to invest $500m in India to prevent the company being affected by broader tension between Indian and China. India has excluded Chinese companies from government tenders or infrastructure projects for national security reasons. In December 2009 New Delhi imposed steep anti-dumping tariffs on certain Chinese telecoms networking gear.

None of the companies represented by Mr Tang's association is well-known, but the thousands of groups that make handsets or their components around Shenzhen have become a force in global markets.

Handsets branded Sunup, Cexco, Dazian, Jugate, Oba, Hantel, Telsda, Aole or Lexun, to name a few. Different from the classical 'bandit' phones, these handsets come with a one-year guarantee and a booklet carrying the address and phone number of the manufacturer. Moreover, these handsets have the blue sticker indicating certification by the Chinese Ministry of Industry and Information Technology. But while many Shenzhen handset makers have indeed started submitting products for government quality testing, they openly admit that they do not do that with handsets destined for export.

'The blue sticker counts for nothing in India or Vietnam, so we're not getting it for phones we sell there,' says Echo Liu, a sales executive at SOP. Concerns have also been raised overseas about the Chinese imitation handset market, as many

Case Study 13.5 *continued*

phones do not carry a legitimate International Mobile Equipment Identity number – a code by which handsets can be traced to stop communication channels for terrorists or other criminals. IMEI numbers are supposed to be allocated only on behalf of the GSM association, the industry body, to manufacturers deemed legitimate.

Although more than 100 Chinese companies have gained that status, many Shenzhen manufacturers have gained a high mastery in faking these codes. Things are further complicated by the fact that the 'bandit' and the legitimate handset makers share the same value chain. 'Most of the

components in an outright fake of an iPhone can be legitimate ones, or the core of a branded Chinese handset can be problematic,' says Sun Wenping, deputy head of the Shenzhen Mobile Communications Association.

Source: from Chinese headset groups look to India, *Financial Times*, 17/02/2010 (Hille, K.), © The Financial Times Ltd

Questions

1 Why are Chinese handset makers seeking to move production to India?

2 What intellectual property right (IPR) and quality control issues are raised by this case study?

A vital aspect of doing business in China is that permission to conduct business is controlled by the government. The host government controls and restricts a foreign company's activities by encouraging and offering support or by discouraging and banning its activities; this depends on the potential benefits the foreign company is likely to deliver. As China is a developing country, a sudden change in policy could seriously affect a firm's business environment.

In the year 2008, all eyes of the world were focused on Beijing, as China became host to the Olympic Games for the first time. The Chinese government invested millions of dollars in reducing the pollution and developing the infrastructure required for staging such an event. Beijingers were actively encouraged by the government to learn English in preparation for the influx of foreign visitors that descended on the city, providing an ideal opportunity for the country to continue to share its culture with the outside world. Although the Chinese government invested billions of dollars into cleaning up the natural environment, especially in Beijing (in time for the Olympics), parts of China continued to suffer from environmental abuse. China already contains several of the world's most polluted cities. A primary cause of this pollution is the country's heavy reliance on coal as its main source of energy.

The long-term rewards that can be gained for foreign firms seeking market development in China are obvious. Joining the WTO and the Olympic Games have provided real investment opportunities. However, the complexity of the market, particularly the cultural and legal factors, cannot be ignored.

Of course, a major issue for China and the world community is the value of the remnimbi and its impacts on global trade. Case Study 13.6 reviews this exchange rate issue and the reasons behind China's increasing share of world exports.

Case Study 13.6   China, exchange rates and exports

Zhong Shan, the country's vice-minister of trade, declared that China will continue to increase its share of world exports, as we move into the second decade of the new millennium. China's exports fell by around 17% in 2009 as a whole, but other countries' slumped by even more. As a result

China overtook Germany to become the world's largest exporter and its share of world exports jumped to almost 10% up from 3% in 1999.

China takes an even bigger slice of America's market. In the first ten months of 2009 America imported 15% less from China than in the same

Case Study 13.6 *continued*

period of 2008, but its imports from the rest of the world fell by 33%, lifting China's market share of imports into the US to a record 19%. So although America's trade deficit with China narrowed, China now accounts for almost half of America's total deficit, up from less than one-third in 2008.

Trade frictions with the rest of the world are hotting up. In December 2009 America's International Trade Commission approved new tariffs on imports of Chinese steel pipes, which it ruled were being unfairly subsidised. This is the largest case of its kind so far involving China. On December 2010 European Union governments voted to extend anti-dumping duties on shoes imported from China for another 15 months.

Foreigners insist that the main reason for China's growing market share is that the government in Beijing has kept its currency weak. But there are several other reasons why China's exports held up better than those of its competitors during the global recession. Lower incomes encouraged consumers to trade down to cheaper goods, and the elimination of global textile quotas in January 2009 allowed China to increase its slice of that market.

How high could China's market share go? Over the ten years to 2008 China's exports grew by an annual average of 23% in dollar terms, more than twice as fast as world trade. If it continued to expand at this pace, China might account for around one-quarter of world exports within ten years. That would beat America's 18% share of world exports in the early 1950s, a figure that has since dropped to 8%. China's exports are likely to grow more slowly over the next decade as demand in rich economies remains subdued, but its market share will probably continue to creep up. Projections in the IMF's World Economic Outlook imply that China's exports will account for 12% of world trade by 2014. Its 10% slice in 2010 will equal that achieved by Japan at its peak in 1986,

but Japans' share has since fallen back to less than 5%. Its exporters were badly hurt by the sharp rise in the yen – by more than 100% against the dollar between 1985 and 1988 – and many moved their factories abroad, some of them to China. The combined export-market share of the four Asian tigers (Hong Kong, Singapore, South Korea and Taiwan) also peaked at 10% before slipping back. Will China's exports hit the same barrier as a result of weakening competitiveness, or rising protectionism?

An IMF working paper published in 2009 calculated that if China remained as dependent on exports as in recent years, then to sustain annual GDP growth of 8% its share of world exports would rise to about 17% by 2020. To consider whether that was feasible, the authors analysed the global absorption capacity of three export industries – steel, shipbuilding and machinery. They concluded that to achieve the required export growth, China would have to reduce prices, which would be increasingly hard to manage, whether through productivity gains or a squeeze in profits. In many export industries, particularly steel, margins are already wafer-thin.

However, China's future export growth is likely to come not from existing industries, but from higher-value products, such as computer chips and cars. Japan's exports also moved swiftly up the value chain, but whereas this was not enough to support durable gains in its market share, China has the advantage of capital controls that will prevent its exchange rate rising as abruptly as Japan's did in the 1980s. When China does eventually allow the yuan to rise, it will do so gradually.

Another big difference is the vastness of China's economy. China consists, in effect, of several economies with different wage levels. As Japan moved into higher value exports, rising productivity pushed up wages, making old industries, such as textiles, uncompetitive. In China, as factories in the richer coastal areas switch to more sophisticated goods, the production of textiles and shoes can move inland where costs remain cheaper. As a result China may be able to remain competitive in a wider range of industries for longer.

Foreign hostility to China's export dominance is growing. Paul Krugman, the winner of the 2008 Nobel economics prize, wrote recently in the

Table 13.7 Share of world exports, % of total

Country	1970	1980	1990	2000	2010
China	1	1	2	4	10
USA	14	12	12	12	8
Japan	6	7	9	6	5
Germany	11	9	12	9	9

New York Times that by holding down its currency to support exports, China 'drains much-needed demand away from a depressed world economy'. He argued that countries that are victims of Chinese mercantilism may be right to take protectionist action.

From Beijing, things look rather different. China's merchandise exports have collapsed from 36% of GDP in 2007 to around 24% in 2010. China's current-account surplus has fallen from 11% in 2007 to an estimated 6% of GDP in 2010. In 2007 net exports accounted for almost three percentage points of China's GDP growth; in 2009 they reduced its growth by three percentage points. In other words rather than being a drain on global demand, China helped pull the world economy along during 2009.

Foreigners look at only one side of the coin. China's imports have been stronger than its exports,

rebounding by 27% in 2009 when its exports were still falling. America's exports to China (its third-largest export market) rose by 13% in 2009, at the same time as its exports to Canada and Mexico (the two countries above China) fell by 14%.

Strong growth in China's spending and imports is unlikely to dampen protectionist pressures, however. China's rising share of world exports will command much more attention. Foreign demands to revalue the yuan will intensify.

Source: The Economist (2010) 9–15 January

Questions

1 Examine the reasons behind China's increasing share of world exports

2 Do you expect this trend to continue? Explain your reasoning.

3 How is China contributing to world economic growth?

International institutions and international business

International business can benefit by being aware of the institutional context in which international trade and investment takes place. In this section we review the roles of some of the important international institutions involved with trade and investment.

The WTO and GATT

General Agreement on Tariffs and Trade (GATT)

The General Agreement on Tariffs and Trade was signed in 1947 by 23 industrialised nations that included the UK, the USA, Canada, France and the Benelux countries. The objectives of the GATT were to reduce tariffs and other barriers to trade in the belief that freer trade would raise living standards in all participating countries. Since 1947 there have been eight 'rounds' of trade negotiations, with the average tariff in the industrialised nations falling from 40% in 1947 to below 5% in 1995 when the GATT was replaced by the World Trade Organization (WTO). Supporters of the role of the GATT point to facts such as the volume of world trade rising by 1,500% and world output by 600% over the years of its existence.

The World Trade Organization (WTO)

The WTO replaced the GATT in 1995 and now has 147 members, with the People's Republic of China, Chinese Taipei and Cambodia being the latest to join. The WTO's members in total account for more than 90% of the value of world trade. The objectives of the WTO are essentially the same as the GATT's, namely to reduce tariffs and other barriers to trade and to eliminate discrimination in trade, and by doing so contribute to rising living standards and a fuller use of world resources.

WTO principles

Both the GATT and its successor, the WTO, have sought to implement a number of principles:

- *Non-discrimination*. The benefits of any trading advantage agreed between two nations (i.e. in bilateral negotiations) must be extended to all nations (i.e. become multilateral). This is sometimes referred to as the 'most favoured nation' clause.

- *Progressive reduction in tariff and non-tariff barriers*. Certain exceptions, however, are permitted in specific circumstances. For example, Article 18 allows for the protection of 'infant industries' by the newly industrialising countries, whereas Article 19 permits any country to abstain from a general tariff cut in situations where rising imports might seriously damage domestic production. Similarly, Articles 21–5 allow protection to continue where 'strategic interests' are involved, such as national security.

- *Solving trade disputes through consultation rather than retaliation*. Again, certain exceptions are permitted. For example, Article 6 permits retaliatory sanctions to be applied if 'dumping' can be proven, i.e. the sale of products at artificially low prices (e.g. below cost). Countries in dispute are expected to negotiate bilaterally, but if these negotiations break down a WTO-appointed working party or panel can investigate the issue and make recommendations. Should any one of the parties refuse to accept this outcome, the WTO can impose fines and/or sanction certain types of retaliation by the aggrieved party.

> **Check the net**
>
> Visit the WTO website (**www.wto.org**) to find a wealth of information on international trade. Free online registration provides regular WTO news sent direct to you by e-mail.

International Monetary Fund (IMF)

The IMF plays a key role in providing foreign currencies and other sources of world liquidity to support the growth of international trade and payments. It also provides specific packages of financial support for economies in times of need. This latter role involves a variety of 'stabilisation programmes', which provide essential funding but only on condition that the countries receiving funds agree to implement specific programmes of change agreed with the IMF.

The main components of typical IMF stabilisation programmes include some or all of the following:

- *fiscal contraction* – a reduction in the public sector deficit through cuts in public expenditure and/or rises in taxation;

- *monetary contraction* – restrictions on credit to the public sector and increases in interest rates;

- *liberalisation of the economy* via reduction or elimination of controls, and privatisation of public-sector assets;

- *incomes policy* – wage restraint and removal of subsidies and reduction of transfer payments.

However, some have criticised these IMF stabilisation programmes. For example, by deflating demand, the IMF has imposed large adjustment costs on borrowing countries through losses of output and employment, further impoverishing the poor and even destabilising governments.

World Bank

The World Bank is, in effect, a grouping of three international institutions, namely the International Bank for Reconstruction and Development (IBRD), the International Development Association (IDA) and the International Finance Corporation (IFC).

International Bank for Reconstruction and Development (IBRD)

The origins of the World Bank lie in the formation of the IBRD in 1946. The IBRD sought to help countries raise the finance needed to reconstruct their war-damaged economies. This often took the form of guaranteeing loans that could then be obtained at lower interest rates than might otherwise have been possible.

International Development Association (IDA)

In 1958 a second international institution was created to operate alongside the IBRD, namely the International Development Association. The main objective of the IDA was to provide development finance for low-income nations which had insufficient resources to pay interest on the IBRD loans.

International Finance Corporation (IFC)

The International Finance Corporation was established in 1959. Unlike the previous two bodies, the IFC concentrates on lending to *private* borrowers involved in development projects. Initially much of this lending was for specific infrastructure projects such as dams, power facilities, transport links etc. More recently, the focus of lending has shifted towards improving the efficiency and accountability of the administrative and institutional structures in the recipient countries.

UN international institutions

Here we consider a number of institutions that operate under the auspices of the United Nations. The UN itself was established by charter in 1945 and consists of 185 member states. Its mission statement is to establish a world order based on peace, prosperity and freedom, and its most visible decision-making body is the UN General Assembly, in which all members participate.

United Nations Conference on Trade, Aid and Development (UNCTAD)

The conference first met in 1964 and has met subsequently at three- or four-year intervals. All members of the UN are members of the conference which has a permanent executive and secretariat. UNCTAD seeks to give particular support to the LDCs in their various trade disputes with the more developed economies. An important contribution of UNCTAD has been to support the introduction of the 'Generalised System of Preferences' (GSP) in 1971 which has helped give some of the exports of LDCs preferential access to the markets of the advanced industrialised economies.

United Nations Industrial Development Organization (UNIDO)

This was established in 1966 to provide technical assistance for developing countries seeking to industrialise. It helps countries to undertake industrial surveys, formulate industrial development strategies, conduct project appraisals and implement productivity and marketing strategies.

Organization for Economic Cooperation and Development (OECD)

The OECD was established in 1961 as a grouping of the advanced industrialised economies. Its main objectives were to encourage high levels of economic growth and employment among its member states, together with a stable financial system. It also seeks to contribute to the economic development in non-member states (including LDCs) and to expand world trade on a multilateral basis.

Group of Seven/Eight/Ten

This refers to the seven major industrial countries within the OECD that meet at fairly regular intervals to consider global economic issues, especially those of a macroeconomic nature. The seven countries involved are Canada, France, Germany, Italy, Japan, the UK and the USA (the Russian Federation has been added to this number on an informal basis in recent times when the G7 became G8). The so-called Group of Ten (G10) countries are the G7 countries plus Belgium, the Netherlands and Sweden.

In recent times many of these international institutions and arrangements have become the focus of criticism and their meetings have often been the occasion for large-scale protest.

Free trade and government protectionism

In this section we briefly review the arguments advanced in favour of both free trade and protectionism, before looking more carefully at the actual techniques used by governments in seeking to protect their key sectors of economic activity.

Arguments in favour of free trade

The main argument advanced by 'free traders' is that countries are better off by *specialising and trading* than being self-sufficient. In terms of the production possibility curve of Chapter 1 (p. 4) we are considering the claim that by engaging in trade, countries can achieve a situation outside that curve. If they remained self-sufficient and engaged in no trade they would only achieve resource allocations on or inside the production possibility curve.

Two particularly important theories have encouraged such specialisation and trade.

Absolute advantage

As long ago as 1776, Adam Smith in his *Wealth of Nations* had suggested that countries could benefit from specialising in products in which they had an *absolute advantage* over other countries, trading any surpluses with those countries. By 'absolute advantage' Smith meant the ability to produce those products at lower resource cost (e.g. fewer labour and capital inputs) than the other countries.

This was an essentially limited view as to the benefits of international business. For example, in a simple two-country, two-product model, each country would have to demonstrate that it was *absolutely more efficient* than the other in one of these products if specialisation and trade were to be mutually beneficial.

Comparative advantage

David Ricardo sought, in 1817, to broaden the basis on which trade was seen to be beneficial by developing his theory of *comparative advantage*. Again we can illustrate by using a simple two-country, two-product model. In this approach, even where a country has an absolute advantage (less resource cost) over the other country in *both* products, it can still gain by specialisation and trade in that product in which its *absolute advantage is greatest*, i.e. in which it has a *comparative advantage*. Similarly, the other country which has an absolute disadvantage (higher resource cost) in both products can still gain by specialisation and trade in that product in which its *absolute disadvantage is least*, i.e. in which it also has a *comparative advantage*.

Taking it further 13.1 outlines the original analysis used by David Ricardo in championing free trade.

Taking it further **Comparative advantage**   13.1

Ricardo used the following example, shown in Table 13.8, to demonstrate his theory.

Table 13.8 **Before specialisation and before trade**

	Labour hours required to produce	
Country	1 gallon wine	1 yard cloth
Portugal	80	90
England	120	100

- Portugal has an *absolute advantage* in both wine and cloth over England, since fewer resources (labour hours) are needed to produce each product.
- England has an *absolute disadvantage* in both products.
- Portugal's absolute advantage compared to England is greater in wine (80 : 120) than in cloth (90 : 100). We say that Portugal has a *comparative advantage* in wine.
- England's absolute disadvantage compared to Portugal is less in cloth (100 : 90) than in wine (120 : 80). We say that England has a *comparative advantage* in cloth.

Provided the terms of trade (i.e. rate of exchange between wine and cloth) are appropriate we can show that *both* countries can gain by specialising according to comparative advantages and trading with one another.

Table 13.9 assumes that Portugal uses all its 170 hours of labour on wine production and England uses all its 220 hours of labour on cloth production (assuming constant returns to labour). No trade has yet taken place.

Table 13.9 **After specialisation and before trade**

Country	Resource	Output of wine	Output of cloth
Portugal	170 hours labour	$2\frac{1}{8}$ gallons	–
England	220 hours labour	–	$2\frac{1}{5}$ yards

We now assume *terms of trade* in which 1 gallon of wine exchanges for 1 yard of cloth. Table 13.10 shows the possible consumption situation for each country, after specialisation and after trade.

Table 13.10 **After specialisation and after trade**

Country	Consumption of wine	Consumption of cloth
Portugal	$1\frac{1}{8}$ gallons	1 yard
England	1 gallon	$1\frac{1}{5}$ yards

We can now compare the *self-sufficiency* situation for each country in Table 13.8 with the situation after specialisation according to comparative advantage and after trade in Table 13.10. Clearly each country is better off, consuming more of one product and no less of the other.

- Portugal has an extra $\frac{1}{8}$ gallon of wine, and no less cloth.
- England has an extra $\frac{1}{5}$ yard of cloth, and no less wine.

Conclusion: Specialisation and trade is preferred to self-sufficiency in Ricardo's theory.

The suggestion that free trade is beneficial to all who participate is one of the strongest arguments used in its favour. By specialising in products in which countries have comparative advantages and trading their surpluses, supporters of free trade argue that world resource allocation is improved to the benefit of all.

Welfare gains from trade

Before turning to criticisms of this viewpoint, we can express the case for free trade using more up-to-date techniques than those of Ricardo in 1817. Here we make use of concepts already introduced earlier in the book, namely that 'economic welfare' can be regarded as the sum of *consumer surplus* (Chapter 2, p. 62) and *producer surplus* (Chapter 3, p. 102).

Figure 13.6 is used to explain this approach. It shows that free trade could, in theory, bring welfare benefits to an economy previously protected.

Suppose the industry is initially *completely protected*. The domestic price P_D will then be determined solely by the intersection of the domestic supply ($S_D - S_D$) and domestic demand ($D_D - D_D$) curves. Suppose that the government now decides to remove these trade barriers and to allow foreign competition. For simplicity, we assume a perfectly elastic 'world' supply curve $P_W - C$, giving a total supply curve (domestic and world) of S_DAC. Domestic price will then be forced down to the world level, P_W, with domestic demand being OQ_3 at this price. To meet this domestic demand, OQ_2 will be supplied from domestic sources, with Q_2Q_3 supplied from the rest of the world (i.e. imported).

- The *consumer surplus*, which is the difference between what consumers are prepared to pay and what they have to pay, has risen from D_DBP_D to D_DCP_W.

- The *producer surplus*, which is the difference between the price the producer receives and the minimum necessary to induce production, has fallen from P_DBS_D to P_WAS_D.

- The gain in consumer surplus outweighs the loss in producer surplus by the area ABC, which could then be regarded as the *net gain* in economic welfare as a result of free trade replacing protectionism.

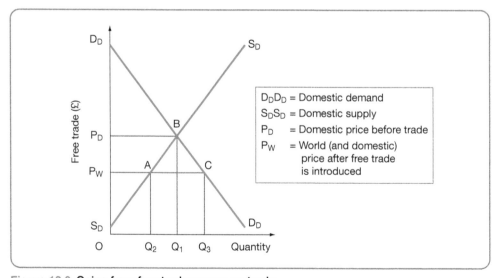

Figure 13.6 Gains from free trade versus no trade

Arguments in favour of protectionism

Not everyone would agree with the suggestion that free trade is necessarily in the best interests of individual countries. A number of arguments have been used to justify the use of tariffs and other means of protection against imported products:

- to prevent dumping (i.e. sale of products at artificially low prices, even below average cost);
- to protect infant industries (i.e. new industries which need support in their early stages in order to grow strong enough to compete with overseas companies);
- to protect strategically important industries (e.g. defence, those which underpin other industries);
- to maintain employment (e.g. protecting major labour intensive industries at risk from overseas competition).

In the next section we consider some of the *policy mechanisms* that governments might use when seeking to protect their domestic industries.

Methods of protection

Those involved in international business face a number of methods by which individual countries or regional trading blocs seek to restrict the level of imports into the home market.

Tariff

A *tariff* is, in effect, a tax levied on imported goods, usually with the intention of raising the price of imports and thereby discouraging their purchase. Additionally, it is a source of revenue for the government. Tariffs can be of two types: *lump sum* (or *specific*) with the tariff a fixed amount per unit; *ad valorem* (or *percentage*) with the tariff a variable amount per unit. There is a general presumption that tariff barriers will discourage trade and reduce economic welfare.

Non-tariff barriers

In recent years there has also been a considerable increase in trade that is subject to *non-tariff* barriers. The main types of non-tariff barrier in use include the following.

- *Quotas*. A quota is a limit applied to the number of units (or the monetary value) of an imported good that may be sold in a country in a given period.

- *Voluntary export restraints (VERs)*. These are arrangements by which an individual exporter or group of exporters agrees with an importing country to limit the quantity of a specific product to be sold to a particular market over a given period of time. VERs are, in effect, quotas.

- *Subsidies*. The forms of protection we have described so far have all been designed to restrict the volume of imports directly. An alternative policy is to provide a subsidy to domestic producers so as to improve their competitiveness in both the home and world markets.

- *Safety and technological standards*. These are often imposed in the knowledge that certain imported goods will be unable to meet the specified requirements.

- *Time-consuming formalities*. During the 1990s the EU alleged that 'excessive invoicing requirements' required by US importing authorities had hampered exports from member countries to the USA.

Check the net

As well as the WTO website (see p. 460), other sources of information on international trade and payments, international institutions and exchange rates include:

www.imf.org

www.oecd.org

www.worldbank.org

www.un.org

www.berr.gov.uk

www.europa.eu.int

www.eubusiness.com

- *Public sector contracts.* Governments often give preference to domestic firms in the issuing of public contracts.

- *Labour standards.* This bears some resemblance to the point made above concerning safety and technological standards but is rather more controversial. Does the enforcement of minimum labour standards represent a source of support for the poorest workers in the developing world or is it simply a hidden form of protection?

Case Study 13.7 investigates the impacts of protectionism in a more globalised economy.

Case Study 13.7 **High cost of anti-dumping tariffs**

Slapping extra tariffs on cheap 'dumped' imports can be counter-productive even when justified, Peter Mandelson, the EU trade commissioner, told a conference in the Netherlands. He argued that anti-dumping tariffs and quotas could harm Europe's own manufacturers, which have increasingly outsourced the production of shoes, textiles, light bulbs and other goods, aiming to maintain a competitive edge against cheaper Asian rivals.

'Imposing punitive measures . . . is often both justified and right. But if it is inhibiting companies from pursuing rational production strategies . . . it can also be counter-productive,' he said. While Europe should tackle unfair trade, globalisation meant the definitions of what was European-made had become blurred.

Mr Mandelson said the European Commission had struggled before finally deciding in late 2007 to phase out anti-dumping duties on energy efficient light bulbs made by European companies in China over a year. He had wanted the punitive duties abolished immediately, but fellow commissioners won more time to protect Osram, the German company that is the sole European-based manufacturer, he said. 'If producing cheaply in China helps generate profits and jobs in Europe, how should we treat these companies when disputes over unfair trading arise?'

A further case was leather footwear, he said. The imposition of tariffs on shoes for two years in 2006 led to duties of 16% for China and 10% for Vietnam. A Swedish government report says the duties have caused heavy losses among shoe importers, although these companies may be generating as much as 80% of each shoe's value in the EU through product design. Surveying five typical EU shoemakers, the Swedish government's National Board of Trade says the companies have become 'globalised', creating jobs and investment in the EU.

Even a €20 ($27, £13.50) pair of women's shoes adds value to the European economy, it says. Intermedium, a Dutch company, pays €4.40 to bring the shoes to Europe, then sells them to retailers for €6.65. By that point, €2.45 of the total cost is classified as European value-added. Intermedium and its Chinese supplier make margins of less than 10% each.

For a more expensive €150 pair of shoes, DC of Milan charges retailers €77.80 of which leather accounts for a third. But €40 of €50 value-added is classed as European, mostly going to research and development. 'The European value-added is 79%,' says the report. 'Is this a European or Vietnamese shoe?'

Italy pushed hardest for the duties. Companies still producing entirely in Europe have benefited. Shoe importers, meanwhile, can simply switch their supply source to another low-cost country. 'Globalised' manufacturers, however, could not be so flexible. Since prices were fixed with retailers, most of those EU-based shoemakers had to absorb cost increases.

Source: from Mandelson warns on hidden cost of anti-dumping tariffs, *Financial Times*, 04/09/2007 (Bounds, A.), © The Financial Times Ltd

Question

What does this case study suggest in terms of the 'free trade versus protectionism' debate?

You try 13.3 provides an opportunity for you to check your understanding of free trade and protection and other aspects of international business.

You try   13.3

1 In a two-product, two-country model, which of the following corresponds to Ricardo's theory of 'comparative advantage'?

(a) Each country specialising in that product in which it is absolutely most efficient.

(b) Each country specialising in that product in which it is absolutely least efficient.

(c) Each country specialising in that product in which it is relatively most efficient (or relatively least inefficient).

(d) Each country specialising in that product in which the terms of trade are most favourable.

(e) Each country specialising in that product in which the terms of trade are least favourable.

2 Which of the following is often said to be a benefit of specialisation and trade?

(a) Reaching a consumption bundle inside the country's production possibility frontier.

(b) Reaching a consumption bundle on the country's production possibility frontier.

(c) Reaching a consumption bundle inside the country's terms of trade.

(d) Reaching a consumption bundle outside the country's terms of trade.

(e) Reaching a consumption bundle outside the country's production possibility frontier.

3 Which *three* of the following are often used to support a policy of protectionism?

(a) Mature industry argument.

(b) Infant industry argument.

(c) Protecting strategically important industries.

(d) Encouraging 'dumping'.

(e) Preventing 'dumping'.

4 True/False

(a) A country has a comparative advantage (in a two-product model) in that product in which it has a lower opportunity cost than the other country.   True/False

(b) The international product life cycle (IPLC) is usually applied to a variety of knowledge intensive products.   True/False

(c) Inter-industry trade refers to situations where a country exports certain terms from a given product range while at the same time importing other items from the same product range.   True/False

(d) A fall in the sterling exchange rate will make UK exports cheaper abroad and imports into the UK dearer at home.   True/False

5 Where member countries reduce or abolish restrictions on trade between each other while maintaining their individual protectionist measures against non-members.

(a) Common market

(b) Economic union

(c) Free trade area

(d) Customs union

(e) Common Agricultural Policy (CAP)

You try 13.3 continued

6 Where, as well as liberalising trade among members, a common external tariff is established to protect the group from imports from any non-members.

  (a) Common market

  (b) Economic union

  (c) Free trade area

  (d) Customs union

  (e) Common Agricultural Policy (CAP)

7 Where the customs union is extended to include the free movement of factors of production as well as products within the designated area.

  (a) Common market

  (b) Economic union

  (c) Free trade area

  (d) Customs union

  (e) Common Agricultural Policy (CAP)

8 Where buffer stock purchases have often been used to achieve the target price for various products.

  (a) Common market

  (b) Economic union

  (c) Free trade area

  (d) Customs union

  (e) Common Agricultural Policy (CAP)

9 Where national economic policies are also harmonised within the common market.

  (a) Common market

  (b) Economic union

  (c) Free trade area

  (d) Customs union

  (e) Common Agricultural Policy (CAP)

Answers can be found on pp. 545–546.

Recap

- Forms of internationalisation may involve direct/ indirect exports, licensing/franchising and alliances/joint ventures and foreign direct investment (fdi).

- A 'multinational' is a company that owns or controls production or service facilities in more than one country.

- The 'transnationality index' is a useful measure of the degree of multinational involvement of a firm.

- Multinationals account for around 30% of GDP in the UK and almost half of manufacturing employment.

- Successful multinational activity from the home base usually depends on the possession of 'ownership-specific' advantages over firms in the host country, together with 'location-specific' advantages which favour overseas production.
- Cost-oriented multinationals mainly focus on reducing costs of production via overseas production (often via vertical integration); market-oriented multinationals mainly focus on easier sales access to overseas markets via overseas production (often via horizontal integration).

Key terms

Foreign direct investment (fdi) Investment across borders involving plant, machinery and other capital items.

Greenfield investment Investment involving the setting up of new buildings and plant.

Multinational enterprise A company that owns or controls production or service facilities in more than one country.

'Piggy backing' Where different companies share resources in order to access foreign markets more effectively.

Shared value-added joint venture Where partners contribute to the same function in the joint venture.

Specialised joint venture Where each partner brings a specific and different competence to the joint venture.

Transnational *see* 'Multinational enterprise'.

Transnationality index A measure of a firm's multinational involvement which uses the average of three different ratios: namely, foreign assets to total assets, foreign sales to total sales and foreign employment to total employment.

Chapter

14

Strategies in a globalised business environment

Introduction

Throughout this book we have already touched on many aspects of strategic business analysis. As early as Chapter 2 we noted the importance of the linkage between price elasticity of demand and revenue to the firm's pricing strategy. In Chapter 3 we reviewed the pricing strategies required in both short-run and long-run time periods for the firm to remain in a particular industry and in Chapter 12 examined the role of price in the marketing mix. Similar strategic implications for price and output policy have been mentioned in most or all chapters of the book. Chapter 13 reviewed a wide range of strategic issues involved in the internationalisation process. However, in this chapter we focus more on the *frameworks* within which the business can refine and develop broad strategic initiatives before examining how businesses seek to implement these strategies in a globalised environment.

What you'll learn

By the end of this chapter you should be able to:

- identify the main stages in developing and operating a strategy, whether at corporate, business unit or functional levels

- examine the more 'conventional' strategic approaches by *businesses* within essentially stable sectors of the economy; these include Porter's 'Five Forces' and 'generic' strategies, Ansoff's matrix, SWOT and PEST analyses, Boston matrix, among others

- examine strategic approaches involving *national* business activity, such as Porter's 'Diamond' and Vernon's 'International product life cycle'

- outline some of the key patterns and trends attributed to globalisation and assess their implications for multinational enterprises (MNEs) which must continually re-evaluate the nature and geographical location of the activities which comprise their value chains

- review the newer approaches to strategy within globalised economies, where previously stable sectors of economic activity are undergoing rapid change, and the contribution of joint ventures and alliances to strategic initiatives

- review further strategies involving reconfiguring value chains in order to remain competitive within the global economy.

Strategic frameworks for corporate activity

As previously mentioned, aspects of the strategic approaches covered here may have been touched on elsewhere. However, in this chapter we adopt a more 'holistic' approach, bringing entire strategic frameworks to bear on particular business problems.

Many definitions have been applied to business **strategy** which, while differing in detail, broadly agree that it involves devising the guiding rules or principles which influence the direction and scope of the organisation's activities over the long term. Johnson and Scholes describe strategy as:

Quote

The direction and scope of an organisation over the long term which achieves advantages for the organisation through its configuration of resources within a changing environment to meet the needs of markets and to fulfil shareholder expectations.

(Johnson and Scholes, 2006)

In this definition, as in many others, there is clearly a focus on:

- long-term direction;
- internal resource allocation;
- external environmental factors.

Levels of strategy

For larger organisations strategy may be developed at three different levels.

- **Corporate (enterprise) level.** Here the strategy involves the *organisation as a whole*, its objectives and mission statement, the sectors of economic activity with which it wishes to be involved, the geographical location of its activities, the mechanisms (e.g. mergers, alliances, joint ventures) by which it might grow, the activities for which highest priority might be given in allocating scarce resources.
- **Business level.** Here the strategy involves a *particular part of the organisation*, such as a particular division or subsidiary, a particular market or industry sector. At the business level the focus is on issues of competitive strategy, such as how the business intends to compete effectively within that particular market or industry.
- **Functional (operational) level.** Here the strategy involves the approach to be adopted within *functional areas* such as marketing, production, finance, human resource management and distribution.

Strategic management

Achieving a consistent approach across these three levels may require careful management, especially for larger, more complex organisations. *Strategic management* is a term widely used to describe this process.

Quote

The term strategic management refers to the managerial process of forming a strategic vision, setting objectives, crafting a strategy, implementing and executing the strategy, and then over time initiating whatever corrective adjustments in the vision, objectives, strategy and execution are deemed appropriate.

(Thompson and Strickland, 1999)

Figure 14.1 provides a visual summary of the five tasks implied by this definition.

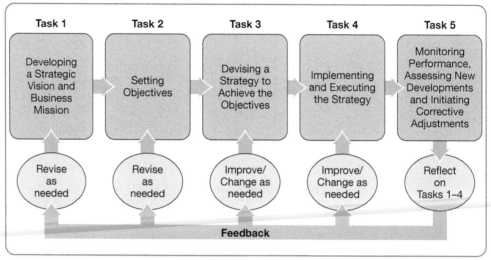

Figure 14.1 The five tests of strategic management

Source: Adapted from *Strategic Management*, 11ed., McGraw-Hill (Thompson, A., and Strickland A. 1999), The five tests of strategic management, reproduced with permission of The McGraw-Hill Companies.

Informing and shaping the five tasks of Figure 14.1 are three key elements (or processes), namely:

● strategic analysis;

● strategic choice;

● strategic implementation and evaluation.

We might usefully look at each of these in rather more detail.

Strategic analysis

This is a key element underpinning Tasks 1, 2 and 3 above. Strategic analysis is concerned with providing information for decision makers to help them better understand the present and future context in which the organisation must operate. Careful analysis of both the *internal* and *external* environments of the organisation will help inform decision makers as to their prospects for meeting previous stated objectives as well as help them set realistic future objectives.

Strategic analysis will seek to respond to questions such as:

● What are the strengths and weaknesses within the organisation itself?

● How is the external environment currently affecting the organisation and what changes, if any, are likely to occur in that environment?

● What opportunities exist or might arise for using the strengths identified?

● What threats exist or might arise from the weaknesses identified?

Responding to questions such as these provides a *context* in which a strategic vision can be developed or refined (Task 1), objectives set or adjusted (Task 2) and a strategy devised to meet those objectives (Task 3).

Strategic choice

This is a key element underpinning Tasks 3 and 4 in Figure 14.1. Strategic choice is concerned with choosing between *alternative courses of action* which have been identified as a result of the organisation's strategic analysis.

Strategic choice will seek to:

- make explicit the policy options which stem from the strategic analysis already undertaken;
- evaluate the benefits and costs to the organisation of the various policy options;
- help in selecting those policy options deemed most appropriate for advancing the organisation's stated objectives;
- help in integrating the policy options selected to form a coherent strategy, guiding the organisation's decision making at the appropriate level (corporate, business or functional).

Taking it further 14.1 reviews Porter's suggestion of three broad themes which might guide the integration of different policy options to form a coherent whole. *Taking it further* 14.1 also reviews Ansoff's suggestion that the integration of policies (strategies) can be given coherence by assessing their impacts on markets and on products.

Taking it further Strategic options   14.1

Porter's generic strategies

Writing in 1980 in his pioneering book on *Competitive Strategy*, Porter described three generic strategies open to firms. These are overall cost leadership, differentiation and focus.

- *Overall cost leadership strategy* requires the business to achieve lower costs than other competitors in the industry while maintaining product quality. This strategy requires aggressive investment in efficient plant and machinery, tight cost controls and cost minimisation in functional areas. An organisation must understand the critical activities in the business's value chain that are the sources for cost advantage and endeavour to excel in one or more of them.

- *Differentiation strategy* is based on creating 'something unique, unmatched by its competitors' which is 'valued by its buyers beyond offering simply a lower price' (Porter, 1985). This entails achieving industry-wide recognition that the business produces different and superior products compared to competitors, which might result from using superior technology or providing superior customer service.

- Focus strategy involves selecting 'a particular buyer group, segment of the product line, or geographic market' as the basis for competition rather than the whole industry. This strategy is 'built around serving a particular target very well' in order to achieve better results. Within the targeted segment the business may attempt to compete on a low cost or differentiation basis.

Figure 14.2(a) illustrates Porter's generic strategies.

Ansoff's product-market strategies

Igor Ansoff (1968) used the implications of policies for markets and for products to define strategic options. He presented the various strategic options in the form of a matrix (Figure 14.2b).

- *Market penetration strategy* refers to gaining a larger share of the market by exploiting the firm's existing products. Unless the particular market is growing, this will involve taking business away from competitors, perhaps using one or more of the 4 Ps (see Chapter 12, p. 386 and Chapter 13, p. 441) in a national or international context respectively.

- *Market development strategy* involves taking present products into new markets, and thus focusing activities on market opportunities and competitor situations.

- *Product development strategy* is where new products are introduced into existing markets, with the focus moving towards developing, launching and supporting additions to the product range.

Taking it further 14.1 *continued*

● *Diversification strategy* involves the company branching out into both new products and new markets. This strategy can be further subdivided into horizontal, vertical and conglomerate diversification.

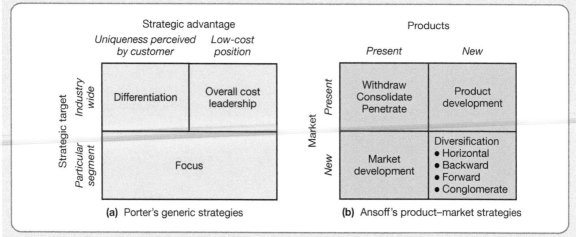

Figure 14.2 **Porter's generic strategies and Ansoff's product–market strategies**

Source: Figure 14.2a from *Harvard Business Review*, Porter's generic strategies; Figure 14.2b from Strategies of diversification, *Harvard Business Review*, 25(5), 113-25 (Ansoff, H.I. 1957), The Harvard Business School Publishing Corporation. All rights reserved

As we shall see, techniques such as SWOT, PEST and scenario planning, among others, can be most useful in helping the business select between different policy options and integrating those selected to form a coherent strategy.

Strategic implementation and evaluation

This is a key element underpinning Tasks 4 and 5 in Figure 14.1. Once the firm has chosen one or more strategies at whatever level (corporate, business or operational), it must seek to put those strategies into effect and continuously monitor and review their impacts.

● *Strategy implementation* is concerned with the processes to be used in carrying out the strategic decisions already made. Strategy implementation will usually involve:

 – deciding on the overall total of resources available;

 – deciding on the precise allocation of that total;

 – confirming lines of responsibility and accountability for using these resources.

 In other words, strategy implementation will usually involve questions of resource allocation and of organisational structure and design.

● *Strategy evaluation* is concerned with monitory performance, assessing new developments and initiating any corrective adjustments involving Tasks 1–4 (Figure 14.1) as may be deemed necessary.

Adopting managerial best practice

A key element for successful strategic management is an awareness of the strengths and weaknesses of new approaches to management and a readiness to modify, where appropriate, existing organisational structures to incorporate managerial 'best practice'.

For example, a major study in the UK examined the contribution of cross-border management approaches to productivity differences in manufacturing. The results of this *Productivity Report* (Proudfoot Consulting, 2003) suggested that manufacturing plants/factories in the UK are only being used to 60% of their capacity. It noted that if productivity could be raised from 60% to 85% capacity, then UK GDP would rise by 10% (£90bn). It concluded that the main source of low manufacturing productivity in the UK involves management-related problems.

Sources of 'lost' productivity:

- insufficient management planning and control (37%);
- inadequate supervision (25%);
- poor worker morale (14%);
- inappropriately qualified workforce (11%);
- IT-related problems (9%);
- ineffective communication (4%).

Conclusions of the report:

- Too many managers lack the skills necessary to deliver a culture of high productivity and don't spend enough time dealing with the barriers we have identified that prevent people working most effectively.
- Managers are too preoccupied with day-to-day matters to make strategic moves to boost productivity.
- Managers are poor at measuring their own performance and benchmarking it against their peers.
- Managers are poor at tackling low workforce morale and matching qualification levels to skill needs.

Clearly an effective strategic management approach will take into account the findings of such studies and re-evaluate existing practices in the light of emerging evidence.

SWOT and PESTLE analyses

As we have already noted, these techniques may be particularly useful, both in conducting a strategic analysis and in making a strategic choice.

During the 1970s Kenneth Andrews proposed a framework for strategy formulation based on the premise that the final strategy adopted by a company should seek a *'fit'* between its internal capabilities (strengths and weaknesses) and the external situation (opportunities and threats). This is commonly known as *SWOT analysis* (Figure 14.3a) and involves undertaking the following.

1 An *internal analysis* which should identify those things that the organisation does particularly well (*strengths*) and those features that inhibit its ability to fulfil its purposes (*weaknesses*). The features to be assessed may include the organisational structure itself together with various functional activities such as personnel, marketing, finance and logistics.

2 An *external analysis* which should highlight the general environmental influences that the organisation must cope with, such as the political, economic, social and technological factors (PEST) already considered in Chapters 9–12. Indeed, we noted in Chapter 12

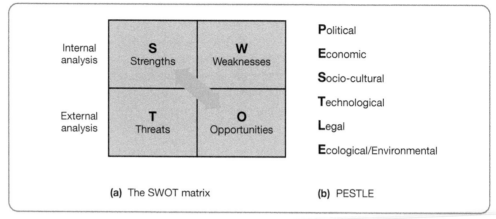

Figure 14.3 **SWOT and PESTLE approaches**

that **PEST** is often expanded to **PESTLE**, bringing the additional legal and ecological external factors into consideration (Figure 14.3b). This analysis of the external environment will lead to the identification of a number of *opportunities* and *threats*.

Strategic alternatives then arise from matching current strengths to environmental opportunities at an acceptable level of risk.

It may be useful at this stage to apply this broad-based approach to a particular business situation, namely to that of GlaxoSmithKline in the pharmaceutical industry. You might usefully read Case Study 14.1 and respond to the questions asked. We will then conduct a **SWOT** and PESTLE analysis of a different company to which most of us are familiar – Starbucks – and analyse Starbuck's situation looking forward from 2010.

Case Study 14.1	The pharmaceutical market and GlaxoSmithKline

The largest pharmaceutical markets are in the USA, Europe and Japan. The total world markets for pharmaceuticals have displayed strong growth over the past years and this trend is set to continue with the ageing of population in the major markets. Table 14.1 provides some details of global pharmaceutical sales by region in 2008.

Table 14.1 **Global pharmaceutical sales (2008)**

Market	Sales ($bn)	% of global sales
North America	311.8	40.3
Europe	247.5	32.0
Japan	76.6	9.9
Asia, Africa and Australia	90.8	11.8
Latin America	46.5	6.0
Total	773.3	100.0

Source: Adapted from IMS (2009) Health Market Prognosis, March

The pharmaceutical market was projected to grow at an average of 8.9% per year over the period 1999–2010 with growth being particularly fast in the USA. This helped the market share of North America to rise from 30% in 1996 to 40.3% of global sales by 2008. However, the annual rate of growth of the markets in Asia, Africa and Australia, as well as Latin America, was projected to reach double figures in each year between 2008 and 2018.

The pharmaceutical market itself is very competitive, with both large and small companies competing to produce the most effective drugs to treat a wide spectrum of illnesses. Many observers have said that the sector is oligopolistic in the sense that large companies (the large 'Pharmaceuticals', i.e. those whose revenues exceed $3bn/year) tend to dominate the industry. The test often used to determine whether the market is oligopolistic involves calculating the 3 firm or 5 firm concentration ratios, which measure the

Table 14.2 **Top 10 pharmaceutical companies 2008**

	Company	Country	Sales ($m)	Market share (%)
1	Pfizer	USA	43,363	6.0
2	GlaxoSmithKline	UK	36,506	5.0
3	Novartis	Switzerland	36,172	5.0
4	Sanofi-Aventis	France	35,642	4.9
5	AstraZeneca	UK	32,516	4.5
6	Roche	Switzerland	30,336	4.2
7	Johnson & Johnson	USA	29,425	4.1
8	Merck & Co	USA	26,191	3.6
9	Abbott	USA	19,466	2.7
10	Eli Lilly	USA	19,140	2.6

Source: Adapted from IMS (2009) Top 15 Global Corporations 2008

market shares of the top three or top five largest firms respectively. Table 14.2 provides information on the world's top 10 pharmaceutical companies for the year 2008. This will help us identify the large pharmaceutical companies and also clarify the structure of the industry itself.

As noted above, Table 14.2 shows the top 10 largest pharmaceutical companies by sales and their respective market share. Here we see that the 3 firm concentration ratio (Pfizer, GlaxoSmithKline and Novartis) was 16%, and the 5 firm concentration ratio (the top three plus Sanofi-Aventis and Astra Zeneca) was 25.4%. These ratios do *not* show an overtly oligopolistic structure since even the top five companies comprise no more than a third of the overall market. However, it is not easy to enter the industry to compete with the large companies because barriers to entry are high. For example, the industry often requires new companies to invest large amounts of capital for research and development in order to develop new drugs, which are the lifeblood of the industry. In addition, patent protection gives the large companies some time to reap the benefits of their expensive research expenditure. In the USA, for example, drugs may be given a 20-year protection, extendable by five years under specific circumstances.

However, competition is still present in the marketplace. In fact there are, in effect, two separate markets; one market in which drugs are still under patent protection and another 'off patent market' in which patent protection has been exhausted, i.e. the so called 'generic market'. Competition actually occurs, but in different ways, in both markets. In the *patent market* competition is usually between large companies which produce their own branded medicines to treat the same disease. These drugs are usually sold at a higher price and profit margin in order to repay the original investment. However, once patents expire, many more companies can produce their own generic version of the drugs and so the initial innovating companies lose their competitive advantage. In this *off-patent market*, prices are lower and various governments across the world often pressurise physicians and hospitals to use generic rather than the more expensive original brand-name medicines. For example, between 2006 and 2009 drugs with sales amounting to $100bn moved out of patent protection, and in 2010 the big pharmaceutical companies still relied on old products (on the market for over five years) for 90% of their revenues. These factors will create increasing competitive pressures in this sector in the future.

GlaxoSmithKline

As can be seen in Table 14.2, GlaxoSmithKline (GSK) was the second largest pharmaceutical company in the world by sales in 2008, with 5% of the global market. By 2010, the company was employing around 100,000 people in 120 countries. Its global manufacturing and supply network includes 78 sites in 33 countries. GSK emerged from a series of mergers after the Second World War. Some of the main mergers included the Glaxo Inc merger with Burroughs Wellcome in 1995 to form GlaxoWellcome in order to be stronger in the medicine market. Similarly, in 1989 SmithKline

Beckman and Beecham merged to become SmithKline Beecham. Eleven years later in 2000, Glaxo Wellcome and SmithKline Beecham merged to form the present company, GlaxoSmithKline.

GSK operates in two segments, namely pharmaceuticals and healthcare. The pharmaceutical sector involves the manufacture of prescription drugs and vaccines in areas which treat diseases of the central nervous system, as well as antiviral, antibacterial and cardiovascular diseases. It produces six of the world's top 60 pharmaceutical products, such as Avandia (diabetes), Lamictal (epilepsy), Advair (asthma), Valtrex (herpes), Wellbutrin (antidepression) and Zofran (anti nausea). The Consumer Health Care segment covers over-the-counter medicines (OTCs), oral care and nutritional healthcare. Products in this segment include Nicorette (anti smoking), Aquafresh (toothpaste), and Lucozade and Ribena (drinks).

The company experiences intense competition from other pharmaceutical companies in two main ways. First, GSK competes with well known competitor brands, e.g. GSK's drug Avodart (urinary) competes directly with Merck's Proscor, while its Advandia (diabetes) drug competes with Takeda Chemical's Actos (which the Japanese company co-promote with Eli Lilly in the USA). Second, some of GSK's well known drugs are out of patent protection and so experience competition from generic producers, as with its drugs Augmentin (antibiotic) and Wellbutrin (antidepressant) which are under pressure from generic producers.

To try to maintain its leading position, GSK's first strategic response has been to continue to invest in research and development. For example, GSK has more than 15,000 R&D staff on 24 sites in 11 countries. By 2009 there were 150 projects in clinical development, including 94 new drugs, 23 vaccines and 41 product line extensions. The company spent around 15% ($6.4bn) of its total turnover of $44bn on R&D in 2009 – equivalent to $18m per day. The second strategic response to competition has been to create alliances with other, often smaller companies, in order to speed up the development of new drugs. For example, in December 2007 GSK entered a strategic alliance with the Danish company, Santaris Pharma, enabling it to access Santaris' advanced technology to combat viral diseases. In January 2008 the company announced a new collaboration with the Swiss

not-for-profit group Medicines for Malaria Venture (MMV), to identify novel new drugs for the treatment of malaria. In June 2009, GSK announced its collaboration with Chroma Therapeutics of the UK designed to develop compounds which will help deliver drugs more effectively to cells damaged by inflammatory disorders and cancer.

Finally, in March 2010 GSK declared its new strategic alliance with Isis Pharmaceuticals, a Californian company. GSK will use the expertise of Isis to help it develop new drugs to target rare diseases including infectious diseases and some conditions causing blindness. Under the agreement, GSK will fund Isis research and will have the option to license any compounds developed from such research. It will also be involved in future development and commercialisation of such compounds.

No pharmaceutical company operates in a riskless environment and GSK is no exception. For example, there are product risks when drugs appear to have serious side-effects, as was the case with Seroxat/Paxil, the antidepressant drug in 2007. In the same year GSK was fined $217,000 for a misleading advertisement which exaggerated the amount of vitamin C in its Ribena drink. There are, of course, many other types of risks which originate from the company operating in a global environment. These range from exchange rate risks involving the use of many currencies across the globe, to political risks when significant regime changes occur in the countries where the company operates. Companies such as GSK do, of course, try to minimise some of these risks by exhaustive drug trials, hedging currencies and consulting experts at assessing political risks. These types of difficulties are often seen when experts undertake SWOT or PESTLE analyses of companies such as GlaxoSmithKline.

Questions

1 Look back at the information in this case study, and, with reference to GSK's website (**www.gsk.com**), clarify further the nature of risk taking at GSK. Suggest how the company could minimise such risks.

2 Explain the role that mergers and alliances have had in enhancing GSK's 'strategic vision' over the last few years.

3 Conduct a SWOT and PESTLE analysis of GSK for the years 2010 onwards.

SWOT and PESTLE applied to Starbucks

It will be a useful exercise to apply the SWOT and PESTLE analyses of Figure 14.3 (p. 476) to a company with which most of us are familiar, namely the present-day Starbucks as it looks towards the future. While the following analysis is illustrative only, it draws wherever possible on established facts and events and possible future scenarios for Starbucks.

In Table 14.3 we identify some strengths and weaknesses from our analysis of the internal environment of Starbucks. However, the boxes for opportunities and threats are left blank for the moment. The PESTLE analysis is conducted *before* these are filled since this will give a useful overview of the *external* environment in which Starbucks is now operating, and is likely to be operating in the near future. After conducting the PESTLE analysis we will be in a better position to match Starbucks' competitive advantages/ disadvantages (strengths/ weaknesses) to the changing external environment. Only then can we be in a position to identify opportunities and threats and to fill in the final two boxes of Table 14.3.

Devising a strategy

Given that we have conducted a *strategic analysis* (see p. 472) via SWOT and PESTLE, we must now move towards *strategic choice* (p. 473) by devising a strategy for Starbucks. Of course the strategy will, as we noted earlier (p. 471), depend on the *level* concerned.

Corporate (enterprise) level

Corporate objectives have been laid down by Starbucks in its 'six guiding principles' involving aspects of the environment, diversity, corporate and social responsibility, as well as profitability. However, these are rather general and may be made more specific by the Starbucks board. For example, the sixth guiding principle 'Recognise that profitability is essential to our future success', might be operationalised as a corporate target in the following ways:

- Achieve x% annual profit growth as an average over the period 2010–2013.
- Achieve y% annual revenue growth as an average over the period 2010–2013.
- Achieve z% market share of the coffee bar market by 2013, and so on.

Table 14.3 **SWOT analysis for Starbucks: strengths and weaknesses only**

S	W
– Strong brand image for quality products and relaxed ambience. 5.4 million followers on Facebook in 2010 and 705,000 followers on Twitter	– Associated by some with the alleged excesses of global capitalism
– High staff motivation and commitment	– Despite some product differentiation via localisation, still largely homogenous in terms of product and ambience
– Reputation for social responsibility (both internally, e.g. treatment of own staff – and externally, e.g. links with Fairtrade organisation)	– Higher staff costs per head than rivals
– 'Capital light' and extensive global coverage of stores	
– 'Local' responsiveness of products and services via use of locally licensed partners	
T	O

Table 14.4 uses a PESTLE approach to assess likely changes in the external environment for Starbucks from 2010 onwards.

Table 14.4 PESTLE analysis for Starbucks

Political	– Threat of terrorism, especially in major cities where most Starbucks are located, may significantly reduce the customer base
	– Pressures for tax-raising schemes by governments on coffee drinking. For example, the so-called 'sin tax' in Seattle in 2003 proposed taxing every cup of coffee drunk to raise money for day care for poor children. While this was defeated in a public referendum, governments are looking more closely at raising revenue by taxing 'luxury' goods and services associated with higher income lifestyles
	– Some developing countries are investigating reviving the International Coffee Agreement which, until its abandonment in 1989, kept coffee prices much higher by setting quotas for production levels in coffee-growing areas
Economic	– More buoyant than expected global growth from 2010 onwards would help to raise real incomes per head in many key markets. However, less buoyant growth (e.g. credit problems with the sub-prime market) could depress sales
	– Some key competitors have withdrawn from the market, e.g. Coffee Republic announced in 2003 that it was moving from the pure coffee bar model to a more food-focused formula involving US-style sandwich delicatessens (Republic Deli)
Social	– Increasing average age because of demographic change in many countries is reducing the market base (young age groups visit Starbucks more frequently than older age groups)
	– Increased use of social networking
	– Anti-obesity drive is focusing on more spartan lifestyles and lower calorific intakes of both food and drink
	– 'Idea' stores are being introduced in UK libraries and museums (and in other countries) selling coffee and other products to create an ambience quite unlike that traditionally associated with such institutions
Technological	– New technologies are increasing the output per acre of coffee growers and the increased supply is reducing world coffee prices
Legal	– Legislation in the UK to lengthen pub opening hours is potentially attracting some customers away from coffee drinking in Starbucks
	– A smoking ban in public places is now UK law, reducing the current competitive advantage Starbucks has as a 'non-smoking' environment among coffee and beverage establishments
Environmental	– There is evidence of an increased public interest in and awareness of issues of corporate social responsibility (see Chapter 4)

The board might then seek to give general direction as to the set of policies which it expects to employ to achieve these corporate objectives.

Here, for illustration, we will seek to describe some possible broad-based *'corporate strategies'* using the terminology of Porter's generic strategies and Ansoff's product-market strategies already encountered (Figure 14.2, p. 474).

For example, in terms of Porter's generic strategies, Starbucks might select:

● *differentiation strategy* whereby further attention is given to developing its existing image of superior high quality products in the coffee bar genre, perhaps by developing new product lines or using new technologies to make existing product lines still more attractive.

We can now return to complete our SWOT analysis for Starbucks, as indicated in Table 14.5.

Table 14.5 **SWOT analysis for Starbucks**

S	W
– Strong brand image for quality products and relaxed ambience. 5.4 million followers on Facebook in 2010 and 705,000 followers on Twitter – High staff motivation and commitment – Reputation for social responsibility (both internally, e.g. treatment of own staff – and externally, e.g. links with Fairtrade organisation) – 'Capital light' and extensive global coverage of stores – 'Local' responsiveness of products and services via use of locally licensed partners	– Associated by some with the alleged excesses of global capitalism – Despite some product differentiation via localisation, still largely homogenous in terms of product and ambience – Higher staff costs per head than rivals

T	O
– Decreased demand in city centre Starbucks locations because of terrorism and because of reduced real incomes if there is a global credit crisis – Higher real price of coffee if either 'sin taxes' are levied or coffee producer cartel is reinstated – Association with USA and global capitalism makes it a target for protests and damages brand image – Association with unhealthy lifestyles and obesity – New ready-to-drink (RTD) coffee substitutes for home use – Rival coffee/tea providing companies are making still greater (and well-publicised) commitments than Starbucks to Fairtrade suppliers	– Higher real incomes are increasing demand for Starbucks products given that they have a high income elasticity of demand ('luxury' category) – Major platform exists for using social networking in promotions and online sales – New coffee bar locations available in city centres as Coffee Republic sells unwanted outlets – Higher output of coffee growers is reducing price of coffee – Gain in 'public esteem' via Fairtrade coffee sales, annual Social Responsibilities reports, etc. strengthens brand image

Since these generic strategies need not be mutually exclusive, Starbucks might at the same time select:

● *focus strategy* whereby, say, it targets attracting a higher proportion of the 'grey market' of older customers who, at present, form a very small proportion of its existing customer base.

In terms of Ansoff's product-market strategies Starbucks might select:

● *market penetration strategy* whereby it seeks to attract customers from rival coffee shops, perhaps using special offers, extensive advertising or other comparative marketing policies.

Again, it might at the same time select:

● *market development strategy* whereby it seeks to take its existing products into new markets, as in seeing the 'grey consumer' as already mentioned. This might also involve new geographical markets, perhaps seeking new outlets in the 12 accession countries which joined the EU since 2004.

Of course, these are merely illustrative ideas at the corporate level of strategy. You might be able to suggest other alternatives based on the earlier materials.

Business level

Business (or competitive) strategy will involve more policy detail as to how Starbucks intends to compete within a *particular* market or industry. For illustrative purposes we now consider the *UK market*.

The SWOT and PESTLE analysis will need to be revisited and more carefully honed to the internal and external environment facing Starbucks UK. The ensuing business strategy might include the following policy components.

Achieving, say, 2010–2013 profit, revenue and market share targets along the lines outlined above (p. 480) but this time refined to the particular situation of the UK market by:

- purchasing 30 of the 50 outlets released by Coffee Republic in the UK, following its withdrawal from the pure coffee bar market;
- raising prices of drinks and food in Starbucks by 5% per year over the period (higher than the predicted rate of inflation of 2.5% per year), given that studies suggest a relatively price inelastic demand and rising UK real incomes;
- responding to a major survey showing high degree of sensitivity of Starbucks' customers to 'social responsibility' by increasing use of Fairtrade products from 10% to 20% (with extensive publicity of this policy);
- using more effective just-in-time delivery systems to distribute drink and food supplies to Starbucks shops, reducing storage costs and 'waste' from time expiry of products;
- developing a major promotional campaign in the national UK media (press, TV, radio, cinemas, Internet);
- providing additional in-store attractions in the UK to attract new target customers (e.g. more newspapers, quality journals for 'grey' market);
- further developing 'loyalty cards' to encourage repeat purchases.

Functional level

The *functional strategy* will be honed to a particular functional area of the organisation. This functional level may involve the whole organisation or be confined to a particular geographical area. Here, for illustrative purposes, we shall use *HRM* in the geographical context of the UK.

The ensuing functional strategy might include the following policy components. Achieving 2010–2013 targets specified for the HRM department of Starbucks UK (x% fall in staff turnover, y% increase in female employees and z% increase in employees from ethnic minorities) by:

- increasing the flexible working conditions available to Starbucks' employees beyond the minimum levels established by the April 2003 UK Act;
- raising hourly wage rates by 2% more than UK inflation in each year;
- extra advertising of job vacancies in media sources widely used by women and ethnic minorities in the UK.

Porter's Five Forces analysis

Porter argued that 'the essence of strategy formulation is coping with competition' and that in addition to undertaking a PEST analysis, it is also necessary to undertake a structural analysis of the industry to gauge the strengths and weaknesses of the opposition

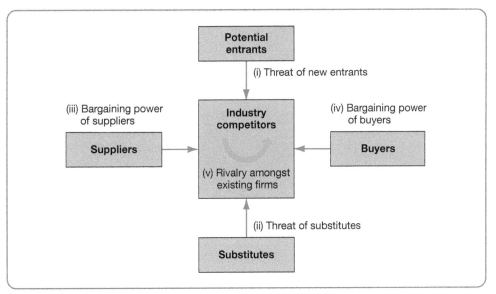

Figure 14.4 Porter's 'Five Forces' analysis

Source: Adapted with the permission of The Free Press, a Division of Simon & Schuster, Inc., from *Competitive Strategy* by Michael E. Porter. Copyright © 1998 by Michael E. Porter. All rights reserved.

and also determine the competitive structure of a given market. The key elements in Porter's Five Forces analysis (Figure 14.4) can be identified as the threat of (i) *potential entrants* and (ii) *substitutes*, as well as the power of (iii) *suppliers* and (iv) *buyers*, together with an exploration of (v) *the degree of competitive rivalry*.

(i) Threat of potential entrants

The threat of new entrants into an industry depends on the barriers that exist in the market and the expected reaction of existing competitors to the entrant. Porter identified six possible sources of barriers to entry, namely economies of scale, differentiation of the product, capital requirements of entry, cost advantages, access to distribution channels and legislative intervention.

(ii) Threat of substitute products

The threat of substitute products can alter the competitive environment within which the firm operates. A new process or product may render an existing product useless. For an individual firm the main issue is the extent to which there is a danger that substitutes may encroach on its activities. The firm may be able to minimise the risks from substitutes by a policy of product differentiation or by achieving a low-cost position in the industry.

(iii) Bargaining power of suppliers

Suppliers have the ability to squeeze industry profits by raising prices or reducing the quality of their products. Porter states that a supplier is powerful if few suppliers exist in a particular market, there are no substitute products available, the industry is not an important customer of the supplier, or the supplier's product is an important input to the buyer's business. Japanese firms have shown the importance of establishing a strong relationship with suppliers so that they 'become an extension of the firm itself'.

(iv) Bargaining power of buyers

In general, the greater the bargaining power of buyers, the greater is their ability to depress industry profitability. Porter identified a number of determinants of bargaining

Chapter 14 Strategies in a globalised business environment

power, including the concentration and size of buyers, the importance of purchases to the buyer in cost terms, the costs of switching between suppliers, and the degree of standardisation of products. Buyers should be treated as rivals but should have a 'friendly relationship based on performance and integrity'.

(v) Rivalry among existing firms

Finally, the extent of rivalry between firms can influence the competitive environment within which the firm operates. Rivalry is influenced by the above forces but also depends on the concentration of firms in the marketplace and their relative market shares, the rate of industry growth, the degree of product differentiation, and the height of exit barriers. Porter refers to the tactics used by firms to seek an advantage over their competitors as 'jockeying for position'. This usually takes the form of policies towards pricing, promotion, product innovation and service level.

According to Porter, strategy formulation requires that each of the above forces be carefully analysed in order to successfully:

1 *position the company* so that its capabilities provide the best defence against the competitive forces;

2 *influence the balance* of the forces through strategic moves, thereby improving the company's position;

3 *anticipate changes* in the factors underlying the forces and respond to them.

Competitive advantage

The strategic focus of Porter and his contemporaries often involves companies being seen as seeking to identify and exploit *competitive advantages* within stable industrial structures. Such competitive advantages were often expressed in terms of the additional 'added value' the more successful firms in an industry were able to generate vis-à-vis the most marginal firm in that industry.

> *Quote*
>
> *Where no explicit comparator is stated, the relevant benchmark is the marginal firm in the industry. The weakest firm which still finds it worthwhile to serve the market provides the baseline against which the competitive advantage of all other firms can be set.*
>
> (J. Kay, 1993)

These competitive advantages could be attributed to a host of potential factors:

● *architecture* (a more effective set of contractual relationships with suppliers/customers);

● *incumbency advantages* (reputation, branding, scale economies etc.);

● *access to strategic assets* (raw materials, wavebands, scarce labour inputs etc.);

● *innovation* (product or process, protected by patents, licences etc.);

● *operational efficiencies* (quality circles, just-in-time techniques, re-engineering etc.).

You could usefully re-read the earlier Case Study 13.3 on IKEA (p. 439). Although that case study was more concerned with marketing aspects, it also provides strategic insights additional to those presented in Case Study 14.2.

> Stop and think   14.1
>
> Use the earlier Case Study 14.1 on GlaxoSmithKline and your own investigations into its operations to conduct a five-forces analysis. What further strategic issues does this raise?

Case Study 14.2 looks at the Swedish furniture group IKEA. It provides a further opportunity for you to use SWOT, PESTLE and 'Five Forces' analysis in devising strategies for IKEA at each of the three levels, corporate, business and functional.

Case Study 14.2   IKEA and growth strategies

It is business as usual at IKEA's Helsingborg office in southern Sweden, where wall signs highlight the company's latest cost-saving initiative: Kill-a-watt. Staff are urged to turn off lights, taps and computers when they are not being used. In fact it is a competition: whichever IKEA store or office round the world saves most electricity between November and January will win a prize.

IKEA's spartan corporate culture stems from Ingvar Kamprad, its founder, who famously drives an old Volvo and buys his fruit and vegetables at afternoon markets when prices are cheaper. IKEA staff always travel economy class and take buses rather than taxis. But cost-cutting has recently been more necessary than usual. The Swedish home furnishings group had its toughest year in 2003 for a decade and Anders Dahlvig, chief executive of IKEA group, did not just blame weak economic conditions internationally. 'The truth is that this year we have not stretched ourselves to the limit. We are less than fully satisfied with what we have achieved,' he says.

IKEA's sales rose 3% to €11.3bn (£7.9bn) in the year to 31 August 2003 – but that was after including the impact of 11 new stores. Like-for-like sales growth was zero. Mr Dahlvig suggested that the stronger euro had had an impact, as sales at constant currencies were 6% higher. He also blamed the economic downturn in central Europe, where the group makes about half its sales. But there were also other issues. There was a greater than expected impact from cannibalisation: the impact that new stores have on the sales of existing stores in countries where IKEA was already present. For example, in 2002 IKEA had opened a fourth store in Toronto and second stores in Washington and San Francisco.

In a year-end report, Mr Dahlvig had also highlighted three other areas where IKEA needed to do better: range, service and product availability. 'Customers should never come to our stores only to find that the product they want is temporarily out of stock. The lines of customers at the check-outs . . . should never be so long that they deter people from visiting the store,' he wrote. IKEA has faced a constant barrage of criticism for the quality of service in its UK stores but Mr Dahlvig insists that the complaints are specific to that market.

In any case, the 2003/4 financial year saw a significant growth of sales of 13.3%, and healthy sales growth continued in 2004/5 (15.6%), 2005/6 (15.6%), 2006/7 (14.4%). However, growth slowed down from 7.0% in 2007/8 to 1.4% in 2008/9 as the global recession began to bite. As a result, the pace of store openings had fallen temporarily to two or three per year by 2010.

Therefore notwithstanding the difficult market conditions of the early millennium, the expansion goes on. In 2007 IKEA had a total of 234 wholly owned stores in 24 countries excluding 30 franchises. By 2006 two new stores had opened at Milton Keynes and Ashton under Lyne in the UK. A year later in 2007 IKEA had increased its presence in Eastern Europe and the Far East with a total of four stores in China, eight stores in Russia and two in Japan. The China connection continued in 2008 as stores in Nanshan (Shenzen province) and Daming (Nanking province) were opened.

Looking to the future, Mr Dahlvig admits that competition is hotting up. He says the group is increasingly being challenged by hypermarkets and DIY retailers – companies such as Wal-Mart and B&Q. In addition, supermarkets such as Tesco of the UK are expanding outside their core areas, while dedicated home furnishing groups such as Conforama of France are developing a regional presence. 'It's understandable. At some point these companies become saturated in food or clothing and they need to expand in other segments if they want to grow,' he says. IKEA is responding with its store expansion programme and with more aggressive pricing. 'We have reduced our prices by 15 to 20% on average over the last five years,' Mr Dahlvig says.

In any case, he is confident that the IKEA concept is hard to imitate. 'Many competitors could try to copy one or two of these things. The difficulty is when you try to create the totality of what we have. You might be able to copy our low prices, but you need our volumes and global sourcing presence. You have to be able to copy our Scandinavian design, which is not easy without a Scandinavian heritage. You have to be able to copy our distribution concept with the flat pack. And you have to be able to copy our interior competence – the way we set out our stores and catalogues.'

Case Study 14.2 *continued*

And what about the long-term challenges facing the group? Mr Dahlvig admits that as the group grows bigger it will become harder for it to remain 'quick, lean and simple'. Being big has advantages – in purchasing, for example – but it can also lead to bureaucracy and slow reactions to consumer change.

Something else is looming. In most countries, IKEA still has plenty of room for growth, with market shares in the 5–10% range. But in some countries the company is now so big that it may be nearing saturation point in terms of its appeal. For example, in Germany, the group's largest market, the group has 43 stores. In Sweden, where it has 17 stores, it has 20% of the home furnishings market. 'The more stores we build and the more we increase our market share, the more we have to find ways to appeal to a broader public. Scandinavian design and style is a niche and it is not to everyone's taste. But we don't want to be just another supplier of traditional furniture. Scandinavian design is what makes us unique. We have to find a balance.'

A weekend trip to an IKEA store is hell, if you believe some sections of the UK media. Long queues and poor product availability in the UK are in danger of overshadowing the company's reputation for low prices and Scandinavian design, critics say. Anders Dahlvig admits that the 'UK experience is not what we would like it to be'. But he says the UK is a special case and there is one overriding reason for the problems. 'Retailing laws in the UK have made it impossible for us to expand because of the restrictions on building out of town. If we had the same situation as in Germany, France and the US, we would have more stores and bigger stores in the UK and the situation would be different.'

IKEA's Brent Park store in north London has acquired a particularly bad reputation – although Mr Dahlvig refused to describe it as the worst store in the group. He insisted that IKEA was doing everything it could to improve things: staying open longer, adding check-outs and encouraging shoppers to come on weekday evenings rather than at weekends. But, he added, 'More stores or extended stores is the only really good way to satisfy fully the capacity problem that we have. The other things just put plaster on the wound.'

As with any successful company, there are always problems during the process of company growth. For example, in 2008 IKEA was criticised for sending an e-mail to customers advising them that the online shop was open all over the UK when it only applied to England and Wales. Similarly, in February 2010 customers in Northern Ireland and Scotland were unable to shop online although some Scottish customers could get items delivered via IKEA's Edinburgh store. However, the scheme called IKEA DIRECT only applied to certain areas and cost between £35 and £120 for delivery depending on the location of the customer's home.

Source: from An Empire Built on a Flat-Pack, *Financial Times*, 24/11/2003, 12 (Brown-Humes, C.), © The Financial Times Ltd

Questions

Again you could remind yourself of extra detail on IKEA by re-reading Case Study 13.3 (p. 439) before answering the following questions.

1 Use as many of Porter's 'five forces' as you can in analysing the situation facing IKEA.

2 What growth strategies might you recommend at a corporate (enterprise) level for IKEA?

3 What strategies might you recommend at the business level for IKEA, where the business unit in question is IKEA UK?

Portfolio analysis

The Boston Consulting Group's portfolio matrix provides a useful framework for examining the balance of the portfolio of products in a multi-product firm. It can therefore be helpful in guiding the strategic direction of that organisation.

The organisation's portfolio of products is subjected to a detailed analysis according to market share, growth rate and cash flow. The four alternative categories of company

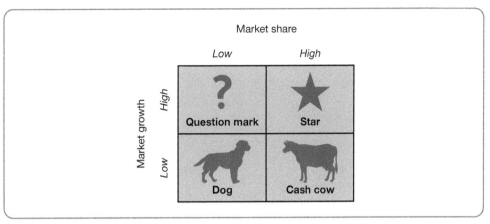

Figure 14.5 The Boston Matrix

Source: The BCG Portfolio Matrix, from the Product Portfolio Matrix, © 1970, The Boston Consulting Group

(or product) that emerge from the model are given the labels of Stars, Cash Cows, Dogs and Problem Children (or Question Marks), as can be seen in Figure 14.5.

- *Stars* have high market share, high growth, but limited cash flow due to the substantial amount of investment required to maintain growth. Successful Stars go on to become Cash Cows.
- *Cash Cows* have a high market share but slow growth. They tend to generate a very positive cash flow that can be used to develop other products.
- *Dogs* have a low share of a slow-growth market. They may be profitable, but only at the expense of cash reinvestment, and thus generate little for other products.
- *Problem Children* have a low share of a fast-growing market and need more cash than they can generate themselves in order to keep up with the market.

However, there have been several criticisms aimed at the **Boston Matrix**, namely that it is prone to oversimplification and that it takes no account of other key variables such as product differentiation and market structure.

National strategic perspectives

In the *national* context, Porter has also examined competitive advantages as a basis for strategic initiatives. Porter identifies six key variables as potentially giving a country a competitive advantage over other countries:

1 *demand conditions*: the extent and characteristics of domestic demand;

2 *factor conditions*: transport infrastructure, national resources, human capital endowments etc.;

3 *firm strategies: structures and rivalries*: the organisation and management of companies and the degree of competition in the market structures in which they operate;

4 *related and supporting industries*: quality and extent of supply industries, supporting business services etc.;

5 *government policies*: nature of the regulatory environment, extent of state intervention in industry and the regions, state support for education and vocational training etc.;

6 *chance*.

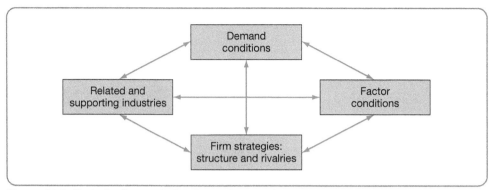

Figure 14.6 **Porter's diamond: the determinants of competitive advantage**

Source: Adapted from M. Porter, *The Competitive Advantage of Nations*, 1990, Palgrave Macmillan, reproduced with permission of Palgrave Macmillan.

Porter's diamond

The first four of these variables form a **diamond** shape, as shown in Figure 14.6, when mapped as the most important determinants of national competitive advantage.

In Porter's view, the four determinants are interdependent. For example, favourable 'demand conditions' will only contribute to national competitive advantage when combined with appropriate 'factor conditions', 'related and supporting industries' and 'firm strategies: structures and rivalries' so that companies are *able* and *willing* to take advantage of the favourable demand conditions. To sustain national competitive advantages in modern, high technology industries and economies, Porter argues that all four determinants in the 'diamond' must be favourable. However, in less technology-intensive industries and economies, one or two of the four determinants being favourable may be sufficient for a national competitive advantage: e.g. natural resource dependent industries may only need favourable 'factor conditions' (presence of an important natural resource) and appropriate infrastructure to extract and transport that resource.

The last two determinants 'government policies' and 'chance' outlined above (p. 487) can interact with the four key determinants of the diamond to open up new opportunities for national competitive advantage. For example, government policies in the field of education and training may help create R&D and other knowledge-intensive competitive advantage for a nation. Similarly, 'chance' events can play a part, as in the case of Russia supporting a greater US presence in Uzbekistan during the war in Afghanistan in 2001/2, thereby creating new opportunities for US oil companies to exploit the huge oil resources in that country.

Example

Britain is attractive to business

A KPMG survey found that Britain was the third cheapest advanced industrialised country in the world in which to do business – better even than the US and outperformed only by Canada and Australia. The survey compared the after-tax cost of starting and operating 12 types of business over a ten-year period, with the UK particularly competitive in the aerospace, automotive, telecommunications and pharmaceutical sectors. Britain had the second lowest effective income tax rates among the advanced economies, the fourth lowest relative labour costs, including wages and salaries, and other employer payments for labour. The report noted, however, that 'cost is not the sole factor for business attraction . . . talent and skills base together with academic support are also major contributors . . . to attracting inward foreign direct investment'.

International product life cycle (IPLC)

The suggestion here (e.g. Vernon and Wells, 1991) is that the pattern of products traded between countries will be influenced by the stage of production reached by a nation in the international life cycle of a variety of knowledge-intensive products. The *new product stage* (invention/development) will typically occur in the (advanced industrialised) innovating country but then the balance between production and consumption (and therefore between export and import) may shift *geographically* as different stages of the product life cycle are reached. In Figure 14.7 we can see a stylised IPLC for a knowledge-intensive product over three stages of the product life cycle (new product, mature product, standardised product) and for three broad geographical regions (innovating country, other advanced countries, less developed countries – LDCs).

- *New product stage*. Here production is concentrated in the *innovating country*, as is market demand. A typical scenario for this stage would be where the (initially) relatively low output is sold at premium prices to a price-inelastic domestic market segment (with few, if any, exports). There may be a small amount of production via subsidiaries in 'other advanced countries' but little or none in the LDCs.

- *Mature product stage*. Both production and consumption typically continue to rise in the *innovating country*, with scale economies beginning to reduce costs and price to a new, more price-sensitive mass market segment. Exports to other countries become a higher proportion of total sales. Output of the generic product also rises in the 'other advanced countries', via the output of subsidiaries or of competitors in these countries which have the knowledge-intensive capability of developing close substitutes. These countries typically import a high proportion of their sales from the innovating country, as do the LDCs.

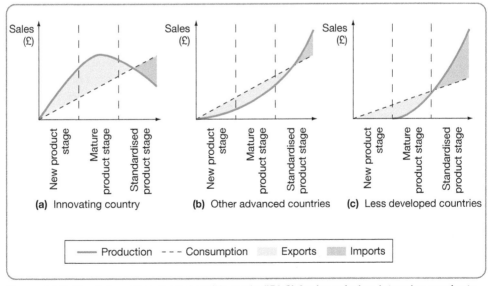

Figure 14.7 **The international product life cycle (IPLC) for knowledge-intensive products**

● *Standardised product stage.* At this stage the technology becomes more widely diffused and is often largely 'embodied' in both capital equipment and process control. Low-cost locations become a more feasible source of quality supply in this stage, often via multinational technology transfer. The LDCs may even become net exporters to the innovating country and to the other advanced countries.

Globalisation and strategic options for MNEs

The multinational enterprise (MNE) was considered in some detail in Chapter 13. Here we first review the key characteristics of globalisation and then focus on the ways in which the *value chain* for MNEs within a globalised environment is continually being appraised as to the *geographical location* of various elements. We also consider the strategic issues of whether or not parts of the value chain currently in-house might be *outsourced* by the MNE.

Globalisation

There is much debate as to what exactly is meant by 'globalisation'. Those who believe that globalisation is something really new tend to point to three key elements.

● *Shrinking space.* The lives of all individuals are increasingly interconnected by events worldwide. This is not only a matter of fact but one which people increasingly perceive to be the case, recognising that their jobs, income levels, health and living environment depend on factors outside national and local boundaries.

● *Shrinking time.* With the rapid developments in communication and information technologies, events occurring in one place have almost instantaneous (real-time) impacts worldwide. A fall in share prices in Wall Street can have almost immediate consequences for share prices in London, Frankfurt or Tokyo.

● *Disappearing borders.* The nation state and its associated borders seem increasingly irrelevant as 'barriers' to international events and influences. Decisions taken by regional trading blocs (e.g. EU, NAFTA) and supra-national bodies (e.g. IMF, World Trade Organization) increasingly override national policy making in economic and business affairs as well as in other areas such as law enforcement and human rights.

Others argue that 'globalisation' is a meaningless term, since world trade and investment as a proportion of world GDP is little different today from what it was over a hundred years ago and that international borders were as open at that time as they are today, with a similar proportion of the world's population migrating between countries.

Globalisation certainly has many dimensions (see *Taking it further* 14.2) which cannot be captured in their entirety using statistical data. However, we have already noted

---

Taking it further **Globalisation**   14.2

New markets

● Growing global markets in services – banking, insurance, transport.
● New financial markets – deregulated, globally linked, working around the clock, with action at a distance in real time, with new instruments such as derivatives.
● Deregulation of antitrust laws and growth of mergers and acquisitions.
● Global consumer markets with global brands.

Taking it further 14.2 *continued*

New actors

- Multinational corporations integrating their production and marketing, dominating world production.
- The World Trade Organization – the first multilateral organisation with authority to force national governments to comply with trade rules.
- A growing international network of non-governmental organisations (NGOs).
- Regional blocs proliferating and gaining importance – European Union, Association of South-East Asian Nations, Mercosur, North American Free Trade Association, Southern African Development Community, among many others.
- More policy coordination groups – G7, G8, OECD, IMF, World Bank.

New rules and norms

- Market economic policies spreading around the world, with greater privatisation and liberalisation than in earlier decades.
- Widespread adoption of democracy as the choice of political regime.
- Human rights conventions and instruments building up in both coverage and number of signatories – and growing awareness among people around the world.
- Consensus goals and action agenda for development.
- Conventions and agreements on the global environment – biodiversity, ozone layer, disposal of hazardous wastes, desertification, climate change.
- Multilateral agreements in trade, taking on such new agendas as environmental and social conditions.
- New multilateral agreements – for services, intellectual property, communications – more binding on national governments than any previous agreements.
- The (proposed) Multilateral Agreement on Investment.

New (faster and cheaper) tools of communication

- Internet and electronic communications linking many people simultaneously.
- Faster and cheaper transport by air, rail, sea and road.
- Computer-aided design and manufacture.

the significant and sustained growth in the 'transnationality index' for MNEs, indicating a greater global involvement. If we look at just three further specific indicators, namely international communications, international travel and international currency transactions, again there would seem to be changes occurring at a pace quite unlike that previously experienced.

- *International communications*. There have been dramatic rises in various modes of international communication. For example, the time spent on international telephone calls has risen from 33bn minutes in 1990 to over 120bn minutes by 2007. Internet usage is also rising exponentially, with the 2010 'Human Development Report' noting that the number of Internet hosts per 1,000 people rose from a mere 1.7m in 1990 to 28.2m in 2007, with cellular mobile phone subscribers per 1,000 people worldwide also rising from only 2 in 1990 to 200 in 2007. Various studies have found a strong and positive correlation between the extent of the telephone network and Internet usage. From this perspective it is important to note that the number of telephone mainlines per 1,000 people has increased in many *developing countries* over this period, from 21 per 1,000 people in 1990 to over 120 per 1,000 people in 2007.

● *International travel.* The number of international tourists more than trebled from 260m travellers a year in 1980 to over 800m travellers a year in 2007. The growth of tourism is closely correlated with the growth of world GDP and is an important source of income and employment for many developed and developing countries alike. However, increases in the perceived and actual risks associated with travel and tourism since 11 September 2001 and its aftermath have been linked to a drop in worldwide tourism of 2.2% from its peak in 2001.

● *International currency transactions.* The daily turnover in foreign exchange markets has dramatically increased from $15bn in the mid-1970s to over $2,400bn in 2007. This has contributed to greater exchange rate volatility, on occasions putting severe pressure on national economies and currencies.

Taking it further 14.2 broadens the discussion on globalisation to embrace a broad set of characteristics which in total represent something quite different from what has gone before.

International business and the value chain

We noted in Chapter 14 that international business is dominated by MNEs which, within the globalised economy, are increasingly transnational in operation, including horizontally and vertically integrated activities more widely dispersed on a geographical basis. This brings into focus the *value chain* in Figure 14.8, which breaks down the full collection of activities which companies perform into 'primary' and 'secondary' activities.

● *Primary activities* are those required to create the product (good or service, including inbound raw materials, components and other inputs), sell the product and distribute it to the marketplace.

● *Secondary activities* include a variety of functions such as human resource management, technological development, management information systems, finance for procurement etc. These secondary activities are required to support the primary activities.

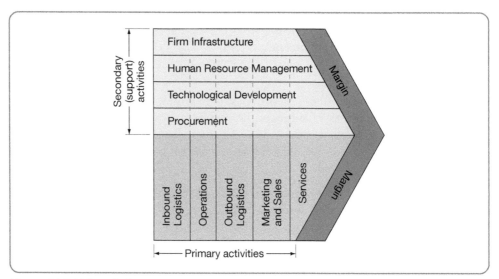

Figure 14.8 **Value chain**

Source: Used with the permission of The Free Press, a Division of Simon & Schuster, Inc., from *Competitive Advantage: Creating and Sustaining Superior Performance* by Michael E. Porter. Copyright © 1985 by Michael E. Porter. All rights reserved.

It is useful to remember that an effective international business strategy must encompass *all* parts of the value chain configuration, wherever their geographical location. Here we concentrate on international strategic approaches which might help the firm maximise the sum of these individual activities. International strategies which yield *global synergies* for the firm over its entire value chain are likely to be of particular interest, where synergies refer to the so-called '2 + 2 > 4 effect' whereby the whole becomes greater than the sum of the individual parts.

International business strategies

The enormous variety of operations embraced by the term 'multinational' has led some writers to distinguish between four key strategies when competing in the international business environment: a global strategy, a transnational strategy, a multidomestic strategy and an international strategy. The appropriateness of the particular strategy selected will depend to a considerable extent on the pressures faced by the international business in terms of both cost and local responsiveness, as indicated in Figure 14.9. These will become clearer as we discuss the nature of these various strategies and their associated advantages and disadvantages.

Global strategy

This is particularly appropriate when the firm faces high pressures in terms of cost competitiveness but low pressures in terms of being responsive to local market conditions. Firms adopting a **global strategy** focus on being cost competitive by securing the various economies of scale, scope and experience outlined in Chapter 3. Production, marketing and R&D activities tend to be concentrated in a few (and in extreme cases a single) favourable geographical locations rather than being widely dispersed. The emphasis of the global firm is on a homogenous, standardised product to maximise these various technical and non-technical economies. Of course, such a low-cost strategy is only possible where few pressures exist to localise either production or marketing. If localisation pressures were high, then shorter production runs of a locally differentiated product would invariably raise both technical (production) and non-technical (function/support services) costs.

The global strategy is best suited to industrial products for which there are high pressures for cost reductions but relatively low pressures for the product to be differentiated

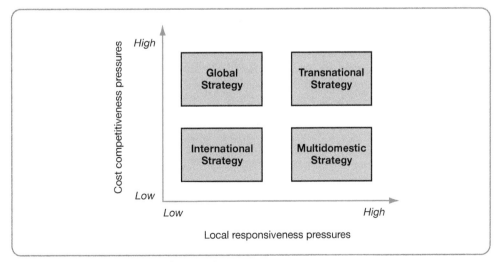

Figure 14.9 **Four international strategies**

to meet local market requirements. The semiconductor industry is widely regarded as suitable for this strategy, with global standards placing a premium on firms such as Intel, Motorola and Texas Instruments producing standardised products at minimum cost. A global strategy does not suit many consumer goods markets where product differentiation is a key to local/cultural acceptability.

Transnational strategy

Transnational strategy is particularly appropriate when the firm faces pressures in terms of both cost competitiveness and responsiveness to local conditions. Of course, such local responsiveness may involve more than the 'local' market acceptability of a differentiated product. It might, for example, also reflect entry barriers which effectively protect the local market from the import of a standardised product, however locally acceptable to consumers.

Firms adopting the *transnational strategy* cannot depend on cost reductions via scale economies from producing a standardised product in a few selected geographical locations. Rather they must seek cost reductions by exploiting *location economies* appropriate to a particular element of the value chain; for example, locating labour-intensive component production in countries where relative labour costs are low. Another cost reduction mechanism open to a transnational strategy might involve benefiting from *experience economies* related to cumulative production across a larger number of geographical locations. *Global learning* may be a further mechanism yielding cost reductions, as when foreign subsidiaries themselves add value to any core competencies transferred from the parent company. The foreign subsidiaries may go on to develop the expertise to become the primary centres for further, initially unforeseen, value added activities, thereby increasing global efficiency. Foreign subsidiaries may then be able to use this 'global learning' to transfer their own (newly acquired) core competencies to other foreign subsidiaries or back to the parent company itself.

These cost reduction outcomes via a transnational strategy must, of course, remain consistent with the high pressure towards local responsiveness. For example, local responsiveness may require product differentiation and non-standardised marketing and HRM approaches appropriate to local socio-cultural sensitivities.

Implementing a transnational strategy is likely to require a high degree of complex organisational coordination across geographically dispersed primary and secondary activities within the global value chain. There is also likely to be an element of conflict between cost reductions via the various mechanisms outlined above and cost increases resulting from an increased local responsiveness which inhibits scale economies of both a technical and non-technical nature. How then can the international business implement a transnational strategy?

There are, of course, many variants, but a widely used method for implementing this strategy involves the idea of 'modularity' in both design and production. This approach is currently being widely used in the car industry as part of a transnational strategy, whereby production activities are progressively broken down into a number of large but separate elements that can be carried out independently in different international locations, chosen according to the optimum mix of factor imports (cost and quality) for each element. Final assembly, characterised by local responsiveness in terms of product differentiation involving design and other features, often takes place at, or near to, the intended market.

Ford is following this approach, making many different models but using the same 'platform' – the basic chassis and other standardised internal parts. Design and technological breakthroughs of this kind permit even the transnational strategy to benefit from scale economies, as in the production of the

Links

The idea of relative unit labour costs (RULCs) will play a part in the firm's decision as to whether and where to relocate any part of its value chain (see *Taking it further* 14.3, p. 497) as part of a transnational strategy.

basic platform. However, Ford plans to produce ten different vehicles from this common platform, with differentiated features reflecting the need to respond to localised consumer preferences.

Multidomestic strategy

This is particularly appropriate when the firm faces low pressures in terms of cost competitiveness but high pressures in terms of local responsiveness. The multidomestic strategy tends to involve establishing relatively independent subsidiaries, each providing a full range of value chain activities (primary and secondary) within each national market. The subsidiary is broadly free to customise its products, focus its marketing and select and recruit its personnel, all in keeping with the local culture and the expressed preferences of its customers in each local market.

Such a strategy is more likely to occur when economies of scale in production and marketing are low, and when there are high coordination costs between parent and subsidiary. A disadvantage of such local 'independence' may also be an inability to realise potential experience economies. A further disadvantage may manifest itself in the autonomous actions of subsidiaries, sometimes paying little regard to broader-based corporate objectives. A classic example in this respect is the decision by the US subsidiary of Philips NV in the late 1970s to purchase the Matsushita VHS-format video-cassette recorders (VCRs) and put its own label on them, when the parent company was seeking to establish its own V2000 VCRs as the industry standard.

International strategy

This is particularly appropriate when the firm faces low pressures as regards both cost competitiveness and local responsiveness. The international strategy places the main focus on establishing the 'core architecture' (e.g. product development and R&D) underpinning the value chain at the home base of the MNE and seeking to translate this more or less intact to the national markets overseas. Some localised production and marketing activities may be permitted, but these will be limited in scope. McDonald's, IBM, Microsoft, Wal-Mart, Kellogg's and Procter & Gamble are often cited as companies pursuing an international strategy in which head office keeps a tight rein over product strategy and marketing initiatives.

Over time, some additional local customisation of product and marketing has tended to accompany the international strategy, not least because of some well-publicised failures from an overly strict adherence to the 'core architecture' at head offices. For example, IKEA, the Swedish furniture retailer, transferred its retailing formula developed in Sweden into other nations. While this transfer proved successful in the UK and elsewhere, it most certainly failed in the US, where product ranges proved inappropriate to the larger American physiques (e.g. beds, sofas were too small), the American preferences for larger storage spaces (drawers, bedroom chests and other containers were too confined), and European-sized curtains were incompatible with the sizes of American windows. After entering the US market in 1985, IKEA had realised by the early 1990s that it would need to customise its product range to the American market if it was going to succeed there, which it has now done with considerable success.

Such celebrated failures, together with a growing awareness of the benefits of at least a limited amount of local responsiveness, have somewhat diluted the international strategy, though it still remains one in which a centralised core architecture persists. It is most appropriate to situations where the parent firm possesses core competencies which are unmatched by indigenous competitors in foreign markets and where the key characteristics of the product are broadly welcomed by consumers in those markets.

Outsourcing

A key strategic decision for many MNEs is whether or not to outsource elements of the value chain which are currently 'in house'. A major attraction of outsourcing is the potential for reducing costs, as we noted in the case of Dyson moving production of its bagless vacuum cleaner from Wiltshire, UK to Malaysia (Case Study 1.4, p. 17) and in the movement of Hyundai vehicle manufacture from South Korea to China (Case Study 3.6, p. 98).

Case Study 14.3 looks more carefully at the strategic implications of outsourcing.

Case Study 14.3	Outsourcing: Competing in a globalised economy	

Emblazoned across the huge blue barns of the Daewoo shipyards on Koje island, off the southern coast of South Korea, are signs declaring 'No change, no future'. Certainly it is a frequent mantra in Korea, as Hyundai Heavy Industries, Samsung Heavy Industries and Daewoo Shipbuilding and Marine Engineering strive to maintain their positions at the top of the global industry. Right now, the top three are in a sweet spot – orders are rolling in fast, deep hedging means they are insulated against the strong Korean won and their share prices have been sky-rocketing. All are frantically extending their docks and building new quays to allow them to increase capacity.

'Korean shipbuilders are enjoying this very bullish market,' says Koh Youngyoul, chief strategy officer at Daewoo, which has a three-year backlog of orders worth $29bn. But how long will it last? Korean shipbuilders are being threatened by China, which is set to have 23 docks for construction of large ships by 2015, many more than Korea's 15. Meanwhile, Chinese manufacturers, already churning out standard container ships, are trying to make high-tech liquefied natural gas carriers and large containers – the Korean industry's bread and butter.

Korean estimates of the time China will take to close the technological gap range from four years to ten years. Industry operators know they must not be complacent. 'At the moment, China is simply building low-value added ships while Korea is making much more high-technological oriented ships,' says Mr Koh of Daewoo, which expected to win orders worth $11bn in 2007 but had to revise this up to $17bn after achieving its target in the first half of the year. 'There is no serious competition from China right now but it is only a matter of time until China catches up with Korea like Korea caught up with Japan ten years ago,' says Mr Koh.

Korea came from nowhere to become the world's biggest shipbuilding country and, thanks largely to Hyundai, Samsung and Daewoo, has a global market share of around 40%. The rise of Chinese industry has caused Korean manufacturers to look at Japan's mistakes and make sure that they do not fall into the same trap. 'Japan failed to diversify,' says Park Chung-Heum, executive vice-president of project planning at Samsung Heavy Industries, which likewise received $10bn in orders in the first half of 2007 and raised its projected orders to $15bn.

About 90% of all Korean orders are for run-of-the-mill container carriers and tankers but the other 10% is made up of vessels such as floating production storage and offloading oil facilities that Korean shipbuilders hope will be their future. Already Daewoo has built the Agbami FPSO vessel for Chevron, the US oil giant, for a record $1.6bn offshore oil production facility for Abu Dhabi Marine. Samsung is increasingly concentrating on offshore vessels such as barge-mounted power plants and drilling rigs. It has also built an Arctic tanker for Lukoil and ConocoPhillips that can break 1.5m-thick ice. 'Six years ago the average price of a Samsung ship was $50m or $80m at today's prices – but now it is $170m,' Mr Park says from his office overlooking the Koje shipyards, illustrating both the sophistication of the ships being built and the recent escalation of prices shipyards can command.

But all this new added value carries a risk, namely technology leakage. Korea's National Intelligence Service has been investigating leaks from Korean companies to Chinese competitors and a former Daewoo employee has been arrested for selling drawings to a Chinese company. 'We are very concerned about this sort of leakage,' says Mr Park of Samsung. 'Now we are putting watermarks on

Case Study 14.3 *continued*

our drawings and we always print them on paper, not on CD. This is a very critical time and China would like to be able to catch up with Korea.'

Sanjeev Rana, a shipbuilding analyst at Merrill Lynch in Seoul, nevertheless says Korean shipbuilders will be able to remain market leaders in high-value ships at least until 2010, although he adds that this is not necessarily a recipe for success.

'Korea will maintain their lead in the value-added segment but they need to maintain conventional shipbuilding in their portfolio – you can't have everything value added,' Mr Rana says. 'So even if they increase the high-tech component of their portfolio to 65%, they will still be 40 or 35% exposed to China.'

Strategy of cheap labour

China might present a threat to Korean shipbuilders, but it also offers significant opportunities. Samsung Heavy Industries and Daewoo Shipbuilding and Marine Engineering, Korea's second and third largest shipbuilders, respectively, have both opened yards across the Yellow Sea. There, Chinese workers construct the blocks that form the basis for Korean ships, which are then transported back to Korea for value-added production. This enables Korean producers to utilise China's cheap labour without – in theory – giving away core technology.

'China is supplying the one-third of the blocks used in our ships, which are put together in the Koje yards,' says Park Chung-heum, executive vice-president of project planning at Samsung Heavy. 'The price of block fabrication in Korea has become very expensive so we are very happy to do this in China.'

Samsung's factory in Ningbo, Zhejiang province, now produces 200,000 tonnes of ship blocks a year, while Daewoo's subsidiary in the north-eastern port city of Yantai, Shandong province, will churn out 220,000 tonnes of ship blocks when it reaches full capacity in 2011. However, Hyundai Heavy Industries, Korea's largest shipbuilder, does not have a joint venture in China and has no plans to open one, says Kevin Chang, a company spokesman. 'Shipbuilding is a very labour-intensive industry and Hyundai Heavy wants to supply jobs for Koreans,' he said.

Source: Adapted from Korean shipbuilders struggle to keep Chinese in their wake, *Financial Times*, 27/07/2007 (Fifield, A.), © The Financial Times Ltd

Questions

1 Why does Korea look to Japan when reviewing its strategies?

2 Consider the opportunities and threats to Korean shipbuilding from globalisation.

This whole issue of outsourcing can be more clearly understood in the context of 'relative unit labour costs' (RULCs). It is this measurement that is the most widely accepted indicator of international competitiveness and that will ultimately determine whether and where any particular part of a firm's value chain will be outsourced. *Taking it further* 14.3 provides further information on RULCs.

Taking it further Relative unit labour costs (RULCs)   14.3

Labour costs per unit of output (unit labour costs) depend on both the wage and non-wage (e.g. employer National Insurance contributions in the UK) costs of workers and the output per worker (labour productivity). For example, if the total (wage and non-wage) costs per worker double, but productivity more than doubles, then labour costs per unit will actually fall.

However, the exchange rate must also be taken into account when considering international competitiveness, and this also is included in the definition of RULC below. For example, for any given value for labour costs per unit, if the exchange rate of that country's currency falls against a competitor, then its exports become more competitive (cheaper) abroad and imports less competitive (dearer) at home.

The calculation of RULC is therefore as follows:

$$\text{RULC} = \frac{\text{Relative labour costs}}{\text{Relative labour productivity}} \times \text{Relative exchange rate}$$

This formula emphasises that (compared to some other country) lower RULC for, say, the UK could be achieved by reducing the UK's relative labour costs, or by raising the UK's relative labour productivity, or by lowering the UK's relative exchange rate, or by some combination of all three.

More information on international labour costs and productivity is given in 'Data response and stimulus questions', question 1 of 'Assessment Practice' on the Student Website accompanying this text.

Table 14.6 **India's low cost advantage**

	Per capita income US$	Salary of educated person as multiple of per capita income	Salary of educated person US$	Salary of educated person, purchasing power parity US$
IT Professional				
US	34,280	2.2	75,000	75,000
UK	25,120	3.8	96,000	93,120
India	460	55.4	26,000	159,380
Graduate				
US	34,280	1.2	45,000	45,000
UK	25,120	1.9	48,000	46,560
India	460	14.1	6,500	39,845

Source: Based on information from National Association of Software and Service Companies, India

The strategic decision as to where to locate any particular element of the value chain must include all three elements. Certainly information such as that for India, shown in Table 14.6, will merit consideration by MNEs adopting a transnational strategy.

However, such information must be considered in the context of exchange rate changes, as indicated in the RULC formula. Indeed, exchange rate changes may themselves influence the international business strategies adopted by companies.

Example

Falling dollar and business strategies

Overseas MNEs seeking to compete effectively in the USA were facing, whatever strategies they employed, still further problems in 2007/8 with the then low value of the dollar. For example, the dollar fell in value against the pound sterling by around 20% in 2007. Investment bank Morgan Stanley calculated that a 10% fall in the dollar against the pound would disadvantage UK trade with the USA by over £1.4bn per year, with US exports to the UK cheaper in sterling and UK exports to the USA dearer in dollars. For UK-based MNEs operating in the USA with a 'transnational strategy', whereby elements of the value chain are located outside the USA with, say, manufacture or assembly of the finished item inside the USA, this had major disadvantages. The prices of components imported into the USA were rising, increasing their cost base. A 'global strategy' faced similar problems, where the finished item was produced *outside* the USA and then imported for US consumers to buy. In some respects the low dollar at that time was encouraging a 'multidomestic strategy' for non-US MNEs whereby the entire value chain, or at least the major part of it, would be best located in largely independent subsidiaries inside the USA. Exports from the US subsidiaries to the rest of the world would then benefit from the low dollar, while expensive imports of components etc. would be minimised under such a strategy. Of course, since 2008 the situation has reversed, with the pound falling significantly against the dollar.

Stop and think   14.3

What other factors need to be taken into account other than that shown in Table 14.4 (p. 480) to gain a better idea of international competitiveness between the UK, USA and India?

New dimensions of strategic choice

C. Prahalad, an authority on globalisation, has suggested that the changes this is bringing to the competitive landscape are changing the basis for strategic choice. He suggests that industrial and service sectors are no longer the stable entities they once were:

● Rapid technology changes and the convergence of technologies (e.g. computer and telecommunications) are constantly redefining industrial 'boundaries' so that the 'old' industrial structures become barely recognisable.

● Privatisation and deregulation have become global trends within industrial sectors (e.g. telecommunications, power, water, healthcare, financial services) and even within nations themselves (e.g. transition economies, China).

● Internet-related technologies are beginning to have major impacts on business-to-business and business-to-customer relationships.

● Pressure groups based around environmental and ecological sensitivities are progressively well organised and influential.

● New forms of institutional arrangements and liaisons are exerting greater influences on organisational structures than hitherto (e.g. strategic alliances, franchising).

In a progressively less stable environment there will arguably be a shift in perspective away from the previous strategic focus of Porter and his contemporaries in which companies are seen as seeking to identify and exploit *competitive advantages* within stable industrial structures. Instead, in the 'discontinuous competitive landscapes' which characterise today's global economy, Prahalad (1999) suggests four key 'transformations' which must now take place in strategic thinking.

1 *Recognising changes in strategic space.* Deregulation and privatisation of previously government controlled industries, access to new market opportunities in large developing countries (e.g. China, India, Brazil) and in the transitional economies of Central and Eastern Europe, together with the rapidly changing technological environment, are creating entirely new strategic opportunities. Take the case of the large energy utilities. They must now decide on the extent of integration (power generation, power transmission within industrial and/or consumer sectors), the geographical reach of their operations (domestic/overseas), the extent of diversification (other types of energy, non-energy fields) and so on. Powergen in the UK is a good example of a traditional utility with its historical base in electricity generation which, in a decade or so, has transformed itself into a global provider of electricity services (generation and

transmission), water, gas and other infrastructure services. Clearly the strategic 'space' available to companies is ever expanding, creating entirely new possibilities in the modern global economy.

2 *Recognising globalisation impacts.* As we discuss in more detail below, globalisation of business activity is itself opening up new strategic opportunities and threats. Arguably the distinction between local and global business will itself become increasingly irrelevant. The local businesses must devise their own strategic response to the impact of globalised players. Nirula, the Indian fast food chain, raising standards of hygiene and restaurant ambience in response to competition from McDonald's, is one type of local response, and McDonald's providing more lamb and vegetarian produce in its Indian stores is another. Mass customisation and quick response strategies require global businesses to be increasingly responsive to local consumers. Additionally, globalisation opens up new strategic initiatives in terms of geographical locations, modes of transnational collaboration, financial accountability and logistical provision.

3 *Recognising the importance of timely responses.* Even annual planning cycles are arguably becoming progressively obsolete as the speed of corporate response becomes a still more critical success factor, both to seize opportunities and to repel threats.

4 *Recognising the enhanced importance of innovation.* Although innovation has long been recognised as a critical success factor, its role is still further enhanced in an environment dominated by the 'discontinuities' previously mentioned. Successful companies must still innovate in terms of new products and processes but now such innovation must also be directed towards providing the company with faster and more reliable information on customers as part of mass customisation, quick response and personalised product business philosophies.

These factors are arguably changing the context for business strategy from positioning the company within a clear-cut industrial structure, to stretching and shaping that structure by its own strategic initiatives. It may no longer be sensible or efficient to devise strategic blueprints over a protracted planning time-frame and then seek to apply the blueprints mechanically, given that events and circumstances are changing so rapidly. The *direction* of broad strategic thrust can be determined as a route map, but tactical and operational adjustments must be continually appraised and modified along the way.

Nor can the traditional strategy hierarchies continue unchallenged – i.e. top management creating strategy and middle management implementing it. Those who are closest to the product and market are becoming increasingly important as well-informed sources for identifying opportunities to exploit or threats to repel. Arguably the roles of middle and lower management in the strategic process are being considerably enhanced by the 'discontinuities' previously observed. Top managers are finding themselves progressively removed from competitive reality in an era of discontinuous change. Their role is rather to set a broad course, to ensure that effective and responsive middle and lower management are in place to exercise delegated strategic responsibilities, and to provide an appropriate infrastructure for strategic delivery. For example, a key role of top managers in various media-related activities may be to secure access to an appropriate broadband wavelength by successfully competing in the UK or German auctions. Such access is likely to be a prerequisite for competitive involvement in a whole raft of Internet-related products for home and business consumption via mobile telephony.

Figure 14.10 provides a useful summary of the traditional and emerging views of international business strategy.

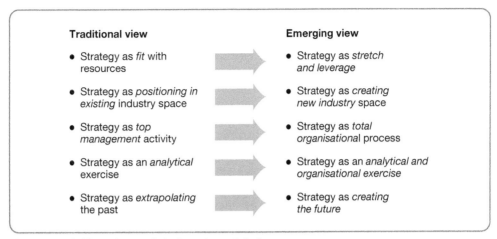

Figure 14.10 **New views of strategy in a global economy**

Strategic joint ventures and alliances

In a global economy in which rapid technological change is a fact of life, even the larger companies often find it beneficial to undertake strategic joint ventures or alliances with other companies. Sometimes these arrangements might even take place with rivals, as for example Ford and Honda undertaking a joint venture involving expensive R&D in advanced engine development, but competing aggressively against each other's vehicles which contain the same engine specifications.

Strategic joint ventures or alliances between companies are more likely when both companies see the benefit of coming together but when a more formal merger or acquisition is ruled out. For example, when two companies merging would give them too high a share of the market for regulatory bodies to allow the merger to go ahead, then a joint-venture or alliance may be an acceptable alternative.

Joint ventures

Joint ventures (unlike alliances) involve creating a new identity in which both the initiating partners take active roles in formulating strategy and making decisions. Joint ventures can help:

- share and lower the costs of high-risk, technology-intensive development projects;
- gain economies of scale and scope in value-adding activities that can only be justified on a global basis;
- secure access to a partner's technology, its accumulated learning, proprietary processes or protected market position;
- create a basis for more effective future competition in the industry involved.

Joint ventures are particularly common in high-technology industries where hugely expensive R&D is often required to remain at the cutting edge of high technology. Joint ventures usually take one of two forms, namely specialised or shared value-added.

Specialised joint ventures

Here each partner brings a specific competency; for example, one might produce and the other market. Such ventures are likely to be organised around *different functions*. One specialised joint venture has involved JVC (Japan) and Thomson (France). JVC contributed the specialised skills involved in the manufacturing technologies needed to produce optical and compact discs, computers and semiconductors, while Thomson contributed the specific marketing skills needed to compete in fragmented markets such as Europe.

The major benefits of *specialised joint ventures* include an opportunity to share risks, to learn about a partner's skills and proprietary processes and to gain access to new distribution channels. However, they carry risks as well, perhaps the greatest being that one partner's exposure of its particular competences may result in the other partner gaining a competitive advantage which it might subsequently use to become a direct competitor. This happened to GE when it entered into a specialised joint venture with Samsung to produce microwave ovens. Samsung now competes with GE across the whole range of household appliances.

Shared value-added joint ventures

Here both partners contribute to the *same function* or value-added activity. For example, Fuji-Xerox is an example of a shared value-added joint venture with the design, production and marketing functions all shared.

Shared value-added joint ventures pose a slightly different set of risks: partners can more easily lose their competitive advantage since the close working relationships involve the same function. If the venture is not working, it may be more difficult to exit since coordination costs tend to be much higher than they are in specialised joint ventures, with the more extensive administrative networks having usually been established.

Critical success factors for any type of joint venture or indeed alliance might include the following.

- *Take time to assess the partners.* Extended courtship is often required if a joint venture of either type is to be successful; Corning Incorporated of the US formed its joint venture with CIBA-GEIGY only after two years of courtship. Being too hurried can destroy a venture, as AT&T and Olivetti of Italy discovered when they formed a joint venture to produce personal computers which failed because of an incompatibility in management styles and corporate cultures as well as in objectives.

- *Understand that collaboration is a distinct form of competition.* Competitors as partners must remember that joint ventures are sometimes designed as ways of 'de-skilling' the opposition. Partners must learn from each other's strengths while preserving their own sources of competitive advantage. Many firms enter into joint ventures in the mistaken belief that the other partner is the student rather than the teacher.

- *Learn from partners while limiting unintended information flows.* Companies must carefully design joint ventures so that they do not become 'windows' through which one partner can learn about the other's competencies.

- *Establish specific rules and requirements for joint venture performance at the outset.* For example, Motorola's transfer of microprocessor technology to Toshiba is explicitly dependent on how much market share Motorola gets in Japan.

- *Give managers sufficient autonomy.* Decentralisation of decision making should give managers sufficient autonomy to run the joint venture successfully. Two of the most successful global value-adding joint ventures are those between Fuji-Xerox and Nippon-Otis which are also among those giving management the greatest autonomy.

It has been found that extensive training and team building is crucial if these joint ventures are to succeed. There are three ways in which effective HRM may be critical:

- developing and training managers in negotiation and conflict resolution;
- acculturation (i.e. cultural awareness) in working with a foreign partner;
- harmonisation of management styles.

Case Study 14.4 investigates the 2010 strategic alliance involving Daimler and Renault-Nissan.

Case Study 14.4   Daimler and Renault-Nissan create strategic alliance

The Franco–Japanese alliance between Renault and Nissan in 1999 involved a nearly bankrupt Nissan. Ever since Carlos Ghosn made his reputation by turning round the Japanese carmaker, he has been looking for a third partner to achieve even greater economies of scale. General Motors rejected Renault-Nissan's offer to join them in 2006, but on 7 April 2010 Mr Ghosn announced a deal with Daimler, effectively creating a three-way car-making alliance.

The Renault-Nissan-Daimler alliance is but one more example of recent agreements between large-scale car producers seeking ways to benefit from greater economies of scale and to share high up-front costs for innovative developments such as hybrid electric cars. The tie-up with the German luxury car and truck firm falls some way short of the kind of full-blown alliance that Mr Ghosn would prefer. The new alliance will focus on sharing resources in four main areas: platforms for small cars and light commercial vehicles; small petrol and diesel engines; technology for fully electric and hybrid cars; and bigger diesel engines. The first benefit of the collaboration is likely to be the development of a new platform for the little Renault Twingo that will also be used by Mercedes for the next two- and four-door Smart cars, due in 2013.

Renault holds a 44% stake in Nissan which, in turn, has a 15% (non-voting) share in the Renault company, Daimler will take a much more modest 3.1% stake in each of them, and they will each take a tiny 1.55% stake in Daimler. Mr Ghosn believes that cross-shareholdings are a critical signal to employees, especially engineers, that the partnership is both long-term and strategic. Dieter Zetsche, Daimler's boss, was reluctant to go further in that direction, perhaps still unnerved by the disastrous Daimler-Chrysler merger.

Benefits to Daimler include the fact that its Mercedes brand urgently needs to find a better way

of producing small cars. The world's drivers are increasingly turning to smaller, more efficient vehicles as environmental regulations are strengthened and the average age rises in many developed countries. Mercedes already makes small cars, but its efforts have been undermined by products that are too expensive and over-engineered. It has lost huge amounts on its Smart, A-Class and B-Class programmes – perhaps as much as €7 billion ($9 billion) over the past decade, according to Max Warburton of Bernstein Research.

His research also indicated that in terms of compact car sales (Global C-segment), Mercedes fell far behind its competitors. Mercedes only produced 0.2 million such cars in 2009, well below the 2.1 million of VW, 1.5 million of Toyota, 1.1 million of Renault-Nissan, 0.8 million of Peugeot Citroen and the 0.7 million of Ford in this small car category. Our earlier (p. 93) data showed the disadvantages in terms of unit production costs of a volume of car output below 2 million units per annum. It also showed (p. 94) the disadvantages in terms of non-production costs such as R&D, finance, etc. of lower volumes of car output.

In an attempt to turn things around Daimler has talked to Volkswagen and Fiat as well as its great rival, BMW. However, Renault-Nissan's experience in making partnerships work and the complementary nature of the firm's products made the pair a good fit for the German firm.

Renault will not benefit as much from technology sharing, but Nissan will get Mercedes diesel engines for its high-end Infiniti range, which is struggling to establish itself in Europe without a diesel option. According to insiders, the three partners will also earn around €2 billion from the deal in the form of cost savings and additional sales over the next five years.

Perhaps more important to Mr Ghosn is the apparent vote of confidence from Daimler. For

Case Study 14.4 *continued*

much of the past decade Renault has been a disappointingly mediocre performer, bolstered by substantial dividends from the more successful Nissan. Thanks to the launch last year of the new Megane hatchback and Scenic minivan, Renault's market share in Europe is rising. But despite (or perhaps because of) Renault's bold attempt to be the first volume maker of purely electric vehicles, investors, according to Mr Warburton, still see the firm as 'a long-term structural loss'. Mr Zetsche's cautious endorsement could shift that perception, but only if he and Mr Ghosn can convincingly show how they will make their tie-up work.

Source: Based on information from *The Economist* (2010) 10–16 April

Questions

1 What is the attraction of this new alliance to both Renault-Nissan and to Daimler?

2 What are likely to be the factors which will determine whether the alliance will be judged a 'success' or 'failure'?

Recap

- Corporate strategy is defined as involving the direction and scope of an organisation over the long term.
- 'Competitive advantage' refers to the strengths of the more successful firms in an industry vis-à-vis the most marginal firm in that industry.
- SWOT (Strength, Weakness, Opportunities, Threats) analysis emphasises both external and internal environmental factors.
- PEST (Political, Economic, Social and Technological) analysis focuses on the external environment in which the firm operates, to which law and ecology are sometimes added to make PESTLE. It may be used in support of SWOT analysis.
- The stage reached in the product life cycle both nationally and internationally can have important implications for price and non-price strategies undertaken by the firm.
- The Boston matrix uses categories such as 'Question Marks', 'Stars', 'Cash Cows' and 'Dogs' to support a balanced portfolio approach by multi-product firms.
- The Ansoff matrix uses 'new' and 'present' categories of product and market to identify strategic direction.
- Porter's 'Five Forces' analysis can be used to help the firm 'position' itself in terms of the appropriate strategic responses to those forces, while Porter's 'diamond' emphasises national rather than firm competitiveness.
- Porter's 'generic' strategies involve broad directions of strategy such as overall cost leadership, product differentiation and focus strategies.
- In a global context MNEs must continually reconfigure their value chains to reflect both cost-competitive opportunities and pressures towards local responsiveness.
- MNEs may adopt global, multidomestic, transnational and national strategies.
- 'Relative unit labour costs' (RULCs) are a key index of international competitiveness and play an important role in strategic choice.

Key terms

Boston Matrix A device by which products can be rated according to sales growth and market share. Developed by the Boston Consulting Group in the US and involving categories such as 'problem children', 'stars', 'cash cows' and 'dogs'.

Focus strategy Where the company identifies a segment in the market and tailors its strategy to serve that market, excluding all other segments.

Generic strategies Porter identified three such strategies; namely, cost leadership (emphasis on cost reduction), differentiation strategy (emphasis on superior product characteristics) and a focus on strategy in which the company identifies a segment in the market and tailors its strategy to serve that market, excluding all other segments.

Global strategy Emphasises large-scale production of a standardised product securing economies of scale, scope and experience.

International strategy 'Core' architecture located in home base with limited aspects of the value chain only located overseas.

Multidomestic strategy Emphasises responsiveness to the different conditions in each national market by establishing relatively independent subsidiaries with a full range of value chain activities.

PEST An analysis involving the political, economic, social and technological environment in which the firm operates.

PESTLE Political, economic, social, technological, legal and environmental.

Porter's diamond Highlights four interdependent determinants of national competitive advantages, namely demand conditions, factor conditions, related and supporting industries and firm strategies, structures and rivalries.

Porter's Five Forces An analysis involving an assessment of the threat of (1) potential entrants and (2) substitutes, as well as the power of (3) suppliers and (4) buyers, together with an exploration of (5) the degree of competitive rivalry.

Strategy Guiding 'rules' or principles influencing the direction and scope of the organisation's activities in the long term.

SWOT An analysis of the strengths, weaknesses, opportunities and threats facing the company from both internal and external sources.

Transnational strategy Emphasises establishing each element in the value chain in the most appropriate geographical setting.

APPENDICES

Indifference curves, budget lines and the 'law of demand'

Indifference curves are lines representing different combinations (bundles) of products that yield a constant level of utility or satisfaction to the consumer. The consumer is therefore *indifferent* as between the various consumption possibilities denoted by the line.

Figure A1.1(a) can be used to illustrate the properties of an indifference curve.

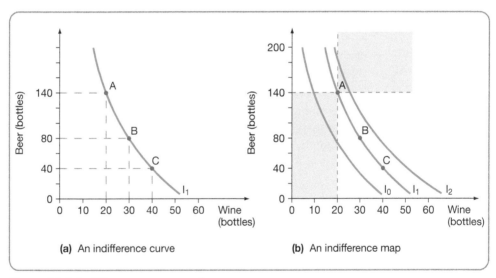

(a) An indifference curve

(b) An indifference map

Figure A1.1 **Indifference curves and maps**

In addition to diminishing marginal utility, suppose our consumer is indifferent between three different combinations of bottles of wine and beer, namely A (20 wine, 140 beer), B (30 wine, 80 beer) and C (40 wine, 40 beer). In other words, these three combinations of wine and beer yield the same level of utility to the consumer as in fact do all the combinations of wine and beer on the curve I_1. We call this curve connecting all the combinations (bundles) of products that yield a constant level of utility, an indifference curve.

Indifference maps

As we can see from Figure A1.1(b), indifference maps show *all* the indifference curves that rank the preferences of our consumer as between the two products. Indifference maps are drawn on the basis of three key assumptions.

1 *Non-satiation.* The consumer is not totally satisfied (satiated) with the amounts of the products already obtained, but prefers to have more of either. In other words, 'a good is a good', with any extra units of either product (good or service) adding some positive amount to total utility.

2 *Transitivity.* Consumers are consistent in their ranking of various consumption bundles.

3 *Diminishing marginal rate of substitution between products.* This assumption is related to our earlier idea of 'diminishing marginal utility'. However, this time it refers to the fact that as more of any one product (X) is consumed, the consumer will be willing to sacrifice progressively less of some other product (Y) for utility to remain unchanged.

Let us now examine the relevance of these assumptions to our indifference map.

- The first assumption of non-satiation implies that more of one product and no less of some other product is a preferred position, so that indifference curves above and to the right must represent higher levels of utility/satisfaction. In Figure A1.1(b) the indifference curve I_2 includes consumption bundles in the shaded box above and to the right of consumption bundle A on indifference curve I_1. These shaded consumption bundles all include having more beer and no less wine, or more wine and no less beer, or more beer and more wine than A, and are therefore preferred consumption bundles to A. It follows that all the consumption bundles on I_2 that go through this shaded area must correspond to a higher level of satisfaction than the consumption bundles on I_1.

- The second assumption, that consumers are *consistent* in their preference orderings, implies that it is impossible for separate indifference curves to intersect one another. For example, suppose we have the following consumer ranking of three bundles of products A, B and C.

$$A > B$$
$$B > C$$

Then, via consistent consumer behaviour we can say that

$$A > C$$

If this assumption holds true, then indifference curves could not intersect. However, if consumer preferences are *not* consistent, then indifference curves can intersect, as they do in Figure A1.2.

In Figure A1.2:

$A > B$ (more of Y, same X)
$A = C$ (on same indifference curve)
$B = D$ (on same difference curve)
$C > D$ (via consistency assumption)

But $D > C$ (more of Y, same X)!

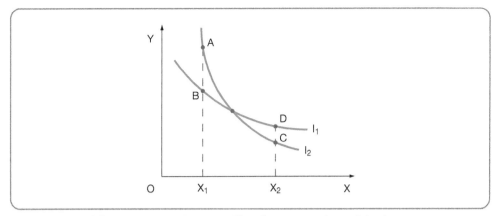

Figure A1.2 Indifference curves intersect if preferences not consistent

Clearly, when indifference curves intersect this indicates that consumers are not exercising consistency in their ranking of different bundles of product.

● The third assumption of diminishing marginal rate of substitution between the products implies that we draw indifference curves convex to (bowed towards) the origin. In other words, the more of one product you are consuming, the progressively less of the other product you are willing to give up in order to consume an extra unit of that product. This means that slope of an indifference curve diminishes as we move from left to right along its entire length.

Deriving the demand curve: indifference analysis

We can use indifference curve analysis to predict the downward sloping demand curve, just as we used marginal utility analysis previously (see *Taking it further* 2.4, p. 65). However, before doing this we must become familiar with the idea of the budget line of the consumer.

Budget line

In much of the analysis involving indifference curves we assume that consumers wish to maximise utility subject to a number of constraints, such as the level of household income and the prices of the products bought. These particular constraints can be represented by the *budget line* showing the various combinations of two products, X and Y, which can be purchased if the whole household income is spent on these products.

● The *slope* of the budget line will depend upon the relative prices of the two products.
● The *position* of the budget line will depend on the level of household income.

Figure A1.3 usefully illustrates these points.
   Let us suppose the following:

   Household income   = £200
   Price of product X (P_x) = £20
   Price of product Y (P_y) = £25

In Figure A1.3(a), if all the income is spent on X, then we are at point B (10X, 0Y); if all the income is spent on Y then we are at point A (0X, 8Y). The line AB is therefore the

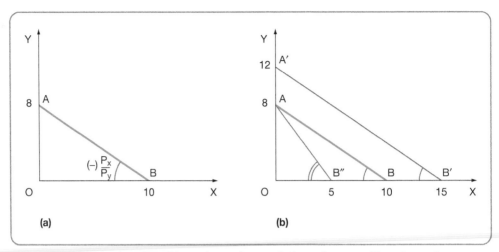

Figure A1.3 **The budget line. Slope depends on relative prices; position depends on household income**

budget line and represents the various combinations of X and Y that could be purchased if the *whole* household income was spent on these products.

The *slope* of this budget line depends on the relative price ratio:

$$\text{Slope} = (-)\frac{8}{10} = (-)\frac{20}{25} \quad i.e. \ (-)\frac{P_x}{P_y}$$

The *position* of this budget line depends on the level of household income.

We can use Figure A1.3(b) to make this last point clear.

(a) A′B′ shows what happens to the budget line AB if there is a 50% increase in household income from £200 to £300. Notice that a rise in household income leads to a *parallel* outward shift in the budget line. The new and old budget lines have the same slope because the price ratio is unchanged.

(b) AB″ shows what happens to the budget line AB if the household income remains at the original £200 but the price of product X (P_x) rises from £20 to £40 with the price of the product Y (P_y) unchanged at £25. Notice that a change in the relative price ratio means that the slope of the new budget line is different from that of the old budget line. In this case the slope is steeper since only five units of X can now be purchased from an income of £200 if its price rises from £20 to £40, whilst it is still possible to purchase eight units of Y at its unchanged price of £25. Notice that a rise in the price of product X leads to the budget line pivoting inwards around point A.

Consumer equilibrium

We assume that the consumer seeks the maximum utility (highest indifference curve) subject to the constraints imposed on him/her. These constraints involve the level of household income (*position* of budget line) and the relative prices of the products (*slope* of budget line).

Figure A1.4 brings together our work on indifference curves and budget lines to identify the particular consumption bundle that corresponds to maximum consumer utility subject to these constraints. Given the position of the budget line AB in Figure A1.4 and its slope $(-)\ P_x/P_y$, the highest indifference curve the consumer can reach is I_2 at point E. By consuming 30 units of X and 80 units of Y the consumer has maximised utility subject

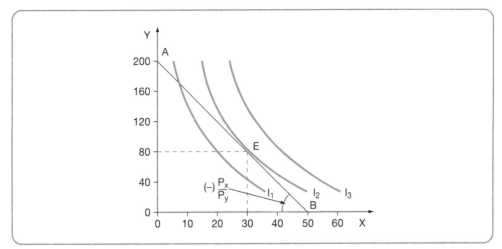

Figure A1.4 Consumer equilibrium. Reaching the highest indifference curve attainable, at point E

to the constraints he faces. I_3 is, of course, an indifference curve yielding still higher satisfaction, but is unattainable under present circumstances.

Notice that this consumption bundle of 30X and 80Y, which corresponds to 'consumer equilibrium', represents a situation of *tangency* between the budget line and the highest attainable indifference curve. In other words, consumer utility is maximised when the slope of an indifference curve is exactly equal to the slope of the budget line (i.e. the price ratio).

Price–consumption line

Figure A1.5 uses this idea of 'consumer equilibrium' to derive the so-called *price–consumption* line, showing tangency points between budget lines with different prices of product X (P_x) and the highest attainable indifference curves.

Suppose our household has a weekly income of £48, with the initial price of X (P_x) at £16 and price of Y (P_y) at £4. This gives us the initial budget line AB' and the equilibrium point at E for maximum utility of I_1. At P_x = £16, one unit of good X is demanded. Suppose now that P_x falls first to £8 and then to £4, other things equal (i.e. household income and P_y). We can represent this by pivoting the budget line to AB' (P_x = £8) and AB" (P_x = £4) respectively. This gives us new equilibrium points of E' and E" where the consumer reaches the highest attainable indifference curves of I_2 and I_3 respectively.

From this, we can derive the individual demand curve in the bottom part of Figure A1.5. So at P_x = £16 we have one unit of X demanded, at P_x = £8 we have three units of X demanded and at P_x = £4 we have seven units of X demanded.

As we shall see, the demand curve for normal commodities will always have a negative slope, denoting the law of demand, namely that the quantity demanded rises (expands) as price falls.

Example

Sales of the iPhone would seem to follow the 'law of demand'. The price of the iPhone was cut by Apple by a third in the USA in September 2007 in an effort to boost sales. At an unveiling of a new line of its music and video players in San Francisco, the Chief Executive of Apple, Steve Jobs, indicated that the price of its most popular iPhone, with 8GB of storage, would be cut from $599 to $399 in the expectation that this price cut would so expand the quantity sold that the revenue from the iPhone would increase. In the event the sales growth was less than in proportion to the price cut.

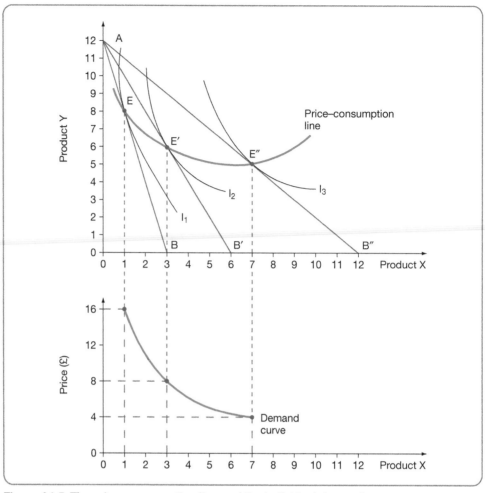

Figure A1.5 **The price–consumption line and the individual demand curve**

Taking it further A1.1 investigates the conditions which are necessary for this law of demand to hold true.

Taking it further **The 'law of demand'**   A1.1

A reduction in the price of X has, in our analysis, resulted in an overall rise in the quantity demanded of good X, as for instance in the move from E to E', along the price–consumption line in Figure A1.5 and along the corresponding demand curve. However, this rise in the quantity demanded is the *total price effect* which may be split into two separate parts, the *substitution effect* and the *income effect*. We now examine each part in turn (see Figure A1.6).

- **Substitution effect**. This refers to the extra purchase of product X now that it is, after the price fall, relatively cheaper than other substitutes in consumption.

- **Income effect**. This refers to the rise in real income (purchasing power) now that the price of one product is lower within the bundle of products purchased by the consumer. This extra real income can potentially be used to buy more of all products, including X.

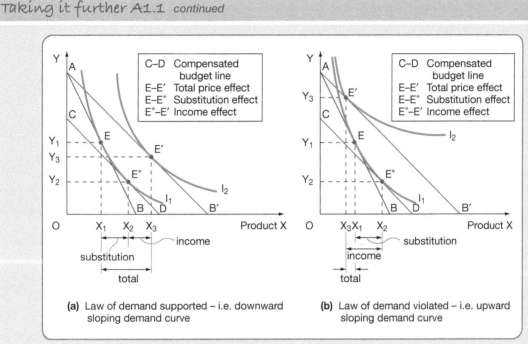

Figure A1.6 Income and substitution effects

For analytical purposes it is helpful to deal separately with each effect and we do this by making use of the *compensated budget line*. In Figure A1.6 above the fall in P_X has caused the budget line to pivot from AB to AB', representing the new price ratio between X and Y.

The *total price effect* is shown in the movement from E to E', i.e. the rise in quantity demanded of X from X_1 to X_3. To derive the *compensated budget line* we reduce the consumer's real income, but retain the new price ratio after the fall in P_X so that the consumer is still only able to achieve the same level of utility as before. We show this by shifting the budget line AB' inwards and parallel to itself (thereby retaining the new price ratio) until it is a tangent to the original indifference curve I_1. This occurs with the budget line CD at point E*.

We can now say that the movement from E to E* is the pure *substitution effect*, i.e. the extra amount $(X_2 - X_1)$ of X purchased solely as a result of X being cheaper relative to Y, the income effect having been compensated, i.e. eliminated.

If we now allow the income effect to be restored, the budget line returns to AB', moving outwards and parallel to CD. We can now say that the movement from E* to E' is the *income effect*. In this case the income effect is positive $(X_3 - X_2 > 0)$, with still more of X being purchased as a result of a rise in the consumer's real income.

We can therefore state that:

$$\text{Total price effect} \equiv \text{Substitution effect} + \text{Income effect}$$

The income effect can be positive, zero or negative, depending on the type of product in question. For *normal* products, the income effect will be positive; for inferior products, the income effect may be negative over certain ranges of income. Inferior products are cheap, but poor quality, substitutes for other products. As real incomes rise beyond a certain level, consumers will tend to replace such inferior products with more expensive but better quality alternatives.

Taking it further A1.1 *continued*

We can now explore the situation which will result in the law of demand operating in the conventional manner, i.e. more of X being demanded at a lower price.

- Clearly, when *both* substitution and income effects are positive, as in Figure A1.6(a), the total price effect will be positive and the law of demand holds.

- However, if the product is inferior, then the total price effect may include a positive substitution effect but a negative income effect, and the overall outcome will be in doubt.

- Where the product is so inferior that the income effect is sufficiently negative to more than outweigh the positive substitution effect, the total price effect will be negative. In this case a fall in P_x will result in a fall in the demand for X and the law of demand will be violated, with the demand curve sloping upwards from left to right.

Just such an occurrence is shown in Figure A1.6(a). The negative income effect $(X_2 - X_3)$ more than outweighs the positive substitution effect $(X_1 - X_2)$. The fall in price of X causes demand to contract from X_1 to X_3.

Inferior products and Giffen products

- **Inferior products**. These are cheap but poor quality substitutes for other products. As real incomes rise above a certain 'threshold', consumers tend to substitute the more expensive but better quality alternatives for them. In other words, inferior products have negative income elasticities of demand over certain ranges of income. However, not all inferior products are Giffen products.

- **Giffen products**. These are named after the nineteenth-century economist, Sir Robert Giffen, who claimed to identify an upward sloping demand curve for certain inferior products. Of course, we should now be in a position to explain exactly when an inferior product will become a Giffen product. Remembering our identity:

$$\text{Total price effect} \equiv \text{Substitution effect} + \text{Income effect}$$

the total price effect will be negative when the positive substitution effect is more than outweighed by the negative income effect. This has already been illustrated in Figure A1.6(b) so that this inferior product is also a Giffen product. For an inferior product where the degree of inferiority is rather small, however, the negative income effect may be outweighed by the positive substitution effect, so that the law of demand will still hold. In other words, a fall in P_x will still result in a rise (expansion) in the quantity of X demanded and this inferior product is not a Giffen product.

Table A1.1 summarises the various possibilities.

Table A1.1 **Inferior and Giffen products**

Type of product	Substitution effect	Income effect	Total effect
Normal	Positive	Positive	Positive
Inferior (but not Giffen)	Positive	Negative	Positive
Giffen	Positive	Negative	Negative

Imperfect information and loss of consumer welfare

We noted above that the consumer will maximise utility (satisfaction) when there is tangency between the budget line and the highest attainable indifference curve. The *slope* of that budget line is given by the price ratio of the two products involved, X and Y. But what if one consumer has information that a product can be bought cheaply, and another consumer does not! Here we examine the implications of such imperfect information ('information asymmetry') on consumer welfare.

Figure A1.7 usefully summarises this situation. For simplicity, we assume that both consumer A and consumer B have exactly the same level of income. However, suppose consumer A is *less aware* (perhaps via less search activity) of the availability of a cheaper source of product Y than is consumer B, so that he faces a higher price for Y and therefore a *lower* product price ratio (P_X/P_Y) than does consumer B. This implies a flatter budget line (AM) for consumer A as compared to B. This is because when they spend their identical income on product Y, consumer B, who goes to the lower priced source, is able to obtain more Y than consumer A. This is *not* the case for product X, where each is equally aware of the lowest prices available.

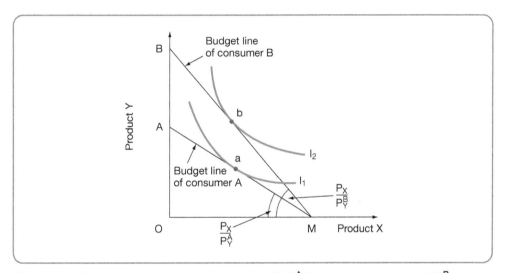

Figure A1.7 Consumer A pays more for product Y (P_y^A) than does consumer B (P_y^B)

Clearly, from Figure A1.7 we can see that in maximising utility by equating their respective budget lines with the highest attainable indifference curves, consumers A and B are in a different situation from each other. Consumer B, who is aware of the cheaper price available for product Y, is able to reach a higher level of utility (I_2) than consumer A (I_1).

Isoquants, isocosts and production

Isoquants

Iso means constant and isoquant means constant quantity. The 1X isoquant refers to the different combinations of factors of production able to produce one unit of a product in a technically efficient manner. Let us examine isoquants a little further, using an example. In producing a given amount of a particular type of knitted garment, the firm may be able to choose between different processes of production, i.e. different combinations of capital and labour technically available to the producer. In the table the firm might be able to produce one sweater (i.e. one unit of product X) using any one of the processes outlined, where K represents units of capital and L units of labour.

Alternative processes for producing one sweater (1X) are shown in the table below:

Process	K	L
a	18	2
b	12	3
c	9	4
d	6	6
e	4	9
f	3	12
g	2	18

If we plot the points from the table, then connect them together we get the curve shown in Figure A2.1.

This curve is the 1X *isoquant*, i.e. it shows all the processes that can produce one sweater (1X) in a *technically efficient* manner.

Isoquant lines above and to the right of 1X (e.g. 2X isoquant) correspond to more of both factor inputs, so will represent higher levels of output of product X.

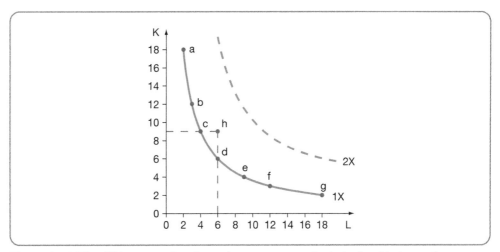

Figure A2.1 The 1X isoquant; i.e. the various processes technically able to produce 1 unit of X

Isocost lines

Just as isoquants are lines of constant quantity, so isocosts are lines of constant costs. They are similar to the budget lines of consumer behaviour except that this time they tell us the different quantities of the factors of production that producers can purchase for a given expenditure (instead of the different quantities of products that consumers can purchase for a given expenditure).

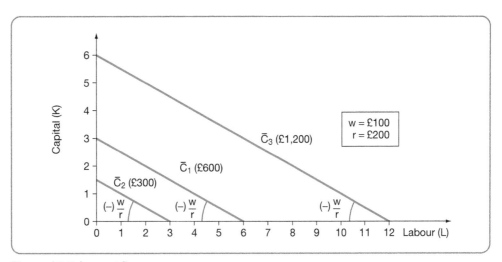

Figure A2.2 Isocost lines

The isocost line $\bar{C}_1$ in Figure A2.2 shows the various combinations of capital and labour that can be purchased for an expenditure of £600, where the price of capital (r) is £200 per unit and the price of labour (w) is £100 per unit.

- The *position* of the isocost line is determined by the value of the total expenditure of the firm on factor inputs. If expenditure halved to £300 with factor prices unchanged, the isocost line would shift inwards to $\overline{C}_2$ and if expenditure doubled to £1,200 the isocost line would shift outwards to $\overline{C}_3$. Notice that these are parallel shifts since the factor price ratio is unchanged.
- The *slope* of the isocost line is given by the factor price ratio.

$$\frac{\text{Price of labour}}{\text{Price of capital}} = (-)\frac{w}{r} = \frac{100}{200} = \frac{1}{2}$$

Strictly this factor price ratio is negative, but we usually ignore the sign, as indicated by the use of brackets around the sign.

Economic efficiency

From all the technically efficient processes of production shown as available on the isoquant, a profit-maximising producer is likely to select that process which is most *economically efficient* (or 'productively efficient'), i.e. the least-cost process (see Figure A2.3).

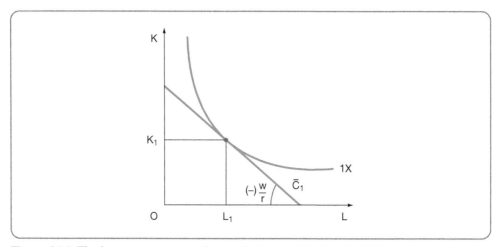

Figure A2.3 **The least-cost process for producing 1 unit of product X**

From all the technically efficient processes of production defined by the isoquant, this economically or least-cost-efficient process will occur where there is a *tangency* between isoquant and isocost. In other words, for any given output, the profit-maximising firm will select that process which is on an isocost line nearest the origin. This will indicate which, of all the technically efficient processes indicated by the isoquant, is the least-cost process (given the current factor price ratio).

If 1X is the desired level of output, the lowest cost of producing 1X at the current factor price ratio (w/r) is $\overline{C}_1$. This 'least cost' process will involve using capital to labour in the ratio K_1/L_1.

Changing the process of production

Suppose the price of capital now falls from r_1 to r_2 in Figure A2.4, with the isocost line now becoming steeper (since $w_1/r_2 > w_1/r_1$).

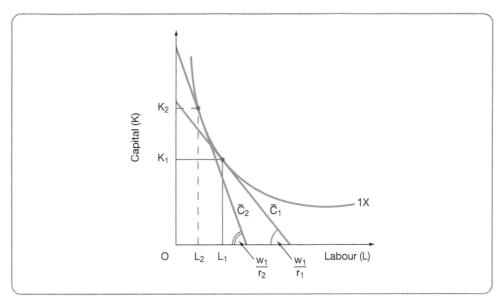

Figure A2.4 **Factor substitution under changing factor–price ratio**

The new minimum cost of producing 1X is $\bar{C}_2$ (i.e. tangency between the 1X isoquant and the nearest isocost line to the origin with the new slope w_1/r_2), giving a capital/labour ratio K_2/L_2. Not surprisingly, standard theory has predicted an increased use of the cheaper capital input (K_2 instead of K_1) and a decreased use of the now relatively more expensive labour input (L_2 instead of L_1).

References

Akerlof, G. and Shiller, R. (2010) *Animal Spirits: How Human Psychology Drives the Economy, and Why It Matters for Global Capitalism*, Princeton University Press

Ansoff, H. I. (1968) *Corporate Strategy*, Penguin

Armstrong, M. (2009) *Handbook of Human Resource Management Practice*, 11th edn, Kogan Page

Bacon, R. and Eltis, W. (1978) *Britain's Economic Problem: Too Few Producers*, 2nd edn, Macmillan

Barkema, H. G. and Gomez-Meija, L. R. (1998) Managerial compensation and firm performance, *Academy of Management Journal*, 41, 2

Baumol, W. J. (1959) *Business Behaviour, Value and Growth*, Macmillan

Bebchuk, L. (2004) in 'Special Report on Mergers and Acquisitions', *Economist*, 21 February

Beer, M. *et al.* (1984) *Managing Human Assets*, Free Press; Collier Macmillan, New York

Berle, A. A. and Means, G. C. (1934) *The Modern Corporation and Private Property*, Macmillan

Black, G. (2007) *Introduction to Accounting and Finance*, Financial Times/Prentice Hall

Blankenhorn, D. (2008) *Thrift: A Cyclopedia*, Templeton Foundation Press

Brindley, B. and Buckley, M. (2004) *Business Studies: A-Level Study Guide*, Pearson Education

Buckingham, L. and Atkinson, D. (1999), 'Whisper it . . . takeovers don't pay', *Guardian*, 30 November

Capron, L. (1999) 'Horizontal acquisitions: the benefits and risk to long-term performance', *Mastering Strategy*, p. 202, Financial Times/Prentice Hall

Conyon, M. and Gregg, P. (1994) Pay at the top: a study of the sensitivity of top director remuneration to company specific shocks, *National Institute Economic Review*, August

Conyon, M. and Leech, D. (1994) Executive compensation, corporate performance and ownership structure, *Oxford Bulletin of Economics and Statistics*, 56, 229–47

Conyon, M. and Nicolitsas, D. (1998) Does the market for top executives work? CEO pay and turnover in small UK companies, *Small Business Economics*, 11, 2

Cosh, A. and Hughes, A. (2000) *British Enterprise in Transition: Growth, Innovation and Public Policy in the Small and Medium Sized Enterprise Sector 1994–1999*, Cambridge: ESRC Centre for Business Research

Cyert, R. M. and March, J. G. (1963) *A Behavioural Theory of the Firm*, Prentice Hall

Dunning, J. (1993) *Multinational Enterprise and the Global Economy*, Addison Wesley

Economist, The (2004) 'Special Report on Mergers and Acquisitions', pp. 79–82, 21 February

European Commission (2002) Observatory of European SMEs 2002/No. 2

Ezzamel, M. and Watson, R. (1998) Market compensation earnings and the bidding up of executive cash compensation: evidence from the United Kingdom, *Academy of Management Journal*, 41, 2

Fuller, E. (2007) 'Mergers and acquisitions in the growth of the firm' in *Applied Economics*, 11th edn, Griffiths, A. and Wall, S. (eds), Financial Times/Prentice Hall

Gerstner, L. (2005) *Who Says Elephants Can't Dance? Leading a Great Enterprise Through Dramatic Change*, Harper Collins

Gregg, P., Machin, S. and Szymanski, S. (1993) The disappearing relationship between directors' pay and corporate performance, *British Journal of Industrial Relations*, 31, pp. 1–9

Griffiths, A. (2000) Corporate objectives, risk taking and the market: the case of Cadbury Schweppes, *British Economy Survey*, 29(2), Spring

Griffin, R. Y. and Pustay, M. (2010) *International Business*, 6th edn., Pearson Education, Inc., Upper Saddle River, NJ

Hall, E. T. (1960) The silent language in overseas business, *Harvard Business Review*, 38, 3, pp. 87–96

Hendry, J. and Pettigrew, A. (1990) Human resource management: an agenda for the 1990s, *International Journal of Human Resource Management*, 1, 1

Hofstede, G. (1980) *Cultural Consequences; International Differences in Work Related Values*, Sage

Hornby, W. (1994) *The Theory of the Firm Revisited: A Scottish Perspective*, Aberdeen Business School

Jensen, M. C. and Murphy, K. J. (1990) Performance pay and top management incentives, *Journal of Political Economy*, 98

Jobber, D. and Hooley, G. (1987) Pricing behaviour in UK manufacturing and service industries, *Managerial and Decision Economics*, 8, pp. 167–77

Johnson, G. and Scholes, K. (2006) *Exploring Corporate Strategy*, 7th edn, Financial Times/ Prentice Hall

Jones, P. and Dickerson, A. (2007) Poor returns, winners and losers in the job market, *Equal Opportunities Commission Working Paper Series*, No. 52

Kay, J. (1993) 'The structure of strategy', *Business Strategy Review*, 01, June

Kessapidou, S. and Varsakelis, N. (2000) 'National culture, choice of management and business performance: the case of foreign firms in Greece', in *Dimensions of International Competitiveness: Issues and Policies*, Lloyd-Reason, L. and Wall, S. (eds), Edward Elgar

Keynes, J. M. (1936) *The General Theory of Employment, Interest and Money*, Macmillan

Larner, R. J. (1970) *Management Control and the Large Corporation*, Dunellan, Cambridge, Mass.

Laurent, A. (1986) 'The cross-cultural puzzle of international human resource management', *Human Resource Management*, 25

Leech, D. and Leahy, J. (1991) Ownership structure, control type classification and the performance of large British companies, *Economic Journal*, 101

Maslow, A. H., Frager, R. D., Fadiman, J. (1987) *Motivation and Personality*, 3rd edn., Pearson Education, Inc., Upper Saddle River, NJ

Moeller, S., Schlingemann, F. and Stulz, R. (2004) Wealth destruction on a massive scale? A study of acquiring-firm returns in the merger wave of the late 1990s, *Journal of Finance*, 60, 2

Newman, K. and Nollen, S. (1996) in *Dimensions of International Competitiveness: Issues and Policies*, Lloyd-Reason, L. and Wall, S. (eds), Edward Elgar

Nyman, S. and Silberston, A. (1978) 'The ownership and control of industry', *Oxford Economic Papers*, Vol. 30, No. 1, March

Porter, M. (1980) *Competitive Strategy*, Free Press, New York

Porter, M. (1985) *Competitive Advantage*, Free Press, New York

Prahalad, C. K. (1999) 'Changes in the competitive battlefield', *Financial Times*, 4 October. In *Mastering Strategy* (2000) Financial Times/Prentice Hall

Proudfoot Consulting (2003) *Global Productivity Study*

Shipley, D. D. (1981) Primary objectives in British manufacturing industry, *Journal of Industrial Economics*, 29, 4 June

Shipley, D. D. and Bourdon, E. (1990) Distributor pricing in very competitive markets, *Industrial Marketing Management*, 19

Simon, H. A. (1959) Theories of decision making in economics, *American Economic Review*, 69, 3 June

Smith, A. (1776) *An Enquiry into the Nature and Causes of the Wealth of Nations*

Storey, D. (1982) *Entrepreneurship and the New Firm*, Croom Helm

Storey, D. (1994) *Understanding the Small Business Sector*, Routledge

Storey, D., Keasey, K., Watson, R. and Wynarczyk, P. (1987) *The Performance of Small Firms*, Croom Helm

Storey, D., Watson, R. and Whynarczyk, P. (1995) The remuneration of non-owner managers in UK unquoted and unlisted securities market enterprises, *Small Business Economics*, 7

Thompson, A. and Strickland, A. (1999) *Strategic Management*, 11th edn, McGraw-Hill

TUC (2000) Small Business – Myths and Reality, March

Vernon, R. and Wells, L. T. (1991) *The Manager in the International Economy*, Prentice-Hall, Upper Saddle River, NJ

Williamson, O. E. (1963) Managerial discretion and business behaviour, *American Economic Review*, 53, December

Answers to Stop and think and You try

Chapter 1

Stop and think

1.1 Fall in price of substitute in consumption; rise in price of complement in consumption; fall in income; change of tastes against oranges; fall in advertising expenditure on oranges (and/or increase in advertising expenditure on substitutes in consumption); etc.

1.2 Rise in price of substitutes in production; fall in price of complement in production; rise in costs of production; change of tastes of producer against wheat; tax increase on wheat; subsidy reduction on wheat; unfavourable weather conditions; etc.

1.3 Less orthodox ways might include letting special groups which can be authenticated (e.g. pensioners; consumers in developing countries; etc.) purchase the excess supply at discounted prices. The aim is to avoid excess supply depressing price in the market as a whole.

You try 1.1

1 If the recording studio chooses to operate at point R' on the production possibility curve then it can produce a combination of A_2 albums per year and S' singles per year.

2 By moving from R to R' the studio has had to forgo $A_1 - A_2$ albums. If more singles are produced, then resources will have to be shifted away from producing albums. This means that the opportunity cost of producing more singles is the number of albums that have had to be forgone, i.e. $A_1 - A_2$ albums.

3 A movement from N to R does not involve an opportunity cost in terms of albums forgone to the studio. This is because at N the studio is not using all its resources fully. If it used all its resources it would be able to produce at R on the production possibility curve. In other words, it could produce the same amount of albums as before (A_1) *and* more singles (S_1). The number of albums has not decreased so there is no opportunity cost in terms of albums in the movement from N to R.

4 The possibilities are that the studio could produce more albums and the same singles (M to R), more singles and the same albums (M to R') or more of both (anywhere north-east of M). The optimum set of combinations of singles and albums would be between R and R' on the production possibility curve since all the resources would then be fully employed.

You try 1.2

1 (a) True (b) True (c) False (decrease) (d) False (contraction)

2 I D I I D I D D

3 (a) True (b) True (c) False (fits together with) (d) True (e) False (rival with)

You try 1.3

1 (i) (c) A to E (ii) (d) A to D (iii) (a) A to B (iv) (b) C to D

2 (ii) and (iv) both increase the supply of the petrol, the complement in production (jointly supplied product) with oil.

3 (ii) and (iv) both decrease the supply of petrol.

4 (a) (v)   (b) (iii)   (c) (ii)   (d) (iv)   (e) (i)

You try 1.4

1 (a) False (P_1)   (b) False (excess supply)   (c) True   (d) False (fall)   (e) True (move along D)
   (f) False (contract)   (g) True   (h) True

2 (a) Rise: Rise (via increase in demand)   (b) Fall: Fall (via decrease in demand)
   (c) Fall: Rise (via increase in supply)   (d) Rise: Fall (via decrease in supply)

3 When the demand for Microsoft XBox increases from D to D_1 then, under normal circumstances, the demand for Sony PlayStation 2 will decrease from D to D_1 because they are in competition with each other, i.e. it is a competitive demand situation. This means that when the demand for XBox increases it will take customers away from PlayStation 2, causing the demand for PlayStation 2 to decrease.

4 As the demand for wool increases from D to D_1, the price of wool rises and the quantity of wool supplied expands from Q to Q_1. To supply more wool requires more sheep so that more mutton is (eventually) supplied at any given price of mutton, i.e. wool and mutton are jointly supplied. As a result of the increase in supply of mutton, the price of mutton falls and the quantity rises.

5 As the demand for cars increases from D to D_1 then at any given price of tyres, more tyres are now demanded. In other words, the demand for tyres will also increase from D to D_1 as cars and tyres are complements in consumption.

You try 1.5

1 USA, UK, France, Poland, China, Cuba

   Cuba is a highly regulated economy with little in the way of a free market, and is therefore the closest to a pure command economy. The USA is at the opposite end of the spectrum, with private enterprise dominating its economy. The UK is the closest to the USA in terms of free market activity, with France having relatively more state support and regulation than the UK. China is closest to Cuba, though substantial parts of its economy have been opened to free enterprise in recent years. This has been still more true of the economy of Poland.

2 (a) Some aspects which could be discussed include:

   – The free market brings buyers and sellers together in their own self-interest. The interaction of buyers and sellers will result in the determination of price.
   – When products or services are scarce (plentiful), the price mechanism will rise (fall) and resources will then be moved towards (away from) the product or services concerned.
   – The free market is a decentralised system which permits many solutions to be tried. Hence if competition is strong it creates challenges to find the best ways of producing good and services.
   – Freedom for individuals to take risks and to try to create new products or new business ventures.
   – Maximises producer and consumer surpluses.
   – The possibility of maximising profits encourages entrepreneurs to invest in new products and techniques.
   – No major barriers to entry of firms so that competition can be enhanced.

(b) Some of the areas that could be discussed are:

- If the market is left free, then the competition between firms may become limited. In other words, freedom may allow a few large firms to dominate the industry. The results could be higher prices and abnormally large profits.
- In the free market, entrepreneurs may be encouraged to persuade consumers to buy their goods by advertising. The information from advertising firms may not be 'perfect' and may be designed to persuade consumers', i.e. choice is not totally 'free'.
- Lack of competition and high profits may remove the incentive for firms to be efficient.
- The practices of some firms may be socially undesirable, e.g. pollution.
- Power and property may be unequally distributed, i.e. those who have power will gain at the expense of those who have no power.
- Free market can lead to macroeconomic instability as entrepreneurs may be tempted towards the 'herd' instinct – leading to over-investment and then resulting in a reversal, i.e. the boom and slump cycle.
- Free markets may reward self-interest behaviour and can encourage selfishness and materialism.

Chapter 2

Stop and think

2.1 The scales used for the axes in (b) may be different from those in (d). For example, if the scales for the vertical axes were the same but for the horizontal axis the scale was 1 cm = 1,000 units for (b) but 1 cm = 10 units for (d), then (b) might actually be the more elastic demand curve.

2.2 Price increase along a unit elastic demand, no change in total revenue.

- Price increase along a relatively elastic demand, total revenue will decrease.
- Price increase along a relatively inelastic demand curve, total revenue will increase.

2.3 (a) marginal utility is positive but falling   (b) marginal utility is zero
(c) marginal utility is negative

2.4 Total utility is now a maximum with 2 units of A and 7 of B so that $12/2 = 12/2$ for the respective marginal utility/price ratios. The fall in price of B means 4 extra units demanded (and 1 less of A).

You try 2.1

1 (a)

Quantity (units)	AR (£)	TR (£)	MR (£)
1	100	100	100
2	95	190	90
3	90	270	80
4	85	340	70
5	80	400	60
6	75	450	50
7	70	490	40
8	65	520	30

(b) From the diagram we can see that as AR (price) falls, quantity demanded expands so that the demand curve slopes downwards from left to right. The MR curve also slopes down from left to right but is below the AR curve throughout the length of AR. Both AR and MR curves are linear in this example (i.e. straight lines).

2 (a) (ii)   (b) (iv)   (c) (iii)   (d) (v)   (e) (i)

3 (a) True   (b) False (raise total revenue)   (c) True   (d) True

4 (a) (i) and (iv)   (b) (iii)   (c) (i) and (iv)   (d) (i)   (e) (ii)

You try 2.2

1 (b) and (c)

2 (a) and (c)

3 (a) (ii)   (b) (v)   (c) (i)   (d) (iii)   (e) (iv)

4 (c)

5 (b) Football boots (complement)

6 Beer (substitute)

You try 2.3

1 (c) and (d)

2 (a)

3 (c) and (e)

Chapter 3

Stop and think

3.1 Some costs will not vary with the number of students or number of lectures undertaken, e.g. costs related to the building or infrastructure of the university. Energy costs, wage bill (lecturers, support staff), cost of teaching materials, etc. may vary with the number of students/lecturers.

3.2 Many possibilities here. Silicon Glen (computer industries in Clydeside), Silicon Fen (computer industries in Cambridge) and many other examples are possible.

3.3 New entrants into a sector of economic activity might seek to merge with or take over these (often small) firms which have learned over time how to reduce costs.

You try 3.1

1

No. of workers (L)	Total product (TP)	Average product (AP)	Marginal product (MP)
1	40	40	40
2	140	70	100
3	255	85	115
4	400	100	145
5	600	120	200
6	720	120	120
7	770	110	50
8	800	100	30
9	810	90	10
10	750	75	−60

(a) (i) Diminishing marginal returns sets in after the employment of five workers.
    (ii) Diminishing average returns sets in after the employment of six workers.

(b) Your diagram should show the marginal product curve *above* the average product curve until six workers (when they are the same). After six workers the marginal product curve is *below* the average product curve. Your diagram should look something like that in the top part of Figure 3.3.

2 (a) In the top diagram, both average product (AP) and marginal product (MP) curves rise to a peak and then fall. When the MP curve is above the AP curve, then AP will continue to rise even when MP is falling. When they both intersect, the AP curve will be at a maximum. As soon as MP is below AP then AP must fall.

(b) In the bottom diagram, both average variable cost (AVC) and marginal cost (MC) curves are U-shaped. When the MC curve is below the AVC curve then it pulls down the AVC curve. The minimum point on the AVC curve is where both AVC and MC curves intersect. For further increases in output the MC curve is above the AVC curve and therefore it pulls up the AVC curve.

(c) The two diagrams are linked because costs are a reflection of productivity. In other words, an increase in MP (i.e. increase in productivity of the last person) will lead to a fall in the marginal costs of production (MC). On the other hand, a decrease in MP (i.e. decrease in productivity of the last person) will lead to a rise in the marginal costs of production. The same principles hold for the AP and AVC curves, i.e. when AP rises/falls, the AVC curve falls/rises. The link between the two diagrams is that improving/worsening productivity will result in decreasing/increasing costs. This linkage also means that when MP and AP are at maximum values, MC and AVC respectively are at minimum values.

3

Output	TFC	TVC	TC	AFC	AVC	ATC	MC
0	50	0	50	–	–		
1	50	40	90	50	40	90	40
2	50	75	125	25	37.5	62.5	35
3	50	108	158	16.7	36	52.7	33
4	50	138	188	12.5	34.5	47	30
5	50	170	220	10.0	34	44	32
6	50	205	255	8.3	34.2	42.5	35
7	50	243	293	7.1	34.7	41.8	38
8	50	286	336	6.3	35.8	42.1	43
9	50	335	385	5.6	37.2	42.8	49
10	50	390	440	5.0	39	44	55

From the diagram (which should be similar to Figure 3.2(b), p. 80) we can see that the average fixed costs (AFC) falls continuously as output increases because the fixed costs are spread over more and more output. Both the AVC and the ATC curves are U-shaped, with the AVC being below the ATC. The difference between the two curves represents the average fixed costs (AFC). Notice that the marginal cost curve (MC) falls and then rises – it also intersects both AVC and ATC at their lowest points. This is because the MC curve determines whether AVC and ATC rise or fall. For example, if MC is below AVC, then AVC will fall; but when MC is above AVC, AVC will rise. Similarly, if MC is below/above ATC, then ATC will fall/rise.

4 (b) and (c)

5 (b) and (c)

You try 3.2

1   The first table shows that costs of production per car (i.e. average production costs) decreases as production of cars increases. The optimum number of cars that should be produced in this car plant in order to achieve lowest average production costs is 2m per year. This table is looking at technical scale economies. Note that a car company producing only 100,000 cars per year is at a 34% cost *disadvantage* compared to one producing 2m cars per year.

   The second table shows that the optimum number of cars that should be produced to minimise the various non-production costs under five categories of activities (which are related to the car industry) are quite different. It shows that if the car plant produces 2m cars per year then this output is also sufficient to meet (or more than meet) the optimum output in the sales, advertising and risk activities. However, the 2m cars per year is not large enough to meet the optimum outputs for Finance and Research and Development. This means that at 2m cars per year, the cost of Finance per car and the R&D costs per car will not be at their lowest (optimum). These non-technical (enterprise) economies are different from the technical (production) economies.

2   (a) (ii)   (b) (i)   (c) (iii)   (d) (i)   (e) (iv)   (f) (v)

3   (a) (iv)   (b) (iii) (c) (vi) (d) (i) (e) (ii) (f) (vii) (g) (v)

4   (a) and (c)

5   (a)

6   (e)

7   (e)

8   (b)

9   (a) False (just sufficient)   (b) False (diseconomies of scale)
    (c) False (economies of experience)   (d) True   (e) True

You try 3.3

1   (a) (iv)   (b) (iii)   (c) (v)   (d) (ii)

2   (a) False (relatively elastic)   (b) True   (c) True   (d) False (+0.75)

3   (b)

4   (b)

5   (c)

Chapter 4

Stop and think

4.1   Marginal revenue and marginal cost curves would have intersected at Q_p, the output where total profit is a maximum.

4.2   Consumer tastes shifting progressively towards more ethical/environmental aspects may increase demand for companies/products more closely aligned to these values. Stricter government regulations in these areas may favour companies/products which already meet these standards (those failing to comply may be excluded from major markets).

4.3   There may still be a small number of highly committed purchasers with extremely in-elastic demand characteristics. Charging these purchasers a high price may well result in increased revenue.

You try 4.1

1 Many local possibilities here.

2 This table provides a breakdown of the number of different types of business organisations by sector. First, it can be seen that the service sector contains the largest number of VAT-based enterprises in total, accounting for some 76% of all such enterprises. It also has the largest number of enterprises in all business categories. This is not surprising, because the service sector in the UK accounts for over 70% of total UK output. Second, sole proprietors are well represented in agriculture and construction, with many single owners of small farms in agriculture and many self-employed carpenters, bricklayers, plumbers etc. in construction. Partnerships are also well represented in agriculture and services, construction and production sectors. Third, when we investigate the larger firms we see that in the production sector, some 69% of enterprises are companies or public corporations as the larger size helps them to attain economies of scale and compete in an increasingly dynamic environment. The service sector also has around 60% of its enterprises in the large-scale category of companies and corporations. Note also the high percentage of general government and non-profit-making enterprises in the service industry. This should not be surprising since it covers many local government-run offices and charity organisations across the country.

You try 4.2

1 (a) Q_2 with total profit Q_2X (b) Q_3 with total revenue Q_3C.
   (c) Total revenue equals total costs, so that profit levels are zero (break-even outputs).
   (d) Q_3 with the minimum profit constraint of (1) since total revenue is a maximum at point C and more than the minimum profits are being earned. But the output level would move to Q_2' if the minimum profit constraint rises from (1) to (2) and total revenue would fall below C.

2 Arguably only 15.9% of firms are 'true profit maximisers' since only 15.9% of firms answered with *both* 1(a) and 2(d), which you would expect from a true profit maximiser. Profit is clearly the most important single objective, with 85% of firms regarding it as either 'very important' or 'of overriding importance'.

3 (b) and (c)

4 (a) and (d)

5 (b) and (d)

6 (a) and (e)

7 (b) and (d)

8 (b) and (c)

9 (b) and (d)

Chapter 5

Stop and think

5.1 Accounting, solicitors and various legal practices, hairdressing and personal services, agriculture etc.

5.2 Organic growth is more likely to reflect the firm's existing core competencies, to be incremental rather than high value/high risk, to avoid cultural 'shocks' via mergers/acquisitions etc. Disadvantages may be that it may take longer than mergers to achieve any desired results and may be delayed by a lack of internal core competencies or lack of internal finance etc.

5.3 Many possibilities here. Check the student website which accompanies this text where current examples are given.

5.4 Many possibilities here. Check the student website which accompanies this text where current examples are given.

You try 5.1

1 (a) The table shows many interesting aspects of UK business. First, the growing importance of self-employment (sole proprietor and partnerships) in that 77.8% of businesses do not employ any workers. However, this type of business only employs around 14% of the total employees and contributes just over 8% of total turnover. If we look at the whole SME sector, i.e. those firms employing fewer than 250 employees, then the picture changes in that the whole SME sector accounts for 99.8% of all businesses, employs 48.4% of all employees and accounts for 47.9% of total turnover. The SME sector therefore accounts for about half the turnover and half the employment in the UK, often acting as stepping stones on the way to becoming larger businesses.

(b) The UK has a very small number of particularly large firms. For example, while only 0.2% of all businesses are defined as large (employing more than 250 employees), they account for as much as 51.6% of all employees and 52.1% of total turnover. These large firms are to be found mostly in manufacturing and services where intense competition and the importance of economies of scale have led to the growth of large-scale businesses.

2 (b)

3 (d)

4 (e)

5 (d) (larger firms are more likely to experience a separation between ownership and control)

You try 5.2

1 (a) (v)   (b) (iv)   (c) (vii)   (d) (i)   (e) (vi)   (f) (iii)   (g) (ii)

2 (a) (ii)   (b) (v)   (c) (i)   (d) (iii)   (e) (iv)

3 (a) False (backward)   (b) False (forward)   (c) False (horizontal)   (d) True
(e) True   (f) True   (g) False   (h) False

Chapter 6

Stop and think

6.1 Many possibilities here, but examples are unlikely to include highly branded oligopolistic product markets where entry barriers are considerable.

6.2 Again many possibilities, but this time extensively branded products will be good examples of entry barriers, as will substantial economies of scale (technical and non-technical), tariffs, legal requirements, geographical distance etc.

6.3 Railways and water industries are often mentioned, as are gas and electricity supply.

6.4 (1) Monopolists will benefit directly from their own advertising which, if successful, will increase demand for their output. Perfectly competitive firms already have infinite demand at the going market price and can only benefit via advertising on behalf of the industry as a whole (which may raise the market price).

(2) If economies of scale (technical and non-technical) shift the marginal cost curve further downwards than MC', in Figure 6.10, then the profit-maximising output is higher and price lower than in perfect competition. The 'classical case' against monopoly would no longer hold true.

6.5   Thirty years if Bob confesses and five years if Bob doesn't confess.

6.6   Thirty years if Alf confesses and five years if Alf doesn't confess.

6.7   If A adopts a maxi–min decision rule, then it selects 'price cut' strategy as this is the best of the worst possible outcomes (60% of market share). If B adopts a mini–max decision rule, then it selects 'Extra advertising' since this is the worst of the best possible outcomes (45%, i.e. 100% – 55% of market share).

6.8   (1) No, since there is no single policy option that is best for Beta regardless of how Alpha reacts.
(2) Beta is likely to select a low price since (£m) 140 is better than 100 for Beta.

You try 6.1

1   (a) P_1/Q_1
(b) P_3/Q_3
(c) Q_2
(d) b (where MR is zero, suggesting that total revenue is unchanged for price changes around P_2)
(e) Within the total area of 'deadweight loss' of agc, aec of consumer surplus is lost and ecg producer surplus is lost. However, you could have mentioned that area P_3aeP_1 was also lost from consumer surplus but was exactly matched as a gain in producer surplus – so this area has a zero *net* effect on economic welfare and does not appear in 'deadweight loss'.
(f) P_2/Q_2 (total revenue is a maximum where marginal revenue is zero).

2   Letters, in vertical order: (d), (f), (b), (e), (a), (c)

3   (a) and (e)

4   (b) and (c)

5   (a) and (d)

6   (b) and (d)

You try 6.2

1.

Perfect competition	Monopolist competition
(b) (d) (e) (g) (i)	(a) (c) (f) (h) (j)

2   (e)

3   (a)

4   (a)

You try 6.3

1   (a) (iii)   (b) (vii)   (c) (ii)   (d) (v)   (e) (iv)   (f) (i)   (g) (vi)

2   (c)

3   (d)

4   (d)

Chapter 7

Stop and think

7.1 More elastic demand for the product; becomes easier to substitute labour with capital or with another type of labour; becomes less easy to pass on wage increases to consumers as higher prices; etc.

7.2 An increase in DD (e.g. rise in MRP_L via rise in marginal physical productivity or rise in price of product produced) and/or decrease in SS (e.g. less labour supplied to the market).

Depends on the reasons – if entirely an increase in DD, employment rises; if entirely decrease in SS, employment falls; otherwise indeterminate employment outcome.

Some workers may now switch to being bus drivers from being lorry drivers or from other occupations; supply increases and equilibrium wage falls.

7.3 There is a higher proportion of women part-time workers, so over the year their annual earnings are significantly less than for men.

7.4 Perhaps ensuring that interviews for jobs have an equal number of male and female applicants etc.

7.5 Labour supply shortages may occur, increasing the demand for older workers who may bring higher productivity to some jobs via greater experience. Payouts on company pension schemes will also be deferred.

You try 7.1

1 (a) The table provides information about the marginal revenue product (MRP), which is, in effect, the demand curve for labour in a perfectly competitive market. Your MRP_L diagram should show the MRP_L rising and then falling; the effective demand curve is that part of the MRP_L which is falling.

(b) (i) At a wage rate of £250, the number of workers employed will be 8.

(ii) At a wage of £80, the number of workers employed will be 11. These solutions are arrived at by equating MRP_L (where it is downward sloping) with MC_L in each situation, where wage $= MC_L$ in a competitive labour market.

(c) The demand curve for labour could become more elastic if it became easier to substitute one type of worker by another type of worker (e.g. more occupational or geographical mobility of labour) or by capital equipment. A given percentage rise in wages for this occupation would then result in a bigger percentage fall in the quantity of that type of labour demanded. Also, since demand for a factor is derived from demand for the product it makes, anything which makes the demand for the product more elastic will make the (derived) demand for the factor more elastic.

(d) (i) If the price of the product produced by labour rose from £5 to £8 then the marginal revenue product (MRP_L) curve would be greater because $MRP_L = MPP_L \times Price$. The demand curve for labour would therefore shift to the right and there would be an increase in demand for labour at each wage rate.

(ii) The answers to the questions in part (b) will not necessarily remain the same because although the given wage rates are the same, the MRP_L values will be different and hence the equilibrium position in the labour market. In fact, with product price of £8 and wage of £250, nine people will be employed (one more than before). If the wage is only £80 then 11 people will be employed (same as before).

You try 7.2

1 (a)

Wage rate (AC$_L$) (£)	Number of workers supplied (per day)	Total cost of labour (£)	Marginal cost of labour (MC$_L$) (£)
50	1	50	50
60	2	120	70
70	3	210	90
80	4	320	110
90	5	450	130
100	6	600	150
110	7	770	170
120	8	960	190

(b) This plots the first column of the table on the vertical axis and the second column on the horizontal axis. It should look like S$_L$ in Figure 7.3(b) (p. 210).

This plots the fourth column of the table on the vertical axis and the second column on the horizontal axis. The MC$_L$ curve should lie above the S$_L$ = AC$_L$ curve, as in Figure 7.3(b) (p. 210).

(c) From the figure we can see that the AC$_L$ and MC$_L$ curves are upward sloping, with the MC$_L$ curve lying above the AC$_L$. In other words, the marginal cost of hiring workers increases as more workers are employed and is above the average cost (wage) as employers bid the wage rate up against themselves.

(d) Under monopsony, the equilibrium level of wages and employment will be achieved where MC$_L$ is equal to MRP$_L$. The monopsonist will employ fewer workers than in a competitive market and also pay them less than the competitive wage (again see Figure 7.3(b) (p. 210).

2 (a) Your sketch diagram should look like Figure 7.3(a) (p. 210), showing the union forcing the employer off his/her MRP$_L$ curve (point A). In other words, by raising wages to W$_3$ in Figure 7.3(a), the union is able to keep employment constant at L$_1$ (point A).

(b) The union will be able to achieve increases in both wages and employment if it has sufficient bargaining power. For example, if the union is strong and controls the total supply of labour into the industry then it can, to some extent, dictate the bargaining outcome. Also, if the demand for the product which labour is making is inelastic, then managers might be prepared to pay a higher wage *and* keep the same number of workers if they can shift this increase in costs onto the price of their product.

Chapter 8

Stop and think

8.1 For each unit of output up to OQ$_2$, each unit adds more to social benefit than to social cost, thereby raising total social surplus. For each unit of output beyond OQ$_2$, each unit adds less to social benefit than to social cost, thereby reducing total social surplus. Social surplus can only be maximised at output OQ$_2$.

8.2 Your diagram could look like that in Figure 8.1 (p. 228) but this time the MSC and MPC labels could be reversed, so that MSC is now below MPC. Social surplus would now be maximised at the higher output (OQ$_1$), and to give the private producer the profit incentive to produce OQ$_1$ a *subsidy* (opposite of tax) will be needed to shift the new MPC vertically downwards to match the lower MSC curve. Now MPC (=MSC) would equal MSB at output OQ$_1$.

Alternatively, your diagram could this time have MSB above MR (MPB), rather than equal to MR (MPB) as in Figure 8.1.

8.3 As just mentioned, this time MSB should be drawn above MR (MPB) to indicate the presence of a merit good. The higher output now needed for social surplus to be a maximum could be achieved by subsidising the merit good.

You try 8.1

1 (a) (ii)   (b) (v)   (c) (iv)   (d) (vi)   (e) (i)   (f) (iii)

2 (a) P   (b) P   (c) P   (d) M   (e) M   (f) P   (g) M

3 (b) and (c)

4 (a) and (d)

5 (b)

Chapter 9

Stop and think

9.1 (1) Withdrawals are savings, imports and taxes. As national income rises, so does that of individuals and businesses, giving more scope to save out of higher incomes (for business this saving will be undistributed profit). Also, as national income rises there will be more spending on imports and more money will be taken by the government in the form of taxes (both via income taxes and expenditure taxes).

(2) The idea here is that some consumer spending still occurs at zero national income and this is financed from past savings (i.e. negative savings or *dissaving*).

9.2 Injections are investment, government spending and exports. In fact as national income rises and consumers spend more, businesses will be more optimistic about the future and are likely to invest more. Government spending may be able to increase, since tax revenues will have risen. Exports might also be encouraged – since the stronger domestic economy may allow domestic firms to produce more output, perhaps growing to reach the minimum efficient size (where average total cost is a minimum) for their sector and therefore being better able to compete on foreign markets.

9.3 (1) aps = total savings divided by total national income
apt = total tax revenue divided by total national income
apm = total spending on imports divided by total national income
(2) aps = 1.5/20 = 0.075
apt = 4/20 = 0.2
apm = 6/20 = 0.3
(3) (a) mps > aps   (b) mpt = apt   (c) mpm = apm

9.4 Any vertical straight line from the horizontal axis to the 45° line creates a right-angled triangle with two (base) angles equal at 45°. This is an isosceles triangle and therefore the two sides are equal, i.e. Y and E.

9.5 (1) At Y_1 injections now fall short of withdrawals. National income (Y) must fall, and as Y falls so too does withdrawals (W). National income continues to fall until W falls sufficiently to match the new and lower level of injections at V_2. This occurs at Y_2, the new equilibrium value.

(2) (a) Your diagram should look like that in the top part of Figure 9.9 (p. 288), with the E (C + J) schedule intersecting the 45° line at a higher level of national income, following the increase in injections.

(b) The opposite will now occur, with a lower level of national income in the new equilibrium.

9.6 (1) The decrease in withdrawals from W_1 to W_2 means that withdrawals now fall short of injections at Y_1. National income now rises and withdrawals also rise along the new schedule W_2. National income continues to rise until withdrawals and injections are again equal at V_1, with national income Y_2 the new equilibrium value.

(2) On the 45° diagram a change in withdrawals would be captured by a change in the consumption function (C). For example, a rise in W will mean that there is an equivalent fall in C at any given level of national income Y ($Y \equiv C + W$). This will shift the aggregate expenditure (E) schedule downwards, since $E = C + J$.

9.7 It could shift J vertically downwards to go through point B, i.e. reduce injections J, perhaps by cutting G. Alternatively, it could increase taxes (T) and shift the withdrawals schedule upwards to go through point A. Or it could shift both J and W curves in these same directions (but not by as much) so that they intersect at Y_F.

9.8 It could shift J vertically upwards to go through point C (e.g. increase G) or shift W vertically downwards to go through point D (e.g. reduce T), or some of both so that J and W intersect at Y_F.

You try 9.1

1 (a) (iv)   (b) (i)   (c) (vii)   (d) (ii)   (e) (v)   (f) (iii)

2 (a) (iii)   (b) (i)   (c) (viii)   (d) (vi)   (e) (ii)   (f) (vii)

3 (a) (v)   (b) (ii)   (c) (iii)   (d) (iv)   (e) (i)

4 (a)

National income (Y)	Tendency to change in national income
0	0
1,000	Increase
2,000	Increase
3,000	Increase
4,000	Increase
5,000	Increase
6,000	No change
7,000	Decrease
8,000	Decrease

(b)

National income (Y)	Withdrawals (W)	Injections (J)
0	−1,000	2,000
1,000	−500	2,000
2,000	0	2,000
3,000	500	2,000
4,000	1,000	2,000
5,000	1,500	2,000
6,000	2,000	2,000
7,000	2,500	2,000
8,000	3,000	2,000

(c) Your diagram should look like that in Figure 9.4 (p. 278) but with W intersecting J at a value of Y of 6,000. J will be a horizontal line at 2,000 and W will intersect the vertical axis at $-1,000$ and will intersect the horizontal axis when Y = 2,000.

(d) Savings (S) = $-1,000 + 0.2Y$

Taxes (T) = $0.2Y$

Imports (M) = $0.1Y$

Withdrawals (W) = $-1,000 + 0.5Y$

(e)

National income (Y)	Consumption (C)	Injections (J)	Aggregate expenditure (E)
0	1,000	2,000	3,000
1,000	1,500	2,000	3,500
2,000	2,000	2,000	4,000
3,000	2,500	2,000	4,500
4,000	3,000	2,000	5,000
5,000	3,500	2,000	5,500
6,000	4,000	2,000	6,000
7,000	4,500	2,000	6,500
8,000	5,000	2,000	7,000

(f) Your diagram should look like that in Figure 9.9 (p. 288). The E = C + J + J schedule should intersect the 45° line at Y = 6,000. The E schedule intersects the vertical axis at a value of 3,000.

(g) The equilibrium level of national income is where the 45° line intersects the aggregate expenditure line, i.e. at the 6,000 level of national income. It can be seen from the various tables created in this exercise that the equilibrium level of national income is 6,000 whether the W = J approach or the Y = E approach to equilibrium is taken. This confirms the nature of the relationships between the variables discussed in the chapter.

Chapter 10

Stop and think

10.1   See discussion of business cycle on p. 313.

10.2   (1) (a) Reduces national income equilibrium via extra withdrawals/reduced consumption expenditure.

(b) As for (a) except that the impacts will be mainly on those purchasing particular products which now are more expensive.

(2) By raising the marginal propensity to tax (mpt), the national income multiplier would be reduced in value.

10.3   (1) Reduces national income equilibrium via cutting injections (J) or cutting aggregate expenditure (E = C + J).

(2) Lower national income is likely to mean cuts in output and employment. It may bring about a deflationary gap situation, curbing price increases. The balance of payments may improve as less spending goes on imports.

10.4   Extra benefits for those unemployed; higher taxes for those with higher incomes (individuals and companies); etc.

10.5   Too much or too little change in injections or withdrawals may take place – overshooting or undershooting the planned change in national income.

10.6   (a) Extra money available may stimulate higher consumer spending and perhaps less saving (fall in W). Rise in national income.
        (b) As above, this time shifting E = C + J upwards. Rise in national income.

10.7   Businesses which are more highly geared, depending more on borrowings (e.g. from financial institutions, issues of company bonds/debentures) than on their own funds or funds raised from share issues, will be more at risk from interest rate rises.

10.8   For example for price levels *below* P_1, AD exceeds AS putting upward pressure on prices and National Output. As the general price level rises, aggregate demand (AD) contracts (e.g. negative 'real balance effect' reducing C via reductions in the real value of wealth holdings) and aggregate supply (AS) expands (profitability is increased as prices rise faster than the less flexible input costs for producers). Only at P_1/Y_1 do we have an equilibrium outcome.

10.9   The sterling exchange rate has been falling in recent years against the US dollar, making UK exports to the US cheaper there, and making UK imports from the US more expensive in the UK. This with help the UK balance of payments. The sterling exchange rate has also been falling against the euro, making UK exports to the eurozone cheaper in euros and imports from the eurozone dearer in sterling. This will help the UK's balance of payments with the eurozone, which is actually more important for UK trade than for the USA.

10.10   (a) A fall in the exchange rate will make exports cheaper abroad, which is likely to increase exports (X) in the aggregate demand schedule. It may also increase investment (I) in the export sector of the UK. Consumers in the UK may also switch to domestically produced products which are now cheaper than the more expensive imports from abroad, thereby raising consumer expenditure (C) and reducing imports (M). All these factors will tend to shift the aggregate demand (AD) curve to the right, raising the price level and national output, as in Figure 10.9(a) on p. 330. However, the rise in import prices may also cause the aggregate supply (AS) curve to shift upwards and to the left due to cost-push pressures, as in Figure 10.9(b) on p. 330.
        (b) Reverse the arguments in the answer above as the higher exchange rate will this time make exports dearer abroad and imports cheaper at home.

10.11   You could show a shift in AD upwards and to the right matched by a shift in AS downwards and to the right. You could show them intersecting at the same price level as before the shifts, but at a higher level of National Output.

You try 10.1

1

Objective	Fiscal policy	Monetary policy
Increase in economic growth	(a) (d) (e) (f) (h) (j)	(b) (l) (m)
Reduce inflationary pressures	(h) (j)	(c) (k) (n)
Reduce balance of payments deficit	(g) (i)	(c) (k) (n)
Reduce unemployment	(a) (d) (e) (f) (h) (j)	(b) (l) (m)

2   When trying to increase the growth rate of the economy, a decrease in interest rates could help to stimulate investment and consumption expenditure. However, if the economy is near full capacity this could create inflationary tendencies in the economy. An increase in tax allowances would provide more income to spend, but it could also lead to less tax revenue for the government which could increase the government's budget deficit and cause it

to reduce future government spending. A reduction in the top rate of tax could act as an incentive to work and result in more growth; however, it could also lead to a more unequal distribution of income as people in the higher tax brackets benefit at the expense of other wage earners.

3   The table shows the effect of indirect taxes on different income groups. It is clear that indirect taxes (e.g. VAT) are regressive, i.e. affect those on lower incomes more than those on higher incomes. Since all people who buy products or services have to pay the tax irrespective of their income, indirect taxes will take a higher proportion of the income of the poorest groups. For example, the bottom 20% of income earners pay 31.3% of their disposable income in the form of indirect taxes, while the top 20% of income earners pay only 13.3% of their income in indirect taxes.

You try 10.2

1   (a) (iv)   (b) (vi)   (c) (i)   (d) (iii)   (e) (v)

2   (a) False; prices are rising less quickly   (b) True   (c) True   (d) True
    (e) False; lower levels of wage and price inflation

3   (a) RPI   (b) RPIY   (c) RPIX

4   (a) (vi)   (b) (ii)   (c) (iv)   (d) (i)   (e) (vii)   (f) (v)   (g) (iii)

Chapter 11

Stop and think

11.1   The rise in taxes and cuts in government expenditure will increase withdrawals and therefore the withdrawals and injections schedules will intersect at a lower level of national income. In terms of the 45° diagram there will be a reduction in aggregate demand, both because of a reduction in consumer spending C (since disposable income for households after tax will be reduced) and in government expenditure G.

There are many other examples of macropolitical risk, e.g. the loss of investor confidence in Spain and Portugal in 2010 as a result of high budget deficits and resistance of trade unions to various measures including a freezing of wages, later retirement age, etc.

11.2   Many possibilities of micropolitical risk, e.g. damage to oil exploration in the USA and elsewhere as a result of the major oil spill for BP in the Gulf of Mexico.

11.3   There are many possibilities here. For example, Toyota was able to restrict the damage to its reputation in the US following accidents linked to faulty design and parts in some models, because it had become so embedded in the US economy over many decades that many US citizens and politicians regarded it as, in effect, an 'American' company because of its major investment and job creating activities in the US over many years.

11.4   A downgrading in the credit rating of either country would make it more expensive (higher interest rates) for the US or UK to borrow to finance their respective budget deficits. It would also make it more difficult to borrow as lenders become more concerned that their loans might not be repaid. This may discourage investment in each country and reduce National Income below the levels it might otherwise have reached.

11.5   Many possible examples. There is much debate on attempts to patent the human genome in recent times.

11.6   Premium prices are being successfully charged for a wide range of products which advertise themselves as being produced by environmentally sensitive procedures, e.g. wood, rugs, washing powders etc.

11.7   The response here depends on your own selection and research.

You try 11.1

1   There are certainly aspects of micropolitical risk involved in that the major impacts of the Chinese government policy on milk for children is impacting the dairy industries in both the EU and China, stimulating more milk production and rearing of dairy cattle. However, there are also aspects of macropolitical risk in that the impact of a significant increase in output for a major industry (dairy) in Europe will increase employment, incomes, consumer spending and investment, all tending to raise the equilibrium level of National Income. Similarly the rise in prices may cause cost-push inflation, another macropolitical risk.

2   (d)

3   (b) (d) and (e)

4   (b)

5   (a) (ii)   (b) (v)   (c) (iv)   (d) (vi)   (e) (i)   (f) (iii)

You try 11.2

1   (a) The sugar beet type of product produces as much sugar as conventional sugar cane, in half the time and with one third of the water. It is a crop that has been developed to specifically suit the Indian climate and has a further benefit that, by producing a very high sugar content per unit of land, it frees up other land for food production.

    (b) Syngenta is seeking to establish itself as a major company in the Indian agricultural market – one of the largest in the world. This high profile and profitable technological advance in sugar production will help position the company with the Indian government and Indian farmers in ways which will help it develop and market other agricultural products. The product is also extremely profitable in its own right with nearly 20% of Syngenta's total sales in the Asia-Pacific region currently linked to this product, and more Indian farmers are being attracted to its future production.

2   (b) (d) and (e)

Chapter 12

Stop and think

12.1   It can raise price and raise total revenue, since consumers are less focused on price when purchasing that product.

12.2   UK promotional activity may well involve greater use of the Internet for many products, since the UK makes more use of the Web than other EU countries and the time spent by the average UK resident on the Internet each day has almost trebled since 2002. Younger age groups make the most use of the Internet, but even 20% of the over-65 age group use the Internet and those who do so use it more intensively than any other age group. Of course, other patterns will need to be taken into account for promotional activity, e.g. the fact that 22% of UK households have a digital video recorder and 84% of these use it to fast-forward through adverts.

12.3   Many arrangements and practices involving groups and interactions in the workplace can be guided by the principles of Mayo, Maslow and Herzberg. Even functional areas such as recruitment and promotional policy are impacted, for example giving higher priority to those with good interpersonal skills given the importance of the social interactions highlighted by motivational theorists.

12.4   Many stakeholders may potentially benefit. The information in the profit and loss account, balance sheet and cash flow statements will help investors and analysts decide whether to continue investing in the company, withdraw or even deepen such investments. Employees can also gain some insights into corporate prospects, especially important where pension entitlements are company related.

You try 12.1

All responses depend on the products you have selected for each question.

You try 12.2

1, 2 Again, all responses depend on your individual selections.

3 (a) There are both similarities and differences. David is placing more emphasis on the factor input aspect of the human resource and its contribution to corporate objectives ('hard' HRM). Sarah is perhaps adopting a more employee-centred approach, giving more emphasis to the 'fulfilment of potential' aspects of the human resource ('soft' HRM).

   (b) David is less likely than Sarah to see the objectives of the human resources as being necessarily aligned with those of the employer. Incentive structures, both rewards and penalties, and more employer-directed activities in line with the corporate strategy are likely to feature in David's HRM approach. Sarah is more likely to develop activities seen by employees themselves as beneficial, being more ready to assume that their desire for self-improvement is already well established and closely aligned to the interests of the employer.

   (c) There are many possibilities here. In the context of training, David would tend to focus on prescriptive training courses which seek to develop specific employee competencies seen as being directly relevant to achieving corporate objectives. Sarah on the other hand would probably support more 'reflective' employee centred training courses whereby employees seek to identify and develop personal attributes and competencies that they themselves see as relevant, with less concern for 'external' corporate priorities.

You try 12.3

1 (c)

2 (a)

3 (d)

4 (b)

5 (a)

6 (a) Your break-even charts should capture the following and look something like Figure 12.4(b) on p. 412.

- **Price** = £5

$$\text{Budgeted profit (at 10,000 units)} = \text{TR} - \text{TC}$$

$$\text{TR} = £5 \times 10,000 = £50,000$$

$$\text{TC} = \text{TFC} + \text{TVC} = £10,000 + (£3 = 10,000)$$

$$\text{i.e. Budgeted profit} = £50,000 - £40,000 = £10,000$$

$$\text{Contribution per unit (C/U)} = \text{Price} - \text{AVC}$$

$$= £5 - £3$$

$$\underline{\text{C/U} = £2}$$

$$\text{BEP} = \frac{\text{Total fixed cost}}{\text{Contribution per unit}}$$

$$\text{BEP} = \frac{£10,000}{£2}$$

$$\underline{\text{BEP} = 5000 \text{ units}}$$

$$\text{Margin of safety} = \text{Budgeted output} - \text{BEP}$$

$$= 10,000 - 5,000$$

$$\text{Margin of safety} = 5000 \text{ units}$$

As a percentage:

$$\text{Margin of safety} = \frac{\text{Budgeted output} - \text{BEP}}{\text{Budgeted output}} \times 100$$

$$= \frac{10,000 - 5,000}{10,000} \times 100$$

$$\text{Margin of safety} = 50\%$$

In summary, for £5 price scenario

$$\text{Budgeted profit} = £10,000$$

$$\text{BEP} = 5,000 \text{ units}$$

$$\text{Margin of safety (\%)} = 50\%$$

● **Price** = £4

$$\text{Budgeted profit (at 15,000 units)} = \text{TR} - \text{TC}$$

$$\text{TR} = £4 \times 15,000 = £60,000$$

$$\text{TC} = \text{TFC} + \text{TVC} = £10,000 + (£3 = 15,000)$$

$$= £55,000$$

$$\text{Budgeted profit} = £60,000 - £55,000$$

$$\text{Budgeted profit} = £5,000$$

$$\text{Contribution per unit (C/U)} = \text{Price} - \text{AVC}$$

$$= £4 - £3$$

$$\text{C/U} = £1$$

$$\text{BEP} = \frac{\text{TFC}}{\text{C/U}}$$

$$\text{BEP} = \frac{£10,000}{£1}$$

$$\text{BEP} = 10,000 \text{ units}$$

$$\text{Margin of safety} = \text{Budgeted output} - \text{BEP}$$

$$= 15,000 - 10,000$$

$$\text{Margin of safety} = 5,000 \text{ units}$$

As a percentage:

$$\text{Margin of safety} = \frac{\text{Budgeted output} - \text{BEP}}{\text{Budgeted output}} \times 100$$

$$= \frac{15,000 - 10,000}{15,000} \times 100$$

$$\text{Margin of safety} = 33\frac{1}{3}\%$$

In summary, for £4 price scenario

$$\text{Budgeted profit} = £5,000$$

$$\text{BEP} = 10,000 \text{ units}$$

$$\text{Margin of safety (\%)} = 33\frac{1}{3}$$

(b) The £5 price scenario would appear to be the most attractive for the firm. Setting a price of £5 would give it a higher budgeted profit, a lower break-even point and a higher margin of safety, than would setting a price of £4. The £5 price would seem to be both more profitable and less risky for the firm than the £4 price. As well as an *extra* £5,000 in expected profit, the firm need produce and sell 5,000 *fewer* units in order to break even. The margin of safety reinforces this aspect of reduced risk, in that at a price of £5 it can experience a fall in its sales of up to 50% below its budgeted (expected) output before losses are actually incurred. In contrast, at a £4 price the firm can only see sales fall 33% below expectation before losses are actually incurred.

Of course, all this break-even analysis is based on the linearity assumption. This may *not* actually be valid in practice. For example, the assumption that variable cost per unit (AVC) is constant at all levels of output may be unrealistic. If various economies of scale occur, then AVC might *fall* as output increases, raising contribution per unit (Price – AVC) at the £4 price scenario with its higher budgeted output. In this case the TVC and TC curves would cease to be straight line (linear).

Further, the TR curves may not be linear in practice! In order to sell more output it may be that the firm may have to *reduce price*. It may therefore make little sense to draw a TR curve as a straight line with a constant slope representing a given and unchanged price as output varies.

For these and other reasons the break-even analysis may be too simple. Nevertheless, the linearity assumption may have some validity for *relatively small changes in output*, which is often the most likely result of policy changes by a firm.

Chapter 13

Stop and think

13.1 Many possibilities depending on your choice.

13.2 Again, depends on your choice. Some US-based multinationals have started out following this approach, but many are becoming more sensitive to local concerns, e.g. Coca Cola, McDonald's etc. Where cultural distance (e.g. Hofstede) is significant, there may be good reasons to use local nationals in key positions.

13.3 Depends on your choice.

You try 13.1

1 (1) You will need to conduct market research in Northern Ireland – using primary (focus groups/questionnaires, etc.) or secondary sources to establish market potential for such a move. For example, whether there is less competition from other training providers in Northern Ireland and/or greater demand for training services there than in and around Liverpool. Northern Ireland also has its own governmental agencies and funding mechanisms to support SME development. You might seek to establish whether there is access to grants and other financial supports for Wilona itself or for the users of its services.

(2) This could involve looking at establishing a presence (e.g. office) in Northern Ireland, probably via using intermediaries to act part-time on Wilona's behalf, given the limited financial resources of Wilona. Alternatively alliances might be made with established training providers in Northern Ireland, or there might be other possible linkages which could be of mutual benefit (e.g. working within large companies, providing customised training services, etc.).

(3) See the various sources of funding for SMEs identified in Chapter 5.

2 (1) HPP should internationalise for many reasons. First, it has concentrated on the home market too much. If it could expand overseas, it would be able to reap economies of scale to a much greater extent. Second, the promotional gifts market in the UK is stagnant so that if it wishes to be more dynamic and to grow, it must find other markets outside the UK. Third, as the incomes of countries such as Eastern Europe and China rise as a result of more rapid growth than in the past, the demand for gifts sold by the company will grow, since this type of product is relatively income elastic.

(2) HPP could enter the foreign markets by franchising the sales of gifts to a foreign country. It could also form a joint venture with a similar company abroad. This company could act as the distribution arm of HPP while benefiting from a new range of gift products from HPP to complement its own range of products. It may also be possible for HPP to take over the foreign company and 'internalise' its operations. In other words, HPP could use its skills in product design etc. in other countries without worrying that the partner company might break the agreement etc.

(3) An interesting example of a joint venture was that between the two giant pharmaceutical companies, Astra and Merck Inc. of the UK, in 1994. The background for the joint venture was a licensing agreement between the two companies which began in 1984, whereby Merck had exclusive rights to most Astra products in the USA and Astra could benefit from Merck's marketing muscle in the USA. In 1994 a free-standing joint venture was formed between the two companies called Astra-Merck Inc., which focused exclusively on marketing, sales and drug development. This joint venture was popular for a time because it brought together expertise in the development of new drugs (Astra) with marketing strength (Merck). The joint venture lasted until 1998 when Astra wanted to look for another long-term partner with a merger in mind. Astra wanted to merge with the UK company Zeneca because they both had a complementary range of products and they both had similar management philosophies and were strong on R&D. The merger did take place in December 1998 but Astra had to pay Merck compensation for the break-up of their existing joint venture.

You try 13.2

1 (a) (iv)   (b) (iii)   (c) (i)   (d) (v)   (e) (ii)

2 (a) This example shows the nature of the *risks* which multinationals experience when they operate outside their own home environment. For example, the change in government policy which removed tariff protection led to a significant increase in Panasonic's costs. However, the decision as to whether to stay in Mexico also depended on other powerful benefits. The lower labour costs, relatively high labour productivity plus the massive high income market of California on its doorstep (i.e. low transport costs) were strong reasons for the company to remain in Mexico.

(b) An advanced industrial country such as the USA would be affected by the decision to locate the Panasonic plant in Mexico in many ways. For example, it could lead to unemployment in competing electronics industries in the USA. It could also bring down wages in US electronics industries as they fight to compete with low wage countries. On the other hand, it could lead US companies to go 'upmarket' by making more expensive electronic equipment so that they would not be in direct competition with Panasonic.

3 (c) and (e)

4 Attractiveness for multinational: (1) Denmark   (2) Netherlands   (3) France   (4) UK

5 (1) The responses to these questions can reflect the discussions earlier in the chapter on the international marketing mix and those later in the chapter on the characteristics of the EU and US markets. For example, the new international marketing mix for European and US sales is likely to be quite different from that in Hong Kong, Malaysia, South Korea and southern China, but experience in Australia might provide useful insights. There may be opportunities for new (higher!) pricing strategies in Europe and the USA, and existing promotional strategies will need to be adapted to correspond to 'drivers' of European and US consumer behaviour in the toy market. Of course, 'place' strategies will need adapting, with logistical development of supply chains to Europe and the USA as well as to South East Asia. Products may also need adaptation, e.g. in order to comply with regulations such as those for health and safety in the EU and the USA.

(2), (3) and (4) As with (1) there are no 'correct' answers. Your market research into the characteristics of the new (EU/US) markets will help you decide which international marketing 'tools' (techniques) and strategies to adopt, and which market segments to address. Internet media are likely to be important 'communication' devices in these new markets; the households with *x* children under *y* years with an income level above *z* in the EU and USA are likely to be a key target (*x*, *y* and *z* to be determined by market research). Some of the issues discussed in (1) above will also apply to any planned entry into the UK market.

6 (1) The concerns over food health and safety for Chinese shoppers after highly publicised failings, is giving branded food and other products, with their widely respected quality standards, an advantage in the market place.

(2) The study emphasises the huge geographical, cultural and religious diversity across China, with tastes and preferences varying considerably in different regions. Carrefours, for example, has recognised this by giving considerable flexibility to local managers to sell products more appropriate to local tastes and preferences. Logistical problems in reaching stores in the interior of China may also influence the types of products that can be sold in such regions.

You try 13.3

1 (c)

2 (e)

3 (b), (c) and (e)

4 (a) True   (b) True   (c) False; intra-industry trade   (d) True

5 (c)

6 (d)

7 (a)

8 (e)

9 (b)

Chapter 14

Stop and think

14.1 Many possibilities here, with earlier analysis refocused into a five-forces structure involving potential entrants, substitutes, buyers, suppliers and industry competitors for Glaxo-SmithKline.

14.2 From a national perspective 9/11 has caused lower growth rates in global and national GDP so that most countries 'demand conditions' will be less favourable, with possible adverse consequences for 'factor conditions' and 'related and supporting industries'. Of course, nations with competitive advantages in sectors such as defence and security industries may be relatively better placed than others after 9/11.

14.3 As well as the relative labour costs between these countries, we need to know more about the relative productivities of these different types of labour in each country. We also need to know more about changes in the relative exchange rates between the currencies of these countries. In other words we need to know more about all the items in relative unit labour costs (RULCs) between these countries (see p. 498) if we are to gain a better understanding of international competitiveness between the countries.

Index